MICROPROCESSOR-BASED DESIGN

MICROPROCESSOR-BASED DESIGN
A Comprehensive Guide to Hardware Design

MICHAEL SLATER
President, Gryphon Engineering

PRENTICE HALL PTR, Englewood Cliffs, NJ 07632

Library of Congress Catalog Card Number: 86-063293
International Standard Book Number: 0-87484-706-0

 © 1989 by Prentice Hall PTR
Prentice-Hall, Inc.
A Simon & Schuster Company
Englewood Cliffs, New Jersey 07632

Printed in the United States of America

15 14 13 12 11 10

ISBN 0-13-582248-3

Prentice-Hall International (UK) Limited, *London*
Prentice-Hall of Australia Pty. Limited, *Sydney*
Prentice-Hall Canada Inc., *Toronto*
Prentice-Hall Hispanoamericana, S.A., *Mexico*
Prentice-Hall of India Private Limited, *New Delhi*
Prentice-Hall of Japan, Inc., *Tokyo*
Simon & Schuster Asia Pte. Ltd., *Singapore*
Editora Prentice-Hall do Brasil, Ltda., *Rio de Janeiro*

To my parents
For instilling in me the belief
That what I set out to accomplish
I can

CONTENTS

3   BUS STRUCTURES   97

4   MEMORY   173

PREFACE

In the course of designing and teaching seminars about microprocessor-based products over the past ten years, I have found that the books available were too basic or too academic to be directly applicable to product design; they also lacked coverage of many important topics. I have written this book to fill those gaps.

Written from a design engineer's perspective, this book emphasizes the optimal selection of components and design approaches for each application. The goal is to take the reader from an understanding of basic concepts to design-level competence. The wide range of integrated circuits available presents the designer with many opportunities and also makes selecting components and designing the system a challenging task. By tying together the alternatives and possibilities into a cohesive unit, the book provides a basis for evaluating new devices and making intelligent design decisions.

The book is intended for use as a reference for practicing engineers and as a text for an upper-level design course on microprocessor-based systems. In a two- or three-semester course sequence, an introductory text could be used for the first semester and this volume for the following semester(s). For courses that cover both hardware and software, it can be supplemented with a programming text. For many courses it will be useful to provide manufacturer's literature for one or more microprocessors. The book is also well-suited for continuing education courses and professional development seminars.

Approach

Designing microprocessor-based systems requires an understanding of several areas. I've assumed that readers understand basic digital logic and the concepts of buses and stored-program computers. Some knowledge of programming is helpful, too, although not absolutely necessary. These topics are the heart of most introductory texts on microprocessors.

This book focuses on the more advanced topics of designing hardware for microprocessor-based systems. To allow for detailed coverage of selected areas, several topics have been excluded. Software is not covered, except in the context of programming considerations for the hardware discussed. User interface devices and data communication interfaces are covered, but physical interface devices such as analog-to-digital and digital-to-analog converters, power control, and motor control circuits are not. These topics are separate from the core of microprocessor-based design and are well covered in other texts.

A key feature of this book is its design orientation. Many texts describe the technology but fail to provide perspective and an understanding of trade-offs. This text is application-oriented rather than technology-oriented. Although the technology is described, it is always within the context of "What is this useful for and at what cost?" The reader should understand not only what the devices are, but also why there are so many alternatives and when one is more desirable than others.

Topics Covered

A variety of topics appear here in more detail than in most other books. These include:

Chapters 2 and 3: the full range of microprocessor architectures, from low-end single-chip microcomputers to high-performance 32-bit microprocessors.

Chapter 4: all principal memory types, including not just static RAM and EPROM, but also EEPROMs, nonvolatile RAMs, and dynamic RAMs, with complete interfacing details and selection guidelines.

Chapter 5: peripheral chips to assist the microprocessor, including DMA controllers, programmable counter/timers, watchdog timers, and clock/calendar circuits.

Chapter 6: user interface approaches, including dedicated function keys, soft keys, general-purpose keyboards, and menus; user interface devices, including mice, touch screens, and speech input and output.

Chapter 7: flat-panel display types and interfacing, including liquid crystal, vacuum fluorescent, gas discharge, and electroluminescent displays; CRT displays, including CRT controller design and techniques for monochrome and color graphics.

Chapter 8: serial interfaces, including the widely-used RS-232 standard and more advanced standards such as RS-422, RS-423, and RS-485.

Chapter 9: mass storage devices, including floppy disks, hard disks, cartridge tape drives, and bubble memory; both the technology of the storage devices and their interfacing requirements are described.

Chapter 10: techniques for using more than one microprocessor in a system to improve performance and flexibility.

Each chapter has been designed to be as independent of the others as possible. Most courses will cover at least the first five chapters; material can then be selected from the last five chapters based on the time available and the course orientation.

Learning Aids

This book contains several learning aids to help readers reach design-level competence. These include the following:

An overview of each problem and the merits of possible approaches encourage problem-solving skills.

Fundamental principles and system requirements, supplemented with specific implementation examples, enable readers to develop a basis for understanding new devices and approaches as they are introduced on the market.

Real-world examples support sections on how to select from available components and design approaches.

A complete design example illustrates the application of the concepts presented and provides an example of the trade-offs and detailed design considerations required in any design.

Exercises at the end of each chapter reinforce the concepts and allow readers to test their understanding.

A selected bibliography at the end of each chapter directs readers to sources of more detailed information on particular topics. References to the manufacturer's literature and other information sources enable readers to obtain the most up-to-date information.

In addition to a subject index, a part number index allows readers to easily find all information related to a particular device.

The companion newsletter *Microprocessor Report* provides an ongoing technology update. Be sure to send in the form at the back of the book for a *free* trial subscription.

Acknowledgments

First and foremost, many thanks are due to my wife Irene Stratton, who not only put up with several years of lost evenings and weekends, but also proofread the entire manuscript and handled the permissions correspondence for the many figures from other sources, as well as numerous other tasks. I couldn't have done it without her.

Many people have read all or part of the manuscript in its various versions, and I am grateful to them all for their comments and suggestions. They include Ken Cuyle, Bob Weiman, John Nichols, Rob Walker, John Wakerly of Stanford University, Walter Higgins of Arizona State University, and Charles H. House of Hewlett-Packard. Ken L. Rothmuller of Hewlett-Packard and William M. Parrott of Anchor Automation, Inc. provided particularly thoughtful reviews. David Schwartz provided technical assistance on a variety of topics and originally created some of the figures for use in a seminar we taught together. The students in my evening class used the manuscript for course notes, and found the last few errors (I hope); Walter Miller was especially helpful in this regard. Any remaining errors are, of course, my fault alone, and I would greatly appreciate being notified of any that you find.

I would also like to thank Steve Bakkee and John Martindale of Omation, Inc., for creating the Schema schematic-capture software that I used to produce the design example schematics.

The entire staff at Mayfield has been consistently friendly, competent, and helpful. Jan Beatty has been especially helpful in recruiting excellent reviewers and in shepherding the book out of the development mode and into production. Alice Goehring, who copyedited the manuscript, brought a level of consistency that was much appreciated; any remaining inconsistencies are most likely due to my stubbornness. Jan de Prosse, the production editor, accepted my last-minute changes without complaint. Cynthia Bassett managed the art production process, one of the most challenging production tasks, and was always most supportive. The illustrations themselves (except those credited to other sources) were drawn by George Samuelson, whose skill and care is apparent to all.

Michael Slater
Palo Alto, California

MICROPROCESSOR-BASED DESIGN

INTRODUCTION

1.1 HISTORICAL PERSPECTIVE

The development of the microprocessor has revolutionized every major area of electronics. The vast majority of electronic instruments now incorporate at least one microprocessor. Consumer electronics have become increasingly microprocessor-based, and *microprocessor* has become an advertising buzzword. The microprocessor made personal computers economically practical. Its impact has been comparable to that of the vacuum tube, the transistor, or the integrated circuit. Yet the microprocessor is a relatively recent invention, having been introduced commercially in 1971.

The microprocessor resulted from a merging of integrated-circuit technology and computer architecture. The first commercial integrated circuit (IC), a flip-flop, was introduced in 1961. With only a few transistors per IC, general-purpose building blocks such as flip-flops and logic gates were easy to define. In the following years, the number of transistors that could be integrated on a single IC increased rapidly. Integrated circuits are commonly divided into classes, based on the number of transistors per chip:

Small-scale integration (SSI): up to 100

Medium-scale integration (MSI): 100 to 1000

Large-scale integration (LSI): 1000 to 10,000

Very large scale integration (VLSI): 10,000 or more

These definitions are not universally agreed upon. The number quoted for the complexity of an IC is often the number of gates (or equivalent), which is of course smaller than the number of transistors. *Small-scale integration (SSI)* is often defined as less than 10 to 12 gates. Typical examples of SSI devices are gates and flip-flops. *Medium-scale integration (MSI)* made possible more complex building blocks, such as counters, shift registers, multiplexers, and registers. Examples of *large-scale integration (LSI)* devices are the 8080, Z80, and 6800 8-bit microprocessors. Examples of *very large scale integration (VLSI)* are 32-bit microprocessors such as the 68020 and 80386.

With the development of LSI, custom ICs became widely used. Custom ICs are specifically designed for a particular application and thus can make efficient use of large numbers of transistors fabricated on a single chip. However, the cost of developing such ICs is high, limiting their use to high-volume applications. Before the introduction of the microprocessor, it was not clear what standard IC (other than a memory chip) could use hundreds of gates and still be sufficiently general-purpose to have a large market.

A breakthrough came when Intel designed a custom chip set for a customer who was building calculators. The original design was very complex, and it occurred to Intel's designers that minicomputers had all the necessary capabilities and were architecturally much simpler. The chip set was thus designed as a stored-program computer, which could be customized with a program to perform the desired functions. When the customer declined to purchase the chip set because it was too slow, Intel introduced it as the 4004 family and the microprocessor was born.

Had Intel's designers been looking for a way to reduce the number of components required to build a minicomputer, the microprocessor would have been the logical conclusion. However, even though microprocessors perform the functions of a computer's *central processing unit (CPU)*, they were not originally intended as computer building blocks. They were designed to replace *hard-wired* digital logic, in which the interconnections determine the function. Microprocessor-based *programmed logic* uses standardized functional blocks and interconnections; the software (program) determines the functions. While early microprocessors were too primitive and slow to be useful as general-purpose computers, today they are widely used both in general-purpose computers and in *dedicated* control applications.

The ability to customize the functions performed by a microprocessor by modifying only the program stored in a memory device was the key to its success. It met the need for a complex building-block IC that could be used in a wide variety of applications. In the years since its introduction, increasingly complex microprocessors have been introduced and have become the standard method for implementing control and computational functions.

Microprocessors need memory and peripheral chips, and the progress in these areas has been equally important. The software-based architecture of microprocessor systems would not be practical without large, dense, low-cost memory ICs. Peripheral circuits, which interface the microprocessor to mass-storage and input/output (I/O) devices, are equally important. Many memory and peripheral-interface ICs rival their companion microprocessors in complexity.

1.2 FUNDAMENTALS REVIEW

In this text, we assume that the reader has some knowledge of digital logic and microprocessor fundamentals. For those lacking this background, one of the introductory texts listed in the Selected Bibliography at the end of this chapter should be studied. This section is intended to provide both a brief review of these fundamentals and a common vocabulary and basis of understanding for the remainder of the text. It may be skimmed by more experienced readers.

Microprocessor-based hardware is by its very nature closely tied to the programs that guide the system's operation. These programs are commonly called *software,* or, if stored in a nonvolatile semiconductor memory, *firmware.* The purpose of much of the hardware is simply to execute the software. Thus, it is necessary for the reader to have a basic understanding of microprocessor software. Knowledge of at least one microprocessor's assembly language is desirable. This review section does not provide this background; the texts listed in the Selected Bibliography at the end of this chapter cover the area well.

1.2.1 Basic Digital Logic Concepts

Gates and De Morgan's Equivalents

The basic digital logic structure is the *gate.* All digital logic systems, including microprocessors, are composed of gates. While the major functions in a microprocessor system are performed by the LSI and VLSI microprocessors, peripherals, and memory devices, SSI and MSI "glue" devices (such as gates, flip-flops, and decoders) serve to connect the more complex devices together and to translate control signals from one device to match those required by another.

The basic AND, OR, NOT, and exclusive-OR (XOR) gates are shown in Fig. 1.1, along with the *truth tables* that define their operation. A truth table shows the state of the output for each possible combination of inputs. The figure also shows the *Boolean algebra* equations describing each function. In Boolean algebra, the plus sign (+) is used to indicate the OR function, and the multiplication dot (·) is used to indicate the AND function. XOR is indicated by a circled plus sign ($\oplus$). A bar over a signal name indicates inversion.

A NOT gate has only one input and is usually called an *inverter.* An inverter can be combined with an AND or OR gate to form a NAND or NOR gate, as shown in Fig. 1.2. The "bubble" on a gate's input or output indicates an *active-low* signal. Active-low means that the active ("true") state is logic 0, or the lower voltage level. The function of a gate depends on the input polarity. For example, consider the NAND gate. The function of this gate, which has active-high inputs and an active-low output, can be described as "if both inputs are high, then the output is low." Alternatively, it can be described as "if either input is low, then the output is high"; this describes an OR gate with active-low inputs and an active-high output. Thus, the same physical gate can be viewed as two different logical devices, as shown in the figure. These are formally known as *De Morgan's equivalents.*

ɟgure **1.1.**   Basic
ogic gates: *(a)* AND, *(b)*
OR, *(c)* NOT (inverter),
and *(d)* XOR (EXCLUSIVE-
OR).

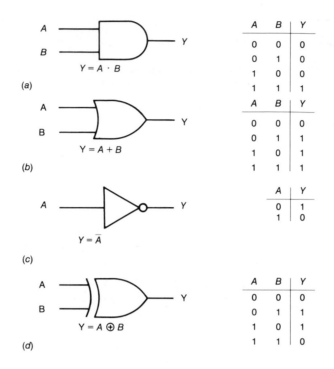

A	B	Y
0	0	0
0	1	0
1	0	0
1	1	1

A	B	Y
0	0	0
0	1	1
1	0	1
1	1	1

A	Y
0	1
1	0

A	B	Y
0	0	0
0	1	1
1	0	1
1	1	0

Figure 1.2.   *(a)* NAND
and *(b)* NOR gates and
their De Morgan's
equivalents.

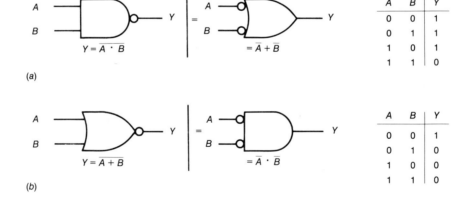

A	B	Y
0	0	1
0	1	1
1	0	1
1	1	0

A	B	Y
0	0	1
0	1	0
1	0	0
1	1	0

Both symbols represent the same physical circuit, and while IC gates are generally named by their positive-logic function (the function with active-high inputs), gates are best drawn according to their function in the circuit, rather than their databook symbol. For example, when a NAND gate is used to OR together two active-low signals, it should be drawn as an OR gate with active-low inputs. This makes logic diagrams easier to read, since the functions are apparent. Microprocessor systems frequently use active-low control signals, so the active-low versions of gates are often used.

To make it clear whether a signal is active-low or active-high, active-low signal

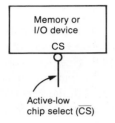

Figure 1.3. "Bubble" indicating active-low input on LSI device.

names are written with a bar over them. Because the bar is not easily typed or produced by a word processor or computer-aided design system, other symbols are sometimes used, such as a slash (/) or asterisk (∗) before or after active-low signal names, or an "H" or "+" (active-high) or "L" or "−" (active-low) at the beginning or end of each signal name.

The "bubble" similarly represents active-low inputs and outputs on LSI devices. Most microprocessors generate active-low control signals, and most memory and peripheral ICs have active-low enable inputs, often called $\overline{\text{CHIP SELECT}}$ ($\overline{\text{CS}}$), as shown in Fig. 1.3.

Three-State and Open-Collector Buffers

The *three-state buffer* is a special type of buffer that is particularly important in microprocessor-based systems. (*Tri-state,* a trademark of National Semiconductor, has the same meaning as three-state.) Three-state buffers (also called *three-state drivers*) have a third output state in addition to high and low: off, or high-impedance (also called *tristated,* or *floating*). This state is implemented by disabling both the pull-up and pull-down transistors in a device's output stage. This effectively disconnects the driver from the output pin and allows the output pins of numerous drivers to be connected together, as long as only one is enabled at a time.

Figure 1.4 shows the symbol and truth table for a three-state buffer. Often, three-state buffers are used in groups (typically of eight) with a common enable line and are drawn as shown in Fig. 1.5. The 74LS244 is an example of such a chip and is widely used in microprocessor systems. Three-state drivers are also included internally in many devices, including microprocessors, memory ICs, and peripheral ICs.

Open-collector drivers have only two states: low and off. A resistor from the output to the power supply pulls the output high when the driver is off. Open-collector drivers are most commonly used in microprocessor systems for interrupt, bus request, and ready/wait signals. *Open-drain* drivers are the same as open-collector drivers, but implemented in MOS rather than bipolar technology.

Figure 1.4. Three-state driver symbol and truth table.

$\overline{\text{ENABLE}}$	IN	OUT
0	0	0
0	1	1
1	0	3-state
1	1	3-state

High-impedance

Figure 1.5. Symbol for multiple three-state drivers with common enable.

Flip-Flops and Registers

Gates have no memory; their output is a function only of the current state of the inputs. The basic memory element is the *flip-flop,* as shown in Fig. 1.6. The flip-flop shown is a *D-type;* the 74LS74 is a common IC containing two flip-flops of this type. The symbol at the clock input that looks like a sideways "V" indicates that this input is *edge-triggered.* When this clock signal changes from low to high, the level at the data (D) input is stored in the flip-flop. This stored state appears on the Q output, as shown in Fig. 1.7. As the arrows in the figure indicate, the change in the output is initiated by the low-to-high clock transition and depends on the state of the D input. Note that there is some delay from the clock edge to when the output changes; this is the *propagation delay time.* The output will not change again until the next rising clock edge, regardless of any change in the D input. Thus, the flip-flop can store the state of the input indefinitely.

Some flip-flops have additional inputs and outputs. The $\overline{Q}$ output is simply the complement of the Q output. The $\overline{PRESET}$ and $\overline{CLEAR}$ inputs allow the state of the flip-flop to be set to 1 or cleared to 0 independently of the clock and are typically

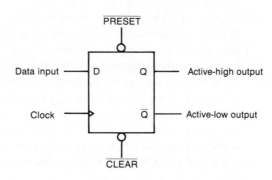

Figure 1.6. D-type flip-flop.

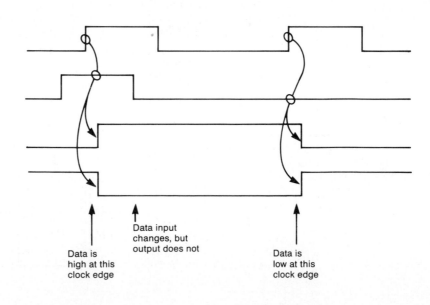

Figure 1.7. D-type flip-flop timing diagram.

Figure 1.8. Multiple flip-flops with common clock and clear.

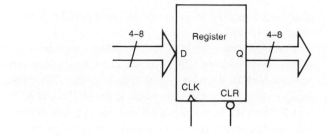

Figure 1.9. Principal process technologies.

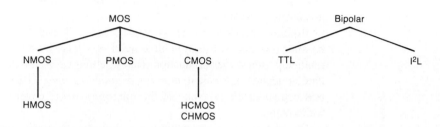

active-low. There are also other types of flip-flops with different inputs instead of the D inputs; the most common is the *J-K flip-flop,* such as the 74LS112. The additional input makes J-K flip-flops more flexible for logic (rather than data storage) applications.

Flip-flops are often used in groups to store more than 1 bit of data. A group of flip-flops with a common clock and often a common clear input is called a *register.* The symbol is shown in Fig. 1.8. The 74LS273 is an example of an 8-bit register. (The terms "register" and "latch" are sometimes used interchangeably, although a true latch is different. In a latch, such as a 74LS373, the clock input is replaced by an enable input, which is not edge-triggered; see Sec. 3.4.) Registers and latches are available with standard or three-state outputs.

Various terms are used to describe the transitions of a signal. The low-to-high transition is called the *rising,* or *positive,* edge, while the high-to-low transition is called the *falling,* or *negative,* edge. The terms *leading* and *trailing* edge are also used, but they can be ambiguous. The leading edge is the edge that begins a pulse, and the trailing edge ends the pulse. Depending on whether the pulse is low-going or high-going, the leading edge may be either the rising or falling edge.

1.2.2 Process Technologies

Figure 1.9 shows the relationships among the principal process technologies used for microprocessors and related components. There are two broad process types: *metal-oxide semiconductors (MOS)* and *bipolar* semiconductors. There are several different MOS technologies. *P-channel MOS (PMOS),* the first LSI technology, is relatively slow. It is now used only for a few large memories and low-end microcomputers for which speed is not critical. *N-channel MOS (NMOS),* the dominant technology for many years, is used for many of the most popular parts, from the 8048 and Z80 to the 8086 and 68000.

Complementary MOS (CMOS), which uses both p-channel and n-channel transistors, is overtaking NMOS as the mainstream technology. CMOS versions of most popular NMOS microprocessors (such as the Z80, 8086, and 68000) are available. Many newer microprocessors (such as the 80386 and NEC's V-series) were designed in CMOS from the beginning. CMOS is best known for its very low power consumption. The power consumption of a CMOS device is a function of the clock rate, however, and at high speeds the difference between CMOS and NMOS is not as great. CMOS devices are capable of wider output voltage swings, resulting in larger noise margins and greater noise immunity.

Bipolar technology is used primarily for small- and medium-scale logic ICs and for bit-slice processors. It is difficult to build very large bipolar chips, partially because the relatively high power dissipation makes getting rid of the heat troublesome. A type of bipolar technology called *integrated injection logic (I^2L)* is used for some peripheral controller chips. None of the microprocessors covered in this text uses bipolar technology.

For each of the major technologies, there are many variants, often proprietary to one vendor. Examples include National's P^2CMOS and Intel's HMOS (high-performance NMOS) and CHMOS (high-performance CMOS). Processes are continually improved, and a number is often added after the name to signify the version (such as HMOS III). New versions of older parts are often designed using the newest process and smaller dimensions; the user may be unaware of the change. Specifications or prices may improve, and the vendor's profit margin may increase.

In most cases, different speed versions of a memory, microprocessor, or peripheral chip are simply "sorts" from the production runs. Wide performance variations are common both within each production run and in successive production runs. The manufacturer tests the parts, and those that happen to perform better are so marked and sold at a premium. Sometimes faster versions are the result of a redesign or a *shrink,* in which the dimensions (transistor sizes and width of interconnect lines) are reduced. In addition, as the manufacturer gains experience with the process and the device, performance is often improved.

The process technology used is important to the system designer because of its impact on power consumption, speed, noise immunity, drive capability, and cost. To achieve very low power consumption, it is necessary to use CMOS throughout the system, not only for the microprocessor and memory but also for all peripheral chips and logic "glue" chips.

1.2.3   Logic Families

SSI and MSI logic ICs, such as gates, flip-flops, and registers, are available in several logic families. The most common devices are the 74xxx series. (The 54xxx series is equivalent, but is specified for operation over the military temperature range.) The last two, three, or sometimes four digits specify the function of the device. For example, 00 specifies a quad NAND gate, 02 a quad NOR gate, and 244 an octal three-state buffer. The original transistor-transistor logic (TTL) family included no other characters in the device number; a quad NAND gate in standard TTL is a 7400. Standard TTL logic has been obsoleted in new designs by several newer families, which offer lower power consumption and/or higher speed operation. The major families are as follows:

74xxx   The original TTL family. Now obsolete.

74Lxxx   Low-power version of standard TTL. Very slow and now obsolete.

74LSxxx   Low-power Schottky TTL. Lower power and higher speed than standard TTL. Widely used in microprocessor systems.

74Sxxx   Schottky TTL. High speed and high power consumption. Now obsoleted by newer families.

74ALSxxx   Advanced low-power Schottky TTL. An improved version of LS TTL, providing faster speed, lower power, and better-defined specifications.

74ASxxx   Advanced Schottky TTL. A replacement for Schottky TTL, with higher speeds and lower power.

74Fxxx   Fairchild Advanced Schottky TTL. A competitor of AS.

There are also several families of CMOS logic that are pin-compatible with the TTL families and use the same type number designations. CMOS logic has the advantage of very low power consumption. Unlike TTL, however, the power consumption of CMOS logic increases linearly with switching frequency. At high frequencies (above several megahertz), CMOS logic can consume as much power as ALS TTL. However, many devices in a typical system operate at much lower frequencies, and for these devices the use of CMOS logic significantly decreases power consumption.

There are several major families of CMOS logic, as follows:

4xxx   The original CMOS logic family, now largely obsoleted in micro-processor-based systems by newer families.

74Cxxx   CMOS equivalents of standard TTL devices, but considerably slower. Obsoleted by newer families.

74HCxxx   High-speed CMOS logic. Speeds comparable to LS TTL.

74HCTxxx   High-speed CMOS logic with TTL-compatible input thresholds. Widely used as a low-power LS TTL replacement.

74ACxxx   Advanced CMOS logic, with higher speeds than HC. This nomenclature is used for several families, including Fairchild's FACT family and the ACL family from TI, Signetics, and Phillips.

74ACTxxx   Same as 74AC, with TTL-compatible thresholds.

The need for CMOS devices with TTL-compatible thresholds is explained in Sec. 1.2.4.

In this text, we have used 74LS designations in most places for brevity. 74ALS or 74HCT devices can generally be substituted. When higher speed (shorter propagation delay) is needed, 74AS, 74F, or 74ACT can be used. Choosing among these families requires comparison of the power consumption, speed, output drive capability, input loading, and pricing for the specific device of interest.

Figure 1.10. TTL-compatible logic levels.

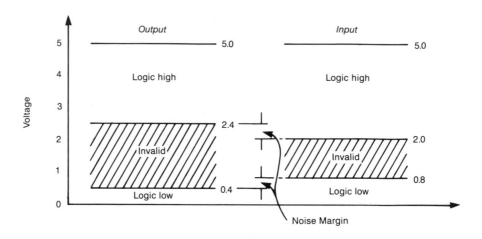

1.2.4   Logic Levels

Because we must continually deal with a mix of active-low and active-high signals, we will generally use the terms *asserted* (or true) and *negated* (or false) rather than high and low. An active-high signal is asserted when it is high and negated when it is low. An active-low signal, on the other hand, is asserted when it is low and negated when it is high.

For most of this text, we deal with high and low logic levels (or asserted and negated signals) rather than actual voltage levels. Figure 1.10 shows the standard TTL levels. A TTL output low is 0.4 V or lower, and a high is 2.4 V or higher. A TTL input will accept any voltage up to 0.8 V as a low level and any voltage over 2.0 V as a high level. Thus, up to 400 mV of noise can be tolerated without error; this is one of the fundamental advantages of digital systems. Most devices used in microprocessor systems are compatible with these standard TTL levels, which we can thus refer to simply as high and low, or asserted and negated, or 1 and 0.

The designer must keep in mind that these are real electrical signals, however, and not pure ones and zeros traveling through the wires. Each logic output has a maximum load that it can drive, and exceeding this may cause invalid levels. In addition, the frequency of the signals in microprocessor systems is commonly in the 1- to 20-MHz range. Since these are sharp-edged pulse signals, their high-frequency components extend far beyond the fundamental frequency. Propagation characteristics and signal distortion can thus become important and are discussed in Chap. 3.

CMOS logic, unlike TTL, has an input threshold of one-half the supply voltage (2.5 V for a system with a standard 5-V supply). CMOS outputs switch from very near ground for a logic low to very near the positive supply for a logic high. This is a result of the symmetrical internal structure of CMOS devices and provides greater noise immunity than TTL. However, it also means that the standard TTL logic high output level of 2.4-V minimum will not be seen as a logic high by a CMOS input. This can be remedied by adding a pull-up resistor from the CMOS input to the positive supply, which raises the logic high level above the CMOS input threshold. Alternatively, the 74HCT and 74ACT CMOS logic families provide TTL-compatible input thresholds, eliminating the need for the pull-up resistors. Their outputs provide CMOS levels, so they can drive standard CMOS inputs without requiring pull-up resistors.

1.2.5 Number Systems

Digital systems operate on strings of high and low logic levels, or ones and zeros. These are naturally represented as binary numbers. For notational convenience, we will refer to binary numbers by their *hexadecimal (hex),* or base-16, representation.

Hexadecimal is useful because it allows four binary digits *(bits)* to be represented with one character. If there are more than four bits to be represented, each group of four can be treated independently. Since four binary digits have sixteen possible combinations, the numerals 0 through 9 are not sufficient, and the six letters A through F are called into service. The hexadecimal representation for each possible 4-bit binary pattern is shown in Table 1.1.

If you are not yet used to counting 0, 1, 2, . . . , 8, 9, A, B, C, D, E, F, 10, 11, . . . , then you will be soon. Many programming languages and other texts use an "H" suffix or a "$" prefix to indicate that a number is hexadecimal. In this text, the number base is assumed to be hexadecimal when discussing binary numbers or bit patterns, and no suffix or prefix is used. When necessary for clarity, hexadecimal numbers are identified by the word *hex* following the number.

Memory sizes are generally powers of 2, since the number of addressable memory locations is 2 to the power of the number of address bits. There are two abbreviations frequently used for large binary values:

$$1K = 2^{10} = 1024 \text{ decimal} = 400 \text{ hex}$$

$$1M = 2^{20} = 1,048,576 \text{ decimal} = 100000 \text{ hex}$$

Thus, a device with 10 address lines has 1024, or 1K, addressable locations.

Unfortunately, the symbols K and M are used in other engineering, scientific, and financial contexts to mean 1000 and 1,000,000. A 65,536-bit memory has sometimes been called a 65K device, meaning "approximately" 65,000 bits. In the context of digital systems, however, K is defined as *exactly* 1024. A 65,536-bit memory thus has

Table 1.1   Binary and Hexadecimal Equivalents

Binary	Hex	Binary	Hex
0000	0	1000	8
0001	1	1001	9
0010	2	1010	A
0011	3	1011	B
0100	4	1100	C
0101	5	1101	D
0110	6	1110	E
0111	7	1111	F

12

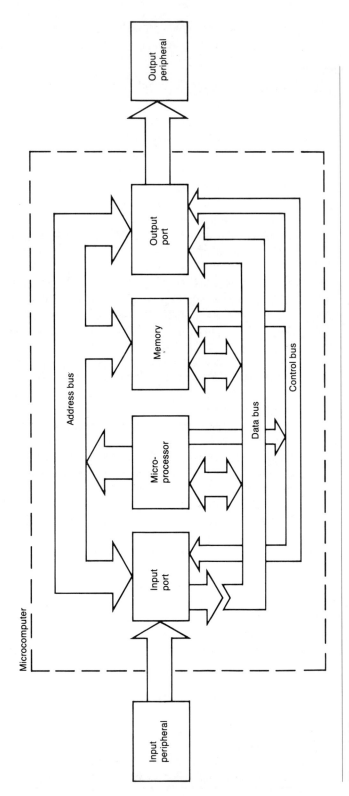

Figure 1.11. Basic microprocessor system block diagram.

exactly 64K bits. In this text, a lowercase k is used for the traditional "kilo" (1000) and an uppercase K for 1024.

1.2.6 Microprocessor System Architecture

All microprocessor systems include a microprocessor, memory, and I/O devices interconnected by address, data, and control buses, as shown in Fig. 1.11. A microprocessor cannot do anything by itself; it must be connected to memory and I/O devices. A complete, functional system is called a *microcomputer*. A *single-chip microcomputer* is a complete system on a single IC.

The basic operation of all microprocessor systems is the same, regardless of the type of microprocessor or the task being performed. The microprocessor reads an instruction from the memory, executes that instruction, and then reads the next instruction. This sequence repeats indefinitely as long as the system is running. Reading an instruction from memory is called the instruction *fetch,* and the sequence described above is called the *fetch-execute* sequence. (Some microprocessors use *prefetch*; they fetch a few instructions ahead of the instruction to be executed.)

Figure 1.12 illustrates the signals that connect to a typical microprocessor. This example shows an 8-bit microprocessor, which has eight wires in the data bus. The data bus signals are bidirectional, since data can flow into or out of the microprocessor. The address signals are outputs only, since the microprocessor generates the address for all operations. Most 8-bit microprocessors have 16-bit address buses, which allows them to address 64K (2^{16}) memory locations. Input and output ports are addressed similarly; subtle differences in I/O addressing techniques are described in Secs. 5.2.1 and 5.2.5.

The two fundamental control signals are $\overline{\text{READ}}$ and $\overline{\text{WRITE}}$, often called the *read strobe* and *write strobe*. The read strobe is asserted by the microprocessor to read data from a memory location or input port. The write strobe is asserted to write data to a memory location or output port. There are many variations of these signals, as described in Chap. 3, but the basic function is always the same. Additional control signals, including RESET, CLOCK, READY/$\overline{\text{WAIT}}$, BUS REQUEST, BUS ACKNOWLEDGE, and various types of interrupts are described briefly in Sec. 1.2.7, and in detail in Chap. 3.

Many types of memory devices are used in microprocessor systems. *Main memory* is directly addressed by the microprocessor and is required in all microprocessor systems. Chap. 4 describes types of main memory in detail. *Mass-storage* devices, such as disk drives, are not directly addressable but have large storage capacities at a relatively low cost. Mass-storage devices are covered in Chap. 9.

The two principal types of main memory are *read-only memory (ROM)* and *read/write memory (RAM)*. ROMs are programmed with the desired data pattern before being installed in the application system. ROMs that are programmed by the IC manufacturer as part of the manufacturing process are called *mask-programmed*. The microprocessor cannot write data to a ROM; it is used only for permanent programs and unchanging data. *EPROMs* are erasable and programmable read-only memories that can be erased with ultraviolet light and programmed by the user with an instrument called an *EPROM programmer*.

With a read/write memory (RAM), the microprocessor can write data into the memory and read it back later. RAM is *volatile,* however: the contents are retained only as

Figure 1.12. Basic microprocessor signals.

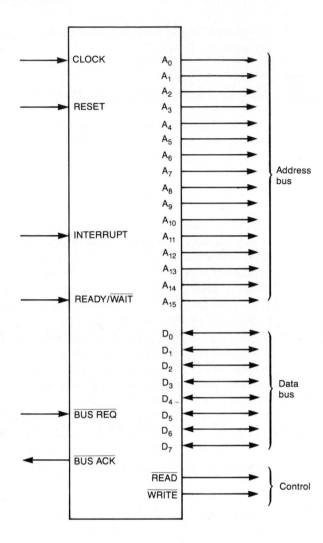

long as power is present. (Note that RAM seems like a strange acronym for read/write memory. RAM actually stands for random-access memory, but the term is misleading because ROMs are also random-access memories. However, RAM is widely used to designate read/write random access memory.)

The buses link the microprocessor to the rest of the system. The microprocessor selects a particular device via the address bus and then reads or writes data via the data bus. The data bus is a common, bidirectional bus used for all data transfers. Each *bus cycle* consists of a transfer of a word of data between the microprocessor and a memory or I/O device.

Each bus cycle begins when the microprocessor outputs an address to select one memory location or I/O port, as shown in Fig. 1.13. In this timing diagram, the address and data buses are each represented by a pair of lines. These indicate that the information on the bus is stable; when the lines on the timing diagram cross, it indi-

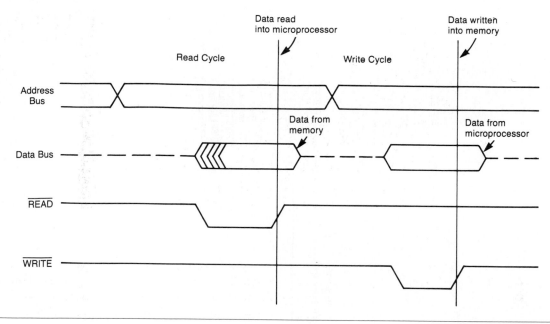

Figure 1.13. Basic bus timing.

cates that the data has changed. A single dashed line is used to show when the data bus is not being driven by any device and is therefore floating.

The address is decoded by an *address decoder,* as shown in Fig. 1.14, which generates an address select signal for each device in the system. Every I/O port and memory location has a unique address, and the address decoder ensures that only one device is selected at a time.

Because all devices share the same data bus, when a device's address is not present on the address bus (along with the proper control signals), the device must be electrically removed from the data bus. This is accomplished with three-state drivers. Three-state drivers are included in all devices intended to directly drive the data bus, such as microprocessors, memories, and input ports. These drivers are enabled by the device's chip select input. This signal is sometimes called *OUTPUT ENABLE (OE)* if its only function is to control the output drivers. When a device's output drivers are enabled, it is said to be *driving* the bus.

If two devices attempt to drive the data bus at the same time, a *bus conflict* occurs and neither device is likely to control the bus successfully. If a bus conflict occurs while the data on the bus must be valid, invalid data can be read from or written to memory. Even a bus conflict that occurs when data does not need to be valid can cause problems. If one driver is trying to pull a line low and another is trying to pull it high, large currents can flow through both devices. This can cause a drop in the system's power supply voltage, which can, in turn, cause memory errors and many other mysterious failures.

After the microprocessor outputs the address, it asserts either $\overline{\text{READ}}$ or $\overline{\text{WRITE}}$ to

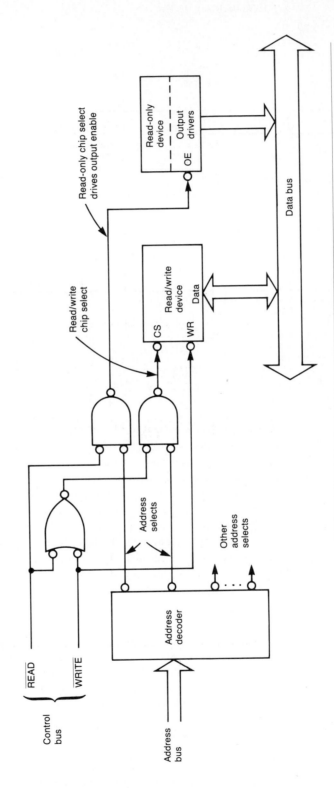

Figure 1.14. Generation of address select and chip select signals.

indicate when the addressed device should drive data on (or read data from) the data bus. For a read-only device, $\overline{\text{READ}}$ is ANDed with $\overline{\text{ADDRESS SELECT}}$ to generate the $\overline{\text{CHIP SELECT}}$ ($\overline{\text{CS}}$) signal. $\overline{\text{CS}}$ enables the device's output drivers, which thus are enabled only when the device's address is present on the address bus and the read strobe is asserted.

For read/write devices, $\overline{\text{ADDRESS SELECT}}$ is ANDed with $\overline{\text{READ OR WRITE}}$. Thus, $\overline{\text{CS}}$ is asserted whenever either operation occurs. $\overline{\text{WRITE}}$ also connects directly to the I/O or memory device. If $\overline{\text{CS}}$ is asserted and $\overline{\text{WRITE}}$ is false, the device's output drivers are enabled. However, if $\overline{\text{WRITE}}$ is also asserted, then the device reads data from the bus instead of outputting data to it.

The actual data transfer occurs as $\overline{\text{READ}}$ or $\overline{\text{WRITE}}$ is negated to allow as much time as possible for the addressed device to decode the address and prepare to perform the read or write operation. The addressed device needs time to decode the address, select the desired memory location, and drive the data onto the bus (for a read cycle) or accept data from the bus (for a write cycle).

1.2.7 System Control Signals

Most microprocessors have a number of control signals in addition to the basic read and write strobes. This section provides brief descriptions of the basic functions of these signals; more detailed descriptions are included in Chap. 3.

The CLOCK input to the microprocessor paces the operation of the system. This signal is typically generated by a crystal oscillator. Each instruction execution requires a fixed number of clock cycles as determined by the design of the microprocessor.

The RESET input starts (or restarts) the microprocessor. It causes the microprocessor to begin executing instructions from a predefined memory location. With some microprocessors, execution begins from address zero when RESET is asserted; others use a different reset address, but in some way it is always well defined.

Interrupts are input signals that force a change in the software execution sequence. When an INTERRUPT input is asserted, the software is forced to jump from whatever program it is executing to a special program called the *interrupt service routine*. Interrupts are useful because they allow the system to provide fast response to real-time events. Many microprocessors have two or more interrupt inputs and an interrupt acknowledge output.

The $\overline{\text{WAIT}}$ input allows memory and I/O devices to force the microprocessor to lengthen the bus cycle. This is necessary when the memory or I/O device is too slow to respond to the microprocessor in the time it normally allows. When $\overline{\text{WAIT}}$ is asserted, the microprocessor freezes the state of the buses for one clock cycle; this is called a *wait state*. If the $\overline{\text{WAIT}}$ input is kept asserted, additional wait states are generated. When $\overline{\text{WAIT}}$ is negated, the microprocessor continues operation. This signal is called READY on some microprocessors.

The $\overline{\text{BUS REQ}}$ (bus request) input forces the microprocessor to relinquish control of the address, data, and control buses so that another microprocessor or other device (such as a direct memory access controller, as described in Sec. 5.7) can take control. The microprocessor asserts the $\overline{\text{BUS ACK}}$ (bus acknowledge) output to indicate that it has released the buses and the requesting device can take over.

Figure 1.15. Basic
output port.

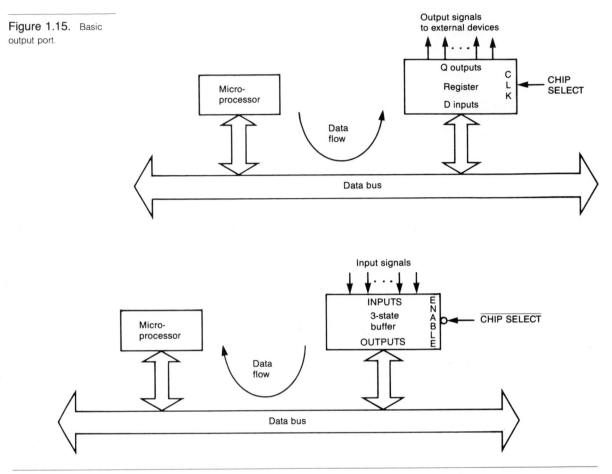

Figure 1.16. Basic input port.

1.2.8 Basic I/O Ports

Input and output ports interface the microprocessor to devices that cannot connect directly to the buses. An output port is fundamentally just a register, as shown in Fig. 1.15. When the microprocessor writes to the address assigned to the port, the port stores the data from the data bus. Thus, it provides latched outputs to external devices, which are changed whenever the microprocessor writes to the port.

An input port is fundamentally just a three-state driver, as shown in Fig. 1.16. When the microprocessor reads from the address assigned to the port, the three-state driver drives the data from the external inputs onto the data bus. The microprocessor then reads the signals from the bus.

The output-port register and input-port three-state driver may be implemented with standard TTL or CMOS devices. They may also be incorporated with additional logic on larger ICs. A simple example is a parallel I/O chip, such as Intel's 8255 (see Chap. 5). More sophisticated examples in which the I/O ports themselves are only a fraction of the chip's functions are floppy disk controllers (Chap. 9) and data communications controllers (Chap. 8).

1.3 APPLICATION EXAMPLES

Applications for microprocessors can be found in virtually any type of electronic equipment. In some products, a single-chip microcomputer incorporating memory and I/O on the same chip as the microprocessor is the only active component required. In others, the microprocessor is surrounded by semiconductor memory, mass storage, and I/O interfaces, resulting in a complex system with the microprocessor at its core.

1.3.1 Instrumentation

The digital voltmeter is an example of a traditional instrument that has been enhanced through the use of microprocessors. Traditional voltmeters, as shown in Fig. 1.17, are completely analog. The voltage input is amplified, and the resulting signal deflects the meter needle. A rotary switch allows the amplifier gain to be selected for various input signal ranges.

Digital voltmeters have gradually replaced analog meters in most applications, providing more accurate readings and easier use. A microprocessor is not needed, and many digital voltmeters do not include one. Fig. 1.18 shows the block diagram for a basic digital voltmeter (DVM). The analog input is amplified or attenuated to bring it within a reasonable range and is then converted to digital representation by an analog-to-digital (A/D) converter. The output of the converter drives the display. (Typically, digital voltmeters are also multimeters, which can measure current and resistance in addition to voltage. For simplicity, this discussion refers only to the voltmeter function.)

Figure 1.17. Analog voltmeter block diagram.

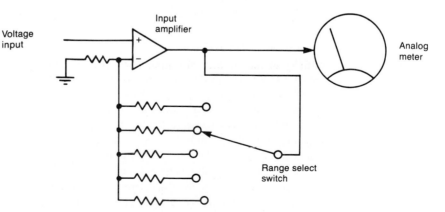

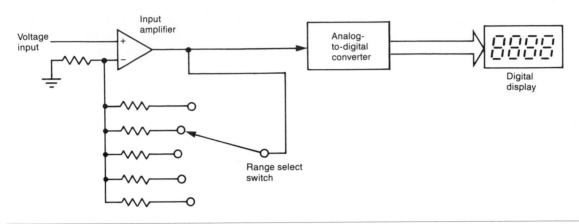

Figure 1.18.   Basic digital voltmeter block diagram.

The addition of a microprocessor allows new features to be added and results in a fundamental change in the internal design of the instrument. Figure 1.19 shows the block diagram for a microprocessor-based digital voltmeter. The A/D converter connects not to the display but to the microprocessor's buses. The microprocessor executes a program that causes it to read the data from the A/D converter and output it to the display. Thus, the data flow is determined by the software, which must instruct the hardware to read from the A/D converter and then write to the display.

The rotary switch for setting the range is replaced with momentary push buttons. To select a voltage range the user presses a button, which is sensed by the microprocessor via an input port. The microprocessor then writes data to an output port, which in turn controls the gain of the input amplifier. The push-button switches are less expensive and more reliable than the rotary switch, but this approach has more important advantages as well. The switches do not directly control the gain but provide inputs to the microprocessor system, which in turn sets the gain. This allows the software to decide what to set the gain to, based on the setting of the switches and any other data.

Now that the microprocessor has control of the gain, automatic range selection *(autoranging)* can be implemented with only some additional software. The microprocessor begins by selecting minimum gain. It then reads the A/D converter output, and if the value read is small, the gain is increased. Thus, via a procedure implemented in software (called an *algorithm*), the microprocessor can automatically select the optimum gain setting. The software can also perform additional calculations, allowing such functions as display of the reading as a percentage of a previously stored value.

Remote control is another feature made practical by microprocessor-based design. A microprocessor-based voltmeter can connect to a computer that can read the voltage and also send commands to the meter to select the range and other functions. During remote control operation, the voltmeter's control software takes its commands from (and sends data to) the remote control interface rather than the front panel.

This example illustrates the advantages typically gained from microprocessor-based design: improved user interface, more automatic measurements, remote control capability, and the ability to perform calculations on raw measurement data before it is displayed.

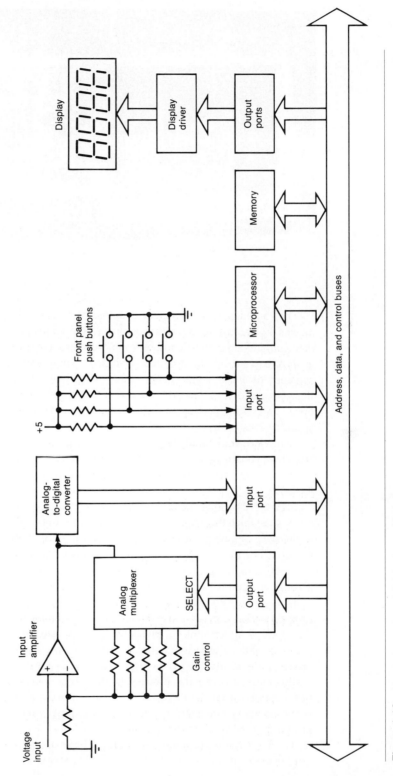

Figure 1.19. Microprocessor-based digital voltmeter block diagram.

Figure 1.20. Micro-
processor-based logic
analyzer. *(Photo courtesy
of Hewlett-Packard.)*

Figure 1.20. Micro-processor-based logic analyzer. *(Photo courtesy of Hewlett-Packard.)*

The logic analyzer is another example of an instrument that has been greatly enhanced by the use of microprocessors. Logic analyzers capture sequences of digital data and are an invaluable aid in troubleshooting complex digital systems. Early logic analyzers were not microprocessor-based. Their front panels contained dozens of switches to allow trigger patterns and other controls to be set. With the advent of microprocessors, the need for sophisticated triggering setups and data analysis developed. The switch-per-function approach is extremely cumbersome for complex trigger specifications.

A modern logic analyzer, such as the one shown in Fig. 1.20, uses a relatively simple keyboard to allow complex measurement setups to be entered. The display shows the user the choices for a particular function, eliminating the need for a switch for every function. Setup and trace information can also be stored on a floppy disk.

Figure 1.21 shows the block diagram for a logic analyzer. Because of the high frequency at which the inputs are sampled, the microprocessor cannot be directly involved in the data capture process. Special control logic is therefore used to control the data capture. The microprocessor provides trigger patterns and other setup information to the control logic via output ports. During the data capture, the control logic provides address and control signals to the high-speed data capture memory. After the memory is filled, effectively taking a "snapshot" of the data activity at the inputs, the microprocessor takes control of the capture memory. The software analyzes and manipulates the captured information for presentation to the user on the CRT display.

Thus, although the microprocessor is too slow to be involved in the data capture process, it is invaluable for the user interface. It not only allows complex setups to be easily entered but can also process the data after it is captured. For example, information captured from the data bus of a microprocessor system can be disassembled to show assembly language instructions. A remote interface can transfer the data to a printer or another computer system.

The basic hardware requirements for a logic analyzer as described above are a microprocessor, memory for program and data storage, a keyboard and display, a disk

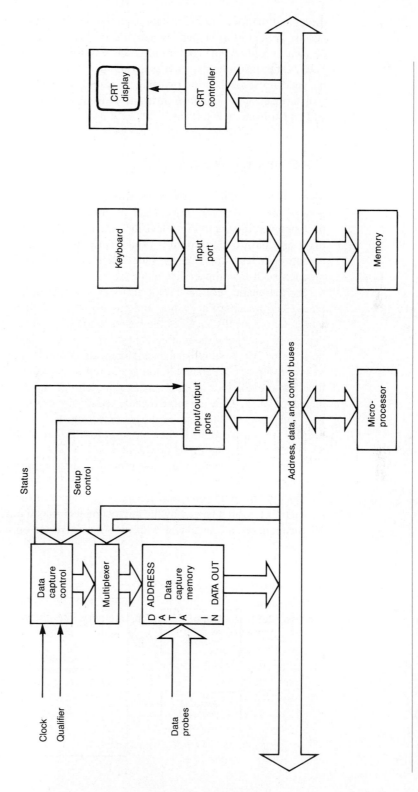

Figure 1.21. Logic analyzer block diagram.

drive, and the logic analyzer data capture logic. All these components except for the last are present in a personal computer such as an IBM PC. Thus, a logic analyzer can be built by adding data capture logic and control software to a standard personal computer. Other instruments, such as digitizing oscilloscopes, pattern generators, and signal generators, can be built by using the same approach. The personal computer is thus transformed into a universal instrument, whose characteristics are determined by the add-on hardware and software.

1.3.2   Consumer Electronics

Many audio and video products, such as televisions and stereo equipment, have incorporated microprocessors for control functions. For example, microprocessor control has improved the quality of television pictures, provided radio tuners with digital displays and push-button controls, and improved tape transport control for faster operation with less stress on the tape. Microprocessors are essential for digital audio products such as compact disc players.

The automatic setback thermostat is an example of how microprocessors can replace electromechanical designs and provide many additional features. A setback thermostat automatically changes the heater thermostat setting at preset times during the day, saving energy without affecting user comfort by decreasing the amount of time the heater is on. Units with mechanical timers are available, but they are generally limited to two different temperature settings and repeat the same cycle every day. Electronic units can provide four or more temperature settings and different time settings for each day of the week. They are more reliable and require less power. Some take advantage of the "intelligence" that can be programmed into the microprocessor to anticipate the need to turn on the heat. If the unit is set for 72°F at 6:00, it may turn on the heat at 5:30 or 5:50, depending on how cold it is.

Figure 1.22 shows the block diagram for a setback thermostat. A single-chip microcomputer, which includes a microprocessor, ROM, RAM, and I/O ports, is the central component. An A/D converter translates the output of the temperature sensor to a binary number, which is read by the microcomputer via an input port. (Some single-chip microcomputers are available with an A/D converter on-chip.) The microcomputer

Figure 1.22. Setback thermostat block diagram.

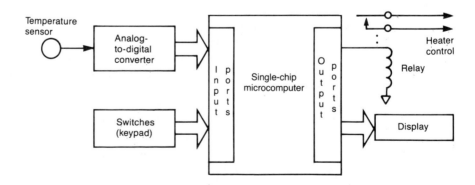

drives the display, which can show either time or temperature. The switches allow the user to program the times and temperatures. The heater is controlled by the microcomputer via a relay (or triac) driven from an output port bit.

Automobiles are gradually being filled with microprocessor-based electronics. The first use was for convenience features, such as temperature controls and trip computers. In some cars, the traditional analog dashboard displays have been replaced with electronic displays and push buttons.

Microprocessors are now taking on increased importance in automotive engine control. A microprocessor-based engine control system senses engine rpm, temperature, position of the gas pedal, and other parameters and sets the fuel flow, fuel mixture, and spark timing for optimum engine performance. The result is improved gas mileage and less pollution.

Automotive applications have provided many challenges, although not so much for the microprocessor itself. The difficulties lie in the sensors and actuators and in making a system that can handle the wide operating-temperature range and high-electrical-noise environment. In addition, reliability must be high, and automotive service personnel must be able to maintain the system.

Video games are one of the most conspicuous microprocessor applications. Although the earliest video games did not use microprocessors, they were relatively expensive and could not be reprogrammed to change the game. Microprocessor-based games greatly reduced the cost and made it possible to change the game by changing the cartridge that holds the ROM with the program.

One of the most significant products made possible by the microprocessor is the personal computer. Before microprocessors, personal computers were the province of a very few dedicated computer scientists and hobbyists. Now, the time is not far off when personal computers will be as common as televisions, and personal-computer-based word processing is nearly obsoleting typewriters. Figure 1.23 shows the block diagram for a typical personal computer. Compared to the previous applications described, the memory size is likely to be relatively large: at least 64 Kbytes, and typically 512 Kbytes or more. A single-chip microcomputer scans the keyboard and sends a serial key code to the main microprocessor whenever a key is pressed. The serial link allows the keyboard to be physically detached, connected to the main system via a cable with only a few wires. A cathode-ray-tube (CRT) controller provides the display interface. The floppy-disk controller interfaces the system to floppy disk drive(s) for mass storage. The CRT controller and floppy-disk controller are both very complex, although much of the complexity may be hidden in an LSI controller IC. The serial I/O port can connect to an external terminal, a modem, another computer, or a printer. Some printers use a parallel interface provided by a parallel I/O port. Each of these interfaces is described in detail in this text.

1.3.3 Computer Peripherals

Nearly all computer peripherals, from terminals to printers and modems, are now microprocessor-based. While earlier versions of these products did not use microprocessors, the microprocessor provides increased performance, a significant reduction in the number of parts and physical size, and new features.

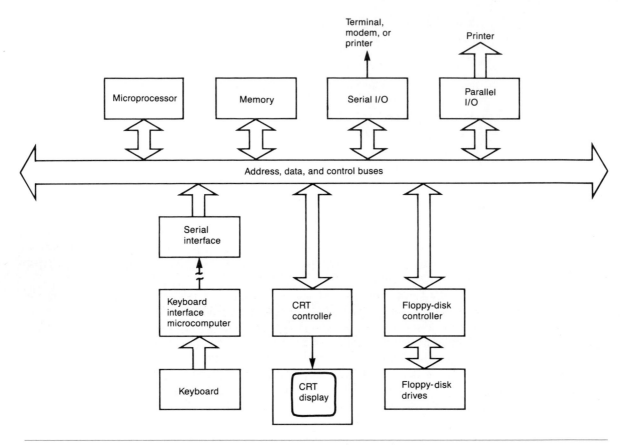

Figure 1.23. Personal computer block diagram.

In a CRT terminal, the microprocessor reads data from the keyboard, updates the CRT display, and sends and receives data on the communications link. Although such terminals were built for years without the benefit of microprocessors, their use reduces cost while adding features. Features such as editing of data before it is transmitted and software-definable function keys are easily added. In so-called intelligent terminals, programs can be executed to pre- or postprocess data, relieving the host computer of some of the computing burden.

In printers, the microprocessor takes on a variety of tasks. It accepts data from the host computer, controls the paper feed motor and the print-head positioning, and controls the printing of each dot or character. The microprocessor's memory can store the character generation tables for dot matrix printers, allowing type fonts to be changed by software command. Before microprocessors, much more circuitry was required to accomplish these tasks.

1.3.4   Medical Devices and Aids for the Handicapped

The microprocessor has had a significant impact on medical equipment. Nearly all new analytical equipment used in hospitals and medical laboratories is microprocessor-based, providing faster and more accurate measurements in addition to a range of capabilities never before available.

An example of a "consumer" medical instrument is the hand-held blood glucose meter shown in Fig. 1.24. This device allows diabetics to monitor their blood glucose level and adjust their insulin dosage according to their actual condition, thus reducing the harmful side effects of varying glucose levels on the body's organs.

The instrument works by measuring the light reflected from a chemically treated test strip onto which the user has placed a drop of blood. The chemistry of the strip causes

Figure 1.24. Hand-held blood glucose meter. *(Courtesy of Lifescan, Inc.)*

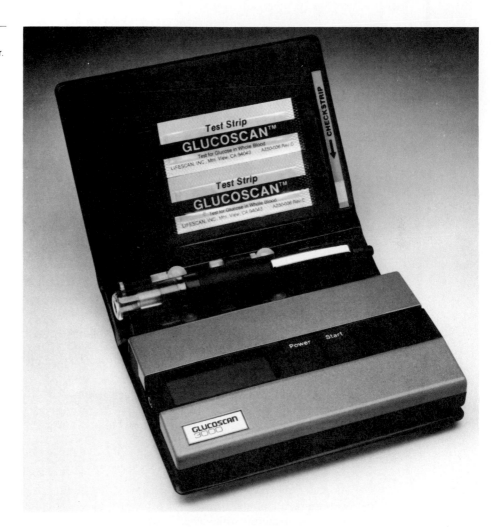

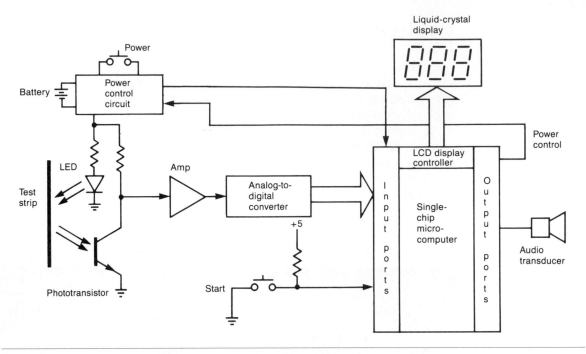

Figure 1.25. Blood glucose meter block diagram. *(Courtesy of Lifescan Inc.)*

it to darken in proportion to the glucose level in the blood. Figure 1.25 shows the block diagram of the meter. A light-emitting diode (LED) illuminates the strip, and a phototransistor detects the reflected light. The signal from the phototransistor is amplified and fed to an A/D converter. A CMOS single-chip microcomputer reads the data from the A/D converter, calculates the blood glucose level, and displays the value on a liquid crystal display (LCD). The microcomputer times the operations for the user and prompts for the necessary actions. The entire unit is ½ in. thick, fits in a shirt pocket, and operates from its internal battery for over a year.

A wide variety of microprocessor-based devices are increasing the mobility and communication abilities of many handicapped people. One example is the Optacon reading device. Using an optical scanner, it reads printed text, which is then spoken by a speech synthesizer. This device allows blind people to "read" normally printed books. Working in the opposite direction, a variety of devices have been developed to translate sound patterns into tactile or visual patterns as an aid to lipreading for deaf people.

1.3.5 Applications Summary

As is evident from the preceding examples, the microprocessor has revolutionized a wide range of product areas. Some products were more subtly improved in performance and features, while others were almost completely changed.

The list of applications goes on and on. A few of the common ones not mentioned are industrial control systems, robots, military systems, and numerous other consumer and instrumentation products.

Microprocessor applications can be divided into three broad categories, those whose applications were:

Previously implemented with digital logic or analog circuits

Previously implemented with electromechanical devices

Not previously possible or practical

The benefits of microprocessor-based products can also be generalized:

Simplified user controls

Prompting and menus to make complex operations easier

Algorithmic control of processes

Postprocessing of acquired data

1.4 WHEN NOT TO USE MICROPROCESSORS

Despite the nearly universal applicability of the microprocessor, there are some applications for which it is *not* the best solution. One class of applications is those that are completely analog in nature, such as a power supply, a radio receiver, or an amplifier. Even in these applications, a microprocessor is often useful for controlling the analog functions. If the analog information is not very high in frequency, such as in a telephone system, it can be digitized and then processed by a microprocessor.

Another area in which microprocessors are not always appropriate is in very high-volume products. Designs based on custom or semicustom ICs are often less expensive to manufacture than microprocessor-based designs, since many chips are typically replaced by a single custom IC. However, the cost of developing a custom IC is much higher than the cost of developing an equivalent product using standard ICs. To be able to amortize these costs, annual production volume typically must be in the tens of thousands of units for semicustom devices and in the hundreds of thousands for full-custom ICs. Another consideration with custom ICs is the long development time required, delaying the product's introduction. Nevertheless, consumer products such as calculators, repertory-dialing telephones, and some electronic toys are most cost-effectively implemented with custom ICs. The custom IC has the added advantage of protecting the design from being easily copied.

Various approaches to custom and semicustom IC design are used to minimize the development time and cost. Examples of such approaches include gate arrays, standard cells, and silicon compilation. [Custom or semicustom ICs are often called *application-specific integrated circuits (ASICs)*.] These techniques reduce the development cost and time and thus make custom ICs competitive in more applications. Frequently, they do not compete with microprocessors but rather supplement them by providing support logic, interface circuitry, and other special functions.

In some applications, microprocessors simply cannot provide the performance required. Bit-slice processors or high-speed discrete logic implementations must then be used, although the price paid in development difficulty and production cost is substantial. Typical examples are mainframe computer systems, radar signal processors, and high-end graphics processors.

1.5   ASPECTS OF MICROPROCESSOR-BASED DESIGN

The design of a microprocessor-based product can be divided into several phases, as shown in Fig. 1.26.

Figure 1.26. Microprocessor-based system development tasks.

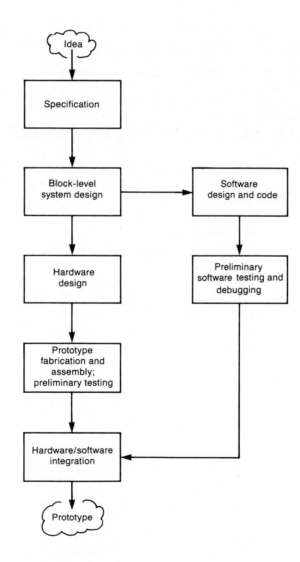

The first step in any product design is the system specification. This specification states the functions that the system must perform but does not necessarily cover how the functions are implemented. The next step is the block-level system design, which includes the selection of a microprocessor type, determination of I/O and memory requirements, and division of tasks between hardware and software. Hardware/software tradeoffs are discussed in Sec. 1.6.

Once the block-level system design is complete, the design process divides into two paths: hardware design and software design. The hardware design consists of the selection of the microprocessor, memory, and peripheral ICs and the design of the circuitry to connect them together to form the system. This is the principal topic of this text.

The software design often proceeds in parallel with the hardware design. The software may be written in the microprocessor's assembly language or in a high-level language, or in a combination of the two. Depending on the type of computer used for the software development, it may be possible to debug parts of the software without the prototype hardware.

Hardware debugging usually begins by testing the system with short test programs. After the hardware is able to execute these test programs, the hardware/software integration phase begins. The test programs are replaced by the the actual application software, and the complete system is debugged. This can be a challenging task, since there are often both hardware and software problems to be found, and it is not always clear which is which. Several types of test equipment are available for assisting in this process. The most common is the in-circuit emulator, which plugs into the microprocessor socket and allows the operation of the system to be controlled and monitored. In-circuit emulators usually include memory that can be used in place of the prototype's memory. Another useful test instrument is the logic analyzer, which captures a "trace" of the bus activity and displays the sequence of bus cycles that were executed. Most in-circuit emulators also provide this function, which is invaluable for both hardware and software debugging.

1.6 COST-EFFECTIVE DESIGN

Throughout this text, cost-effective design is emphasized. Cost-effective design means optimizing for overall cost, including design, tooling, and manufacturing costs. It also includes balancing the benefits of alternative implementations with their costs. Chap. 2 describes how these considerations affect microprocessor selection.

Hardware/software tradeoffs is an area where the designer can have a significant impact on cost-effectiveness. In the design of a microprocessor-based product, numerous choices must be made among alternative implementation approaches. Often, a decision must be made between a hardware-intensive solution and a software-intensive solution. Every situation must be examined on an individual basis, starting from the design and production costs of each approach and the performance differences.

As an example, consider the implementation of a serial data interface. This function can be implemented with an IC called a UART (see Chap. 8). The cost of the IC is typically $2 to $10. Implementation is straightforward, requiring only simple interface logic and I/O driver software. Performance is very high, with full-duplex (simultaneous communication in both directions) and high-speed communication easily attainable.

The UART function can also be implemented with software. The software UART reads the serial data on one bit of an input port, measures the bit times with software loops, and shifts the bits together to form a complete character. The transmit side is similar, using one bit of an output port. In many applications the I/O port bits and ROM space required are "leftovers," so there is no incremental hardware cost to add the function.

However, the software UART is limited in performance. It can typically handle only slow data rates and cannot transmit and receive simultaneously. The microprocessor is kept busy performing the serial I/O operation and has little time available for other tasks. In addition, while the hardware cost may be low, the software development cost is significantly increased.

As this example illustrates, hardware/software tradeoffs are complex, and many factors must be taken into consideration. Hardware-intensive approaches inevitably have more hardware and therefore a higher production cost. Performance is higher, and software development is reduced. Software-intensive approaches, on the other hand, require more software development and are slower. In return, flexibility may be enhanced and production cost is reduced.

Performance is usually better with hardware implementations for a variety of reasons. The microprocessor is a general-purpose device, and some speed is sacrificed to generality. Microprocessors act sequentially, performing one action on one word at a time. They must continually fetch instructions in order to know what to do. Logic circuits, on the other hand, can be configured to provide any number of data paths of any width and to provide parallel paths and additional logic for simultaneous operations. In addition, most logic functions occur in tens of nanoseconds. Microprocessor instruction execution times, on the other hand, range from several hundred nanoseconds to tens of microseconds, and many instructions may need to be executed sequentially to perform the desired function.

In evaluating hardware/software tradeoffs, the ability of a software solution to provide the required performance should be examined first. If the software solution lacks the performance required, then a hardware approach is mandatory. If the software's performance is adequate, then a careful cost tradeoff must be made. On the software side is lower production cost, while on the hardware side is (possibly) decreased development cost. This tradeoff depends on anticipated production volumes and other economic factors and is discussed further in Sec. 2.7.11. In low-volume applications, the development cost dominates and hardware implementations are often preferred, while high-volume applications justify higher development costs.

Another consideration for cost-effective design is the use of readily available parts. The most conservative approach is to use only *second-sourced* parts that are available from at least two independent vendors. Often, the newest devices are *sole-sourced* (available from only a single manufacturer). If the manufacturer later stops making the part (or never reaches full production), an expensive redesign could be needed. In addition, having multiple sources helps drive down prices and increase availability. However, when a product is pushing performance limits and therefore needs the very latest devices, it is often necessary to use sole-sourced parts.

1.7 CHIPS, BOARDS, AND BOXES

In designing any system, the designer must decide which functions to develop from basic components and which to purchase as subassemblies from another company. The most detailed level at which most microprocessor-based system designers work is the IC, or component level. Systems using custom or semicustom ICs have an additional level of detail: the inside of the ICs.

Microprocessor-based systems can also be assembled from standard printed circuit boards, such as a CPU board, a memory board, and an interface board. These boards are connected via a system bus, as described in Chap. 3. Building systems with board-level components greatly decreases the design effort (as compared to a component-level design) but generally increases the material cost of the system. The physical size of such systems is typically much larger than for custom systems designed at the component level. In low-volume applications, standard boards are the best alternative if the size and capability requirements can be met. When production volume is higher, investing in the engineering to build the system from the component level results in lower costs in the long run.

For some applications, the hardware design can be limited to interfacing peripherals to a standard personal computer. Specialized capabilities can be added with add-in interface boards, such as data acquisition systems. This approach reduces the hardware design task to a minimum. Most applications that use an ASCII keyboard, alphanumeric display, disk drive, and printer can be most effectively implemented by using a personal computer as a base. Standard system-level computers without keyboards and CRT displays are also available for applications using other forms of I/O.

This text emphasizes component-level design. Although not all systems are designed at this level, understanding component-level design is critical to effectively selecting board-level products. Unless there are unusual interfacing requirements, designing systems using "box"-level microcomputers does not require this detailed understanding. ➤

1.8 DESIGN EXAMPLE

Figure 1.27 shows the block diagram for a microprocessor-based instrument controller that is used as an example throughout this book. The design example sections of Chapters 2 to 8 each present a detailed circuit design for one section of this system. The aspects covered in each chapter are as follows:

Chap. 2: Microprocessor, clock and reset logic

Chap. 3: Bus interface, timing, interrupt logic

Chap. 4: Memory

Chap. 5: Multifunction peripheral, including programmable timers

Chap. 6: Keypad interface

Chap. 7: Display module interface

Chap. 8: Serial I/O interface

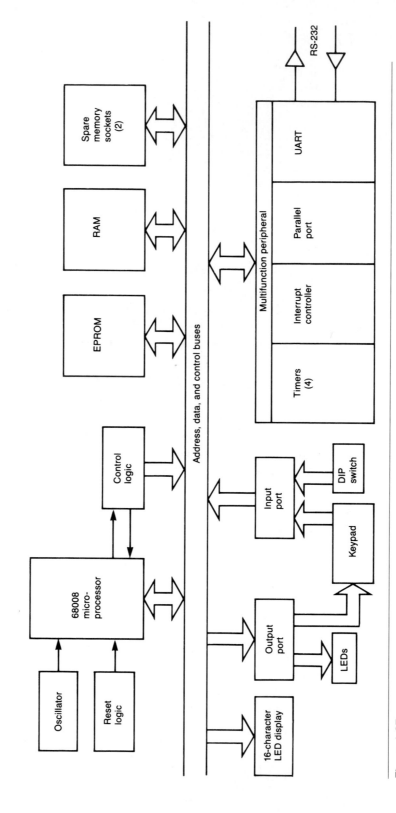

Figure 1.27. The 68008 design example block diagram.

This design example is representative of a variety of dedicated instrumentation and control applications. By adding the appropriate sensor interfaces (and software), it can be transformed into an intelligent DVM, an automatic weather station, a temperature control system, or an analytical chemistry instrument. With additional I/O circuitry, it can be used as a machine tool controller, a waveform synthesizer, or an EPROM programmer. The possible functions are nearly limitless and are determined by the I/O devices and the software.

One example of a real product that uses a similar design is the STS-4040 Slice Tracking System from Slicing Specialists, Inc. The front panel of this instrument, which is used with a wafer saw (a machine that slices silicon ingots into wafers), is shown in Fig. 6.12. It monitors the position of the saw blade as it passes through the ingot in order to measure the flatness of the wafer being cut. In addition to the circuitry described in the design example, it includes an analog "front end" that interfaces to the sensor, a high-resolution A/D converter, and a thermal printer. The printer plots the blade displacement during the cut. Several parameters are monitored and compared to preset limits, and if a limit is exceeded, an alarm output is set. A variety of information for all cuts in the current lot is stored in memory and formatted into reports on request.

The 68008 is used as the microprocessor in this example. This is a version of the 68000 with an 8-bit-wide external data bus. The design can be easily modified to use any of the other microprocessors in the 68000 family, such as the 68000, 68010, or, with somewhat more effort, the 68020. Most of the memory and peripheral circuits shown can be adapted to other microprocessor families as well.

The purpose of this design example is to present a complete, detailed example of one possible system. Although some variations are mentioned, the example system is not intended to show all possible alternatives. The example system is designed for dedicated applications requiring moderate performance. The design alternatives chosen represent a middle-of-the-road approach that has proven useful in many applications; there are both simpler and more complex alternatives for most aspects of the system.

1.9 SUMMARY

Microprocessors have had a profound impact on the design of electronic systems. Software is stored in standard memory devices, enabling systems with identical hardware to perform different functions. The hardware design determines the facilities available to the software, such as memory and I/O, while the software determines the functions performed.

Several benefits of microprocessor-based design are common to the wide range of applications. Software control allows easier modification and allows complex control functions to be implemented far more simply than with other implementations. The computational capabilities allow analysis and interpretation of data to be performed by instruments that previously could only display raw data.

The fundamental microprocessor-based system structure is the connection of microprocessor, memory, and I/O devices with address, data, and control buses. The remainder of this text describes many of the available devices in each of these three functional categories and the design of the interconnections between them.

1.10   EXERCISES

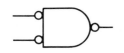

Figure 1.28. AND gate with active-low inputs and outputs.

1.1.   When was the first microprocessor introduced? How many years earlier was the first IC introduced? The first semiconductor device?

1.2.   Describe the reasons why the microprocessor caused a major change in the way electronic systems are designed.

1.3.   Figure 1.28 shows an AND gate with active-low inputs and outputs. What is an alternative way to draw the same physical gate? When should it be drawn that way?

1.4.   An active-low signal is asserted. Is it high or low? What is the corresponding voltage range for TTL-compatible devices?

1.5.   Translate the following hexadecimal numbers to binary and to decimal:

a.   07   c.   1B   e.   FFFF

b.   17   d.   FF   f.   FFFFFF

1.6.   Since all devices share a common data bus, control logic must ensure that only one device is enabled at a time. What are the inputs to this control logic? What is the output called?

1.7.   What is the purpose of three-state drivers in a microprocessor system?

1.8.   Describe the function of an input port. If a peripheral device *outputs* data to an input port, why is it called an *input* port?

1.9.   What benefits of using microprocessors are common to most of the applications described in this chapter?

1.10.   Section 1.3.5 lists three categories of microprocessor applications.

a.   Describe one product you are familiar with in each category.

b.   List the advantages of using a microprocessor in each product.

c.   Sketch a block diagram for a possible implementation of each product.

1.11.   Describe a product that would *not* benefit from a microprocessor-based design. List the reasons why a microprocessor is not suitable (or optimal).

1.12.   When highest performance is desired, is a hardware-intensive or software-intensive approach usually the best choice? When production cost is paramount? When development time is limited?

1.11   SELECTED BIBLIOGRAPHY

Additional references in specific areas are included at the end of each chapter.

Microprocessor History
Faggin, F., and M. E. Hoff. "Standard Parts and Custom Design Merge in Four-Chip Processor Kit," *Electronics*, Apr. 24, 1972, pp. 112–116. An early technical article on the first microprocessor, Intel's 4004.

Intel. *A Revolution in Progress,* Santa Clara, CA, 1984. Describes the history of Intel and the development of the microprocessor and related products.

————. "10th Anniversary of the Microprocessor," *Solutions,* November/December 1981, pp. 2–5. Describes the invention of the microprocessor and briefly summarizes the first 10 years of developments.

Morse et al. "Intel Microprocessors—8008 to 8086," *IEEE Computer,* October 1980, pp. 42–60. A detailed review of Intel's microprocessor evolution. Shows how architecture of earliest microprocessors is still evident in more recent devices.

"Fiftieth Anniversary Issue," *Electronics,* Special Commemorative Issue, Apr. 17, 1980. (Also available as a book reprint, *The Age of Innovation,* New York: McGraw-Hill, 1980.) Series of articles provides comprehensive coverage of the development of modern electronics.

Introductory Texts

Blakeslee, Thomas R. *Digital Design with Standard MSI and LSI,* 2d ed., New York: Wiley-Interscience, 1979. Describes digital design using hard-wired logic and microprocessors.

Ferguson, John. *Microprocessor Systems Engineering,* Reading, MA: Addison-Wesley, 1985. Provides a good balance of hardware and software coverage. Covers the 6502, Z80, 8086, and 68000. Also describes development tools and local area networks.

Osborne, Adam. *An Introduction to Microcomputers, Volume 1,* 2d ed., Berkeley, CA: Osborne/McGraw-Hill, 1981. Updated version of one of the first books on microprocessors. Covers basic hardware and software principles.

Peatman, John B. *Microcomputer-Based Design,* New York: McGraw-Hill, 1977. Describes design techniques for microprocessor-based instruments.

Pooch, U. W., and R. Chattergy. *Designing Microcomputer Systems,* Rochelle Park, NJ: Hayden, 1979. A basic text oriented towards personal computers.

Uffenbeck, John. *Microcomputers and Microprocessors: The 8080, 8085, and Z80 Programming, Interfacing, and Troubleshooting,* Englewood Cliffs, NJ: Prentice-Hall, 1985. Although limited to these somewhat obsolete microprocessors, this text provides comprehensive coverage of microprocessor basics. The 8086 is also covered in a supplemental chapter.

Wiatrowski, Claude A., and Charles H. House. *Logic Circuits and Microcomputer Systems,* New York: McGraw-Hill, 1980. Covers digital logic, state machines, and basic microprocessor system design.

Zaks, Rodnay. *Microprocessors from Chips to Systems,* Berkeley, CA: Sybex, 1977. A basic introduction to microprocessor systems, with real-world examples.

Intermediate Texts

Artwick, Bruce A. *Microcomputer Interfacing,* Englewood Cliffs, NJ: Prentice-Hall, 1980. General coverage of interfacing techniques. Aimed at the personal computing field.

Eccles, William J. *Microprocessor Systems: A 16-Bit Approach,* Reading, MA: Addison-Wesley, 1985. A software-oriented text covering the 68000 and 8086, with some hardware coverage as well.

Lesea, Austin, and Rodnay Zaks. *Microprocessor Interfacing Techniques,* 3d ed., Berkeley, CA: Sybex, 1979. Describes many common microprocessor peripherals and basic interface circuits. Somewhat dated, but still useful for basic concepts.

Peatman, John B. *Digital Hardware Design,* New York: McGraw-Hill, 1980. Covers non-microprocessor digital systems plus the circuits that surround microprocessors. Includes descriptions of self-test and signature analysis implementations and state machine design.

Roberts, Steven K. *Creative Design with Microcomputers,* Englewood Cliffs, NJ: Prentice-Hall, 1984. Covers microprocessor basics, using a variety of industrial applications as examples. Also covers development and debugging approaches.

Savitsky, Stephen R. *Real-Time Microprocessor Systems,* New York: Van Nostrand Reinhold, 1985. Software-oriented text, provides detailed coverage of software design for real-time applications.

Short, Kenneth L. *Microprocessors and Programmed Logic,* Englewood Cliffs, NJ: Prentice-Hall, 1981. An 8085-oriented text, covers microprocessor hardware and software basics.

Stone, Harold. *Microcomputer Interfacing,* Reading, MA: Addison-Wesley, 1982. Covers basic microcomputer hardware, memories, I/O ports, mass storage, and CRT controllers and concludes with a section on software.

Wakerly, John F. *Microcomputer Architecture and Programming,* New York: Wiley, 1981. An extensive treatment of microprocessor software, including both assembly language and Pascal. Describes several microprocessors' assembly languages.

Microprocessor Applications

Gosh, J. "Aids for Blind 'Read' Books, Speak Temperatures," *Electronics,* Sept. 11, 1980, pp. 77–78. Describes two applications for handicapped people.

Hamilton, P. "Communicators Help the Handicapped," *Electronics,* June 8, 1978, pp. 94–97. Describes a device that allows speech-disabled people to form messages on a keyboard, which are then spoken by the machine.

Lerner, E. J. "Micros in 'White Goods'," *IEEE Spectrum,* April 1982, pp. 50–54. Discusses the pitfalls and possibilities for microprocessor-based home appliances, with several examples.

Stout, David (ed.). *Microprocessor Applications Handbook,* New York: McGraw-Hill, 1982. A collection of technical papers describing microprocessor applications.

MICROPROCESSOR TYPES AND SELECTION

2.1 INTRODUCTION

2.1.1 Microprocessor Selection

A bewildering variety of microprocessors and microcomputers are available. There are, in fact, many more than can be justified on purely technical grounds. The selection of a microprocessor is influenced by many factors, some technical, some economic, and some circumstantial. For most applications there are several acceptable microprocessors, with no significant technical advantage in choosing one over the other. There are also a number of processors that are poorly matched to any given application, and selecting one of these would likely result in increased development time and expense, increased production cost, or reduced performance.

Technical considerations include speed, input/output capabilities, power consumption, instruction set, and register set. Economic factors include not only the unit price of the device but ease of programming, ease of debugging, existence of alternate sources, and expected production volume for the application. Economic considerations generally eliminate from consideration processors that are significantly more powerful (and thus more expensive) than necessary.

The final selection often depends on circumstantial considerations. If the engineering staff has experience with a particular microprocessor family, and the lab has the development tools for it, the decision will be heavily weighted toward microprocessors in that family. The efficiency of using existing tools and building on past experience often overwhelms other considerations. For low-volume applications, this is appropriate. However, for products that are to be produced in high volume, the selection of the least expensive microprocessor that will do the job is justified, even if it involves additional development costs.

This chapter aims to give the reader an understanding of the various processor types and advantages and disadvantages of each. For each type, several popular devices are described. The intent is not to substitute for manufacturers' data sheets but to provide an overview of the origins of the device, its particular strengths and weaknesses, and the types of applications in which it is used. The final sections of this chapter discuss the selection process.

Details of several common microprocessors' control signals and bus structures are described in Chap. 3. In keeping with the hardware orientation of this text, registers and instruction sets are not discussed in detail. For a software perspective on a variety of microprocessors, refer to Wakerly's *Microcomputer Architecture and Programming* (New York: Wiley, 1981). For detailed hardware specifications and instruction set descriptions, refer to the manufacturer's documentation. For each microprocessor, the manufacturer publishes a detailed data sheet, and usually a separate user's manual. For more complex microprocessors, there are often separate hardware and software reference manuals. This documentation is available from the manufacturers at no charge if you are an established customer (or viable prospect); otherwise, there is often a small charge.

2.1.2   Overview of Processor Types

Microprocessors are commonly characterized by the number of bits they process in a single instruction, which is generally determined by the width of the data path. Another major distinction is between single-chip microcomputers, which include a microprocessor, memory, and I/O on the same chip, and general-purpose microprocessors, which require external memory and I/O circuits. Table 2.1 lists each possible combination of these categorizations and typical part numbers for each category.

Some microprocessors have internal data paths or registers that are wider than their external data path. For example, the 8088 has a 16-bit architecture internally but interfaces to an 8-bit data bus. The 68000 has 32-bit registers and can perform 32-bit operations but uses a 16-bit data bus.

Microprocessors whose internal and external data path widths differ can be classified by either width. From a software point of view, the internal architecture is what is important; from a hardware point of view, the external bus width is more significant. Another factor is the width of the arithmetic and logic unit (ALU) in the microprocessor. The 68000's ALU is only 16 bits wide, and 32-bit operations are automatically performed as a two-step process. In this respect, it is really a 16-bit processor, even though it has 32-bit registers and can perform 32-bit operations with a single instruction.

Marketing forces also come into play: the 8088 has been marketed as a powerful 8-bit microprocessor (rather than a slow 16-bit microprocessor). However, computer

Table 2.1   Single-chip Microcomputer and General-purpose Microprocessor Types

	4-bit	8-bit	16-bit	32-bit
Single-chip microcomputer	TMS1000￼ COPS	8048/49/50￼ 8051/52￼ 6801/04/05￼ Z8	8096/97￼ 68200	
General-purpose microprocessor	4004￼ 4040￼ (both obsolete)	8085￼ Z80￼ 6802￼ 6809￼ 6502	8086￼ 80186￼ 80286￼ Z8000	80386￼ 68020￼ 32032
		8088￼ 80188￼ 68008￼ 32008	68000/10￼ 32016	

manufacturers using 8088 microprocessors prefer to call their systems 16-bit computers. Perhaps the best solution is to use both numbers: the 8088 is an 8/16-bit microprocessor, and the 68000 is a 16/32-bit microprocessor. The system designer must consider all aspects of the microprocessor's architecture, including internal and external bus widths, register widths, ALU width, and instruction set, and not rely on simplistic labels.

Microprocessors have evolved in two basic directions. One direction is toward more powerful microprocessors with wider data paths and better instruction sets; the other is toward highly integrated systems, combining the microprocessor with memory and I/O on the same chip to form a single-chip microcomputer. In this text, we use the terms *microcomputer* to mean single-chip microcomputers and *microcomputer system* to refer to a multichip system built with a microprocessor. Single-chip microcomputers are often called *microcontrollers,* since they are generally used in control applications.

The 8-bit and 16-bit microprocessors have obsoleted the early 4-bit microprocessors, and now dominate the market. The very high-end market is served by 32-bit microprocessors. Eight-bit processors are not dying, however; they will not go the way of the early 4-bit devices. Many applications do not need the increased power of the 16-bit processors, which inevitably are more expensive. Many tasks involve 8-bit data, and in these applications the 16-bit machines have less of an advantage. However, 16-bit microprocessors are not merely wider-word versions of the 8-bit devices; their architecture and instruction sets are considerably more sophisticated and they can address much more memory, which makes them attractive even in applications involving only 8-bit data. Their more flexible instruction and register sets also allow high-level languages to be more easily and efficiently implemented.

Single-chip microcomputers are available in 4-, 8-, and 16-bit versions. The 4-bit devices are used in large volume in low-end applications such as toys and appliances. Their relatively limited power is adequate, and their low cost makes them a common choice for reasonably simple high-volume applications. The 8-bit microcomputers are widely used in applications that demand more processing power. As the prices of 8-bit microcomputers fall, the range of applications in which 4-bit microcomputers make sense is reduced.

Some classes of processors are not covered in this text. *Bit-slice* processors are "slices" of a CPU that can be used to make processors of any width. For example, four 8-bit bit-slice-processor chips can be used to make a 32-bit processor. Bit-slice processors, such as AMD's 2901 family, are significantly different from the microprocessors covered in this text. They are most commonly fabricated in bipolar technology rather than in MOS or CMOS and are faster and consume more power.

One major difference between standard microprocessors and bit-slice processors is the location of the *microcode,* which tells the microprocessor every detailed step required to execute each machine language instruction. Microcode is thus at an even more detailed level than machine language, and in fact it defines the machine language. In a standard microprocessor, the microcode is stored in a ROM or programmed logic array (PLA) that is part of the microprocessor chip and cannot be modified by the user. The manufacturer has designed an instruction set, written the microcode to implement it, and made that microcode a permanent part of the microprocessor.

Bit-slice processors, on the other hand, require external microcode ROMs which the user must program. For maximum performance, the software can be written entirely in microcode. For larger programs, microcode can be written to execute a higher-level instruction set. The bulk of the application software can then be written with these higher-level instructions. This reduces the task of writing and maintaining the application software. However, the task of designing an instruction set and writing and debugging the microcode is formidable and must be done before any application software can be executed.

Bit-slice processors are therefore more complicated to implement than most microprocessor systems. They are used in applications where very high speed is required; if a standard microprocessor can do the job, a bit-slice processor is needlessly expensive, complex, and power-hungry.

Digital signal processor chips are microprocessors designed to implement filters and other analog signal processing functions using digital techniques. A complete digital signal processing system includes a digital processor with an instruction set optimized for signal processing, memory, and A/D and D/A converters to provide analog inputs and outputs. Some digital signal processor ICs, such as Intel's 2920, include all these functions. Many others, such as TI's TMS32010 and TMS32020, require external converters and/or memory.

2.1.3   Microprocessor Packaging

Figure 2.1 shows the outline of each of the common microprocessor packages and illustrates the differences in circuit board area required. The most common microprocessor package is the 40-pin *dual-in-line package (DIP).* This package has two rows of pins spaced 0.6 in. (600 mils) apart, with 100-mil spacing of pins within the rows, and is available in either ceramic or plastic. The 600-mil-wide DIP is also commonly used in 24-, 28-, and 48-pin sizes. For the 64-pin DIP, a 900-mil-wide package is used.

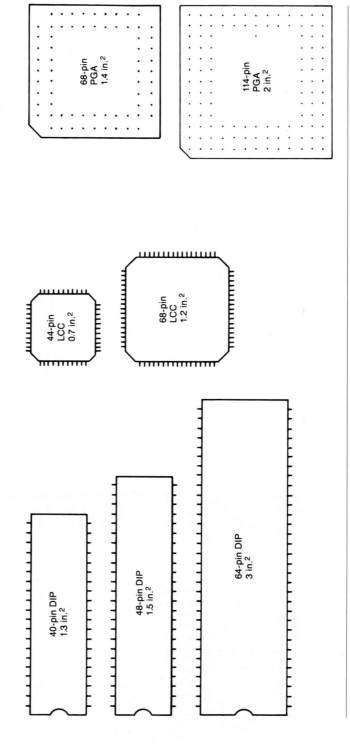

Figure 2.1. Relative size of various IC packages. Note that these area figures are not representative of total circuit board area required since trace area is not included.

Ceramic packages are preferred for high-temperature and high-reliability applications, whereas plastic packages are preferred for low cost. Plastic packages are generally limited to the standard commercial temperature range of 0 to 70°C. Ceramic packages can operate over the full military temperature range of -55 to +125°C, provided, of course, that the IC in the package can also operate over that temperature range. Note that these temperatures refer to the IC temperature, which is generally higher than the air surrounding the IC. In addition, unless there is excellent airflow, the temperature of the air surrounding the IC will be higher than the ambient temperature.

The 64-pin DIP uses a large amount of circuit board area relative to the size of the IC chip itself. Beyond 64 pins, the DIP package is impractical. These problems have led to the development of several other package types.

Figure 2.2 shows a *ceramic leadless chip carrier (LCC)*. This package has metallized pads on all four edges. The spacing between adjacent pads is 0.050 in. (50 mils) center to center. The closer spacing and the use of all four sides provides much higher pin density than a DIP and eliminates most of the wasted package area. The chip carrier can be mounted in a socket, or it can be attached directly to a circuit board by using surface-mount techniques. The sockets provide two staggered rows of pins along each edge to provide a practical pin pattern for conventional pin-in-hole circuit board mounting.

Another variation is the *plastic chip carrier (PCC),* as shown in Fig. 2.3. This package is similar to the ceramic LCC but has J-shaped leads that are bent under the package. (These packages are also called plastic leaded chip carriers, or PLCCs, but this is ambiguous since L can stand for leaded or leadless. The ceramic packages are generally leadless, and the plastic ones leaded.) Surface mounting (or a socket) is used, since the 50-mil lead spacing makes it difficult to use the traditional pin-in-hole approach. The PCC is similar to the *flatpack,* which is widely used for Japanese single-chip microcomputers.

Chip carriers are available in a wide variety of sizes and are commonly used for 32-,

Figure 2.2. A 68-pin ceramic leadless chip carrier (LCC). *(Photo courtesy of Advanced Micro Devices, Inc., Sunnyvale, California.)*

Figure 2.3. A 32-pin plastic leaded chip carrier (PLCC) compared to a 28-pin DIP. *(Courtesy of Intel Corporation.)*

Figure 2.4. A 114-pin pin-grid array package. *(Courtesy of Motorola, Inc.)*

44-, and 68-pin packages. Above 68 pins, however, the package size must be increased or the pad spacing decreased. Since neither of these changes is desirable, another approach is needed.

The *pin-grid array (PGA)* package, as shown in Fig. 2.4, solves this problem by providing more than one row of pins along each side. It also allows standard pin-in-hole mounting techniques to be used and retains the DIP's 100-mil lead spacing. Many different pin configurations are possible. Pin-grid arrays are used for packages with 68 to several hundred pins. Common packages have either 11 or 13 pins on a side. A full

Figure 2.5. Piggyback single-chip microcomputer package with EPROM socket showing internal circuit board. *(Courtesy of Zilog, Inc.)*

13 × 13 array provides 169 pins. Routing all the traces on a printed circuit board to the dense array of pins in a PGA can be difficult. Multilayer boards are required, and the need for trace routing space can increase the effective package area.

Figure 2.5 shows a *piggyback* DIP package that is sometimes used for single-chip microcomputers. This is typically a 40-pin DIP with a 24- or 28-pin socket in the top of the package, allowing a single-chip microcomputer to be used with an external EPROM without using up any of the normal pins for the EPROM's connections. Piggyback packages are used primarily for prototypes of systems that will eventually use mask-programmed single-chip microcomputers, with the EPROM replaced by on-chip ROM.

2.2 THE 8-BIT MICROPROCESSORS

Eight-bit microprocessors are flexible, general-purpose devices that can be easily expanded with a wide range of memory and peripheral devices. Common examples include the Z80, 8085, 6502, 6802, and 6809. They are not stand-alone devices and require the support of additional memory and I/O chips. However, they provide the most versatility for the lowest cost of any processor type. Single-chip microcomputers are less expensive but are more awkward to expand, while 16-bit microprocessors provide greater power at a higher cost. A great number of microprocessor applications are best served by systems based on general-purpose 8-bit microprocessors. While the personal computer market has almost universally adopted 16-bit (or 8/16-bit) microprocessors for new designs, 8-bit microprocessors continue to be used in dedicated control applications.

Most 8-bit microprocessors have an 8-bit data bus and a 16-bit address bus. The 8-bit bus does not limit the system to 8-bit data; it simply requires multiple memory accesses for larger data words. All common microprocessors have some instructions for handling 16-bit data internally. The 16-bit address bus limits the direct addressing range to 64K (2^{16}) bytes, which is more than adequate for many applications.

Figure 2.6 shows a microprocessor "family tree." The first 8-bit microprocessor was

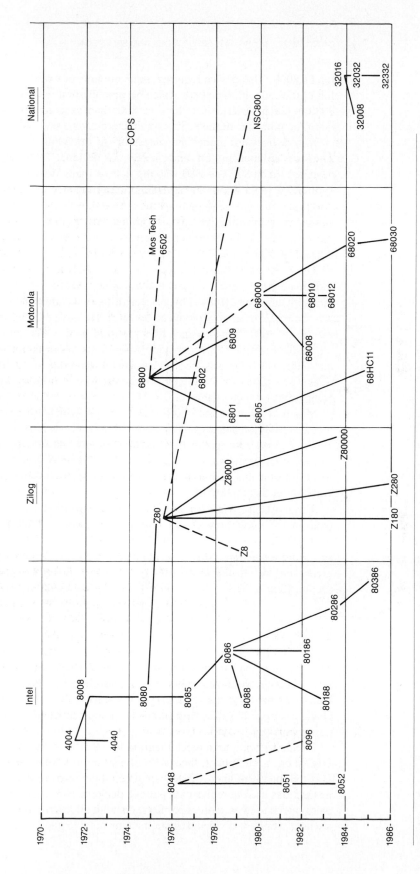

Figure 2.6. Microprocessor family tree. Solid lines link direct descendants; dashed lines link related devices.

Intel's 8008. This device required large amounts of external logic and was quite slow. Intel followed with the 8080, which became the first widely used microprocessor. The 8080 is much easier to use than the 8008 and executes instructions at a much faster rate. The influence of the 8080's architecture can be seen in many more recent devices.

Two devices are immediate successors to the 8080: Intel's 8085 and Zilog's Z80. Zilog was an Intel spin-off, and the Z80 was designed by some of the same people who designed the 8080. The Z80 was the first of many devices to maintain upward compatibility with the 8080; that is, 8080 programs can be executed by a Z80, although the Z80 provides many additional instructions and features. The Intel 8085, while it differs significantly from the Z80, is also an upward-compatible version of the 8080. From these devices came a third generation: the NSC800 from National Semiconductor and the 64180, Z180, and Z280 from Hitachi and Zilog.

The 8080's first major competition was Motorola's 6800. It was introduced at approximately the same time and had a distinctly different architecture. Like the 8080, the 6800 has been followed by a series of more advanced devices. The first outgrowth was the 6502, originally produced by MOS Technology. Following a familiar industry pattern, the 6502 was designed by a group of people who left Motorola after working on the 6800. The 6502 bears many similarities to but is not directly compatible with the 6800. The 6502 was the first low-cost microprocessor (particularly in small quantities), and primarily for this reason it was widely used in Apple and Atari personal computers and video games.

Motorola followed the 6800 with the 6802, which is very similar to the 6800 but includes additional hardware features. The 6801 was then introduced, which is a single-chip microcomputer that is software-compatible with the 6800. The most advanced member of this family is the 6809. The 6809 is architecturally similar to the 6800 but contains many additional features and is not directly software-compatible with any of the other 6800 family parts.

The most recent generation of microprocessors with 8-bit data buses are descendants of 16-bit microprocessors. Examples include the 8088, a variant of the 8086, and the 68008, a variant of the 68000. These devices are identical to their 16-bit predecessors from a software point of view but interface to an 8-bit data bus. Because of the great similarity to the 16-bit devices, these are covered in the 16-bit microprocessor section (Sec. 2.3).

2.2.1   Intel 8085

The 8085 was Intel's immediate successor to the 8080. It executes the 8080 instruction set, with only two minor additions to support new hardware features. The main contributions of the 8085 are reduction of the three-chip 8080 system (8080A CPU, 8224 clock driver, and 8228 system controller) to one chip and operation from a single +5 V power supply.

Figure 2.7 shows the block diagram of the 8085. The register set is the same as the 8080's: one accumulator, the stack pointer, and the six general-purpose registers B, C, D, E, H, and L. (Other registers shown in the figure are not directly accessible.) Some instructions use the registers in pairs to perform 16-bit operations, and the HL and DE pairs can be used as address pointers. As with all microprocessors of this vintage, there are no multiply or divide instructions. One notable gap in the 8085 instruction set is the

Figure 2.7. The 8085 microprocessor block diagram. *(Courtesy of Intel Corporation.)*

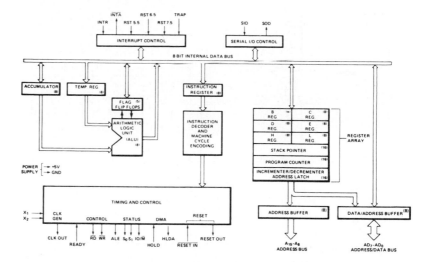

lack of a relative addressing mode; this increases program length and makes position-independent code impossible.

Several innovative hardware features are incorporated in the 8085. The 8080 requires an external system controller chip to generate bus control signals. The 8085 provides these signals directly. This requires more pins on the microprocessor's package. Since economic considerations limit the package size to 40 pins for a device in this price class, Intel chose to multiplex the address and data lines to provide more pins for control functions. The least-significant half of the address bus shares the same pins as the data bus; a control signal called ADDRESS LATCH ENABLE (ALE) indicates when address information is present on the bus. The net savings is thus seven pins: eight address pins freed, and one additional control signal required in their place. (See Sec. 3.4 for a detailed description of multiplexed buses.)

These additional pins provide a variety of functions. A quartz crystal may be connected directly to the 8085's X_1 and X_2 pins, eliminating the need for an external oscillator. (Note that the oscillator frequency is internally divided by 2, so a 10-MHz crystal provides a 5-MHz clock.) Four pins are used for additional interrupt inputs, providing a powerful and easy-to-use set of interrupt capabilities. Finally, two pins called SOD (serial output data) and SID (serial input data) are provided. These are simply 1-bit input and output ports; they are not, as the name implies, supported by serial I/O hardware on the chip.

Standard nonmultiplexed devices can be interfaced to an 8085 by adding an 8-bit latch (such as the 74LS373) to demultiplex the bus. In addition, several memory and I/O chips are available that connect directly to the multiplexed bus. Examples are the 8156 RAM, I/O, and timer, the 8355 ROM and I/O, the 8755 EPROM and I/O, and the 8185 RAM. The multiplexed bus results in a pin savings on the memory or I/O chips, as well as a reduction in the number of bus traces required on the printed circuit board.

Figure 2.8 shows a system based on the chip set. Each of the three chips is in a 40-pin package. The memory/IO chips have a number of pins available for I/O, since multiplexing reduces the number of pins required for the bus interface. The 8156 provides 256 bytes of RAM, a timer, and 22 bits of I/O. The 8355/8755 provides 2 Kbytes of

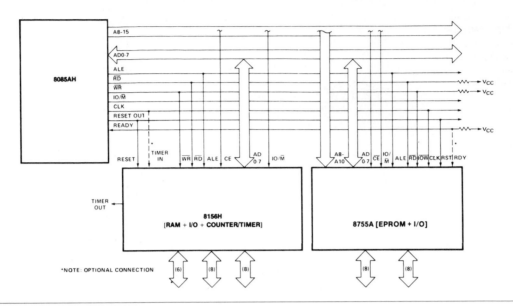

Figure 2.8.   Three-chip 8085 system. *(Courtesy of Intel Corporation.)*

ROM/EPROM and 16 bits of I/O. These three devices make a powerful, compact system. Unfortunately, these memory/IO devices are not usable with most other microprocessors. This results in a lower sales volume, and thus a higher price, as compared to implementing the same functions with nonmultiplexed parts and a demultiplexing latch.

The standard 8085A has a maximum clock rate of 3 MHz; selected parts are available with clock rates of 5 (8085AH-2) or 6 MHz (8085AH-1). The shortest instructions require four clock cycles, resulting in minimum instruction times of 1.33 μs at 3 MHz, 0.8 μs at 5 MHz, and 0.67 μs at 6 MHz. A CMOS version, the 80C85, is available from OKI Semiconductor.

2.2.2   Zilog Z80

Zilog's Z80 is one of the most widely used microprocessors. Before the introduction of the IBM PC, it was the dominant microprocessor in personal computers. It is now used more widely in dedicated control applications. Like the 8085, it follows the 8080's basic architecture and adds a number of improvements. It is, however, quite different from the 8085. While retaining object code compatibility, the instruction set is greatly enhanced. Additions to the 8080 instruction set include bit test, set and reset instructions, block move and search instructions, and improved I/O instructions.

In addition to the enhanced instruction set, the Z80 provides an alternate register set. Only one set of registers, the main or the alternate, is accessible at any moment. However, by executing a single instruction, the register set in use can be changed. This allows fast interrupt response, since the microprocessor can switch register sets instead of pushing registers on the stack.

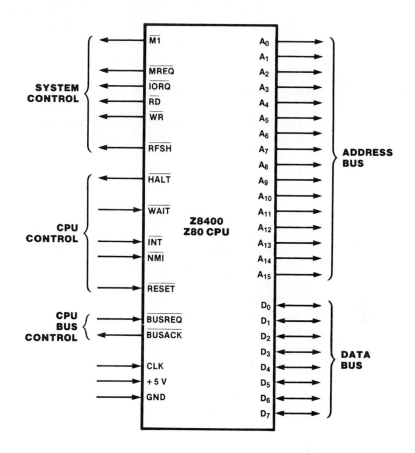

Figure 2.9. *Z80 micro-processor pin functions. (Reproduced by permission. © 1983 Zilog, Inc. This material shall not be reproduced without the written consent of Zilog, Inc.)*

Figure 2.9 shows the Z80 pin functions. The Z80 retains the nonmultiplexed address and data buses of the 8080. This leaves relatively few pins available for additional control functions; the Z80 thus has no I/O pins such as the 8085's SID and SOD, only two interrupt pins, and requires an external oscillator.

The Z80 includes an internal refresh counter to support dynamic RAM refresh. After reading the first byte of each instruction (the *opcode*), the contents of this counter are output on the address bus, and the $\overline{\text{RFSH}}$ signal is asserted. This simplifies the circuitry required to implement a dynamic RAM interface but also takes up some of the time available for the opcode fetch cycle. The Z80 thus requires memory to respond faster (by approximately one-half clock cycle) when reading an opcode than when reading data.

The Z80 is available in several versions with different maximum clock speeds: the Z80, 2.5 MHz; the Z80A, 4.0 MHz; the Z80B, 6.0 MHz, and the Z80H, 8.0 MHz. At 4 MHz, instruction execution times range from 1 to almost 6 μs, depending on the instruction. The Z80 family devices are also available from Thompson/Mostek as the MK3880 series. Most Z80 family components are also available in CMOS versions.

A wide variety of peripheral devices are available for the Z80, including a direct memory access (DMA) controller (Z80-DMA or MK3883), serial I/O controller (Z80-SIO or MK3884), parallel I/O interface (Z80-PIO or MK3881), and programmable counter/timer (Z80-CTC or MK3882). The use of family peripherals is particularly important with the Z80 if interrupts are to be used; it is difficult to support the Z80 interrupt structure with non-Z80-family devices.

2.2.3 Motorola 6800 and 6802

While the 8080, 8085, and Z80 are very similar in architecture, the Motorola 6800 represents a different approach. The 6800 family uses relatively few registers and emphasizes efficient use of main memory for data storage. Only three registers are available for data storage in the CPU: the two accumulators, A and B, and the 16-bit index register. This is in contrast to the numerous registers of the Intel/Zilog-family processors.

The 6800 requires an external clock generator to generate a two-phase clock. The 6802 is software-compatible with the 6800 but includes an on-chip oscillator and clock generator plus 128 bytes of RAM. Figure 2.10 shows the 6802 block diagram and register set. The small on-chip RAM provides all the RAM needed in many small systems that need RAM only for variable storage and program stack.

The 6800 and 6802 use nonmultiplexed buses. The bus control signals are partitioned differently than for Intel-family processors; these signals are described in detail in Chap. 3. A single line, R/$\overline{\text{W}}$ (read/write), indicates the direction of each transfer, and a clock signal provides the timing. The 6800 and 6802 do not provide separate memory and I/O address spaces; all I/O must be memory-mapped.

Figure 2.10. The 6802/6808 microprocessor block diagram. The 6808 has no on-chip RAM. *(Courtesy of Motorola, Inc.)*

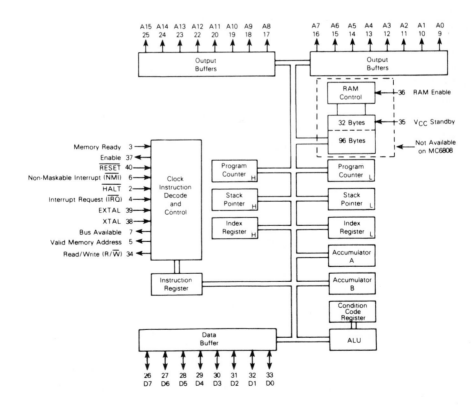

The 6800 and 6802 are available in a variety of clock speeds, indicated by the letters A or B after the first two digits (for example, 68B00). The standard parts (with no letter) have a maximum frequency of 1 MHz; A is 1.5 MHz, and B is 2 MHz. The 6800-family uses a different timing approach than the Intel/Zilog families. The 6800-family microprocessors require only one clock cycle per bus cycle. The Z80, on the other hand, requires three or four clock cycles per bus cycle. Thus, a 1 MHz 6800 has a minimum instruction execution time of 1 μs, and executes instructions at approximately the same rate as a 4-MHz Z80A. Note that to compare the actual processing power, or *throughput,* the relative efficiency of the instruction set for a given application must be considered in addition to clock rate and number of clock cycles per instruction (see Sec. 2.7.9).

2.2.4   Motorola 6809

The 6809 represents the third generation of 6800-family microprocessors. While it follows the same basic architectural approach, it is not directly hardware- or software-compatible with the 6800 or 6802. Compatibility always carries with it limitations, and Motorola chose to sacrifice some degree of compatibility to gain the freedom to produce a completely new design.

Figure 2.11 shows the block diagram of the 6809. The register set includes the same registers as the 6800, plus a second stack pointer and a direct-page base address regis-

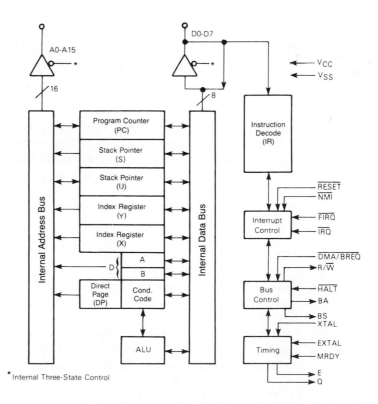

Figure 2.11. The 6809 microprocessor block diagram. *(Courtesy of Motorola, Inc.)*

ter. The second stack pointer allows the programmer to easily maintain two separate stacks, one for subroutine return addresses and another for data. The direct page register is used to determine the high byte of the address for certain load and store instructions. This provides an addressing mode that can be used for any area of memory but requires only 8 bits of the address to be coded as part of the instruction.

The 6809 instruction set is among the most sophisticated available on an 8-bit microprocessor. An integer multiply instruction is included, and a wide variety of addressing modes are available. The instruction set is designed particularly to allow the generation of position-independent object code and for efficient code generation by a high-level language compiler.

The 6809 is source-code-compatible with the 6800. What this means, in essence, is that Motorola provides a translator program that converts 6800 assembly language to 6809 instructions. They are not compatible at the binary, or object code, level.

The 6809 bus interface is very similar to the 6802. The bus timing is improved, the interrupt structure is extended, and a more flexible DMA capability is included, but the basic bus architecture remains unchanged. One interesting feature is a special interrupt line FIRQ, or fast interrupt request, which allows a faster interrupt response time by saving only the program counter rather than all the registers. The major contribution of the 6809 lies not in its hardware aspects but in its instruction set.

The 6809 is available in 1-, 1.5-, and 2.0-MHz versions, called the 6809, 68A09, and 68B09, respectively. Minimum instruction execution time at 1 MHz is 1 μs. All 6800-family peripherals can be used with the 6809.

2.2.5 Other 8-bit Microprocessors

Many other 8-bit microprocessors are available in addition to those described above. While it is beyond the scope of this text to provide detailed descriptions of all available devices, a few of the more important ones are briefly described in this section.

The *6502* was originally developed by MOS Technology and then produced primarily by Synertek (until its shutdown in 1985) and Rockwell. As mentioned previously, this device is similar to the 6800 in many ways. It uses a nonmultiplexed bus, 6800-style control signals, and has a similar instruction set. While it has not been widely used in industrial applications, it is used in several very high-volume products, including the Apple II family, Atari's video games and early personal computers, and Commodore's low-end personal computers. The use of the 6502 in these applications is due primarily to its low cost. At the time these products were developed, the 6502 was much less expensive than other microprocessors.

One innovation that was partially responsible for the 6502 family's success in the video game business is the availability of a number of different packaging options. There are a variety of 28-pin versions that do not provide all the address and control lines. The smaller package reduces the production cost and makes the parts particularly attractive for applications that are cost-sensitive and have relatively modest memory requirements.

National Semiconductor's NSC800 represents an unusual mix of capabilities: it executes the Z80 instruction set and interfaces to the 8085 multiplexed bus structure. In addition, it is implemented in CMOS, so power consumption is very low. National also makes the 8085-family multiplexed bus peripherals in CMOS. This device thus allows users to take advantage of existing software for the Z80, while also gaining the benefits of the multiplexed bus and the low power of CMOS. The standard Z80 is also available in CMOS from Toshiba and Zilog.

Hitachi's HD64180 combines a Z80-compatible microprocessor with additional interface circuits on the same chip. Included with the CPU are a two-channel DMA controller, two UARTs, a serial peripheral chip interface, two 16-bit timers, a memory-management unit to allow a 512-Kbyte addressing range, a wait-state generator, and additional control logic. This 64-pin device can replace eight or more ICs in a typical Z80 system and also provides higher performance. Several new instructions, such as integer multiply, are added, and some Z80 instructions are executed in fewer clock cycles.

The 64180 is also produced by Zilog. *Zilog's Z180* is an enhanced version that is compatible with all Z80-family peripherals. Zilog's *Z280* is a high-performance upgrade of the Z80, which includes a 16-bit bus interface, multiply and divide instructions, on-chip memory management for memory protection and an extended address range, and an on-chip cache memory. (The Z280 is the end result of what was at one time known as the Z800, which was never produced.)

2.3   THE 16- AND 32-BIT MICROPROCESSORS

Microprocessors have evolved from the early 4-bit devices to 8-bit and then to 16- and 32-bit processors. The 16-bit microprocessors not only process 16 bits of data at a time but also have more sophisticated architectures and instruction sets than most 8-bit processors.

The first generations of microprocessors were constrained by the limits of silicon technology. In more recent microprocessors, semiconductor technological advances have provided the power and flexibility to design microprocessors that are user-optimized rather than silicon-optimized. Popular minicomputer architectures, such as DEC's PDP-11, have had a large influence on more recent microprocessor designs.

The first 16-bit microprocessor was Texas Instruments' 9900. For several years, the 9900 was the only 16-bit microprocessor, but more advanced devices made it obsolete. While it does process 16-bit data, it lacks many features now commonly associated with 16-bit microprocessors.

Intel's 8086, introduced in 1979, began a major new family of microprocessors, including the 8088, 80186, 80188, 80286, and 80386. Soon after the introduction of the 8086, Motorola introduced the 68000 and Zilog introduced the Z8000. TI announced the 99000, an upgraded microprocessor based on the 9900. National Semiconductor's 32000 family was the first to be designed from the start as a 32-bit microprocessor and is popular in high-performance applications. The Intel and Motorola families dominate and are available from several alternate sources.

These 16- and 32-bit microprocessors include multiply and divide instructions and a wide variety of addressing modes and data types. The address bus width typically is between 20 and 24 bits, yielding an effective addressing range of 1 to 16 Mbytes.

Motorola's 68000 includes many 32-bit operations and is often called a 16/32-bit microprocessor. The 68020 is an enhanced design with full 32-bit architecture. Like Intel's 80386, the 68020 provides 32 address lines for a mammoth 4-gigabyte address space.

Each of the major 16-bit microprocessors has led to a family of devices, including processors with 8-bit buses and single-chip microcomputers with on-chip memory and I/O. For most families, software is transportable between the various devices, so the user can move up or down in hardware capability without losing the software investment.

2.3.1   Intel 8086 Family

The introduction of the 8086 (also called the *iAPX86*) marked the beginning of a major new microprocessor family as well as a trend toward more sophisticated micro-processor architectures. Intel built upon the foundations of the 8080 and 8085, al-though the 8086 is not directly compatible with them. The 8086 was the first 16-bit microprocessor to be widely used. Its use in the IBM PC firmly established the 8086/88 as the dominant 16-bit microprocessor family. The succeeding 80186, 80286, and 80386 were assured a large following due to their compatibility with software written for the 8086/88.

The 8086 register set is shown in Fig. 2.12. The shaded registers represent equiva-

Figure 2.12. The 8086 register set, 8080/8085 subset shaded. *(Courtesy of Intel Corporation.)*

DATA REGISTERS

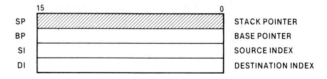

POINTER AND INDEX REGISTERS

SP — STACK POINTER
BP — BASE POINTER
SI — SOURCE INDEX
DI — DESTINATION INDEX

SEGMENT REGISTERS

CS — CODE
DS — DATA
SS — STACK
ES — EXTRA

INSTRUCTION POINTER AND FLAGS

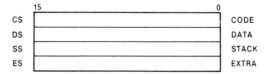

IP — INSTRUCTION POINTER

STATUS WORD OR FLAGS

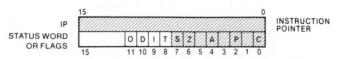

Figure 2.13. Address calculation for 8086-family microprocessors. *(Courtesy of Intel Corporation.)*

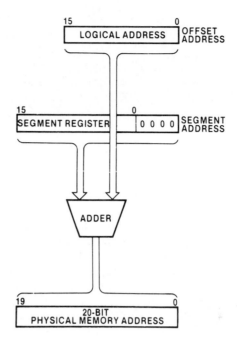

lents to the 8080 register set. Data registers A, B, C, and D can each be used as single 16-bit registers or two 8-bit registers. The stack is managed via a base pointer (BP) in addition to the usual stack pointer. The base pointer locates the bottom of the stack, while the stack pointer locates the top. Two index registers are provided, welcome additions to the 8080 register set.

The 8086 has four *segment registers,* which provide base addresses for addressing memory. Separate segment registers are provided for code, data, and stack. For each memory access, a 20-bit address is calculated by adding the appropriate segment register to an offset specified in the instruction, as shown in Fig. 2.13. The contents of the segment register are left-justified in the 20-bit field, with zeros in the four rightmost bits, while the offset is right-justified. A simpler approach would be for the segment register to provide only the most significant four bits of the address. The advantage of the approach used by the 8086 is that each segment can start at any address that is a multiple of 16; using the simpler approach, all segments would have to start at a multiple of 64K. The 8086 thus has a *segmented* address space; each segment register selects a 64-Kbyte segment of the memory space that can be directly accessed. Program code, data, and stack each have separate segments, which may overlap or not.

This approach provides a number of advantages. A 1-Mbyte addressing range is maintained, but each instruction needs to specify only a 16-bit address offset. Programs can be relocated simply by resetting the segment registers, and the stack and data areas can be kept isolated from program areas.

On the negative side, it is awkward in some applications (particularly those with data arrays larger than 64 Kbytes) to have the entire memory space partitioned into 64K blocks. Programs that fit within a single 64K segment can use "short" jump and call instructions, which require only a 16-bit address offset. For jumps and calls that

Figure 2.14. The 8086 microprocessor block diagram. *(Courtesy of Intel Corporation.)*

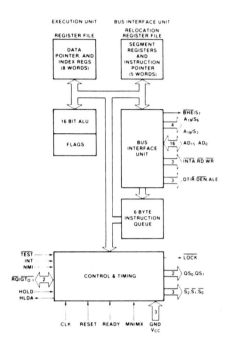

are not within the segment, a longer form of the instruction is required that includes the new 16-bit segment value in addition to the 16-bit offset.

The 8086 does not have separate user and supervisor privilege levels, as do most other 16- and 32-bit microprocessors.

Figure 2.14 shows the block diagram of the 8086. Multiplexed address and data buses allow a 40-pin package to be used. Pins AD_0 to AD_{15} provide both the data bus and the least-significant 16 bits of address. The four most significant address bits, A_{16} to A_{19}, are multiplexed with four status signals. The 8086 requires an external clock generator IC, the 8284, which also provides reset and ready logic.

The 8086 is particularly innovative in the use of control pins. It operates in one of two modes, minimum or maximum, as determined by the level on the MIN/$\overline{\text{MAX}}$ pin. The mode determines the function of several pins. In minimum mode, the 8086 provides 8085-style bus control signals directly, as shown in Fig. 2.15. In maximum mode, as shown in Fig. 2.16, the basic bus control signals are replaced with encoded status lines. These status lines are then decoded by the 8288 system controller IC to generate bus control signals. Maximum mode must be used if the 8289 Multibus arbiter or the 8087 coprocessor are to be used, since they connect to the encoded status lines. (See Chap. 10 for a further description of these devices.) Maximum mode also has the advantage of providing better-defined bus timing. Minimum mode is used primarily in applications in which minimum chip count is important.

The 8086 is divided internally into two sections: the bus interface unit and the instruction execution unit. The bus interface unit performs all address calculations and fetches instructions whenever the bus is available. Fetched instructions are stored in a 6-byte instruction queue from which they are read by the execution unit. This structure

Figure 2.15. The 8086 minimum mode configuration. *(Courtesy of Intel Corporation.)*

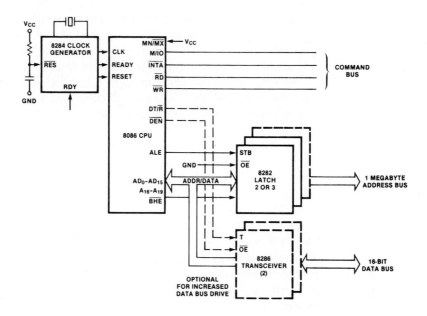

Figure 2.16. The 8086 maximum mode configuration. *(Courtesy of Intel Corporation.)*

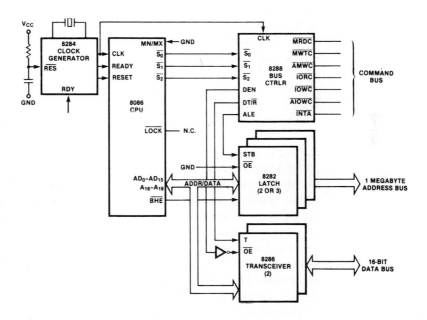

allows the 8086 to *prefetch* up to 6 bytes ahead of the instruction being executed and results in efficient bus utilization. Whenever a jump is executed, the instructions in the queue have to be discarded (called *flushing* the queue), since they are not to be executed.

Instruction prefetching can make debugging more difficult, since the bus activity does not correspond directly to the instruction execution activity. Some instructions that are fetched may never be executed, and instructions may be executed several bus cycles after they are fetched. In maximum mode, two queue status signals (QS_0 and QS_1) indicate when the queue is flushed, allowing debugging tools (such as an in-circuit emulator or logic analyzer) to determine when instructions are actually executed.

The *8087* is an arithmetic coprocessor that is closely coupled to the 8086. It provides hardware support for trigonometric and floating-point operations in accordance with the IEEE floating-point standard, and greatly improves performance in applications that need these functions.

The standard 8086 operates at a maximum clock rate of 5 MHz. Selected versions, the 8086–2 and 8086–1, operate at 8 and 10 MHz, respectively. The minimum instruction execution time is four clock cycles, or 0.5 μs at 8 MHz. Some instructions take much longer, however: a divide instruction takes up to 200 clock cycles, or 25 μs at 8 MHz.

Like the 8080, the 8086 architecture has formed the basis for a family of devices. The *8088* has an 8-bit data bus but is otherwise identical to the 8086. The 8-bit data bus requires the processor to perform two bus cycles for a single 16-bit word. The 8088's instruction execution unit (IEU) is identical to that of the 8086; only the bus interface unit (BIU) is different. The 8088 provides slightly more than half the performance of an 8086, since most bus operations take twice as long for the 8088 and internal operations and single-byte read or write operations execute at the same speed with either processor. The advantage of the 8088 is that low-cost 8-bit memories and buses can be used, along with existing 8-bit peripherals. The physical bus connectors need only eight data pins, and only 8-bit-wide data bus buffers are needed, further reducing the system cost. Should the user need more power, the entire software investment can be maintained by switching to an 8086. The 8088 is designed (i.e., priced and marketed) to compete with the Z80 and 6809. It is used in IBM's PC and XT personal computers and in many IBM-compatible computers.

The second-generation members of the 8086 family are the 80186, 80188, and 80286. The *80186* (also called *iAPX186*) "high-integration" microprocessor includes on-chip many common peripheral functions. Figure 2.17 shows the block diagram. On-chip functions include a clock generator, two DMA channels, an interrupt controller, three programmable timers, programmable chip-select logic, and a wait-state generator. The goal is to provide everything except the memory and I/O devices on the microprocessor chip. The instruction set is fully compatible with the 8086, and 10 new instruction types have been added. Because of the large number of functions performed, many pins are required: the standard package is a 68-pin chip carrier. The 80186 represents a major advance in reducing the number of ICs required for typical applications. The *80188* is a similar device that interfaces to an 8-bit data bus for reduced system cost.

The *80286* (*iAPX286*, often referred to as the *286*) was introduced at the same time as the 80186. While the 186 is designed to reduce parts count, the 286 is intended to provide high performance in larger systems. The 80286 is used in IBM's PC/AT and many other personal computers. Figure 2.18 shows the block diagram of the 286. It includes on-chip the memory management hardware and instruction restarting capabilities necessary for virtual memory. The 286 executes a superset of the 8086 instruction set and uses nonmultiplexed buses for maximum performance. Performance is further enhanced by a more sophisticated ALU.

Figure 2.17. The 80186 microprocessor block diagram. *(Courtesy of Intel Corporation.)*

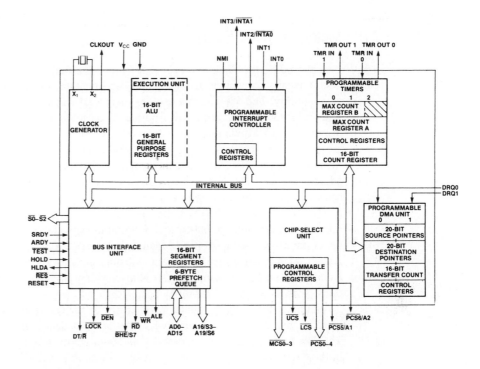

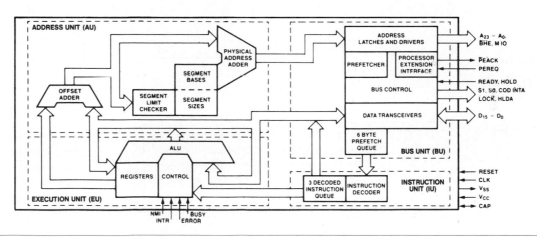

Figure 2.18. The 80286 microprocessor block diagram. *(Courtesy of Intel Corporation.)*

The *iAPX 386* is a full 32-bit microprocessor based on the 8086 architecture. It provides an upgrade path for users who need higher performance than an 80186 or 80286 can provide, and it is upward-compatible with software written for those microprocessors. The address and data buses are both 32 bits wide. The instruction set is extended to support 32-bit addresses and data, and the registers are extended to 32 bits. Sophisticated on-chip caches and pipelining are used to increase performance.

2.3.2   Motorola 68000 Family

Like the 8086, the 68000 was the beginning of a major microprocessor family. The 68000 departs completely from the 6800 architecture, making no attempt at software compatibility. The 68000 can use 6800 peripheral chips, however. The 68000 was the first 16-bit microprocessor to incorporate 32-bit internal registers. It was also the first to provide a 16-Mbyte nonsegmented address space. (Nonsegmented means that there are no segment registers, such as in the 8086, so a single instruction can address any memory location without the need to change the segment register. Since the 68000's address registers are 32 bits wide, each can directly address an even larger address space than the hardware supports.)

Had IBM chosen a 68000-family microprocessor for their personal computer, the relative popularity of the 68000 and 8086 families would likely be quite different. The 68000 family is used in Apple's Macintosh, Atari's 520ST and 1040ST, Commodore's Amiga, high-performance workstations from Sun Microsystems and others, and many Unix-based multiuser computers. It is also widely used in dedicated control applications, such as the design example in this text.

Figure 2.19 shows the 68000 register set. A far cry from the few registers of the 6800, it includes seven address registers and eight data registers, each 32 bits wide. The data registers can also be accessed as 16-bit words or bytes. All internal operations in the 68000 can be performed on 32-bit values; this includes address calculations as

Figure 2.19. The 68000 register set. *(Courtesy of Motorola, Inc.)*

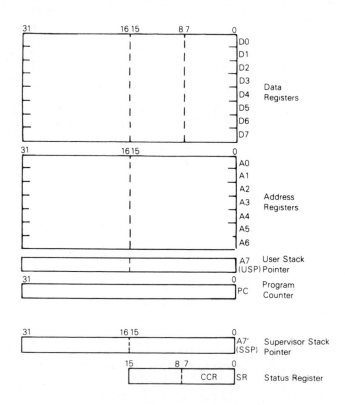

Figure 2.20. The 68000 microprocessor pin functions. *(Courtesy of Motorola, Inc.)*

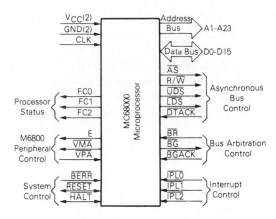

well as data manipulation, although only 24 address bits are provided externally. Instructions for multiplication and division include a 32 × 32 bit multiplication with a 64-bit result. The 68000 thus well deserves the 16/32-bit designation. The 68000's ALU is only 16 bits wide, however, so 32-bit operations must be performed in two steps. This is handled automatically by the microcode in the 68000 but does make these operations slower than in microprocessors with full 32-bit ALUs.

Another important feature is the support of two distinct privilege levels, or modes of operation: user and supervisor. There are two stack pointers, one for each mode. This is designed to support a user program operating under the control of an operating system, and provides protection against a user program run awry (accidentally or purposefully). At reset, the system is in the supervisor mode, in which no restrictions are placed on the operation of the program. In this mode, initialization sequences and operating system programs are normally executed. In dedicated control applications, the user mode is generally not used; the entire program operates in the supervisor mode.

The status register is divided into two bytes. One byte contains the condition codes and is available to all programs. The other byte contains the interrupt mask level and the bit that determines whether the processor is in the user or supervisor mode; this byte cannot be modified by user-mode programs. When the operating system jumps to a user program, it sets the mode control bit to user mode. In this mode, instructions such as STOP and RESET cannot be executed. If an interrupt occurs, either from an external source or from an internal source such as an overflow error (often called a *trap*), the system is forced back to the supervisor mode. All interrupt and error processing is done in the supervisor mode; when the processing is complete, the system may return to the user program.

Figure 2.20 shows the 68000 pin functions. The 68000 provides three function-code outputs that indicate for each memory access whether it is a user or supervisor access and if it is a code, data, or stack access. These function codes can be decoded and used in the chip select logic for the memories, physically separating the memory for each category of access. This makes it impossible for a user program to overwrite the supervisor code or for an improperly controlled stack to creep down and wipe out the program. The function-code outputs are also used by external memory management logic to restrict certain types of accesses to selected memory areas.

The 68000 buses are nonmultiplexed, with 24 address bits and 16 data bits. The program counter and address registers are 32 bits wide; thus, it is only pin limitations that prevent the address bus from being even wider (not that many users have use for an address space over 16 Mbytes). The 68000 does not retain the one-clock-per-access bus timing approach of the 6800 family but rather uses the more common scheme of four clocks for a typical cycle.

The 68000 bus structure is unique in that each bus cycle is truly asynchronous; that is, an acknowledge signal ($\overline{\text{DTACK}}$) from the addressed memory or peripheral must be asserted for every transfer to indicate that the addressed device is ready to read or write data. This allows the speed of the bus to be easily adjusted for accesses to fast or slow devices and also allows the system to be designed to halt if an access is attempted to an unused address. (Asynchronous and synchronous buses are described in detail in Chap. 3.)

All I/O must be memory-mapped; there are no separate I/O instructions or control lines. This is not too restrictive, since a large address space is available.

Because 68000 peripheral chips were not immediately available at the introduction of the 68000, several control signals were included in the 68000 to support 6800 peripheral chips. The $\overline{\text{VPA}}$ (valid peripheral address) input tells the 68000 which type of bus cycle to run. The system address decoder asserts $\overline{\text{VPA}}$ when it recognizes an address for a 6800-family peripheral device; the 68000 then executes a slower 6800-style bus cycle, using the E and VMA outputs, and ignores $\overline{\text{DTACK}}$.

The 68000 is available in various clock speeds, including 8, 10, and 12.5 MHz. The speed is indicated by one or two digits following the package-type code letter. For example, the 68000L10 is a 10-MHz part in the "L" package type (64-pin ceramic DIP). Other package types include the "R" pin-grid array and "ZB" and "ZC" leadless chip carriers. The fastest instructions execute in 4 clock periods, while the slowest requires 174. Thus, at 10 MHz, instruction times range from 0.4 to 17.4 μs.

Several variations of the 68000 are also available. The *68008* is an 8-bit bus version of the 68000, similar in concept to the 8088 8-bit version of the 8086. This microprocessor, which is used for the design example in Chapters 2 to 8, allows the use of 8-bit memory and peripherals while providing full compatibility with 68000 software. The *68010* is very similar to the 68000 but includes an important additional feature: the ability to continue an instruction after it has been suspended by a bus error, which is critical to the implementation of virtual memory (see Chap. 4). Another feature of the 68010 is a "loop mode" that speeds execution of short repetitive loops. The *68012* is a version of the 68010 with a 30-bit address bus for applications requiring a very large addressing range.

The *68020* is a full 32-bit microprocessor based on the 68000 architecture and is packaged in a 114-pin pin-grid array. The 32-bit address bus provides a 4-gigabyte address space. The standard clock rate is 16.67 MHz, and the basic bus cycle is reduced to three clock cycles rather than the four required by previous 68000-family processors. Thus, the minimum instruction time is only 180 ns. The ALU is a full 32 bits wide, so 32-bit operations require fewer cycles than with a 68000. The 68020 includes an on-chip 256-byte instruction cache. The cache stores the most recently executed (or about-to-be-executed) program sequences. This can significantly speed up program execution, since access to the on-chip cache requires only two clock cycles as compared to three cycles for external memory accesses. For successive executions of a program loop, no external memory references are required, since the instructions in the loop are stored in the cache after the first pass through the loop.

An innovative feature of the 68020 is dynamic bus sizing. Two bus signals are driven by the control logic to indicate the data bus width, which can be 8, 16, or 32 bits. The bus width can thus be varied depending on the address being accessed. This allows the use of a single 8-bit-wide EPROM to store the power-up "boot" program and a 32-bit-wide main memory for high-speed program execution.

The 68020 also includes several instruction set enhancements and a coprocessor interface. The coprocessor interface is used for the 68881 floating-point unit and the 68851 paged memory management unit and is described in Chap. 10.

The *Philips/Signetics 68070* is software compatible with the 68000 and includes a two-channel DMA controller, serial interface, timer/counter, memory management unit, and interrupt controller in the CPU chip. It is similar in concept to Intel's 80186 and Hitachi's 64180.

2.3.3 Other 16- and 32-bit Microprocessors

Zilog's Z8000 family was an early competitor to the 8086 and 68000. While it has not achieved the sales volume of the Intel and Motorola families, the Z8000 family is comparable in power. The Z8001 segmented version provides a 7-bit segment number in addition to a 16-bit address, for an effective addressing range of 8 Mbytes. The Z8002 nonsegmented version is software-compatible but is limited to a 64-Kbyte addressing range. The Z8003 supports virtual memory when used with a Z8020 memory management unit.

Zilog's Z80000 is a 32-bit microprocessor aimed at high-performance applications. Although it was announced before most other 32-bit microprocessors, a several-year delay in shipping fully functional chips made it a late entry.

Digital Equipment Corporation's LSI-11 was one of the first 16-bit microcomputers available. Since it is software-compatible with the PDP-11, a large software base was immediately available. The original LSI-11 was a set of three to five chips, depending on the version. The chip set is microprogrammed to emulate the PDP-11 instruction set. The T11 is a more recent single-chip implementation of the basic PDP-11 instruction set. The J11 is a more powerful version that includes hardware multiply/divide and floating point instructions. It is actually a hybrid, consisting of two chips mounted on a ceramic substrate. The major use of these microprocessors is in applications where there is existing software or expertise for the PDP-11.

TI's 99000 is a second-generation enhancement of the 9900. Rather than competing head-on with the 68000 and 8086 families for general computing applications, the 99000 is aimed at the high-performance control market.

National's 32000 family is one of the most advanced, having been designed from the start as a 32-bit microprocessor with virtual memory support. Like the 68000, it has 32-bit internal registers (although only 24 address bits are used) and an unsegmented 16-Mbyte address space. The addition of the 32082 memory management unit provides full virtual memory capability, with a 32-Mbyte segmented address space. The optional 32081 floating-point unit provides high-performance arithmetic functions.

Several different CPUs are available in the 32000 family. The 32032 has 32-bit internal and external data buses. The 32016 has a 16-bit external data bus, and the 32008 has an 8-bit data bus. The 32332 is an enhanced version of the 32032 which includes full 32-bit addressing and a variety of improvements for increased performance. All family members use a multiplexed address/data bus.

NEC's V Series microprocessors are enhanced 8086-type microprocessors. The V20 and V30 are pin-compatible with the 8088 and 8086, respectively. Their instruction set is a superset of the 8086's, so they are code-compatible but also provide additional functions. Internal design improvements reduce the number of clock cycles needed for some instructions and result in a modest performance increase (NEC claims "5 to 100 percent, depending on the application") even if the new instructions are not used. The V40 and V50 are similar to Intel's 80188 and 80186 and include a four-channel DMA controller, interrupt controller, three counter/timers, and a serial interface. They also include additional instruction set enhancements. All V-series microprocessors are implemented in CMOS.

AT&T's WE 32100 is a 32-bit microprocessor that is the heart of AT&T's Unix Microsystem, a chip set that (as the name implies) is specifically designed to be used in Unix-based computers.

Fairchild's Clipper is a very high-performance CMOS three-chip set sold mounted together on a small printed circuit board. It uses a *reduced instruction set computer (RISC)* architecture and operates at a clock rate of 33 MHz. A floating-point processor is included on the CPU chip, unlike most other microprocessors that require an external floating-point coprocessor. The two chips on the module in addition to the CPU are identical cache/memory management chips, one for data and one for instructions. In both price and performance, this chip set is out of the range of the microprocessors covered in this text.

The *Inmos T212 and T414 Transputers* are specialized 16-bit and 32-bit microprocessors, respectively, designed for use in multiple processor networks. Each CPU chip includes four high-speed (10 Mbits/s) serial interfaces for connection to other CPUs. Each CPU chip also includes 2 Kbytes of high-speed on-chip RAM.

2.4 THE 4-BIT SINGLE-CHIP MICROCOMPUTERS

The previous sections have described a variety of microprocessors. While some perform more functions than others and a few provide some internal RAM, all require additional memory and I/O devices to form a minimum functional system. The 16- and 32-bit devices represent an evolution toward very high-performance microprocessors.

A separate evolutionary path has led to complete single-chip microcomputers. Single-chip microcomputers (also called *microcontrollers*) include ROM, RAM, and I/O on a single chip, in addition to the processor itself.

The pioneering 4-bit microprocessors have become extinct. However, 4-bit single-chip microcomputers have not, and are used in very high volume. They are very inexpensive, single-chip solutions to multitudes of control tasks, including toys, appliances, and simple instruments. Most of these devices are mask-programmed and have relatively crude architectures and instruction sets. The expense of the mask charge combined with the relative difficulty of programming make these devices unattractive for low- to moderate-volume applications. However, for high-volume applications where every penny of production cost counts, the design time and mask cost are easily justified.

Four-bit single-chip microcomputers typically have an 8-bit-wide instruction memory and a separate 4-bit-wide data memory. Four bits are insufficient to encode a reasonable instruction set; 8-bit-wide program memory is therefore required to allow instructions to be fetched in a single read cycle. For bit-oriented or decimal-oriented applications, the 4-bit data word is convenient. The smaller size of the ALU, registers, and data memory is partially responsible for the decreased cost. The simpler instruction set also makes the chips smaller and therefore less expensive than more powerful 8- and 16-bit microprocessors and single-chip microcomputers.

Most 4-bit microcomputers are proprietary devices that are available only from a single manufacturer. Most of the successful microcomputer families include many versions with slightly different capabilities. For those families that are second-sourced, usually only a few members of the family are included.

As prices of 8-bit single-chip microcomputers fall, there is less and less incentive to suffer with the limited capabilities of 4-bit microcomputers. Thus, these devices will gradually be replaced by 8-bit microcomputers in all but the simplest, most cost-sensitive applications.

TI's TMS1000 was the first single-chip microcomputer. It is implemented with PMOS technology and includes 1024 bytes of ROM, sixty-four 4-bit words of RAM, a simple CPU, a 4-bit input port, and 19 output bits. It is available only as a mask-programmed device and cannot be expanded with external memory. Several different versions are available, including some in CMOS. While it is very primitive by today's standards, it was for many years the most cost-effective solution to many simple control tasks. Although it is less well known than devices such as the Z80 or 8048, it has in fact been produced in much higher volume due to its use in a number of very high-volume applications.

The TMS1000 was designed at a time when it was necessary to make optimal use of the available silicon area, since the limits of chip size and complexity presented severe constraints. While this device is now technologically obsolete, it continues to be used in some high-volume applications where the very low chip cost is the overwhelming consideration.

National Semiconductor's COPs (Controller Oriented Processors) family is a group of 4-bit microcomputers aimed at a wide range of control and timing applications. The family includes many different versions, including NMOS and CMOS devices and mask-programmed and ROM-less parts. Memory size varies from 512 bytes to 4 Kbytes of ROM and from 32 to 256 nibbles (4-bit words) of RAM. The ROM-less devices have external buses that allow external EPROMs to be connected for low volume applications.

Many other 4-bit microcomputers are available. Most are specialized in some way, such as providing direct drive for LCDs or vacuum fluorescent displays. The COPs family described above is distinguished by the large number of family members, allowing the user to choose a part with just the required capabilities and thus minimize the cost. Many other 4-bit microcomputers are available, primarily from Japanese manufacturers.

2.5   THE 8-BIT SINGLE-CHIP MICROCOMPUTERS

While 4-bit microcomputers have the advantage of being low-cost single-chip systems, they are limited in their computational power and speed and are often awkward to program. Eight-bit single-chip microcomputers provide significant computational resources and powerful instruction sets, yet still can operate as stand-alone devices. They are also capable of operating in expanded modes, which provide external buses in addition to the on-chip resources.

Several generations of 8-bit microcomputers are now available. The two major first-generation families are Intel's 8048 and Fairchild's and Mostek's 3870. The 8048 does not follow the architecture of any previous microprocessor. Because of the limits of the silicon technology at the time of the device's design, the instruction set and architecture are somewhat awkward. Nevertheless, the 8048 provides a flexible single-chip control system and is used in many diverse applications. Although the 8048 family is now technologically obsolete, it remains in fairly wide use due to its low cost, large number of alternate sources, and existing base of trained programmers. CMOS versions are also available, providing lower power consumption.

The 3870 is a single-chip version of Fairchild's early microcomputer, the F8. It has a crude instruction set and never gained much favor among programmers. It did achieve wide usage for a time, as it was less expensive than the 8048 and used less power. However, it has largely been superseded by more sophisticated microcomputers.

The Motorola 6801 was the first of the second-generation microcomputers. The 6801 is unusual in the single-chip arena in that it is software-compatible with a standard 8-bit microprocessor, the 6800. The 6801 led to the 6804 and 6805 families, which use a subset of the instruction set to reduce the chip size and cost. There is a large family of devices with varying I/O and memory configurations, including both CMOS and NMOS versions. Other second-generation devices include Zilog's Z8 and Intel's 8051. These include an on-chip serial I/O interface and timer.

Most single-chip microcomputers are available in ROM-less versions, which allow an external ROM to be connected. This provides the flexibility to use standard EPROMs or ROMs and to add external data memory or I/O. The ROM-less versions are widely used, often accounting for up to half the family's sales volume. (Most so-called ROM-less parts are not actually ROM-less; the ROM is simply disabled. They are often mask-programmed parts with an error in the ROM. As a result, the power consumption of the ROM-less parts is the same as that of the mask-programmed parts.) Typically, one or more control inputs are read by the microcomputer at power-up to determine whether internal or external ROM should be used. Thus, by connecting this control input appropriately, a mask-programmed device can be used with an external EPROM, and the on-chip ROM ignored.

Many single-chip microcomputers are also available in a piggy-back version with an EPROM socket in the top of the microcomputer package. This allows the use of EPROMs for prototyping while retaining all the I/O pins. Another approach is to provide a version in a package with enough pins to provide connections for the internal buses as well as the I/O signals.

Several single-chip microcomputers are available with a high-level language interpreter in their on-chip ROM. The high-level language program (typically BASIC or FORTH) is stored in external RAM. The interpreter program reads each high-level instruction from the external RAM and performs the indicated operation. From an external point of view, the single-chip microcomputer is operating as a high-level language processor. Inside the microcomputer, however, many machine language instructions must typically be executed for each high-level instruction, and program execution is quite slow.

2.5.1   Intel 8048 Family

The design of the 8048 family represents a compromise between the desire to produce a complete single-chip system and the limits of what could be economically implemented at the time it was designed. Figure 2.21 shows the block diagram. The 8048 includes 1 Kbyte of ROM, 64 bytes of RAM, and 27 I/O lines in a 40-pin package. Other family members provide up to four times as much memory. A simple 8-bit programmable

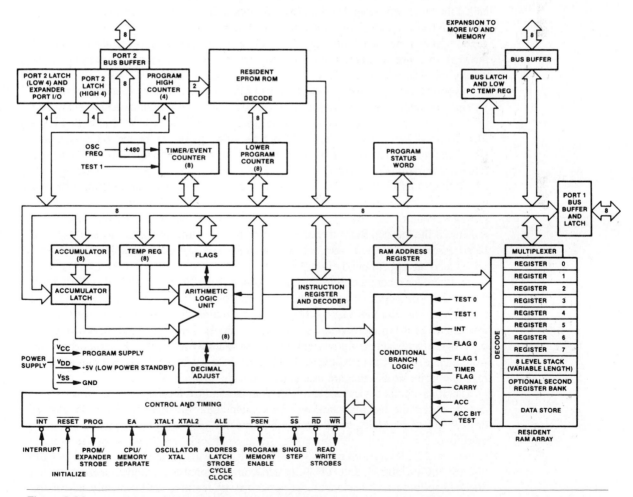

Figure 2.21.   The 8048 family 8-bit microcomputer block diagram. *(Courtesy of Intel Corporation.)*

timer is included. A separate power supply pin is provided for the RAM, which can be maintained on as little as 2.2 V.

The 8048's program counter is divided into two parts. The lower 8 bits function as a normal program counter, but the upper bits are changed only by certain instructions. This effectively divides the program memory space into 256-byte pages. The ROM contents can be accessed as data only on the same page as the current instruction, and on page 3. This makes it awkward to access large tables within a program and also makes generating a ROM checksum difficult. In addition, conditional and indirect jumps are limited to locations within the current page. For the 4K ROM version, the ROM is further divided into two 2K banks; jumps between banks require a bank select instruction, followed by a jump instruction.

The 8048 family includes the 8049 with twice the ROM and RAM, the 8748 and 8749 with EPROM on-chip instead of the mask-programmed ROM, and the 8035 and 8039 ROM-less devices. The 8050 has four times the ROM and RAM of the 8048. CMOS versions of most of the devices are also available. All execute the same instruction set. A lower-cost device with a subset of the instruction set and fewer I/O lines is called the 8021 and is supplied in a 28-pin package. The 8022 is a variation of the 8021 that includes an on-chip A/D converter. Most of these devices are produced by several vendors, including Intel, National Semiconductor, NEC, and OKI. There are some differences in power consumption, maximum clock rate, and various special features among the manufacturers.

Several 8048-family devices with on-chip EPROM are available in a plastic package without a window. They are programmed in the same way as a standard EPROM microcomputer, but since there is no window in the package, they cannot be erased. This is ideal for low- to moderate-volume production, since the plastic package is less expensive than the ceramic package with the window and no mask charge is required as with a mask-programmed device.

All 8048-family devices can interface to external memory, even if internal ROM is also used. The program counter is only 12 bits wide, so 4 Kbytes is the upper limit of program memory size. An input pin called EA (external access) is tied high or low to indicate if the internal ROM (if present) should be accessed or if external ROM should be accessed. If EA is low, internal ROM will be accessed as long as the address does not exceed the upper bound of the ROM.

The hardware configuration for connecting external ROM is shown in Fig. 2.22. The "bus" port serves as a multiplexed address/data bus; an external address latch is required to store the address bits. The high-order address bits are output on port 2. The 8048, like the 4-bit microcomputers described earlier, has separate address spaces for the program and data memories. This is implemented by providing the $\overline{\text{PSEN}}$ (program store enable) signal, which acts as the chip select to the program ROM, plus separate read and write strobes that are used only to enable data memory.

The 8048-family devices are available with maximum clock rates from 6 to 11 MHz, depending on the manufacturer and the version. One bus cycle requires 15 clocks, or 1.36 μs at 11 MHz. Most instructions execute in one cycle, although some require two.

Several CMOS versions of 8048-family devices are also available. These include the 80C48, 80C49, 80C35, and 80C39. In addition, National Semiconductor produces the 80CX48 series, which has additional power-saving features, and a piggyback version of the 8050.

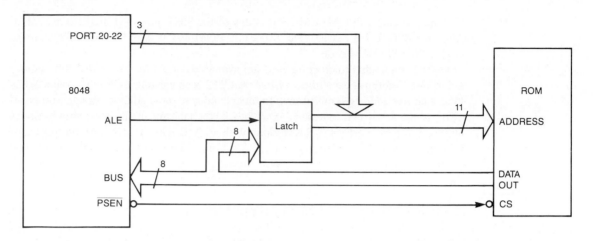

Figure 2.22.   The 8048 interface to external memory.

2.5.2   Intel 8051 Family

The 8051 is an enhanced single-chip microcomputer based on the 8048 architecture. The instruction set is based on the 8048's instruction set, but is significantly enlarged and improved. The awkwardness of the paged memory architecture is eliminated with the addition of nonpaged jumps, and a 16-bit program counter provides direct addressing of a 64-Kbyte memory space to make larger programs practical. Other improvements include twice the number of register banks, a much larger stack space, and subtract, multiply, and divide instructions.

An innovative software facility in the 8051 is the so-called Boolean processor, a set of instructions that operate on single-bit variables. Each bit of the I/O ports, registers, and certain memory locations can be individually addressed. These bits can be set, cleared, complemented, or moved and can be tested with conditional jump instructions. This provides very efficient instruction coding for the numerous single-bit operations typical of control-oriented applications; the masking and shifting instructions typically used to isolate single bits are not needed.

Hardware features of the 8051 include a serial I/O interface and two 16-bit programmable timers. The general hardware design, including off-chip memory expansion, follows the 8048 approach. ROM size is 4 Kbytes, and RAM size is 128 bytes.

The 8052 provides 8 Kbytes of ROM, 256 bytes of RAM, and an additional timer. This larger memory opens up new possibilities, such as the use of higher-level languages and larger application programs, which are too awkward to implement with the 8048 and similar microcomputers. The 8052 is available with a BASIC language interpreter in the on-chip ROM.

The standard 8051 operates at clock rates up to 12 MHz; a high-speed version, the 8051BH-1, operates at up to 16 MHz. A basic bus cycle requires 12 clock cycles, or 1 μs at 12 MHz. Most instructions execute in 1 μs, although some require 2 μs and the multiply and divide instructions require 4 μs. The 8031 is a ROM-less version, and the

8751 has on-chip EPROM. CMOS versions of the 8051 and 8031 are also available, called the 80C51 and 80C31. The 8032 is a ROM-less version of the 8052, and the 8752 is the EPROM version.

Several single-chip microcomputers are available that are based on the 8051 family and include additional capabilities. *Intel's 80C252* is an enhanced CMOS version of the 8052 with five additional multifunction timers and automatic address recognition capability on the serial port. *Siemens' SAB80515* is a superset of the 8051 that includes additional timers, ports, and RAM along with an A/D converter in a 68-pin package. *Signetics' 80C451* is another enhanced 8051 with more ports and other additional features.

2.5.3   Other 8-bit Single-chip Microcomputers

Intel's 8041 and 8042 are variants of the 8048 that are designed for use as slave processors. The *8044* is a variant of the 8051 that includes a special serial interface, which is intended to connect to a host processor. These devices are described in Chap. 10.

Motorola's 6801 family is software-compatible with the 6800 and includes 128 bytes of RAM, 2 Kbytes of ROM, a serial communications interface, and a programmable timer on-chip. It thus provides a way for small 6800-based applications to be implemented in a single chip. It is between the 8048 and the 8051 in capability, having only half the ROM of the 8051, a simpler instruction set, and only one timer.

The 6801 family includes many devices. The 6803 is a ROM-less version, while the 68701 includes an on-chip EPROM. The 6805 is a lower-cost microcomputer with a simpler instruction set and smaller memory. The 6804 is an even lower-cost family, aimed at competing with 4-bit devices. Both these families include many devices with varying memory and I/O capabilities. The version is specified by a letter and a number following the basic part type, such as 6804J2. CMOS versions are also available for many of the devices. A "14" prefix is used to indicate CMOS, while EPROM versions have a "7" after the "68." Thus, the CMOS version of the 6805 is the 146805, which becomes the 1468705 when the on-chip ROM is replaced with an on-chip EPROM. For high-performance CMOS devices, Motorola changed the numbering scheme to use the HC designation. The 68HC11, for example, is an enhanced CMOS version of the 6801, with 512 bytes of on-chip EEPROM, 4 Kbytes of ROM, 256 bytes of RAM, and additional I/O capabilities, including an eight-channel 8-bit A/D converter. The 68HC805C4 is a member of the 6805 family that includes 4 Kbytes of on-chip EEPROM, rather than EPROM or ROM.

Zilog's Z8 is roughly comparable to the 6801 in features and performance. It is not software-compatible with the Z80 or any other microprocessor; it has its own unique instruction set. The original member of the family, the Z8601, includes 2 Kbytes of ROM and 128 bytes of RAM, a serial I/O interface, and two programmable timers. Two prototyping versions are available. The Z8602 is in a 64-pin package with external bus connections in addition to the I/O lines, which allows external memory to be connected without giving up any I/O lines. The Z8603 piggyback version is in a 40-pin package that includes an EPROM socket in the top. A 4-Kbyte ROM version is also available as the Z8611.

The *Fairchild and Mostek 3870 family,* as mentioned earlier, was an early volume leader in 8-bit microcomputers but is not performance-competitive with newer devices.

CMOS versions, a version with on-chip EPROM, and a piggyback version with a built-in EPROM socket are available. In addition, a number of variants provide various memory capacities and I/O capabilities.

Rockwell's 6500/1 is a single-chip version of the 6502, which includes 2 Kbytes of ROM and 64 bytes of RAM. A version of this device is available with a FORTH language interpreter in on-chip ROM. *RCA's 1804* CMOS microcomputer is a single-chip version of the 1805. The 1805 is an enhanced version of the 1802, one of the first CMOS microprocessors, which has a relatively simple architecture. *NEC's 7801* is a high-end device targeted at applications requiring both on-chip resources and off-chip expansion. Supplied in a 64-pin package, it provides full 8085-type buses in addition to the on-chip I/O ports. It includes a 4-Kbyte ROM, and the instruction set is similar to the Z80's. The 7802 is a 6-Kbyte ROM version. *TI's TMS7000* series allows user customization of the chip features, including redefinition of the instruction set.

2.6   THE 16-BIT SINGLE-CHIP MICROCOMPUTERS

With the ability to build larger and larger chips has come the 16-bit single-chip microcomputer. These devices are the very high end of the single-chip field and are not as widely used as the simpler and less expensive 8- and 4-bit devices. Most single-chip applications simply do not need the increased performance these devices offer. However, there are some high-performance control applications for which these devices provide a very compact solution.

The first single-chip 16-bit device was TI's 9940, based on the 9900 architecture. Like the 9900, this device was not a big enough step above the 8-bit devices to gain much popularity. Two more recent devices, Intel's 8096 and Thompson/Mostek's 68200, are described in the following sections.

2.6.1   Intel 8096

Intel's 8096 evolved from a chip set designed for Ford Motor Company called EEC-IV, Ford's fourth-generation electronic engine control system. This system monitors all engine parameters and adjusts the engine controls to optimize performance, fuel economy, and emissions, which demands fast arithmetic capabilities and precise I/O timing.

Figure 2.23 shows the block diagram of the 8096. The 8096 is designed for applications such as closed-loop servo control that require high-speed I/O and computation capability. It does not follow the instruction set or architecture of any previous microprocessor family. It is available with an on-chip 8-Kbyte mask-programmed ROM (as the 8396), or external program memory can be used. The maximum clock rate is 12 MHz; this rate is internally divided by 3 to provide a basic state time of 250 ns. Simple instructions require four states, or 1 µs. The instruction set includes multiply and divide instructions, which execute in 6.5 µs with a 12-MHz clock. The 8097 is the same as the 8096 but includes an on-chip 10-bit A/D converter. Each device is available in a 48-pin DIP or a 68-pin flatpack; the 68-pin version provides additional I/O lines.

The 8096 includes a serial interface similar to that in the 8051, plus the usual parallel I/O lines. Two of the 8-bit parallel ports can operate as a multiplexed address/data

Figure 2.23. The 8096 16-bit microcomputer block diagram. *(Courtesy of Intel Corporation.)*

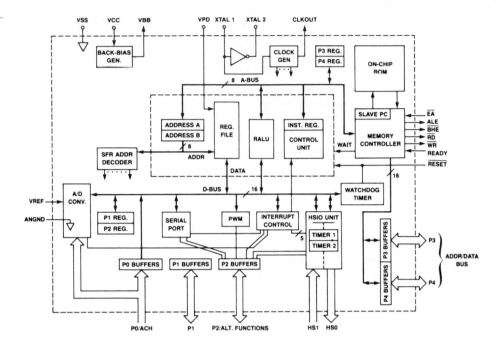

Figure 2.24. The 8096 high-speed input unit. *(Courtesy of Intel Corporation.)*

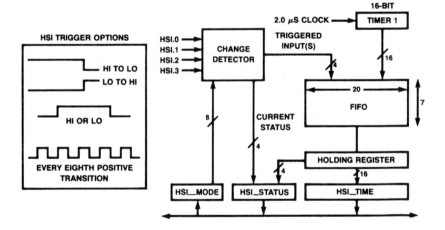

bus for connecting external program or data memory. The most innovative aspect of the 8096 is its high-speed I/O (HSIO) unit. Figure 2.24 shows the block diagram of the high-speed input unit. Timer 1 is a free-running timer that is incremented every eight states (2.0 μs at 12 MHz). The four high-speed input pins are sensed by the change detector. When a change is detected, the state of the inputs and the state of the timer are stored in a seven-level-deep first-in-first-out (FIFO) buffer. The mode can be set to detect only selected edges on selected inputs. An interrupt can be generated when the first word is written to the FIFO buffer or when the FIFO buffer is full. The software then reads the data in the FIFO buffer that indicates which signals changed and when the change occurred. Thus, this allows the timing of input signals to be determined with good resolution (2 μs with a 12-MHz clock) without requiring the software to rapidly poll the inputs.

The high-speed output unit performs a similar function for output signals. The software can specify up to eight events to occur at specified times. The time for each event can be determined by either of two timers. Events that can be programmed include setting or clearing any of the six high-speed output lines, generating an interrupt, clearing a timer, or starting an A/D conversion.

Another unusual output capability is the pulse-width modulated (PWM) output. This output signal has a fixed period of 256 states. The pulse width can be set to any value from 0 to 255 states by simply loading a register; the output signal is generated continuously with no software intervention. This provides an effective motor speed control with very little software overhead.

The 8096 includes an on-chip watchdog timer. This is a 16-bit counter that is incremented every state time. If the timer reaches its maximum count value, the processor is reset. Normally, software resets this timer periodically to prevent it from reaching the maximum count. If for any reason the software fails, the timer overflows and the processor is restarted.

The 8x9xBH is an improved version of the 8096 family. The 809xBH parts have no on-chip program memory; 839xBH devices have 8 Kbytes of on-chip ROM, and 879xBH devices have 8 Kbytes of on-chip EPROM. The last digit indicates whether or not the A/D converter is included and, if so, how many channels are available.

2.6.2   Thompson/Mostek 68200

While the 8096 uses a specialized architecture aimed specifically at high-speed control applications, the 68200 is a more traditional single-chip microcomputer. Figure 2.25 shows the block diagram of the 68200. The architecture of the 68200 is similar to single-chip microcomputers such as the 6801, except that there is more of everything: more sophisticated instructions, more bits processed at a time, more timers, and a more powerful serial interface.

The 68200 CPU is based on the 68000 architecture, modified to provide more efficient handling of byte-wide data and to improve performance in control-oriented applications. The instruction set is a subset of the 68000's, so the two devices are not directly code-compatible. The 68200-family devices include 4 Kbytes of ROM (2K × 16), 256 bytes of RAM, three 16-bit interval timers, and up to 40 bits of parallel I/O. A sophisticated serial interface provides synchronous or asynchronous communications and is more powerful than the serial interface found in most other single-chip microcomputers. The interrupt structure is also more sophisticated than usual for a single-chip microcomputer and includes up to 15 vectored interrupts.

Like most 8-bit single-chip microcomputers, the 68200 can operate as a self-contained single-chip device or it can connect to an external system bus. In the external bus mode, the pins used for parallel I/O lines in the single-chip mode are redefined to serve as a multiplexed address/data bus and control signals. The 68200 can be the master of the external bus, allowing the bus to be used to expand the memory and I/O capabilities.

Alternatively, the 68200 can be configured as a slave processor. In this mode, it

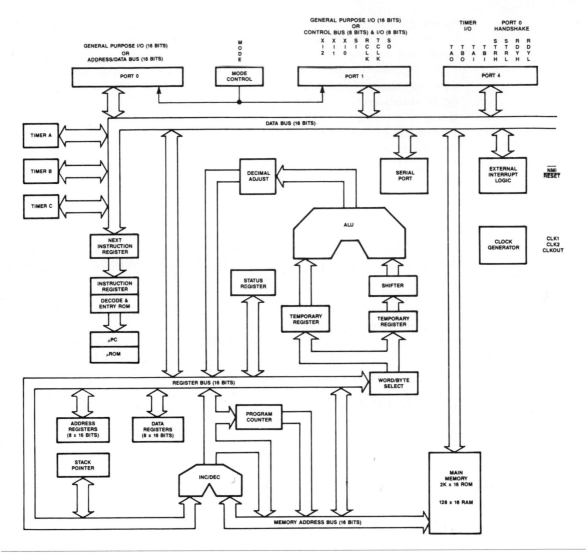

Figure 2.25.   The 68200 16-bit single-chip microcomputer block diagram. *(Courtesy of Thompson Components-Mostek Corp.)*

operates as a single-chip device but also connects to the system bus of a host processor. It operates independently except when it needs to communicate with the host system. It then requests the use of the host processor's buses and acts as a temporary bus master to transfer data to and from the host system's memory and I/O.

The maximum clock rate for 68200 family devices is 12 MHz. This clock is internally divided by 2, so the effective clock rate is 6 MHz. Basic instructions execute in three clock periods, or 0.5 μs. A 16 × 16 multiply instruction requires 21 clock periods, or 3.5 μs.

The 68200 family consists of several versions. The 68201 is packaged in a 48-pin DIP, and in the external bus mode is compatible with 68000-family microprocessors.

The 68E201 is an "emulator" version packaged in an 84-pin leadless chip carrier. The internal buses are connected to the additional pins, allowing memory and I/O expansion without sacrificing any I/O pins. The 68211 is similar to the 68201, except that the external bus is a general-purpose bus designed for use with microprocessors other than the 68000. The emulator version of the 68211 is the 68E211. ROM-less versions of the 68201 and 68211 are also available, designated by "/44" after the base part number.

2.7 MICROPROCESSOR AND MICROCOMPUTER SELECTION

The selection of a particular microprocessor or microcomputer cannot take place in a vacuum—it must be done with the application in mind. The quantity to be produced and the experience and capabilities of the designers must also be considered. Various aspects of the application's needs may have conflicting influences on the selection process, so it is also important to determine which characteristics are most important. This section describes each aspect of the selection process.

2.7.1 Matching Processors and Applications

Table 2.2 shows various classes of applications and typical processor types for each. Single-chip microcomputers are commonly used in control applications. In more complex control applications requiring large amounts of I/O, memory, or high-speed processing, 8- and 16-bit microprocessors are used. Data processing applications, such as personal computers, require more memory and I/O than a single-chip microcom-

Table 2.2 Typical Device Types for Various Application Classes

Application classes			Typical device types					
			Single-chip microcomputer			Microprocessor		
Type	Speed and complexity	Typical example	4-bit	8-bit	16-bit	8-bit	16-bit	32-bit
Control	Low	Automatic thermostat	X	X				
	Medium	Digital multimeter		X		X		
	High	Engine control		X	X	X	X	
Data processing	Low	Home computer				X		
	Medium	Midrange personal computer					X	X
	High	Engineering workstation; multiuser computer					X	X

puter can handle. The 32-bit microprocessors are used in single-user systems that require high performance, such as engineering workstations, and in multiuser computer systems.

2.7.2   Defining the Application

Determining microprocessor requirements is often difficult at the early stages of a project. When the microprocessor selection is being made, many features and various interfaces may be under consideration, and the speed at which functions must be performed and the size of the program required to implement them may not be clear. These ambiguities should serve as a warning that perhaps the project is not adequately defined for the microprocessor selection to be made.

A syndrome familiar to anyone who has been through a few product development cycles is "creeping featurism": one by one, features are added to the product during its development that by the end have significantly increased the scope of the software's tasks. After all, "it'll only take a few more lines of code." One of the problems associated with this syndrome is that the microprocessor or microcomputer originally selected (on the basis of the original requirements) may turn out to be marginally adequate by the time all the features have been added.

Another common situation is the project which is begun with only a vague idea of what the final product should be. It may be clear in someone's mind but often not in the mind of the people who make the final decisions (or the people who must implement them). Often even the originator of the product idea finds that as the implementation proceeds, many details crop up that were not considered in the beginning. To a certain extent, this type of product development is the most creative and has a place in a research environment. In a product development environment, however, the results can be disastrous.

Each of these situations results in substantial change in the definition of the product over the course of its development. While some change is unavoidable, it is clearly impossible to make an intelligent selection of a particular microprocessor when the characteristics of the end product are not well known at the outset. It is therefore important that the product be thoroughly thought out and defined before hardware or software development work begins. The user interface should be fully defined, including descriptions of typical interactions between the user and the product. Any tasks that must be performed within a time limit must be carefully analyzed to determine just how much processing must occur and how much time is available.

There is a great temptation among engineers and programmers to jump into the details of the design before all the analysis and definition work is completed. In some cases, the pressures of time or the unknown nature of the problem may make a complete definition impossible until some development work is completed. In these cases the microprocessor selection must be made before adequate information is available, and the risks involved in doing so must be recognized. The safest course of action is to pick a microprocessor more flexible and more powerful than seems necessary; by the time the project is complete, the microprocessor will likely be pushed closer to its limits than initially envisioned. When production volume is high and the cost of the end product is critical, a redesign for cost savings when the initial implementation is com-

Table 2.3   Application Characterization Checklist

Estimated size and complexity of program
Speed requirements: time-critical functions
Language to be used
Arithmetic functions needed
Memory requirements: ROM, RAM, mass storage
Input/output requirements
Data transfer rate: DMA requirements
Interrupt sources and response time required
Power available
Production volume
Price sensitivity

plete should be anticipated. This is least painful if the microprocessor selected for the initial product is part of a family that includes a lower-cost, lower-performance device.

In summary, the best approach is to design the product as fully as possible before selecting a microprocessor and to always expect that the demands placed on the microprocessor will increase substantially during the development.

Table 2.3 summarizes the characteristics of an application that should be considered when selecting a microprocessor or single-chip microcomputer. The following sections discuss each of these considerations.

2.7.3   Software Requirements

Software factors that affect microprocessor selection include the length and complexity of the programs required and the speed at which they must be executed. The length of a program is often difficult to judge from a set of product specifications. The only real guideline is experience; someone who is familiar with the programs required in previous applications can compare the new application to others and make an educated guess. The size of the program is important not only because of the amount of memory required but also because the longer the program the more important the ease of programming becomes.

Execution speed is often an important software criterion. It must be determined what the time-critical functions are and how many instructions are required to implement those functions. For example, if a program is required to receive data from a peripheral device at a certain rate, it must be able to read and process the data at that rate. If a motor or other mechanical device is under software control, the program must be able to execute the control algorithm quickly enough to keep up with the physical motion. When most of the system interfaces are to a human user, speed is usually less critical. In this case, the system must only be fast enough so that the product does not frustrate the user.

The selection of assembly language or a higher-level language can have a dramatic impact on memory usage and execution speed. Most high-level language programs use substantially more memory than equivalent assembly language programs. The exact multiple is highly dependent on the application, the language, and the programmer, but ratios of 2:1 to 5:1 are common. Many considerations enter into the selection of a language, and the details of this selection process are beyond the scope of this text.

High-level languages are becoming more and more common, since they allow programmers to develop software more quickly. They are most useful in larger applications, where the programming time (and thus the savings from the use of a high-level language) is substantial. They are also important when the software is likely to undergo many revisions and enhancements and must be easily understood and modified by programmers who were not involved in the initial development. Programs written in a high-level language are generally slower than assembly language programs, but speed-critical routines can be written in assembly language and linked to the high-level language program.

Another benefit of high-level languages is that the program is microprocessor-independent. A program written in assembly language is difficult to convert for use on another microprocessor. For a program written in a high-level language, on the other hand, the conversion consists primarily of passing the source code through a compiler for the new target microprocessor. (There are also a number of other potential complications. Peripheral chips are likely to change when the microprocessor is changed, and the software must be modified accordingly. The stack, interrupt vectors, and other special memory areas may have to be set up differently for different microprocessors.)

The need for fast arithmetic functions can significantly affect microprocessor selection. Sixteen-bit microprocessors typically provide multiply and divide instructions, which are much faster than algorithms based on addition and subtraction as must be used with most 8-bit microprocessors. If trigonometric or floating-point functions are required, coprocessors such as the 8087 provide greatly improved performance.

2.7.4 Memory Requirements

The amount of memory needed has two aspects: program memory requirements and data memory requirements. In a disk-based system, the program is stored on the disk and loaded into RAM. Thus, both program and data reside in RAM. The RAM does not necessarily need to be as large as the program, since the program can be broken up into sections (called *overlays*) that are loaded from the disk as needed. However, this reduces the speed of operation, so a tradeoff must be made between memory size and execution speed.

In a dedicated application without mass storage such as a disk drive, program memory is typically ROM or EPROM. In this case, RAM is used only for stack space (subroutine return addresses and saved registers) and temporary data storage. For many applications only 100 to 200 bytes of RAM are required. Particular requirements can greatly increase this, of course. A system that stores large amounts of temporary data, such as characters waiting to be printed or transmitted, may require much more data memory. Common RAM sizes in disk-based systems are 64 Kbytes to 1 Mbyte.

Program memory requirements are relatively difficult to estimate and are best estimated from experience. However, a few examples may serve to provide some feel for typical sizes. Typical video game cartridges contain 2 to 4 Kbytes of ROM. These programs are written in assembly language and are often carefully coded to minimize memory size. Many simple control applications also fall in this size range. A complex test instrument, such as a logic analyzer, may have 16 to 64 Kbytes of assembly language code. Programs that use alphanumeric displays and which have "user friendly" features such as prompts, error messages, and "help" functions can quickly grow into many tens or even hundreds of kilobytes. These programs are usually written in a high-level language.

Memory requirements must be very carefully evaluated when a single-chip microcomputer is under consideration. If the device is to be used in its single-chip mode, the program must fit in the on-chip ROM, and the on-chip RAM must be adequate for data storage. If the needs grow beyond the limits of the device, then it must be used in an expanded mode (if such a mode is available), resulting in a significantly different system architecture for which the "single-chip" microcomputer may not be the best choice. The expansion buses of most single-chip microcomputers offer little timing flexibility, so peripheral and memory interfacing can be more difficult than with conventional microprocessors. Some microcomputers have limits on the program memory even in the expanded mode; the 8048-family devices, for example, are limited to 4 Kbytes of program memory. Many a program has been painstakingly compressed to fit the available memory, and while this type of programming has its place, it can wreak havoc with schedules, budgets, software reliability, and product features.

2.7.5 Interfaces

The devices with which the microprocessor must interface, such as displays, keyboards, and storage devices, have a great impact on the hardware design of the system. As not all microprocessors are equal in their interfacing abilities, the interfaces required should be determined before a microprocessor is selected. This is particularly important if a single-chip microcomputer is to be used, since its I/O capabilities are relatively limited.

In the simplest case, it is only the number of I/O pins that are required that must be determined. This will show, for example, if a particular microcomputer can provide the I/O as a single-chip system. If serial I/O is required, the speed and type of data transfer are important. For low speeds and half-duplex, the serial interface can be implemented in software. If high speed or full-duplex operation is required, then a microcomputer with a built-in serial interface (or a serial interface IC) will be needed.

If high-speed data transfers are required, then the speed at which the transfers must occur may be critical. For example, if parallel transfers must occur at 100,000 transfers per second (10 μs per transfer), some microprocessors may be able to do the transfers under program control, while slower devices would require a DMA controller.

Most microprocessors can be interfaced to a variety of peripheral chips, including those in its own family, those in other families, and processor-independent devices. One area where this is generally not true is DMA controllers. Since the DMA controller must manipulate the buses in exactly the same way as the microprocessor, it must be designed to work with a particular microprocessor type. Interrupts are another area where the microprocessor characteristics are important. If a large number of interrupt sources are present and require fast response time, then a microprocessor with a good vectored interrupt structure is a must.

2.7.6   Coprocessors

For applications that require floating-point or trigonometric calculations, the availability of a math coprocessor that is designed to function with the selected microprocessor can be important. Such a coprocessor provides much faster execution of such functions than is possible with software subroutines. Although microprocessor-independent math processors are available that can be interfaced to any microprocessor, coprocessors designed to work with a specific microprocessor family are generally easier to use and provide higher performance. Common examples include Intel's 8087 for the 8086 and 8088, 80287 for the 80286, Motorola's 68881 for the 68020, and National's 32081 for the 32000 family. Coprocessors are discussed in detail in Chap. 10.

2.7.7   Future Needs and Expandability

The expected lifetime of a product and the degree of change and enhancement anticipated can be of considerable importance in microprocessor selection and system design. If the product design is likely to be fixed for its lifetime, and never modified or upgraded, then the expandability of the system is not important. In this situation it is also less of a problem if the program is compressed to fit in a limited memory space, since it will not need to be expanded. However, in applications that will evolve with customer feedback and the developer's experience, the memory and I/O must be expandable and the program readable and easily modified.

These requirements tend to lead the selection away from single-chip microcomputers. Many single-chip devices do not have any high-level languages available, and the limited memory size often conflicts with the desire for clean, straightforward programming. If a single-chip microcomputer is used in an application expected to undergo enhancement and modification, it is helpful to choose one of the devices that are part of a family with various memory capacities. Multichip systems are, of course, the most flexible, since it is relatively simple and inexpensive to add additional memory, I/O ports, and peripheral controllers.

2.7.8   Power Requirements

Portable applications require that the system have very low power consumption. Most hand-held products must operate from a small battery for long periods of time. Even if an ac power source is available, low power consumption is desirable since it means a less expensive power supply, less heat dissipation, and simpler packaging and cooling.

CMOS is the obvious choice when power considerations are paramount. In the early years of microcomputers, using a CMOS device meant significant sacrifices in speed and capability. Today, however, many of the common NMOS families also have CMOS equivalents. Speed is generally at least as high as the NMOS versions. The only penalty paid is increased system cost. As CMOS devices become more common, this penalty is becoming smaller and smaller and is often offset by decreased power supply and cooling costs. CMOS is becoming the dominant technology for most applications.

Most CMOS microcomputers include power-saving halt modes in which current drain typically drops to a few microamps. These modes are initiated under program control and terminated by an interrupt or by an internal timer reaching its count limit. If the application is such that the processor need not always be active, this can reduce average power consumption to very low levels.

There is a wide range in power consumption among CMOS microprocessors and microcomputers. The 80C48, for example, requires 10 mA when active, while NEC's 7502 consumes less than 900 μA. Thus, attaining low power consumption requires more than just using CMOS; it must be determined how powerful a processor is required, and power consumption specifications must be carefully compared. The percentage of time that can be spent in a halt or stop mode can have a dramatic effect on average current drain. Power consumption of CMOS devices is also a function of clock speed, so slowing the execution rate may be desirable when power consumption is critical.

Note that keeping the system power low requires more than just a CMOS microprocessor: memory, peripheral, and logic "glue" circuits must also be CMOS. If some NMOS or TTL components are used, pull-up resistors may be required where NMOS or TTL outputs drive CMOS inputs, as described in Chap. 1.

2.7.9 Analyzing Processor Performance

Determining the relative performance of various microprocessors is a complex matter. Many factors affect overall performance. The number of clock cycles per instruction can vary widely, so clock speed is only the beginning. For example, the 6809 executes instructions in as little as a single clock cycle, whereas the Z80 requires a minimum of four clock cycles per instruction. Furthermore, the capabilities of instruction sets vary widely. Obviously the width of the data paths is important, but this also depends on the type of data being handled. If the data is all 7-bit ASCII codes, or single-bit control signals, a 16-bit microprocessor may not be any better than an 8-bit microprocessor. However, the more sophisticated instruction set of a 16-bit processor may be an advantage even for such applications. Addressing modes and register sets also come into play. Some microprocessors have only a few registers, and others have over a dozen. Some have very limited arithmetic instructions, while others have extensive arithmetic instruction sets.

Many applications do not begin to push the limits of the microprocessor's performance, and in these situations an analysis of the relative performance of several candidate devices is not necessary. (Such applications are also a good candidate for implementation in a high-level language.) However, some applications need all the performance they can get, and it is then critical to make an accurate appraisal of the alternative microprocessors. This is typically done with programs called *benchmarks*. A benchmark is a well-defined program, such as a bubble sort or a search routine, that can be written for each microprocessor under consideration. The length and execution speed of each implementation can then be compared to get some indication of how the processors compare in memory efficiency and performance. Since each program does exactly the same function, it is supposed to be a fair comparison. Another aspect that can be measured with benchmarks is the interrupt response time, which includes the time required to save the registers (called a *context switch*).

Unfortunately, benchmarks are often misleading. Nearly every microprocessor manufacturer provides benchmarks showing that their device is better than the competition's. Some processors are much better at some tasks than at others; the comparison can thus be slanted by the selection of the task. It is therefore important to use a variety of benchmarks, and for the benchmarks to be typical of the tasks needed by the specific application. For example, the Z80 will score high on block search and move programs, since special instructions for these functions are part of the Z80 instruction set. The 6809, on the other hand, does much better than the Z80 for multiplications, since it includes a multiply instruction.

The expertise and attitude of the programmer also play a critical role. If one person writes the benchmarks for several microprocessors and is an experienced 8086 programmer (or happens to work for Intel), then the 8086 version is likely to be better written. The best solution is for an expert on each microprocessor to write the benchmark for that microprocessor. This is generally impractical, however. Next best is to have one person write all the benchmarks, assuming that this person is (1) unbiased, (2) equally experienced (or more likely inexperienced) with each microprocessor, and (3) a good enough programmer to quickly learn the various instruction sets and do a good job on each version. It is difficult to find such an individual.

Yet another factor that biases benchmarks is the range of microprocessor speeds available. For example, the 8086 is available with a maximum clock speed of 5, 8, or 10 MHz, while the 68000 is available with maximum clock speeds of 8, 10, or 12.5 MHz. Which do you select for the comparison? One alternative is to use the fastest part available in each case, but this often changes with time as faster versions are introduced. Picking equal clock frequencies is not a good solution, since different processors require different numbers of clock cycles per instruction. Further complicating the issue is that different processors operating at identical clock rates may have very different memory access time requirements; thus, for the same memory devices, one microprocessor may require a wait state while another microprocessor does not. Perhaps the best choice is to use the maximum clock speed that allows each microprocessor to operate with a given speed of memory with no wait states.

To generate truly valid benchmarks, it is therefore necessary for users to write their own (or hire someone to write them). This involves a substantial effort. The tasks or algorithms to be implemented must be carefully chosen to be representative of the needs of the application. Each microprocessor must then be studied, and the benchmark programs carefully written and checked. The clock speeds must be selected, and it must be determined if any of the processors will require wait states to work with the desired memory devices. The execution time of each routine can then be calculated by counting the total number of clock cycles required, or if a working system is available, execution time can be measured.

Execution time is not the only parameter of interest, however. The length of the program is also important, since this determines the amount of memory that will be required. It is generally possible to write a program for optimum execution speed or minimum length, but not both. Another variable is the amount of data memory required. Thus, the importance of each of these factors in the particular application must be weighed and the benchmarks written accordingly.

The use of high-level languages further complicates the issue. Some processors may do very well with carefully coded assembly language, but the available compilers are not likely to generate code of comparable efficiency. If a high-level language is to be used for the application program, it is therefore necessary to compare the size of the code generated and the speed of execution for a given high-level language program when using the compilers available for each of the processors.

Clearly, generating useful benchmarks is a great deal of work. Very few projects can afford the time and budget required for such a study. Fortunately, for most applications any of the processors within a given class will have adequate performance. The importance of benchmarks is frequently overstressed; performance is often not the key issue.

Published benchmarks can be used to get some idea of relative performance. They must be examined very carefully, however, for all the variables just discussed. If published benchmarks are taken at face value, the user is likely to be led astray by the biases (conscious or unconscious) of the programmer or differences between the benchmark situation and the actual application. If a variety of benchmarks from different sources are available, an average can be used to obtain a more accurate appraisal.

Another aspect of benchmarking is evaluating microprocessors based on their architecture and instruction set. Table 2.4 lists characteristics to be considered when evaluating a microprocessor. Software factors that can be compared include the number and

---

Table 2.4 Microprocessor Characteristics Checklist

Instruction set
    Data types: bit operations, long words
    Arithmetic functions: multiply and divide
    Encoding efficiency
Register set
    Number of registers
    Width of registers
    Regularity/orthogonality; special-purpose registers
Addressing
    Number of modes: indirect, indexed, etc.
    Segmented or linear addressing
    Memory and I/O address ranges
    Memory management
Buses and control signals
    Bus timing and control signal architecture
    Interrupts
    DMA/bus arbitration control signals
    Data and address bus width
    Clock speed and bus cycle time
Miscellaneous
    Prefetch, cache memory
    Privilege levels
    Coprocessor support: floating-point, I/O processors
    Power requirements
    Additional on-chip functions: interrupt controller, DMA, etc.
Nontechnical considerations
    Vendor reputation and alternate sources
    Documentation quality and availability
    Application notes and design guides
    Development tools: emulators, debuggers
    Software support: operating system, compiler, assembler, utilities

Table 2.5   Additional Characterization Checklist for Single-chip Microcomputers

Parallel I/O
    Number of bits
    Control flexibility: single-bit access
    Drive capability
Serial I/O
    Data rates
    Modes of operation: synchronous, asynchronous
    Software support required
Timers
    Number of timers
    Number of bits in each timer
    Flexibility: number of operating modes
    Expansion capabilities
Family members
    Compatible devices with more or less memory
    Emulator or piggyback devices for prototyping
    Devices with special display drive (for example, LCD)

size of the registers, addressing modes, and instruction set capabilities. The encoding efficiency of the instruction set (the number of bytes of code to represent a given instruction) can significantly affect program size. If needed by the application, high-level language and operating system support is important. The *regularity* or *orthogonality* of a register set and instruction set refers to the degree to which all registers are general-purpose. A very regular architecture (such as the 68000's) allows any register to be used for any function, whereas a nonregular architecture (such as the 8086's) has special functions associated with specific registers. Regular architectures make programming easier and make it easier for compilers to produce good code.

Hardware factors include the width of the address and data buses, bus cycle times, control signals, and clock speed. Interrupt structures and bus arbitration signals are also important. For 16- and 32-bit microprocessors, microprocessor evaluation is complicated by the need to consider memory management methods, coprocessors, and the effect of caches and instruction prefetching. In addition to the technical characteristics, the vendor's reputation, alternate sources, documentation support, and software support are important.

Table 2.5 lists additional factors to be considered when evaluating single-chip microcomputers. These include the power and flexibility of parallel and serial I/O ports, timers, and off-chip expansion capabilities. The existence of other family members is important, both for prototyping purposes and for future expansion.

2.7.10   Nontechnical Considerations

Considerations other than the technical virtues of a microprocessor often dominate the selection process. For any given application, many devices are technically acceptable. Price is, of course, an important consideration, but it must be viewed in the proper light. If the anticipated production volume is low, development time and cost are more important than unit cost. The cost must also be evaluated not just for the micro-processor by itself but for the entire system.

In many cases, development cost is an important consideration. It is strongly affected by the tools available and by the expertise of the designers. A good develop-ment system will often substantially reduce development time and thus reduce engi-neering costs. However, if the development system must be purchased specifically for a single project, it may be difficult to amortize the expense. Thus, the choice of a micro-processor is often strongly influenced by existing development tools. This is entirely appropriate as long as the anticipated production volume is fairly low. For high-volume applications, it pays to select the most optimal device, even if it means buying addi-tional support equipment.

The experience of the designers often sways the selection more than it should. Engi-neers and programmers with limited experience are likely to choose the device they are most comfortable with or interested in. This may not be the optimal device, but if it will do the job for a reasonable cost, it may be acceptable. It is important, however, for major projects, or products to be produced in high volume, that a broader view be taken.

The reputation of prospective vendors must also be considered, particularly if a sole-sourced device is under consideration. The ability to obtain parts in the required volume, at a good price, and in a timely manner is critical. Many economically unsuc-cessful microprocessors have been discontinued or been produced in such low volume that the prices have risen while more successful devices have become cheaper. The decision to use a just-introduced device, or one that does not have much of a following, must thus be made very carefully. Some vendors have a reputation for standing behind whatever they introduce; others have often dropped products that failed to meet sales expectations.

Much support is needed for an efficient development effort. The availability of good development tools, high-level language compilers, software manuals, and application notes varies considerably from one device to another and from one vendor to another. Much of this support typically evolves over a period of years after the introduction of a device, and not everything that is advertised is always actually available. Peripheral chips are also often slow to follow microprocessor introductions, particularly for ad-vanced 16- and 32-bit devices. Selecting the latest and greatest microprocessor can thus be fraught with peril. Often an older, less glamorous microprocessor will do the job equally well at a lower price.

2.7.11 Economics of Production Volume

Throughout this chapter, production volume has been mentioned as a consideration in the selection of a microprocessor or microcomputer. The number of units to be produced affects the selection process in many ways. At one end of the spectrum is a one-of-a-kind application, in which only one or a few units are ever produced. In gen-eral, such applications use standard single-board computers or multiboard systems based on a standard system bus, such as the Multibus. The cost to develop custom hardware cannot be justified in this case, unless for some reason (such as severe physi-cal size constraints) standard boards are not usable. Only the interface hardware unique to the application needs to be custom-built.

The selection of a microprocessor in these very low-volume applications is relatively noncritical. The most important factors are performance and ease of programming. The cost of the microprocessor hardware is relatively unimportant; for any but a trivial program, the cost of the programming will exceed the hardware cost by a wide margin. Availability of the desired standard hardware and software tools is also of key importance.

At the other extreme, for applications to be produced in very high volumes, the unit cost is the paramount consideration. Most very high-volume applications are consumer products whose production volume often exceeds 100,000 units per year. This means that an additional engineering expense of $100,000 will pay for itself in the first year if it saves $1 on unit production cost.

Most applications fall somewhere between these two extremes. A *break-even chart*, as shown in Fig. 2.26, is helpful in making tradeoffs between development and production costs. A horizontal line shows the development costs for each alternative. Since development cost is a one-time expense, it remains constant regardless of the pro-

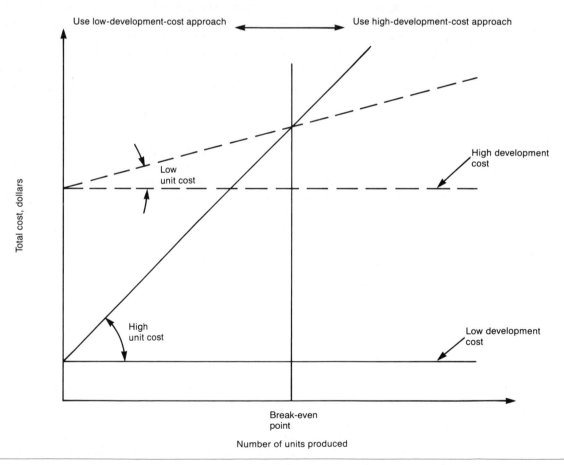

Figure 2.26.   Break-even chart for comparing development alternatives.

duction volume. The figure shows two possible implementations for a hypothetical product: one approach with high development costs, using a mask-programmed microcomputer, and another with lower development costs, using a standard single-board computer. The high-development-cost approach results in a lower unit cost, so the total costs increase more slowly with production volume. Where the two sloped lines cross is the break-even point; the total production volume must exceed this level to justify the high development cost approach.

Of course, real life is not so simple, and many other factors come into play. The cost-vs.-volume relationship is not really linear; the higher the volume, the lower the unit cost. Another factor is the time value of money; it is not worth spending $100,000 just to save $100,000 over the lifetime of the product. In addition, the risk factor and amount of capital available come into play. High volumes may be hoped for, but if the risk is high or the developer is cash poor, the lowest-cost development approach may be the only realistic solution. The product can always be redesigned for cost reduction if it proves to be a smashing success.

The selection of a particular microprocessor or microcomputer affects these costs in many ways. Mask-programmed single-chip microcomputers generally increase development costs. Special development tools are often required, the instruction sets and architectures are often more difficult to work with, high-level languages are often unavailable, and debugging tools are often primitive. Four-bit single-chip microcomputers are cost-effective only when production volume is high; 8-bit microcomputers may be more cost effective for moderate-volume applications, even if a less expensive 4-bit device could do the job.

For mask-programmed microcomputers, a mask charge must be paid. This charge is typically between $1000 and $4000. Depending on the supplier and part type, the time from submitting the program code to delivery of first samples varies from 6 to 20 weeks. Any program change means another mask charge must be paid and another 6- to 20-week delay. While many single-chip microcomputers are available in EPROM or piggyback versions, these are generally more expensive than multichip systems and are used primarily for prototyping.

For products to be produced in low volume, ease of programming and debugging becomes a primary concern. For example, it would be foolish in a low-volume application to use an 8048; a Z80, 6809, or perhaps even an 8086 or 68000 could reduce the programming costs, and the total increase in production cost would be relatively small. For intermediate volumes, a ROM-less microcomputer with an external EPROM is often a cost-effective choice.

2.8 DESIGN EXAMPLE

In this section, we begin the presentation of the complete 68008-based dedicated controller design example. In Chap. 1, the block diagram was presented, and various applications were described. In this chapter, we describe the most basic support circuits for the microprocessor: the clock oscillator and reset circuits. In Chap. 3, the bus interface and control logic are added. The complete schematic consists of five pages: Figs. 3.42, 4.44, 6.25, 7.55, and 8.35.

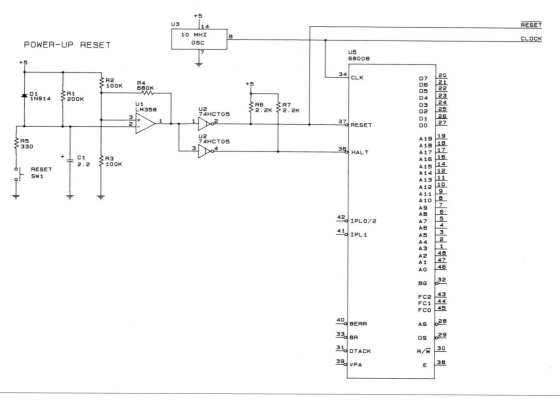

Figure 2.27.   The 68008 design example: processor, clock, and reset circuits.

The 74ALS logic family is used for most of the "glue" logic in the design example. In some cases, the speed of ALS (as compared to LS) is required; these situations are noted in the timing descriptions. The ALS family is used even when speed is not critical, since it has lower power dissipation than LS and the price premium is small. For octal latches and buffers, which have relatively high power consumption even in ALS, the HC and HCT families are used. High speed is not required for these devices. To reduce the power consumption of the system even further, some of the ALS TTL could be replaced with HCT, but the savings would be minor.

Figure 2.27 shows the 68008 microprocessor with its clock and reset circuits. The clock circuit is very simple: a hybrid clock oscillator module connected to the microprocessor's CLK input. The hybrid clock oscillator module includes a quartz crystal, load capacitors, and an oscillator IC. These modules occupy the same space as a 14-pin IC and relieve the designer from concern with crystal specifications and oscillator design. Depending on the output drive capability of the oscillator module and the number of other devices using the clock signal, it may be desirable to buffer its output with a high-speed buffer. The 68008 specification calls for minimum clock rise and fall times of 10 ns. If several capacitive loads are placed on the oscillator output, the rise and fall times may be slowed beyond these limits.

The clock circuit should be placed as close to the microprocessor as practical to minimize electromagnetic radiation emitted by the system, and also to keep the clock signal as "clean" as possible. Microprocessors can behave very strangely if there are noise glitches, poor logic levels, or slow rise and fall times on the clock signal.

The reset circuit is slightly more complex. The operational amplifier (*op amp*), operating as a comparator, provides the power-up reset pulse. Many different types may be used, but the op amp or comparator must be able to operate on a +5-V supply and provide valid logic levels at its output. The LM358 op amp shown can drive CMOS inputs but is marginal with TTL. When power is first applied, capacitor C_1 is discharged. Thus, the voltage at the minus input of the comparator is initially at 0 V but rises as the capacitor is charged through R_1. Resistors R_2 and R_3 provide a threshold of approximately 2.5 V at the positive input of the comparator. When the capacitor charges to this voltage, the comparator output goes low, terminating the reset pulse. Resistor R_4 adds a small amount of hysteresis to the threshold: when the comparator output is high, R_4 increases the threshold voltage, and when the comparator output is low, R_4 decreases the threshold voltage. This helps prevent glitches on the reset signal if there is noise on the power supply line as the voltage on the capacitor reaches the comparator threshold.

Diode D_1 is included to discharge the capacitor quickly when power is turned off. This reenables the reset circuit to generate another power-up reset pulse after a short power interruption.

The push button is included to allow a manual reset. In most applications, this is not needed, but it is often useful during debugging. Resistor R_5 limits the current through the switch to protect its contacts; otherwise, when the switch is pressed, the current would be limited only by the capacitor's internal resistance, the switch's contact resistance, and the wiring resistance.

The 68008 specification calls for a reset pulse of at least 10 clock cycles, except at power-up. At power-up, the specification calls for a reset pulse of at least 100 ms. The values shown in the figure provide a nominal power-up reset pulse of 250 ms, providing more than adequate margin for component tolerances.

While most microprocessors require that the reset pulse be applied only to a single $\overline{\text{RESET}}$ input, 68000-family microprocessors require that both $\overline{\text{RESET}}$ and $\overline{\text{HALT}}$ be asserted. These are bidirectional pins and are asserted by the microprocessor under certain conditions. Thus, they must be driven with open-collector drivers.

The pull-up resistors provide the high level when the line is not being driven. The value of these pull-up resistors must be low enough to provide the high-level input current required for all the inputs connected to the line while maintaining a valid logic high, and high enough so that they do not require that the driver sink more current than it is capable of at a logic low. As long as the second limit is not exceeded, a lower value provides better performance in terms of greater high-level drive capability and faster switching from low to high (although switching speed is not of importance in this application). Power consumption is increased as the resistance is decreased. The low-level current required by the 2.2 kΩ pull-up resistors to provide a 0.4 V logic low is

$$\frac{5 \text{ V} - 0.4 \text{ V}}{2.2 \text{ k}\Omega} = 2.1 \text{ mA}$$

Figure 2.28. Simpler reset circuit

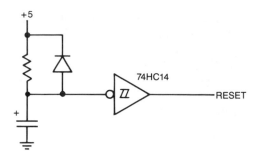

This is easily within the 4-mA drive capability of the 74HCT05. The 2.2-kΩ resistor can provide a high-level current (assuming a logic high of 2.4 V) of

$$I = \frac{5\ V - 2.4\ V}{2.2\ k\Omega} = 1.2\ mA$$

This is well in excess of the combined input currents of all the loads, so 2.2 kΩ is a safe value.

The $\overline{HALT}$ output is asserted when the microprocessor stops executing instructions due to an unrecoverable failure, such as a *double bus fault*. An example of a double bus fault is when an error such as an illegal address occurs and another error occurs when the microprocessor attempts to execute the exception-processing routine.

Figure 2.28 shows an alternative power-up reset circuit that, although widely used, is not as effective as the one described above. Using a Schmitt-trigger inverter (an inverter with hysteresis) instead of a comparator eliminates the need for the three threshold-setting resistors, and the inverter may be essentially "free" if the other inverters in the IC are used elsewhere in the circuit.

The problem with this circuit occurs when there is a brief power failure. The inverter's input threshold when its output is high may be as low as 0.9 V. Thus, when a power failure occurs, the capacitor must be discharged below this voltage for a power-up reset pulse to be generated when power returns. Diode D_1, which is responsible for quickly discharging the capacitor in this situation, has a voltage drop of 0.7 V. Thus, the capacitor charge asymptotically approaches 0.7 V after a power failure, and several seconds without power are typically required for a power-up reset pulse to be generated when power returns. Discharge below 0.7 V occurs relatively slowly, since the only path is through the pull-up resistor. Also note that if the capacitor is discharged to only 0.7 V, the power-up reset pulse will be shorter than expected and may cause erroneous microprocessor operation.

Thus, the higher threshold voltage of the comparator circuit provides several benefits. The capacitor can be smaller for a given value of reset pulse width and pull-up resistor, since it is charged for a longer time before the threshold is reached. The capacitor is quickly discharged below the threshold when power fails, providing a more reliable reset pulse after short power interruptions.

These circuits are equally applicable to systems using the 68000, 68010, and 68020 microprocessors. The basic power-up reset circuit can be used with virtually any microprocessor.

2.9 SUMMARY

The selection of the optimal microcomputer or microprocessor for a particular application is a challenging task. The higher the anticipated production volume, the more important it is that the lowest-cost device be selected. In low-volume applications, it is most important to have a device that has more than enough power and is easy to program and debug.

The selection must begin by narrowing the field. First, the needs of the application must be carefully analyzed. Second, a class of device (i.e., microprocessor or microcomputer) is selected. Third, the word size is selected, and finally, the field is narrowed to a few devices that are compared in detail. Other considerations, such as the experience of the staff, the development tools and peripheral chips available, and the reputation of the vendor, are also important.

Completing this selection effectively requires knowledgeable, unbiased personnel and a significant amount of time and energy. The selection should always take into account the anticipated needs of the application and the fact that these needs are likely to increase during the development. Unless cost is very critical, it is always better to have too much capability than too little.

2.10 EXERCISES

2.1. The devices discussed in this chapter fall into two classes: microprocessors and single-chip microcomputers.

    a. What are the characteristics required for a device to be a single-chip microcomputer?

    b. The 6802 includes many of these characteristics. Is it a single-chip microcomputer? If not, what is missing?

    c. What are the major advantages and disadvantages of single-chip microcomputers?

2.2. Which semiconductor process technologies are the most widely used for microprocessors? Which has the lowest power consumption?

2.3. What is the key characteristic that differentiates an 8-bit microprocessor from a 16-bit microprocessor? What other differences typically exist between the two classes that are not specifically related to word size?

2.4. The 8085 and Z80 are both upgrades of the original 8080. What are the differences between these two devices? What are the similarities? Describe an application for which the 8085 would be a better choice.

2.5.   Most 8-bit microprocessors have 16-bit address buses, while most 16-bit microprocessors have address buses from 20 to 24 bits wide. What is the reason for the increased number of address bits? Is it related to the word size?

2.6.   List the major differences between the 8086 and 68000. Which can address more memory? Which uses a multiplexed bus? Which has a segmented address space?

2.7.   Four-bit single-chip microcomputers usually have an 8-bit-wide instruction memory and no external buses. Why then are they called *4-bit* microcomputers?

2.8.   List the most important differences between the first-generation single-chip microcomputers, such as the 8048, and the second-generation devices, such as the 8051 and 6801.

2.9.   CMOS microcomputers have inherently lower power consumption as compared to NMOS microcomputers. What other features do they often include to further reduce power consumption?

2.10.   List the key characteristics of any application that should be known before making a microprocessor selection.

2.11.   The XYZ Company is developing a new product line and needs to select a microprocessor or microcomputer. The new products are stand-alone test instruments, and the program size required is estimated to be 2 to 4 Kbytes. There are no particularly time-critical tasks. Production volume is estimated to be 100 units a year for each of four different products.

    a.   Should they use a microprocessor or a single-chip microcomputer? What are the pros and cons of each for this application? What other information about the products is needed to make a fully informed decision?

    b.   Should they use a 4-, 8-, or 16-bit device? Why?

    c.   The engineers have decided to use an 8051, but the lab manager complains about the cost and wants to consider an 8048. How do the engineers justify their decision?

    d.   One of the products has a number of features added, and the program size is now estimated to be 12 Kbytes. How does this affect the device selection?

    e.   One of the simpler products is a great success and now looks like it will sell 10,000 units a year if the cost can be reduced. Can a different microprocessor or microcomputer help lower the cost? What type should they consider?

    f.   One product has been respecified by the marketing department and now needs a remote control interface, an internal floppy disk, and easy expandability. What type of microprocessor or microcomputer would you now recommend?

2.12.   Define a task to serve as a benchmark, and code the benchmark program for at least two different microprocessors. Compare the execution time and number of bytes of program and data memory required by each. Then rewrite each program to optimize for program size rather than speed, and repeat the comparison.

2.13. A one-of-a-kind system requires a moderately long and complex program. What type of microprocessor should be used? Would the selection be different if 100 units were to be built? For 100,000 units?

2.11 SELECTED BIBLIOGRAPHY

Microprocessor and Microcomputer Surveys

Electronic Design magazine and *EDN* magazine. Each of these magazines produces annual microprocessor survey issues, usually in the late fall, that summarize all available devices.

IC Master, Hearst Business Communications. This massive reference work is published annually and lists virtually all commercially available ICs. Listings are sorted by part number and by function, and a second-source directory is also included.

Greenfield, Joseph D. (ed.). *Microprocessor Handbook,* New York: Wiley, 1985. Includes a general introductory section, followed by chapters on the 8080, 8085, 6502, 6800, 6809, Z80, 8086, Z8000, and 68000.

Lister, Paul (ed.). *Single-Chip Microcomputers,* New York: McGraw-Hill, 1984. Describes the 6801, TMS1000, TMS7000, Z8, COPs, and 68200 single-chip microcomputers.

General Microprocessor and Microcomputer Data Books

Advanced Micro Devices. *MOS Microprocessor Data Manual,* Sunnyvale, CA. Covers the 8085, 8086, and Z8000 families and a variety of peripherals.

Intel. *Microsystem Component Handbook,* Santa Clara, CA. Includes data sheets and applications information for all Intel microprocessors and peripherals, including 8085 and 80x86 families.

Thompson Components-Mostek. *Microelectronic Data Book,* Carrollton, TX. Includes data sheets on Z80, 3870, and 68000 families.

Zilog. *Data Catalog,* Campbell, CA. Includes data sheets on Z8, Z80, Z800, and Z8000 families.

8-bit Microprocessors

Intel. *MCS-85 User's Manual,* Santa Clara, CA.

Motorola. *Eight-Bit Microprocessor and Peripheral Data,* Phoenix. Covers the 6800, 6802, and 6809 families.

National. *NSC800 Microprocessor Family Handbook,* Santa Clara, CA.

Thompson Components-Mostek. *Z80 Designer's Guide,* Carrollton, TX.

Zilog. *Z80 CPU Technical Manual,* Campbell, CA.

16- and 32-bit Microprocessors

Goody, Roy W. *The 16-Bit Microprocessor: An 8086/8088 Based Product Development Approach,* Sunnyvale, CA: CompuTech Publishers, 1986. A software-oriented text covering systems design with the 8086 family. Includes a section on development tools.

Intel. *iAPX 86/88/186/188 User's Manual Hardware Reference* and *iAPX 86/88/186/188 User's Manual Programmer's Reference,* Santa Clara, CA. The primary reference documents for 8086/80186-family microprocessors; also cover the 8087 and 8089.

————. *iAPX 286 Hardware Reference Manual,* Santa Clara, CA.

————. *iAPX 286 Programmer's Reference Manual,* Santa Clara, CA.

Motorola. *M68000 8-/16-/32-bit Microprocessors Programmer's Reference Manual,* Phoenix. (Also published by Prentice-Hall.) Software reference for the 68000, 68008, 68010, and 68012.

————. Detailed individual data sheets are published for the 68000, 68008, and 68010. These data sheets are the primary hardware reference documents.

————. *MC68020 User's Manual,* Phoenix. (Also published by Prentice-Hall.) This is both the hardware and software reference for the 68020.

National. *NS32000 Family Data Book,* Santa Clara, CA.

Triebel, Walter A., and Avtar Singh. *The 68000 Microprocessor Architecture, Software, and Interfacing,* Englewood Cliffs, NJ: Prentice-Hall, 1986. The emphasis of this text is on architecture and software, but a basic hardware example is included.

4-bit Microcomputers

National. *COPS Microcontroller Databook,* Santa Clara, CA.

Texas Instruments. *TMS1000 Series Data Manual,* Dallas.

————. *TMS1000 CMOS Family Data Manual,* Dallas.

8-bit Microcomputers

Intel. *Microcontroller Handbook,* Santa Clara, CA. Includes data sheets and applications information for all Intel single-chip microcomputers, including the 8048, 8051, and 8096 families.

Motorola. *Single-Chip Microcomputer Data,* Phoenix. Includes data sheets on the 6801, 6803, 6804, 6805, and 68HC11 families.

————. *MC6801 Reference Manual,* Phoenix.

National. *48-Series Microprocessors Handbook,* Santa Clara, CA. Reference book for 8048-family devices.

16-bit Microcomputers

Intel. *Microcontroller Handbook,* Santa Clara, CA. Includes data sheet and application notes for the 8096.

————. *MCS-96 User's Manual,* Santa Clara, CA. Detailed reference for the 8096 family.

Thompson Components-Mostek. *Microelectronic Data Book,* Carrollton, TX. Includes the 68200 data sheet.

CHAPTER 3

BUS STRUCTURES

3.1 INTRODUCTION

A *bus,* in the context of a microprocessor system, is a group of signals that communicates among devices and that typically connects multiple devices in parallel. Buses can exist at several levels in microprocessor-based systems. The lowest level is the component-oriented bus defined by the microprocessor and peripheral chips. In a single-board system, this may be the only bus present. In a single-chip microcomputer, the buses are hidden inside the chip and may not be externally accessible, but they are still present.

In a multiboard system, a higher-level bus is present: the backplane bus, also called the system bus. A *backplane* is typically a circuit board with a number of identical connectors connected in parallel. Each board in the system plugs into one connector and is thus connected to the other boards in the system via the backplane. (The backplane is sometimes called a *motherboard*.) The specification for a backplane bus defines the physical connector and circuit board size, as well as the function and timing of each of the bus signals.

The signal definitions of a backplane bus are not necessarily tied to any particular microprocessor, as component-level buses generally are. Logic on the CPU board translates microprocessor-specific signals to general-purpose backplane bus signals. This logic can be very simple or quite complex, depending on the particular microprocessor and system bus.

At an even higher (i.e., more abstract) level are intersystem buses. These buses connect independent systems and operate over longer distances than backplane buses. One common example of such a bus is the General Purpose Interface Bus (GPIB), also known as IEEE-488. Because this bus is used for communication between systems rather than for interconnections within a system, it is covered in Chap. 8 (Data Communication).

Local area networks (LANs) are another type of intersystem bus. Since most LAN connections consist of a single pair of wires (signal and ground), they are often not thought of as buses. Because LANs do not use separate signal wires for control, they are considerably different from conventional parallel buses. (For additional information on LANs, see Sec. 10.4.3.)

Other types of buses may also be present within a microprocessor-based system. Expansion buses allow limited I/O or memory functions to be added to a circuit board but are less general-purpose than backplane buses. An example of such a bus is the iSBX bus, also known as IEEE-595, which is used primarily with Multibus boards.

Additional buses are sometimes added within a system to improve performance. When a single backplane bus is used to fetch instructions from memory and also for transferring data to or from I/O boards, the performance of the system is often limited by the bus' maximum data rate, called the *bus bandwidth*. One way to increase performance is to use a "private," or local, memory bus to connect processor and memory boards, leaving the backplane bus free for I/O operations. This also relieves the local processor-to-memory bus from the timing restrictions of the system bus and thus allows faster memory cycles. Examples of local memory buses include Intel's iLBX (used with the Multibus) and the VMXbus (used with the VMEbus).

Alternatively, a separate I/O bus can be used to remove I/O activity from the backplane bus, leaving it free for processor-to-memory transfers. Intel's Multichannel is an example of a high-speed I/O bus.

Yet another type of specialized bus is the interprocessor message bus. This is a serial bus used as a supplement to a parallel system bus, and allows messages to be passed between processor modules in multiprocessor systems without using the main system bus. Examples include Intel's iSSB and the VMSbus.

Most buses can be divided into address, data, and control sections; each of these is commonly referred to as a bus. (Address and data can be multiplexed on a single bus, as described later in this chapter.) These three buses are the fundamental structures that tie all microprocessors to memory and interface circuits. The address bus specifies one memory location or I/O port to communicate with the microprocessor, the data bus carries the data, and the control bus provides timing and direction control. Additional control signals provide interrupts and bus-sharing capability. Other than the number of bits in each bus, address and data buses are quite standardized; the most variation occurs in the control signals.

This chapter describes each of the common bus functions. For each function, such as data transfer control, synchronization, or interrupts, the approach used by each of several common microprocessors is described. Table 3.1 lists key bus characteristics for a variety of common microprocessor types. Each of the characteristics listed is described in the following sections.

Following the description of microprocessor-specific bus structures, several common system (backplane) buses are described. Finally, the electrical considerations necessary for reliable bus operation are discussed.

Table 3.1   Bus Characteristics of Various Microprocessors

	6809	**6502**	**8085**	**Z80**	**8086**	**80186**
Data bus, bits	8	8	8	8	16	16
Address bus, bits	16	16	16	16	20	20
Multiplexed	No	No	Yes	No	Yes	Yes
Transfer control	Semisync	Semisync	Semisync	Semisync	Semisync	Semisync
Transfer control signals	E, R/$\overline{\text{W}}$	Φ2, R/$\overline{\text{W}}$	$\overline{\text{RD}}$, $\overline{\text{WR}}$, IO/$\overline{\text{M}}$	$\overline{\text{RD}}$, $\overline{\text{WR}}$, $\overline{\text{MREQ}}$, $\overline{\text{IORQ}}$	$\overline{\text{RD}}$, $\overline{\text{WR}}$, M/$\overline{\text{IO}}$, $\overline{\text{BHE}}$	$\overline{\text{RD}}$, $\overline{\text{WR}}$, M/$\overline{\text{IO}}$, $\overline{\text{BHE}}$
External interrupt inputs	3	2	5	2	2	4

	80286	**80386**	**68008***	**68000/10**	**68020**
Data bus, bits	16	32	8	16	32
Address bus, bits	24	32	20	23	32
Multiplexed	No	No	No	No	No
Transfer control	Semisync	Semisync	Async	Async	Async
Transfer control signals	$\overline{\text{RD}}$, $\overline{\text{WR}}$, M/$\overline{\text{IO}}$, $\overline{\text{BHE}}$	$\overline{\text{RD}}$, $\overline{\text{WR}}$, M/$\overline{\text{IO}}$, $\overline{\text{BHE}}$	$\overline{\text{DS}}$, R/$\overline{\text{W}}$	$\overline{\text{UDS}}$, $\overline{\text{LDS}}$, R/$\overline{\text{W}}$	$\overline{\text{DS}}$, R/$\overline{\text{W}}$ SIZ0, SIZ1
External interrupt inputs	2	2	2 (3 levels)	3 (7 levels)	3 (7 levels)

*48-pin DIP version.

3.2 CONTROL SIGNAL ARCHITECTURES

The primary function of bus control signals is to indicate the direction and control the timing of each data transfer. The most basic control signals are a read strobe and a write strobe, which exist in some form in virtually every system. In this section, common implementations of these signals are described. Other control signals, including interrupts, synchronization signals, and bus request and acknowledge signals, are discussed later in this chapter.

3.2.1 Intel-style Control Signals

Intel's 8080 established a basic set of control signals that, with minor variations, has been used for most of Intel's and Zilog's later designs. The original 8080 signals are $\overline{\text{MEMRD}}$ (memory read), $\overline{\text{MEMWR}}$ (memory write), $\overline{\text{IORD}}$ (I/O read), and $\overline{\text{IOWR}}$ (I/O write). These signals are all active-low, as are most bus control signals.

Figure 3.1 shows the basic bus timing. Each bus cycle begins when the microprocessor outputs an address. For a read cycle, the microprocessor then asserts $\overline{\text{MEMRD}}$ or $\overline{\text{IORD}}$. The addressed memory or I/O device decodes the address, gets the data from the requested location, and drives the data onto the data bus. When the microprocessor negates the read signal, it reads the data from the bus. Most micro-

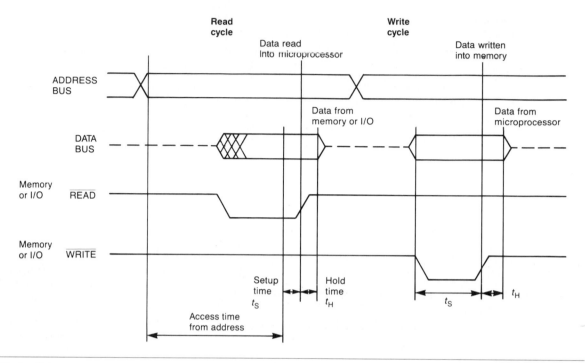

Figure 3.1.   Basic Intel-style bus timing.

processors require that the data be valid some time before the termination of $\overline{\text{READ}}$; this is called *setup time*. The maximum *access time* allowed by the microprocessor is therefore the time from when the address is output to the start of the setup time. Data may also be required to remain valid for some time after the negation of $\overline{\text{READ}}$; this is called *hold time*. Hold time is rarely a problem for read cycles.

The write cycle is similar, except that now the microprocessor is supplying the data to the data bus, and $\overline{\text{MEMWR}}$ or $\overline{\text{IOWR}}$ is asserted. When the microprocessor negates the write signal, the addressed device is expected to capture the data from the bus and store it at the addressed location. The microprocessor outputs the data early in the cycle, so there is a long setup time available to the memory. The hold time provided by the microprocessor can be quite short, however, and this is often a critical timing parameter.

The I/O control lines $\overline{\text{IORD}}$ and $\overline{\text{IOWR}}$ provide, in effect, an I/O address space that is separate from the memory address space. When an IN or OUT instruction is executed, $\overline{\text{IORD}}$ or $\overline{\text{IOWR}}$ is asserted. The address bus is then interpreted as an I/O address rather than as a memory address. I/O transfers often use only 8 bits of address, limiting the number of ports that can be addressed to 256. This number is more than adequate for nearly all applications.

Many systems do not use separate memory and I/O control lines but rather address the I/O ports as memory by using the memory control signals. This is called *memory-mapped I/O*. From the programmer's point of view, an input port is a read-only memory location and an output port is a write-only memory location.

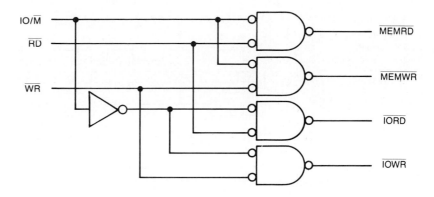

Figure 3.2. The 8085 control signal gating.

Memory-mapped I/O can also be used with microprocessors that have separate I/O and memory control signals by simply ignoring the I/O control signals and I/O instructions. One motivation for memory mapping I/O ports with a microprocessor such as the 8085 lies in the weakness of its I/O instruction set. The IN and OUT instructions can transfer data to or from only the accumulator, and direct addressing is the only mode available. This makes many programs awkward, since all data must pass through the accumulator, creating a bottleneck. In addition, programs that must dynamically change port addresses must resort to self-modifying code, since the port address must be embedded in the instruction. (A *self-modifying* program, as the name implies, modifies itself as it is executing. This is an undesirable technique, since it can be difficult to debug and cannot be used with programs stored in read-only memory.) Memory read and write instructions, on the other hand, allow for data transfer to or from any register using a variety of addressing modes. Using memory-mapped I/O allows all these memory read and write instructions to be used for I/O.

The 8085 control signals are $\overline{RD}$ (read), $\overline{WR}$ (write), and IO/$\overline{M}$ (IO/memory). The read and write strobes are used for both memory and I/O transfers, and IO/$\overline{M}$ indicates the type of transfer. This organization reduces the number of signals from four to three, saving one pin on the microprocessor. External logic, as shown in Fig. 3.2, is often used to generate the four basic control signals. If memory-mapped I/O is used, IO/$\overline{M}$ can be ignored.

The 8086 16-bit microprocessor uses the same basic control signals as the 8085 except that the polarity of the IO/memory signal is inverted (M/$\overline{IO}$). Several additional 8086 bus control signals provide additional features and are described in a later section.

The Z80 uses another variation. As with the 8085, read and write strobes common to both I/O and memory transfers are used. However, rather than the single IO/$\overline{M}$ signal, memory request ($\overline{MREQ}$) and I/O request ($\overline{IORQ}$) signals are used. These signals thus need four pins on the microprocessor as compared to three pins with the 8085 approach. External gating is typically required to AND together pairs of signals; for example, $\overline{MREQ}$ AND $\overline{RD}$ generates a memory read strobe. The use of four signals rather than three can eliminate some external gating: $\overline{MREQ}$ is equivalent to memory read ORed with memory write, which is often needed to enable RAM memories.

The Z80 memory read and write timing is shown in Fig. 3.3. Φ is the system clock.

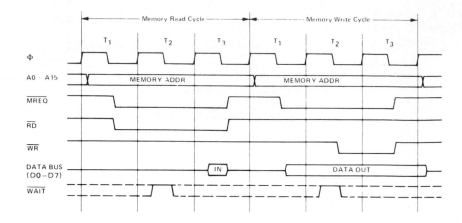

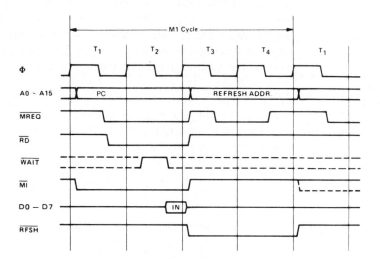

$\overline{\text{RD}}$ and $\overline{\text{MREQ}}$ are asserted simultaneously for memory read cycles. For I/O read cycles, $\overline{\text{RD}}$ and $\overline{\text{IORQ}}$ are asserted. For write cycles, $\overline{\text{WR}}$ is asserted after $\overline{\text{MREQ}}$. $\overline{\text{MREQ}}$ is asserted as early as possible to indicate that the address is valid, while $\overline{\text{WR}}$ is not asserted until the data is valid.

Figure 3.4 shows the Z80's opcode fetch cycle. This cycle is called the *M1 cycle* because it is the first machine cycle of every instruction cycle. It begins just like a normal memory read cycle, except that the $\overline{\text{M1}}$ output is asserted to identify it as an opcode fetch cycle. The $\overline{\text{RD}}$ pulse is approximately one-half clock period shorter than for normal memory reads, however, resulting in a faster access time requirement for opcode fetches as compared to normal memory reads. This is a peculiarity of the Z80 and is due to the built-in dynamic memory refresh support. After each opcode fetch, while the Z80 is internally decoding the opcode, it performs a memory refresh cycle. The contents of the Z80's internal refresh register are output on address bits 0 to 6, and the refresh control signal ($\overline{\text{RFSH}}$) is asserted. $\overline{\text{RD}}$ is not asserted, so this cycle is ignored by normal bus devices. (See Sec. 4.7.3 for further information about dynamic memory refresh.)

3.2.2 Motorola-style Control Signals

Motorola uses an alternative approach to bus control signals. This approach was first used by the 6800, and it is used by all subsequent Motorola microprocessors and by the 6500-family devices. Intel-style read and write strobes convey both direction control and timing in the same signals. Motorola separates these into a data strobe (called $\overline{\text{DS}}$, E, or $\Phi 2$ depending on the microprocessor) that is asserted for transfers in either direction and a read/write ($\text{R}/\overline{\text{W}}$) direction control line that conveys no timing information. There are no separate I/O control signals; all I/O must be memory-mapped.

Figure 3.5 shows the timing diagram for the 6809. (The same basic timing also applies to the 6802.) The E (enable) signal serves as the data strobe. If $\text{R}/\overline{\text{W}}$ is high, indicating a read operation, the addressed device drives the data bus while E is high, and at the falling edge of E the 6809 reads the data from the bus. If $\text{R}/\overline{\text{W}}$ is low, indicating a write operation, the 6809 drives the data bus while E is high, and the addressed device stores the data from the data bus at the falling edge of E. The transitions of $\text{R}/\overline{\text{W}}$

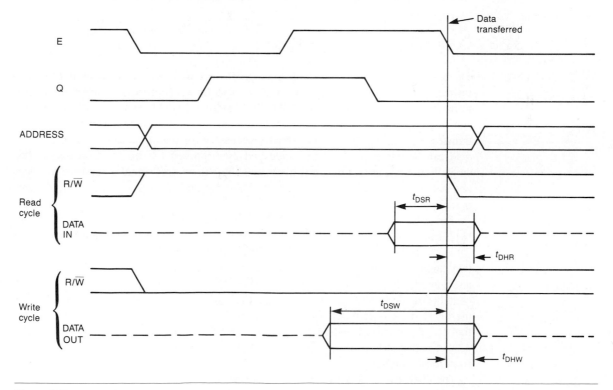

Figure 3.5. The 6809 bus timing.

Figure 3.6. The 6809
control signal gating.

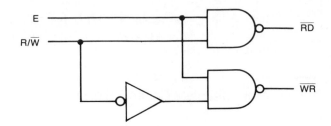

have no timing significance, and R/$\overline{\text{W}}$ is always stable while E is high. The 6809 also provides a Q (quadrature) signal, whose leading edge indicates when the address is valid.

Figure 3.6 shows the simple gating required to generate separate read and write strobes. This logic is typically required in any system that uses non-6800/68000-family peripherals.

The Motorola 6802 and the MOS Technology 6502 use very similar control signals. The first device to use this control signal approach, the 6800, required an external two-phase clock generator. The two clock phases were called Φ1 and Φ2. Φ2 performs the enable function as described above. The 6502 provides this clock generator on-chip and is driven by a single clock signal called Φ0. The 6502 then generates an output called, for historical reasons, Φ2, which is the same as the 6809's and 6802's E signal.

3.2.3   Control Signals for 16-bit Buses

The basic control signals for 16-bit microprocessors are generally very similar to those for the 8-bit microprocessors. However, most 16-bit microprocessors retain the ability to perform single-byte operations, and they address memory as a series of bytes that can be paired to form 16-bit words. Thus, some mechanism for selecting 8- or 16-bit transfers is required. This is not strictly necessary for read operations, since a 16-bit read can be performed and the undesired byte ignored by the microprocessor. For single-byte write operations, however, an additional control signal is required to select one half of the 16-bit word. As usual, Motorola and Intel have taken different approaches to this problem.

The 8086 addresses memory as 2^{20} (1,048,576) individual bytes. Any two adjacent bytes can be treated as a 16-bit word. A signal called $\overline{\text{BHE}}$ (bus high enable) is asserted if the upper half of the data bus (D_8 to D_{15}) is to be used. The memory is divided into two banks, as shown in Fig. 3.7. The lower bank connects to data bus lines D_0 to D_7 and contains the even-numbered bytes, while the upper bank connects to D_8 to D_{15} and contains the odd-numbered bytes. When the least-significant address line (A_0) is low, the lower bank is enabled. $\overline{\text{BHE}}$ enables the upper bank. Thus, to perform a 16-bit transfer, A_0 is set low and $\overline{\text{BHE}}$ is asserted. Single bytes can be transferred by setting A_0 to 1 and asserting $\overline{\text{BHE}}$ or by setting A_0 to 0 and negating $\overline{\text{BHE}}$. Table 3.2 summarizes these combinations.

The 8086 can thus perform 16-bit transfers in a single bus cycle only if the lower byte is at an even address (an address in which A_0 is 0). Figure 3.8 shows an even-

Figure 3.7. Division of
8086 memory into high
and low banks. *(Courtesy
of Intel Corporation.)*

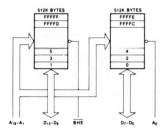

Table 3.2   The 8086 Memory Addressing Control

$\overline{\text{BHE}}$	A_0	Operation
0	0	16-bit transfer
0	1	Upper-byte (odd-address) transfer
1	0	Lower-byte (even-address) transfer
1	1	None

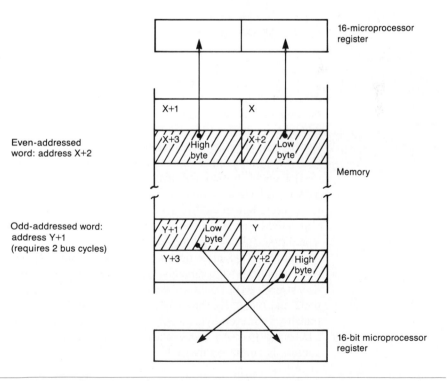

Figure 3.8.   Intel-style even- and odd-addressed words in memory.

Figure 3.9. The 68000
memory organization.
*(Courtesy of Motorola,
Inc.)*

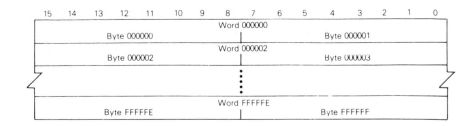

Figure 3.10. The
68000 bus timing for byte
and word transfers. *(Courtesy of Motorola, Inc.)*

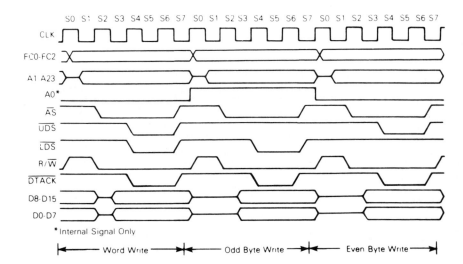

addressed and an odd-addressed word. The even-addressed word is read in a single 16-bit transfer. The 8086 will accommodate 16-bit operations even if the low byte is at an odd address. In this case, the 8086 automatically performs two bus cycles, one to read each byte. This appears to the programmer as a single 16-bit operation, except for the slower execution speed since two bus cycles are required.

The 68000 uses a different scheme. The memory address space consists of 16 Mbytes, which are individually accessible. Figure 3.9 shows the organization of data in memory. Individual bytes are addressed with the reverse convention as Intel's; even-numbered bytes are the upper half of a 16-bit word (i.e., the most-significant byte is stored first, followed by the least-significant byte).

The 68000's control signals are straightforward. A read/write signal, similar to the 6800's, indicates the direction of the transfer. Two data strobe signals, $\overline{\text{UDS}}$ (upper data strobe) and $\overline{\text{LDS}}$ (lower data strobe), take over the function performed by E on the 6802 and 6809. As shown in Fig. 3.10, both $\overline{\text{UDS}}$ and $\overline{\text{LDS}}$ are asserted for 16-bit transfers. For even-byte transfers only $\overline{\text{UDS}}$ is asserted, and for odd-byte transfers only $\overline{\text{LDS}}$ is asserted. Address strobe $(\overline{\text{AS}})$ is asserted at the start of each cycle when the new address is output on the address bus, and it can be used to enable address decoding circuits.

The least-significant address bit (A_0) exists only inside the 68000; the external address bus begins with A_1. The state of A_0 is reflected in $\overline{UDS}$ and $\overline{LDS}$. For 16-bit transfers, A_0 must be zero. Unlike the 8086, the 68000 does not allow 16-bit transfers beginning at an odd address; if such a transfer is attempted, an error trap (internal interrupt) occurs. For single-byte transfers, A_0 determines whether $\overline{UDS}$ or $\overline{LDS}$ is asserted. The design example section (Sec. 3.10) describes the 68000-family bus timing in detail.

3.3 TRANSFER SYNCHRONIZATION

Whenever data is exchanged between two devices in a system, such as a microprocessor and a memory device, the system design must ensure that the two devices are synchronized. For example, when the microprocessor reads data from a memory device, the microprocessor outputs an address, asserts a data strobe signal (such as $\overline{RD}$, E, or $\overline{UDS}$ and/or $\overline{LDS}$), holds the strobe asserted for some time, and then reads the data from the bus as the strobe signal is negated. This is called a *synchronous* transfer because no "ready" signal is required from the memory, and it is expected to operate synchronously with the microprocessor's control signals.

A fully synchronous bus is generally undesirable in a microprocessor system. Not all memory and peripheral devices have access times faster than that required by the microprocessor. The microprocessor's clock can be slowed, but this requires the entire system to run at the rate of the slowest device. Some devices (such as ROMs and peripheral chips) may be slower than others (such as RAMs), so slowing the clock may not make efficient use of all components. Some mechanism for varying the bus timing of the microprocessor for each access is needed. The following sections describe several approaches to this problem.

3.3.1 Synchronous Buses

Motorola's 6800 is one example of a microprocessor with no facilities for varying the bus timing. As a result, early users of the 6800 often built special clock generators that could vary the clock speed. These circuits divide down a high-speed clock to generate the microprocessor clock and change the divisor when accessing slower memory or peripheral devices. Motorola eventually produced a clock generator chip that performs this function and also integrated a similar "clock stretch" circuit into the 6802 and 6809.

One weakness of the clock stretching approach is that the bus cycles cannot be indefinitely lengthened. Most NMOS microprocessors are dynamic devices internally, which means that there is a minimum clock speed required to guarantee proper operation. (CMOS microprocessors are usually fully static.) For any standard memory interfacing application, adequate stretching can be obtained. However, clock stretching cannot be used to single-step or slow-step the microprocessor for debugging or to synchronize the microprocessor with very slow I/O devices.

Most single-chip microcomputers are fully synchronous when operating in their expanded mode with off-chip memory or I/O devices. Because they typically connect directly to a quartz crystal and include their own clock oscillator, it is awkward to dynamically vary the clock frequency. It is thus generally necessary to use a slow enough clock rate to work with all the external memory and peripheral devices.

3.3.2 Semisynchronous Buses

Most microprocessors use a semisynchronous approach to bus timing control. The microprocessor normally requires no response from the memory or peripheral device. However, a "wait" input can be asserted if the memory or peripheral device needs to stretch the bus cycle. Because the microprocessor's clock is not stopped, the bus cycle can be stretched indefinitely.

A typical example of this approach is the Z80. Figure 3.11 shows the timing diagram for a read or write cycle with two wait states. The Z80 bus cycle is divided into T states. A T state is one period of the system clock. Early in the cycle, the address is output, and shortly thereafter $\overline{\text{MREQ}}$ and $\overline{\text{RD}}$ are asserted. The system's address decoder then decodes the address to determine which memory is to be selected. If the memory selected is one that requires a wait state, then the $\overline{\text{WAIT}}$ line is asserted. The Z80 samples this line at the middle of T2, the second clock cycle of the bus cycle. Thus, the decoding and control logic has approximately one clock period to assert the $\overline{\text{WAIT}}$ line to prevent the cycle from completing at full speed.

If the $\overline{\text{WAIT}}$ line is asserted when sampled by the Z80, the buses are frozen and the Z80 goes into a *wait state* rather than into T3. At the middle of the wait state, the $\overline{\text{WAIT}}$ line is sampled again, and if it is still asserted, then another wait state is entered. This process can continue indefinitely. When the $\overline{\text{WAIT}}$ line is negated, the microprocessor continues with T3 in the following clock cycle. Note that the $\overline{\text{WAIT}}$ line is sampled only at specific times and that bus cycles can be stretched only by integral numbers of clock cycles.

Figure 3.12 shows a circuit for generating one wait state in a Z80 system. When

 **Figure 3.11.** Z80 bus cycle with two wait states. *(Courtesy of Thompson Components-Mostek Corp.)*

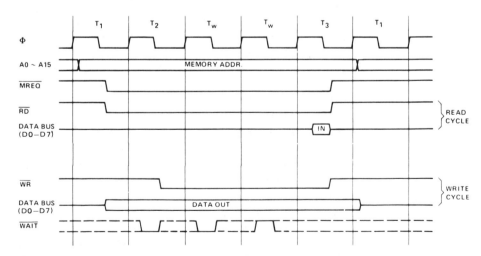

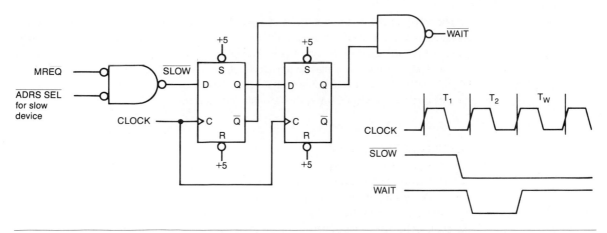

Figure 3.12. Z80 wait-state generator.

$\overline{\text{MREQ}}$ is negated (high), both flip-flops are set, with the Q output high and the $\overline{\text{Q}}$ output low. At the first rising clock edge after $\overline{\text{MREQ}}$ is asserted, the first flip-flop is cleared and the $\overline{\text{WAIT}}$ output is asserted. At the next rising edge of the clock, the second flip-flop is cleared and the $\overline{\text{WAIT}}$ output is negated.

Most other microprocessors provide a similar wait-state mechanism. The 8085's READY input functions similarly to the Z80's $\overline{\text{WAIT}}$; only the name is changed. The 8086 also uses a similar READY input. The 8284 clock generator chip for the 8086 synchronizes READY with the system clock. It also provides two separate ready inputs, which are selected by the AEN (address enable) inputs. This allows the selection of a local ready signal or a system bus ready signal in multiple bus systems. (See Chap. 10 for an example of such an application.)

The Z80, 8085, and 8086 all require that the ready input be synchronized to the system clock. This is to avoid the possibility of a *metastable* state in the microprocessor. A metastable state occurs if the data input to a flip-flop changes just before the clock edge occurs. Flip-flop specifications require a setup time for the data input, and if this specification is met, then this situation cannot occur. (The actual time window during which a data transition will cause a metastable state is shorter than the setup time, and is shortest for very fast flip-flops such as those in the AS and F families.) In the metastable state, the flip-flop's output may be high or low or at an invalid logic level, and this condition can persist for much longer than the normal propagation delay of the device.

The standard solution to this problem when an asynchronous input must be synchronized to the system clock is to use two flip-flops in series, both clocked by the system clock (or by opposite polarities of the clock). If the first flip-flop does enter a metastable state, then the system will operate properly as long as the metastable state ends before the next clock edge when the second flip-flop is clocked.

In most microprocessor systems the ready signal is produced by counting pulses of the system clock, so it is inherently synchronized to that clock. However, if a memory or peripheral interface produces a ready signal with an independent clock or an analog delay, then the synchronization problem must be addressed.

The 80186 includes two ready inputs, ARDY (asynchronous ready) and SRDY (synchronous ready). The SRDY input, like the ready input of most other microprocessors, must be synchronized to the system clock. The 80186 includes an on-chip synchronizer for the ARDY input, so it can be asynchronous to the system clock. The synchronizer adds a one-half clock cycle delay to the signal, however, so it must be asserted earlier in the bus cycle than SRDY for zero-wait-state operation.

3.3.3 Asynchronous Buses

Asynchronous buses require an acknowledge signal from the addressed device on every bus cycle for operation to continue. Fast devices assert the acknowledge immediately after decoding the address, while slower devices wait until they are ready to terminate the cycle. The effect is similar to using the READY/$\overline{\text{WAIT}}$ signal previously described. The major difference is that every device must supply the acknowledge, rather than only slow devices. Asynchronous buses allow the acknowledge signal to be asynchronous to the system clock, so the microprocessor or its associated circuitry must handle the synchronization problem.

One benefit of this approach is increased system security; if the software accesses a nonexistent memory location or I/O port, the system will automatically stop, since it will wait forever for an acknowledge. A bus time-out "watchdog" (as described later in this section) can be used to cause execution of an error routine in this situation.

An asynchronous bus can be implemented with microprocessors using a READY/$\overline{\text{WAIT}}$ signal by using additional logic. The READY input to the microprocessor is normally held low, and it is set high when an acknowledge has been received from the addressed device. This is sometimes called the *normally-not-ready* mode. In a normally-ready system, in which the peripheral or memory interface circuit must negate READY to cause a wait state, READY must be negated within a fixed time or the cycle will continue without wait states. Thus, normally-not-ready and asynchronous bus systems can tolerate longer buses and slower ready logic.

The Motorola 68000 is one of the few microprocessors that directly provides an asynchronous bus interface. The $\overline{\text{DTACK}}$ (data transfer acknowledge) input replaces the READY/$\overline{\text{WAIT}}$ line used on most other microprocessors. The 68000 begins a bus cycle by outputting an address and asserting $\overline{\text{AS}}$ (address strobe) and $\overline{\text{UDS}}$ and/or $\overline{\text{LDS}}$. As shown in Fig. 3.13, $\overline{\text{DTACK}}$ is sampled at the end of state S4. If $\overline{\text{DTACK}}$ is not asserted by this time, a wait state is executed. As long as $\overline{\text{DTACK}}$ remains false at each falling clock edge, wait states are executed. When $\overline{\text{DTACK}}$ is asserted, the cycle continues in the next clock cycle.

If all devices in the system can operate at the maximum (no-wait-state) bus speed, the $\overline{\text{DTACK}}$ input can simply be grounded. However, most systems include some devices that are slower, and it is then necessary to assert $\overline{\text{DTACK}}$ at different times for different devices. Figure 3.14 shows a circuit that accomplishes this. The shift register is held cleared when $\overline{\text{AS}}$ is not asserted. At the first rising clock edge after $\overline{\text{AS}}$ is asserted (the start of S4), the shift register's Q_A output is set high. The Q_A output is thus asserted before the end of S4 and serves as a no-wait $\overline{\text{DTACK}}$. ($\overline{\text{AS}}$ can also be used directly as a no-wait $\overline{\text{DTACK}}$. The Q_A signal has the advantage that it allows time for the address decoder outputs to stabilize before they are used for $\overline{\text{DTACK}}$ generation.)

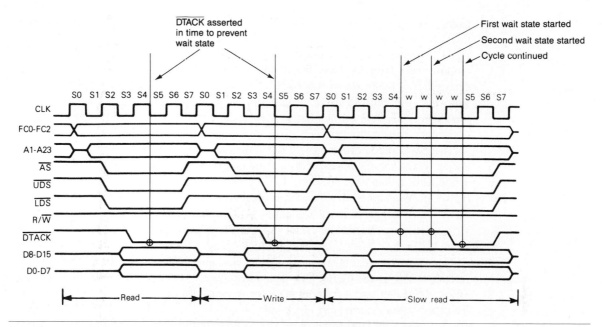

Figure 3.13. The 68000 timing for normal and slow bus cycles. *(Courtesy of Motorola, Inc.)*

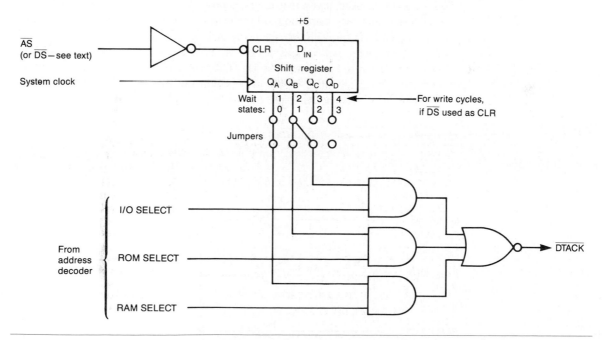

Figure 3.14. Basic circuit for 68000 $\overline{\text{DTACK}}$ generation.

Each successive output is then set in turn at each rising clock edge. Q_B generates $\overline{\text{DTACK}}$ for devices requiring one wait state, Q_C for two wait states, and so on. The $\overline{\text{DTACK}}$ signals for various devices are ORed together to produce $\overline{\text{DTACK}}$ for the microprocessor. Jumpers allow the number of wait states for each device to be easily changed. The figure shows RAM set for zero wait states and ROM and I/O set for one wait state. An equivalent circuit can also be implemented in a programmable array logic (PAL) IC, with the number of wait states selected by the PAL programming pattern rather than by jumpers.

There is a subtle problem with the simple $\overline{\text{DTACK}}$ generation approach described above. When the 68000 executes a read/modify/write (RMW) cycle, $\overline{\text{AS}}$ is held asserted while a data strobe ($\overline{\text{UDS}}$ or $\overline{\text{LDS}}$) is pulsed twice, once for the read and once for the write. A separate $\overline{\text{DTACK}}$ pulse is required for each part of the cycle. Since the circuit above is triggered from $\overline{\text{AS}}$, only one $\overline{\text{DTACK}}$ will be generated. As a result, the write portion of the RMW cycle will execute without wait states regardless of the memory timing.

One way to correct this is to use $\overline{\text{UDS}}$ ORed with $\overline{\text{LDS}}$ (or simply $\overline{\text{DS}}$ for a 68008) instead of $\overline{\text{AS}}$ as the CLEAR for the shift register. However, this has the additional effect of causing one more wait state for write cycles than for read cycles, since the data strobes are asserted one clock later on write cycles. This is sometimes desirable, since it results in data strobe pulse widths that are the same for read or write cycles. Another solution is to add additional logic (which could be part of a $\overline{\text{DTACK}}$ generation PAL) to handle the special case of the RMW cycle $\overline{\text{DTACK}}$.

This is less of an issue than it may at first appear, since the RMW cycle is used only by the TAS (test and set) instruction, which is often not used. In addition, if the program is executed from no-wait-state memory, then there is no problem.

The $\overline{\text{DTACK}}$ signals from various devices are often combined by using open-collector drivers, as shown in Fig. 3.15. The $\overline{\text{DTACK}}$ line can be pulled low by any of the open-collector drivers; if none of the drivers pull the line low, the pull-up resistor causes it to float to the inactive level. Thus, the open-collector drivers function as a

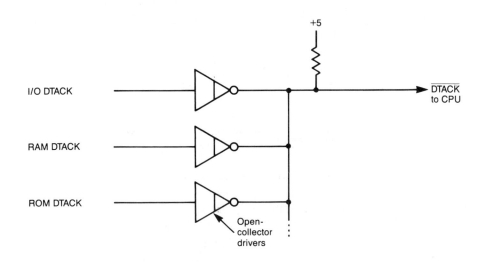

Figure 3.15. Combining $\overline{\text{DTACK}}$ signals by using open-collector bus line.

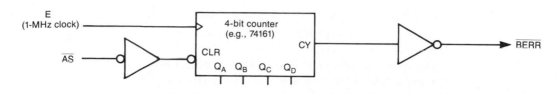

Figure 3.16. Watchdog timer for bus error generation.

wire-OR, ORing together the various $\overline{\text{DTACK}}$ sources. This approach is commonly used in multiboard systems, since it requires only a single $\overline{\text{DTACK}}$ signal on the backplane. A similar wire-OR is also commonly used for interrupt and bus request lines.

Because the 68000 will wait indefinitely for $\overline{\text{DTACK}}$, the system will stop if $\overline{\text{DTACK}}$ is never asserted in response to a bus cycle. This can happen if a software error causes a nonexistent memory location to be accessed. Because interrupts are not acknowledged until the instruction cycle is completed, they cannot be used to get out of this situation. To allow termination of a bus cycle, the 68000 includes an input called $\overline{\text{BERR}}$ (bus error). When $\overline{\text{BERR}}$ is asserted, it aborts the cycle in progress and directs the CPU to a special error handling routine. The address that caused the error is passed to the error routine on the system stack to provide diagnostic information. If the address is one that is not used by any device in the system, then a software error has occurred. If the address is that of an existing device, then the $\overline{\text{DTACK}}$ circuit for that device has failed or is not installed.

$\overline{\text{BERR}}$ is typically driven from a *watchdog timer*. This is a "one-shot" or counter circuit that is reset each time either $\overline{\text{UDS}}$ or $\overline{\text{LDS}}$ is asserted. (A counter is strongly preferred to a one-shot, since one-shots are notoriously unreliable and have inherent timing variability.) It is designed so that it will never "time out" as long as the memory and I/O devices respond within a predetermined time limit. If no $\overline{\text{DTACK}}$ occurs within this time, the watchdog times out and asserts $\overline{\text{BERR}}$ to abort the cycle. The error routine then handles the failure in an orderly manner.

Fig. 3.16 shows a typical bus error watchdog circuit. The counter is cleared between cycles, just like the shift register used to generate $\overline{\text{DTACK}}$. The E output of the 68000, which free-runs at one-tenth the processor clock rate, is a convenient source for the watchdog timer clock. The 4-bit counter's carry (CY) output produces $\overline{\text{BERR}}$. Since this is asserted after 16 clock pulses, and the clock rate is one-tenth that of the processor clock, the bus error is asserted after 160 processor clocks. With a 10-MHz processor clock, this corresponds to a 16 μs time-out period, which is considerably slower than the slowest device in nearly all systems.

The $\overline{\text{BERR}}$ input has other uses as well. If some form of error detection (such as parity or an error detection and correction code) is used on the memory, this signal can be asserted to abort a cycle in which the data read is not valid. For systems that include memory management hardware (described in Chap. 4), the $\overline{\text{BERR}}$ input is asserted when an invalid or disallowed access is attempted or when a *page fault* occurs. Note, however, that a 68000 or 68008 cannot continue the instruction after the page fault; a 68010 or 68020 must be used.

If $\overline{\text{BERR}}$ and $\overline{\text{HALT}}$ are both asserted, then the 68000 reruns the bus cycle when $\overline{\text{BERR}}$ and $\overline{\text{HALT}}$ are negated. This feature can be used to allow a re-try for automatic recovery from soft errors.

The term *watchdog timer* is also used for a timer that is periodically reset by software and that resets the system if it ever reaches the time limit. Unlike the $\overline{\text{BERR}}$ timer, this is intended to allow the system to continue operating after a hardware or software fault (assuming, of course, that the fault is intermittent or a one-time event). This type of watchdog timer is described in Sec. 5.5.

3.4 MULTIPLEXED ADDRESS/DATA BUSES

Many of the pins on a typical microprocessor are used for the address and data buses. *Multiplexing* the address and data buses on the same set of pins reduces the number of pins required for the buses. This saving in the number of pins allows an 8-bit microprocessor to provide several additional interrupt inputs or control signals and still fit in a 40-pin package. For a 16-bit microprocessor, it allows a 16-bit data bus and 20-bit address bus to be accommodated in a 40-pin package. All else being equal (which it rarely is), nonmultiplexed buses are faster since the information on the buses does not have to be switched from address to data during each cycle. Most Intel microprocessors use multiplexed buses, while most Motorola microprocessors do not.

At the beginning of each bus cycle, the multiplexed bus is used for address information. Because the address does not change during a bus cycle, there is no need for the microprocessor to supply it continuously. However, most memory and I/O devices require that the address be present for the entire cycle, so the address must be stored in a latch external to the microprocessor. Once the address has been written to the latch, the multiplexed bus operates as a standard data bus for the remainder of the cycle.

The 8085 is the most common 8-bit microprocessor that uses a multiplexed bus. Since the 8085 has an 8-bit data bus, only eight address lines are multiplexed. The most significant eight address bits are not multiplexed and are output on dedicated pins.

Figure 3.17 shows the timing diagram for an 8085 fetching and executing an OUT instruction. Two memory read cycles are performed to read the opcode and the port address. An I/O write cycle is then performed to execute the instruction.

The microprocessor outputs the address at the beginning of each cycle. The high half is output on the A_8 to A_{15} pins, and the low half on the AD_0 to AD_7 pins (the multiplexed bus). The ALE (address latch enable) signal is then pulsed. When ALE is negated, the low half of the address is stored in the external address latch. The address is then removed from the multiplexed bus, and it becomes a standard data bus. ALE also indicates that a new bus cycle has started, and it can be used by other control logic.

As mentioned in Chap. 2, several memory and peripheral chips are available that interface directly to the 8085's multiplexed bus. However, most systems use nonmultiplexed memory and peripheral devices because they are generally less expensive and more widely available, and therefore require an external address latch. The address latch should be a transparent latch such as a 74LS373 and not an edge-triggered register (such as a 74LS273 or 74LS374). As shown in Fig. 3.18, the transparent latch

Figure 3.17. The 8085 multiplexed bus timing. *(Courtesy of Intel Corporation.)*

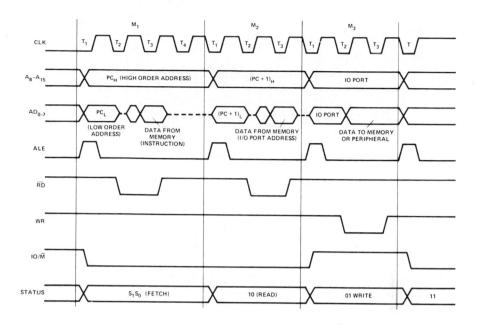

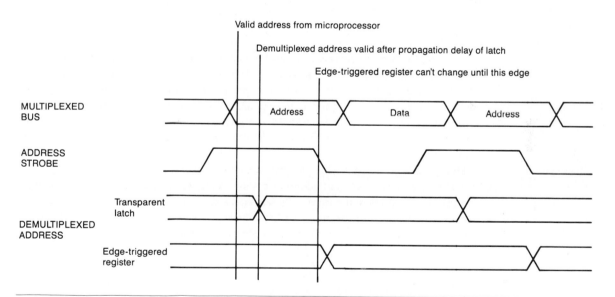

Figure 3.18. Timing advantage of transparent latch for address demultiplexing.

passes the input data to the outputs when the enable is active and freezes the outputs when the enable is negated. An edge-triggered register, on the other hand, would have to be triggered on the trailing edge of ALE (since the address is not generally valid at the leading edge), resulting in an unnecessary delay in the presentation of the address to the rest of the system.

Figure 3.19. Demultiplexing latches for 8086.

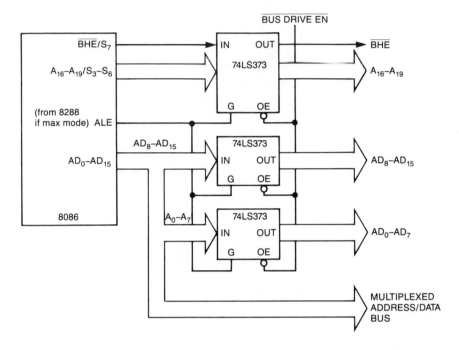

The 8086 16-bit microprocessor also uses a multiplexed bus. Figure 3.19 shows the demultiplexing latches. The 8086 uses 16 bits of data and 20 bits of address. The 16-line multiplexed bus thus serves as the data bus and all but the four most significant address lines. An ALE signal is generated just as with the 8085, and a 20-bit latch (physically three 8-bit latches) stores the address on each cycle and drives the demultiplexed address lines. For systems that use multiple processors or have other bus masters such as a DMA controller, latches with three-state outputs are used, and the output enable is negated when bus acknowledge is asserted (see Sec. 3.7).

The four most significant address lines are multiplexed with status signals S_3 to S_6, and $\overline{\text{BHE}}$ is multiplexed with S_7. These status signals are primarily for diagnostic purposes and are not used in most applications. However, since these address lines and $\overline{\text{BHE}}$ are not stable throughout the cycle, they must also be latched.

3.5 PRIVILEGE MODES AND ADDRESS MODIFIERS

Many 16- and 32-bit microprocessors, including the 68000, Z8000, and 80286, provide two or more distinct modes of operation. At the most privileged level, called *system* or *supervisor* mode, no restrictions are placed on program execution. In the less privileged, or *user* modes, various instructions are prohibited, including halt, reset, and interrupt control instructions. In addition, all interrupts and error traps (such as divide by zero or invalid opcode) cause a return to supervisor mode and a jump to a service routine. This division of privilege levels allows multiuser systems to cleanly isolate operating system functions from user programs and protect the system from undesirable actions by user programs.

Microprocessors that support these modes provide an output signal that indicates, for each bus access, whether it is a supervisor or a user access. This signal can be used as an additional address line or memory bank select. This can make the operating system memory physically separate from the user memory and thus prevent any possibility of inadvertent (or intentional) modification of system programs or data by user programs. In the case of the 80286, there are several privilege levels, and the level indication for each access is used by the on-chip memory management logic to provide protection functions.

Table 3.3 shows the 68000's function code outputs, which can be thought of as address modifiers. FC2 is high during supervisor accesses and low during user accesses. FC2 can therefore be used to select between supervisor and user memory banks, as shown in Fig. 3.20. FC1 can be used in a similar manner to separate program and data memory. Using both these signals can thus increase the 68000's normal 16-Mbyte address space to 64 Mbytes (16 Mbytes each for supervisor program, supervisor data, user program, and user data) while providing increased protection. The function-code signals can also be used as inputs to memory management logic (see Sec. 4.11).

Table 3.3   The 68000 Function Code Signals

FC2	FC1	FC0	Access type
0	0	0	Not used
0	0	1	User data
0	1	0	User program
0	1	1	Not used
1	0	0	Not used
1	0	1	Supervisor data
1	1	0	Supervisor program
1	1	1	Interrupt acknowledge

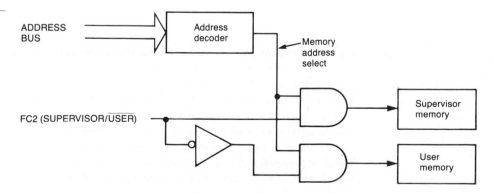

Figure 3.20. Separation of user and supervisory memory.

3.6   INTERRUPT STRUCTURES

Interrupts provide a mechanism for a hardware signal to force the software to change its path of execution. While each microprocessor has its own method for implementing the details of interrupt processing (called the *interrupt structure*), there are several features that are common to all. Interrupts are acknowledged only between instructions; the microprocessor cannot be interrupted out of the middle of an instruction (except by a bus error signal, if available).

Nearly all microprocessors include an interrupt enable flag (or equivalent). If this flag is cleared, interrupts are ignored (except a nonmaskable interrupt, as described later). This flag is cleared at power-up, so interrupts are disabled until the system is initialized. It is also cleared whenever an interrupt is acknowledged, so additional interrupts will not be processed until they are enabled by the interrupt service routine (by executing an enable interrupts instruction). The software can also disable interrupts at any time by executing a disable interrupts instruction. This is useful for sections of the program that must operate uninterrupted either because they are time-critical or because they are sharing programs or data also used by interrupt service routines.

The first step the microprocessor takes to process an interrupt is to save the program counter (usually on the stack, an area of memory pointed to by the microprocessor's stack pointer register that operates in a last-in-first-out fashion). This allows the software to return to normal program flow at the point at which it was interrupted by loading the saved value from the stack into the microprocessor's program counter. Some microprocessors automatically save other registers (such as the accumulator or index pointer) in addition to the program counter. Finally, the actual interrupt processing begins when the microprocessor jumps to the *interrupt service routine*. Interrupts are automatically disabled when interrupt service begins but can be reenabled in the service routine if desired.

The service routine must first save any processor registers that it may modify, unless they have been saved automatically by the microprocessor. It then performs whatever function is dictated by the interrupt and concludes by restoring the registers and executing a return from interrupt instruction. The microprocessor now returns to executing the program where it left off prior to the interrupt, just as if nothing had happened.

If the microprocessor hardware cannot distinguish between various interrupt sources, then the interrupts are called *nonvectored*. With nonvectored interrupts, the interrupt service routine must test (poll) each of the possible interrupt sources to determine which device generated the interrupt. A faster scheme is *vectored interrupts*, which provides a hardware mechanism to select a separate service routine for each interrupt source. One common approach is for the interrupting device to identify itself by driving an ID code on the data bus during an *interrupt acknowledge* cycle, which takes place at the beginning of interrupt processing. The microprocessor then executes the indicated interrupt service routine.

Most microprocessors also have a *nonmaskable interrupt (NMI)* that cannot be disabled by software. This interrupt is always processed at the end of the current instruction execution. It is typically used for high-priority error interrupts, such as an abort signal or power-fail detection. The NMI input can be gated externally with an enable signal from an output port if it is necessary to disable it at times.

Most single-chip microcomputers, such as the 8048, 8051, and 6801, have a number of internal interrupt sources. Typical examples are timer interrupts and serial I/O interrupts. There may also be external interrupt sources. However, no vector is read; each interrupt source has a fixed service routine address associated with it. Thus, these interrupts are vectored in that each internal interrupt source and the external interrupt input(s) can have separate interrupt service routines. However, no interrupt acknowledge cycle is performed, and multiple external devices connected to the same interrupt input cannot select separate service routines. Interrupts processed in this manner are called *autovectored*. Many microprocessors include both autovectored and externally vectored interrupt modes.

Interrupt inputs can be either *level-sensitive* or *edge-triggered*. Most microprocessors' interrupt inputs are level-sensitive, which means that the interrupt signal must be held asserted until the interrupt is acknowledged, or it will be ignored. If the interrupt is asserted and then negated while interrupts are disabled, the interrupt is lost. The peripheral generating the interrupt therefore must keep the interrupt asserted until it is acknowledged. In some cases the interrupt signal is held asserted until the interrupt service is complete.

An edge-triggered interrupt input responds to either the rising or the falling edge of the interrupt signal. The interrupt request is latched when the edge is detected, and the interrupt signal may be negated at any time. When the interrupt is acknowledged, the latched interrupt request is cleared. External interrupt controller ICs often provide edge-triggered interrupt inputs, allowing the selection of either the rising or the falling edge.

3.6.1 Nonvectored Interrupts

Motorola's 6802 is an example of a microprocessor with nonvectored interrupts. There are two interrupt inputs: $\overline{\text{NMI}}$ and $\overline{\text{IRQ}}$. $\overline{\text{NMI}}$ is a nonmaskable interrupt, while the $\overline{\text{IRQ}}$ interrupt can be disabled by the software. Four bytes of memory near the top of the address space are reserved for the jump addresses for these two interrupts. When $\overline{\text{IRQ}}$ is asserted, the microprocessor saves the program counter and the registers on the stack. It then reads the memory locations FFF8 and FFF9, forms a 16-bit address from the two bytes, and jumps to that address. In other words, a subroutine call is performed by using FFF8 as the indirect address (the address of the memory location that contains the address) of the subroutine. The RTI (return from interrupt) instruction restores the registers and returns to the instruction following the one executed just before the interrupt. The $\overline{\text{NMI}}$ interrupt causes the same sequence, except that the service routine address is fetched from locations FFFC and FFFD.

3.6.2 The 6809 Interrupt Structure

The 6809 provides an improved interrupt structure that allows, but does not require, external interrupt vectoring. Like the 6802, the interrupt service routine address (the interrupt vector) is fetched from a memory location near the top of the address space. Unlike the 6802, however, status outputs are provided that can be decoded to indicate when an interrupt vector is being read. The four least significant address lines indicate which interrupt type is being serviced. Additional logic can thus be added to disable the memory when the interrupt vector is being read and substitute the address of interrupt service routine for a particular peripheral.

Another unusual feature of the 6809's interrupt structure is the existence of a "fast" interrupt request $\overline{\text{FIRQ}}$, in addition to the regular interrupt request $\overline{\text{IRQ}}$. In response to an $\overline{\text{IRQ}}$ interrupt, the 6809 saves all the microprocessor's registers on the stack. In most cases this is convenient, but it does slow the interrupt response. For situations in which all the registers need not be saved and fast response is important, the $\overline{\text{FIRQ}}$ input is used instead. $\overline{\text{FIRQ}}$ interrupts cause only the program counter and condition code register (flags) to be saved. This speeds up the response, since the interrupt service routine can then save only those registers that it uses. (Note that the $\overline{\text{FIRQ}}$ interrupt is equivalent to the normal interrupt input on most other microprocessors.)

3.6.3 The 8080 and 8085 Interrupt Structures

The 8080 microprocessor, while now obsolete, has had a significant influence on subsequent designs. The 8080 has a single interrupt input INT and an interrupt acknowledge output $\overline{\text{INTA}}$. ($\overline{\text{INTA}}$ is actually provided by the 8228 system controller chip, which is included in most 8080 systems.)

When the 8080 begins processing an interrupt, it asserts $\overline{\text{INTA}}$. The interrupting device then supplies an instruction onto the data bus, which is fetched and executed by the microprocessor. Typically, the instruction supplied is one of the 8080's eight "restart" instructions, which are single-byte subroutine calls with fixed addresses. A standard subroutine CALL instruction can also be supplied, in which case the 8080 automatically performs two additional interrupt acknowledge cycles to fetch the subroutine address. This is an awkward scheme in that the "vector" read from the interrupting device is treated not as an address or an interrupt number but as an instruction.

The 8085 provides an enhancement of the 8080's interrupt structure. There are five interrupt inputs: INTR, TRAP, RST 5.5, RST 6.5, and RST 7.5. The INTR input functions just like the 8080's INT, and the 8085 provides an equivalent $\overline{\text{INTA}}$ output. TRAP is a nonmaskable interrupt that causes a call to a fixed address (0024). No acknowledge cycle is performed for a TRAP interrupt.

The three RST inputs are autovectored. Each has a fixed service routine address associated with it; no acknowledge is generated, and no response from the peripheral is required. These interrupts are prioritized, with RST 7.5 having the highest priority. Each interrupt can also be selectively disabled by the software by using the SIM (set interrupt mask) instruction. The RST interrupt inputs allow many systems to operate without an external interrupt controller such as the 8259A. The RST 7.5 input is edge-triggered; a rising edge on this signal sets an internal latch. Thus, if RST 7.5 is pulsed while interrupts are disabled, the interrupt will be serviced as soon as interrupts are enabled. The other interrupt inputs are not edge-triggered, and must be held asserted until they are acknowledged.

3.6.4 The Z80 Interrupt Structure

The Z80 retains compatibility with the 8080 approach but provides a more powerful and flexible interrupt structure. There are two interrupt inputs, $\overline{\text{INT}}$ and $\overline{\text{NMI}}$. $\overline{\text{NMI}}$ is a nonmaskable interrupt input that causes a call to a fixed address (0066). No acknowledge cycle is performed for $\overline{\text{NMI}}$ interrupts.

The Z80 has no interrupt acknowledge output pin. Instead, the simultaneous assertion of $\overline{\text{M1}}$ (which normally indicates an opcode fetch cycle) and $\overline{\text{IORQ}}$ is used to indicate an interrupt acknowledge. This combination of control signals cannot occur in normal bus cycles, since opcodes cannot be fetched from I/O. Neither $\overline{\text{RD}}$ nor $\overline{\text{WR}}$ is asserted during interrupt acknowledge cycles, so memory and I/O devices (other than the one that generated the interrupt) are not enabled.

The Z80's $\overline{\text{INT}}$ input can operate in one of three software-selected modes. Mode 0 emulates the 8080 structure described previously. In mode 1, the $\overline{\text{INT}}$ input operates as a nonvectored interrupt and causes a call to address 0038. As with $\overline{\text{NMI}}$, no acknowledge cycle is performed.

Mode 2 is the most powerful and provides table-driven vectored interrupts. It is used by all Z80-family peripheral chips and is thus used in most Z80-based systems. Figure 3.21 shows the registers and memory locations involved and the method used to determine service routine addresses. A table in memory called the *interrupt vector table* contains the starting address of each interrupt service routine. The Z80's I register contains the upper byte of the table address and thus determines the area of memory where the table is stored. Each peripheral capable of generating an interrupt contains an interrupt vector register. Both the I register and the interrupt vector register(s) must be set by software before interrupts can be processed.

In response to an interrupt acknowledge from the Z80 (indicated by the assertion of $\overline{\text{IORQ}}$ AND $\overline{\text{M1}}$), the interrupting device places the contents of its interrupt vector register on the data bus. This provides the least significant byte of the table address. The combination of the microprocessor's I register and the peripheral's vector register form a 16-bit address, which points to an entry in the interrupt vector table. The selected table entry then provides the address of the interrupt service routine.

The Z80 interrupt structure also provides a method for prioritizing interrupts without requiring an interrupt controller chip. Interrupt priority determines which interrupt gets acknowledged first if two occur simultaneously and which interrupts can interrupt other interrupt service routines. A *daisy chain* is used to implement the priority structure, as shown in Fig. 3.22. Each Z80 peripheral chip has an input called IEI (interrupt enable in), and an output called IEO (interrupt enable out). The highest-priority device has its IEI tied high, so it is always enabled to generate interrupts. Its IEO drives the IEI of the next-highest-priority device, and so on. The IEO of the lowest-priority device is not used. When a peripheral is not requesting an interrupt, it copies the signal on its IEI to its IEO. A peripheral may generate an interrupt only if its IEI is high. When requesting an interrupt, it first waits for its IEI to be high and then sets its IEO low. This action prevents all lower-priority devices from generating an interrupt.

The peripheral device must detect when its interrupt service is complete so that it can set its IEO high again. It does this by monitoring the data bus, watching for an RETI (return from interrupt) instruction. When it detects this instruction being fetched while its IEI input is high, it sets its IEO output high.

In the example shown in Fig. 3.22, device 3 makes the first interrupt request. It sets its IEO low, preventing device 4 from generating interrupts. Devices 1 and 2 are of higher priority, so they can still generate interrupts. When device 2 requests an interrupt, it sets its IEO low, indicating to device 3 that its interrupt service has been suspended. Device 2 monitors the flow of instructions on the data bus, and when the RETI

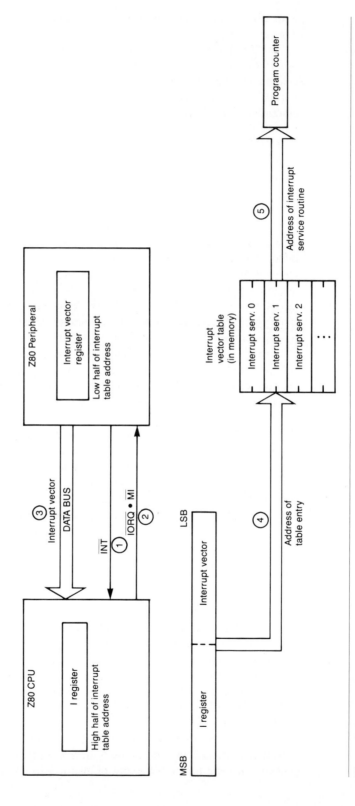

Figure 3.21. Z80 mode 2 interrupt vectoring.

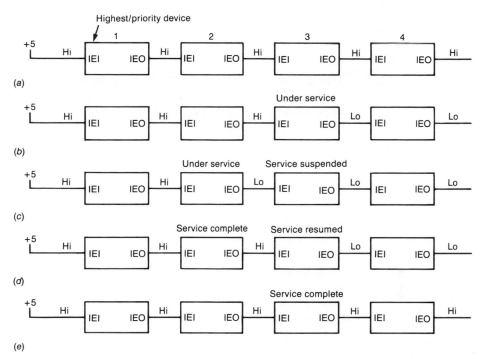

Figure 3.22. Z80 interrupt priority daisy chain operation. *(a)* Priority interrupt daisy chain before any interrupt occurs. *(b)* Device 3 requests an interrupt and is acknowledged. *(c)* Device 2 interrupts, suspends servicing of device 3. *(d)* Device 2 service routine complete, RETI issued, device 3 service resumed. *(e)* Second RETI instruction issued on completion of device 3 service routine.

instruction is fetched, it sets its IEO high again. Device 3 ignores this RETI, since its IEI is low. The processor now resumes device 3's service routine, and when the RETI at the end of this routine is fetched, device 3 sets its IEO high, and all devices are again enabled to generate interrupts.

While this structure is complex to explain, it is simple to implement because the Z80-family peripheral chips provide all the required logic internally. It does make it difficult to use non-Z80-family devices to generate Z80-mode-2-compatible interrupts. (The Z80-CTC or Z80-PIO chips can be used to process interrupts from incompatible devices.) The table-driven scheme is very flexible, allowing both the table and the service routines to be located anywhere in the memory space while requiring only an 8-bit vector from each peripheral. All interrupt control logic is placed in the peripherals. This is in contrast to Intel's approach, which does not require any special logic in the peripherals but requires either an external interrupt controller chip or a microprocessor such as the 80186 with an on-chip interrupt controller.

The Z80 automatically saves only the program counter at the beginning of the interrupt service. Because the Z80 has many registers, it slows the interrupt response significantly to save them all on the stack. To help alleviate this problem, the Z80 provides a second set of registers called the *alternate register set*. The software can swap register sets with a single instruction. Thus, the main program can use one register set while the interrupt service routine uses the other. This allows all the registers to be used by the interrupt service routine and still have fast interrupt response.

Care must be exercised in using this feature if there is more than one interrupt source. If more than one service routine uses the alternate register set, it must keep interrupts disabled while in the interrupt service routine (unless it is the highest-priority interrupt). Otherwise, if an interrupt service routine was interrupted, the register bank would be switched twice and the original set of registers would be lost.

3.6.5   The 8086 and 80186 Interrupt Structures

The 8086 departs completely from the 8080 and 8085 interrupt structures, although the interrupt request and acknowledge signals are similar. The external interrupt inputs are INTR and NMI. NMI is a nonmaskable interrupt with a fixed vector address, and $\overline{\text{INTR}}$ is the vectored interrupt input. In response to an INTR request, the 8086 asserts $\overline{\text{INTA}}$ (interrupt acknowledge, supplied directly by the 8086 in minimum mode and by the 8288 bus controller in maximum mode). The interrupting device then places its interrupt "type" number on the data bus. The microprocessor reads this number and transfers control to the corresponding interrupt service routine.

Intel's 8259A priority interrupt controller chip provides the logic to prioritize eight interrupt inputs and to provide a unique interrupt type code for each. Figure 3.23 shows the block diagram for this device. Before any interrupts can be processed, the 8259A must be initialized by the microprocessor by writing a series of bytes to the 8259A's internal registers. The interrupt mask register allows each of the eight interrupt inputs to be selectively enabled or disabled. Additional control registers (not explicitly shown in the block diagram) are written to select the mode of operation and the addresses to be generated in response to an interrupt acknowledge.

The 8259 interrupt controller was designed for use with the 8080. It was then modified slightly to become the 8259A, which can be used with the 8080/8085 or the 8086 family. When the 8259A is initialized, one of the control bits specifies 8080 or 8086

Figure 3.23. The 8259A interrupt controller block diagram. *(Courtesy of Intel Corporation.)*

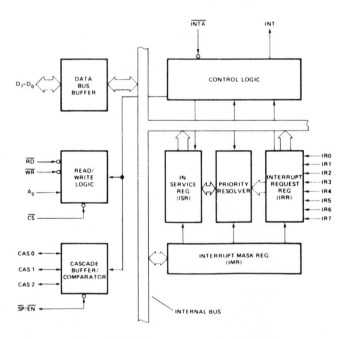

Figure 3.24. The
8086 interrupt vector
table. *(Courtesy of Intel
Corporation.)*

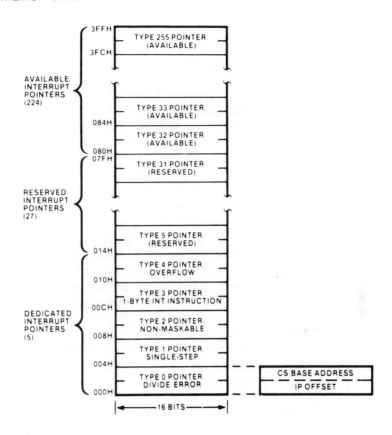

mode. In 8080 mode, the interrupt acknowledge response consists of the 8080's CALL instruction opcode, followed by the interrupt service routine address. In 8086 mode, 8259A supplies only a single-byte interrupt type number in response to the interrupt acknowledge.

When an interrupt input is asserted, it is latched into the interrupt request register. Interrupts that have been masked by the initialization are ignored, and if more than one interrupt is asserted, the one with highest priority is processed first. When an unmasked interrupt is detected, the 8259A asserts INT to the microprocessor. When the microprocessor responds with $\overline{INTA}$, the interrupt type code is driven onto the data bus.

Multiple 8259As can be interconnected for up to 64 interrupt inputs. One 8259A acts as the master and processes interrupts from up to eight other 8259As. The three cascade lines CAS 0, 1, and 2 form a private interrupt control bus that is driven by the master 8259A and received by each of the slaves. The SP/$\overline{EN}$ pin is tied high on the master and low on the slaves to set each device's mode.

Figure 3.24 shows the 8086's interrupt vector table. There are 256 interrupt types, and each type pointer requires 4 bytes, so a total of up to 1 Kbyte (from 00000 to 003FF) may be used by the table. Most applications use many fewer interrupts and correspondingly less memory for the table. Four bytes (two 16-bit words) are required for each interrupt vector because the 8086 addresses instruction memory by adding a 16-bit instruction pointer (program counter) to a 16-bit base value, called the code segment (CS) base address. Since the program executing may be in any part of the 1-Mbyte address space, it is necessary to load both the instruction pointer and the CS base address register to perform the jump to the interrupt service routine. Thus, each interrupt pointer includes two bytes for the CS base address and two bytes for the instruction pointer value. After the interrupt type number is read by the 8086 during the interrupt acknowledge cycle, it is internally multiplied by 4 to produce the address of the first of the four bytes that contain the address for the interrupt service routine.

The 8086 has several internal interrupt sources. Interrupt type 0 is generated when a divide error occurs (such as an attempt to divide by zero), and type 4 is generated when an overflow occurs. Two other internal interrupts provide debugging facilities. The 8086 status register includes a bit called the *trap flag*. The trap flag can be set by the software to enter *single-step mode*. In this mode, a type 1 interrupt occurs after each instruction execution. The service routine for this interrupt is typically a monitor program, which displays the registers and allows them to be modified. The user program can be continued by executing a return from interrupt instruction. The microprocessor will execute the next instruction in the program, and the trap interrupt will then cause a jump back to the monitor. Thus, the register contents can be easily traced during the execution of a program.

The 1-BYTE INT. interrupt (type 3) occurs whenever an INT 3 breakpoint instruction is executed. This is a single-byte instruction that is used to replace a program instruction at the point where the user wants to stop a program and examine registers or memory. Its function is similar to the single-step interrupt, except that any number of instructions can be executed before the breakpoint occurs.

Interrupt types 5 to 31 are reserved for future features (of these, types 5 to 19 are used in the 80186), leaving interrupt types 32 to 255 available for the user's external interrupts. Thus, interrupting devices should supply a type number between 32 and 255 in response to the interrupt acknowledge. This allows for up to 224 different interrupt service routines, more than enough for virtually any application.

In summary, the 8086 reads a single byte of data from the interrupting device to determine which one of 224 possible interrupt service routines should be called. The 8086 multiplies this number by 4 to provide a pointer to a four-byte entry in the interrupt vector table. The table entry provides the address of the interrupt service routine.

The 80186 uses a superset of the 8086's interrupt structure. The interrupt vector table occupies the same 1 Kbyte at the bottom of memory, and the same internal interrupt sources are present. There are also several additional internal interrupt sources, including timer and DMA interrupts, array index out-of-range interrupt, and undefined opcode interrupt.

The equivalent of the 8259A interrupt controller is included in the 80186 to minimize the need for external hardware. Four interrupt input pins are provided, each of which is automatically vectored via its own interrupt vector table entry. Thus, no interrupt acknowledge cycles are required. If more than four interrupt inputs are needed, two of the interrupt pins can be programmed as interrupt acknowledge outputs. These can be used in conjunction with an 8259A interrupt controller IC to provide additional interrupt inputs.

(Note that the 8088's interrupt structure is the same as the 8086's, and the 80188's is the same as the 80186's.)

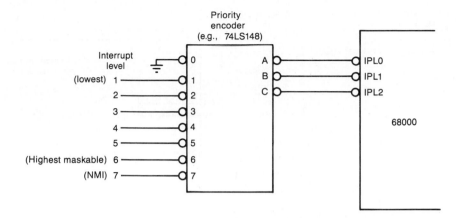

Figure 3.25. The 68000 interrupt encoding circuit.

3.6.6 The 68000 Interrupt Structure

The 68000 family has a relatively sophisticated interrupt structure. The interrupt inputs to the 68000 are the three *Interrupt Priority Level* lines $\overline{IPL0}$, $\overline{IPL1}$, and $\overline{IPL2}$. These are not individual interrupts but a binary interrupt number. The normal no-interrupt condition is indicated by interrupt priority level 000 (i.e., all three lines negated). Interrupt priority level 111 (i.e., all three lines asserted) is a nonmaskable interrupt. The six other possible combinations (001 to 110) represent six different interrupt levels. A decimal-to-binary encoder (also called a *priority encoder* IC because only the highest-numbered active input is encoded) encodes individual inputs into their binary representation, as shown in Fig. 3.25.

The 68000's processor status register includes a 3-bit interrupt mask. Interrupts of priority levels below or equal to the interrupt mask value are inhibited. Thus, some interrupts are ignored while others are processed, depending on the interrupt mask value. When an interrupt service routine is entered, the interrupt mask is set to the priority level of the interrupt. At the end of the interrupt service routine, an RTE (return from exception) instruction is executed that restores the status register (which includes the interrupt mask) to its previous state.

When an interrupt is of a higher level than the interrupt mask value, it is acknowledged by the 68000 as soon as the instruction in progress is complete. The 68000 performs a read cycle with the function code outputs FC0, FC1, and FC2 set to 111 to indicate an interrupt acknowledge cycle. Interrupt vectoring can now be completed in either of two ways: autovectoring or external vectoring.

Autovectoring provides one of seven different vector addresses, one for each of the seven interrupt priority levels. This mode is selected by asserting $\overline{VPA}$ when an interrupt acknowledge cycle occurs (indicated by FC = 111), as shown in Fig. 3.26. No vector is required from the interrupting device. Thus, each interrupt priority level is treated as an individual interrupt with its own interrupt service routine. This mode is the natural one to use if seven or fewer interrupt sources are present.

For maximum flexibility, the interrupting device can supply an 8-bit vector on the data bus during the interrupt acknowledge cycle. Figure 3.27 shows the timing diagram

Figure 3.26. The 68000 interrupt acknowledge and autovector circuit.

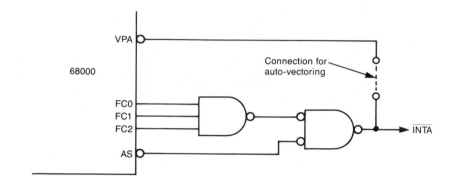

68000

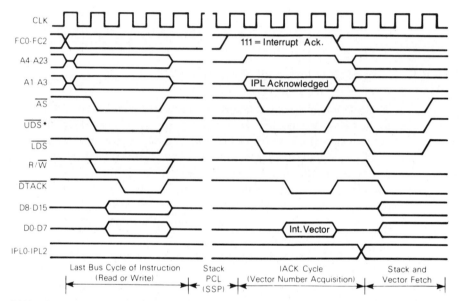

111 = Interrupt Ack.

IPL Acknowledged

Int. Vector

| Last Bus Cycle of Instruction (Read or Write) | Stack PCL (SSP) | IACK Cycle (Vector Number Acquisition) | Stack and Vector Fetch |

* Although a vector number is one byte, both data strobes are asserted due to the microcode used for exception processing. The processor does not recognize anything on data lines D8 through D15 at this time.

Figure 3.27. The 68000 bus timing for externally vectored interrupt acknowledge. *(Courtesy of Motorola, Inc.)*

for an externally vectored interrupt acknowledge cycle. The 68000 sets the function code outputs to 111 and outputs the interrupt priority level (IPL) being acknowledged on A1, A2, and A3. These lines are decoded to provide an interrupt acknowledge signal for each level. In response, the interrupting device supplies the interrupt vector on the data bus. This vector selects an entry in the interrupt vector table. Each entry in the table is four bytes long, although only three bytes are needed to store the 24-bit interrupt service routine addresses.

The interrupt vector table is part of what Motorola calls the *exception vector* table, shown in Table 3.4. Like the 8086, the 68000 has a number of other exception conditions, which are internal interrupt sources. These include a *trace* vector that operates similarly to the 8086's single-step interrupt and a *trap* vector that is similar to the 8086's breakpoint interrupt. Also included are divide by zero, illegal instruction, and bus error exceptions. Autovectored interrupt addresses are also in this table. Vectors 64 to 255 are available for use as external interrupt vectors.

Whenever an exception (such as an interrupt) occurs, the 68000 switches to supervisor mode. Supervisor programs then direct the interrupt to the appropriate service routine. This allows common service routines to be used for all programs in a multi-

Table 3.4   The 68000 Exception Vectors *(Courtesy of Motorola, Inc.)*

Vector Number(s)	Dec	Address Hex	Space	Assignment
0	0	000	SP	Reset: Initial SSP[2]
1	4	004	SP	Reset: Initial PC[2]
2	8	008	SD	Bus Error
3	12	00C	SD	Address Error
4	16	010	SD	Illegal Instruction
5	20	014	SD	Zero Divide
6	24	018	SD	CHK Instruction
7	28	01C	SD	TRAPV Instruction
8	32	020	SD	Privilege Violation
9	36	024	SD	Trace
10	40	028	SD	Line 1010 Emulator
11	44	02C	SD	Line 1111 Emulator
12[1]	48	030	SD	(Unassigned, Reserved)
13[1]	52	034	SD	(Unassigned, Reserved)
14	56	038	SD	Format Error[5]
15	60	03C	SD	Uninitialized Interrupt Vector
16-23[1]	64	040	SD	(Unassigned, Reserved)
	95	05F		—
24	96	060	SD	Spurious Interrupt[3]
25	100	064	SD	Level 1 Interrupt Autovector
26	104	068	SD	Level 2 Interrupt Autovector
27	108	06C	SD	Level 3 Interrupt Autovector
28	112	070	SD	Level 4 Interrupt Autovector
29	116	074	SD	Level 5 Interrupt Autovector
30	120	078	SD	Level 6 Interrupt Autovector
31	124	07C	SD	Level 7 Interrupt Autovector
32-47	128	080	SD	TRAP Instruction Vectors[4]
	191	0BF		
48-63[1]	192	0C0	SD	(Unassigned, Reserved)
	255	0FF		—
64-255	256	100	SD	User Interrupt Vectors
	1023	3FF		—

NOTES:
1. Vector numbers 12, 13, 16 through 23, and 48 through 63 are reserved for future enhancements by Motorola. No user peripheral devices should be assigned these numbers.
2. Reset vector (0) requires four words, unlike the other vectors which only require two words, and is located in the supervisor program space.
3. The spurious interrupt vector is taken when there is a bus error indication during interrupt processing.
4. TRAP #n uses vector number 32 + n.
5. MC68010 only. This vector is unassigned, reserved on the MC68000, and MC68008.

user or multitasking system. At the end of the interrupt service routine, the RTE instruction restores the status register (which includes the user/supervisor flag and the interrupt mask) to its state prior to the interrupt.

The 68008 8-bit bus version of the 68000 is available in two packages: a 48-pin DIP and a 52-pin chip carrier. Due to pin limitations, the DIP version has only two interrupt inputs: $\overline{IPL1}$ and IPL0/$\overline{2}$. $\overline{IPL0}$ and $\overline{IPL2}$ are connected together internally to produce the IPL0/$\overline{2}$ input. Thus, there are only four possible interrupt levels: 0 (no interrupt), 2, 5, and 7 (nonmaskable interrupt). As illustrated in the design example in Sec. 3.10, this is more than adequate for many applications.

3.7 BUS ARBITRATION

The microprocessor is normally the only device that drives the address and control buses. However, there are situations in which another device drives these buses, and the microprocessor's bus drivers must then be disabled. The most common example is direct memory access (DMA), in which a DMA controller takes over the buses to perform high-speed data transfers (typically between a peripheral and memory). Other examples are systems with coprocessors that need access to the buses, and multiple microprocessor systems in which more than one microprocessor share the same buses. Normally the microprocessor controls the buses and is thus the *bus master*. When another device such as a DMA controller takes control of the buses, it becomes the *temporary bus master*.

(DMA is described in detail in Chap. 5, and multiple processor systems are described in Chap. 10.)

3.7.1 Basic Bus Request/Bus Grant Logic

Most microprocessors include a *bus request* input to allow other devices to request that the microprocessor not use the buses. When this input is asserted, the microprocessor completes the instruction in progress and then stops instruction execution, disables its bus drivers, and asserts the *bus grant* output. Bus grant is monitored by the other device(s) capable of controlling the bus to determine when the microprocessor has released the buses. Bus grant is also used to disable external bus buffers, if present. The device that requested the buses then controls them for as long as is needed. It then negates bus request, and the microprocessor takes control of the buses and resumes normal operation.

Many microprocessors use this basic two-wire bus control scheme, although different names are used. The 8085 and 80186 call these signals HOLD and HLDA (hold acknowledge). The Z80 calls them $\overline{BUSRQ}$ (bus request) and $\overline{BUSAK}$ (bus acknowledge). The 6802 calls them $\overline{HALT}$ and BA (bus available). The 6802 does not place its address bus in a high-impedance state, however, so external three-state drivers are required. This is not unreasonable, since most systems using DMA or multiple processors are likely to need address bus buffers anyway to provide increased bus drive.

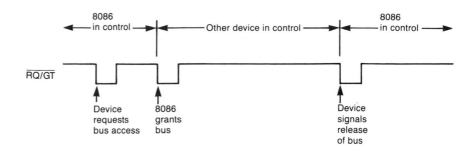

Figure 3.28. The 8086 bus request/bus grant operation.

3.7.2 The 8086 Request/Grant Operation

The 8086 uses two different techniques to implement bus request/bus grant functions. In minimum mode, HOLD and HLDA signals as previously described are used. In maximum mode, a different approach is used. Rather than using one pin for request and another for grant, one pin serves both functions. There are two request/grant pins, $\overline{RQ}/\overline{GT0}$ and $\overline{RQ}/\overline{GT1}$, which are bidirectional. Each operates in the same manner, although $\overline{RQ}/\overline{GT0}$ has higher priority.

Control of the buses is requested by asserting one of the $\overline{RQ}/\overline{GT}$ inputs for one clock period, as shown in Fig. 3.28. Note that the line is not held asserted but only pulsed. Open-collector or three-state drivers are used, so that when the line is not asserted it floats to the inactive state. The 8086 then issues the bus grant by outputting a pulse on the same pin. To terminate the sequence, the temporary bus master pulses the same $\overline{RQ}/\overline{GT}$ pin again to indicate to the 8086 that the buses are now available.

While this approach complicates the logic required to perform bus arbitration, it reduces the number of lines required from two to one. This allows the 8086 to provide two separate request inputs in maximum mode and allows the 8087 math coprocessor to request and be granted use of the bus using only one pin.

For those applications that don't need this feature and don't want the complications, the 8086's minimum mode provides the simpler two-wire control approach. The two $\overline{RQ}/\overline{GT}$ pins are replaced with HOLD and HLDA pins, identical to those used by the 8085 and 80186.

3.7.3 The 68000 Bus Arbitration

The 68000 uses a three-wire approach to bus arbitration. Figure 3.29 shows the bus exchange operation. As usual, a bus request signal (called $\overline{BR}$) indicates to the microprocessor that another device wants access to the bus. The microprocessor responds by asserting $\overline{BG}$ (bus grant), but this bus grant functions differently than the signals previously discussed. $\overline{BG}$ is asserted as soon as the 68000 has internally synchronized the $\overline{BR}$ input. The buses are not actually available until the completion of the cycle, so the device requesting bus control must wait not only for $\overline{BG}$ to be asserted but also for the address and data strobe signals to be negated.

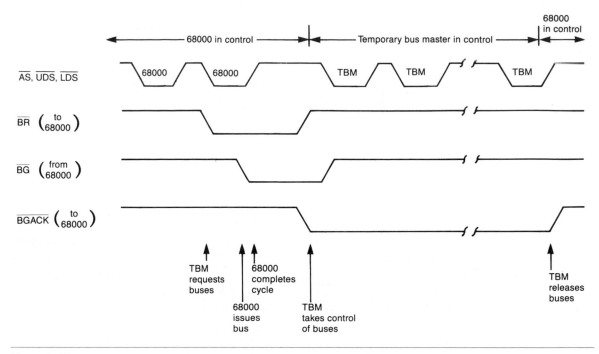

Figure 3.29.   The 68000 bus request/bus grant operation.

The device requesting the buses responds to the bus grant by asserting $\overline{\text{BGACK}}$ (bus grant acknowledge) and negating $\overline{\text{BR}}$. The temporary bus master holds $\overline{\text{BGACK}}$ asserted for as long at it needs the bus and then negates it. The 68000 then resumes operation. This is in contrast to most other microprocessors, which have no bus grant acknowledge. In such systems, the temporary bus master simply keeps bus request asserted until it is done using the buses.

The reason for $\overline{\text{BGACK}}$ is to allow bus requests from multiple devices to be ORed into the $\overline{\text{BR}}$ input. Thus, when one or more of the devices are requesting the bus, $\overline{\text{BR}}$ is asserted. $\overline{\text{BGACK}}$ is needed so that the temporary bus master can indicate when it is done. If it simply held $\overline{\text{BR}}$ asserted while it was using the bus, and if another device was also requesting the bus, then the 68000 would see no change in $\overline{\text{BR}}$ when the first device was done, and the second device would not know that it could take over the bus.

When the temporary bus master is ready to release the bus, it negates $\overline{\text{BGACK}}$. If $\overline{\text{BR}}$ is still asserted, indicating that another device is also requesting control of the buses, the 68000 asserts $\overline{\text{BG}}$ again.

External priority logic is required if multiple bus requests are ORed into $\overline{\text{BR}}$. When the bus grant is issued, it must be accepted only by the highest priority device currently requesting the bus.

Due to pin limitations, the 48-pin DIP version of the 68008 does not include the $\overline{\text{BGACK}}$ signal. Instead, more conventional bus request and bus grant signals are used.

3.7.4   Bus Arbitration with Multiple Bus Requesters

The bus arbitration schemes discussed above are those provided directly by the micro-processors. If there is more than one potential bus requester, however, additional logic is required. If multiple bus requests are simply ORed together to provide the bus request to the processor, a problem can occur if two devices request the bus at the same time: both requesters will see the acknowledge, and both will attempt to take control of the bus. The result is a bus conflict, and neither requester will be able to effectively control the bus. The end result is generally a system "crash."

It is thus necessary that a priority be assigned to each potential bus master, so that when two or more requests are received simultaneously the higher-priority device is granted the bus before the lower-priority device(s). Two common approaches are *serial* and *parallel* arbitration.

Serial arbitration, as shown in Fig. 3.30, uses a daisy chain similar to the Z80's interrupt priority control discussed in Sec. 3.6.4. Each possible bus master has a bus priority in and a bus priority out pin. The highest-priority device is at the start of the chain and can always request the bus. Normally, each device copies the level on its bus priority input to its bus priority output. When a device wants to access the bus, it first checks the state of BUS ACK. If BUS ACK is asserted, indicating that the main processor has already granted the bus to a temporary bus master, then the bus requester must wait for this device to complete its bus activity and release the bus. The requester then negates its bus priority output and asserts BUS REQ. If more than one requester does this at the same time, the lower-priority device will know that it has been overridden because its bus priority in will be negated. The lower-priority device therefore ignores the BUS ACK, and the higher-priority device takes control of the buses.

There are several disadvantages of serial arbitration. It is slow if there are many potential bus masters, since the bus priority signal must pass through each of them

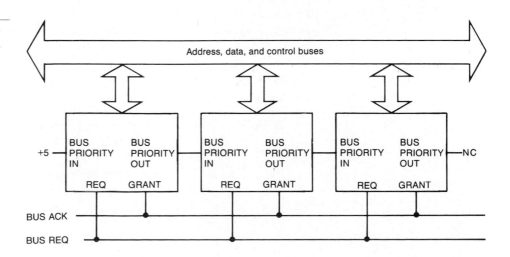

Figure 3.30. Serial bus arbitration using priority daisy chain.

Figure 3.31. Daisy-chained priority signals on backplane.

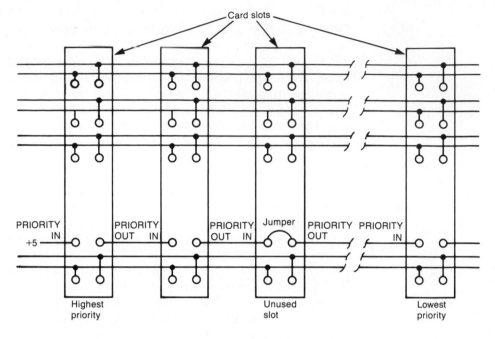

Figure 3.32. Parallel bus arbitration using central arbiter.

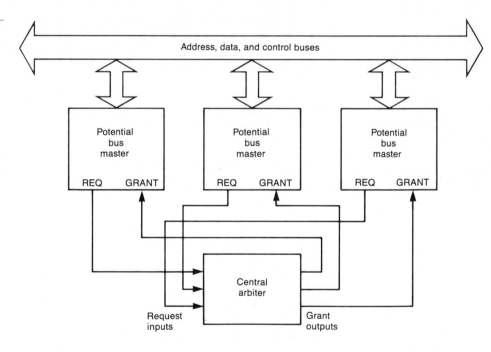

before it is valid at all points. The priority chain signal cannot be wired to all connectors on the backplane in parallel but must be connected as shown in Fig. 3.31. The priority of each board is thus determined by its physical position in the backplane and cannot be dynamically changed. Any open slots between occupied slots must have a jumper to provide continuity for the priority daisy chain signal. The primary advantage of the serial technique is that it is simple and inexpensive to implement since no central arbiter is needed.

Parallel arbitration, as shown in Fig. 3.32, uses a separate bus request and grant signal for each potential bus master. A central arbiter, which is typically part of the backplane, receives all bus requests, decides which is the highest priority, and grants the bus to that device. This technique is faster, since additional levels of logic are not needed for each possible bus master.

The most common central arbiter implementation assigns a fixed priority to each bus request input (in effect, each backplane connector). More sophisticated arbitration algorithms are also possible with a central arbiter. One example is *round-robin* priority, in which the priority of each device changes each time the bus is granted. Round-robin priority is less commonly used than fixed priority due to the additional logic required.

3.8 SYSTEM BUSES

In a single-board system, the bus structure provided directly by the microprocessor is the natural one to use. In multiboard systems, the interface between the various boards must be defined; this is the purpose of standard system buses. This section describes several common system buses.

3.8.1 Motivations for System Buses

In systems that are not processor-based, there is generally no standard interface between boards. Each board's interface signals are specific to the function of the card, and a multiboard system is configured by interconnecting the boards for the signal flow required by the particular application. The backplane, which consists of connectors for the boards and all the interconnecting wires, is therefore customized according to the signal flow and combination of boards required for each application.

In microprocessor-based systems, the address, data, and control buses provide the most effective interconnection. Microprocessor system buses provide a standardized set of bus signals. This allows a wide variety of board types, including processor boards, memory boards, and interface boards, to be easily combined to configure a customized system. A good bus standard provides the guidelines necessary for independent designers to design various boards that will all work together. System buses generally include address, data, and control signals, plus additional signals for bus arbitration, system control, and power.

The backplane in a microprocessor system consists primarily of connectors wired in parallel; that is, each pin of each connector is connected to the corresponding pin on all other connectors. Thus, any board can be plugged into any slot. (The major exceptions to this rule are bus arbitration and interrupt priority signals.) Each memory or peripheral board must decode a unique range of addresses. Switches or jumpers on each board allow the user to set the range of addresses to which it will respond. This permits multiple boards of the same type to work together by setting the address decoding switches on each board differently.

The use of a standard bus also lets a system designer avoid re-inventing standard functions. For many applications, standard off-the-shelf CPU, memory, and I/O cards can be used to provide the basic system. The designer's efforts can then be concentrated on any unique functions required by the system, adding one or more custom cards to a set of standard boards and a standard backplane and card cage. In many systems, no custom cards are required at all; the system is configured from an assortment of standard cards, and the main contribution is in the software.

Several industry standard buses have emerged, such as the STD bus, Multibus, and VMEbus, which allow many manufacturers to make products that can be combined to configure complete systems. Another set of bus standards has evolved from personal computers: for example, the S100 bus, the Apple II bus, and the IBM PC bus. There are also many specialized system buses, which are typically used by a single manufacturer for a product line or group of products.

3.8.2 Characterizing System Buses

Table 3.5 lists the basic characteristics of several system buses. Like native microprocessor buses, the dominant classification is by the number of bits in the data bus. Other important characteristics include the width of the address bus, type of interrupts, and type of data transfer control (synchronous or asynchronous). System buses may be multiplexed or nonmultiplexed and may follow the Motorola or Intel style. Motorola-style buses typically have a read/write line and a data strobe and use memory-mapped I/O, while Intel-style buses have separate read and write strobes and provide separate memory and I/O strobes.

Performance of a system bus is often specified as the bus bandwidth in bytes per second. This is the maximum performance that the bus is capable of (within its specified timing parameters), and any real system is likely to perform at a lower rate. Since bus bandwidth is most commonly specified in bytes per second, it takes into account both the width of the data bus and the time to perform a transfer. For example, an 8-bit data bus capable of a transfer every 500 ns has a bandwidth of 2 Mbytes/s. A 32-bit data bus with the same transfer time has a bandwidth of 8 Mbytes/s.

System buses are also rated by their ability to handle multiple bus masters. A bus that is not designed for multiple processor applications will typically allow for one temporary bus master, which is generally a DMA controller. A single-processor bus of this type does not require any arbitration logic other than that provided directly by the microprocessor. A *multimaster* bus, on the other hand, allows several processors to share the system bus and requires additional arbitration logic.

Buses with data paths wider than 8 bits generally allow for data transfers that use only part of the data path. A bus with a 32-bit data path, for example, may allow transfers of single bytes or 16-bit words in addition to full 32-bit transfers. There are two approaches to the alignment of data for these partial-width data transfers. A *justified*

Table 3.5   System Bus Characteristics

	STD bus	Multibus	VMEbus	IBM PC/AT	Multibus II	Futurebus
IEEE Standard	P961	796	1014	None	P1296	P896
Data bus, bits	8	16	16 w/P1 only 32 w/P2	PC: 8 AT: 16	32	32
Address bus, bits	16 24 w/mux	24	23 w/P1 only 31 w/P2	PC: 20 AT: 24	32	32
Bus control	Semisync	Async	Async	Semisync	Semisync	Async
Multiplexed	No (yes for 20-bit adrs)	No	No	No	Yes	Yes
Interrupt levels	1	8	7	6	SW poll	SW poll
Multimaster arbitration	Some bus versions	Yes, serial or parallel	Yes, 4 levels w/serial arb.	No, DMA only	2 levels, 20 per level	Yes
Connector(s)	56-pin	P1: 86-pin P2: 60-pin	P1: 96-pin P2: 96-pin	PC: 62-pin AT: +36-pin	96-pin 96-pin aux.	96-pin
Connector type	Card edge	Card edge	Pin-in-socket	Card edge	Pin-in-socket	Pin-in-socket
Board size(s)	4.5 × 6.5 in.	6.75 × 12 in.	100 × 160 mm 233.35 × 220 mm	PC: 4.2 × 13.2 in. AT: 4.8 × 13.2 in.	233.35 × 220 mm	336.7 × 280 mm
Bus transfer rate (max), MHz	1.3	5	8.3	PC: 1.2 AT: 2.6	Normal: 5 Block: 10	Normal: 10 Block: 24
Bus bandwidth, (Mbytes/s)	1.3	8 bit: 5 16-bit: 10	16-bit: 16 32-bit: 32	PC: 1.2 AT: 5.2	Normal: 20 Block: 40	Normal: 37 Block: 95

transfer always uses the least significant portion of the data bus; an 8-bit transfer, for example, always uses data lines D_0 through D_7. This requires additional logic on boards that use the full bus width, since they must be able to shift bytes that normally would be transferred on upper data lines (as part of a full-width transfer) to the lower data lines. An *unjustified* transfer does not perform this shifting, and partial-width transfers can therefore occur on any portion of the bus. The advantage of justified buses is that memory and I/O boards can be designed to work with a variety of processor boards with different data bus widths. Unjustified buses save the additional logic required to shift bytes of data to the lower part of the bus but require that all boards in the system be able to transfer data over the full bus width.

The following sections describe several common buses. For detailed specifications on these buses, refer to the references listed in the Selected Bibliography at the end of this chapter.

In describing these buses, we have followed the nomenclature used in the official bus specifications. Thus, while an overbar is used to designate active-low signals in most of this book, in this section different styles are used to match that used in specification for the bus being described. For the same reason, subscripts are not used for some numbered signals (such as address and data lines).

3.8.3   STD Bus

The STD bus, or "standard" bus, is designed to allow low-cost semicustom systems to be built. It was originally defined by Pro-Log and Mostek. After several years of use, the bus specification was formalized first by the STD Manufacturer's Group (STDMG) and then as IEEE-P961 (a proposed standard as of this writing). It is most widely used in instrumentation and control systems. The boards are relatively small (4.5 × 6.5 in.), and a wide variety of functions are available. Several different microprocessors are available in STD bus CPU cards, including the Z80, 8085, 6809, 6502, and 8088. Interface cards available include almost everything imaginable, from simple I/O ports to stepper motor controllers, disk interfaces, display controllers, and fiber-optic communication interfaces. An example of an STD bus board is shown in Fig. 3.33.

Table 3.6 lists the signal assignments. It uses a relatively small 56-pin connector and is limited to 8 data lines and 16 address lines. To adapt the bus for use with the 8088, Ziatech Corporation devised a method for multiplexing 8 additional address bits on the data bus to provide a total of 24 address lines. The control signals RD∗, WR∗, IORQ∗, and MEMRQ∗ reveal a bias toward Z80 systems, although equivalent signals can be generated from most microprocessors. The presence of the REFRESH∗ control signal for dynamic RAM on the bus is also due to the Z80's influence (the Z80 provides this signal directly); normally, such a signal would not exist on a system bus. Interrupts are supported by the INTRQ∗ request and INTAK∗ acknowledge signals, along with the PCI and PCO priority daisy chain signals. The exact usage of these signals depends on the type of microprocessor. For Z80-STD systems, the Z80 mode 2 interrupts (described in Sec. 3.6.4) are generally used, and PCI and PCO connect to the IEI and IEO pins of Z80-family peripheral chips.

The original bus definition left several signals loosely defined, to be used in differ-

Figure 3.33. STD bus 8088 CPU board. *(Courtesy of Ziatech Corp.)*

Table 3.6   STD Bus Signals

		Component side				Circuit side	
	Pin	Signal name	Description	Pin	Signal name	Description
Logic power bus	1	V_{CC}	Logic power (+5 V dc)	2	V_{CC}	Logic power (+5 V dc)
	3	GND	Logic ground	4	GND	Logic ground
	5	V_{BB} #1/VBAT	Logic bias #1/bat pwr	6	V_{BB} #2/DCPD*	Logic bias #2/Pwr dwn
Data bus	7	D3/A19	Data bus/address extension	8	D7/A23	Data bus/address extension
	9	D2/A18		10	D6/A22	
	11	D1/A17		12	D5/A21	
	13	D0/A16		14	D4/A20	
Address bus	15	A7	Address bus	16	A15	Address bus
	17	A6		18	A14	
	19	A5		20	A13	
	21	A4		22	A12	
	23	A3		24	A11	
	25	A2		26	A10	
	27	A1		28	A9	
	29	A0		30	A8	
Control bus	31	WR*	Write to memory or I/O	32	RD*	Read memory or I/O
	33	IORQ*	I/O address select	34	MEMRQ*	Memory address select
	35	IOEXP	I/O expansion	36	MEMEX	Memory expansion
	37	REFRESH*	Refresh timing	38	MCSYNC*	CPU machine cycle sync.
	39	STATUS 1*	CPU status	40	STATUS 0*	CPU status
	41	BUSAK*	Bus acknowledge	42	BUSRQ*	Bus request
	43	INTAK*	Interrupt acknowledge	44	INTRQ*	Interrupt request
	45	WAITRQ*	Wait request	46	NMIRQ*	Nonmaskable interrupt
	47	SYSRESET*	System reset	48	PBRESET*	Pushbutton reset
	49	CLOCK*	Clock from processor	50	CNTRL*	AUX timing
	51	PCO	Priority chain out	52	PCI	Priority chain in
Auxiliary power bus	53	AUX GND	AUX ground	54	AUX GND	AUX ground
	55	AUX + V	AUX positive (+12 V dc)	56	AUX − V	AUX negative (−12 V dc)

ent ways by different processors. Signals used differently by different CPU boards include MCSYNC* STATUS1*, and STATUS0*. In addition, bus timing was not specified. Thus, not all STD bus boards will work together. For example, many peripheral cards designed for use in Z80-based STD bus systems use the Z80 peripheral chips to provide interrupt support logic, and depend on the presence of the Z80's $\overline{M1}$ signal on the STATUS1* line. These boards will work only with a Z80 CPU board.

The original STD bus definition allowed for one temporary bus master (such as a DMA controller) via BUSRQ* and BUSAK*. However, no provision was made for arbitration among multiple bus masters. Multiple processor systems have been implemented in several ways. Additional signals can be added on the edge of the board opposite the backplane for serial or parallel arbitration. The signals are connected between boards with ribbon cable. Another approach, which is used by Pro-Log Corporation in their 8088 CPU boards, is to use the PCI and PCO lines (originally intended for interrupt priority) as serial arbitration signals.

The power supply connections (other than $+5$ V and ground) are also not fully standardized. Pins 5 and 6 can be used for a -5 V supply (used primarily in older boards) or for a battery-backed supply. The auxiliary power supply is not always used and is sometimes ± 15 V instead of ± 12 V as nominally specified.

The STD-Z80 bus is a subset of the STD bus, which was originally designed by Mostek for systems using the Z80 microprocessor. All bus signals and timing are fully specified, so that any two cards designed to the standard should work together. Several manufacturers make lines of boards that conform to this standard.

There is also a CMOS version of the STD bus for low-power applications. The signal functions are the same, but the electrical levels are redefined to use CMOS's higher switching thresholds for greater noise immunity.

The STE bus is a variation of the STD bus that uses the Eurocard size and pin-and-socket connector type (see VMEbus description, Sec. 3.8.5).

3.8.4   Multibus

The Multibus was designed by Intel to provide a system bus for the 8080. It was carefully designed, however, so that it would not be limited to the 8080. The bus has been enhanced several times since its original definition to add control features and increase the width of the address bus. A typical Multibus CPU board, such as the one shown in Fig. 3.34, is a complete single-board computer that is expanded via the Multibus. CPU

Figure 3.34.   Multibus 80286 CPU board. *(Courtesy of Intel Corporation.)*

boards are available with most popular microprocessors, although the 8085, Z80, and 8086/186/286 families predominate. Memory boards are available up to several megabytes. Multibus boards are relatively large and expensive as compared to STD bus boards. The Multibus is used primarily in high-performance applications, including both dedicated systems and general-purpose computers.

The Multibus has been formalized as an IEEE standard, IEEE-796. This standard allows for various levels of compliance, such as 8- or 16-bit data buses. Within these limits, all Multibus boards that meet the IEEE specification should be compatible. Older Multibus products may not meet all details of the IEEE specification.

Multibus boards have two separate edge connectors, called P1 and P2. Table 3.7 lists the Multibus signals on the P1 connector. The P2 connector has four additional address lines for applications requiring a 24-bit address bus; the remainder of P2's 60 pins are used for application-dependent signals or auxiliary buses.

The Multibus includes a 16-bit data bus and a 24-bit address bus, although not all applications use the full width of either bus. (The original Multibus included only 16 address lines. It was then extended to 20 lines by using free pins on P1, and to 24 lines by using P2.) All signals on the Multibus, including the address and data buses, are active-low. The data transfer control signals are MRDC* (memory read), MWTC* (memory write), IORC* (I/O read), and IOWC* (I/O write). Data transfers are asynchronous; XACK* must be asserted by the addressed device when the transfer is complete. Since Intel's microprocessors use semisynchronous control signals, logic is required on the CPU board that inserts wait states until XACK* is asserted. Ironically, the 68000's $\overline{\text{DTACK}}$ signal is a closer match to XACK* than the ready/wait signals provided by Intel's microprocessors.

There are significant differences between the timing of the Multibus's XACK* and the 68000's $\overline{\text{DTACK}}$. XACK* cannot be asserted until the slave device (memory or I/O) has completed the bus transfer (for a read transfer, when valid data is on the bus). However, the 68000 does not read the data until one clock cycle after $\overline{\text{DTACK}}$ is asserted. Thus, using the Multibus XACK* for $\overline{\text{DTACK}}$ will generally cause an unnecessary wait state.

The signals BCLK*, BPRN*, BPRO*, BREQ*, BUSY*, CBRQ*, and LOCK* are used for multimaster arbitration. These signals are described in Chap. 10 (Multiple Microprocessor Systems).

The Multibus includes eight interrupt request lines and an interrupt acknowledge line. Interrupts may be processed in one of two ways. For *non-bus-vectored* interrupts, the interrupting device does not provide a vector, and each of the eight interrupt request signals initiates a specific interrupt service routine. For *bus-vectored* interrupts, the interrupting device supplies a vector on the data bus in response to INTA*.

The two inhibit signals INH1* and INH2* allow memory to be selectively enabled or disabled. A typical application is a disk-based system that has an EPROM used only for *boot-up* (reading the operating system from the disk). After the boot-up is complete, the EPROM is no longer needed, and it is desirable to have RAM in the same address space. This is implemented by using INH1* to control the RAM enable and INH2* to control the EPROM enable. These signals are driven from output port bits, which are asserted or negated by control software at the appropriate times to select one memory type or the other to occupy the memory space.

Several auxiliary buses have been defined for use with the Multibus. The iSBX bus

Table 3.7   Multibus Signals

		Component side				Circuit side	
	Pin	Mnemonic	Description	Pin	Mnemonic	Description
Power supplies	1	GND	Signal GND	2	GND	Signal GND
	3	+5 V	+5 V dc	4	+5 V	+5 V dc
	5	+5 V	+5 V dc	6	+5 V	+5 V dc
	7	+12 V	+12 V dc	8	+12 V	+12 V dc
	9		Reserved, bused	10		Reserved, bused
	11	GND	Signal GND	12	GND	Signal GND
Bus controls	13	BCLK*	Bus clock	14	INIT*	Initialize
	15	BPRN*	Bus priority in	16	BPRO*	Bus priority out
	17	BUSY*	Bus busy	18	BREQ*	Bus request
	19	MRDC*	Memory read command	20	MWTC*	Memory write command
	21	IORC*	I/O read command	22	IOWC*	I/O write command
	23	XACK*	XFER acknowledge	24	INH1*	Inhibit 1 (disable RAM)
Bus controls	25	LOCK*	Lock	26	INH2*	Inhibit 2 (disable PROM
and address	27	BHEN*	Byte high enable	28	AD10*	or ROM)
	29	CBRQ*	Common bus request	30	AD11*	Address bus
	31	CCLK*	Constant clock	32	AD12*	
	33	INTA*	Interrupt acknowledge	34	AD13*	
Interrupts	35	INT6*	Parallel interrupt	36	INT7*	Parallel interrupt
	37	INT4*	requests	38	INT5*	requests
	39	INT2*		40	INT3*	
	41	INT0*		42	INT1*	
Address	43	A14* (ADRE*)	Address bus (see *Note*)	44	A15* (ADRF*)	Address bus (see *Note*)
	45	A12* (ADRC*)		46	A13* (ADRD*)	
	47	A10* (ADRA*)		48	A11* (ADRB*)	
	49	A8* (ADR8*)		50	A9* (ADR9*)	
	51	A6* (ADR6*)		52	A7* (ADR7*)	
	53	A4* (ADR4*)		54	A5* (ADR5*)	
	55	A2* (ADR2*)		56	A3* (ADR3*)	
	57	A0* (ADR0*)		58	A1* (ADR1*)	
Data	59	D14* (DATE*)	Data bus (see *Note*)	60	D15* (DATF*)	Data bus (see *Note*)
	61	D12* (DATC*)		62	D13* (DATD*)	
	63	D10* (DATA*)		64	D11* (DATB*)	
	65	D8* (DAT8*)		66	D9* (DAT9*)	
	67	D6* (DAT6*)		68	D7* (DAT7*)	
	69	D4* (DAT4*)		70	D5* (DAT5*)	
	71	D2* (DAT2*)		72	D3* (DAT3*)	
	73	D0* (DAT0*)		74	D1* (DAT1*)	
Power supplies	75	GND	Signal GND	76	GND	Signal GND
	77		Reserved, bused	78		Reserved, bused
	79	−12 V	−12 V dc	80	−12 V	−12 V dc
	81	+5 V	+5 V dc	82	+5 V	+5 V dc
	83	+5 V	+5 V dc	84	+5 V	+5 V dc
	85	GND	Signal GND	86	GND	Signal GND

Note: All reserved pins are reserved for future use and should not be used if upward compatibility is desired. Address and data mnemonics in parentheses are for historical reference.

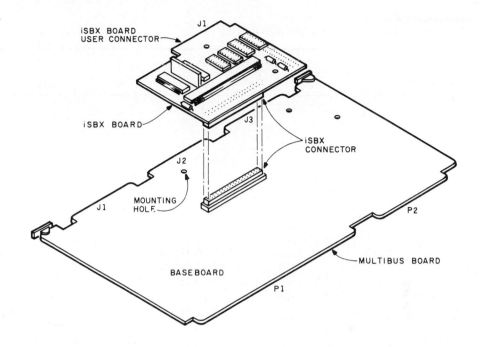

(IEEE-P959) is a simple expansion bus for adding I/O functions. The motivation for this bus is that the large size and multimaster interface of the Multibus makes even the simplest Multibus I/O card relatively expensive. The iSBX boards are small and have a simple bus interface, making them an inexpensive way to add a small amount of specialized I/O circuitry to a Multibus board.

Figure 3.35 shows the physical configuration and Table 3.8 lists the bus signals for the iSBX bus. Intel calls the iSBX boards *Multimodules,* which is the reason for the "M" prefix on many of the signal names. The iSBX bus cards mount as piggyback cards onto another PC board called the *baseboard,* which is typically (but not necessarily) a Multibus board. Only one iSBX bus card mounts on one connector, but a single Multibus board can have up to three iSBX connectors. Because the bus is intended only for I/O expansion, there are only three address lines and only I/O read and write signals.

The baseboard provides two chip select signals, MCS1∗ and MCS0∗, each of which is asserted for a range of eight addresses. The address lines MA0, MA1, and MA2 provide the addressing within the range determined by the chip select signals. The iSBX specification specifies different address ranges for each of the two chip select signals on each of up to three iSBX connectors. Eight-bit baseboards use a 36-pin connector with an 8-bit data bus. Sixteen-bit baseboards can use a 44-pin connector to provide a 16-bit data bus. DMA control signals allow an iSBX board to perform DMA transfers using a DMA controller on the baseboard. The MPST∗ (module present) signal is tied to ground on the iSBX board and pulled high through a resistor on the baseboard, indicating to the baseboard if a module is installed in the connector.

The performance of Multibus-based systems is often limited by the bus bandwidth.

Table 3.8   iSBX Expansion Bus Signals

Component side			Circuit side		
Pin	Mnemonic	Description	Pin	Mnemonic	Description
1	+12V	+12 V	2	−12V	−12 V
3	GND	Signal ground	4	+5V	+5 V
5	RESET	Reset	6	MCLK	Expansion module clock
7	MA2	Address 2	8	MPST*	Expansion module present
9	MA1	Address 1	10	—	Reserved
11	MA0	Address 0	12	MINTR1	Interrupt 1
13	IOWRT*	I/O write command	14	MINTR0	Interrupt 0
15	IORD*	I/O read command	16	MWAIT*	Expansion module wait
17	GND	Signal ground	18	+5V	+5 V
19	MD7	Data bit 7	20	MCS1*	Chip select 1
21	MD6	Data bit 6	22	MCS0*	Chip select 0
23	MD5	Data bit 5	24	—	Reserved
25	MD4	Data bit 4	26	TDMA	Terminate DMA
27	MD3	Data bit 3	28	OPT1	Option 1
29	MD2	Data bit 2	30	OPT0	Option 0
31	MD1	Data bit 1	32	MDACK*	DMA acknowledge
33	MD0	Data bit 0	34	MDRQT	DMA request
35	GND	Signal ground	36	+5V	+5 V
37	MD14	Data bit 14	38	MD15	Data bit 15
39	MD12	Data bit 12	40	MD13	Data bit 13
41	MD10	Data bit 10	42	MD11	Data bit 11
43	MD8	Data bit 8	44	MD9	Data bit 9

Note: MD8–MD15 used only on 16-bit systems.

The Multibus setup, pulse width, and hold time specifications, along with the requirement that XACK* not be asserted until the data transfer is complete, make it impossible for a high-speed microprocessor to operate without wait states when performing a transfer via the bus. In multiprocessor systems, each CPU can spend considerable time waiting for the bus to become available. High-speed DMA transfers to disk controller or communications interfaces can also consume much of the available bandwidth, limiting the CPU's access to the bus.

One solution to these limitations is to provide separate buses for each type of access. Intel's iLBX is a "private" memory bus for connecting CPU and memory boards. This bus is used primarily for expanding the CPU's "local" memory and is both faster than the Multibus and isolated from the I/O transfers occurring on the Multibus. The iLBX bus uses the P2 connector, which is selectively connected to the CPU and memory boards using the bus. There can be several independent iLBX buses in a single Multibus system, as shown in Fig. 3.36.

High-speed I/O transfers can also be given their own private bus to remove this traffic from the main system bus. Intel has defined a bus for this purpose called the *Multichannel*, which uses a ribbon-cable connector at the edge of the board opposite from the backplane.

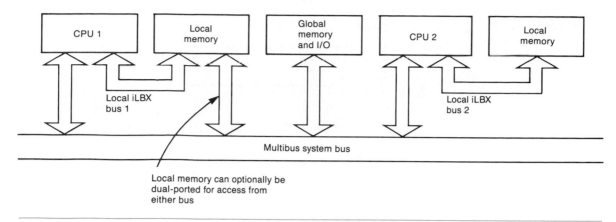

Figure 3.36. Multiple bus system using local memory buses.

3.8.5 VME Bus

The VME bus (commonly merged into one word as VMEbus) is the most complex and powerful of the buses described here. It was designed by Motorola, Mostek, and Signetics/Phillips to provide a high-performance bus for 68000-based systems. It is also used for other high-performance 16- and 32-bit microprocessors, such as National's 32000 family. The VMEbus evolved from the VERSAbus defined by Motorola for its first board-level 68000 products, and stands for Versa Module Europe. It has been formalized as IEEE-P1014, a proposed standard at this writing.

The size of the VME boards originates from a European standard called the Eurocard. There are two standard physical sizes for VME bus boards, called *single height* and *double height,* as shown in Fig. 3.37. The single-height board is 160 × 100 mm (approximately 6.3 × 3.9 in.) and has a single 96-pin connector called P1. The double-height board is 160 × 223.35 mm, slightly more than twice the width of the smaller board, and has a second 96-pin connector called P2. Figure 3.38 shows a typical double-height board. The Eurocard standard also specifies standard cards of triple- and quad-height, and with extended depth. Some VMEbus system manufacturers use the extended-depth (220 or 280 mm) and/or the triple-height boards to increase the board size and number of connector pins.

Another mechanical aspect of the VMEbus that differs from the Multibus and STD bus is that each card carries with it a slice of the front panel, which is used for switches, indicators, and connectors, and as a board stiffener and handle.

The DIN-type connectors used also follow a European standard. They are the pin-and-socket type, requiring a male connector on each board and female connectors on the backplane. While these connectors are more expensive than the edge connectors used with most other buses, they provide higher reliability and longer life. They also provide more pins in the same area, since three rows of pins are used as compared to two sets of contacts on a printed circuit board.

Figure 3.37. VMEbus and Eurocard board dimensions (in millimeters)

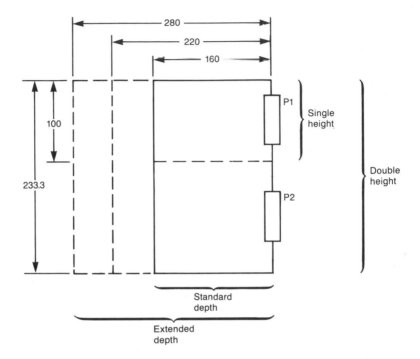

Figure 3.38. VMEbus 68020 CPU board. *(Courtesy of Motorola, Inc.)*

Table 3.9 lists the P1 signals, and Table 3.10 lists the P2 signals. The P1 connector includes all the signals required for a 16-bit microprocessor such as the 68000. The optional second connector provides expansion of both address and data buses to 32 bits and also provides 96 pins for user I/O lines or an auxiliary bus. This expanded configuration is intended for microprocessors such as the 68020 and 32032 with full 32-bit buses. Note that it is not necessary for a double-height board to use both connectors; it is common for double-height boards to use only P1.

The VMEbus specification divides the bus into four sub-buses: the data transfer bus (DTB), arbitration bus, interrupt bus, and utility bus. The DTB is very similar to the 68000's native buses, using AS∗, DS0∗ ($\overline{\text{UDS}}$), DS1∗ ($\overline{\text{LDS}}$), and DTACK∗. LWORD∗ (long word) is asserted for 32-bit transfers.

Table 3.9 VMEbus Signals on P1 Connector

Pin number	Row A signal mnemonic	Row B signal mnemonic	Row C signal mnemonic
1	D00	BBSY∗	D08
2	D01	BCLR∗	D09
3	D02	ACFAIL∗	D10
4	D03	BG0IN∗	D11
5	D04	BG0OUT∗	D12
6	D05	BG1IN∗	D13
7	D06	BG1OUT∗	D14
8	D07	BG2IN∗	D15
9	GND	BG2OUT∗	GND
10	SYSCLK	BG3IN∗	SYSFAIL∗
11	GND	BG3OUT∗	BERR∗
12	DS1∗	BR0∗	SYSRESET∗
13	DS0∗	BR1∗	LWORD∗
14	WRITE∗	BR2∗	AM5
15	GND	BR3∗	A23
16	DTACK∗	AM0	A22
17	GND	AM1	A21
18	AS∗	AM2	A20
19	GND	AM3	A19
20	IACK∗	GND	A18
21	IACKIN∗	SERCLK (1)	A17
22	IACKOUT∗	SERDAT (1)	A16
23	AM4	GND	A15
24	A07	IRQ7∗	A14
25	A06	IRQ6∗	A13
26	A05	IRQ5∗	A12
27	A04	IRQ4∗	A11
28	A03	IRQ3∗	A10
29	A02	IRQ2∗	A09
30	A01	IRQ1∗	A08
31	−12V	+5V STDBY	+12V
32	+5V	+5V	+5V

Table 3.10   VMEbus Signals on P2 Connector

Pin number	Row A signal mnemonic	Row B signal mnemonic	Row C signal mnemonic
1	User I/O	+5V	User I/O
2	User I/O	GND	User I/O
3	User I/O	RESERVED	User I/O
4	User I/O	A24	User I/O
5	User I/O	A25	User I/O
6	User I/O	A26	User I/O
7	User I/O	A27	User I/O
8	User I/O	A28	User I/O
9	User I/O	A29	User I/O
10	User I/O	A30	User I/O
11	User I/O	A31	User I/O
12	User I/O	GND	User I/O
13	User I/O	+5V	User I/O
14	User I/O	D16	User I/O
15	User I/O	D17	User I/O
16	User I/O	D18	User I/O
17	User I/O	D19	User I/O
18	User I/O	D20	User I/O
19	User I/O	D21	User I/O
20	User I/O	D22	User I/O
21	User I/O	D23	User I/O
22	User I/O	GND	User I/O
23	User I/O	D24	User I/O
24	User I/O	D25	User I/O
25	User I/O	D26	User I/O
26	User I/O	D27	User I/O
27	User I/O	D28	User I/O
28	User I/O	D29	User I/O
29	User I/O	D30	User I/O
30	User I/O	D31	User I/O
31	User I/O	GND	User I/O
32	User I/O	+5V	User I/O

Two features provided by the DTB that are not present in most other buses are the 6-bit address modifier (AM0 to AM5) and the bus error signal (BERR*). The address modifier allows the type of access (such as user or supervisor, and code, data, or stack) to be specified. Three of these bits are typically used for the 68000's function code outputs. The bus error signal is typically used to indicate a memory error.

The interrupt bus has seven interrupt request lines (IRQ1* to IRQ7*), an interrupt acknowledge (IACK*), and a daisy-chained priority signal (IACKIN* and IACKOUT*). Each of the seven lines corresponds to an interrupt priority level. Within each level there can be up to 256 different vectors. The interrupt vectoring scheme is basically the same as the 68000's bus-vectored interrupt method as described in Sec. 3.6.6. The addition of the interrupt daisy chain ensures that if more than one board issues an interrupt at the same time at the same priority level, then only one will respond to the acknowledge.

The arbitration bus provides four levels of arbitration. For each level, there is a bus request signal (BR0* to BR3*) and a bus grant daisy chain (BG0IN* to BG3IN*, BG0OUT* to BG3OUT*). A parallel arbiter processes each of the bus requests and produces a bus grant. The bus grant daisy chain implements serial arbitration among multiple bus masters at the same priority level.

The utility bus consists of SYSCLK (system clock), SYSRESET* (system reset), SYSFAIL* (system fail), ACFAIL* (ac fail), and power supplies. The 16-MHz SYSCLK signal can be used by any bus module, but bus transactions are not necessarily synchronized to the clock. SYSFAIL can be driven by any board to indicate that a failure has occurred.

The *VME Subsystem Bus (VSB)* is a local expansion bus, similar in concept to Intel's iLBX bus, that uses the undefined pins on the P2 connector to expand the resources of a CPU board without using the VMEbus and to provide higher-speed memory access than is possible over the main bus. The *VMXbus* is a more limited expansion bus that has been replaced by the VSB for most applications. The *VMSbus* is a two-line serial bus (signals SERDAT and SERCLK on the P1 connector) for passing messages among multiple CPUs.

3.8.6 IBM PC Bus

Unlike the buses described previously, the IBM PC bus was not designed as a true backplane bus but as an expansion bus for a single-board personal computer. The physical bus connectors are typically part of the main "system board," which includes the processor, some memory, and some I/O. The bus was originally used in the IBM PC and has since been used in IBM's XT and in many compatible computers. It is also used in an extended form in IBM's AT. Although IBM calls the bus the *I/O Channel,* it is also used for memory expansion. In fact, the bus design can be used with a passive backplane, with the CPU on one of the "expansion" boards.

The IBM PC bus is a straightforward bus that is very close to the native 8088 microprocessor buses. Table 3.11 lists the bus signals. A "+" at the start of a signal name indicates an active-high signal, and a "−" indicates an active-low signal. There are 20 address lines and 8 data lines, plus typical Intel-style control signals. The signal +I/O CH RDY (I/O channel ready) is an open-collector signal that is pulled low by slow devices on the bus to request a wait state. The −I/O CH CK (I/O channel check) signal causes a nonmaskable interrupt and is intended for indicating expansion memory parity errors. The normal interrupts are +IRQ2 to +IRQ7. Each of these interrupts is associated with an individual vector location. (IRQ0 and IRQ1 are used on the system board, and are thus not available on the expansion bus.)

The PC bus does not include any multimaster arbitration but does allow for DMA transfers. The DMA controller is included on the system board and has four DMA channels. Channel 0 is used for memory refresh; channels 2, 3, and 4 are available for use by expansion boards. Channel 2 is typically used by the floppy-disk controller, and channel 3 by the hard-disk controller. DMA transfers are requested via +DRQ1, +DRQ2, and +DRQ3 and are acknowledged by the DMA controller via the corresponding DACK signals. (See Sec. 5.7 for more details on DMA operation.)

Table 3.11   IBM PC Bus Signals

Component side			Circuit side		
Pin	Mnemonic	Description	Pin	Mnemonic	Description
A1	−I/O CH CK	I/O channel check	B1	GND	Ground
A2	+D7		B2	+RESET DRV	System reset
A3	+D6		B3	+5 V	Power
A4	+D5		B4	+IRQ2	Interrupt request
A5	+D4		B5	−5 V	Power
A6	+D3	Data bus	B6	+DRQ2	DMA Request
A7	+D2		B7	−12 V	Power
A8	+D1		B8	−CARD SLCTD/0WS	See *Note*
A9	+D0		B9	+12 V	Power
A10	+I/O CH RDY	I/O channel ready	B10	GND	Ground
A11	+AEN	Address enable	B11	−MEMW	Memory write
A12	+A19		B12	−MEMR	Memory read
A13	+A18		B13	−IOW	I/O write
A14	+A17		B14	−IOR	I/O read
A15	+A16		B15	−DACK3	DMA acknowledge
A16	+A15		B16	+DRQ3	DMA request
A17	+A14		B17	−DACK1	DMA acknowledge
A18	+A13		B18	+DRQ1	DMA request
A19	+A12		B19	−DACK0	DMA acknowledge
A20	+A11		B20	CLOCK	Processor clock
A21	+A10		B21	+IRQ7	
A22	+A9	Address bus	B22	+IRQ6	
A23	+A8		B23	+IRQ5	Interrupt requests
A24	+A7		B24	+IRQ4	
A25	+A6		B25	+IRQ3	
A26	+A5		B26	−DACK2	DMA acknowledge
A27	+A4		B27	+T/C	DMA terminal count
A28	+A3		B28	+ALE	Address latch enable
A29	+A2		B29	+5 V	Power
A30	+A1		B30	+OSC	14.31818-MHz clock
A31	+A0		B31	GND	Ground

Note: This signal is CARD SELECTED only for slot J8 of the IBM XT. For operation in this slot, this signal must be asserted when the card recognizes its address. For the PC and other slots in the XT, this signal is not used. For the AT, this pin is the 0WS signal, which is asserted by the card to request a zero-wait-state cycle.

The IBM PC/AT uses the 80286 microprocessor and extends the bus for 16-bit data transfers and a wider addressing range. The AT bus slots consist of two connectors, one that is the same as the PC bus and an additional connector. Table 3.12 lists the signals on the additional connector.

The additional connector has eight data lines (SD08 to SD15), seven address lines (LA17 to LA23), a few control signals, and additional DMA and interrupt signals. The LA17 to LA19 signals carry the same information as the A17 to A19 signals available on the original bus connector; LA20 to LA23 provide four additional address lines to increase the addressing range to 16 Mbytes. (The LA signals are not latched and must be latched on expansion boards at the falling edge of ALE.) By using signals on both connectors, 16-bit AT expansion boards have access to a 16-bit data bus and a 23-bit

Table 3.12 Signals on Additional Bus Connector for IBM AT

Component side			Circuit side		
Pin	Mnemonic	Description	Pin	Mnemonic	Description
C1	SBHE	Bus high enable	D1	−MEM CS16	16-bit memory CS
C2	LA23 ⎫		D2	−I/O CS16	16-bit I/O CS
C3	LA22		D3	IRQ10 ⎫	
C4	LA21		D4	IRQ11	
C5	LA20 ⎬	Unlatched address	D5	IRQ12 ⎬	Interrupt requests
C6	LA19		D6	IRQ15	
C7	LA18		D7	IRQ14 ⎭	
C8	LA17 ⎭		D8	−DACK0	DMA acknowledge
C9	−MEMR	Memory read	D9	DRQ0	DMA request
C10	−MEMW	Memory write	D10	−DACK5	DMA acknowledge
C11	SD08 ⎫		D11	DRQ5	DMA request
C12	SD09		D12	−DACK6	DMA acknowledge
C13	SD10		D13	DRQ6	DMA request
C14	SD11 ⎬	Data bus high byte	D14	−DACK7	DMA acknowledge
C15	SD12		D15	DRQ7	DMA request
C16	SD13		D16	+5 V	Power
C17	SD14		D17	−MASTER	DMA bus control
C18	SD15 ⎭		D18	GND	Ground

address bus. Most standard PC bus boards can also be used in an AT by using only the original connector.

The −MEM CS16 or −I/O CS16 signal on the expansion connector is pulled low by boards that use the 16-bit data bus when they recognize their address on the address bus. In response, the system board performs a 16-bit transfer. If neither of these signals is pulled low, the system board performs only 8-bit accesses. In this case, two 8-bit cycles are performed for 16-bit transfers. This is similar to the dynamic bus sizing performed by Motorola's 68020. The 80286 does not include this function, however, so the AT's system board implements it with TTL logic.

An 8-bit board that uses only the original connector does not have access to the upper four address lines on the additional AT connector. Therefore, the −MEMR and −MEMW signals on the original bus connector are disabled unless the top four address lines are all zero (i.e., the access is to the lower 1 Mbyte of the address space) to prevent an 8-bit board from erroneously responding to an address in the upper 15 Mbytes. The −MEMR and −MEMW signals on the additional connector are not disabled; 16-bit boards use these signals, rather than the ones on the original connector.

One problem with IBM's PC and AT buses is that they are not official standards but only IBM internal standards that have become de facto standards. Thus, there is no official specification, and the bus definition is subject to change whenever IBM introduces a new product. Although IBM's technical reference manuals list the signal names and descriptions, no bus timing information is supplied, and many other details that are part of any proper bus specification are omitted. This can make these buses more difficult to design with than fully documented industry standards such as the Multibus, STD bus, or VMEbus.

3.8.7   Other System Buses

The *S-100 bus* is one of the earliest microprocessor system buses. It was originally used in the Altair 8800, the first general-purpose microcomputer based on the 8080 microprocessor. The Altair 8800 bus was not designed to be a standard; it was simply the interconnection scheme for a particular set of boards. Other manufacturers began making boards to plug into the Altair computer, and before long other manufacturers began producing computers that could use the same boards. Thus, the de facto standard S-100 bus was born.

The IEEE-696 standard formalizes the S-100 bus definition, eliminates the direct ties to the 8080, and adds additional features. This bus standard was widely used in personal computer systems, but it has been replaced by newer personal computer architectures such as the IBM PC. In the industrial area, the Multibus, VMEbus, or STD bus is generally preferred.

The *IEEE-P896 Futurebus* is a sophisticated 32-bit bus designed for high-performance applications. Despite its sophisticated features, its use has been restricted by its late definition.

The *Multibus II* is a 32-bit bus designed by Intel as a replacement for the original Multibus in high-performance 32-bit applications. It is expected to be widely used for 80286- and 80386-based systems, whereas 68000-family systems are likely to stay predominantly with the VMEbus.

3.9   ELECTRICAL CONSIDERATIONS

While it is convenient to think of digital signals as simple logic levels, electrical realities must be kept in mind if reliable operation is to be achieved. The primary areas of concern are signal loading and distortion. Loading considerations limit the number of devices that can be connected to the bus, while distortion limits the speed at which operations can occur and the physical length of the buses.

3.9.1   Bus Loading

All digital signal outputs have a maximum load they are capable of driving to maintain proper logic levels. Two types of loading are important: dc, or static, loading, and ac, or capacitive, loading. DC loading is the constant current required by an input in either the high or the low state. It limits the ability of a device driving the bus to maintain proper logic levels. Capacitive loading is caused by the input capacitance of each device and limits the speed at which a device driving a bus signal can change the state from high to low or low to high.

In a multiple-board system, each board should buffer all connections to the buses to limit the load it places on the system bus and to ensure that it has adequate bus drive capability. This is done with bidirectional buffers (also called *bus transceivers*) for the data bus and with unidirectional buffers (three-state drivers) for the address bus and control signals, as shown in Fig. 3.39. The buffers should be placed as close to the

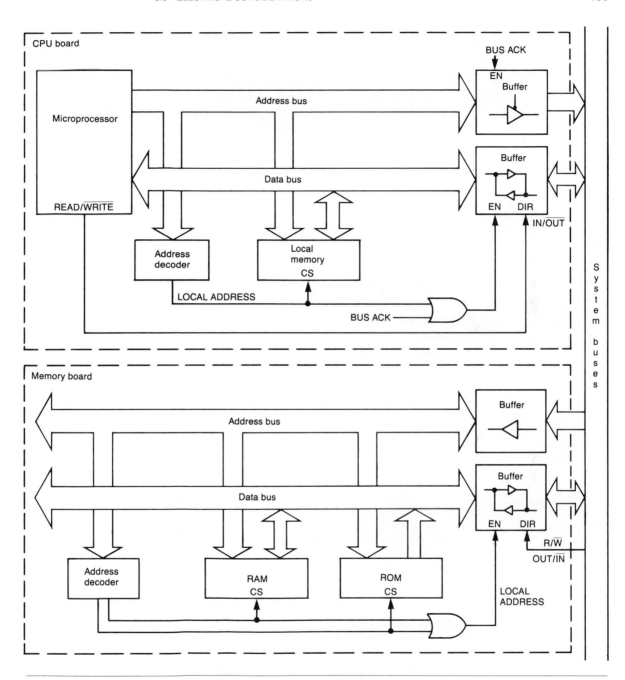

Figure 3.39. System bus buffering on CPU and memory boards.

connectors as possible to minimize the capacitance and noise added to the bus signals. The address and data bus drivers on the processor board are disabled when the bus is granted to another bus master. The data bus buffer is also disabled when memory or I/O ports on the processor board are accessed, so that the bus buffer will not conflict with the on-board device. The direction of the data bus buffer is controlled by the read (or read/write) control signal. Some microprocessors, such as the 8086, provide specific signals to control the data bus buffers.

The data bus buffer on memory and I/O boards is enabled only when an address for a device on the board is present on the address bus, preventing the board from conflicting with other boards in the system. The system bus generally has only TTL devices connected to it, so capacitive loading is not usually a problem. Common TTL buffers such as the 74LS245 have a sufficiently large drive capability that dc loading is rarely a limitation in a system bus.

In a single-board system, buffers are often unnecessary. A careful analysis must be performed, however, to ensure that in a worst-case situation no loading limits are exceeded. If a bus is loaded slightly beyond its worst-case limit, the prototype may work fine. In production, however, this is likely to cause problems. Sooner or later, a batch of parts whose input loading is close to the maximum is likely to be encountered. Proper logic levels will then fail to be maintained, and unreliable operation may result. Marginal loading problems are particularly insidious, since the effect is often erratic operation and nonrepetitive errors that are extremely difficult to track down.

For both the high and low logic levels, the sum of the currents required by all the inputs and the leakage currents of all outputs (drivers) on the bus must be added together. This sum must be less than the output capability of the weakest driver. Most microprocessor system components are MOS devices, which have very little dc loading (typically 10 μA). The main contributors to dc loading are TTL devices. On the data bus, TTL ICs are used as output port latches, demultiplexing latches, and buffers. On the address and control buses, buffers and address decoders are the most common TTL loads.

Capacitive loading is often the most important consideration in a small, unbuffered system. The input capacitance of MOS devices typically is between 5 and 20 pF. MOS outputs are typically rated to drive 100 to 150 pF of load capacitance. If this load is exceeded, the output will switch states more slowly than specified. Many data sheets specify the effect of increased load capacitance. For example, the Mostek Z80 data sheet specifies all timing parameters with a maximum load of 50 pF. A 10-ns delay must be added for each additional 50 pF of load capacitance, up to a maximum of 200 pF for the data bus and 100 pF for address and control lines. Typical MOS memory and peripheral chips have an input capacitance of approximately 10 pF, so the 50-pF maximum load for full-speed operation translates to approximately five devices on the data bus.

It is difficult to guarantee that capacitive loading calculations accurately represent the actual conditions, so it is best to have some margin in capacitive drive capability. Input capacitance is often specified as "sample tested only, and not guaranteed." In addition, the printed circuit traces themselves contribute some capacitance (approximately 2 pF/in.). Since capacitive loading slows down signal transitions, keeping the loading under the specified limit is particularly important when the timing margin is small.

The data bus must be driven not only by the microprocessor but also by memories,

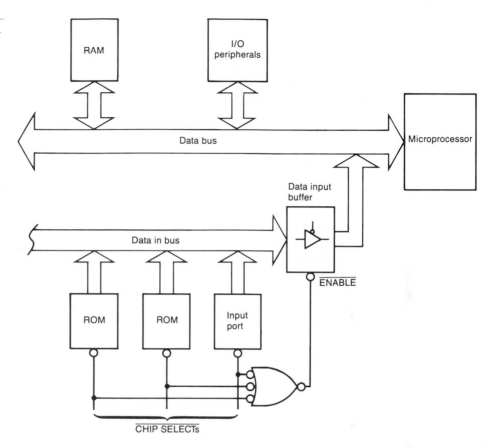

Figure 3.40. Bus buffering for read-only devices.

input ports, and other peripheral chips. Thus, in evaluating bus loading, the weakest output is the limiting case. If ROMs or input ports are the limiting factor, they can be grouped together and buffered with a three-state driver, as shown in Fig. 3.40. Bidirectional devices such as RAMs and most peripheral chips must, of course, be buffered with bidirectional buffers.

For an example of bus loading calculations, see Sec. 3.10.2.

3.9.2 Reflections and Termination

It is convenient to assume that the voltage at all points along a wire is the same and that a change at one end of a wire appears instantly and identically at the other end. While this assumption is reasonable for short wires and low frequencies, it is unfortunately not the case for relatively high frequencies or long wires.

Electrical signals travel at speeds approaching the speed of light. The exact speed depends on several factors, but is typically 1 to 2 ns/ft. In large, high-speed systems this delay can be significant and must be taken into consideration when calculating access times. However, this propagation velocity is of most importance in analyzing the *reflections* that occur at the end of bus lines.

Consider the simple case of a single output driving a long wire with one load at the end. When the output changes from low to high, the new voltage level travels down the wire at approximately 2 ns/ft. The problem occurs when the transition reaches the far end of the wire. If the impedance of the wire and the load are not perfectly matched (as described below), some of the signal is reflected back down the wire to the driving end. Some of this reflected signal is then reflected back to the opposite end, and this process repeats until the energy has died down to an insignificant level. The result is an oscillation, called *ringing*, added to the signal whenever it changes state. This can cause errors if the signal is assumed to be valid during the oscillation time.

To analyze this reflection, the wire must be treated as a *transmission line*. A full explanation of transmission line theory is beyond the scope of this book, but a few simple observations will suffice for this analysis. A key parameter is the *characteristic impedance* of the wire. The characteristic impedance of a wire suspended an infinite distance above the ground is approximately 377 ohms. As the wire and ground are brought closer together, the characteristic impedance is reduced. Typical values are 50 to 75 ohms for coaxial cable, 100 ohms for a twisted pair, and 50 to 150 ohms for traces on a PC board (depending on the trace widths and PC board materials).

The magnitude of the reflection is proportional to the difference in the impedances. The fraction of the signal reflected is called the *reflection coefficient*, and is calculated as follows:

$$\text{reflection coefficient} = \frac{V_R}{V_O} = \frac{Z_L - Z_O}{Z_L + Z_O}$$

where V_R = magnitude of the reflected signal

V_O = magnitude of the original signal

Z_L = impedance of the load

Z_O = characteristic impedance of the wire

Thus, if the impedance of the load at the end of a wire is equal to the characteristic impedance of the wire, there will be no reflection when a signal transition reaches the load, so it is desirable to match the load impedance to the wire as closely as possible. This is done by *terminating* the wire with a fixed impedance. One simple way to do this is with resistors, as shown in Fig. 3.41. While the resistors do not perfectly match the impedance, terminating in this manner greatly reduces the ringing on bus lines. These

Figure 3.41. Resistive termination.

resistors also ensure that the lines will float to the high level (inactive state for most control signals) if not driven.

Deciding where to put the terminators can be difficult. Ideally, the driver should be at one end of the line and the terminator at the other. In a microprocessor system, however, the data bus may be driven from any board, which may be in any physical position on the backplane. The VMEbus deals with this problem by using terminators (330 Ω to +5 and 470 Ω to ground) at both ends of each bus line. This technique is effective but requires high-current drivers due to the loading from the terminators and increases power dissipation.

The speed of the signals and the length of the wires are the major factors in determining the need for termination. Ringing will typically die down to insignificant levels by the third or fourth reflection. Thus, for a 1-ft-long bus, the ringing will stop within 3 to 8 ns (1 to 2 ns/ft $\times$ 1 ft $\times$ 3 to 4 reflections). This effectively adds a small delay before bus signals are valid; since the bus signals are required to be valid only at specific times, this ringing can be tolerated as long as the delay caused is taken into consideration. If the system is pushing the limits of the bus timing, ringing can cause data to be sampled when it is not valid. Ringing is most critical for clock and control signals. If the ringing causes the voltage level to cross the logic threshold, then more than one transition will occur at the receiver for a single transition at the driver.

3.9.3 Crosstalk

Interaction between signal lines that are not electrically connected is called *crosstalk*. Physically adjacent signal lines are both inductively and capacitively coupled. When a rapid transition occurs on one signal line, a pulse is generated on nearby lines. The magnitude of the crosstalk is determined by the speed of the transition, the physical distance between the lines, and the presence of shielding or a ground plane. If the magnitude is large enough to cause a change in logic level, errors can be caused.

Transitions of address and data lines do not by themselves carry any significance; only the state of the lines is important, and this is important only at specific times. For example, when the microprocessor changes the address on the address bus at the start of a cycle, the address bus is not valid until all the lines have settled to their new state. Crosstalk between address lines during this settling time is not important; once the address stabilizes, no address lines will be changing so there cannot be any crosstalk. Thus, crosstalk among address and data bus lines is usually not of concern.

Control and clock lines are much more critical, however. For example, if the read control line is adjacent to a data line, it can disturb the state of that line at the very moment when it must be valid. If the read line is adjacent to the write line, an erroneous write pulse can be generated when a read is performed.

Following a few simple guidelines generally eliminates crosstalk problems:

1. Avoid long parallel traces on printed circuit boards when one or more of the signals is a clock or control line.

2. Never bundle together groups of wires on wire-wrapped boards. This is a common mistake, since bundling the wires together makes the board look neater.

3. Use numerous ground traces or a full ground plane on backplanes. If there is no ground plane, use ground traces at least on each side of the clock and control lines. A ground plane reduces the electromagnetic field generated by each wire, and thus crosstalk is also reduced.

4. Use ground wires for isolation on ribbon cables. Ribbon cables are one of the worst offenders, since the wires are parallel and close together and the cables are often relatively long. The wire on each side of each control or clock line should be grounded to provide isolation. A common practice is simply to ground every other wire in the entire cable, although this is not generally necessary. Flat cables with a wire mesh or foil ground plane are available, which reduce crosstalk at the expense of higher cable capacitance. Flat cables composed of twisted pairs are also available.

5. Limit the rise and fall times of critical signals when possible. High-speed Schottky (S, AS, and F) and advanced CMOS (AC and ACT) drivers produce very fast transitions, and should be avoided whenever possible. Low-power Schottky (LS or ALS) is much better, and standard CMOS (HC or HCT) is better still. Special bus buffers called *trapezoidal drivers* are also available that have fast propagation delay times but controlled rise and fall times.

3.10   DESIGN EXAMPLE

Since our design example is a single-board system, there is no backplane bus. In this system, many of the 68008's more-sophisticated capabilities are not needed. For example, since there are no other bus masters in the system, $\overline{BR}$ is tied high and the $\overline{BG}$ output is not used. The $\overline{BERR}$ input is also not used and is tied high. These and other simplifications reduce the cost of the system without sacrificing performance and are typical of the type of design used in dedicated control applications.

3.10.1   Interrupt and $\overline{DTACK}$ Logic

Figure 3.42 shows the 68008 processor circuit with the reset and clock logic from Chap. 2, plus the interrupt acknowledge and $\overline{DTACK}$ generation logic. The interrupt acknowledge logic is quite simple and was described in Sec. 3.6.6. This system uses the 68901 multifunction peripheral (MFP), which serves as the interrupt controller. It provides an interrupt vector in response to the interrupt acknowledge, so autovectoring is not used and the $\overline{VPA}$ input is tied high. (The 68901 and its interface circuitry are described in Chap. 5.) The interrupt output from the MFP, called $\overline{MFPINT}$ on the schematic, connects directly to the $\overline{IPL0/2}$ input, and the $\overline{IPL1}$ input is tied high. Thus, the MFP produces a level 5 interrupt, and the other levels are not used.

This system uses a different approach to $\overline{DTACK}$ generation than the general technique described in Sec. 3.3.3. It is designed to operate with no wait states for memory accesses or I/O reads and one wait state for I/O writes, except for accesses to the 68901 MFP. The 68901 MFP is designed as a 68000-family peripheral and provides an open-drain $\overline{DTACK}$ output (shown on the schematic as the $\overline{MFPDTACK}$). This output is as-

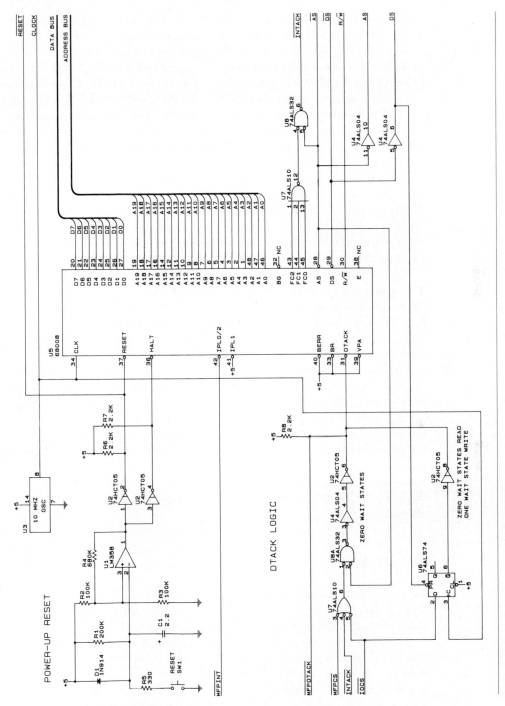

Figure 3.42. Design example 68008 CPU circuit.

serted only if the MFP is selected (by either its chip select or interrupt acknowledge input). Thus, it can directly drive the 68008's $\overline{\text{DTACK}}$ input.

Since all other devices in the system operate with no wait states, $\overline{\text{DTACK}}$ is asserted as soon as it is known that a cycle has been started and that the address is not that of an I/O device or the MFP. The gate U8a produces this no-wait $\overline{\text{DTACK}}$, which is asserted when $\overline{\text{AS}}$ is asserted and neither $\overline{\text{MFPCS}}$ (MFP chip select), $\overline{\text{IOCS}}$ (I/O chip select), nor $\overline{\text{INTACK}}$ (interrupt acknowledge) is asserted. (The chip select signals are generated by the address decoder, as described in Chap. 4.) The no-wait $\overline{\text{DTACK}}$ must be inhibited when $\overline{\text{INTACK}}$ is asserted, since the 68901 MFP provides the interrupt vector and will assert $\overline{\text{DTACK}}$ when it is ready.

The U6 flip-flop generates the $\overline{\text{DTACK}}$ for I/O devices. This flip-flop is held set when $\overline{\text{DS}}$ is negated. (Since the $\overline{\text{Q}}$ output is inverted to produce $\overline{\text{DTACK}}$, setting the flip-flop negates $\overline{\text{DTACK}}$.) For non-I/O accesses, the D input remains high, and no $\overline{\text{DTACK}}$ is generated by this circuit. For I/O accesses, $\overline{\text{DTACK}}$ is generated at the first rising clock edge after $\overline{\text{DS}}$ is asserted. This produces no wait states for read cycles and one wait state for write cycles. (This timing is explained in Sec. 3.10.3.)

Since $\overline{\text{DTACK}}$ is asserted for any access, a bus error watchdog timer is not needed. The system could be made slightly more secure by adding a watchdog timer and changing the $\overline{\text{DTACK}}$ logic to assert $\overline{\text{DTACK}}$ only if a valid address is present on the address bus. This is not necessary in typical dedicated control applications.

This approach can be less than optimal during software debugging, however. If a software error causes an access to an unused address, $\overline{\text{DTACK}}$ will be asserted since it is asserted for all addresses except those assigned to the MFP. Thus, the microprocessor will read undefined data or write to a nonexistent memory location, and there is no direct indication that this error has occurred (except, of course, that the software will not work as desired). If the access is an instruction fetch, this is likely to produce an illegal instruction, which causes a trap, indirectly indicating that an erroneous access has occurred. However, a data access to an unused location will not produce any error trap. A system that generates $\overline{\text{DTACK}}$ only for valid addresses and includes a bus time-out watchdog timer makes finding this type of software error easier, since the bus error exception routine is executed when an access to an unused address is attempted.

3.10.2   Bus Loading

Since this design example is a small, single-board system, it seems likely that no address or data bus buffering is needed. The following analysis demonstrates that this is indeed the case, although the data bus does not have much capacity for expansion.

Table 3.13 shows the drive capabilities of each of the devices that drive the data bus. (Each of these devices is described in later chapters; we are concerned here only with their bus drive and loading specifications.) Note that, by convention, currents are specified as positive when they flow into a device. Thus, the current sourced in the high state is shown as negative. The 68901 MFP is the weakest driver for both the high and low levels and is tied with several others for the lowest specified capacitive load. Thus, its drive specifications are the limiting factor.

Finding these specifications in the data sheet can be a challenge. The I_{OL} and I_{OH} specifications are often listed only as test conditions for the V_{OH} and V_{OL} (output voltage high level and output voltage low level) specifications. The load capacitance is generally listed as part of the loading condition for the ac (timing) specifications. For the 74HC244, two sets of timing specifications are provided: one with a 50-pF load, and one with a 150-pF load. Although the propagation delay time with the 150-pF load is much larger, it is still fast enough for this application.

Table 3.14 shows the load presented by each device on the data bus. Note that even devices such as the EPROM that do not input data from the bus are nevertheless bus loads due to their output leakage current and capacitance. All the ICs on the data bus are MOS devices, so the input currents are very low—they are leakage currents only and are generally specified as a single value, regardless of the logic level. As can be seen by comparing the totals at the bottom of this table with the 68901's output drive

Table 3.13 Data Bus Drivers Drive Capability

	Low-level output current I_{OL}, mA	High-level output current I_{OH}, μA	Load capacitance C_L, pF
68008 processor	5.3	−400	130
2764/128/256 EPROM	2.1	−400	100
6264/256 RAM	2.1	−1000	100
68901 MFP (weakest driver)	2.0	−120	100
74HC244 3-state buffer (input port)	6.0	−6000	150

Table 3.14 Data Bus Loads

Device	Quantity	Low-level input current I_{IL}, μA		High-level input current I_{IH}, μA		Input capacitance C_{IN}, pF	
		Per device	Total	Per device	Total	Per device	Total
68008 processor	1		−20		20		20
2764/128/256 EPROM	2	−10	−20	10	20	12	24
6264/256 RAM	2	−2	−4	2	4	8	16
68901 MFP	1		−10		10		10
74HCT273 register (output port)	2	−1	−2	1	2	10	20
74HC244 3-state buffer (input port)	1		−1		1		10
Totals			−57		57		100

Table 3.15   Address Bus Loads

Device	Quantity	Low-level input current I_{IL}, μA		High-level input current I_{IH}, μA		Input capacitance C_{IN}, pF	
		Per device	Total	Per device	Total	Per device	Total
2764/128/256							
EPROM	2	−10	−20	10	20	6	12
6264/256 RAM	2	−2	−4	2	4	6	12
68901 MFP	1		−10		10		10
74ALS138							
decoder	1		−100		20		5
74HCT74	1		−1		1		10
Totals			−135		55		49

capability, the total dc loading is well within the available drive capability. The capacitive loading, however, is right at the limit. This could be reduced by using ALS instead of HCT devices for the output port register and the input port three-state buffer (at the expense of increased power consumption) or by isolating the EPROMs and input port with a unidirectional buffer.

In any case, the system can not be expanded much further before data bus loading becomes a problem. Note that simply adding a data bus buffer at the 68008 does not help, since the 68008's drive capability is not the limiting factor. One approach for system expansion is to leave all the devices in the design example on the unbuffered data bus and add a buffered data bus for additional devices.

The 68008 is the only device that drives the address bus. It can provide a low-level output current of 3.2 mA, a high-level output current of −400 μA, and drive a capacitive load of 130 pF. Table 3.15 shows the address bus loads. All are MOS devices except for the 74ALS138 address decoder. No input capacitance is specified for the 74ALS138 (or most other bipolar devices), but 5 pF is a reasonable assumption. As can be seen from the totals at the bottom of the table, address bus loading is not a problem, and there is room for expansion. If buffering is needed, it is easy to add: 74ALS244 buffers on the 68008's address outputs provide enough drive for a very large system.

3.10.3   The 68008 Bus Timing

As we proceed with the design example, we will need to know the 68008's bus timing so that compatibility with memory and peripheral chips can be determined. In this section, the 68008 timing diagrams are presented, and key timing parameters are calculated. (Most of these timing diagrams and calculations are also applicable to the 68000 and 68010, although there are minor differences.)

Figure 3.43 shows the 68008's read cycle timing, and Fig. 3.44 shows the write cycle timing. The timing parameters, which are indicated by circled numbers in the diagrams, are specified in Table 3.16.

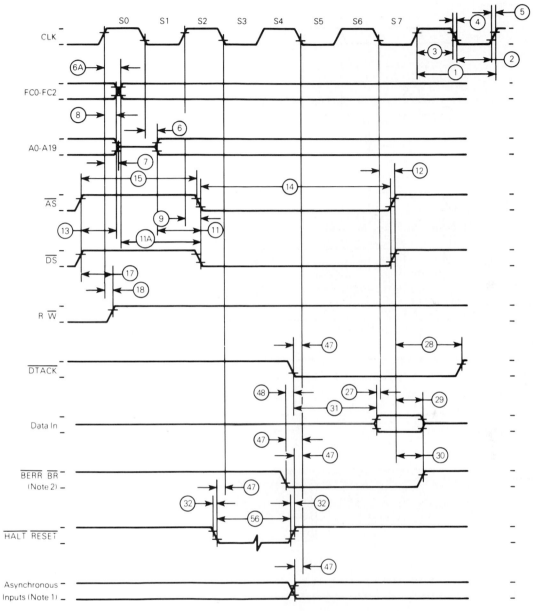

NOTES:
1. Setup time for the asynchronous inputs IPL0/2, IPL1, and VPA guarantees their recognition at the next falling edge of the clock.
2. BR need fall at this time only in order to insure being recognized at the end of this bus cycle.
3. Timing measurements are referenced to and from a low voltage of 0.8 volt and a high voltage of 2.0 volts, unless otherwise noted.

Figure 3.43. The 68008 read cycle timing. *(Courtesy of Motorola, Inc.)*

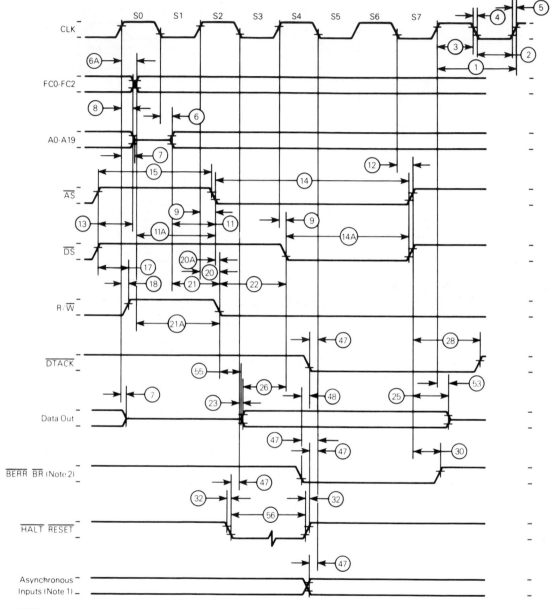

NOTES:
1. Timing measurements are referenced to and from a low voltage of 0.8 volt and a high voltage of 2.0 volts, unless otherwise noted.
2. Because of loading variations, R/$\overline{W}$ may be valid after $\overline{AS}$ even though both are initiated by the rising edge of S2 (Specification 20A)

Figure 3.44. The 68008 write cycle timing. *(Courtesy of Motorola, Inc.)*

Table 3.16   The 68008 Timing Parameters (*Courtesy of Motorola, Inc.*)

Num.	Characteristic	Symbol	8 MHz Min	8 MHz Max	10 MHz Min	10 MHz Max	Unit
1	Clock Period	t_{cyc}	125	500	100	500	ns
2	Clock Width Low	t_{CL}	55	250	45	250	ns
3	Clock Width High	t_{CH}	55	250	45	250	ns
4	Clock Fall Time	t_{Cf}	–	10	–	10	ns
5	Clock Rise Time	t_{Cr}	–	10	–	10	ns
6	Clock Low to Address Valid	t_{CLAV}	–	70	–	60	ns
6A	Clock High to FC Valid	t_{CHFCV}	–	70	–	60	ns
7	Clock High to Address, Data Bus High Impedance (Maximum)	t_{CHADZ}	–	80	–	70	ns
8	Clock High to Address, FC Invalid (Minimum)	t_{CHAFI}	0	–	0	–	ns
9[1]	Clock High to $\overline{AS}$, $\overline{DS}$ Low	t_{CHSL}	0	60	0	55	ns
11[2]	Address Valid to $\overline{AS}$, $\overline{DS}$ Low (Read)/$\overline{AS}$ Low (Write)	t_{AVSL}	30	–	20	–	ns
11A[2,7]	FC Valid to $\overline{AS}$, $\overline{DS}$ Low (Read)/$\overline{AS}$ Low (Write)	t_{FCVSL}	60	–	50	–	ns
12[1]	Clock Low to $\overline{AS}$, $\overline{DS}$ High	t_{CLSH}	–	35	–	35	ns
13[2]	$\overline{AS}$, $\overline{DS}$ High to Address/FC Invalid	t_{SHARI}	30	–	20	–	ns
14[2,5]	$\overline{AS}$, $\overline{DS}$ Width Low (Read)/$\overline{AS}$ Low (Write)	t_{SL}	270	–	195	–	ns
14A[2]	$\overline{DS}$ Width Low (Write)	t_{DSL}	140	–	95	–	ns
15[2]	$\overline{AS}$, $\overline{DS}$ Width High	t_{SH}	150	–	105	–	ns
16	Clock High to Control Bus High Impedance	t_{CHCZ}	–	80	–	70	ns
17[2]	$\overline{AS}$, $\overline{DS}$ High to R/$\overline{W}$ High (Read)	t_{SHRH}	40	–	20	–	ns
18[1]	Clock High to R/$\overline{W}$ High	t_{CHRH}	0	40	0	40	ns
20[1]	Clock High to R/$\overline{W}$ Low	t_{CHRL}	–	40	–	40	ns
20A[6]	$\overline{AS}$ Low to R/$\overline{W}$ Valid (Write)	t_{ASRV}	–	20	–	20	ns
21[2]	Address Valid to R/$\overline{W}$ Low (Write)	t_{AVRL}	20	–	0	–	ns
21A[2,7]	FC Valid to R/$\overline{W}$ Low (Write)	t_{FCVRL}	60	–	50	–	ns
22[2]	R/$\overline{W}$ Low to $\overline{DS}$ Low (Write)	t_{RLSL}	80	–	50	–	ns
23	Clock Low to Data Out Valid (Write)	t_{CLDO}	–	70	–	55	ns
25[2]	$\overline{AS}$, $\overline{DS}$ High to Data Out Invalid (Write)	t_{SHDOI}	50	–	20	–	ns
26[2]	Data Out Valid to $\overline{DS}$ Low (Write)	t_{DOSL}	35	–	20		ns
27[5]	Data In to Clock Low (Setup Time on Read)	t_{DICL}	15	–	10	–	ns
28[2,5]	$\overline{AS}$, $\overline{DS}$ High to $\overline{DTACK}$ High	t_{SHDAH}	0	245	0	190	ns
29	$\overline{AS}$, $\overline{DS}$ High to Data In Invalid (Hold Time on Read)	t_{SHDII}	0	–	0	–	ns
30	$\overline{AS}$, $\overline{DS}$ High to $\overline{BERR}$ High	t_{SHBEH}	0	–	0	–	ns
31[2,5]	$\overline{DTACK}$ Low to Data Valid (Asynchronous Setup Time on Read)	t_{DALDI}	–	90	–	65	ns
32	$\overline{HALT}$ and $\overline{RESET}$ Input Transition Time	$t_{RHr, f}$	0	200	0	200	ns
33	Clock High to $\overline{BG}$ Low	t_{CHGL}	–	40	–	40	ns
34	Clock High to $\overline{BG}$ High	t_{CHGH}	–	40	–	40	ns
35	$\overline{BR}$ Low to $\overline{BG}$ Low	t_{BRLGL}	1.5	90 ns + 3.5	1.5	80 ns + 3.5	Clk.Per.
36[8]	$\overline{BR}$ High to $\overline{BG}$ High	t_{BRHGH}	1.5	90 ns + 3.5	1.5	80 ns + 3.5	Clk.Per.
37	$\overline{BGACK}$ Low to $\overline{BG}$ High (52-Pin Version Only)	t_{GALGH}	1.5	90 ns + 3.5	1.5	80 ns + 3.5	Clk.Per.
37A[9]	$\overline{BGACK}$ Low to $\overline{BR}$ High (52-Pin Version Only)	t_{GALBRH}	20	1.5 Clocks	20	1.5 Clocks	ns
38	$\overline{BG}$ Low to Control, Address, Data Bus High Impedance ($\overline{AS}$ High)	t_{GLZ}	–	80	–	70	ns
39	$\overline{BG}$ Width High	t_{GH}	1.5	–	1.5	–	Clk.Per.
41	Clock Low to E Transition	t_{CLET}	–	50	–	50	ns
42	E Output Rise and Fall Time	$t_{Er, f}$	–	15	–	15	ns
44	$\overline{AS}$, $\overline{DS}$ High to $\overline{VPA}$ High	t_{SHVPH}	0	120	0	90	ns

Continued

Table 3.16   *Continued*

Num.	Characteristic	Symbol	8 MHz Min	8 MHz Max	10 MHz Min	10 MHz Max	Unit
45	E Low to Control, Address Bus Invalid (Address Hold Time)	t_{ELCAI}	30	—	10	—	ns
46	$\overline{BGACK}$ Width Low (52-Pin Version Only)	t_{GAL}	1.5	—	1.5	—	Clk.Per.
47[5]	Asynchronous Input Setup Time	t_{ASI}	10	—	10	—	ns
48[3]	$\overline{BERR}$ Low to $\overline{DTACK}$ Low	t_{BELDAL}	20	—	20	—	ns
49[10]	$\overline{AS}$, $\overline{DS}$ High to E Low	t_{SHEL}	−80	80	−80	80	ns
50	E Width High	t_{EH}	450	—	350	—	ns
51	E Width Low	t_{EL}	700	—	550	—	ns
53	Clock High to Data Out Invalid	t_{CHDOI}	0	—	0	—	ns
54	E Low to Data Out Invalid	t_{ELDOI}	30	—	20	—	ns
55	R/$\overline{W}$ to Data Bus Impedance Driven	t_{RLDBD}	30	—	20	—	ns
56[4]	$\overline{HALT}$/$\overline{RESET}$ Pulse Width	t_{HRPW}	10	—	10	—	Clk.Per.
57	$\overline{BGACK}$ High to Control Bus Driven (52-Pin Version Only)	t_{GABD}	1.5	—	1.5	—	Clk.Per.
58[8]	$\overline{BG}$ High to Control Bus Driven	t_{GHBD}	1.5	—	1.5	—	Clk.Per.

NOTES:
1. For a loading capacitance of less than or equal to 50 picofarads, subtract 5 nanoseconds from the values given in these columns.
2. Actual value depends on clock period.
3. If #47 is satisfied for both $\overline{DTACK}$ and $\overline{BERR}$, #48 may be 0 nanoseconds.
4. For power up the MPU must be held in $\overline{RESET}$ state for 100 milliseconds to allow stabilization of on-chip circuitry. After the system is powered up, #56 refers to the minimum pulse width required to reset the system.
5. If the asynchronous setup time (#47) requirements are satisfied, the $\overline{DTACK}$ low-to-data setup time (#31) requirement can be ignored. The data must only satisfy the data-in to clock-low setup time (#27) for the following cycle.
6. When $\overline{AS}$ and R/$\overline{W}$ are equally loaded ($\pm 20\%$), subtract 10 nanoseconds from the values in these columns.
7. Setup time to guarantee recognition on next falling edge of clock.
8. The processor will negate $\overline{BG}$ and begin driving the bus again if external arbitration logic negates $\overline{BR}$ before asserting $\overline{BGACK}$.
9. The minimum value must be met to guarantee proper operation. If the maximum value is exceeded, $\overline{BG}$ may be reasserted.
10. The falling edge of S6 triggers both the negation of the strobes ($\overline{AS}$ and x$\overline{DS}$) and the falling edge of E. Either of these events can occur first, depending upon the loading on each signal. Specification #49 indicates the absolute maximum skew that will occur between the rising edge of the strobes and the falling edge of the E clock.

Most 68008 timing parameters are specified with respect to an edge of the system clock. A 68008 bus cycle consists of a minimum of four clock cycles. Each half-cycle is considered a state, labeled S0 to S7. Most system-level timing parameters, such as the available access time from address to data, must be calculated from the times shown in Figs. 3.43 and 3.44. By specifying the parameters in this manner, the system-level parameters can be calculated for any clock frequency.

It is important to note that the timing diagrams are not drawn to scale and must be used only to locate the timing parameter of interest. Figure 3.45 shows a simplified timing diagram that *is* drawn to scale for a system operating at 10 MHz. Drawing such a diagram is a good way to begin analyzing the timing for a particular system.

Tables 3.17 and 3.18 show the equations used to calculate the major system-level timing parameters, and the calculated value for a system with a 10-MHz clock (such as this design example). The equations are determined by examining the timing diagram, counting the number of half-clock cycles between the times of interest, and subtracting the appropriate delay parameters. For example, consider the available access time from address out to data in. The 68008 outputs the address after the delay, shown as time 6, following the start of S1. The data must be valid by time 27 before the end of S6. Thus,

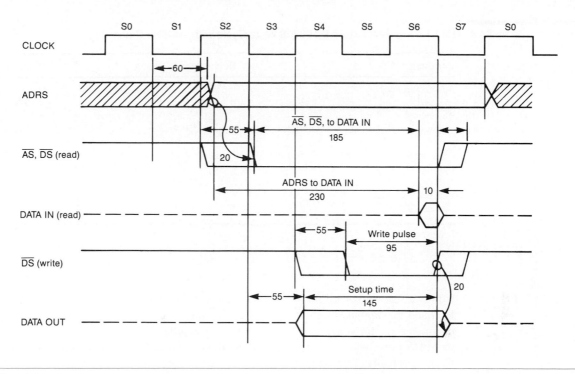

Figure 3.45. The 68008 timing at 10 MHz. All times are given in nanoseconds.

Table 3.17   Key Timing Parameters for 68008 Read Cycle with 10-MHz Clock

Parameter	Derivation	Time, ns
Address out to data in required	3 clock cycles − ⑥ − ㉗ = 300 − 60 − 10 =	230
$\overline{AS}$, $\overline{DS}$ asserted to data in required	2.5 clock cycles − ⑨ − ㉗ = 250 − 55 − 10 =	185
$\overline{DS}$ asserted	⑭ = 2.5 clock cycles − ⑨ = 250 − 55 =	195
Data in hold time required	㉙	0

for a cycle with no wait states, the time from when the address is output to when data in is required is

  3 clock cycles − parameter 6 − parameter 27

Other timing values are calculated in a similar manner. Some interpretation is sometimes necessary to determine which parameters to use to calculate the worst-case timing. Consider the length of the $\overline{DS}$ pulse during a read cycle, for example. Parameter 9 specifies the maximum delay from the start of S2 to the assertion of $\overline{DS}$, and parameter 12 specifies the maximum delay from the start of S7 to the negation of $\overline{DS}$.

Table 3.18   Key Timing Parameters for 68008 Write Cycle with 10-MHz Clock

Parameter	Derivation	Time, ns
Address out to $\overline{\text{DS}}$ negated	3 clock cycles $-$ (6) $= 300 - 60 =$	240
$\overline{\text{AS}}$ asserted to $\overline{\text{DS}}$ negated	2.5 clock cycles $-$ (9) $= 250 - 55 =$	195
$\overline{\text{DS}}$ asserted	(14A) $= 1.5$ clock cycles $-$ (9) $= 150 - 55 =$	95
Data out setup to $\overline{\text{DS}}$ negated	2 clock cycles $-$ (23) $= 200 - 55 =$	145
Data out hold after $\overline{\text{DS}}$ negated	(25)	20

However, the worst-case $\overline{\text{DS}}$ low time is determined by the maximum value of parameter 9 and the *minimum* value of parameter 12. Since there is no minimum specified for parameter 12, for worst-case analysis we must assume it to be zero. Thus, the minimum $\overline{\text{DS}}$ pulse width is 2.5 clock cycles minus parameter 9. Although it is very unlikely (probably impossible) for parameter 12 to be zero while parameter 9 is the maximum allowed, there is no other basis for a worst-case calculation. The $\overline{\text{DS}}$ asserted time is specified directly as parameter 14, which surprisingly does not guarantee any more time than that determined by the worst-case calculation just described.

It is also important to note that some timing parameters are not referenced to the system clock. For example, judging solely on the basis of parameters 6 and 9, it would be possible for $\overline{\text{AS}}$ to be asserted before the address was valid if parameter 6 was near its maximum value and parameter 9 was near its minimum. However, parameter 11 guarantees that the address will be valid for some time before $\overline{\text{AS}}$ is asserted. This is, in effect, a guarantee of the worst-case relative values of parameters 6 and 9.

For write cycles, the $\overline{\text{DS}}$ pulse width is one clock shorter than for read cycles. This is done to provide valid data at the leading edge of $\overline{\text{DS}}$. The worst-case $\overline{\text{DS}}$ pulse width for a write cycle at 10 MHz is only 95 ns, so most peripheral devices will require one or more wait states. One of the most critical parameters for the write cycle is the data hold time provided at the end of the cycle; this is only 20 ns for the 10-MHz 68008. Approaches to increasing the available hold time are described in Chap. 5.

Another timing path to consider is the assertion of $\overline{\text{DTACK}}$. For zero wait states, $\overline{\text{DTACK}}$ must be asserted at least 10 ns (parameter 47) before the end of S4. The zero-wait $\overline{\text{DTACK}}$ for memory accesses is asserted two gate delays after the assertion of $\overline{\text{AS}}$. The time available from the assertion of $\overline{\text{AS}}$ to when $\overline{\text{DTACK}}$ must be asserted is

$$1.5 \text{ clock cycles} - \text{parameter } 9 - \text{parameter } 47$$
$$= 150 \text{ ns} - 55 \text{ ns} - 10 \text{ ns} = 85 \text{ ns}$$

This is more than enough for two gates in almost any modern logic family. Note that an additional timing requirement is that the MFPCS OR IOCS signal must be valid in time to ensure that this zero-wait DTACK is *not* asserted during accesses to those devices.

For I/O read cycles, $\overline{\text{DTACK}}$ is asserted following the rising clock edge that begins S4. Since $\overline{\text{DTACK}}$ must be asserted 10 ns before the end of S4, the time available is

$$0.5 \text{ clock cycles} - \text{parameter } 47 = 50 \text{ ns} - 10 \text{ ns} = 40 \text{ ns}$$

The combined delay of the the 74ALS74 and the 74HCT05 is 37 ns, leaving 3 ns of margin. Note that a 74HC74 or 74LS74 is too slow. For I/O write cycles the timing is the same except that $\overline{\text{DTACK}}$ is asserted one clock cycle later.

3.11 SUMMARY

Buses are the link between the various components of a microprocessor system. All buses include address signals, data signals, and control signals. The variations are in the width of the address and data paths and in the operation of the control signals. Each microprocessor type in effect defines a bus by the signals that it generates and expects in return. The basic bus control signals control the direction and timing of data transfers. Other functions performed by the bus control signals include interrupts, error handling, timing control, and bus arbitration.

While each manufacturer has a different style of implementing these signals, the basic functions performed are equivalent. Most microprocessor bus designs can be classified as Intel-style, using separate read and write strobes, or as Motorola-style, using a read/write line combined with a direction-independent data strobe. Intel-style buses also provide separate control lines for I/O, while Motorola-style buses require I/O to be memory-mapped.

System buses allow a wide variety of boards to be easily designed to work together. The STD bus provides a simple, low-cost method for implementing specialized instrumentation and control systems. The Multibus provides higher performance, larger boards, and the ability to support multiple processors. The VMEbus provides higher performance and is oriented toward 16- and 32-bit microprocessors. The IBM PC bus is widely used in personal computers. Newer bus designs such as the Futurebus and Multibus II provide the highest performance for demanding 32-bit microprocessor applications.

While digital signals are generally treated as pure ones and zeros, their electrical characteristics must be kept in mind. At low speeds and with short wires there are rarely any problems, but the high-speed signals common in microprocessor systems require that reflections and crosstalk be taken into consideration.

3.12 EXERCISES

Note: Several of these exercises require access to detailed data sheets for specific microprocessors.

3.1. The text describes Intel-style and Motorola-style control signals, and shows how to generate the former from the latter. Design a circuit to do the reverse conversion; i.e., translate a read strobe and write strobe to a read/write signal and a data strobe.

3.2.   Name the type of cycle performed when the following Z80 control signals are asserted:

    a. $\overline{\text{RD}}$ and $\overline{\text{IORQ}}$ d. $\overline{\text{M1}}$ and $\overline{\text{IORQ}}$

    b. $\overline{\text{RD}}$ and $\overline{\text{MREQ}}$ e. $\overline{\text{WR}}$ and $\overline{\text{IORQ}}$

    c. $\overline{\text{M1}}$, $\overline{\text{RD}}$ and $\overline{\text{MREQ}}$

3.3.   Buses with 16-bit data paths often have an additional control signal to allow individual bytes to be read or written.

    a.   The 8086 uses the signals $\overline{\text{BHE}}$ and A_0. What combination of signals is used to perform an access to the lower byte (D_0 to D_7)? The upper byte (D_8 to D_{15})?

    b.   The 68000 does not generate A_0, but uses the two data strobes $\overline{\text{UDS}}$ and $\overline{\text{LDS}}$. Which signals are asserted for (1) an upper- or lower-byte access or (2) a word (16-bit) access? What is the state of the internal A_0 signal for an upper-byte access?

3.4.   An 8086 system running at 8 MHz is using memory with an access time (including all buffers) of 300 ns. Are wait states required? If yes, how many? What is the slowest memory access time that allows operation with no wait states?

3.5.   Repeat Exercise 3.4 for the 68000, Z80, or other microprocessor for which you have a data sheet. Repeat for each processor, using memory with access times of 200 and 400 ns.

3.6.   Calculate the time from when the data strobe is asserted to when $\overline{\text{DTACK}}$ must be asserted for a 10-MHz 68000 to operate at maximum speed.

3.7.   What are the main reasons for the use of multiplexed buses?

3.8.   Suppose 74LS374 edge-triggered registers were used to demultiplex an 8086 bus instead of 74LS373 transparent latches. What is the effect on the system timing? What is the magnitude of the timing difference?

3.9.   List the benefits of separate user and supervisory modes such as those provided by the 68000 microprocessor.

3.10.   A system design requires four separate interrupt inputs which are generated from non-microprocessor-compatible peripherals. For each of the following microprocessors, what external hardware (if any) is required to process the interrupts? Draw a circuit diagram for each. Which microprocessor would you recommend, all other factors being equal? What if 10 interrupt inputs were required?

    a.   6802   d.   Z80   g.   80186

    b.   6809   e.   68000

    c.   8085   f.   8086

3.11.   An industrial control system is being designed. Only a few units are expected to be built. The designer has determined that a Z80 will provide adequate computational power, that 8 Kbytes of RAM and 16 Kbytes of ROM will be required, and that 128 TTL output lines and 32 TTL input lines are needed, along with a stepper motor interface and an RS-232 interface. Which system bus would you recommend? Why?

3.12. A system has a 2-ft-long unterminated backplane. How much timing margin should be allowed for ringing to stop?

3.13. Modify the design example's $\overline{\text{DTACK}}$ generation logic to allow zero, one, or two wait states to be selected individually for each of four EPROM or RAM ICs. Assume that a chip select signal is provided for each memory device.

3.14. Design an expansion bus for the design example system. Be sure to consider the following areas:

a. Signals needed on the expansion bus.

b. Buffering of address and data buses, including buffer enable and direction control signals.

c. Buffering of clock and control signals.

d. $\overline{\text{DTACK}}$ generation. Devices on the expansion bus should be able to request wait states.

3.13 SELECTED BIBLIOGRAPHY

For information on specific microprocessors, refer to the references listed at the end of Chap. 2.

Buses: General

Borrill, Paul L. "Microprocessor Bus Structures and Standards," *IEEE Micro*, February 1981, pp. 84–95. A good discussion of bus principles and problems but does not include newer buses such as the VMEbus. Discusses desirable characteristics for a system bus standard.

Gustavson, David B. "Computer Buses—A Tutorial," *IEEE Micro*, August 1984, pp. 7–22. Describes general bus operation and arbitration and data transfer protocols.

Stone, Harold S. "Bus Interconnections," Chap. 3 in *Microcomputer Interfacing*, Reading, MA: Addison-Wesley, 1982. Provides a general treatment of bus principles, with examples from selected microprocessor and system buses.

System Buses

Control Engineering, P.O. Box 2176, Clinton, IA 52735, publishes annual buyer's guides for each of the major system buses, listing all available products and their key characteristics.

STD Bus

Pro-Log. *STD Bus Specification and Practice*. Monterey, CA, 1984. Reference for the general STD bus. Produced by the STD Bus Manufacturer's Group and distributed by Pro-Log.

Thompson Components-Mostek. *System Design Using the Mostek MD-STD-Z80 Bus*, Carrollton, TX, 1980. Reference for the Z80 subset of the STD bus.

Ziatech. *System Designer's Guide: 8088 Family on the STD Bus*, San Luis Obispo, CA. Describes system design and bus timing for the 8088 STD bus.

Multibus

IEEE. *IEEE-796 Bus Specification,* Piscataway, NJ, 1983. Reference for the full IEEE version of the Multibus.

Intel. *AP-28A: Multibus Interfacing,* Santa Clara, CA, 1979. Tutorial description of the Multibus. Does not include all enhancements in IEEE specification.

————. *Multibus II Bus Architecture Specification Handbook,* Santa Clara, CA. The comprehensive Multibus II reference. For a more general description, see the following reference.

————. *OEM Systems Handbook,* Santa Clara, CA. Includes descriptions of and application notes for the Multibus and Multibus II, along with data sheets for Intel's board-level and systems products.

Johnson, James B., and Steve Kassel. *The Multibus Designer's Guidebook,* New York: McGraw-Hill, 1984. A comprehensive reference guide to the Multibus and the associated iSBX bus, iLBX bus, and Multichannel bus. Includes example designs for bus interface logic.

VME Bus

Balph, Tom. "VMEbus—A μP Bus for the Future," *Digital Design,* August 1982.

Motorola. *VMEbus Specification Manual,* Phoenix, 1985. Reference for the VMEbus. Also available from Signetics (Sunnyvale, CA) and Thompson Components-Mostek (Carrollton, TX).

Other System Buses

Eggebrecht, Lewis C. *Interfacing to the IBM Personal Computer,* Indianapolis: Sams, 1983. Describes the IBM PC bus and basic interface circuits. Also covers software requirements for expansion boards to use interrupts and DMA.

IBM. *IBM PC Technical Reference Manual* and *IBM PC/AT Technical Reference Manual,* Boca Raton, FL. These reference manuals include brief bus descriptions and schematics for the system boards and common IBM expansion boards. Unfortunately, they do not provide timing information, and there is no definitive technical reference for these buses.

IEEE. *IEEE-696 Bus Specification,* Piscataway, NJ, 1983. Reference for the enhanced S-100 bus.

Levy, John V. "Buses, The Skeleton of Computer Structures," Chap. 11 in *Computer Engineering: A DEC View of Hardware Systems Design,* Bedford, MA: Digital Press, 1978. Describes the bus structures used in DEC's minicomputers.

Libes, Sol, and Mark Garetz. *Interfacing to S-100/IEEE-696 Microcomputers,* Berkeley, CA: Osborne/McGraw-Hill, 1981. A tutorial treatment of the S-100 bus and simple interfaces.

Electrical Considerations

Balakrishnan, R. V. "Eliminating Crosstalk over Long-Distance Busing," *Computer Design,* March 1982. Describes National's DS3662 trapezoidal bus transceiver and its effects on bus noise and crosstalk. Adapted from National's Application Note 259.

Blakeslee, Thomas R. "Nasty Realities II: Noise and Reflections," Chap. 12 in *Digital Design with Standard MSI and LSI,* 2d ed., New York: Wiley, 1979. A detailed treatment of transmission line problems as applied to digital systems.

Davidson, Malcolm. "Understanding the High-Speed Digital Logic Signal." *Computer Design,* November 1982. Describes transmission line theory for digital systems.

Stone, Harold S. "Shielding, Grounding, and Transmission-Line Techniques," Chap. 2 in *Microcomputer Interfacing,* Reading, MA: Addison-Wesley, 1982. Good coverage of the stated topics.

4

MEMORY

4.1 INTRODUCTION: MEMORY TYPES

Memory is at the heart of all microprocessor systems, since it stores both programs and data that determine the operation of the system. Figure 4.1 shows the hierarchy of memory types. Memory that is the fastest and closest to the processor is at the top of the pyramid. The fastest storage is in the microprocessor's registers, since these can be accessed without using external buses and do not require explicit addressing. At the middle of the pyramid is main memory, which includes standard RAM, ROM, EPROM, and EEPROM. Main memory is directly addressed by the microprocessor. It must be *random-access* memory, which means that each memory location can be accessed in a time roughly equivalent to any other memory location. (Note that we are using random access here in its true sense, and not to imply read/write memory or RAM.) All programs and data in use by the microprocessor at any moment must be stored in the main memory. This chapter describes the various types of main memory used in microprocessor systems.

Mass storage refers to relatively large amounts of memory that are not directly addressed by the microprocessor. For example, to read data from a magnetic disk, the microprocessor must first issue a command to the disk controller to position the read/write head over the desired track, and then wait for the desired data to pass under the head. This is in contrast to a random-access memory, in which the microprocessor simply places the desired address on the address bus, asserts the $\overline{\text{READ}}$ or $\overline{\text{WRITE}}$ control signals, and then reads or writes the selected data. Mass storage is typically lower in cost per bit, has a relatively large storage capacity, and is nonvolatile.

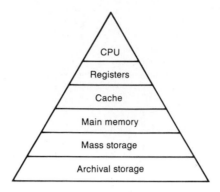

Archival storage refers to long-term memory that may require user intervention for access. Magnetic tape is the most common archival medium; a library of magnetic tapes can store a massive amount of information. Access can be very slow, since the user may have to find a tape in the library and mount it on the tape drive. Optical disks are increasingly used for archival storage when very large capacity is required. Mass storage and archival storage devices and interfacing are covered in Chap. 9.

There is sometimes a level of memory between the main memory and the microprocessor's registers called a *cache memory*. A cache is a relatively small, fast memory that contains copies of frequently used locations in main memory. For each word in a cache memory, there is one location to store the data and a *tag* location that identifies the location in main memory with which the data is associated. When the microprocessor outputs an address at the beginning of a cycle, it is compared to the tags in the cache memory. If a match is found, then the microprocessor reads or writes the byte in the cache, and main memory is not accessed. The cache control logic must keep main memory updated according to changes made in the cache and read new locations into the cache as required.

A cache memory thus allows some processor cycles to execute more quickly by eliminating the need to access relatively slow main memory. The effectiveness of the cache is measured by the *hit rate*, which is the percentage of accesses for which the requested address is found in the cache. Many different algorithms are used to attempt to keep the cache full of the locations most likley to be used, thus maximizing the hit rate. The hit rate is also dependent on the size of the cache. Cache memory is relatively expensive to implement and is used only in high-performance systems whose CPUs are faster than the main memory.

4.2   MEMORY INTERFACING

Interfacing any memory IC to a microprocessor requires control signals and some form of address decoding. This section describes the control signals for basic memory devices, various methods of address decoding, and the analysis of memory access timing.

4.2.1 Internal Structure of Memory Devices

Figure 4.2 shows the internal structure of a typical semiconductor memory device. Each bit of storage requires one memory cell. This cell may be a flip-flop, a capacitor, or a fuse, depending on the memory type. The memory cells are arranged as an array. The address inputs are decoded to produce row select and column select signals, with which any memory cell can be selected.

Memory cells are arranged in arrays for several reasons. A square array provides dense packing of the cells and allows them to be addressed with a minimum number of select lines. Many memory ICs use rectangular arrays, either to make the IC physically narrower so it will fit in the IC package's cavity or for special functional reasons (as with dynamic RAMs, described in Sec. 4.7.3).

The memory chip is enabled only when its $\overline{CS}$ (chip select) input is asserted. To read data from the memory, $\overline{CS}$ and $\overline{OE}$ (output enable) are asserted to enable the output three-state drivers. To write data to the memory, data is provided on the data inputs, $\overline{CS}$ is asserted, and $\overline{WE}$ (write enable) is pulsed low. The data in and data out signals may share the same pins or may be on separate pins.

Some memories do not have a separate chip select and output enable. In this case, the output drivers are enabled whenever $\overline{CS}$ is asserted and $\overline{WE}$ is negated.

The chip select signal is often called $\overline{CE}$ (chip enable). The $\overline{CE}$ designation usually,

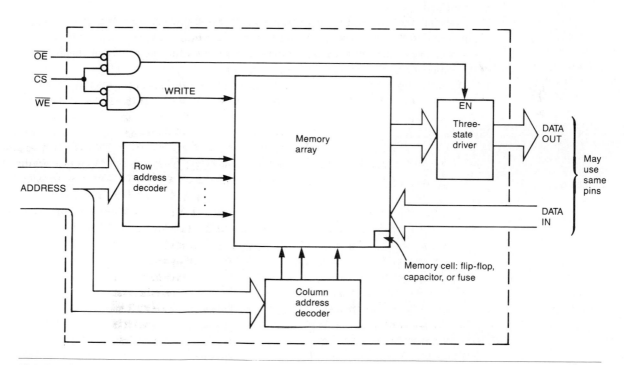

Figure 4.2. Internal structure of typical memory IC.

but not always, indicates that the chip enters a low-power standby mode when the enable is negated.

4.2.2   Basic Bus Interface

Figure 4.3 shows the basic memory interface. This example shows a read/write memory (RAM) chip with 8192 locations of 1 byte each (i.e., an 8K × 8, or 64-Kbit, RAM). The least significant 13 address lines connect directly to the memory chip and select one of the 8K locations within the chip. The *address decoder* decodes the most-significant address lines and provides an address select signal to enable the RAM. The address select signal enables the memory chip to respond to a particular range of addresses. The design of the address decoder thus determines at what addresses each memory device appears, which is called the *memory map*. I/O devices may be addressed as part of the memory map, or there may be a separate I/O map and I/O address decoder.

The address select output from the address decoder provides the chip select signal for the memory. Since the $\overline{WE}$ and $\overline{OE}$ inputs are internally gated with $\overline{CS}$, they can be connected directly to the $\overline{WRITE}$ and $\overline{READ}$ control signals from the microprocessor.

For memories without a separate output enable, the address select signal must be gated so that it is asserted only when $\overline{READ}$ or $\overline{WRITE}$ is asserted. If $\overline{WE}$ is asserted when $\overline{CS}$ is asserted, then a write cycle is performed; otherwise, a read cycle is performed.

The interface for a read-only memory (ROM) is similar, except there is no $\overline{WE}$ input. Most ROMs and EPROMs have a chip select and an output enable, so the chip select can be connected directly to the address select signal and the output enable to the microprocessor's $\overline{READ}$ signal.

Later in this chapter, several actual memory chips and their bus interface requirements are described. While there may be an extra signal or two, the basic structure described above is used for nearly all memory chips.

Figure 4.3. Basic memory interface circuit.

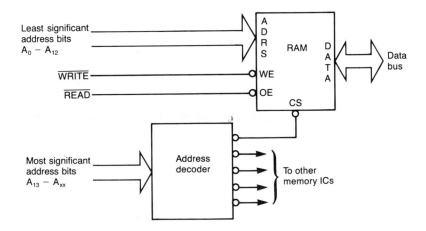

Figure 4.4. Relationship of address decoding to memory map.

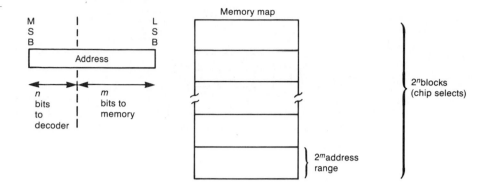

4.2.3 Address Decoding

The task of the address decoder is to decode the most significant address bits and generate address select signals for each device in the system. In effect, it breaks the address space up into blocks; each address select signal indicates that the address on the address bus is within a predetermined range. In general, the desired block size is the amount of address space used by each memory chip. For example, if each memory chip contains 8K memory locations, then an address select signal is needed that is asserted for any address within an 8K range.

The range of addresses for which an address select signal is asserted is determined by which address lines are decoded. Figure 4.4 shows the relationship between the address decoding and the memory map. If the top n bits are decoded by the address decoder, then 2^n separate address select signals can be produced. Each address select signal is asserted for a range of 2^m addresses, where m is the number of less significant address lines not decoded by the address decoder. For example, if the address decoder decodes A_{13} through the most significant address bit, then the least significant 13 address bits A_0 to A_{12} are ignored by the address decoder. This leaves 2^{13}, or 8K, possible addresses for which each address select is asserted.

Some microprocessors, such as the 80186 and 80188, include address decoding logic in the microprocessor IC. The 80186 and 80188 provide six memory chip select signals and seven peripheral (I/O) chip select signals. The address range for each is set by software by writing to control registers. At power-up, one of the memory chip selects is asserted for addresses at the top of the address space, allowing access to ROM at the top of the address space so the initialization software that programs the chip select ranges can be executed.

Decoding with Binary-to-One-of-Eight Decoder ICs

Figure 4.5 shows an address decoding circuit that generates eight separate address select signals, each of which corresponds to an 8K block of addresses. The IC that performs the decoding function is called a *binary-to-one-of-eight* decoder. Only one

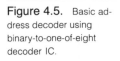

Figure 4.5. Basic address decoder using binary-to-one-of-eight decoder IC.

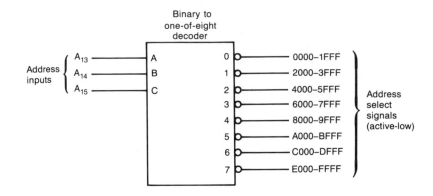

Binary to
one-of-eight
decoder

Address inputs { A_{13} — A   0 — 0000–1FFF
A_{14} — B   1 — 2000–3FFF
A_{15} — C   2 — 4000–5FFF
      3 — 6000–7FFF
      4 — 8000–9FFF
      5 — A000–BFFF
      6 — C000–DFFF
      7 — E000–FFFF }

Address
select
signals
(active-low)

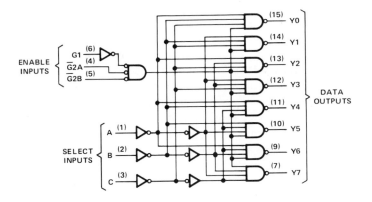

'LS138, 'S138
FUNCTION TABLE

INPUTS				OUTPUTS							
ENABLE		SELECT									
G1	$\overline{G2}$*	C	B	A	Y0	Y1	Y2	Y3	Y4	Y5	Y6	Y7
X	H	X	X	X	H	H	H	H	H	H	H	H
L	X	X	X	X	H	H	H	H	H	H	H	H
H	L	L	L	L	L	H	H	H	H	H	H	H
H	L	L	L	H	H	L	H	H	H	H	H	H
H	L	L	H	L	H	H	L	H	H	H	H	H
H	L	L	H	H	H	H	H	L	H	H	H	H
H	L	H	L	L	H	H	H	H	L	H	H	H
H	L	H	L	H	H	H	H	H	H	L	H	H
H	L	H	H	L	H	H	H	H	H	H	L	H
H	L	H	H	H	H	H	H	H	H	H	H	L

*$\overline{G2}$ = $\overline{G2A}$ + $\overline{G2B}$

H = high level, L = low level, X = irrelevant

Figure 4.6. The 74LS138 decoder internal logic and truth table. *(Courtesy of Texas Instruments.)*

output is asserted at any given time, corresponding to the binary number present at the A, B, and C inputs.

A common TTL IC that performs this function is the 74LS138. It functions exactly as described above, except that it has three enable inputs, two active-low ($\overline{G2A}$ and $\overline{G2B}$) and one active-high (G1). All three enable inputs must be asserted, or the outputs will all be negated. Figure 4.6 shows the internal logic and the truth table that defines the function of this device. All the outputs are active-low, so the selected output is low and all others are high.

Figure 4.7 shows how decoders can be cascaded to generate more select signals and how the enable inputs can be used to AND in the necessary control signals. This example is for a 24-bit address bus and Intel-style control signals, but it is easily adapted to other system configurations.

The first decoder is enabled when A_{19} to A_{23} are all low and when the control signals indicate a memory (rather than I/O) access. Thus, the outputs of the decoder are dis-

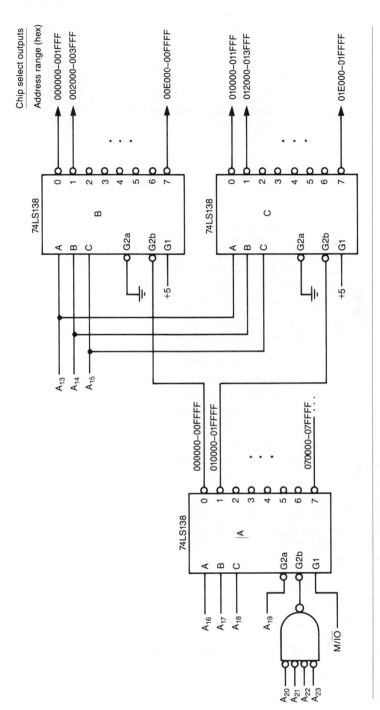

Figure 4.7. Address decoder using cascaded 74LS138s.

abled except for memory accesses in which the most-significant address bits are 00000. Each output of the decoder is asserted for a 64K range of addresses.

The outputs of decoder A are used to enable decoders B and C, each for a 64K range of addresses. Thus, decoder B is enabled when A_{16} to A_{23} are 00000000, and decoder C is enabled when A_{16} to A_{23} are 00000001. Decoders B and C further divide the address space into 8K segments. Additional decoders could be cascaded to further subdivide the address space. However, it must be kept in mind that each decoder introduces a delay (which is doubled if two decoders are cascaded) from when the microprocessor outputs the address to when the address select output is asserted. As we will see in Sec. 4.2.4, this delay may or may not affect the memory system access time, depending on the particular microprocessor, memory chip, and control logic.

If memory devices without separate output enables are used, one enable on decoders A and B can be connected to $\overline{READ}$ OR $\overline{WRITE}$, ensuring that no address select output is asserted unless one of the data transfer control signals is also asserted. However, the data transfer control signals are asserted some time after the address is output by the microprocessor, so this delays the assertion of the address select signals and can affect the access time of the memory system. For Motorola-style microprocessors, the address strobe can be used to enable the decoder but this, too, delays the decoder outputs.

Address decoding for input and output ports is similar and is discussed in Chap. 5.

Address Decoding with Bipolar PROMs

Another address decoding technique is to use a specially programmed bipolar PROM as the address decoder. Figure 4.8 shows a 256×4 PROM used as an address decoder. Two of the PROM's address bits are connected to jumpers. These jumpers effectively select one of four 64×4 areas of the PROM, each of which can contain a different memory map. This is particularly useful in systems designed to support several different sizes of memory chips.

Address bits A_{10} to A_{15} select one of 64 locations in the PROM. Address bits A_0 through A_9 from the microprocessor are ignored by the PROM, so each PROM location

Figure 4.8. Bipolar PROM used as an address decoder.

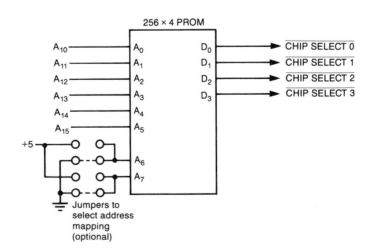

Table 4.1   Address Decoding PROM Programming Pattern

Address	Contents	Address range	Block size
000000	1110	0000–03FF	1K
000001	1111	0400–07FF	1K, unused
000010	1101	0800–0FFF	2K
000011	1101		
000100	1011	1000–1FFF	4K
000101	1011		
000110	1011		
000111	1011		
001000	0111	2000–3FFF	8K
001001	0111		
001010	0111		
001011	0111		
001100	0111		
001101	0111		
001110	0111		
001111	0111		
010000	1111	4000–FFFF	48K, unused
.	.		
.	.		
.	.		
111111	1111		

is accessed for a range of 1K addresses. Table 4.1 shows an example of how the PROM could be programmed. The first memory location is programmed with 1110; thus, the D_0 output will be low (asserted, since address selects are active-low) when this location is accessed. Since this is the only memory location with a zero in the D_0 bit position, the D_0 output is asserted for a range of 1K addresses. The next location contains all ones, so this address range is unused. The next two locations both contain 1101; thus, the address select signal at output D_1 will be asserted for a range of 2K addresses. The range of addresses decoded by each output can be easily extended by programming more PROM locations with the same data pattern, as shown in the table.

Most PROMs are available with either open-collector or three-state outputs. The three-state versions are preferable, since their low-to-high transitions are much faster and output pull-up resistors are not required. (In some applications, the PROM's chip select input is connected to an address strobe signal to ensure that the outputs are always valid. Since the PROM's outputs are in the high-impedance state when chip select is negated, pull-up resistors are required on the outputs even if the PROM has three-state outputs.)

Bipolar PROMs are available from many vendors, and although many are pin-compatible, nearly all vendors use completely different part numbers. For example, MMI's 256 × 4 PROM with three-state outputs is the 63S141. The equivalent device from AMD is the 27S21, National's is the 74S287, and Signetics' is the 82S129. Examples of a 512 × 8 PROM include MMI's 6349, AMD's 27S29, National's 74S472, and Signetics' 82S147.

The advantage of the PROM decoder approach is that, with a single IC, a number of address select signals can be generated with different block sizes. In addition, the memory decoding can be completely changed simply by replacing the PROM with a differently programmed PROM. Thus, this approach has great flexibility and very low chip count. By using a PROM with 8-bit words, eight chip select signals can be generated. By using a PROM with more words, more address bits can be decoded.

Inevitably, there are disadvantages as well. Bipolar PROMs are generally slower, more expensive, and consume more power than decoder ICs. For example, the 74ALS138 decoder has a maximum propagation delay of 18 ns and consumes 10 mA maximum. MMI's 63S141 has a maximum delay of 45 ns and consumes 130 mA maximum. These disadvantages become more severe with larger PROMs. A PROM programmer is required to program the PROM, increasing the design support equipment required. (For production quantities, many electronic component distributors will program the PROMs when you buy them.) In addition, because the PROM is custom-programmed, an additional manufacturing step is required, and the PROM cannot be replaced in the field with parts from a distributor.

Another similar device that is useful for address decoding is the *programmable array logic* (PAL) chip. A PAL is an AND-OR logic array that is programmed like a PROM. PALs can perform address decoding and control logic gating in a single chip and are useful for replacing small-scale TTL logic chips to reduce total chip count. They are more flexible than PROMs, and are thus often preferable. The *Programmable Array Logic Handbook* (listed in the references at the end of this chapter) provides several examples of PALs used for address decoders and memory interface logic.

Address Decoding with Comparators

Another useful IC for building address decoders is the comparator. Figure 4.9 shows an 8-bit comparator connected as an address decoder. The comparator has two sets of inputs, P and Q, and a P=Q output. The output is asserted only when $P_0 = Q_0$, $P_1 = Q_1$, . . . , and $P_7 = Q_7$. The user selects the address range to be decoded by setting the switches connected to the Q inputs. In this example, the comparator decodes the upper 8 bits of a 24-bit address bus; thus, the setting of the switches selects any one of 256 possible 64-Kbyte ranges. The output of the comparator can be used directly to provide a single address select signal or to enable another address decoder that further decodes the address (as in this example). This technique is commonly used on memory boards, since it allows a single system to contain several identical boards. Setting the switches differently on each board places each in a different part of the address space.

Minimizing Decoding: Effects of Undecoded Address Bits

In the preceding examples, the address bus is completely decoded; that is, no address bits are ignored. The least-significant bits are decoded by the memory's internal decoder, and the most-significant bits are decoded by the system's address decoder. Decoding logic can often be simplified by ignoring certain address bits.

Figure 4.9. Address decoder using comparator for bank select.

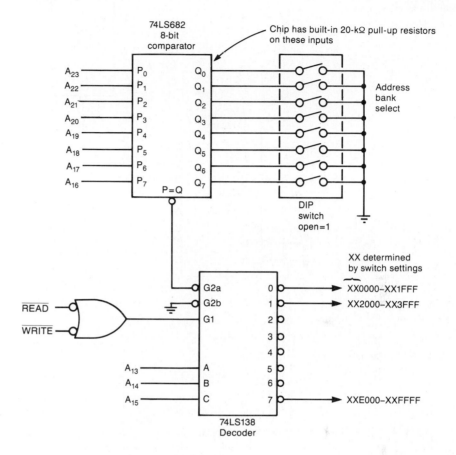

For example, let us reconsider the address decoder shown in Fig. 4.7. A four-input AND gate was required to enable the decoder only when address bits A_{20} through A_{23} were all zero. This selects, in effect, the lowest 1 Mbyte of the 16-Mbyte address space. If the maximum memory (and memory-mapped I/O) in the system is under 2 Mbytes, then this gate is unnecessary. The A_{20} signal can be connected directly to the active-low enable input, and A_{21} to A_{23} can simply be ignored. The effect of this simplification is that all the memory and I/O in the system will repeat at eight different addresses, since the upper three address bits can be in any of eight different combinations. Thus, the usable address space has been reduced by a factor of 8 to 2 Mbytes. One megabyte is decoded by the decoder shown in the figure; the other megabyte can be decoded by a decoder that is enabled when A_{20} is high.

There is another situation in which address bits are often ignored. Consider a system that uses three 32-Kbyte EPROMs and one 8-Kbyte RAM. The address decoding circuit is simplest if each address select corresponds to a 32K address range. This allows the entire decoder to be implemented with a single decoder IC, such as the 74LS138 shown in Fig. 4.10. Three of the decoder outputs are used for the EPROMs and one for the RAM. Figure 4.11 shows the memory map for this system. Each EPROM decodes address bits A_0 to A_{14}, and the decoder decodes A_{15} to A_{19} (for a 20-bit address bus). However, because the RAM is one-fourth the size of the EPROM, it decodes two fewer

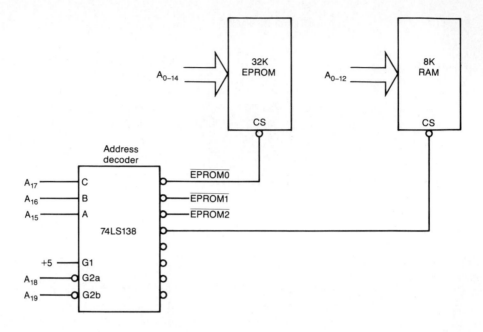

Figure 4.10. Address decoder for mixed memory sizes using partial decoding.

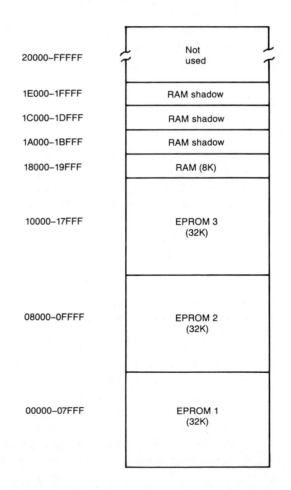

Figure 4.11. Memory map for system in Fig. 4.10.

address lines, and A_{13} and A_{14} are left undecoded when the RAM is accessed. The result is that each RAM location appears at four addresses. For example, addresses 18000, 1A000, 1C000, and 1E000 all access the same location.

A similar effect occurs when using memory-mapped I/O. A single-byte I/O port may be enabled by an address select signal that is asserted for an 8K range of addresses. The effect of this is that the port appears at all the addresses within the range.

Another method for simplifying address decoding, called *linear select,* is to use address lines directly as address select signals. For example, one memory can be enabled when A_{15} is high, another when A_{14} is high, and another when A_{13} is high. This reduces the address decoding hardware to zero but has several drawbacks. If the microprocessor reads an address in which more than one of these bits is high, then more than one memory device would attempt to drive the bus and a bus conflict would occur. This should not happen if the software is operating properly but may happen during software development. Linear select decoding also uses up address space rapidly. The first device (enabled by the most significant address bit) uses half the address space, the second device uses half the remaining space, and so on. With three devices, only one-eighth of the total address space is left unused. Thus, linear select decoding is limited to small, cost-critical systems.

These simplified decoding schemes do "waste" address space, but when there is more address space available than is needed, this is not of concern. Often, a simplified address decoding approach will still leave plenty of address space available for future expansion, and there is then no reason not to take the economy of minimized decoding. Future needs must be kept in mind, however, and it is foolish to make expansion difficult just to save a few gates.

4.2.4 Memory Timing

A key specification of any memory device is its *access time*. For a read cycle, access time is the time from when a new address is presented to the memory to when the memory provides the correct data at its outputs. For a write cycle, it is the time from when the address is presented to when the $\overline{\text{WRITE}}$ pulse can be terminated and the data removed. Access time from address is the most commonly quoted parameter, but there are several other timing specifications of importance.

A related specification is the *cycle time,* which is the time from the start of one memory cycle to start of the next. For most memory types, another access can begin as soon as the previous access is complete, so the minimum cycle time is the same as the access time. For dynamic RAMs, as described in Sec. 4.7.2, the minimum cycle time is longer than the access time. The actual cycle time in any real system is always greater than the access time, since it takes the microprocessor some time to end the cycle and output the new address for the next cycle.

When reading from memory, the microprocessor allows a fixed amount of time for the memory to respond with valid data after an address is output. This is the access time required by the microprocessor for full-speed operation and is determined by the design of the microprocessor and by its clock rate. If the memory device cannot respond in that time, a wait state must be inserted or errors will result. The access time of the memory must be less than the access time required by the microprocessor (including wait states if used).

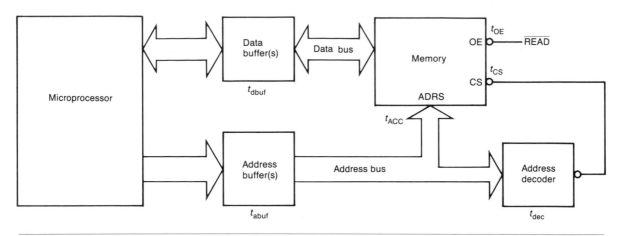

Figure 4.12.   Delay paths in microprocessor-to-memory interface.

Figure 4.12 shows a typical microprocessor-to-memory interface. The address and data buses are both buffered at the microprocessor, which adds additional delays. In a multiple-board system, both buses are also likely to be buffered on the memory board. Thus, there can be up to four buffer delays that add to the access time of the memory chip itself.

As shown graphically in Fig. 4.13, the total access time of the memory system is the sum of the buffer delays and the access time of the memory IC. The access time required by the microprocessor minus the actual access time of the memory system is the timing margin. This margin must, of course, always be positive for proper system operation.

The chip select signal is generated by the address decoder, so it is delayed from the change in address by the decoder's propagation delay time. For most memory devices, access time from chip select (t_{CS}) is equal to the access time from address (t_{ACC}). Thus, the memory access time does not begin until $\overline{CS}$ is asserted. For higher-speed operation, the memory's chip select input can be grounded and all control performed via the $\overline{WE}$ and $\overline{OE}$ signals. In this case, the access time t_{ACC} begins as soon as the address is presented to the memory, as shown by the dashed line in the figure. The EPROM interfacing section later in this chapter provides an example of this situation.

The response of the memory to the output enable signal (t_{OE}) is much faster than its access time from address. (As shown in Fig. 4.2, $\overline{OE}$ controls only the output drivers.) Thus, even though $\overline{OE}$ is asserted later in the cycle, the memory will have its output drivers enabled before the valid data is available. This is the desirable situation: the memory is driving the bus before the access time elapses, so that when the data comes trickling through it will be driven onto the bus as quickly as possible. That the memory will drive invalid data on the bus during the cycle is irrelevant; only the data at the end of the cycle matters.

The data hold time provided by the memory is determined by the speed at which the outputs are disabled when $\overline{OE}$ is negated plus the minimum propagation time of the data bus buffer(s). Most microprocessors require little or no hold time, so this parameter rarely causes problems for read cycles. For multiplexed address/data bus systems

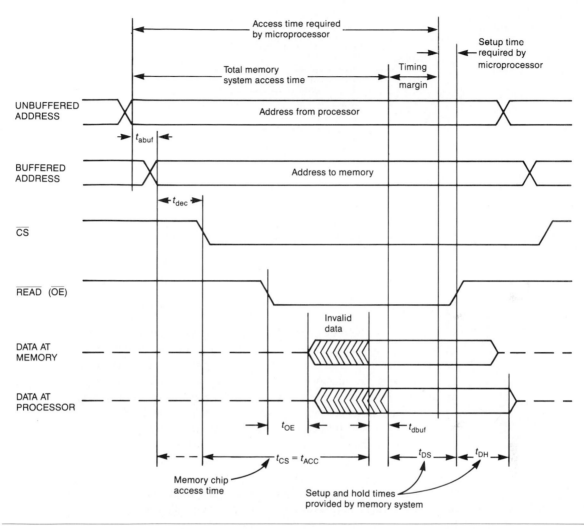

Figure 4.13. Memory read timing.

without data bus buffers, the maximum time for the memory output to be disabled after $\overline{OE}$ is negated must be short enough to ensure that the memory has stopped driving the bus when the microprocessor outputs the address at the start of the next cycle.

Figure 4.14 shows the timing for a typical memory write cycle. The actual write operation is performed when $\overline{WE}$ is negated at the end of the cycle. The equivalent of the read access time is the parameter t_{AW}, the time that the address must be valid before $\overline{WE}$ is negated. As for the read cycle, the address is ignored until $\overline{CS}$ is asserted, so t_{CW} is equal to t_{AW}. Unless $\overline{CS}$ is grounded for maximum speed operation, the limiting parameter will always be t_{CW}. Another limiting parameter is the minimum write pulse width, t_{WP}. The time that the address must be valid before the assertion of $\overline{WE}$ (t_{AS}) is typically zero, which simply means that $\overline{WE}$ cannot be asserted before the address is valid.

Figure 4.14. Memory
write timing.

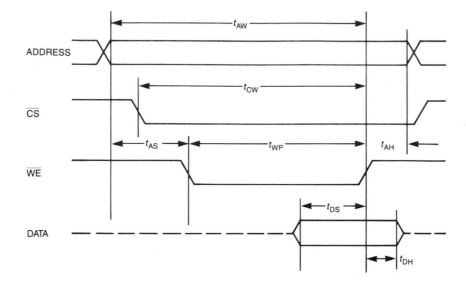

Figure 4.14. Memory write timing.

The data must be provided to the memory for the setup time t_{DS} before the negation of $\overline{WE}$, and it must remain for the hold time t_{DH} after the negation of $\overline{WE}$. The setup time is not generally a problem, since the microprocessor provides the data early in the cycle. Meeting the memory's data hold time can be difficult when using a microprocessor that provides only a short hold time. If gating or buffers delay the $\overline{WE}$ signal from the microprocessor more than the data is delayed by the data buffers (if any), the available hold time is further reduced. Thus, careful attention must be paid to the speed of all devices in the $\overline{WE}$ generation path. Note that data bus buffers help this problem slightly, since they delay the change in the data at the end of the cycle and therefore provide additional hold time for the memory.

Some memories require that the data be valid when $\overline{WE}$ is asserted, and thus have additional timing considerations. Dynamic RAMs also have a variety of additional timing considerations, as described in Sec. 4.7.

How much timing margin is enough? This depends on the type of specifications used in the calculations and on the cost and reliability needs of the application. If all delays used in the calculations are true worst-case values (as they should be), and if all delays are taken into consideration, then a timing margin of zero is acceptable. However, *all* delay factors must be accounted for, including propagation time of the signals through wires and printed circuit traces. As a practical matter, designing for a margin of 10 ns or so (not including trace delays) allows enough margin to eliminate the need to consider trace delays explicitly. All specifications used should be absolute maximums over temperature and supply voltage variations. "Typical" specifications, while widely advertised, are of no use in the design of reliable systems. Even the "worst-case" specifications of standard S and LS TTL devices and some peripheral chips are at 25°C and with little capacitive loading. Thus, additional margin must be allowed if the system is expected to operate over a wide temperature range or if the capacitive loading limits are exceeded. (Newer logic families such as the AS, ALS, and F series of TTL devices and HC and AC CMOS devices do provide timing specifications that are valid over the full temperature range and with a moderate capacitive load.)

The worst-case value for a particular delay is not always its maximum value; in some situations it is the minimum value. For example, the additional data hold time for a write cycle provided by a data bus buffer is the minimum delay of that buffer. For standard S and LS TTL devices, no minimum delays are specified. The most conservative value to use in this case is 0, but ⅓ or ½ of the specified typical is often used. Many newer logic families provide minimum delay specifications. Be careful, however, that the minimum delay is specified with a capacitive load comparable to or less than that in the application; if specified with a larger capacitive load, it will not be a true minimum.

In some cases, full worst-case design may be too conservative. The application and the market must be considered; for a consumer product, cost is critical and reliability, while always important, is not as critical as in a machine control computer or a medical instrument. Most devices will perform much better than their worst-case specifications. Many existing designs of successful products are found to not work worst-case if they are carefully analyzed, and often no problems occur. However, this has the potential to cause production and service nightmares.

See Sec. 4.12.2 for an example of a detailed memory timing analysis.

4.3 EPROM

Erasable programmable read-only memories (EPROMs) are widely used for program storage in microprocessor systems. They are nonvolatile and can be erased and reprogrammed when changes are necessary. Thus, they are useful during product development when they can be repeatedly erased and reprogrammed with new software versions. They are also used for low- to moderate-volume production.

4.3.1 EPROM Nomenclature

All common EPROMs are 8 bits wide, but their size is typically rated by the total number of bits. The first commercial EPROM was Intel's 1702. This chip had a 2-Kbit (256-byte) capacity, required three power supply voltages, and was very slow. Despite these disadvantages, the 1702 provided a capability never before available and was widely used until larger devices were introduced. It was followed by the 2704, the 2708, and the 2716. (For most EPROMs, the last two digits of the part number, or three digits for larger sizes, indicate the size in kilobits.) The 2716 2K-byte device was the first to offer single power supply operation and dominated the market for several years. It has since been replaced by larger and faster devices, such as the 2764, 27128, 27256, and 27512.

Not all manufacturers use identical part numbers. The 27xxx series is used by Intel and several other manufacturers. However, other numbers are also used, most commonly a prefix of 25 instead of 27. Many, but not all, manufacturers' devices of a given type are pin compatible. Chip "shrinks" to a design with smaller dimensions are often done to reduce chip size and increase speed, and these are often designated with an "A" suffix.

EPROMs are available in NMOS and CMOS. CMOS EPROMs are commonly designated 27Cxxx. They are more expensive than their NMOS counterparts and are used primarily in systems in which low power consumption is critical.

4.3.2   EPROM Programming

EPROMs are programmed by an instrument called a *PROM programmer,* and are then inserted into the application system. Programming typically takes from 1 to 5 min, depending on the type of programmer and the size of the memory. EPROMs retain their contents for years without power. The contents can be erased by shining an ultraviolet light into the window in the top of the IC package. The EPROM can then be reprogrammed, and this cycle can be repeated many times.

To program an EPROM, a programming voltage of typically 12 to 25 V (depending on device type) is applied to the V_{PP} pin. The address pins are driven with the address of the memory location to be programmed, and the data to be programmed is applied to the data lines. Finally, the $\overline{CE}$ pin is pulsed low, and the data is stored internally. Note that only during programming do the data pins serve as inputs; during normal operation, the memory is a read-only device and the data pins are outputs only.

Early EPROMs required a 25-V programming voltage. This was reduced in succeeding generations to 21 V and then 12.5 V. For several of the basic device types (such as the 2764), there are versions available requiring each of these three voltages. It is important to verify the correct programming voltage (from the manufacturer's data sheet) before programming the device, since damage can occur to the EPROM and the EPROM programmer if the wrong voltage is used. A common side effect of a chip "shrink" is a reduced programming voltage, so "A" versions often require a lower voltage.

4.3.3   EPROM Interfacing: Using the Standby Mode

Figure 4.15 shows the circuitry to connect a 27256 EPROM to a microprocessor bus. The 27256 is a 32K $\times$ 8 device, so it has 15 address lines and 8 data lines. These connect directly to the system buses. The $\overline{CE}$ input controls the state of the entire chip; when $\overline{CE}$ is false, the chip is disabled and enters a standby mode. In this mode, power consumption is greatly reduced: the maximum supply current for Intel's 27256 is 100 mA in active mode and 40 mA in standby mode. (Power consumption and timing specifications for equivalent memory ICs from other manufacturers may be different.) Thus, it is desirable to enable the EPROM only when it is being accessed. This is accomplished by connecting $\overline{CE}$ to the address select signal from the address decoder; the chip is then selected only when its address is present on the address bus. No control signals need to be gated into the $\overline{CE}$ signal. The bus timing is provided by $\overline{READ}$, which drives $\overline{OE}$. The $\overline{OE}$ signal is ignored unless $\overline{CE}$ is asserted, so the EPROM's outputs are enabled only when the address select signal and $\overline{READ}$ are both asserted.

The separation of the chip select function into two components, output enable and chip enable, has several timing implications. Figure 4.16 shows the timing diagram for

Figure 4.15. Standard EPROM interface circuit.

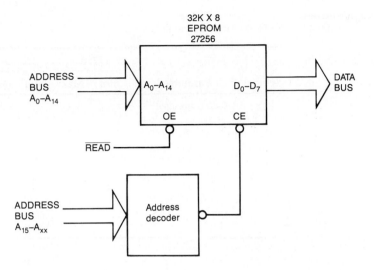

Figure 4.16. EPROM timing diagram. *(Courtesy of Intel Corporation.)*

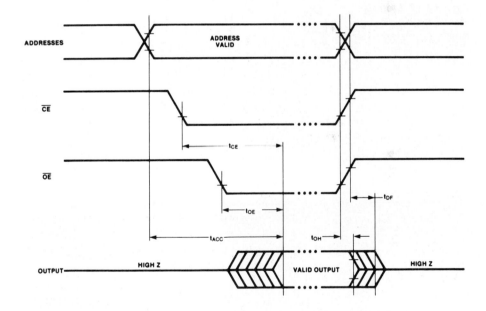

the 27256, and Table 4.2 lists the timing specifications. The main specification is the access time from address to data, t_{ACC}, which is 250 ns for the standard part (faster and slower versions are available, as shown in the table). Note that the access time from chip enable, t_{CE}, is the same as the access time from address. This means that the access time does not begin until the valid address is present and chip enable is asserted. Because $\overline{CE}$ is generated by the address decoder, whose input also comes from the address bus, there is a delay from when a valid address is available to when $\overline{CE}$ is asserted. Thus, the delay time of the address decoder must be added to the access time of the EPROM to calculate the effective access time of the system. For example, if the

Table 4.2   EPROM Timing Specifications

Symbol	Parameter	27256-1		27256-2		27256		27256-3	
		Min	Max	Min	Max	Min	Max	Min	Max
t_{ACC}	Address to output delay		170		200		250		300
t_{CE}	$\overline{CE}$ to output delay		170		200		250		300
t_{OE}	$\overline{OE}$ to output delay		65		75		100		120
t_{DF}	$\overline{OE}$ or $\overline{CE}$ high to output data float	0	55	0	55	0	60	0	105
t_{OH}	Output hold from address, $\overline{CE}$ or $\overline{OE}$, whichever occurs first	0		0		0		0	

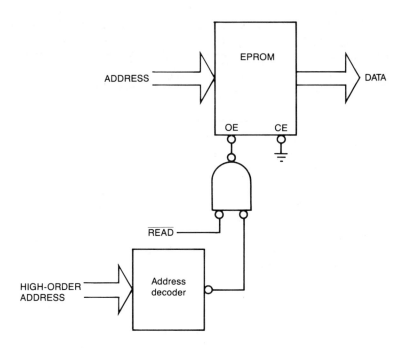

Figure 4.17. EPROM interface for maximum speed.

address decoder is a 74LS138, worst-case delay from address to $\overline{CE}$ is 41 ns; the effective memory access time is therefore 250 ns + 41 ns = 291 ns. (A 74ALS138 decoder can be used to reduce the decoder delay to 18 ns.)

Thus, a speed penalty is paid for the lower-power benefit of the standby mode. For applications in which speed is the paramount consideration, $\overline{CE}$ can be grounded as shown in Fig. 4.17. The EPROM is then always in the active mode. The address decoder output is ANDed with $\overline{READ}$, and the result provides the $\overline{OE}$ control. (Alternatively, $\overline{READ}$ can be used as an enable to the address decoder.) Because the response time to output enable is much faster than the response time to address (100 ns vs. 250 ns), the delay of the address decoder does not add to the effective access time. As long as $\overline{OE}$ is asserted within 150 ns after the address becomes valid, the 250 ns access time will be met.

In choosing such a configuration, the designer must keep in mind the power consumption consequences. If there is only a single EPROM, the difference is not so great. If we assume that the EPROM is enabled 30% of the time, then the average current drain if standby mode is used is

$$I_{CC(av)} = I_{CC(active)} \times 30\% + I_{CC(standby)} \times 70\%$$

For Intel's 27256, $I_{CC(active)} = 100$ mA
$$I_{CC(standby)} = 40 \text{ mA}$$

so $I_{CC(avg)} = 58$ mA

Using the high-speed configuration results in a continuous power drain of 100 mA, or an increase of 42 mA.

With more EPROMs in the system, the power savings become more significant. If the standard configuration is used, only one EPROM is enabled at any time. The current drain for an eight-EPROM system in this configuration is:

$$I_{CC} = I_{CC(avg)} + 7 \times I_{CC(standby)} = 338 \text{ mA}$$

If the high-speed configuration were used, total power consumption would be 8×100 mA $= 800$ mA. Thus, the power savings in this case is 462 mA, or approximately 2.3 W.

4.3.4 EPROM Sizes and Pin Assignments

The 2732A is the largest EPROM available in a 24-pin package. For larger sizes, a 28-pin package is needed for additional address lines. (There is no standard 26-pin package.) To provide pin compatibility for both package sizes, the pinout for the 28-pin EPROMs is the same as the 24-pin devices in the "lower" 24 pins, as shown in Fig. 4.18. A 24-pin EPROM can thus be plugged into a 28-pin socket. (Note, however, that this configuration provides another way to plug the chip in wrong; it must be at the proper end of the socket.)

The programming voltage V_{PP}, which shares the output enable pin on the 2732A, is moved to pin 1 for the larger devices. Pin 28 is assigned to V_{CC} to maintain the standard "corner power" configuration. On the 2764, pin 26 (which corresponds to pin 24 on a 24-pin device) is left as a "no connect" so that power can be connected to both pins 26 and 28 for compatibility with both device sizes. For the 27128 and 27256, however, this pin is needed as an address line, so a jumper that connects pin 26 to V_{CC} or to A_{13} is required for full compatibility. The 27512 needs pin 1 (used by V_{PP} in smaller 28-pin devices) for A_{15}, so it returns to the 2732A technique of using pin 22 for both $\overline{OE}$ and V_{PP}.

The 2764 and 27128 EPROMs use pin 27 to provide an additional control line for programming. This pin must be at logic high during read operations. On the 27256 and

Figure 4.18. Byte-wide EPROM pin assignments.

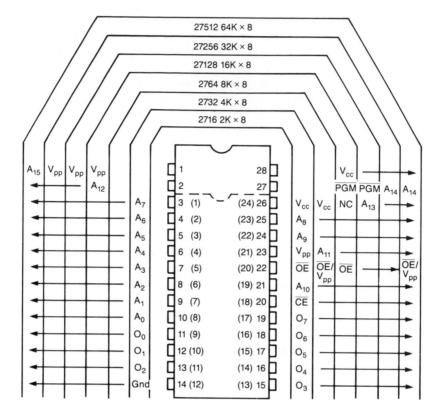

27512, this pin is needed as an address line, and the programming control is performed with $\overline{\text{CE}}$. Thus, to allow use of all EPROMs including the 27256 and 27512, there must be a jumper to allow pin 27 to be connected to V_{CC} or to A_{14}. Other than these pinout changes, the timing and other interface details are similar for all EPROM sizes.

A 27512 EPROM has a capacity of 64 Kbytes, which entirely fills the address space of a microprocessor with a 16-bit address bus. Some address space is needed for RAM and possibly I/O. One solution to this problem is Intel's 27513 paged EPROM. This device is organized as four pages of 16 Kbytes each. At power-up, page zero is selected. A different page is selected by writing to the 2-bit page select register. Thus, only 16 Kbytes can be addressed directly, but the total memory is 64 Kbytes. This leaves 48 Kbytes of address space available for RAM. The page register is written by pulsing the $\overline{\text{WR}}$ input on pin 27. This is the standard pin assignment for a byte-wide static RAM, as described in Sec. 4.5. One disadvantage of a paged EPROM is that software must write to the page register to access any location beyond the currently selected page. This is simple for data accesses but can be awkward when the EPROM is used for program storage.

The 1-Mbit EPROMs, with a 128-Kbyte capacity, are likely to be used primarily with 16-bit microprocessors. Thus, a 16-bit-wide organization is natural. This requires a 40-pin package, unless address and data pins are multiplexed. AMD's 27C1024 is an example of such an EPROM.

Intel makes 1-Mbit EPROMs in three different organizations. The 27210 is a 40-

pin, 64K × 16 device similar to AMD's 27C1024. The 27010 is a 128K × 8 device in a 32-pin package. The pinout is compatible with standard 28-pin EPROMs except for the additional four pins, so a circuit board designed for this chip can also accommodate smaller EPROMs and other byte-wide memories. The 27011 is a paged device similar to the 27513 described previously. It is organized as eight pages, each 16K × 8, allowing it to be packaged in a standard 28-pin DIP.

4.4 MASK-PROGRAMMED ROMS

The erasability of EPROMs is a great benefit during product development when the program is likely to be changed frequently. In production, however, erasability is of no use. EPROMs are relatively expensive because they require a special package with a transparent lid, and because the chip itself is large. Mask-programmed ROMs, which are programmed during the manufacture of the chip itself, are generally less expensive. Many different types are available, including versions that are pin-compatible with each of the EPROM types.

There are several disadvantages associated with the use of mask-programmed ROMs, however. Because they are programmed as part of the IC manufacturing process, the manufacturer must make special masks for each pattern. There is a charge for this, typically $1000 to $5000, and a lead time before parts can be delivered (typically 3 to 10 weeks). For low-volume production, the amortized mask charge makes mask-programmed parts more expensive than EPROMs, and the minimum order quantity can also be a problem. In addition, if a bug is found in the program, all the ROMs in inventory must be scrapped if they are mask-programmed. Mask-programmed ROMs are thus justified only for high-volume applications in which the program has been well-tested. It is best to use EPROMs for the first production run so that some customer feedback and production experience can be obtained before freezing the program in silicon (the modern version of "cast in concrete").

Another option is the *one-time-programmable (OTP)* EPROM. This is a standard UV-erasable EPROM that is packaged in plastic rather than in the special ceramic package with the clear window. Thus, it is programmed like an EPROM but cannot be erased by a standard EPROM eraser. (Technically, it is therefore a PROM and not an EPROM, but the term PROM is generally used for fusible-link bipolar devices.) The reduced package cost results in a total cost between that of mask-programmed and erasable devices. The mask charge and lead times are eliminated, and the parts can be inventoried in their unprogrammed state and programmed just prior to final assembly. Waste due to program changes is thus minimized, and only one part type must be purchased for any number of different programs.

The final selection of the proper memory type for program storage thus depends on several factors. The basic analysis is to divide the mask charge by the expected production volume to determine the amortized mask cost, and add that figure to the unit price of the ROM. Unless the result is significantly less than the price of an EPROM, mask programming is not justified. For example, suppose that the mask charge is $3000 and that a one-time programmable EPROM costs $1 more than the ROM. At a volume of 100 units, the amortized mask charge is $30 each, and the EPROM is clearly the better choice. At 3000 units, the amortized mask charge is $1, so the cost is equal.

At 50,000 units, the amortized mask charge is only $0.06, so the ROM is clearly less expensive.

The real cost of the mask-programmed part is more difficult to calculate and requires estimating how many times the program might need to be changed and how many old ROMs would have to be scrapped. The difference in cost between mask-programmed and user-programmed devices has steadily shrunk as EPROM technology has matured, thus requiring higher volumes to justify mask programming. The one-time programmable EPROM raises even higher the minimum production volume for which mask programming is desirable.

The 1-Mbit and larger ROMs raise the possibility of storing major application programs in a single IC. A large ROM in a cartridge is an alternative to a floppy disk for program distribution and has the advantages of being much more difficult to copy illicitly and not needing to be read into RAM to be executed. However, the ROM cost is higher, and committing a megabyte of code to mask-programmed ROM requires a great deal of confidence in the quality and stability of the program. New versions (with bugs fixed and perhaps new features) are much more expensive to produce when using ROMs for software distribution. One of the principal application areas for large ROMs is for data storage, such as character font memory for laser printers.

4.5 THE BYTE-WIDE STANDARD: DESIGN FOR INTERCHANGEABILITY

The previous sections described the standard pinout configuration for EPROMs and ROMs and showed how it makes upgrading to a larger device possible without circuit board changes. In fact, this basic pin configuration is used by a variety of devices, including RAMs, ROMs, and EEPROMs. Table 4.3 lists some of the compatible devices and shows the pin functions that change from one to another. The pins not shown are the same for all devices, except that the data pins are, of course, bidirectional for read/write devices. This pinout standard is often called the *byte-wide* format or the *universal 28-pin site*.

As the table shows, there are four pins whose functions change among the various "compatible" devices. Complete compatibility with all devices in a single socket thus requires jumpers on each of the four pins so that each can be connected to any of the required signals. Note that there are two numbers for each socket pin, depending on whether a 24-pin or 28-pin device is installed.

Figure 4.19 shows a circuit that allows the use of any of the RAMs or EPROMs in this table. Note that 32-Kbyte static RAMs use a different pin for A_{14} than do 32-Kbyte EPROMs in order to keep the same $\overline{WE}$ pin as used in smaller RAMs. In most applications, the range of desired devices is limited to a subset of the devices listed in the table, and fewer jumpers are used. The design example in Sec. 4.12 provides several examples of jumper configurations.

Electrically erasable PROMs (EEPROMs) and nonvolatile RAMs (NVRAMs) are also available in the byte-wide standard pinout. Some are pin-compatible with static RAMs, but many require additional control signals. These devices are described in Sec. 4.9.

While these jumper configurations allow the same socket to support a variety of

Table 4.3   Pin Assignments for Universal 28-pin Site*

Device type	Size, bytes	No. of pins in package	Pin 1	Pin 23 (21)	Pin 26 (24)	Pin 27
EPROMs:						
2716	2K	24		V_{PP}	V_{CC}	
2732	4K	24		A_{11}	V_{CC}	
2764	8K	28	V_{PP}	A_{11}	NC	$\overline{PGM}$
27128	16K	28	V_{PP}	A_{11}	A_{13}	$\overline{PGM}$
27256	32K	28	V_{PP}	A_{11}	A_{13}	A_{14}
27512	64K	28	A_{15}	A_{11}	A_{13}	A_{14}
RAMs:						
6116	2K	24		$\overline{WE}$	V_{CC}	
6264	8K	28	NC	A_{11}	CS_2	$\overline{WE}$
62256	32K	28	A_{14}	A_{11}	A_{13}	$\overline{WE}$
EEPROMs:						
X2816A	2K	24		$\overline{WE}$	V_{CC}	
2817A	2K	28	RDY/$\overline{BUSY}$	NC	NC	$\overline{WE}$
X2864A	8K	28	NC	A_{11}	NC	$\overline{WE}$
28256	32K	28	A_{14}	A_{11}	A_{13}	$\overline{WE}$
NVRAMs:						
X2001	128	24		$\overline{WE}$	V_{CC}	Pin 19=$\overline{NE}$
X2004	512	28	$\overline{NE}$	NC	NC	$\overline{WE}$

*Pins not shown are the same for all devices (see Fig. 4.18). NC = no connect; $\overline{NE}$ = nonvolatile enable.

Figure 4.19. Jumpers for universal byte-wide socket to support EPROM from 2K to 64K and RAM from 2K to 32K.

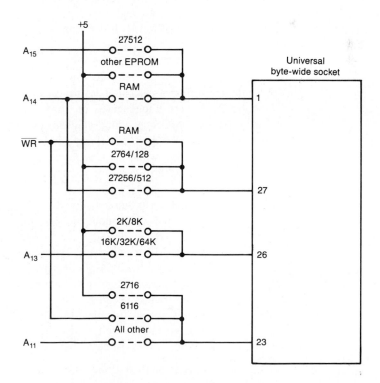

devices, the address decoding logic must also be considered. The address decoder outputs must reflect the size of the memory devices being selected. The simplest and most flexible way to accomplish this is with a PROM or PAL address decoder. The memory chip size can thus be changed by programming a new PROM or PAL or by selecting one of several decoding configurations via jumpers on inputs to the PROM or PAL.

4.6   STATIC RAM

Read-only memories are useful for permanent program storage but cannot provide all of a system's memory needs. Data and programs that change during the operation of the system must be stored in a read/write memory (RAM). (As described in Chap. 1, RAM originally stood for random-access memory but is generally used to refer to semiconductor read/write memory.) In a small system with all software stored in ROM, only a small amount of RAM may be needed to store data and the program stack. In systems using mass-storage devices such as disk or tape drives, relatively large amounts of RAM are needed to store programs and data read from the mass-storage device.

A *static* RAM is one that retains its data as long as power is applied, without any action from the control logic. The basic storage element in a static RAM is a flip-flop, which is stable in either of two states as long as power is present. *Dynamic* RAM, on the other hand, uses a capacitor as the basic storage element. Because charge leaks off the capacitor, dynamic RAM requires continual refreshing to maintain its contents. Static RAM is simpler to use and is more cost-effective than dynamic RAM in systems using a small amount of RAM. It can also be battery-backed for nonvolatility, as described in Sec. 4.9.6.

The most common static RAM sizes for use in microprocessor systems are 2K $\times$ 8, 8K $\times$ 8, and 32K $\times$ 8. Common part numbers are 6116, 6264, and 62256, respectively, although different part numbers are used by various manufacturers. Most byte-wide static RAMs are implemented in "mixed-MOS" technology and use NMOS memory cells and CMOS decoding, control, and interface circuits, even though they are often labeled as CMOS RAMs. The NMOS memory cells require fewer transistors and thus less chip area, while the CMOS support logic reduces power consumption. Full CMOS RAMs are also available for applications requiring extremely low power consumption.

Figure 4.20 shows the pin functions for the 6116, 6264, and 62256, which are compatible with standard byte-wide pinout conventions. The 6264 has two chip selects: the normal active-low $\overline{\text{CS}}$ on pin 20 and an active-high CS on pin 26. Both must be asserted to enable the RAM. In a universal byte-wide socket, pin 26 must have a jumper to connect it to V_{CC} for use with 24-pin devices. This configuration keeps the active-high chip select always asserted, and the active-low $\overline{\text{CS}}$ is connected to the address select signal from the address decoder.

The 62256 requires two additional address lines. Thus, the second chip select input is sacrificed, and pins 1 and 26 are used for the two most significant address lines.

Static RAM timing follows the basic memory timing described in Sec. 4.2.4. Com-

Figure 4.20. Byte-wide static RAM pin assignments.

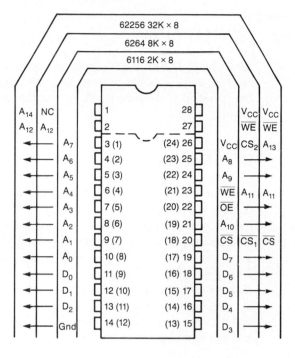

mon static RAMs have access times of 120 or 150 ns; high-speed versions are available with access times below 100 ns. Access from $\overline{OE}$ (t_{OE}) is relatively fast. For Hitachi's HM6264P-15, access from address is 150 ns, and t_{OE} is 70 ns.

Most CMOS static RAMs are available in low-power versions (often designated by an "LP" suffix). The low-power versions may not have lower operating current, but they have a much lower standby current for applications with battery-backup. Power consumption is typically reduced from 200 mW in active mode ($\overline{CE}$ asserted) to under 100 μW in standby. Full CMOS (not mixed-MOS) RAMs have standby power consumption as low as a few microwatts.

Static RAMs are available in many other densities and configurations. Byte-wide RAMs have the advantage of compatibility with a wide range of other devices, such as EPROMs and EEPROMs. However, the 600-mil-wide package used in this configuration requires a substantial amount of board space. Thus, they are also available in "skinny" 300-mil-wide packages for applications in which physical size is more important than compatibility with other memory types.

In addition, having eight data pins on every memory chip is inefficient in a large memory array. One-bit-wide static RAMs are often used for large, high-speed memories. Having only one data bit per RAM chip reduces the pin count and allows use of an 18-pin package, significantly reducing the board space. High-speed static RAMs are available in 1-, 4-, and 8-bit-wide configurations with access times commonly ranging from 15 to 85 ns. They are often used in high-speed 16- and 32-bit microprocessor systems that need fast memory for no-wait-state operation.

4.7   DYNAMIC RAM

While static RAM is much simpler to interface, large memory systems almost universally use dynamic RAM due to its lower cost and greater density. This section describes the operation of dynamic RAM, its interface requirements, and an example interface circuit.

4.7.1   Basic Operation

Dynamic RAMs use the charge on a capacitor, rather than the state of a flip-flop, to indicate if a memory cell contains a 1 or a 0. The benefit of this approach is a drastic reduction in the chip area required for each cell. A static memory cell requires four to six transistors, whereas a dynamic cell requires only one. Thus, there is approximately a 4:1 ratio in chip size for a given number of memory cells. Because chip cost is closely related to chip size, this same ratio applies to cost per bit. Another effect of this ratio is that the largest available dynamic RAM chips tend to have four times the capacity of the largest static RAM chips.

Intel's pioneering 1103 dynamic RAM, introduced in 1970, had a capacity of 1 Kbit and was advertised as the first semiconductor memory to be less expensive than magnetic cores. It was followed with a succession of larger and easier-to-use RAMs. Small dynamic RAMs (under 64 Kbits) have been replaced in new designs by static RAMs or larger dynamic RAMs. The 16-Kbit dynamic RAM was the first very high-volume RAM chip and for several years was the mainstay of computer memory systems. It has now been replaced by 64-Kbit, 256-Kbit, and 1-Mbit RAMs.

In large memory systems with tens or hundreds of ICs, it is most efficient to use 1-bit-wide memory ICs, since this minimizes the number of data pins required on each IC. Thus, the most common dynamic RAMs are one bit wide. One-bit-wide memory ICs are a disadvantage in small systems, since a minimum of eight chips are needed for an 8-bit-wide memory. Thus, the smallest memory system that can be built with 64K × 1 dynamic RAMs is 64 Kbytes. For 16-bit systems, 16 chips are needed and the minimum memory system size is 128 Kbytes. With 256K × 1 dynamic RAMs, the minimum system size is 256 Kbytes for 8-bit systems and 512 Kbytes for 16-bit systems.

Dynamic RAMs are also available in 4- and 8-bit-wide configurations. However, since wider-word RAMs are less desirable in large memory systems, they are used in lower volume. In addition, more pins are required. Thus, they are more expensive than 1-bit-wide RAMs with the same capacity. Their advantage is that they allow, for example, a single 256-Kbit chip to be used as a 32-Kbyte RAM. They are also used in graphics applications in which very wide word memory systems are needed (see Chap. 7).

The internal circuits of dynamic RAMs are designed to consume power only during the brief period during which that circuit is in use. For example, the address input buffers are enabled only when the transition of a control input indicates that a new address is being presented. This reduces the average power consumption significantly, but has another, less desirable, effect: the power supply current is not steady but has sharp peaks during access to the RAM. This means that the impedance of the power supply must be very low so that the current spikes do not cause a voltage drop. Because

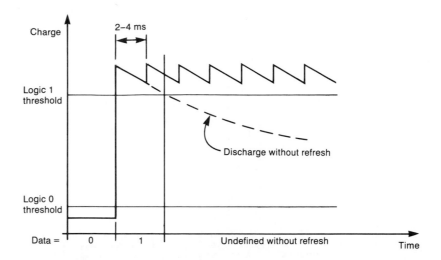

Figure 4.21. Dynamic memory cell discharge and refresh.

the rise time of the current pulses is very fast, a decoupling capacitor with good RF performance must be connected directly from power to ground on each chip.

The major disadvantage of dynamic RAM is that the charge stored on the capacitors leaks off, and unless the memory is *refreshed* the cells that once contained ones will change to zeros. Figure 4.21 illustrates the process of cell discharge and refresh. A discharged cell represents a 0. When a 1 is written to the cell, it is charged to a level somewhat above the minimum charge threshold for a 1. The cell then immediately begins to discharge due to leakage. As long as the charge stays above the threshold, no data is lost. If the cell is allowed to discharge for too long, however, the 1 will turn into a 0. Most dynamic RAMs are guaranteed to hold data for only 2 to 4 ms before such errors may occur. (The actual time the data will remain is much longer for typical devices, but this cannot be depended upon.)

Thus, to prevent data loss, each cell must be refreshed every 2 to 4 ms. The refresh process consists of reading the data from the cell and then writing it back, thereby bringing the cell back to full charge. Dynamic RAMs are designed so that they automatically rewrite the data whenever it is read. Thus, all that is necessary for refresh is a simple read. It is also not necessary to refresh every cell individually or to perform a full read cycle, as explained in the following section.

4.7.2 Addressing and Control

A simplified block diagram of a dynamic RAM chip is shown in Fig. 4.22. The memory cells are organized into a square or rectangular array. An individual memory cell is selected by a column address and a row address. The address is presented to the chip in two parts, as shown in the read cycle timing diagram in Fig. 4.23. (This timing diagram is simplified for clarity, and does not include all timing parameters.) First the row address is driven on the address inputs, and the $\overline{\text{RAS}}$ (row address strobe) control line is asserted. This clocks the row address into an internal row address latch. The row address must be stable for some time before $\overline{\text{RAS}}$ is asserted (setup time, t_{ASR}), and also

Figure 4.22. Dynamic
RAM addressing sim-
plified block diagram.

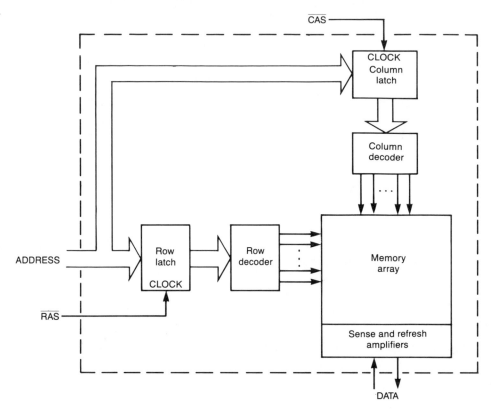

Figure 4.22. Dynamic RAM addressing simplified block diagram.

for some time after $\overline{\text{RAS}}$ is asserted (hold time, t_{RAH}). The address inputs are then changed to the column address, and $\overline{\text{CAS}}$ (column address strobe) is asserted. $\overline{\text{CAS}}$ also serves as the output enable; whenever $\overline{\text{CAS}}$ is asserted, the three-state driver on the data out pin is enabled. The time when $\overline{\text{CAS}}$ can be asserted is determined by the minimum RAS-TO-CAS delay, t_{RCD}. In addition, setup and hold times for the column address must be met.

The data is available after the access times from $\overline{\text{RAS}}$ (t_{RAC}) and $\overline{\text{CAS}}$ (t_{CAC}) have both been met. The limit of performance is determined by the access time from $\overline{\text{RAS}}$. If the assertion of $\overline{\text{CAS}}$ is delayed further than required, then maximum performance will not be obtained and access time from $\overline{\text{CAS}}$ will determine the overall access time.

There is another timing specification that is of importance: the $\overline{\text{RAS}}$ precharge time, t_{RP}. The precharge time is required for the memory circuits to recover from the previous access; another cycle cannot be started the instant the data is available. Thus, the cycle time for dynamic memories is greater than the access time. The difference between the access time and the cycle time is the precharge time. A dynamic RAM with an access time of 150 ns typically has a cycle time of 260 ns.

Figure 4.24 shows the timing diagram for the write cycle. The addressing sequence is the same; the only difference is that $\overline{\text{WRITE}}$ is asserted, and data is supplied by the microprocessor on the DATA IN pin. There are two types of write cycles, depending on the timing relationship of $\overline{\text{WRITE}}$ and $\overline{\text{CAS}}$. The timing diagram shows an *early write,*

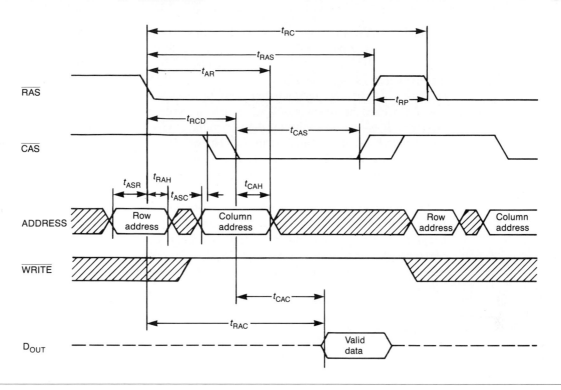

Figure 4.23.   Dynamic RAM read cycle timing.

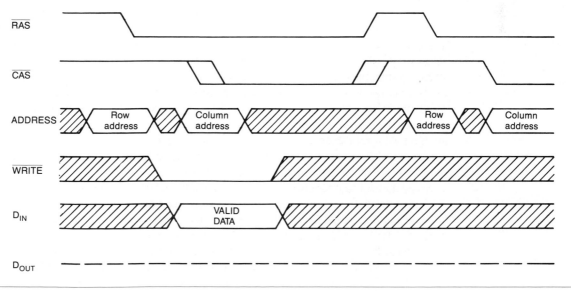

Figure 4.24.   Dynamic RAM write cycle timing.

in which $\overline{\text{WRITE}}$ is asserted before $\overline{\text{CAS}}$. In this case, setup and hold time specifications for the write pulse and the data are referenced to the falling edge of $\overline{\text{CAS}}$. In a *late write*, $\overline{\text{WRITE}}$ is asserted after $\overline{\text{CAS}}$. If $\overline{\text{WRITE}}$ is negated when $\overline{\text{CAS}}$ is asserted, the RAM enables its output driver. (This is the normal condition in a read cycle.) Thus, in a late write cycle, the output buffer is briefly enabled for the time between the assertion of $\overline{\text{CAS}}$ and the assertion of $\overline{\text{WRITE}}$. If a late write cycle is used, the RAM's DATA OUT pin should not be connected directly to the DATA IN pin or to the system's data bus, since a bus conflict would occur. In a late write cycle, setup and hold time specifications for the write pulse and the data are referenced to the falling edge of $\overline{\text{WRITE}}$. Note that, unlike most memory types, dynamic RAMs store the data at the leading edge of the control signal.

Presenting the address in two parts has the advantage of reducing by 50 percent the number of address pins required. Eight address pins provide 16 address lines for 64K dynamic RAMs, and nine pins provide 18 address lines for 256K RAMs. This is important because it reduces the package size. Dynamic RAMs are widely used in large systems with many memory chips, in which the physical chip size has a significant impact on system size.

4.7.3   Dynamic RAM Refresh

Whenever a row in a dynamic RAM is selected by providing its address and pulsing $\overline{\text{RAS}}$, *all cells in that row* are refreshed in parallel. In fact, no $\overline{\text{CAS}}$ pulse at all is required for refresh cycles. The entire dynamic RAM can be refreshed by providing each possible row address in sequence, pulsing $\overline{\text{RAS}}$ for each. This type of refresh is thus called *RAS-only* refresh. Since the RAM's output buffer is enabled only when $\overline{\text{CAS}}$ is asserted, the data bus is not affected during refresh cycles.

The most natural internal organization for a 64K dynamic RAM is 256×256. Devices with this organization require 256 refresh cycles (that is, 256 different refresh addresses). However, 16K dynamic RAMs (now obsolete) are organized as 128×128, and thus require only 128 refresh cycles. For compatibility with existing 16K RAM refresh logic designs, many 64K dynamic RAMs are organized internally as 128×512, and therefore require only 128 refresh cycles. The address is nevertheless multiplexed as two 8-bit portions, but the most significant bit of the row address is used internally as part of the column address. During refresh, only a 7-bit row address is required; the most significant address line is ignored. Some 64K RAMs, however, require an 8-bit refresh address and 256 refresh cycles every 4 ms. A similar situation occurs with 256K dynamic RAMs. They use a 256×1024 internal organization, so only 256 refresh cycles are required.

Some dynamic RAMs also allow *hidden* refresh cycles, as shown in Fig. 4.25. Hidden refresh cycles are performed during a normal read cycle. After $\overline{\text{RAS}}$ and $\overline{\text{CAS}}$ are asserted and the desired location addressed, $\overline{\text{RAS}}$ is negated, the refresh address is supplied, and $\overline{\text{RAS}}$ is asserted again. The output data remains valid while the refresh cycle occurs, which is why this is called a hidden refresh cycle. Multiple refresh cycles can be executed and are limited only by the maximum time that $\overline{\text{CAS}}$ may be held asserted.

To simplify refresh requirements, some dynamic RAMs include an on-chip refresh counter, eliminating the need to supply a refresh address to the RAM. An additional

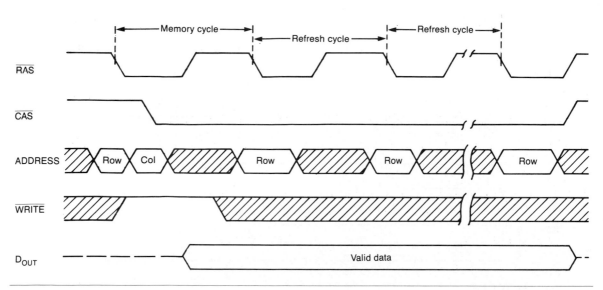

Figure 4.25. Dynamic RAM hidden refresh timing.

control pin that initiates a refresh cycle is used on 64K RAMs with this feature. For 256K RAMs, this pin is needed as an address line. Thus, a different method is used. If $\overline{\text{CAS}}$ is asserted before the leading edge of $\overline{\text{RAS}}$, then a refresh cycle is started. This does not occur in normal operation, since normally $\overline{\text{RAS}}$ is always asserted first. This is called $\overline{\text{CAS}}$ *before* $\overline{\text{RAS}}$ refresh.

4.7.4 Special Dynamic RAM Operating Modes

The previous section described the basic access mode that virtually all common dynamic RAMs support. In addition, there are a number of special features provided in some dynamic RAMs.

Most devices support a read-modify-write cycle, as shown in Fig. 4.26. This allows a byte to be read from memory, modified, and then written back without repeating the addressing sequence. $\overline{\text{RAS}}$ and $\overline{\text{CAS}}$ are held asserted after the data has been read, and when the modified data is available to be written, $\overline{\text{WRITE}}$ is pulsed. Note that since there are separate data in and data out pins, the old data is still available while the new data is being written. This mode is used for byte-write operations on 16-bit-wide memory when using error correcting codes, as described in Sec. 4.10.5.

Several special modes are available for decreasing effective access times. *Page mode* allows a number of locations within an area of memory to be accessed without repeating the entire address. After providing the row address and asserting $\overline{\text{RAS}}$, the column address can be changed a number of times to access a series of locations. Each time a new column address is provided, $\overline{\text{CAS}}$ is pulsed. $\overline{\text{RAS}}$ must be kept asserted throughout the process, and the number of cycles that can be performed is limited by the maximum $\overline{\text{RAS}}$ pulse width allowed. The addresses need not be sequential, and any

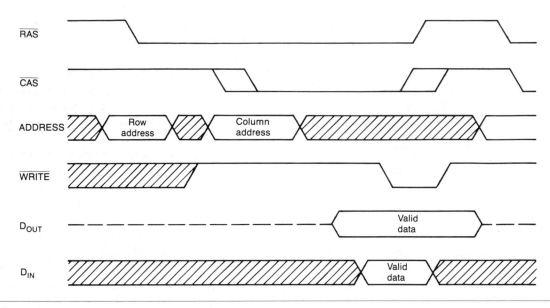

Figure 4.26.   Dynamic RAM read-modify-write cycle timing.

combination of read, write, and read-modify-write cycles is allowed. The access time for the first location in page mode is the same as for a normal access, but successive locations are accessed in approximately half the time of a normal access. This mode can significantly decrease the average access time in memories used for program storage, since typical program execution sequences involve many accesses to sequential, or at least nearby, locations. However, the system control logic to implement page mode is relatively complex. Page mode is therefore not used in most microprocessor systems, since the standard access time is fast enough for most microprocessors.

A number of other special access modes have been devised to decrease effective access time. The most common is *nibble mode,* in which four successive bits are read by simply pulsing $\overline{CAS}$ four times. Only one address is supplied; the column address is internally incremented automatically.

A *static-column* RAM uses a transparent latch for the column address. The row address is strobed in as usual, but the column address flows through the RAM's column address latch if $\overline{CAS}$ is negated. When $\overline{CAS}$ is asserted, the column address is latched, and for a read cycle, the output buffer is enabled. The column access time begins as soon as the column address is supplied to the RAM; in a normal dynamic RAM, the column access time does not begin until $\overline{CAS}$ is asserted. [In some static-column RAMs, $\overline{CAS}$ is renamed $\overline{CS}$ (chip select) to reflect its different function.] The column address can be changed as soon as the desired data is available, allowing rapid access to any location within the same page (all locations with the same row address). This is similar to page mode but provides even faster access times. It is most useful in video display systems and other applications in which minimum access time is critical.

4.7.5 Dynamic RAM Pin Configurations

Figure 4.27 shows the pin configurations for 64K and 256K dynamic RAMs. Although early 16K dynamic RAMs required three power supply voltages, all 64K and larger dynamic RAMs require only a single 5-V supply. Note that although dynamic RAMs use the same power pins as standard TTL devices, the polarity is reversed: V_{cc} on pin 8, and ground on pin 16. For most 64K dynamic RAMs, pin 1 is not used. Some 64K RAMs with internal refresh counters use pin 1 to initiate a refresh cycle. The 256K RAMs use pin 1 for an address pin; since the address is multiplexed, adding one address pin provides two additional address bits, and thus quadruples the address range.

Because of the similar pin configurations, it is relatively simple to design printed circuit boards that can accommodate either 64K or 256K dynamic RAMs. Since pin 1 is not used on most 64K dynamic RAMs, connecting it to the address signal required by 256K RAMs allows operation with either RAM size. However, use of 64K RAMs that use pin 1 as a refresh control requires a jumper to disconnect the address line. Designing the system to use either memory size also affects the multiplexing and address decoding logic.

Unlike byte-wide RAMs, most 1-bit-wide RAMs provide separate data in and data out pins. The pins can be tied together or can be buffered separately. Keeping data input and output paths separate allows late write and read-modify-write cycles to be used. For RAMs that are only 1 bit wide, only one additional pin is required for separate data in and out pins. For wider-word RAMs, this flexibility is usually sacrificed for the sake of a smaller package.

While most dynamic RAM manufacturers follow this standard pin configuration, there are sometimes significant differences between "compatible" parts. When comparing timing specifications for various devices, it is important to look further than the overall access time specification. Even if two RAMs are both specified to have 150 ns access time, for example, the detailed timing (such as access from $\overline{CAS}$ and setup and hold times) may be significantly different. (There is considerably more uniformity among 256K RAMs than among 64K RAMs.) Therefore, specific manufacturers must be kept in mind when designing a system. If multiple sources are desired (as is generally the case), the designer must make up a composite data sheet that shows the worst-case specification for each timing parameter, including all manufacturers that are to be

Figure 4.27. Pin functions for 64K × 1 and 256K × 1 dynamic RAMs.

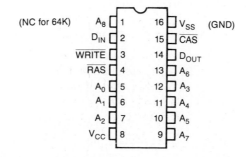

listed as approved vendors. If the system is not pushing the performance of the RAMs, it may be possible to use almost any "compatible" chip. In higher-performance applications, however, it is sometimes necessary to limit the selection to a few manufacturers. If multiple RAM sizes (such as 64K and 256K) are to be supported, then timing parameters for all memory sizes must be considered.

One-megabit dynamic RAMs are available in a variety of configurations. The 16-pin package cannot be used, since there are no pins available for the additional address pin. An 18-pin package is commonly used for $1M \times 1$ RAMs. Larger packages are used for $256K \times 4$ and $128K \times 8$ versions.

4.7.6   Alpha-Particle Noise

Dynamic RAMs have an additional problem that does not appear in static devices. As dynamic RAM density increases, the amount of charge present in each cell becomes smaller and smaller. A high incidence of soft errors was observed in early 16K and 64K dynamic RAMs. (A *soft error* is an error that does not repeat; that is, although the data in a cell has been erroneously changed, the cell is not defective and will work properly when the data is rewritten.) After lengthy investigations, it was determined that the cause of these errors was a type of radiation called *alpha particles*. Alpha particles are helium nuclei that are naturally present in the environment in very small numbers. A major source is radioactive impurities in the IC package itself. If an alpha particle hits a storage capacitor, it can cause the cell to change state.

Alpha particles cannot be eliminated, but a variety of techniques are used to minimize their effects. Decreasing signal impedances and increasing cell capacitance reduces the effect of alpha particles. Special chip coatings that absorb alpha particles are used by some manufacturers, and packaging materials have been improved to minimize radioactive impurities. The most foolproof (but expensive) technique is to implement full error detection and correction, as described in Sec. 4.10.

4.7.7   Dynamic RAM Interfacing

Dynamic RAM Interface Functions
As is apparent from the preceding discussion, interfacing dynamic RAMs to a microprocessor system is far more complex than interfacing static RAMs. The dynamic RAM interface must perform a variety of tasks:

1.   Multiplex the row and column addresses.
2.   Translate the microprocessor's $\overline{\text{READ}}$ and $\overline{\text{WRITE}}$ signals into $\overline{\text{RAS}}$, $\overline{\text{CAS}}$, and $\overline{\text{WRITE}}$ signals compatible with the dynamic RAM's timing.
3.   Keep the RAM refreshed.

The first task is relatively simple, requiring only a multiplexer to select either the lower or upper address bits, as shown in the block diagram in Fig. 4.28. The refresh multiplexer and the row/column multiplexer can be combined into one three-input mul-

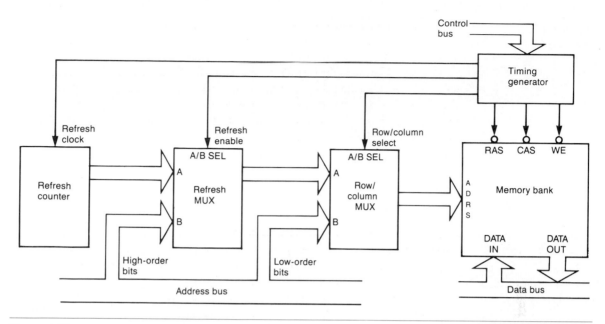

Figure 4.28. Basic dynamic RAM interface block diagram.

tiplexer. (Multiplexer ICs, however, are generally available only as two-input or four-input, so four-input multiplexers are used with one input left open. If software refresh techniques or RAM chips with on-board refresh counters are used, then two-input multiplexers can be used.) Multiplexing can also be implemented with three-state drivers, as shown in Fig. 4.29. For 64K × 1 dynamic RAMs, the row and column addresses are 8 bits each, which is convenient for use with 8-bit three-state drivers. For 256K × 1 dynamic RAMs, the row and column addresses are 9 bits each. Some 9-bit-wide three-state drivers are available, but an 8-bit driver IC plus a single additional driver from part of a second IC is a common solution. If a PAL chip is used to implement the refresh control logic, then it can also include the extra multiplexer bit.

During a refresh cycle, the refresh counter is selected as the address source, and $\overline{\text{RAS}}$ is pulsed. The refresh counter is then incremented to prepare for the next refresh cycle.

When the microprocessor asserts $\overline{\text{READ}}$ or $\overline{\text{WRITE}}$, the control and timing logic must perform a sequence of operations:

1. Wait for the row address to propagate through the multiplexer and for the setup time to elapse.

2. Assert $\overline{\text{RAS}}$.

3. Wait for the row address hold time to elapse.

4. Switch the multiplexer to select the column address.

5. Wait for the multiplexer's propagation delay time and the RAM's column address setup time.

Figure 4.29. Three-
state drivers used to
multiplex dynamic RAM
address sources.

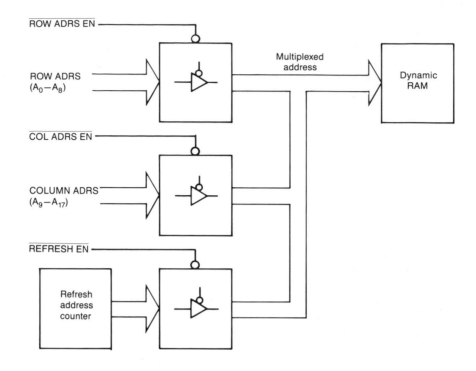

6. Assert $\overline{CAS}$.

7. At the completion of the cycle, negate $\overline{CAS}$ and $\overline{RAS}$ and ensure that the pre-charge time is allowed to elapse before another cycle is attempted.

Each of these events must be precisely timed. If the timing elements depend on one-shots or gate delays, there is a wide variation between minimum and maximum delays. The minimum delay of the delay elements must be sufficient to meet the timing requirements of the memory chip, but the maximum delay of the delay elements determines the worst-case access time. The difference between the minimum and maximum delays is therefore effectively added to the memory IC's access time. Thus, an accurate timing source is required for optimum performance. The timing is often derived from a special component called a *delay line,* which provides delays with an accuracy of ± 1 or 2 ns. Another common approach is to derive the timing from a high-speed clock signal, such as the CPU clock. This can be less expensive but does not provide as much flexibility in optimizing the timing.

Since the RAMs cannot be read or written while a refresh cycle is occurring, the microprocessor cannot always have access to the RAM. The refresh logic must decide when to execute a refresh cycle, and coordinate the refresh with the microprocessor's activities so that a conflict does not occur. The simplest way to do this is to halt the microprocessor every 2 ms and perform a burst of 128 refresh cycles; this is called *burst refresh.* (For some 64K and all 256K dynamic RAMs, the refresh burst is 256 cycles every 4 ms.) Burst refresh can degrade the performance of the microprocessor system. The percentage of time that the microprocessor is halted for refresh is not large, but the length of the burst refresh period increases the system's latency time in responding to an asynchronous event, such as a request for service from a peripheral interface.

The other approach is *distributed refresh,* in which a single refresh cycle is performed every 15 μs resulting in a total of 128 cycles in a 2-ms period (or, for some 64K RAMs and all 256K RAMs, 256 cycles in a 4-ms period). If the refresh cycles are triggered by a refresh timer independent of the microprocessor system timing, then a conflict will sometimes occur when both the refresh logic and the microprocessor require access to the RAM at the same time. If a refresh cycle is in progress, the microprocessor must wait for it to be complete; this is easily accomplished by delaying the "ready" signal to the microprocessor to cause one or more wait states. The refresh control logic must also handle the situation in which both the refresh request and the microprocessor's access request occur simultaneously. Highest performance is obtained by granting the cycle to the microprocessor in this situation, as long as refresh is not delayed too long. The arbiter that performs this function requires careful design, or else reliability problems can result due to the metastable condition that can occur when a flip-flop input is changed during its setup or hold time.

If the microprocessor and the refresh logic can be coordinated so that the refresh logic accesses the RAM when the microprocessor does not need it, then no wait states are required and there is no need for arbitration. This is called *synchronous,* or *transparent,* refresh. The ease of implementing this approach depends on the particular microprocessor and system design, since it requires finding times when the microprocessor is guaranteed not to be accessing the RAM. It is most easily implemented with microprocessors such as the 6502 and 6800 families, in which the microprocessor uses the bus only for one half of each clock cycle; the other half of the clock cycle can be used for refresh.

Dynamic RAM Interface Electrical Considerations

The electrical characteristics of dynamic RAM address and control inputs must be considered when designing the interface circuits. Dynamic RAM inputs are primarily capacitive, and in most applications many RAM chips are wired in parallel. This presents a large capacitive load on the address and control lines. To keep ringing to a minimum, a resistor is often placed in series with the output of the address and control line drivers. The value of this resistor is typically 15 to 33 Ω. Ideally, the value should be selected by experimentation to minimize ringing. An alternative to series termination resistors is to use a special driver, such as AMD's 2966, that is designed to drive dynamic RAM inputs. Dynamic RAM controllers, as described in the following section, often include such drivers internally.

Because of the large input capacitance of the RAM array, the transitions of address and control signals are slowed by the need to charge and discharge this capacitance. Drivers designed for use with dynamic RAMs often specify the propagation delay with a large capacitive load to account for this. If a standard TTL driver is used with a series termination resistor, the resistor-capacitor delay must be added to the normal propagation delay of the driver. The speed of a memory system can be improved by breaking the memory array into smaller groups, with separate drivers for each group. This reduces the capacitive load on each driver and thus reduces the delay time of the address and control signals.

Power supply bypassing is also critical for dynamic RAMs. A 0.1 μF or larger high-frequency capacitor (typically a ceramic type) connected between power and ground must be placed as close as possible to each RAM chip. IC sockets with integral decoupling capacitors are available and provide the shortest possible lead length for the capacitor while reducing the printed circuit board area required. The best way to distribute power is with power and ground planes on a multilayer printed circuit board. A more economical alternative using standard double-sided printed circuit boards is to "grid" the power and ground traces, so that each chip is connected to a matrix of power and ground traces.

Dynamic RAM Controller Chips

To implement dynamic RAM control and refresh logic using standard TTL devices typically requires 8 to 12 chips. Several LSI chips are available that provide most, if not all, of the required circuitry in a single IC. As an example, we will describe Intel's 8208, which supports either 64K or 256K RAM chips.

Figure 4.30 shows a block diagram of the 8208. It includes the refresh counter, refresh timer, and address multiplexers to select the row, column, or refresh address. It also includes arbitration and control logic to coordinate refresh cycles with microprocessor accesses and provides the control signals required to directly drive the dynamic RAMs. The 8208's address, $\overline{\text{RAS}}$, and $\overline{\text{CAS}}$ outputs are designed to directly drive the RAM array, so termination resistors are not required.

The 8208 can be programmed to operate with a variety of different microprocessors and memories. To minimize the 8208's pin count, configuration data is transferred serially on a single pin (program data input, PDI). At the falling edge of RESET, the WE/PCLK pin is pulsed nine times. At each pulse, one bit is read on the PDI pin. By connecting a shift register to these pins, nine different configuration bits can be controlled. For use with an 8-MHz 8086/88 or 80186/88 microprocessor, all configuration

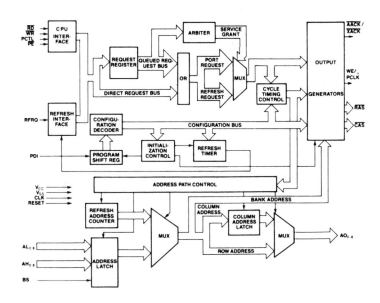

Figure 4.30. The 8208 dynamic RAM controller block diagram. *(Courtesy of Intel Corporation.)*

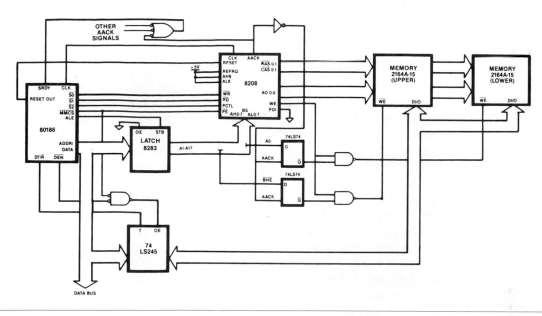

Figure 4.31. Dynamic RAM interface circuit using 8208. *(Courtesy of Intel Corporation.)*

bits are zero, so the PDI pin is simply grounded and no external shift register is required.

Figure 4.31 shows a dynamic RAM system interfaced to an 8086 microprocessor. The 8208 derives the dynamic RAM timing from its CLK input. This can be connected to an external oscillator or to the microprocessor's clock signal, depending on the configuration. The 8208 (and thus the dynamic RAM) is accessed by asserting the port enable ($\overline{PE}$) signal and either $\overline{RD}$ or $\overline{WR}$. If a refresh cycle is in progress, the 8208 waits for the cycle to complete and then begins the cycle requested by the microprocessor.

When used with 8086/88 or 80186/88 microprocessors, the 8208 is configured to accept the encoded status lines rather than separate read and write strobes from the microprocessor. This provides the memory controller with the earliest possible indication of the start of a cycle and thus improves the performance.

The $\overline{AACK}/\overline{XACK}$ output indicates when the cycle is complete and is used to produce the READY signal for the microprocessor. One of the configuration bits determines which signal is produced. For most applications, $\overline{AACK}$ (advanced acknowledge) is used. $\overline{AACK}$ is asserted a fixed time before the cycle is completed, indicating to the microprocessor that the data will be available when it is needed (or for a write cycle, that the data will be stored by the time the microprocessor removes the data).

$\overline{XACK}$ is a Multibus-compatible acknowledge signal. Because it is not asserted until the data has been stored for a write cycle, or is available for a read cycle (as the Multibus specifications require), it will usually result in more wait states than necessary if used to control the READY input to the microprocessor.

The memory access time depends on whether a refresh cycle was in progress when the access was requested, and if so, how far along the refresh cycle was. If the controller is idle (no refresh in progress), the circuit shown operates with no wait states with an 8-MHz 80186 and 150-ns RAMs.

For a 128-Kword memory system built with 64-Kbit dynamic RAMs, address bits A_0 to A_{17} provide the inputs to the address multiplexers in the 8208. A_1 provides the BS (bank select) input that determines which of the two $\overline{RAS}$ outputs is asserted and therefore selects one of the two memory banks. Using A_1 for the bank select means that when accessing successive locations each bank will be accessed in turn. This allows faster access, since it eliminates the need for a delay between cycles to ensure that the $\overline{RAS}$ and $\overline{CAS}$ precharge times are met; if each bank is used only on alternate cycles, then it has one entire bus cycle time for precharge. If nonsequential accesses cause successive accesses to the same bank, the 8208 automatically inserts the required precharge delay.

A_0 is not used to address the RAMs directly because the 8086/186 uses this address bit to enable the low byte of the word addressed by the address bits beginning with A_1. (See the description of the 8086 in Chap. 2.) The 8086/186's $\overline{BHE}$ output enables the high byte. For read cycles, these two signals can be ignored, since the microprocessor will look only at the half of the data bus that it is interested in. For write cycles, however, the write enable to the RAMs must be gated with the signals. If they were not, then a byte write instruction would cause unintentional modification of the adjacent byte. A_0 and $\overline{BHE}$ are latched at the leading edge of $\overline{AACK}$ to ensure that they remain valid for the duration of the cycle.

In the normal configuration, the 8208's REFRQ (refresh request) input is tied high, and the 8208 automatically generates refresh cycles at a rate sufficient to guarantee 128 cycles every 2 ms (256 every 4 ms). Alternatively, the REFRQ input can be used to externally trigger refresh cycles, which is useful for implementing transparent refresh if there is some time available when the system can guarantee that no normal RAM accesses will occur. When using external refresh control, a fail-safe option can be selected. When this option is enabled (via a configuration bit), REFRQ resets the internal refresh timer, but does not disable it. Thus, if the external refresh control fails to maintain an adequate refresh rate, the internal timer will automatically initiate additional refresh cycles.

Other Methods for Implementing Refresh

Memory controller ICs reduce the number of ICs required to implement a dynamic memory system. However, implementing the controller with small-scale TTL (or high-speed CMOS) ICs often provides better control of timing parameters and shorter propagation delay times. Since the address must pass through the memory controller, the propagation delay of the controller adds to the access time of the memory.

A variety of other methods can be used to implement refresh at a lower hardware cost. Software refresh is the least expensive method. A programmable timer or a simple counter chain generates a nonmaskable interrupt to the microprocessor every 4 milliseconds. The interrupt service routine consists of 256 no-operation (no-op) instructions, which cause 256 read cycles to successive addresses. These read cycles refresh the dynamic RAM. If there is more than one memory bank, the refresh timer output can be ORed with the $\overline{RAS}$ logic for each bank so that $\overline{RAS}$ is asserted to all banks during refresh cycles, regardless of the address. Alternatively, the RAM circuitry can be designed to always assert $\overline{RAS}$ to all banks for all memory cycles, but this increases the power consumption.

The overall performance degradation caused by software refresh depends on the particular microprocessor and how long it takes to execute the refresh routine. Typically, 3 to 5 percent of the processor time is consumed by software refresh. (For example, assume that the no-op instruction requires 400 ns to execute. 400 ns $\times$ 256 cycles = 102.4 μs = 2.6 percent of 4 ms. The interrupt response and return times must be added to this figure.) This is not a serious degradation in overall performance. However, it has the same problem as any burst refresh technique: there is a relatively long period of time (the length of the refresh routine) when the microprocessor cannot respond to normal system events. In a system that has tight loops or that needs to respond very quickly to some event, this can be a fatal problem. Software refresh can also lead to difficult debugging problems, since a software error can cause the memory refresh to fail. The RAM contents may also be lost when the system is reset if the reset pulse width exceeds 4 ms, or if the processor is halted for any reason. However, this is an economical way to implement refresh in many applications.

A variation of this technique is to use a DMA controller to provide the refresh cycles. This is most economical in systems that include a multiple-channel DMA controller (or a microprocessor with an on-chip DMA controller) and have an extra channel not needed for normal operation. The microprocessor initializes the DMA controller channel to be used for refresh to read successive bytes from the dynamic RAM. The DMA controller is programmed for a single-cycle mode in which it performs a single transfer at each DMA request. A programmable timer generates a DMA request (and thus a refresh cycle) every 15 μs. One system that uses this technique is the IBM personal computer.

Zilog's Z80, Z180, and Z8000 series microprocessors include some refresh support on the CPU chip. After each opcode fetch, while the microprocessor is decoding the opcode, a refresh address is output on the address bus and the $\overline{REFRESH}$ control signal is asserted. This provides transparent refresh and reduces the interface requirements to only address multiplexing and control. This approach has many of the same disadvantages as software refresh. If the processor stops executing instructions, such as when RESET or BUSREQ is asserted, no refresh occurs. If long DMA transfers occur, memory contents can be lost unless the DMA transfer itself provides sufficient refresh.

Using dynamic RAM chips with built-in refresh counters also simplifies the refresh logic, but still leaves it up to the system designer to decide when to assert the refresh enable input to guarantee the required number of cycles in each 2- or 4-ms period. Dynamic RAMs with on-chip refresh counters are less silicon-efficient in large memory arrays since the refresh counter is replicated in each IC, whereas one external counter can serve an entire memory array using standard RAMs.

4.8 PSEUDO-STATIC RAM

While static RAM is easy to use, the amount of chip area required by each memory cell is much larger than for dynamic RAMs. Dynamic RAM provides greater density and lower cost per bit but is more difficult to interface. One approach that aims to provide the best of both worlds is the *pseudo-static* RAM, a RAM that uses dynamic storage cells but contains all the refresh logic on-chip so the device appears static to the user. This approach is used only for relatively large memories (64 Kbits and up), since the refresh circuitry requires a substantial amount of chip area. For a small memory, the savings in memory cell area would be more than offset by the additional area required for refresh logic. Examples of pseudo-static RAMs include NEC's 42832C and Hitachi's 65256 32-Kbyte RAMs, and Hitachi's 658129 128-Kbyte RAM.

Pseudo-static RAMs are nearly, but not quite, as easy to use as fully static RAMs. Because they must execute internal refresh cycles periodically, there is the potential for a conflict between an external access request and an internal refresh cycle. Two approaches to this problem have been used:

1. Include a refresh control input on the RAM, which must be periodically asserted by the system control logic to tell the RAM when it can execute a refresh cycle without any chance of a conflicting access request.

2. Include a "ready" output on the RAM so that it can tell the system to wait if an access request conflicts with a refresh cycle.

The pseudo-static RAMs mentioned above use the first of the two refresh control approaches. The two 32-Kbyte devices use the standard 28-pin byte-wide pin configuration. Pin 22, normally used for output enable, is used for both output enable and refresh control functions. When $\overline{CS}$ is asserted, pin 22 functions as the output enable; when $\overline{CS}$ is negated, pin 22 is the refresh control input. The 128-Kbyte 658129 is in a 32-pin package and uses a separate pin for refresh control.

The motivation for making pseudo-static RAMs is in their potential for lower cost and lower power per bit. It may also be possible to build larger pseudo-static RAMs with a given level of technology, as compared to standard static RAMs. On the negative side, pseudo-static RAMs require more complicated control logic, occasionally require extra wait states, and are slower than fully static RAMs.

4.9   NONVOLATILE READ/WRITE MEMORY

All current RAM technologies share a common weakness: they are volatile, so all data is lost when power is turned off. ROM and EPROM technologies provide nonvolatility but cannot be erased and reprogrammed in the application system. The ideal memory is a nonvolatile RAM, which would perform like a normal static RAM but retain its contents indefinitely without power. Unfortunately, such a device is not yet available. (Actually, there is a technology that has these characteristics: core memory. However, this is not a semiconductor technology and is not economically viable for most applications.) This section describes the types of nonvolatile memory and their interfacing considerations.

4.9.1   Applications for Nonvolatile Memory

Nonvolatile read/write memory has a wide range of applications. It can be used to store setup information, such as baud rate and data formats for CRT terminals. This allows the setup to be performed by using the keyboard, with prompts on the screen, rather than by setting DIP switches. They can store calibration information, allowing instruments with built-in self-calibration capabilities to be built. For example, an instrument with an analog voltage input can be calibrated by supplying a known accurate voltage to the input. The value is then read from the A/D converter and a correction factor calculated and stored in the nonvolatile memory.

Nonvolatile read/write memory also has applications for program storage. Using memory that can be modified in the application system, rather than ROMs or EPROMs, allows software updates to be made in the field. Changes can be entered on a keyboard, or sent via telephone lines from the factory for products equipped with a modem.

4.9.2 Nonvolatile Memory Types

Several types of devices approach the ideal of a nonvolatile RAM. This section first introduces the basic types and the technology used and then describes each type in detail. Finally, guidelines for selecting a particular device type are provided.

The most common type of nonvolatile memory is the *EEPROM*, or electrically erasable PROM. (These are often called *E²PROMs*, pronounced "E-squared PROM.") The contents of EEPROMs can be erased and rewritten, but the erase and write times are typically 5 to 10 ms/byte. This is faster than programming a UV-erasable EPROM but is very slow when compared to a typical microprocessor write cycle time of a few hundred nanoseconds. EEPROMs are erasable on a byte-by-byte basis, and no ultraviolet light is required.

A similar device (or sometimes another name for the same device) is the *EAROM*, or electrically alterable ROM. While there is no precise definition for these terms, and some devices have been called by both names, EAROMs generally can be erased only in blocks, and not on a byte-by-byte basis. Most devices called EAROMs are implemented in the older MNOS technology, which is described in the following section.

Another nonvolatile memory type is the *shadow RAM*, also called a *nonvolatile RAM*, or *NVRAM*, which combines normal RAM cells and EEPROM cells on the same chip. These devices avoid many of the problems of EEPROMs, at the expense of a much larger chip size and consequently higher cost for a given capacity.

One approach to implementing nonvolatile RAM is to provide a *battery backup* for a standard CMOS RAM so that the RAM is never without power. This is the most established technique and has several functional advantages over EEPROMs and NVRAMS. There are also a number of disadvantages, mostly related to the battery itself.

4.9.3 EEPROM Technology

There are numerous technical difficulties in building EEPROMs. A storage cell is needed that can be written in a reasonable period of time and with moderate voltages, that will retain its state for a long period of time, and that does not lose its data after many read cycles.

The first technology used to implement such devices was *MNOS* (*not* NMOS!), or metal-nitride-oxide semiconductor. MNOS devices have been plagued by a variety of problems, including data loss over time, limited number of read and write cycles, and requirements for multiple power supplies. Input signals to MNOS devices generally require a voltage swing beyond standard TTL levels. Because of these problems, MNOS EAROMs have not been widely used.

The first devices to use standard silicon-gate NMOS technology to implement nonvolatile storage were Intel's 2816 EEPROM and Xicor's X2201 NOVRAM. All common EEPROMs and NVRAMs are now implemented with NMOS or CMOS technology, and MNOS devices are now obsolete.

The key phenomenon exploited by these devices is called *tunneling,* first described by Fowler and Nordheim in 1924, whereby some electrons will pass through an insulating layer in the presence of a sufficient electric field. This is an ideal phenomenon for reading and writing the storage cells, because it allows the storage capacitor to be surrounded by a very good insulator, so charge will not leak off, but by increasing the electric field strength, current can be passed through the insulator to provide access for reading and writing.

To obtain a sufficiently strong electric field at moderate voltages, a very thin oxide insulating layer is required. The oxide layer is much thinner than that used in conventional MOS devices and is a critical aspect of the process.

From a user's point of view, there are several important consequences of this technology. Because of the strong electric field required to write to the cell, a power supply of approximately 20 V is required for write cycles. Most EEPROMs and NVRAMs require only a 5-V supply and include a *charge pump* on the chip that generates the write voltage from the 5-V supply.

The most significant weakness of this technology is that the devices wear out; the oxide layer is weakened with every write cycle, and retention time gradually decreases. These devices are unique in the semiconductor world in this respect; other semiconductor devices will last for enormous numbers of cycles and show no evidence of wearing out. Most EEPROMs, NVRAMs, and similar devices are rated for approximately 10,000 write cycles, although some are rated for as many as 1,000,000 write cycles. Read cycles are unlimited, so these devices can be thought of as "read mostly memories."

Another effect of the technology used for nonvolatile semiconductor memories is that the write time is relatively long, typically 1 to 10 ms, because the tunneling current through the oxide is small, so it takes time to build up sufficient charge on the storage capacitor. Thus, a special interface (which is usually built into the memory chip) is required for connection to the relatively fast buses of a microprocessor system.

Because nonvolatile memory technology is relatively young and a great deal of research effort is being devoted to it, these specifications can be expected to improve significantly. Two key areas of improvement are a reduction in write time and an increase in the number of write cycles.

4.9.4   EEPROMs

EEPROMs are, as the name implies, electrically erasable versions of the more common EPROMs. Most are pin-compatible with EPROMs, except for the write operation.

Intel's 2-Kbyte 2816 was the first generally available EEPROM. It is pin-compatible with the 2716 EPROM and has a read access time less than that of its EPROM equivalent. For writing, however, it requires a 21-V pulse on the V_{PP} pin with specific rise and fall times. The address and data must be held stable for the entire 10-ms write cycle time, which requires a set of latches to drive these pins unless the microprocessor is to execute thousands of wait states. Before data can be written, the memory location must first be erased by writing all ones to that location. Thus, while the 2816 was an important advance at the time, it required substantial support circuitry and was thus uneconomical in most applications. Intel's 2816A, which has replaced the original 2816, is a similar device that includes an on-chip write voltage generator, so it requires only a 5-V power supply.

Adding additional support logic on the EEPROM chip simplifies the interfacing requirements. Figure 4.32 shows the functions included in a typical EEPROM. A basic EEPROM, such as Intel's original 2816, requires a high-voltage supply and external

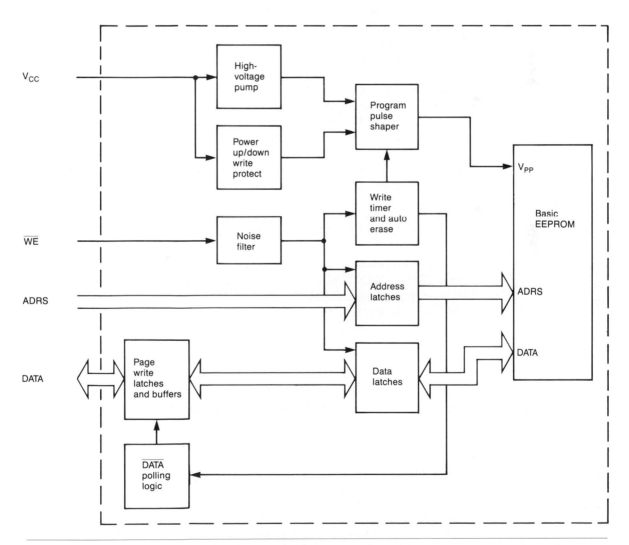

Figure 4.32. Interface circuitry included in full-function EEPROMs.

latches to hold the address and data stable for the duration of the write cycle. Intel's 2817A includes latches and the voltage pump on the chip, along with a write timer that controls the length of the write cycle. The microprocessor can thus write to the EEPROM just as if it were a RAM and continue with other operations during the long write time. The EEPROM cannot be accessed again until the write time has elapsed, but the microprocessor can perform other operations. A READY pin allows the microprocessor to detect when the write cycle is complete, or it can simply wait for the worst-case write time to elapse. Another enhancement in the 2817A is automatic erase before write. The 2817A uses a 28-pin package and is compatible with the byte-wide pinout standard as shown in Table 4.3.

While Intel pioneered the EEPROM, they very soon had numerous competitors, some with more sophisticated parts. Xicor's X2816A, for example, requires only +5 V and includes on-chip latches and automatic erase before write as in Intel's 2817A. The X2816A uses a 24-pin package and does not provide a READY output (since there is no pin available for this function in a 24-pin package). This combination of features makes it fully compatible with $2K \times 8$ static RAMs such as the 6116; the X2816A can plug into a socket intended for a static RAM with no hardware changes at all. The software must be aware, of course, that the memory will not respond normally for 10 ms after a write cycle is initiated.

The X2816A includes a feature called $\overline{DATA}$ *polling* to indicate when a write cycle is complete. If the EEPROM is read while an internal write cycle is in progress, the EEPROM returns the complement of the data last written. Thus, the system software can determine when the write cycle is complete by reading the location last written and comparing the data read to the data written. If the data read and data written match, then the write cycle is complete. Since typical write cycles are shorter than the worst-case write cycle time, using $\overline{DATA}$ polling allows faster accesses than simply waiting for the worst-case write time to elapse.

The X2816A also includes protection against accidental writes at power-up. For a write to occur, $\overline{WE}$ and $\overline{CE}$ must be asserted (low) and $\overline{OE}$ must be negated (high). It is unlikely that this combination would occur during power transitions.

Intel's 2816A, which requires only +5 V, does not include on-chip latches or automatic erase before write, as does Xicor's X2816A. Thus, the designer must be very careful when selecting EEPROMs, as devices with almost identical part numbers can have significantly different features.

EEPROMs are also available in $4K \times 8$, $8K \times 8$, and $32K \times 8$ formats. There is considerably more standardization for these larger EEPROMs than for the 2-Kbyte devices, but still not all devices are the same. Most larger EEPROMs include the address and data latches, write timer, high-voltage generator, $\overline{DATA}$ polling logic, and automatic erase before write. For additional protection against erroneous writes, many EEPROMs include a noise filter on the $\overline{WE}$ input and a voltage sensor that disables the write input when V_{CC} is below the minimum required for normal operation, typically 4.5 V. Xicor's X2864A is a typical $8K \times 8$ EEPROM and is pin-compatible with $8K \times 8$ static RAMs.

The X2864A and many other EEPROMs include a feature called *page write* that speeds the effective write time when writing a series of bytes. Up to 16 bytes can be written in succession, provided that they are all in the same 16-byte page (that is, only A_0 to A_3 change) and they are all written within 200 μs. All 16 bytes are then written in the time normally required to write a single byte. The byte write time is 5 ms. AMD's

Am2864 also includes the page write function and allows 32 bytes per page. The Am2864 provides both a ready pin and $\overline{\text{DATA}}$ polling.

While 64- and 256-Kbit EEPROMs aim at applications requiring large amounts of nonvolatile memory, several smaller devices aim at providing very low cost for low-end applications. One example of such a device is National's COP494 256-bit EEPROM. To keep the package size and interface requirements to a minimum, a serial interface is used. It is packaged in an eight-pin mini-DIP, and only six pins are actually used: power and ground, chip select, serial clock in, serial data in, and serial data out. Internally, the memory is organized as 16 words of 16 bits each. Instructions are sent to the device in a 9-bit serial format, which includes a start bit, a 4-bit operation code, and a 4-bit address. There are six instructions, including read, write, and erase. Interfacing to a serial EEPROM such as this device requires additional software but reduces the hardware interface to a minimum.

4.9.5 Shadow RAM

While EEPROMs solve the volatility problem of normal RAMs, they introduce new problems of limited write cycles and slow write times. One approach to overcoming these deficiencies is the shadow RAM, called *NOVRAM* by its original supplier, Xicor, and commonly called *nonvolatile RAM,* or *NVRAM*. An NVRAM consists of a memory with one normal RAM cell and one EEPROM cell (the "shadow") for each memory location. The RAM can be written at full microprocessor speed, and there is no limit to the number of write cycles. When a power failure is impending, the RAM array is stored in the on-chip EEPROM array. Thus, the EEPROM storage cycle occurs only when power fails, not on every write access.

The first NVRAMs were Xicor's X2210 and X2212, with capacities of 64×4 and 256×4, respectively. Newer devices, such as the 2004 shown in Fig. 4.33, are 8 bits wide and are more natural for use in a microprocessor system. The 2004 is a 512×8 NVRAM and is made by both Xicor (as the X2004) and Intel. (Although Xicor's and Intel's devices are functionally compatible, there are some specification differences.) The static RAM array is accessed just like any other static RAM via the address, data, $\overline{\text{CS}}$, $\overline{\text{OE}}$, and $\overline{\text{WR}}$ pins.

The additional capability of the NVRAM is activated by the $\overline{\text{NE}}$ (nonvolatile enable) pin. With the exception of this pin, the 2004 is compatible with the standard byte-wide pinout. When $\overline{\text{NE}}$ is asserted along with $\overline{\text{WE}}$ and $\overline{\text{CE}}$, the entire RAM array is stored in the EEPROM array. In 10 ms, all 512 bytes are written, with no external signals required. Only a short $\overline{\text{NE}}$ pulse is required, but power must remain for the 10-millisecond store time. Once stored, the data will remain with or without power. The number of "store" cycles is subject to the same limit as the write cycle for an EEPROM (10,000 cycles). The data is recalled from the EEPROM to the RAM by asserting $\overline{\text{NE}}$ along with $\overline{\text{OE}}$ and $\overline{\text{CE}}$. The recall is also performed automatically at power-up. All 512 bytes are restored in under 2.5 µs.

One way to interface the NVRAM to a microprocessor system is to connect $\overline{\text{NE}}$ to an output port bit. To initiate a nonvolatile store operation, the microprocessor sets this port bit low and then writes to the NVRAM. To initiate the recall operation, the microprocessor reads from the NVRAM with the port bit low. The address and data for the NVRAM read or write do not matter when $\overline{\text{NE}}$ is asserted. By adding an additional

Figure 4.33. Xicor
2004 512 × 8 NOVRAM.
(Courtesy of Xicor, Inc.)

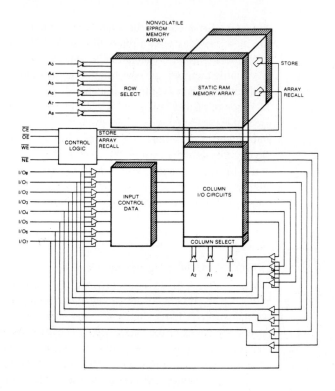

Figure 4.33. Xicor
2004 512 × 8 NOVRAM.
(Courtesy of Xicor, Inc.)

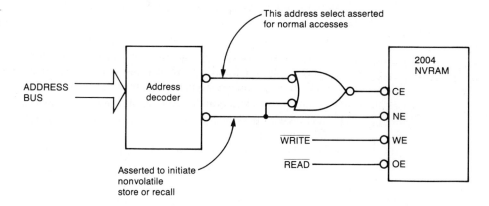

Figure 4.34. Interface
option for 2004 NOVRAM.

gate as shown in Fig. 4.34, the store and recall operations can be initiated by reading or writing a special address.

The store operation is typically initiated when an impending power failure is detected. A power fail signal is produced by sensing when the ac supply, or the dc supply before the voltage regulator, drops below a specified minimum. This power fail signal interrupts the microprocessor, and the interrupt service routine initiates the store operation. Alternatively, logic could be added to the NVRAM interface so that the power fail detect signal would directly cause the $\overline{\text{WE}}$, $\overline{\text{NE}}$, and $\overline{\text{CE}}$ signals to be asserted. Note that at least 10 ms of warning before the dc supply fails must be available. This may require additional capacitance on the output of the dc supply.

Nonvolatile RAMs are also available with a serial interface. Xicor's X2444, for example, is similar to National's COP494 described earlier, except that read and write operations occur on the RAM array so there is no limit to the number of write cycles. The recall and store functions can be initiated via commands sent over the serial link, or via pins dedicated to those functions.

As with EEPROMs, NVRAM compatibility among vendors is problematic. For example, Intel and Xicor both make 128 × 8 NVRAMs, called the 2001 and X2001, respectively. However, these are completely different devices; Intel's is in an 18-pin package and uses a multiplexed address/data bus, while Xicor's is in a 24-pin package and has an interface similar to the 2004.

4.9.6 Battery-backed CMOS RAM

In many respects, adding battery backup to a standard CMOS RAM provides an ideal nonvolatile RAM. Read and write cycles are fast and unlimited in number, and CMOS static RAM chips are readily available from multiple sources. The RAM chips themselves are less expensive per bit then EEPROMs. However, batteries have their disadvantages. They have a relatively limited life and are less reliable than semiconductor devices. Extra circuitry is required to switch the RAMs over to battery power when the main supply fails, and spurious write signals during power transitions must be prevented. Because of this overhead, battery-backed CMOS RAM is most cost-effective when relatively large amounts of memory are needed.

Battery Types

There are two basic battery types: *primary* and *secondary*. Primary batteries use nonreversible chemical processes and therefore cannot be recharged. Secondary batteries use reversible reactions and thus can be recharged. The selection depends on the type of application. Rechargeable batteries are best when the required current is relatively large and when battery power is not required for long periods of time. They typically have a smaller capacity than primary batteries of comparable physical size and cost, but as long as power is available periodically they can be kept charged. Primary batteries are best when the required current is relatively small.

The two most common rechargeable battery types are nickel-cadmium and sealed lead-acid. Nickel-cadmium batteries are available in a wide range of sizes and are widely used in portable equipment. They work best in applications where they are discharged almost completely and then recharged. If they are kept constantly charged, with only occasional shallow discharge, they lose much of their capacity and eventually fail. Thus, they are not well-suited to applications where the battery is rarely used for a short period of time. Another problem with nickel-cadmium batteries is that they have a substantial self-discharge current. Thus, they will not remain charged for a long period of time, even if there is no load on them.

Sealed lead-acid batteries use the same basic chemistry as common automobile batteries but are sealed so that they do not leak or require any maintenance. Most use a gelled electrolyte, so they do not contain any liquid. They tolerate continuous charging and shallow discharging with no loss of capacity or lifetime. Lead-acid batteries are available only in relatively large sizes and are thus most appropriate for applications with relatively large current requirements.

Many types of primary cells are available. The most common are alkaline "flashlight" types. These are useful in some memory backup applications but have a limited life. Many primary batteries are limited by their *shelf life,* which is their life without any current drain at all. Common alkaline batteries have a shelf life of 1 or 2 years. Lithium batteries are widely used in backup applications because of their high power density and long shelf life (typically 10 years).

Another option for short-term power backup is the *double-layer capacitor,* available from NEC as the Supercap and from SOHIO as the Maxcap. These are available with capacitances as high as 1 F, and are much smaller than conventional electrolytic capacitors of comparable capacitance. They can be used as rechargeable "batteries" with the circuits described later in this section. A 1-F supercap, which is approximately 1.1 in. in diameter and 1 in. high, can power a RAM with a 1-μA standby current for over a week.

Battery Lifetime

Battery lifetime is determined by many factors. Batteries are rated by their *amp-hour* (Ah) capacity. This number is often referred to as "C." The amp-hour rating generally assumes a discharge rate of one tenth of C or less. For example, a 10 Ah battery can supply 1 A for 10 hours, or 0.1 A for 100 hours. At discharge rates above 1 A, the capacity is reduced. In addition, the output voltage decreases as it is discharged. The shape of the discharge curve (battery voltage vs. time at a given discharge current) varies depending on the type and size of battery. For some batteries, such as lithium, the curve is very flat (little voltage change) until the battery is almost completely exhausted, at which time the voltage begins dropping rapidly. For others, such as lead-acid, the voltage drops gradually as the battery is discharged. Battery manufacturers supply detailed design manuals, which should be consulted to determine the precise characteristics of any battery to be used as a memory backup supply.

For rechargeable batteries, the amp-hour capacity determines the time the system can operate without a recharge. The overall life of the battery may be determined by the number of charge-discharge cycles it can tolerate, or by its shelf life.

For primary batteries, the amp-hour rating may determine the overall life of the battery. For low-power memories, however, current requirements are often so small that the amp-hour capacity would not be reached for many years. The shelf life of the battery then becomes the determining factor. When used with a low-power CMOS RAM, a moderate-size lithium cell has enough capacity to provide power for its full 10-year shelf life.

Power Switching and Write Protection

In most applications, the battery is intended to provide backup power for the RAM only, not for the rest of the system. It is therefore necessary for the RAM power to be isolated from the rest of the system. In addition, writes to the RAM must be inhibited when V_{CC} is below the normal minimum level, since the microprocessor system may produce erroneous signals. Once power is off, the RAM's chip select input must be isolated from the microprocessor system and pulled high, since the powered-down mi-

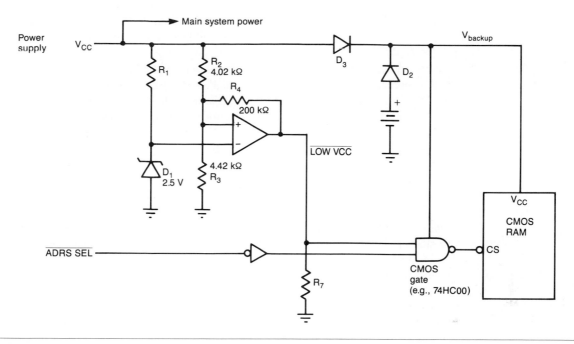

Figure 4.35. Battery backup and write protection circuit for CMOS RAM.

croprocessor system will likely present a low level to all the RAM's inputs. This will produce a write to location zero, if it is not inhibited.

Figure 4.35 shows a battery-backed RAM circuit. Zener diode D_1 (or an IC voltage reference, such as National's LM336) provides a reference voltage. Resistors R_2 and R_3 form a voltage divider. When the voltage produced from this divider is less than the reference voltage, the output of the comparator goes low. R_3 can be replaced with a potentiometer to allow the threshold to be adjusted; if fixed resistors are used, they must be 1 percent tolerance components. R_4 provides positive feedback, and adds hysteresis to the threshold to prevent oscillations of the output as the voltage passes through the transition range. The resistor values shown provide a switching threshold of 4.75 V when V_{CC} is falling and 4.82 V when V_{CC} is rising.

The chip select input to the RAM is gated with $\overline{\text{LOWVCC}}$, so no accesses can occur when the supply voltage is below the threshold. The RAM enters its low-power standby mode when chip select is negated, so this gate also ensures that the RAM is in standby mode when the battery is providing power. The pull-down resistor R_7 ensures that the $\overline{\text{LOWVCC}}$ signal is held asserted if the comparator ceases to drive its output as the voltage drops. (This resistor is not generally required but is an inexpensive precaution.) If only 6264-type RAMs are to be used, the chip select inhibit gate can be eliminated by connecting the $\overline{\text{LOWVCC}}$ signal to the 6264's active-high CS_2 input.

Diode D_3 isolates the battery supply from the rest of the system. The voltage drop across this diode makes the RAM's supply voltage lower than the rest of the system's. If this drop is too large, the supply voltage may be below the RAM's specification. The input logic thresholds are also affected, since they are proportional to the supply voltage. Thus, a Schottky diode is generally used to keep this drop below 0.3 V.

Diode D_2 in series with the battery is necessary when using primary cells to prevent the battery from being charged by the main power supply. Most primary battery types will be permanently damaged by even a small charging current. The diode must therefore have low leakage to protect the battery, particularly if it is a lithium type. Schottky diodes are commonly used because in addition to having low leakage they have a low forward voltage drop, allowing more of the battery voltage to reach the RAM.

For rechargeable batteries, the diode can be replaced with a resistor. When the main power is on, the battery is charged through the resistor. When power fails, the battery supplies the RAM supply current through the resistor. If the RAM supply current is large enough to cause a significant voltage drop in the resistor, a diode in parallel with the resistor can be used to limit the drop to 0.7 V. More complex charging circuits are often used to charge the battery faster. For some battery types, charging current must be shut off when the battery is fully charged to obtain maximum battery life.

Most CMOS RAMs will retain their contents at voltages as low as 2 V in standby mode. Normal access is not possible, but that is not a problem since the rest of the system is generally not powered during battery backup. The battery must be specified at a voltage somewhat higher than that required by the RAM to allow for the drop across the diode (or resistor) and the decrease in battery voltage during discharge.

Figure 4.36 shows an alternative switching circuit. When power is on, $\overline{\text{LOWVCC}}$ is high, Q_2 is on, and Q_1 is on. Thus, the V_{backup} output is equal to the V_{cc} input minus the collector-emitter drop of Q_2. This collector-emitter drop ($V_{\text{CE(sat)}}$) is typically 0.2 V, so the RAM voltage is very close to V_{cc}. When V_{cc} drops below its normal range, $\overline{\text{LOWVCC}}$ is asserted. This shuts off Q_1, which turns off Q_2 by removing the base current. When the V_{backup} voltage drops to one diode drop below the battery voltage, diode D_1 begins conducting and the battery powers the RAM.

There are two additional data integrity problems that can be caused by the automatic write protection as V_{cc} drops below the low V_{cc} threshold. The first problem is that if $\overline{\text{LOWVCC}}$ is asserted during a write cycle, the cycle will be prematurely terminated (from the RAM's point of view), and the data written will be indeterminate. The second problem is that even if the write protect does not occur during a write cycle, multi-

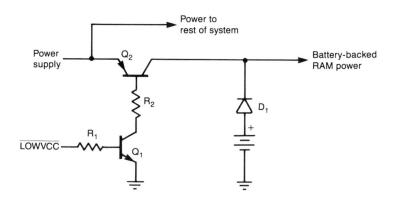

Figure 4.36. Alternative power-switching circuit.

word data structures can be left in a partially modified (and therefore invalid) state. Note that this second problem also applies to any other nonvolatile memory, such as an EEPROM, regardless of any on-chip protection circuitry.

The most general solution to these problems is to provide an interrupt to the microprocessor, providing a warning that power is failing and that writes to the RAM will soon be inhibited. The interrupt service routine then halts the system, ensuring that no write cycles are occurring when $\overline{\text{LOWVCC}}$ is asserted. The service routine can monitor the power fail detect input (if it is connected to an input port as well as to the interrupt input) and continue normal operation via a return from interrupt if the power failure warning is negated. This allows the system to recover from a short power failure or a drop in the ac supply voltage that triggers the power fail warning but does not cause V_{cc} to drop significantly. In a full power failure, the system will be powered down with the microprocessor executing this loop (monitoring the power fail warning input).

Since interrupts are acknowledged only in between instruction executions, this approach ensures that a write cycle will not be prematurely terminated. In addition, any data structure that is always written by a single instruction is guaranteed to be intact. However, there is still a potential problem with data structures that are written by a multiple-instruction sequence. (This can be something as simple as a 16-bit word with many 8-bit microprocessors or as complex as a multifield data base record.) This problem can be solved by disabling the power fail warning interrupt while these data structures are being written. The interrupt must not be kept disabled for so long that a power fail warning which occurred just after the interrupt was disabled could result in $\overline{\text{LOWVCC}}$ being asserted before the interrupt was reenabled. Except for these critical periods when multiword data structures are being written, the power fail warning interrupt should never be disabled.

The power fail warning interrupt signal can be generated in several ways:

1. Monitor the time between zero crossings of the ac line, and assert the warning if the time between crossings exceeds the expected value. This is most commonly done with a one-shot.

2. Monitor the level of the unregulated dc supply. This voltage can usually fall a volt or more before the regulated supply begins to drop.

3. Monitor the regulated power supply line. The warning threshold must be above the write protect threshold, and the time it takes the voltage to drop from one threshold to the other must be greater than the worst-case response time to the warning interrupt.

The first approach provides the most warning but is more difficult to implement since it requires connecting to the ac line and measuring time intervals. The last approach is the simplest to implement in that it does not require any additional power supply connections, but it requires that the two thresholds be close together (and accurately set), and does not provide as much warning.

The need for the power fail warning can be eliminated entirely if the battery-backed memory contains only single-word data structures. In this case, simply synchronizing the $\overline{\text{LOWVCC}}$ signal with the write cycle (using a transparent latch enabled when $\overline{\text{WRITE}}$ is negated) will prevent a write cycle from being prematurely terminated.

Other Interfacing Considerations

CMOS inputs have a high input impedance, and if they are not driven high or low they will float to approximately midway between power and ground. This is undesirable, because the power consumption of CMOS logic increases significantly when the input voltage is in the transition region between high and low. Thus, some provision must be made to ensure that no inputs to a CMOS RAM or other CMOS device are left floating when operating on battery power.

The RAM's $\overline{CS}$ input is never floating, since it is connected to a CMOS gate that is powered by the RAM power. Other inputs may or may not float when power is off, depending on the type of device driving the input and the other devices connected to the same signal. Most low-power Schottky output stages appear as a low impedance to ground when they are not powered, so they will serve to pull the RAM inputs low. Signals that are connected to a TTL input in addition to the CMOS RAM will not float, since the TTL input will pull the line low when power is off.

MOS devices and devices with three-state outputs, however, may have high-impedance outputs when without power. Thus, RAM inputs driven by such drivers and not connected to other TTL inputs should have resistors to ground (*pull-downs*) connected to them. The resistor can be a relatively high value, since the CMOS inputs are high impedance; 10 kΩ is commonly used. Pull-downs are preferable to pull-ups, since if the output stage of the driving device does provide a path to ground, it will increase the power dissipated in a pull-up resistor and thus increase the battery drain.

CMOS RAM with Integral Backup

The design of a reliable battery-backed memory clearly requires more than just adding a battery. Several companies manufacture battery-backed CMOS RAM modules with integral backup control circuitry and lithium battery. On-chip circuitry handles power switching, write protection, and input termination. These modules are typically packaged in a 24- or 28-pin package that is taller than a normal IC package to allow room for the battery, but is compatible with a standard static RAM socket. Thus, a system designed to use standard bytewide static RAMs can be converted to battery-backed RAM by simply plugging in battery-backed modules instead of standard RAMs. The life of the module is typically limited by the battery's shelf life of 10 years.

4.9.7   Selecting a Nonvolatile Memory Type

The selection of a nonvolatile memory type requires an analysis of the needs of the application as well as comparison of currently available devices and pricing. For applications requiring only a small amount of memory, shadow RAMs provide ease of use and relatively low cost. They also have the advantage of allowing unlimited numbers of write cycles, although the number of nonvolatile storage cycles is limited. EEPROMs with on-chip latches, write timers, high-voltage generators, and accidental write protection provide ease of use comparable to static RAMs, and they are a good choice for applications requiring moderate amounts of memory that can tolerate the EEPROM's limitations. For applications requiring large amounts of RAM or large numbers of write cycles, battery-backed CMOS RAM is usually the best choice.

4.10 ERROR DETECTION AND CORRECTION

4.10.1 Reliability of Memory Systems

The error rate for static RAMs, EPROMs, and EEPROMs is sufficiently low that in the quantities that are used in a typical system they are not a serious reliability problem. Dynamic RAMs, however, have significantly higher error rates, due primarily to the alpha-particle problem described earlier in Sec. 4.7.6. For relatively small memories, the system failure rate is still fairly low. The real problem arises when memory size increases, particularly above 512 Kbytes or so. In a large memory system, even memory chips with very low individual failure rates can cause an unacceptable system error rate.

Failure rates are often specified as the percentage of devices expected to fail in each 1000 hours of operation. The average lifetime is called *mean time between failures (MTBF),* and is the reciprocal of the failure rate. A failure rate of 100 percent per 1000 hours means that the MTBF is 1000 hours, while a failure rate of 0.1 percent per 1000 hours (a typical dynamic RAM soft error rate) is equivalent to an MTBF of 1,000,000 hours. To put this in perspective, there are 8760 hours in a year, or over 114 years in 1,000,000 hours.

Since most semiconductor devices do not "wear out" until they get very old, average failure rate statistics are valid for most of a device's life. (EEPROMS, of course, are an exception to this rule.) Failure rate during the initial burn-in period is usually higher, due to "infant mortality," and when a system gets quite old, tnere are "old age" failures. For most of the life of a semiconductor device, however, the failure rate is independent of age.

There are two types of errors: hard and soft. A *hard error* means that the memory cell is permanently defective. *Soft errors,* on the other hand, are temporary; a bit of data has been lost, but the memory cell still functions correctly. Rewriting the data in the cell corrects the error. Soft errors can be caused by alpha particles, noise on power or control signals, temperature extremes, or marginal timing. A soft error may be a read error only, in which case simply rereading the data will correct the problem, but it is more likely that the data has been lost and must be rewritten.

Typical error rates for NMOS dynamic RAMs are 0.10 percent per 1000 hours for soft errors and 0.02 percent per 1000 hours for hard errors. Error rates from different sources are additive, so the overall error rate is 0.12 percent per 1000 hours. The MTBF for a dynamic RAM is thus 1000/0.0012 = 833,333 hours, or over 95 years of full-time operation. That may sound like very high reliability, but that is for a system with only a single RAM chip. The failure rate must be multiplied by the number of chips in the system; or equivalently, the MTBF divided by the number of chips.

A 512-Kbyte memory system requires sixteen 256-Kbit RAM chips. The system MTBF is therefore 833,333/16 = 52,083 hours, or approximately 6 years. This is not an unreasonable number, and memories of this size often do not use error correction.

For a large memory system, the story is quite different. A 4-Mbyte array requires 128 256-Kbit chips, which results in an MTBF of 6510 hours, or approximately 9 months. Thus, at this memory size the error rate becomes significant. For very large memory systems, the problem becomes extreme. A 16-Mbyte array requires 512 256-Kbit chips, resulting in an MTBF of under 10 weeks. This is unacceptable in nearly any application, so some form of error correction must be used.

These MTBF figures are for the RAM chips only and do not include the buffers and other interface circuits. Most interface circuits are small-scale bipolar chips whose failure rate is much lower then that of the RAMs. In addition, for large memory arrays there are many more RAM chips than interface chips. Thus, it is a reasonable approximation to assume (in a properly designed system) that all failures occur in the RAM chips themselves.

The need for some sort of error detection or correction is therefore highly dependent on the memory size. Equally important, however, are the requirements of the application. For the space shuttle controller or a life-support medical instrument, maximum reliability is clearly essential. In a graphics workstation, on the other hand, the needs may not be so extreme; if a single dot erroneously changes from red to blue once every year or two, no one is likely to even notice. In general, data memory is less critical than program memory. The system designer must evaluate the effects of a failure. If it is acceptable for the system to be automatically halted and restarted when a failure occurs, then simple error detection (parity) can be used. The following sections describe several approaches to error detection and their effects on system reliability and performance.

4.10.2   Parity

Parity is the simplest form of error detection. The parity of a word is either even or odd and is determined by the number of ones it contains. For example, 10101111 and 10000010 have even parity, and 10000000 and 10101011 have odd parity. Combining all the bits of the word with XOR gates produces a signal that is high if the word's parity is odd.

To use parity for error detection, a parity bit is appended to each word of memory. The parity bit is chosen to force all data words to have the same parity, either even or odd. Odd parity is the most widely used, because it has the advantage of detecting all zeros as an error. For example, if the data byte is 10101111, the parity bit is set to 1 to force the parity of all 9 bits to be odd. If the data byte is 10000000, then the parity bit is set to 0, again resulting in odd parity for the 9-bit word.

Implementing parity therefore requires one additional memory bit for each byte (or word, although parity is usually implemented separately for each byte in longer words). Figure 4.37 shows a circuit for parity generation and checking. The 74F280 parity generator/checker has nine data inputs (labeled A to I) and provides both even- and odd-parity outputs. (An F-series device is shown because the parity generator's delay adds to the memory access time, so high speed is typically required.) When writing data to the memory, the data to be written drives eight of the data inputs, and the ninth is forced low. If the parity of the original byte is even, the parity bit is set to 1 to force the 9-bit word to have odd parity. Thus, the EVEN output provides the data to be written to the parity bit.

When the data is read, the memory's parity bit drives the ninth input of the 74F280.

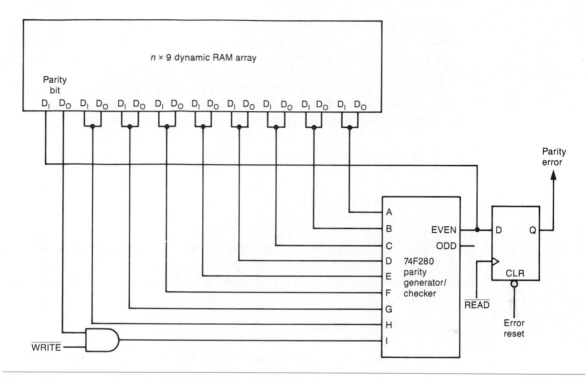

Figure 4.37. Parity generation and checking circuit for dynamic RAM.

If there are no errors, the result should be odd. Thus, the EVEN output signals that there is an error in the data.

As with all error detection schemes, the additional logic introduces additional delays in the memory timing. For write cycles, the data must propagate through the parity generator/checker before the write cycle can be completed. This does not usually affect the access time, since data is available from the microprocessor early in the cycle. For read cycles, the propagation delay time through the parity generator/checker must elapse before it is known if there is an error. The data from the memory must remain valid for the propagation delay time of the parity generator circuit.

Parity cannot be used to correct an error, since there is no way of knowing in which bit the error occurred. Thus, not much can be done when a parity error occurs; usually the safest thing to do is halt the system. This can be done by asserting the microprocessor's halt, wait, or nonmaskable interrupt input. If the interrupt is used, the microprocessor can execute a shutdown sequence or a HALT instruction. This can be risky, however, if the interrupt handler uses the same memory in which the error occurred.

When a parity error is detected, the most common approach is to display a warning to the user, who must manually restart the system. In some applications, it may be desirable to automatically restart the system. In this case, the parity error signal can reset the microprocessor. If the error was a soft error, the system will operate correctly once restarted.

If the memory contains only data, it may be desirable to allow the system to keep running. If the parity error signal generates an interrupt, the software will know that an error has occurred and can choose to return from the interrupt and continue operation. A warning can be displayed and an error log updated for service personnel.

The IBM PC is an example of a system that displays an error and halts if an error occurs, and also illustrates this approach's drawback. The user is likely to lose any data that is in RAM (such as a file being edited) at the time the parity error occurs; if the system were allowed to keep running, probably only one byte of data (such as one character in a text document) would be lost. On the other hand, if the parity error occurred in a program byte, a more serious failure (such as an erroneous disk write) could occur.

Parity cannot detect errors in two or more bits at the same time, since changing any two (or any even number of) bits does not affect the parity. Fortunately, multibit errors are much less frequent than single-bit errors. Two-bit soft errors are very rare in a properly designed system. In systems using 1-bit-wide RAMs, the failure of an entire chip causes only a single-bit error (in many different locations). Thus, hard errors in such a system generally affect only one bit at a time, and since a single error will halt the system when parity is used, the second error will not have a chance to occur.

4.10.3   Error Correcting Codes

Parity adds a single bit to each data word, which allows the detection but not the correction of errors. By using more check bits appended to each word, it is possible to correct errors as well. These check bits are defined by an *error correcting code (ECC)*.

Most error detection and correction (EDC) systems use a modified Hamming code. The original Hamming code was invented by R. W. Hamming at Bell Laboratories and first published in 1950. Modern EDC systems use a modified Hamming code that allows the detection of 2-bit errors, reduces the logic required for implementation, and detects gross errors, such as a word that is all ones or all zeros.

The basic Hamming code requires five check bits for a 16-bit data word. A sixth check bit is required to detect 2-bit errors. Each time the word size is doubled, one additional check bit is needed. As Table 4.4 shows, the check bits represent a considerable amount of overhead. The percent overhead decreases greatly as the word size increases. Since most 8-bit microprocessors cannot address enough memory to require EDC, and because the overhead at 8 bits is so great, EDC is rarely implemented for

Table 4.4   Check Bits Required for Single-bit Error Correction and 2-bit Error Detection

Memory word		Check bit overhead
No. of data bits	No. of check bits	
8	5	38%
16	6	27%
32	7	14%
64	8	11%

Table 4.5   Bit Assignments for Generation of Check Bits
(Courtesy of Advanced Micro Devices, Inc.)

Generated Check Bits	Parity	Participating Data Bits															
		0	1	2	3	4	5	6	7	8	9	10	11	12	13	14	15
CX	Even (XOR)		X	X	X		X			X	X		X			X	
C0	Even (XOR)	X	X	X		X		X		X		X		X			
C1	Odd (XNOR)	X			X	X			X		X	X			X		X
C2	Odd (XNOR)	X	X				X	X	X				X	X	X		
C4	Even (XOR)			X	X	X	X	X	X							X	X
C8	Even (XOR)									X	X	X	X	X	X	X	X

The check bit is generated as either an XOR or XNOR of the eight data bits noted by an "X" in the table.

Figure 4.38. Writing check bits and data to memory.

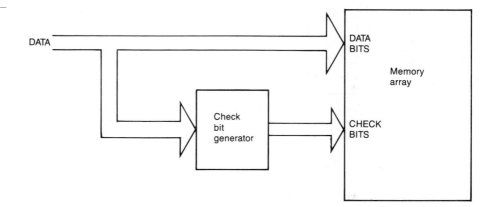

8-bit-wide memory. The most common use of EDC in microprocessor systems is with 16-bit and wider memories.

The key to the code is the algorithm used to generate the check bits. Each check bit is a parity bit for a subset of the data word. Table 4.5 shows which data bits generate each check bit for a 16-bit word. Each check bit is produced by XORing 8 selected bits from the 16-bit word. The C1 and C2 bits are inverted, allowing the detection of the all-zeros and all-ones error conditions.

The check bits are calculated each time data is written to the memory and are written along with the data, as shown in Fig. 4.38. When the data is read back, the check bits are recalculated. To determine if there is an error, and if so where, the recalculated check bits are XORed with the stored check bits, as shown in Fig. 4.39. The result of this operation is called the *syndrome*. If there is no error, both sets of check bits are identical and the syndrome is zero. If there is an error, the syndrome is nonzero, and its value identifies the bit in error. Table 4.6 shows the error indicated by each possible syndrome pattern. The syndrome will identify errors not only in the data but in the check bits as well. All 2-bit and most multibit errors are detected but cannot be corrected.

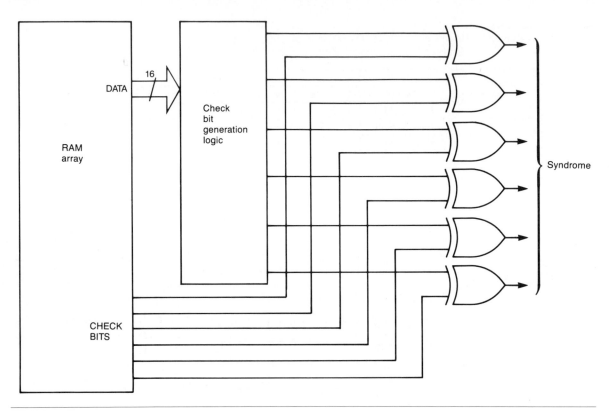

Figure 4.39.   Syndrome generation during read from memory.

Table 4.6   Decoding of Syndrome Bits to Determine Bit in Error
(Courtesy of Advanced Micro Devices, Inc.)

Syndrome Bits			S8	0	1	0	1	0	1	0	1
			S4	0	0	1	1	0	0	1	1
			S2	0	0	0	0	1	1	1	1
SX	S0	S1									
0	0	0		*	C8	C4	T	C2	T	T	M
0	0	1		C1	T	T	15	T	13	7	T
0	1	0		C0	T	T	M	T	12	6	T
0	1	1		T	10	4	T	0	T	T	M
1	0	0		CX	T	T	14	T	11	5	T
1	0	1		T	9	3	T	M	T	T	M
1	1	0		T	8	2	T	1	T	T	M
1	1	1		M	T	T	M	T	M	M	T

* – no errors detected
Number – location of the single bit-in-error
T – two errors detected
M – three or more errors detected

The EDC logic can thus correct the data by decoding the syndrome bits. If the syndrome is zero, the data is correct and no change is necessary. If the syndrome corresponds to one of the cells marked "T" or "M" in the table, then there is a multiple-bit error, which cannot be corrected. In this case, the best that can be done is to provide an error signal to the system. If there is only a single-bit error, then the bit in error (as identified by the syndrome) is simply inverted. An error in a check bit does not need to be corrected for the data to be valid but should be noted since it indicates a problem in the memory.

4.10.4 EDC Implementation

Error detection and correction can be implemented with standard TTL devices, such as parity generator/checkers and XOR gates. Until the development of LSI EDC devices, this was the only practical approach, and its complexity limited the number of systems in which EDC was used. Now, a variety of LSI chips are available that include most of the required logic on a single chip, making EDC more cost-effective in a wider variety of applications.

Figure 4.40 shows the block diagram for an error correcting memory system and the data flow for a write cycle. There are several possible configurations; the one shown is called *check always,* because the data passes through the EDC unit whether there are errors or not. During the write cycle, the data is provided to both the memory and the EDC unit. The EDC unit generates the check bits, which are written to the memory along with the data word.

Figure 4.41 shows the data flow during a read cycle. The data from the memory passes through the correction logic in the EDC unit before being driven on the system data bus. The check bits are recalculated and combined with the check bits read from the memory to form the syndrome, which is then decoded by the *bit-in-error* decoder. This decoder identifies the error bit for the correction logic and provides the ERROR and MULTIPLE ERROR outputs. The correction logic inverts the error bit (if any) and passes the data on to the system bus. The MULTIPLE ERROR output indicates that more than one bit is in error and that the data therefore cannot be corrected. This signal is used to initiate an interrupt, or, for microprocessors such as the 68000, a bus error. If the error was a soft read error, rereading the data may correct the problem.

Figure 4.42 shows the block diagram for AMD's Am2906 error detection and correction unit. During write cycles, the data is stored in the input latches. The check bits are then generated and pass through the syndrome generator (which performs no function during write cycles) and the output multiplexer and are output on the SC_0 to SC_6 pins.

During read cycles, the data from the memory, including the check bits, is stored in the EDC unit's input latches. The syndrome bits are output on the SC_0 to SC_6 pins. These bits, along with the address of the memory location read, identify the defective memory chip. This information can be stored in a diagnostic memory, which allows the system software to log errors for action by the service personnel. The $\overline{ERROR}$ output of the EDC unit serves as a write signal for this data and can also clock a counter to keep track of the number of errors that occur.

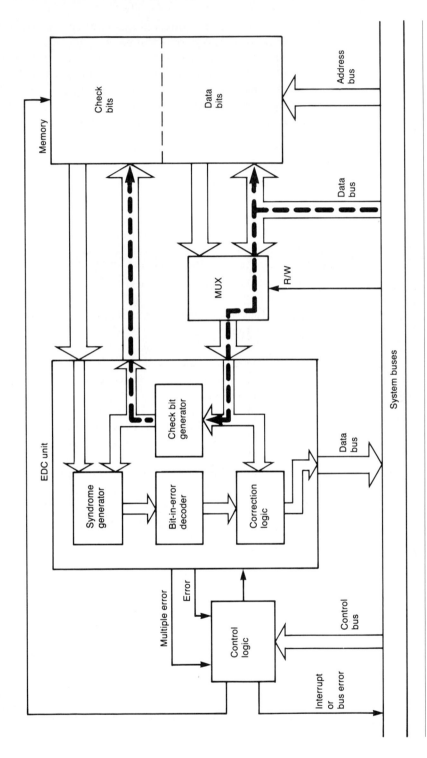

Figure 4.40. Write cycle data flow for memory system with EDC.

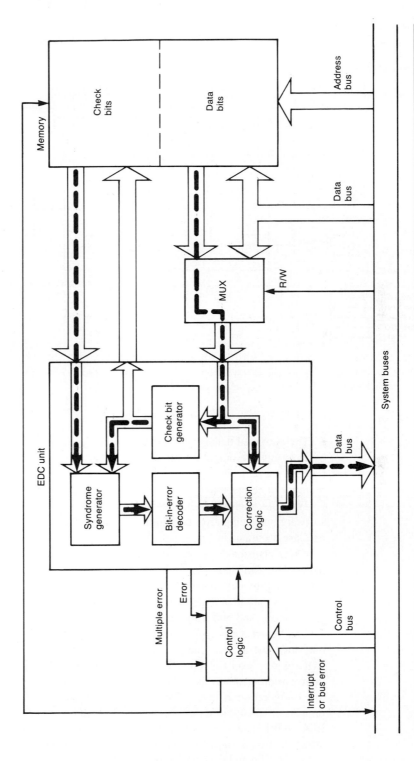

Figure 4.41. Read cycle data flow for memory system with EDC.

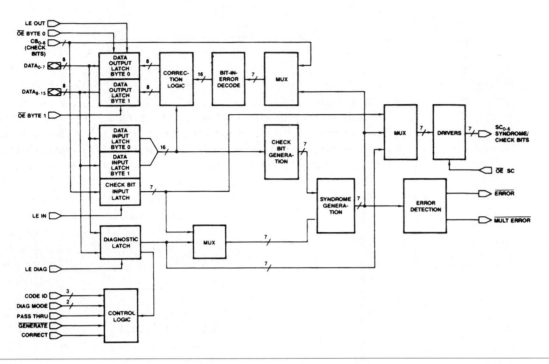

Figure 4.42. Am2960 error detection and correction unit block diagram. *(© Advanced Micro Devices, Inc. 1985. Reprinted with permission of owner. All rights reserved.)*

The corrected data is stored in the output latch, which is gated onto the system bus by asserting the output enable inputs. Separate output enables are provided for each byte to support single-byte read operations. This also allows physical 16-bit-wide memory to be made to appear to the processor as 8-bit-wide memory.

The 2906 includes a diagnostic latch, which allows the unit to be checked by the software by forcing error conditions and verifying that the syndrome and the corrected data are accurate.

AMD also makes a special latch/multiplexer/buffer chip that simplifies the data paths. The Am2961 and 2962 (inverting and noninverting versions) are 4 bits wide. Each chip provides connections for the EDC unit data bus, the system data bus, and the memory's data in and data out lines. Four of these chips thus provide all the data path multiplexing and buffering for a 16-bit system.

The "correct always" configuration described above is the simplest to implement but slows the access time of the memory considerably. The data passes through the EDC unit on every read cycle, so the correction delay is added to all cycles, even if there are no errors in the data. In high-performance applications, a *check only* parallel configuration is used. The data from the memory is read directly by the microprocessor, and at the same time the data is read by the EDC unit. If no error occurs, the EDC unit is not in the data path and does not directly add to the access time. It can affect the timing, however, because the cycle must not be terminated until the ERROR output is valid and the data has been corrected, if necessary. The 2906 requires 32 ns to detect an error and 65 ns to correct it. The $\overline{\text{ERROR}}$ output initiates a wait state when an error does occur, and the microprocessor then waits for the corrected data from the EDC unit.

4.10.5   System Considerations for EDC

While the EDC unit takes care of basic error detection and correction functions, several system-level problems must be considered. When an error occurs, the EDC unit corrects the data sent to the microprocessor, but it cannot correct the data in the memory itself unless an additional write cycle is performed. It is important that soft errors not be left in the memory, however. Although the error will be corrected each time the word is read, the ability to tolerate additional soft errors is lost. If a second error occurs and the data has not been rewritten to correct the first error, then an uncorrectable condition occurs.

There are two ways to handle this problem. With additional control logic, the EDC unit can be directed to automatically write the corrected data back into the memory whenever an error occurs. Alternatively, software can periodically *scrub* the memory by reading all the memory locations and rewriting any that contain errors. This scrubbing can be performed by the microprocessor as a background task, which executes while the system is waiting for some event to occur and thus has some spare time. This technique avoids the additional delay of an extra write cycle whenever an error occurs but requires that the microprocessor has enough slack time to periodically perform the scrubbing process.

Another problem with error correcting memory is that data must always be written an entire word at a time. This is a problem with most 16-bit microprocessors, which have byte write instructions that are intended to modify only half the 16-bit word. For these instructions to operate properly, the memory system control logic must automatically perform a read-modify-write sequence whenever a byte write is requested. The entire word is read, the byte to be written is modified, and then the entire word is rewritten. This is necessary to allow the check bits to be recalculated. Byte write operations are therefore significantly slower than word writes with error-corrected memory.

The system software must initialize the entire memory at power-up. If an attempt is made to read a word that has not been written, the random combination of data and check bits will most likely indicate a multibit error. While it usually indicates an error in the software if a memory location is read that has not previously been written, it is undesirable for this to appear as a memory failure. The problem is easily avoided by having the power-up initialization software write all zeros (or any other data) to all memory locations before any locations are read. Note that the same problem exists even with simple parity, except that there is a 50:50 chance that the parity will come out correct even with random memory contents.

4.10.6   Memory System Reliability with EDC

The calculation of error rates for a system with EDC is complex, because a single-bit error in the memory is not an error from the system point of view. Two failures are required to create a system error, so the system error rate is not simply the sum of the error rates of the components.

Preventive maintenance plays a major role in the reliability of systems with EDC. Errors almost always happen one at a time. Even an entire RAM chip failure is a single-bit error when the RAM chips are only one bit wide. The EDC logic can record each of these errors, so service personnel can replace chips that have failed completely (hard errors) or chips that are showing a large number of soft errors. Thus, the probability of a system error (a multiple-bit error) is proportional to the time it takes after a hard failure occurs for the service personnel to replace the failed device. Scrubbing or automatic rewriting of data virtually eliminates 2-bit soft errors.

Thus, it is difficult to give absolute numbers for the reliability of a system with EDC. As compared to a system with no error detection, reliability is increased by more than a factor of 20, even with no scrubbing or preventive maintenance. With scrubbing and preventive maintenance, reliability can be increased more than two orders of magnitude.

There is another technique that can be used to increase reliability even further. If at least one of the errors is a hard error, 2-bit errors can be corrected with additional software. When the EDC unit signals a multibit error, a special error handling routine is called. The data read is complemented and then written back to the memory and read again. Any bits with hard errors will not change, even though the data has been complemented. The software thus can determine which bit has a hard error. This bit is complemented, and the partially corrected data is written back to the EDC unit. The EDC unit can now correct the one remaining error. National Semiconductor's 8400 EDC chip performs this series of operations without any software assistance.

4.10.7   Selecting the Level of Protection

Error detection and correction clearly provides a high degree of reliability. The costs are considerable, however, and are not justified in many applications. More memory chips are required, additional logic is required to provide the EDC functions, additional software is required to handle errors, and memory access is slowed. Power consumption is increased, resulting in the need for a larger power supply and additional cooling.

Parity is far simpler to implement and will catch the great majority of memory errors. It will not, however, allow the system to keep running when an error occurs (unless the error is ignored). Thus, while parity generally provides an acceptable level of error protection, the need to restart the machine in the case of soft errors or to wait for a service call in case of a hard error may not be acceptable. Parity is also undesirable in very large memory systems, since the increased chip count actually decreases the system's MTBF.

Unchecked memory is used in relatively small systems, in which the small number of devices keeps the error rate low. Systems using mostly static RAM and EPROM or EEPROM do not generally require error detection or correction, since the inherent reliability of these devices is very high and the number of chips is usually small.

4.11 MEMORY MANAGEMENT

In most microprocessor systems, the microprocessor provides an address that directly selects a physical memory location. Adding a *memory management unit* (MMU) to control the microprocessor's access to memory and to translate addresses provides a variety of additional features. This section describes the functions of an MMU and the reasons for its use.

4.11.1 Memory Management Concepts

As shown in Fig. 4.43, the MMU translates the *logical address* from the microprocessor to a *physical address* for the memory. The least-significant bits of the address bus are not processed by the MMU; these bits represent an offset into the section of memory addressed by the upper bits.

Address translation is a basic function of any MMU. With an MMU, application software does not need to be concerned with physical memory locations. This is particularly important when there are multiple programs or tasks in memory at the same time. When the operating system loads a program or task into memory, it sets up the MMU to translate the logical address of the program to the physical address at which the program was loaded. (A *task* is an isolated section of a program.)

Address translation can be used to extend the addressing range of the microprocessor. Many 8-bit microprocessors have only a 16-bit address bus and are thus limited to a 64-Kbyte address space. As memory cost has dropped, it has become economical to have larger amounts of memory. Program sizes have also increased, requiring more memory.

The simplest way to extend the address range is by using *bank switching*. Bits from an output port are used to directly enable separate memory banks or are decoded as the most-significant address bits. A single 8-bit port can provide an additional 8 address bits, multiplying the address space by 256. However, this technique is restrictive. Each of the memory banks is isolated, and only one can be accessed at a time. If each bank is associated with a task, then it is difficult for the tasks to share any code or data; it must be replicated in each bank.

A more sophisticated scheme is to use a few of the upper address bits to select a

Figure 4.43. Translation of virtual to physical address with memory management unit.

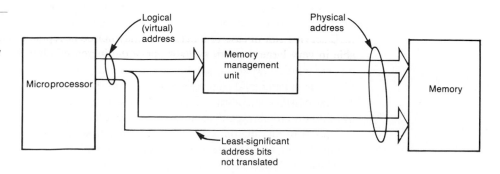

register, which in turn contains the upper bits of the physical address. Examples of memory management ICs that operate in this manner are Motorola's 6829 (intended for use with the 6809) and Texas Instruments' 74610. The 6829 uses the upper five bits of the 16-bit address bus to select one of 32 10-bit registers. The contents of the selected 10-bit register replace the five address bits used to select the register, resulting in a 21-bit physical address. Since the least significant 11 address bits are passed directly to the memory and are not used by the MMU, each possible address mapping affects a block of 2^{11} (2K) addresses. Thus, the smallest block that can be separately mapped is 2K, and the system is said to have a *granularity* of 2K.

When the microprocessor switches tasks, the contents of the mapping registers must be changed to represent the memory assignments for the new task. To speed this process, multiple sets of address translation registers can be included in the MMU. A *task register* stores the number of the task currently executing and selects one set of translation registers. To change tasks, the microprocessor simply reloads the task register, and an entirely new set of translation registers becomes active.

4.11.2   Memory Management Unit Operation

Simple address translation schemes such as those described above are natural approaches to expanding the memory space of older microprocessor architectures. For 16- and 32-bit microprocessors, however, the motivation for memory management is not to expand the address space, but to increase the microprocessor's ability to have many programs in memory at the same time and to protect these programs from interfering with each other.

Minicomputers and mainframe computers have used sophisticated memory management techniques for many years, and most MMUs designed for 16- and 32-bit microprocessors are derived from these designs. The simple translation techniques described previously are replaced by more complex approaches, and additional functions are added. The logical address space can be divided in one of two ways: paging or segmentation. *Paging* divides the address space into many small, fixed-size blocks that do not overlap, while *segmentation* divides the memory into relatively large, variable-size blocks that can overlap. Combined schemes are also used in which segments are divided into pages.

For each page or segment, there is a *descriptor*. The descriptor specifies the physical address to which the block is assigned and also specifies the types of accesses that are allowed. For example, a page or segment can be specified as read-only, execute-only, system-only, etc., and can also be classified as a code, data, or stack area.

Each time the microprocessor outputs an address, the MMU must locate the descriptor for the addressed page or segment. Typically, the MMU has a cache of frequently used descriptors (called a *translation look-aside buffer,* or *TLB*) on-chip, but it must access external memory for the descriptor if it is not in the cache. The descriptor tells the MMU what physical address to provide to the rest of the system and what type of accesses are allowed. The access rights bits are compared to the control and status signals from the microprocessor, and if a disallowed access is attempted, the MMU terminates the cycle by asserting a bus error signal to the microprocessor.

Thus, the MMU allows the operating system to specify what areas of memory can be accessed by a given program, and to restrict the type of accesses that can be performed. This protects one task from interfering with another or with the operating system, since tasks can access only memory that is assigned to them. If a task needs access to a system program, it is given "execute-only" access so that the program cannot be modified.

In addition to protecting tasks from each other, they can also be protected from themselves. By assigning separate areas for data, program code, and stack, common programming errors such as reading code as data or a runaway stack can be automatically detected.

It is also useful for the operating system to know if each block of memory has been accessed or modified. To provide this information, each page or segment descriptor generally includes a "used" bit that is set if any location in the block is read and a "dirty" bit that is set if any location is written. If the dirty bit is set, then the operating system must write the block back to the disk before reusing the associated memory area; if it is not set, then the memory area can be reused immediately.

An MMU delays the presentation of the address to the rest of the system and thus can negatively affect system performance. In some system designs, it is possible to take advantage of the fact that the low-order address bits do not pass through the MMU, and thus are valid earlier than the upper bits. For example, dynamic RAM is addressed in two phases: the row address followed by the column address. Since the row address consists of unmapped address bits, the memory cycle can be started (by asserting $\overline{RAS}$) without waiting for the MMU delay. Intel's 80286 eliminates the address translation delay by including the MMU on the microprocessor chip. The 80286 has an instruction pipeline and performs address calculation in parallel with instruction execution.

Most 16- and 32-bit microprocessor families include one or more optional MMUs. For the 68000 family, Motorola provides the 68451 segmented MMU and the 68851 paged MMU, and Signetics produces the 68910 and 68920 MMUs. The 32082 MMU works with National's 32000-family microprocessors. Zilog's Z8010 and Z8015 provide memory management for Z8000-family microprocessors. Intel does not provide separate MMUs but includes an MMU in the 80286 and 80386 microprocessors.

4.11.3 Virtual Memory

Virtual memory is a memory management technique that allows all memory, including main memory and mass storage devices, to be addressed as part of one large logical address space. The logical address space is larger than the microprocessor's physical address space. When the microprocessor outputs an address, the MMU fetches the descriptor for the addressed page or segment. The descriptor includes a bit that indicates if the requested data is present in main memory or if it is in a mass-storage device. If it is not present in main memory (called a *page fault*), the MMU aborts the current instruction and requests the operating system to read the required page from the mass-storage device. After the page is read into main memory, the instruction can be restarted or continued. Thus, aside from a difference in access time, an application program does not need to distinguish between data or code in main memory and in mass storage. This is called a *demand-paged* system, since pages are read from mass storage on demand. The process of moving pages between main memory and mass storage is called *swapping,* or *paging*.

One advantage of virtual memory is that it allows programs larger than the main memory to be executed. This can be done without virtual memory, but the programmer must divide the program into "overlays" that are loaded explicitly by the application program as needed. The availability of large, inexpensive RAM chips for main memory has reduced the need for virtual memory, and it is used in only the most sophisticated microprocessor-based systems.

Virtual memory requires that the microprocessor have the ability to terminate or suspend an instruction and then restart or continue it after the desired memory block has been read from the mass storage device. Since a page fault can occur on any operand fetch, an instruction may be partially completed when it must be terminated. An interrupt cannot be used to abort an instruction, since interrupts are processed only between instructions. Thus, an "instruction abort" signal (such as the 68000 family's $\overline{\text{BERR}}$) is needed. Two different approaches can be used to continue the instruction after memory is swapped in response to a page fault. In the approach used by the 32000 family, the processor can be restored to its state at the start of the instruction. The 68010 and 68020 use instruction continuation; when a bus error occurs, the processor state is stored on the stack. On returning from the bus error, the processor state is restored from the stack, effectively continuing from the middle of the instruction.

4.12 DESIGN EXAMPLE

In this section, we add the address decoder and memory to our example system. Since most dedicated control applications require relatively modest amounts of RAM, static RAM is the best choice. Since all systems need some RAM and some EPROM, the example system includes one socket for each. In addition, two universal byte-wide sockets are included that can be used for either type of device or for EEPROM.

4.12.1 Address Decoding and Memory Circuits

The address decoder for this system is very simple. A single 74ALS138 provides eight chip select outputs, each of which is active for a 32-Kbyte range of addresses. Figure 4.44 shows the schematic for the memory subsystem, and Fig. 4.45 shows the memory map. $\overline{\text{AS}}$ is not used to enable the decoder, so the outputs are valid as soon as possible in the memory cycle. It must be kept in mind, however, that the decoder outputs are not valid when $\overline{\text{AS}}$ is not asserted. The address decoder also provides chip selects for the 68901 MFP and the I/O ports, which are described in later chapters.

(In general, address decoders in 68000-family systems should be disabled when $\overline{\text{INTACK}}$ is asserted, since the interrupt priority level is output on the low-order address lines. However, the high-order address lines are high during an interrupt acknowledge cycle. Thus, the decoder in the example is disabled by A_{18} and A_{19}.)

The memory at the lowest address range can be a 2764, 27128, or 27256 EPROM. A RAM cannot be used here, since the power-up address pointer and initial stack pointer are read from locations 00000 to 00007. The "top" memory socket is configured for RAM only, which may be an 8- or 32-Kbyte device. To reduce the number of jumpers required, 2-Kbyte devices are not supported. The middle two memory sockets

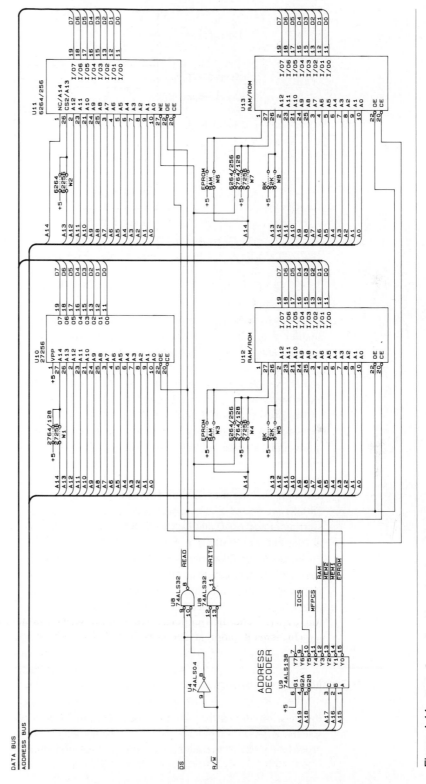

Figure 4.44. Design example address decoder and memory.

Figure 4.45. Design
example memory map.

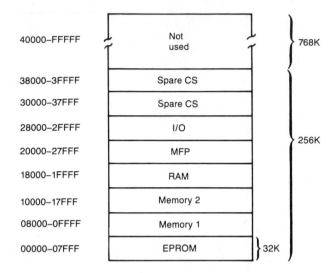

Address	Block	Size
40000–FFFFF	Not used	768K
38000–3FFFF	Spare CS	
30000–37FFF	Spare CS	
28000–2FFFF	I/O	
20000–27FFF	MFP	256K
18000–1FFFF	RAM	
10000–17FFF	Memory 2	
08000–0FFFF	Memory 1	
00000–07FFF	EPROM	32K

include a full complement of jumpers to allow either memory type to be used. (The functions of these jumpers were described earlier in Sec. 4.5.) Note that if memory ICs smaller than 32K are used, the address space occupied will not be contiguous, which must be taken into account in the software.

Two gates and an inverter produce $\overline{\text{READ}}$ and $\overline{\text{WRITE}}$ strobes from the 68008's $\overline{\text{DS}}$ and R/$\overline{\text{W}}$. $\overline{\text{READ}}$ enables the output buffers on each memory chip, and $\overline{\text{WRITE}}$ provides the write strobe for the RAMs.

Because of the addressing modes available in 68000-family processors, not all address ranges are accessible with equal speed. The "short" direct addressing mode requires only a 16-bit address rather than a full 32-bit address, so instructions using this mode execute more quickly than instructions that use 32-bit direct addresses. When using this mode, the microprocessor takes the 16-bit address specified in the instruction and sign-extends it to 32 bits. If A_{15} of this address is 1, then bits A_{16} to A_{23} (A_{19} for a 68008) are set to 1. Thus, this addressing mode can be used for the 32-Kbyte block starting at address 0 and for the 32-Kbyte block at the top of the address space (starting at FF8000 for a 68000, or F8000 for a 68008).

In the design example, an EPROM is located in the bottom 32-Kbyte block. Thus, constants or data tables located in this EPROM can be accessed with the short addressing mode. However, none of the RAM can be accessed with this mode. To take full advantage of this addressing mode, RAM should be located at the very top of the address space. This has not been done in the design example because it complicates the address decoding circuitry.

4.12.2   Memory Timing

Figure 4.46 shows the system timing diagram introduced in Chap. 3, with the chip selects, $\overline{\text{READ}}$, and $\overline{\text{WRITE}}$ added. The chip selects are delayed from when the microprocessor outputs the address by the propagation delay of the 74ALS138, which is

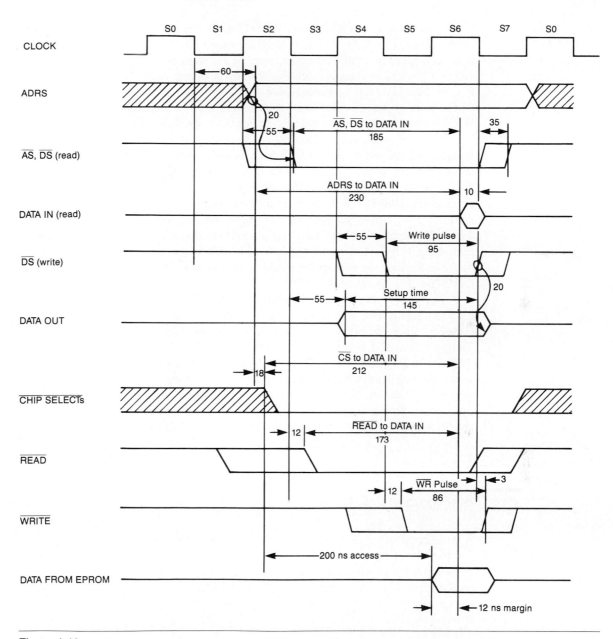

Figure 4.46. Design example timing. All times are given in nanoseconds.

18 ns maximum. Subtracting this 18 ns from the 230-ns address-out-to-data-in time calculated in Chap. 3 yields a chip-select-to-data-in-required time of 212 ns. This is the access time available to the memory chips. Thus, 200-ns devices are adequate. Note that the extra speed of the ALS family is useful here; an HC or LS decoder would make 200-ns EPROMs marginally adequate.

The assertion of the $\overline{\text{READ}}$ and $\overline{\text{WRITE}}$ strobes is delayed from $\overline{\text{DS}}$ by the high-to-low propagation delay of the 74ALS32s, which is 12 ns. Thus, working from the times calculated in Chap. 3, the time from the assertion of $\overline{\text{READ}}$ to data in required is $185 - 12 = 173$ ns. This is much longer than the output enable time of most memory ICs, so there is no timing problem here.

For write cycles, there are two parameters of primary importance: the width of the $\overline{\text{WRITE}}$ strobe, and the data hold time after the negation of $\overline{\text{WRITE}}$. The worst-case $\overline{\text{WRITE}}$ strobe width occurs if the high-to-low delay of the 74ALS32 is the maximum possible (12 ns) and the low-to-high delay is the minimum possible (3 ns). Thus, the absolute minimum $\overline{\text{WRITE}}$ pulse width is the 95 ns provided by the 68008: $- 12$ ns $+ 3$ ns $= 86$ ns. For the Hitachi HM6264, this would require use of the 120-ns access time device (HM6264 – 12), since the minimum write pulse for the slower 150-ns version is 90 ns. However, this fully worst-case analysis is too conservative. No real 74ALS32 could exhibit both the maximum high-to-low delay and the minimum low-to-high delay. If the actual spread between these values is no more than 5 ns, as it is very likely to be, then the write pulse would be 90 ns. Thus, the 150-ns access time 6264 (HM6264 – 15) can be used.

Access time from address is not a problem, since the slowest version of the 6264 has a 150-ns access time and over 200 ns is available. The data setup time is also not a problem, since the 68008 provides 145 ns and the 6264 – 15 requires only 60 ns. Timing for the 32-Kbyte 62256 is similar.

The data hold time provided to the RAM is the hold time from the 68008 (20 ns) minus the maximum low-to-high propagation delay of the 74ALS32 (14 ns), which is only 6 ns. However, most RAMs require zero hold time, and our analysis uses worst-case values, so this is adequate. Note that slower gates such as a 74LS32 or 74HC32 should not be used here, since they would result in a negative worst-case hold time.

4.13   SUMMARY

A wide range of memory types is available for use in microprocessor-based systems. For permanent program storage, ROM, EPROM, or EEPROM is used. Mask-programmed ROM provides the lowest cost for applications with sufficiently high production volume. Ultraviolet-erasable EPROM provides flexibility for a modest cost but cannot be reprogrammed in the application system. EEPROM can be modified by the application system, but it is more expensive, is limited in the number of write cycles, and requires a long write time.

For temporary program and data storage, RAM is used. Static RAM is the easiest to use and is the best choice in small systems. When large amounts of RAM are required, dynamic RAM provides lower cost, lower power, and higher density. However, refresh and control logic is required, and error rates are higher than for static RAMs. For large dynamic RAM systems, error detection and correction is often used to increase reliability. In smaller dynamic memory systems, parity provides a much less expensive alternative and detects the vast majority of errors.

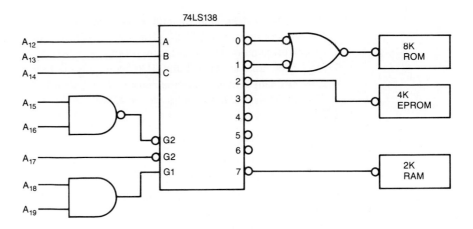

Figure 4.47. Address decoder for Exercise 4.

4.14   EXERCISES

4.1. List the differences between mass storage and main memory. Which is usually nonvolatile? Can both be nonvolatile? Which must be random access?

4.2. A system uses four 8-Kbyte ROMs. Design an address decoder by using a 74LS138 and other gates as necessary, assuming a 16-bit address bus.

4.3. For the memory and address decoder in Exercise 4.2, draw a complete circuit, showing the connection of all address lines and the control logic for the ROM's output enable. Design the additional circuitry necessary to fully decode a 24-bit address bus.

4.4. For the system shown in Fig. 4.47, what address range does each device respond to? Are there any memory locations that appear at more than one address? Which addresses are "used up" by the multiple memory images?

4.5. Design a bipolar PROM-based address decoder to replace the circuit in Exercise 4.2. List the data to be programmed in each PROM location.

4.6. A memory system uses memory ICs with an access time from address of 250 ns. There are two buffers in the data path and two in the address path, each of which has a delay of 20 ns. What is the effective access time of the system as seen by the microprocessor?

4.7. In the memory system described in Exercise 4.6, the memory's access time from output enable is 100 ns. How much delay can be tolerated in the address decoder before it affects the system access time? Does this depend on the memory type or configuration?

4.8. Design a circuit that can support EPROMs of 2, 4, or 8 Kbytes and static RAMs of 2 or 8 Kbytes. List the jumpers required for each memory type.

4.9. An instrument uses an EPROM for program storage. The EPROM costs $4.00

each for 1000-unit quantities, and \$3.50 each for 10,000 units or more. A mask-programmed ROM costs \$2.50 each for 1000 units, and \$2.00 each for 10,000 units or more. The mask charge is \$2000. Which is the best choice if 1000 units are to be built? If 10,000 units are to be built? If the program must be changed twice after the mask is made, what is the minimum quantity for the ROM to cost the same as the EPROM?

4.10.   What is the key difference between static and dynamic RAM? When is dynamic RAM preferable? What are its disadvantages?

4.11.   Design a circuit using standard TTL devices to implement the address multiplexing and refresh logic for a 512-Kbyte array of 256-Kbit dynamic RAMs.

4.12.   Are the memory cells in a pseudo-static RAM static or dynamic?

4.13.   When maximum speed is more important than all else, which RAM technology is preferred? What if cost per bit is most important?

4.14.   A television tuner uses nonvolatile memory for storing the fine tuning setting for each channel. Which memory technology would you recommend?

4.15.   An industrial control system needs 32 Kbytes of memory to store the process parameters and measurement data. This data must not be lost if power fails. Which memory technology would be best? What other information about the system is needed?

4.16.   Design a circuit to interface the 2004 NVRAM to a microprocessor system bus. What special software considerations are required?

4.17.   A battery-backed memory is implemented with a CMOS RAM chip and a lithium battery. The RAM has a current consumption (at the battery voltage) of 10 μA, and the battery capacity is 150 mAh. The shelf life is 10 years. How long will the battery last?

4.18.   Repeat Exercise 4.17, assuming the RAM's current consumption is 5 μA and the battery capacity is 750 mAh.

4.19.   A 1-Mbyte memory system is implemented with 256-Kbit RAMs with an error rate of 0.14 percent per 1000 hours. If no parity is used, what is the MTBF of the system? What is the MTBF with parity?

4.20.   How many additional memory chips are required to add error detection and correction to the system in Exercise 4.19, assuming that the memory is organized as 16-bit words? What if the memory is organized as 8-bit words? Or as 32-bit words?

4.21.   Modify the design example circuit so that one 32-Kbyte EPROM and three 8-Kbyte RAMs can be used, with a contiguous address space for the RAMs.

4.22.   Suppose that the address decoder in the design example were enabled only when $\overline{AS}$ is asserted. How does this affect the memory timing? What speed memory ICs would be needed?

4.23.   Modify the design example circuit to add battery backup for the RAMs.

4.24.   Are any hardware changes required to use EEPROMs in the design example system? Do they affect the software requirements? What are the limitations?

4.25. Modify the design example circuit to allow the use of the 68008's single-word direct addressing mode for both EPROM and RAM.

4.15 SELECTED BIBLIOGRAPHY

For general information on memory types and interfacing, refer to the introductory and intermediate microprocessor texts listed at the end of Chap. 1.

For specific information about a particular memory device, refer to the manufacturer's literature.

General Memory References

Intel. *Memory Components Handbook,* Santa Clara, CA. Includes data on RAM, EPROM, and EEPROM memories and dynamic memory controllers. Also includes many useful application notes and article reprints.

JEDEC. *JEDEC Standard Number 21-A: Configurations for Solid-State Memories,* 1985. The official standard for memory pin assignments. Available from EIA, 2001 Eye St. N. W., Washington, DC 20006.

Monolithic Memories. *Programmable Array Logic Handbook,* Santa Clara, CA. Describes PAL programmable logic devices and includes examples of PALs used as address decoders and memory interface circuits.

Dynamic RAM

Graden, Duane. *AN-816: Software Refreshed Memory Card for the MC68000,* Phoenix: Motorola, 1981. Describes circuitry and software for software refresh.

National Semiconductor. *APPS Handbook 2: Memory Support,* Santa Clara, CA. Includes data sheets and application notes for dynamic RAM controllers and EDC circuits.

Thompson Components-Mostek. *Memory Designer's Guide,* Carrollton, TX. A collection of application notes and article reprints.

Nonvolatile Memory

Hillman, Alfred. "Non-Volatile Memory Selection Mandates Careful Tradeoffs," *EDN,* Apr. 14, 1983, pp. 135–39. Describes each of the nonvolatile memory types and advantages and disadvantages of each.

Vaccarella, R. M. "CMOS with Battery Backup Gives Top Memory Protection," *Electronic Design,* Mar. 31, 1983, pp. 175–80. Covers design considerations for battery-backed memory.

Xicor. *User's Handbook* and *Applications Handbook,* Milpitas, CA. These handbooks describe Xicor's EEPROMS and NVRAMs and include several useful application notes.

Error Detection and Correction

Advanced Micro Devices. *Bipolar Microprocessor, Logic, and Interface Databook,* Sunnyvale, CA. Contains data sheets and application notes for AMD's family of dynamic RAM support chips, including refresh controllers and EDC units.

Intel. *AP-46: Error Detecting and Correcting Codes Part 1,* and *AP-73: Memory Systems Reliability with ECC,* Santa Clara, CA. Describe operation of error-correcting codes and their reliability implications. Provide an example of an EDC implementation with standard TTL devices, which is impractical but useful for illustrating the principles.

Lucy, Drew. "Choose the Right Level of Memory Protection," *Electronic Design,* Feb. 18, 1982, pp. ss37–ss42. Explains basic failure rate calculations as they apply to dynamic RAM systems and discusses the selection of parity or EDC.

Memory Management

Strauss, Edmund. *Inside the 80286,* New York: Brady, 1986. Includes a detailed description of the memory-management unit that is included in the 80286.

Tomplait, Cliff. "Memory Management Boosts Efficiency of Powerful Micros," *Computer Design,* July 1, 1985, pp. 105–109. Describes general memory-management concepts.

Wright, Maury. "Memory-Management Schemes Respond to Super-μC Requirements," *EDN,* Feb. 7, 1985, pp. 97–106. Describes Motorola's, National's, and Zilog's memory-management chips.

CHAPTER 5

BUS PERIPHERALS

5.1 INTRODUCTION

The buses in a microprocessor system are the link that connects all major parts of the system. We have already described how various microprocessors and memories connect to the buses. In later chapters, interfaces for many types of input and output (I/O) peripherals are described. This chapter describes the connection of any peripheral chip to the microprocessor's buses and also covers peripheral chips that are not primarily memory devices or I/O interfaces.

These *bus peripherals* provide additional hardware functions to support the microprocessor. *Programmable counter/timers* can produce periodic interrupts to pace the operation of software. They can also count transitions of external signals, measure time delays, and generate timed output pulses. *Clock/calendar ICs* keep track of time and date and are easily powered by batteries to keep working even when the system is off. *Direct memory access (DMA) controllers* provide fast data transfers.

One attribute shared by each of these functions is that hardware is being used to reduce the burden on the microprocessor and improve performance. In a sense, each device is a slave processor, providing a special function that the main processor cannot perform easily or quickly.

5.2   PERIPHERAL CHIP INTERFACING

Regardless of the particular function performed, most peripheral chips interface to the microprocessor as a group of I/O ports. This section describes the details of this interface.

5.2.1   Basic Peripheral Chip Interface

Figure 5.1 shows the basic interface signals. Some number of address lines, typically two to four, select one of the peripheral chip's internal registers. The $\overline{CS}$ (chip select) input enables the device to read data from or write data to the data bus, as controlled by the $\overline{READ}$ and $\overline{WRITE}$ control signals. For microprocessors that have separate memory and I/O addressing, either memory or I/O read and write signals may be used. Using memory read and write signals to access a peripheral device makes the peripheral appear as a *memory-mapped* device.

Many peripheral chips provide an interrupt output, which is asserted when a response is required from the microprocessor. Depending on the particular microprocessor the chip is designed to work with, it may also have an interrupt acknowledge input or interrupt priority signals. Some peripheral chips are designed to work with DMA controllers, and include signals to coordinate transfers with the controller.

The registers in the peripheral chip may connect directly to I/O pins, as in the case of a parallel I/O chip. In more complex peripheral chips, the registers serve as the interface between the microprocessor and control logic in the peripheral chip. The microprocessor writes commands and data to these registers, and based on these inputs, the chip performs some function. The microprocessor also reads status information and data from the registers. Many chips share a single address for the control and status registers; the control register is write-only, and the status register is read-only.

The number of address lines determines the number of registers that can be directly addressed. However, many peripheral chips use one or more "tricks" to allow access to more registers. One technique is to use a data bit as an extra address bit. A write to a

Figure 5.1.  Basic peripheral chip interface.

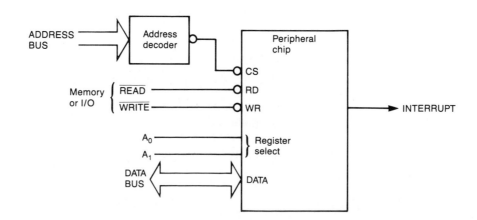

particular address accesses one of two registers, depending on the state of one or more of the data bits. Another approach is to perform a series of accesses to a single address, accessing a group of registers in sequence. One register may also be used as a pointer to select others. These techniques allow the number of address pins to be kept small and also minimize the amount of address space required by the peripheral chip. The peripheral chips described in this chapter and in the remainder of the book provide examples of each of these approaches.

5.2.2 Mixing and Matching Processors and Peripherals

Most peripheral chips are designed to work with a particular microprocessor or family of microprocessors. The control signal definitions and timing are designed to minimize the amount of logic needed to connect the peripheral chip to the microprocessor. Interfacing the peripheral chip to the microprocessor can be almost as simple as connecting all the pins of the same name or following a circuit provided in a data sheet or application note. However, it is limiting to consider only peripheral chips designed explicitly to work with the microprocessor you are using. Often, another microprocessor family includes a peripheral chip that is better suited to the application. In addition, some interface chips are made by companies that do not make microprocessors, and they try to make the bus interface easily adaptable to a wide variety of microprocessors.

When staying within the same family, it is generally not necessary to perform a detailed timing analysis. The peripheral chips are rated by the system clock speed, so if you are using an 8-MHz processor, using 8-MHz peripherals from the same family should guarantee that the timing is compatible.

However, more work is required when crossing family boundaries. Areas that must be checked include the following:

Bus timing for read and write cycles

Control signal polarities

Logic levels

Bus loading

Interrupt structure

Bus timing compatibility, one of the most troublesome areas, is covered in Sec. 5.2.3. Control signal polarities are not usually a problem since active-low control signals are nearly universal. However, some peripherals, such as some Motorola devices, require an active-high data strobe. The reset input is also active-high on some peripherals. These problems are easily corrected with an inverter.

Logic-level incompatibility occurs most commonly when a CMOS peripheral is used with an NMOS microprocessor. Most CMOS peripherals require a logic-high level above the level that an NMOS or TTL device will guarantee. This problem can be corrected by using an HCT-type buffer or pull-up resistors.

Peripherals that generate an interrupt may not be compatible with the microprocessor's interrupt vectoring scheme. Most Intel microprocessors use an external interrupt controller that can be programmed to accommodate an interrupt from nearly any device. The Z80, on the other hand, requires considerable interrupt support logic from the peripheral chip, which makes non-Z80-family peripherals difficult to use when interrupts are required.

5.2.3   Microprocessor and Peripheral Timing Compatibility

It is very common for there to be some degree of timing incompatibility between a microprocessor and a peripheral IC, even when they are from the same manufacturer. Nearly all timing incompatibilities can be overcome by adding wait states and/or additional logic. The major timing parameters that must be checked are as follows:

> Read and write strobe minimum pulse width
>
> Access time from address, from chip select, and from the read strobe
>
> Data setup and hold time for write cycles
>
> Relationships among address, chip select, and read and write strobes

The first two items above are the most easily remedied, since adding wait states will provide arbitrarily long strobe pulses and access times. Data setup and hold times for write cycles can be a more difficult problem. The first specification to check in this regard is whether the data is required to be valid at the leading edge of the write strobe or only at the trailing edge. Some microprocessors, such as the Z80 and 68000, provide valid data before the write strobe is asserted. Others, such as most Intel microprocessors, do not. Most peripheral chips do not require data to be valid at the leading edge of the write strobe, but some do, such as the 8530 serial communications interface.

As long as data is not required at the leading edge of the write strobe, data setup time requirements can be met by adding wait states if needed. Lack of adequate data hold time from the microprocessor is more difficult to correct and is a common problem. Adding wait states does not help, since they only delay the inevitable end of the write cycle, when the hold time problem occurs. There are several approaches to this problem:

1. Latch the data from the microprocessor so that valid data is available to the peripheral after the microprocessor has removed the data. An example of this technique is provided in the design example display interface in Chap. 7.

2. Generate a write strobe that is terminated earlier than the write strobe from the microprocessor.

3. Connect the peripheral to an I/O port rather than directly to the data bus.

Figure 5.2 shows an example of the second technique for 68000-family systems; Fig. 5.3 is the timing diagram. This circuit produces two wait states for write cycles and one wait state for read cycles and adds more than one-half clock cycle of data hold time.

Both flip-flops are held cleared until $\overline{DS}$ is asserted. Q_1 is set by the first rising clock edge after $\overline{DS}$ is asserted, and Q_2 is set on the following rising clock edge. The $\overline{WDS}$ (write data strobe) output is asserted as soon as $\overline{DS}$ is asserted, but it is negated when

Figure 5.2. Circuit for additional hold time in 68000-family systems.

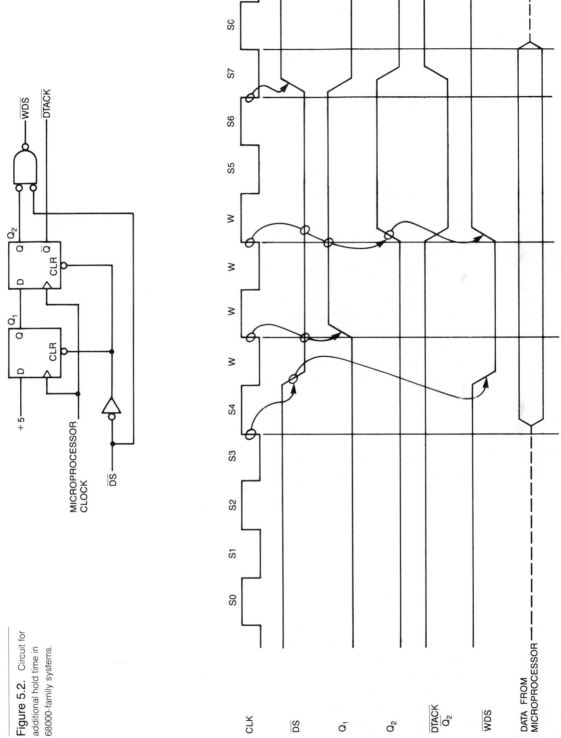

Figure 5.3. Timing diagram for Fig. 5.2.

Q_2 is set, which is 1½ clock cycles before the microprocessor negates $\overline{DS}$. Thus, the additional hold time is approximately 1½ clock cycles. In many 68000-family systems, the flip-flops (or an equivalent shift register) are already present for $\overline{DTACK}$ generation, so the additional circuitry required to generate the special $\overline{WDS}$ signal is only a single gate.

Some peripheral chips place additional timing constraints on the relationships of the control signals. For example, the 8530 serial communications interface requires that the address be valid for a specified setup time before the read or write strobe is asserted. The 68901, as described in the design example in Sec. 5.8, requires that the address input be valid for a specified setup time before the assertion of the chip select input.

5.2.4   Bus Interfacing via I/O Ports

The most general solution to microprocessor and peripheral incompatibilities is to connect the peripheral to I/O ports rather than directly to the bus. Figure 5.4 shows an example in which an Intel peripheral is connected to a Motorola microprocessor (such as a 6809) via a Motorola parallel I/O chip. The data bus connections on the peripheral are connected to I/O lines, as are the read and write strobes, address lines, and chip select input. The software asserts and negates each control line to perform the desired function. For example, the sequence for a write to address 1 of the peripheral is as follows:

1.   Output data to port A.

2.   Output 1 to bit 0, and 0 to bit 1 of port B (this sets the address).

Figure 5.4. Peripheral interfacing via I/O ports.

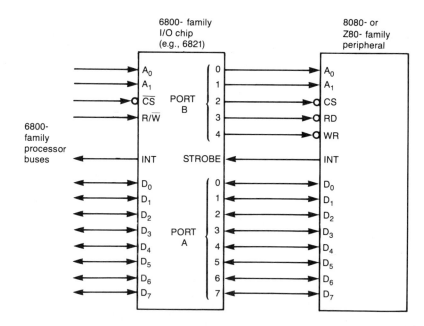

3. Output 0 to bits 2 and 4 of port B (asserts $\overline{CS}$ and $\overline{WR}$).

4. Output 1 to bits 2 and 4 of port B (ncgates $\overline{CS}$ and $\overline{WR}$).

Thus, this four-step sequence replaces what would normally be a write to address 1. The additional software complexity is inconsequential, since it can be confined to a few subroutines through which the rest of the software accesses the peripheral. The peripheral is thus completely isolated from the timing of the microprocessor's buses. The timing seen by the peripheral is quite slow, since at least two bus cycles (one instruction fetch cycle and one write cycle for the write to the I/O port chip) occur between signal transitions. No analysis of the interface between the I/O port chip and the microprocessor is required, since they are designed to work together.

An additional benefit of this approach is that the I/O port chip can serve as an interrupt controller. This is particularly useful if the microprocessor is a device such as the Z80, whose interrupt structure is difficult to support with a non-Z80-family device. The peripheral's interrupt output drives a strobe or data input of the I/O chip, which in turn generates an interrupt to the microprocessor.

While this approach does allow incompatible devices to be used together, it requires additional interface logic and is much slower than a direct bus interface. Use of a more compatible peripheral chip (if available) should be considered to make the interface simpler and faster.

5.2.5 Address Decoding for Peripheral Chips

Address decoding for peripheral chips is very similar to address decoding for memories, which is described in Chap. 4. The primary difference is that the block size (range of addresses) for each address select signal is much smaller. The minimum block size is determined by the number of addresses used by each peripheral chip. In addition, most microprocessors with separate I/O instructions use a shorter address for I/O than for memory; microprocessors with a 16-bit address bus typically use only 8 bits for I/O addresses.

Figure 5.5 shows an address decoder that provides eight outputs with a block size of 16 words. This assumes that the peripheral chips using these address select signals

Figure 5.5. I/O address decoder for 16-word block size, assuming an 8-bit I/O address.

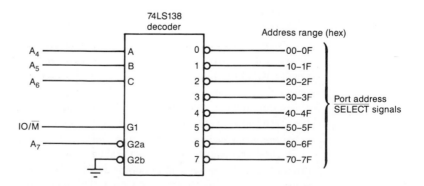

have four or fewer address lines. If one or more of the peripheral chips has fewer than four address lines, its registers will appear repeated within the 16-word block.

If memory-mapped I/O is used, the same address decoder can be used for both memory and I/O devices. This typically results in assigning a much larger block than necessary to the I/O devices, but unless all the address space is used this is not important.

Most peripheral chips have connections for read, write, and chip select signals. For such chips, the address decoder outputs need not be gated with any control signals. Some peripheral chips, however, lack a chip select input. In this case, the address select output is ANDed with the $\overline{\text{READ}}$ and $\overline{\text{WRITE}}$ signals from the microprocessor before they are connected to the peripheral chip. The delay caused by these gates must be considered when analyzing the timing. The delay of the $\overline{\text{WRITE}}$ signal is particularly critical, since it reduces the data hold time available to the peripheral chip.

5.3 PROGRAMMABLE COUNTER/TIMERS

Programmable counter/timer chips provide a variety of capabilities to support the microprocessor in handling time-critical events. Most of the major microprocessor families include a counter/timer chip. While the capabilities vary, the functions performed by most are similar. This section describes the functions of counter/timers and some example devices.

5.3.1 Counter/Timer Functions

At the heart of the device is a *down counter,* as shown in Fig. 5.6. It can operate in either *timer mode* or *counter mode.* In timer mode, the counter's clock is derived from the system clock. The counter is loaded with the "time constant" value (stored in the time constant register) and is then decremented on each clock pulse. When the counter reaches zero, an interrupt (or output pulse) is generated, a status bit is set, and the counter is reloaded with the time constant. Thus, a periodic interrupt (or an output pulse) is generated at a precise frequency selected by the microprocessor. While it is possible to write software loops to create time intervals, this is a tedious method and is impractical in complex applications. The counter/timer chip relieves the software of this burden.

Periodic interrupts allow the software to determine time intervals simply and reliably. Actions that must be performed frequently can be included in the timer's interrupt service routine. To measure longer periods of time, a software counter (stored in the system RAM) is incremented each interrupt. This counter then provides an elapsed time indication that can be used by other parts of the program.

An output pulse generated each time the counter reaches zero provides a signal with a software-programmable frequency. A common use for this output is as a baud rate generator for a serial communications interface.

In counter mode, the clock for the down counter comes from an external input. The microprocessor can reset the counter and then perform other tasks while the counter counts transitions of the external signal. The microprocessor then reads the counter to

Figure 5.6. Programmable counter/timer channel block diagram.

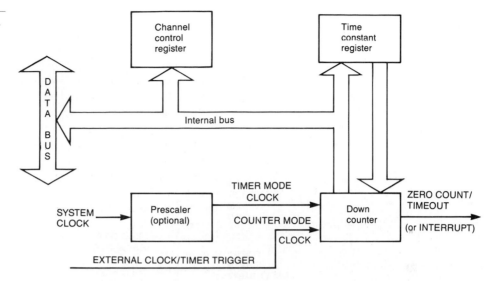

determine the number of transitions detected. This mode is particularly useful for interfacing to optical encoders and other devices that produce streams of pulses that must be counted.

Most programmable counter/timer chips include three to five independent sections, each of which can operate from different clock sources and in different modes. Two or more channels can be cascaded, with the output of one providing the clock for the next, to provide longer timing periods.

It is often useful to use one channel as a timer, generating a periodic interrupt to provide a time base, and another as a counter to count external pulses. For example, if a timer interrupt is generated once per second, then the number of pulses received by the counter channel between timer interrupts is the frequency of the input signal. Thus, a basic frequency counter can be implemented with two channels of a programmable counter/timer and some software. The time base interrupt must occur frequently enough so that the counting channel does not overflow when clocked by the maximum frequency input signal.

5.3.2 Programmable Counter/Timer Example: Z80-CTC

Figure 5.7 shows the pin functions for the Z80-CTC. The two channel select inputs, CS_0 and CS_1, are address inputs that select one of the four channels. Note that all four channels operate all the time; the channel select inputs simply select one channel for interfacing to the system bus. The $\overline{CE}$ (chip enable) input is more properly called chip select since its function is to select the chip for reading or writing bus data. The $\overline{M1}$ and $\overline{IORQ}$ inputs are ANDed together internally to generate the interrupt acknowledge signal. $\overline{IORQ}$ is also internally gated with the chip enable input. Note that there is no connection for the $\overline{WRITE}$ signal, even though it must be possible to write data to the chip. There are not enough pins available for all the desired functions, so the $\overline{WRITE}$ signal was left off. When $\overline{IORQ}$ is asserted and $\overline{RD}$ is negated, the CTC chip assumes

Figure 5.7. Z80-CTC
pin functions. *(Courtesy
of Zilog, Inc.)*

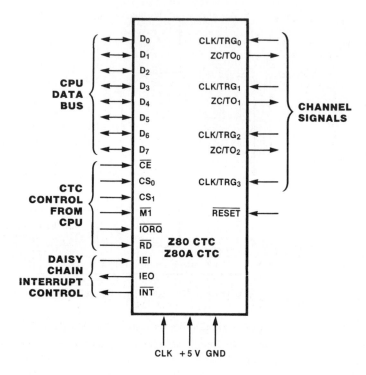

that a write cycle is in progress. This illustrates the redundancy in the Z80 control signals.

The CTC provides an interrupt output and also supports the Z80's interrupt priority daisy chain with IEI and IEO pins. The system clock (CLK) is used for internal timing functions as well as for the counter clock in timer mode.

The pins shown on the right side of the figure are the channel interface signals. There is a clock/trigger input (CLK/TRG) for each of the four channels and a zero count/timer output (ZC/TO) for three of them. The fourth channel does not have a zero count output, simply because there were no pins left. This channel can still be used to generate interrupts.

Each channel is similar to the basic counter/timer structure described earlier. There are three registers for each channel: the down counter, the time constant register, and the channel control register. In addition, there is one interrupt vector register, which is shared by all four channels. Since there is only one address per channel, some "tricks" are required to access all the registers.

The interrupt vector register is written by writing to a channel with data bit $D_0 = 0$. The format of the vector register is shown in Fig. 5.8. Since there is only one interrupt vector register for all four channels, the channel address is irrelevant when writing to this register. Only the five most-significant bits can be set by the user. Bit 0 is forced to 0, and bits 1 and 2 are set by the CTC to indicate which channel generated the interrupt. The channels are internally prioritized, so if multiple channels generate interrupts at the same time, each will be processed in sequence.

To initialize a channel, the channel control word is written to the CTC. The address on CS_0 and CS_1 identifies the channels, and data bit 0 is set to 1 to indicate that it is not an interrupt vector. Figure 5.9 shows the bit definitions for the channel control register. If bit 1 is set, then the channel is reset. Bit 6 selects timer or counter mode. In timer mode, the clock is derived from the system clock, and in counter mode the clock is provided by the signal at the clock/trigger input pin. In timer mode, the clock for the down counter may be either the system clock divided by 16 or the system clock divided by 256; the divisor is selected by bit 5 of the channel control word. In timer mode, the external clock/trigger input may be used to enable or disable the down counter. This feature is enabled by setting bit 3 in the channel control register. The edge that clocks the down counter (either rising or falling) is selected via bit 4 of the channel control word. If bit 7 of the control word is set, then an interrupt is generated whenever the counter reaches zero.

The time constant register is set with a 2-byte sequence:

1. The channel control register is written with bit 2 set. This tells the CTC that the next byte written to this channel is for the time constant register rather than for the control register.

2. The time constant value is written to the channel's time constant register.

To change the value in the time constant register, the control register must be written again with bit 1 set, and the new time constant can then be written.

Only the down counter in each channel can be read. The down counter cannot be

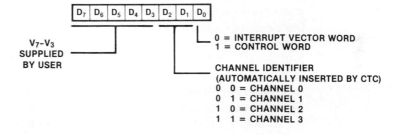

Figure 5.8. Z80-CTC interrupt vector register. *(Courtesy of Zilog, Inc.)*

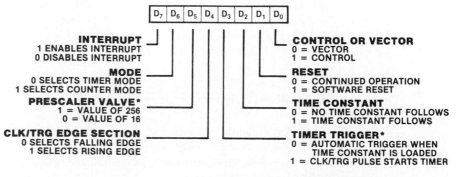

Figure 5.9. Z80-CTC channel control register. *(Courtesy of Zilog, Inc.)*

directly written but must be set via the time constant register. Thus, through a combination of techniques, the CTC's 13 internal registers (4 channel control, 4 time constant, 4 down counter, and 1 interrupt vector) are accessed via only four addresses.

For example, suppose that channel 0 is to be used to provide an interrupt every 10 ms. This interrupt could be used to initiate reading of a keyboard, writing to a display, or reading of another CTC channel used as a pulse counter. If the system clock is 4 MHz, then the down counter clock in timer mode can be either 4 MHz/16 or 4 MHz/256. These correspond to clock periods of 4 or 64 μs, respectively. Using a 4-μs period clock would require 2500 counts for 10 ms, and since the down counter is only 8 bits, a slower clock must be used. Using the divide-by-256 prescaler for a 64-μs clock period, 156.25 counts are required for a 10-ms time period. Fractional counts are not possible, so the best we can do is 156 counts, for a time period of 9.984 ms. Thus, to program the channel, the following bytes are written to channel 0:

10100111   enable interrupts, timer mode, prescaler
             divide by 256, clock on negative edge,
             no external trigger, load time constant next,
             reset channel

10011100   156 decimal, time constant

In addition, the interrupt vector register must be set.

Other programmable counter/timer chips provide similar functions. The Z80-CTC is particularly well-suited to Z80-based systems, since it is compatible with the Z80 bus signals and interrupt structure. Some counter/timer chips, such as Intel's 8253, do not provide any interrupt support. The zero count outputs must be latched and then used to generate an interrupt. The Z80-CTC can also be used in this manner for microprocessors other than the Z80.

One of the most powerful counter/timers is AMD's 9513. It is designed to be compatible with a wide range of microprocessors, and includes five independent channels. A 16-bit data bus allows the 16-bit registers to be written in a single cycle when used with 16-bit microprocessors. Eight-bit microprocessors can also be interfaced to the 9513 by using only half the data pins and writing each register in two steps. Each channel includes a 16-bit down counter, and a 16-bit prescaler can provide eight different prescale values. Longer delays can thus be obtained with a single channel, and the timing resolution is improved. In the example above, an interrupt rate of exactly 10 ms can easily be generated by using a prescale value of 16 and a time constant of 2500.

Counter/timer functions are also available as part of "combo" peripheral chips, as described in the following section.

5.4   COMBINATION PERIPHERAL CHIPS

In an effort to reduce the number of chips needed in a typical system, several manufacturers produce "combo" chips that provide several functions. Various combinations are available; typical elements include programmable counter/timers, RAM or ROM, and serial or parallel I/O lines.

Figure 5.10. The 68230 parallel interface and timer chip block diagram. *(Courtesy of Motorola, Inc.)*

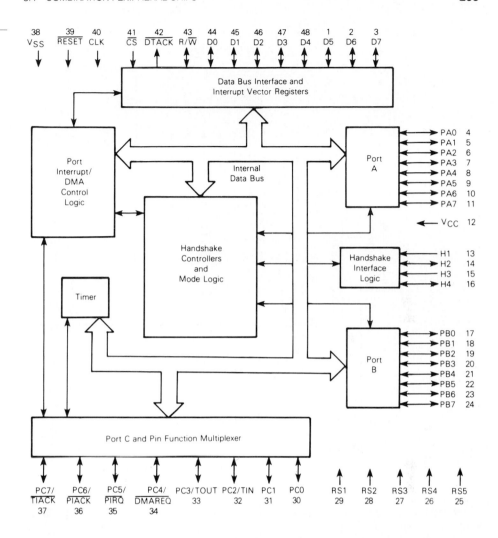

Motorola's 68230 is a combination timer and parallel I/O chip designed for use with 68000- and 6809-family microprocessors. Figure 5.10 shows the block diagram for this device. There are three I/O ports, labeled PA, PB, and PC. Ports A and B always function as parallel I/O ports. Port C can be used as a parallel I/O port and is also used for the timer input and output signals, DMA control signals, and interrupt control signals. Any pins not needed by the timer, interrupt control, or DMA in a particular application can be used as standard I/O pins. The four handshake pins (H1 to H4) can be programmed to operate in any of several modes and can be used as interrupt inputs.

The bus interface is different from the Z80-CTC described previously because it is designed for the 68000 bus structure. Figure 5.11 shows the interface to the 68000. A single R/$\overline{\text{W}}$ input replaces the read and write strobes, and the $\overline{\text{CS}}$ input serves as the strobe for both read and write operations. Since there is no connection for the data strobe ($\overline{\text{DS}}$), this signal must be gated with the address select to produce the chip select signal. The 68230 provides the $\overline{\text{DTACK}}$ signal required by the 68000 microprocessor

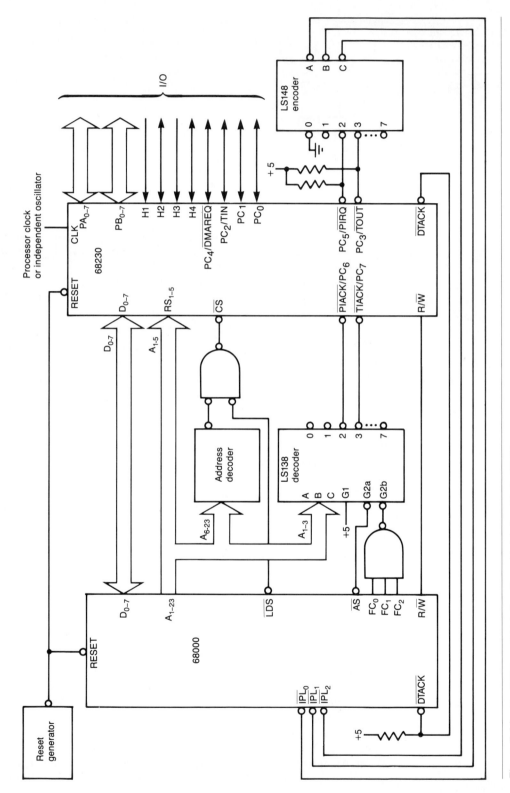

Figure 5.11. The 68230 parallel interface/timer chip interfaced to the 68000.

indicating that the read or write cycle is complete. Five register select inputs (RS_1 to RS_5) allow direct access to any of the 25 internal registers. The relatively large number of address lines eliminates the need for multibyte sequences and flags in the data byte to address a particular register, as required by many other chips. The register select signals are typically connected to address lines A_1 to A_5. (Remember that the 68000 bus structure has no A_0 signal.)

The 68230 uses only eight data lines, so the microprocessor must read and write one byte at a time. This reduces the pin count of the chip and also allows it to be used with the 68008, the 8-bit bus version of the 68000, and also with the 6809 8-bit microprocessor.

The 68230 supports the 68000's vectored interrupt structure. Separate interrupt request and acknowledge signals are provided for the timer and port portions of the 68230. The interrupt vector is written to the 68230 by the system's initialization software. When the timer reaches a count of zero, the $\overline{\text{TOUT}}$ signal is asserted. An interrupt can also be generated on the $\overline{\text{PIRQ}}$ output when a handshake signal is asserted. The figure shows the interrupt encoder required to encode these interrupt request signals to produce the IPL signals for the 68000. The interrupt priority level for each interrupt request signal is determined by the encoder inputs to which the signals are connected; the use of inputs 2 and 3 in the figure is an arbitrary choice. The other encoder inputs can be used for other interrupt sources.

When the 68230 is reset, all port C pins are programmed as input ports. If interrupt outputs are required, the system's initialization software will program PC_5 and PC_3 to perform this function by setting the appropriate bits in the 68230's control registers. The pull-up resistors are required to keep the interrupt request signals negated before the 68230 is initialized.

When the microprocessor detects this interrupt request and asserts interrupt acknowledge (input on the $\overline{\text{TIACK}}$ pin), the 68230 responds by providing the interrupt vector on the data bus. The 68000 indicates an interrupt acknowledge cycle by asserting $\overline{\text{AS}}$ with FC_0, FC_1, and FC_2 all high. The level of the interrupt being acknowledged is output on A_1, A_2, and A_3. The circuit shown in the figure detects this combination of signals to produce interrupt acknowledge signals for the timer and port interrupts.

While the 68230 has a variety of modes for performing parallel I/O, we will describe only the timer portions of the chip. The timer in the 68230 is only a single channel, but it is quite powerful. It includes a 24-bit down counter, a 24-bit preload register (the equivalent of the Z80-CTC's time constant register), and a 5-bit prescaler. The down counter can be clocked by the external timer input (TIN), or by the system clock. The prescaler can optionally be used to divide either clock source by 32. The timer can generate a periodic interrupt or a square wave output via the timer output (TOUT) pin. The TIN input can also be used to enable or disable the counter when using the system clock as the clock source. The large down counter allows time intervals to be generated with high resolution, since it can be clocked directly from the system clock. With an 8-MHz clock, delays of over 2 s can be produced with a resolution of 125 ns. By using the prescaler, the overall delay can be increased to over 67 s, with a resolution of 4 μs.

A variety of other combination peripheral chips are available. The 68901, which is used in the design example in Sec. 5.8, is a 68000-family peripheral that includes four timers, eight parallel I/O lines, an interrupt controller, and a synchronous or asynchronous serial interface (USART). The Z80-STI (also called the MK3801) is a similar device for Z80 systems. Intel's 8155 includes 256 bytes of RAM, 22 parallel I/O lines, and one programmable timer. It uses a multiplexed bus and is compatible with the 8085 and 8088 microprocessors.

5.5   WATCHDOG TIMERS

In many microprocessor applications, it is important that the system run reliably for long periods of time. However, a single misfetched instruction can cause the system to begin executing code from nonexistent or improper memory locations, and it is unlikely to recover on its own. Such an error can be caused by electrical noise from the power line, static electric discharge, or a variety of other causes. Another cause is a brief power line interruption or voltage drop, which is just large enough to cause the system power supply to drop out of regulation but too small to cause a power-up reset. While such errors should be rare in a well-designed system, a single error can cause the entire system to fail.

One solution to this problem is to use a *watchdog timer,* which monitors the operation of the system and forces it back on track if it acts erroneously. Figure 5.12 shows the block diagram for a watchdog timer circuit. The counter is clocked by a free-running clock source, such as the system clock oscillator. This clock must not be under microprocessor control, since stopping the clock would prevent the watchdog timer from detecting an error. The counter is reset by a chip select signal (asserted during a write to a specific memory or I/O address) or an output port bit. The software periodically sets this bit high and then low again to reset the counter.

A chip select signal, which is unlikely to be asserted if the system fails, is a good source for the reset pulse. If the counter reset signal is connected directly to an output port bit, then the counter will be disabled if a system failure occurs while that output bit is asserted. This risk can be minimized by keeping the output negated, except for the very brief (one- or two-instruction) period when the counter is reset. The watchdog reset can be made more selective (and therefore more reliable) by decoding a write of a particular data pattern to a particular address.

If the microprocessor software fails to reset the counter frequently enough, the counter overflows and the carry output provides an indication that there has been a failure. This output can be used to generate a nonmaskable interrupt or to reset the system. The carry output is only one clock period wide and may not be long enough to reset the microprocessor. The last Q output of the counter can be used to generate the reset, which will provide a much longer pulse.

The rate at which the watchdog timer must be reset is determined by the clock frequency and the number of bits in the counter. For example, a 12-bit counter clocked at

Figure 5.12.   Watch-
dog timer circuit.

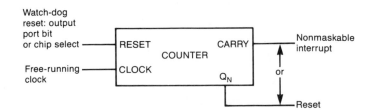

1 MHz will produce a carry output after 4096 μs, or just over 4 ms. (If the Q_{11} output is used instead of the carry, the delay is reduced to 2048 μs.) It is usually desirable that this time interval be relatively long, since resetting the timer frequently is a burden on the software. CMOS counters are available with many stages in a single IC, and they are often good choices for watchdog timers. The 4020 14-bit binary counter is well-suited for this application. If the clock rate is over a few megahertz, a high-speed CMOS counter such as the 74HC4020 is required.

Watchdog timers can also be implemented with retriggerable "one-shots" and other similar analog circuits. As long as the software triggers the one-shot frequently enough, it will never reach the end of its timing period. If it does, its output provides a reset signal. However, counter implementations are generally preferable, since they are less susceptible to noise and do not depend on resistor and capacitor values for their timing.

One channel of a counter/timer chip can also be used as a watchdog timer. This is not as safe as a separate hardware timer, however, since software can easily write an erroneous control word to the counter/timer that would prevent it from operating.

5.6 CLOCK/CALENDAR CIRCUITS

It is often useful to have the time of day and the date available to the system's software. This allows printouts and files to be time-stamped, event times to be recorded, and events to be initiated at a preprogrammed time and date. While it is possible to keep track of the time of day by using a periodic interrupt and appropriate software, this requires that the user enter the current time and date each time the system is turned on. In addition, it adds to the software overhead.

Single-chip clock/calendar circuits are available that relieve the software of keeping the time and also continue keeping time while the rest of the system is turned off. They are implemented in CMOS for low power consumption and can be powered by a small lithium battery for several years.

One example of such a device is Motorola's 146818A; Fig. 5.13 shows the block diagram. A multiplexed address/data bus is used and is intended for connection to microprocessors such as the 8085 and 6801. A flexible control signal design allows the use of either Intel-style or Motorola-style control signals. The three control signals are AS (address strobe), DS (data strobe), and R/$\overline{\text{W}}$ (read write), the names indicating their functions when interfacing to microprocessors using Motorola-style control signals. However, when connected to a microprocessor such as the 8085, the DS pin functions as the read strobe ($\overline{\text{READ}}$), and the R/$\overline{\text{W}}$ pin functions as the write strobe ($\overline{\text{WRITE}}$). This scheme is sometimes called a *Motel* (Motorola-Intel) interface. The MOT pin is tied high or low to indicate which type of signals are used.

Clock/calendar chips such as the 146818A are generally battery-backed so they can continue to keep time when the system is turned off. As with battery-backed RAMs, inadvertent writes to the chip when power is falling must be prevented. The 146818A includes an input called $\overline{\text{STDBY}}$ (standby) that must be high to enable access to the chip. A low-V_{CC} detection circuit similar to the one described in Sec. 4.9.6 for battery-backed CMOS RAM is used to drive this input.

The 146818 "non-A" version does not include the standby or the MOT inputs. The $\overline{\text{CE}}$ input must be inhibited when V_{CC} is below the required minimum voltage. The

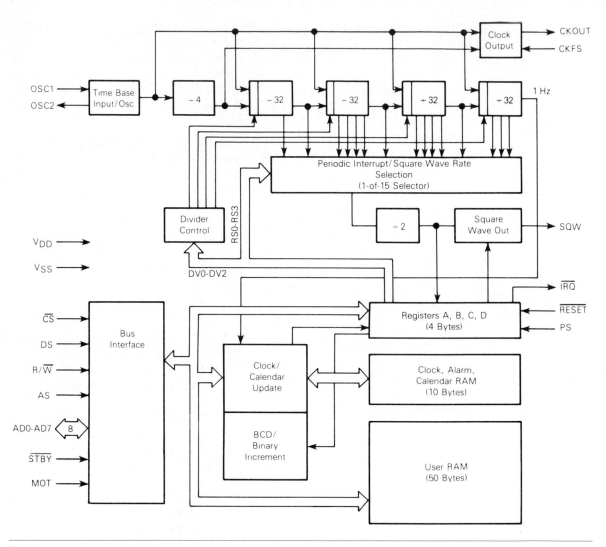

Figure 5.13.   The 146818A clock/calendar IC block diagram. *(Courtesy of Motorola, Inc.)*

Intel or Motorola bus type is determined by the state of the DS input when AS is asserted. The DS input is assumed to be negated when AS is asserted. Since DS is active-high for the Motorola-style bus and active-low for an Intel-style bus, the 146818 can automatically sense to which processor type it is connected.

The heart of the 146818 is a chain of counters, driven by the time base oscillator. The frequency of the oscillator is controlled by an external crystal, as shown in Fig. 5.14. The trimmer capacitor allows the frequency to be fine-tuned for accurate time keeping. This is important, since any error in the oscillator frequency will cause cumulative error in the time. The chain of counters produces a 1-Hz output, which feeds the clock/calendar logic. The clock/calendar logic increments seconds, hours, days, day of

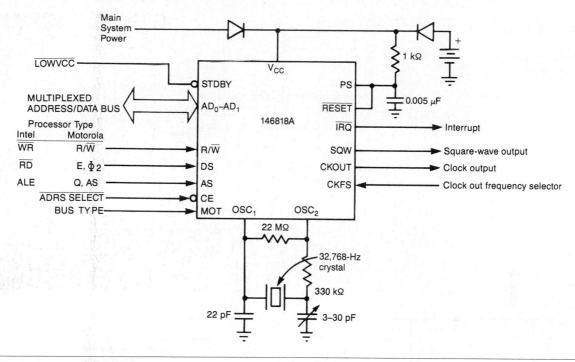

Figure 5.14. The 146818A clock/calendar circuit.

the week, date, month, and year as required. It can automatically account for daylight savings time, leap years, and the different number of days in each month.

The 146818A is powered from the main power supply when ac power is present and from its the battery when it is not. As with battery-backed RAM (as described in Chap. 4), diodes are used to isolate the battery from the main power supply. The power sense (PS) input is high except when a full power-up occurs. This normally happens only when the battery is first installed or when the main power is turned on after the battery has failed. If PS is low, a "time invalid" status bit is set. The resistor-capacitor circuit on the PS input is required so that the PS input does not remain low, to allow the time invalid bit to be cleared when the time is set.

The 146818A can also be interfaced to nonmultiplexed address and data buses, as shown in Fig. 5.15. The address/data inputs are connected to the data bus. AS is asserted for a write to an address with A_0 low, and DS for an address with A_0 high. (The address decoder that generates the chip select should ignore A_0.) The software performs two bus cycles for each access. First, it writes the address of the desired register with A_0 low. (Note that the address is written as a data byte.) It then reads or writes the data for this register with A_0 high.

The 146818A can be programmed to generate interrupts at a periodic rate from every 30.5 μs to 500 ms. This function is similar to that performed by more general-purpose programmable counter/timers. An alarm time can also be programmed to cause an interrupt at a specific time of day.

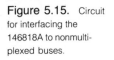

Figure 5.15. Circuit for interfacing the 146818A to nonmultiplexed buses.

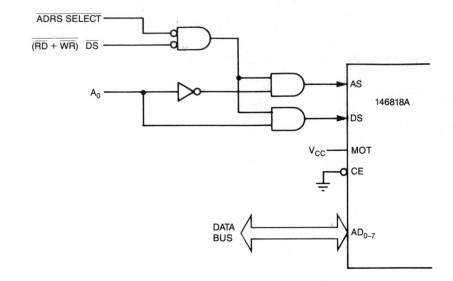

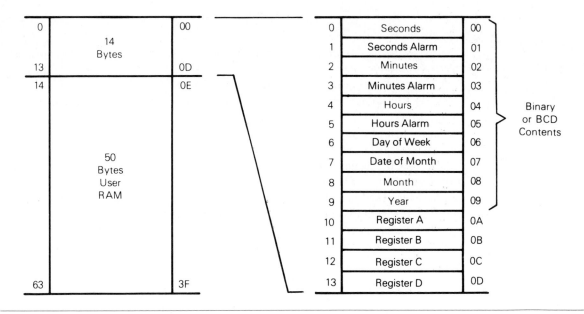

Figure 5.16. The 146818 clock/calendar chip memory map. *(Courtesy of Motorola, Inc.)*

The 146818A appears to the microprocessor as a 64-byte RAM, as shown in Fig. 5.16. The first 10 bytes store the current time and date and the alarm time. To set the time and date, the new values are written to the appropriate locations. To read the time and date, the locations are read, just as if they were regular memory locations. The next 4 bytes are the control registers. These allow the selection of the crystal frequency and periodic interrupt rates. In addition, the various interrupt sources can be enabled or disabled, and either binary or BCD (binary-coded decimal) can be selected for the time and date registers. The automatic adjustment for daylight savings time can also be enabled or disabled.

If the time and date are read while they are in the process of being incremented, the data may not be valid. One of the control registers includes an "update in progress" flag, which is set when an increment is occurring or will occur soon. When the microprocessor wants to read the time, the software first reads this flag. If the flag is clear, then the time and date are guaranteed to be stable for at least 244 μs. If the flag is set, then the software must wait for the flag to be cleared.

The last 50 bytes of RAM are not used by the clock/calendar functions and are available for use as general-purpose RAM locations. They are nonvolatile, since the clock/calendar chip is powered by a battery when the main power has failed. This small amount of nonvolatile storage is often all that is needed for critical system data or setup parameters to be saved when power fails.

5.7   DIRECT MEMORY ACCESS CONTROLLERS

Direct memory access *(DMA)* controllers allow data to be transferred faster than is possible under program control. A common example of a DMA application is reading from or writing to a disk drive that must transfer data at a rate determined by the disk's speed of rotation and other characteristics. Another example is an arbitrary waveform generator that synthesizes analog waveforms by repetitively writing a series of data bytes to a D/A converter. This section describes the types of DMA transfers and several example DMA controller chips.

5.7.1   DMA Controller Operation

Consider the problem of writing a block of memory to an output port, one byte at a time. The following tasks must be performed:

1.   Initialize memory and output port addresses.

2.   Repeat until all bytes transferred:
     a.   Read byte from memory.
     b.   Write byte to output port.
     c.   Increment memory address.
     d.   Check to see if all bytes transferred.
     e.   Wait until output port ready for next byte.

To implement this transfer with software, the microprocessor must fetch one or more instructions to perform each of these steps. Since several instructions must be fetched and executed to transfer a single byte of memory, only a fraction of the memory cycles are used for the actual data transfer. Thus, the speed of the data transfer is much less than the maximum rate at which data can be read from the memory.

A *DMA controller (DMAC)* can be thought of as a very specialized microprocessor, with the program to transfer data implemented in hardware. The DMAC includes counters to provide the memory and port addresses and to count the number of words transferred. Before a transfer can occur, the microprocessor must initialize the DMAC to specify the direction and type of transfer, the source and destination addresses, and the number of bytes or words to be transferred. Once this initialization is completed, the DMAC takes control of the system buses and performs the entire transfer.

Unlike a data transfer performed by the microprocessor, no instructions need be fetched during the transfer to tell the DMAC how to perform the transfer. Thus, all memory cycles are available for transferring data, and the transfer can occur at the maximum speed possible. The peripheral device generally operates at a slower data rate than this maximum, so the DMAC can allow the microprocessor to run for a few cycles in between transfers while the DMAC waits for the peripheral to be ready to transfer the next byte.

DMA controllers add hardware to the system and generally provide only one benefit: faster data transfers. They are therefore used primarily when the data rate possible under program control is insufficient. Even if the data rate is low enough so that the transfer can be performed under program control, the use of a DMA controller increases the amount of time available for other tasks by minimizing the time spent transferring data. This performance improvement can justify the use of a DMAC in some applications. The increase in performance must be weighed against the additional hardware cost of the DMAC and associated circuits.

After the DMA controller has been initialized by the microprocessor, the peripheral (such as a disk controller) can initiate the transfer at any time by asserting the DMA REQUEST input to the DMAC. The DMAC then asserts BUS REQUEST to the microprocessor (this signal is called HOLD on some microprocessors). The microprocessor completes the instruction it is currently executing, disables its address, data, and control bus outputs, and asserts the BUS ACKNOWLEDGE signal. The DMAC then takes control of the buses to perform the transfer. The DMAC controls the buses in the same manner as the microprocessor.

One benefit of DMA transfers is that the transfer can begin very quickly after the peripheral asserts the DMA REQUEST signal. The microprocessor needs only to complete the bus cycle then executing, and the transfer can begin. Since the microprocessor's operation is suspended during the transfer, there is no need for the registers to be saved, as in the case of an interrupt. The time from the request to the beginning of the transfer is called the *latency time*. The worst-case latency for a DMA transfer is the length of the longest bus cycle plus the relatively short time required for the microprocessor to disable its bus outputs and assert BUS ACKNOWLEDGE. One important exception to this is a system with multiple DMA channels, in which case the latency can be as long as the longest DMA transfer occurring on a higher-priority channel.

5.7.2   DMA Transfer Types

The simplest mode of DMA transfer is *burst* mode, in which the entire transfer is completed without interruption. If the peripheral cannot accept data at the maximum transfer rate, then the DMAC keeps the bus idle between transfers. In *cycle-stealing* mode, a single transfer is initiated for each DMA request from the peripheral. This is useful if the data rate from the peripheral is slower than the maximum DMA transfer rate; it allows the microprocessor to execute instructions while waiting for the next byte from the peripheral.

Transparent DMA uses a dual-port RAM to allow both the DMAC and the microprocessor to access the memory concurrently. The microprocessor's bus request input is not used, since it never has to release its buses. This provides the highest performance but its additional cost is generally not justified.

Two-Cycle DMA Transfers

There are two basic types of DMA transfers: one-cycle and two-cycle. Figure 5.17 illustrates a memory-to-output-port transfer using the two-cycle approach. The DMA controller begins the transfer by reading the first memory location to be transferred and storing the data byte in a temporary register in the DMAC. It performs the read in the same manner as a microprocessor; it places the memory address on the address bus, asserts the MEMRD (memory read) control signal, and reads the data from the data bus. When the DMAC has completed the read cycle, it drives the data back onto the data bus, addresses the output port, and asserts the IOWR (I/O write) control signal. Thus, one word of data is read from the memory and written to the output port. The memory address is then incremented, and the process is repeated to transfer the next

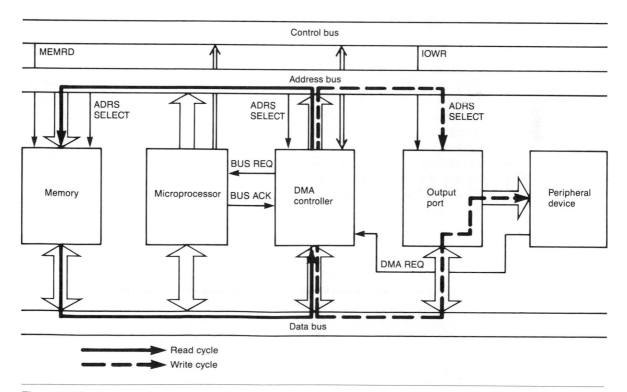

Figure 5.17. Two-cycle DMA transfer from memory to output port. The solid paths indicate the read cycle; the dashed paths indicate the write cycle.

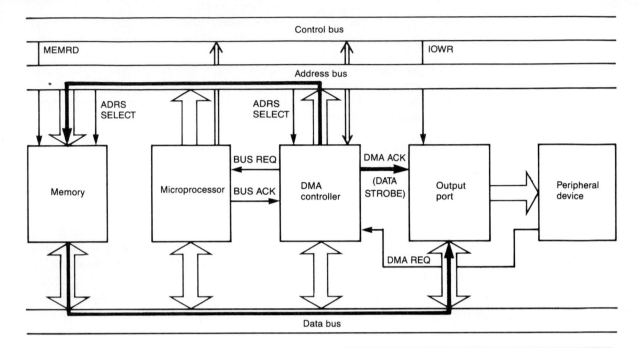

Figure 5.18.   One-cycle DMA transfer from memory to output port.

word. When the specified number of words has been transferred (or after each word in cycle-stealing mode), the DMAC negates the BUS REQUEST signal to the microprocessor and the microprocessor continues operation from the point at which it was halted.

With the two-cycle approach just described, memory-to-memory transfers can also be performed. In this case, the microprocessor initiates the transfer via a software command to the DMAC, allowing the DMAC to be used to speed up programs that require moving blocks of data. Some DMA controllers also have the capability to search for a particular data pattern while transferring or to only search and not transfer at all. This feature can be used to improve the performance of programs that search large blocks of data.

One-Cycle DMA Transfers

While the two-cycle transfer provides maximum flexibility, the transfer rate is only one-half the highest possible rate, since two bus cycles are required for each transfer. To implement one-cycle transfers, a DMA ACKNOWLEDGE signal is added, as shown in Fig. 5.18. This signal replaces the address select signal for the I/O port and allows the DMAC to select an I/O port while simultaneously addressing memory.

To transfer from memory to an output port, the DMAC places the memory address on the address bus and asserts the DMA ACKNOWLEDGE signal to select the port. The DMAC then asserts both the MEMRD and IOWR control signals. The memory provides the data on the data bus, which is read directly by the output port. The data does not pass through the DMA controller.

The main benefit of this technique is the high transfer speed. However, it is much more limited than the two-cycle approach. Since only one device can be addressed at a time via the address bus, a DMA ACKNOWLEDGE signal must be connected to each I/O port that can be used in a DMA transfer. The port addresses cannot be changed by the system software, as with the two-cycle approach. In addition, memory-to-memory transfers cannot be performed.

5.7.3 Am9517A DMA Controller

AMD's Am9517A is an example of a DMA controller that can perform either one- or two-cycle transfers. (This device is also made by Intel as the 8237A.) It was originally designed for use with the 8080 and 8085, although it can also be used with other microprocessors. It includes four independent DMA channels. Figure 5.19 shows the block diagram of the 9517.

The 9517 is a complex device, with numerous registers and operating modes. This section provides an overview of the device's operation. For detailed information, refer to the manufacturer's data sheets.

Figure 5.20 shows the 9517 interfaced to a microprocessor system. The four bus control lines are inputs to the 9517 when the microprocessor is initializing it and outputs from the 9517 when a DMA transfer is taking place. Similarly, address pins A_0 to A_3 are inputs to the 9517 for selecting registers during initialization and are outputs from the 9517 for addressing memory during DMA transfers. Address lines A_0 to A_7

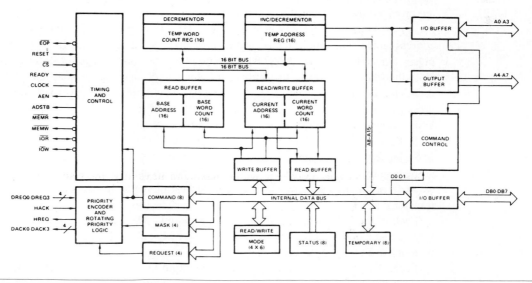

Figure 5.19. Am9517A DMA controller block diagram. *(Courtesy of Advanced Micro Devices, Inc.)*

Figure 5.20.
Am9517A DMA controller
interface. *(Courtesy of
Advanced Micro
Devices, Inc.)*

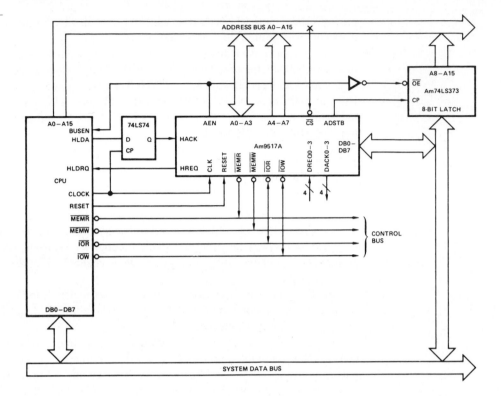

are driven directly by the 9517 during DMA transfers. Because of pin limitations, the upper 8 bits of the address bus are not driven directly by the 9517. These address bits are provided by an external 8-bit latch, which is kept updated by the 9517. Whenever the upper 8 bits of address change during a DMA transfer, the 9517 outputs the new address on the data bus (which is used as a multiplexed bus during DMA transfers) and pulses the address strobe (ADSTB) signal to clock the address into the external latch. Note that this is similar to the manner in which some microprocessors multiplex address and data information, except that the 9517 multiplexes the most-significant address bits, rather than the least-significant bits, with the data. This is done because DMA transfers generally consist of many accesses to successive locations. Thus, the high-order half of the address does not change very often: on the average, once every 256 transfers. Unlike multiplexed-bus microprocessors that perform an address cycle at the beginning of every bus cycle, the 9517 updates the address latch only when necessary. This increases the transfer rate by eliminating the address latch update on most transfer cycles.

Each of the four channels in the 9517 has its own DMA request and acknowledge signals and its own set of control registers. Each channel can perform an independent memory-to-I/O or I/O-to-memory transfer.

Each channel is assigned a priority. If multiple DMA requests occur at the same time, or if one channel's DMA request is asserted while another channel is performing a transfer, the highest-priority channel is serviced first. Thus, the highest-priority channel has a very short worst-case latency time, while the others can have much longer latency if a higher-priority channel is performing a lengthy transfer.

Each channel has a 6-bit Mode register, and four 16-bit registers:

> Base Address register
>
> Base Word Count register
>
> Current Address register
>
> Current Word Count register

Because the address and word count registers are 16 bits wide but the data bus is only 8 bits wide, each register must be written in two parts. The first time a byte is written to a particular register address, it is written to the low-order half of the register, and an internal flip-flop (indicating that the low half has been written) is set. The next byte written to that register address is written to the high half, and the internal flip-flop is cleared.

The Mode register allows various types of transfers to be selected, such as read or write and incrementing address or decrementing address. The Base Address register stores the address of the first memory location to be read or written, and the Base Word Count register indicates the number of bytes to be transferred. When a transfer begins, the Current Address and Current Word Count registers are loaded from the base registers. As the transfer proceeds, the Current Word Count register is decremented, and the Current Address register is incremented or decremented, depending on the mode selected. The transfer is terminated when the current word count reaches zero or when the external end of process ($\overline{\text{EOP}}$) signal is asserted. The base registers are not modified during the transfer. If "autoinitialize" mode is selected (by writing the appropriate value to the Mode register), then the Current Address and Current Word Count registers are automatically loaded from the base registers when the transfer is terminated. This allows another transfer to occur without the microprocessor reinitializing the 9517.

When performing single-cycle transfers, the Current Address register addresses the memory location to be read or written, and the I/O port to be read or written is selected by the DMA acknowledge (DACK) signal for that channel. Thus, while the memory address can be programmed when the microprocessor initializes the 9517, the I/O port to be used in the transfer is determined by the hardware connections.

The 9517 also allows two channels to be used together to perform two-cycle transfers. A read cycle is performed using channel 0, and the data read is stored in a temporary register in the 9517. A write cycle is then performed using channel 1, and the data from the temporary register is driven on the data bus. This allows memory-to-memory transfers to be performed, and also allows DMA transfers to or from memory-mapped I/O ports.

The 9517 does not decode the WAIT or READY control signal, so it will not work properly with very slow memory. The memory must be fast enough to meet the 9517's timing, since the 9517 will not insert wait states as the microprocessor would. For fast memory, there is a "compressed" transfer mode that increases the transfer rate.

Although it was designed for 8-bit microprocessors with 16-bit address buses, the 9517 can be adapted for microprocessors with a wider address bus, such as the 8088. (In fact, it is used in the IBM PC, XT, and AT.) Since the 9517 produces only 16-bit addresses, a "DMA page" register must be added to provide the most-significant address bits during DMA transfers. This register must be set by the microprocessor before the transfer is initiated. Thus, transfers are limited to locations within the 64-Kbyte page selected by this register.

5.7.4 Other DMA Controllers

Most microprocessor families include at least one DMA controller. Most use the two-cycle transfer method. The Z80 is supported by the Z80-DMA (also known as the MK3883 or Z8410). Motorola's 6844 DMAC is designed for use with the 6800- and 6809-family microprocessors and can also be used in a limited manner with the 68000. In addition to the 8237A, which is the same as the Am9517A, Intel manufactures a simpler DMAC, the 8257. This device operates only in the one-cycle transfer mode.

Most DMA controllers for 16- and 32-bit microprocessors are considerably more complex than those for 8-bit microprocessors. In addition to wider address registers (typically 24 bits) and data paths (16 or 32 bits), they include a variety of additional features. Typical features include the ability to read a 16-bit word from a memory location and then perform two byte writes to a peripheral (or vice versa), and automatic "chaining" of a series of data transfers that can be performed without processor intervention. AMD's Am9516 is a "universal" DMAC designed for use with the 8086- or 68000-family microprocessors. Intel's 82258 is a high-performance DMAC that is designed for use with the 80286 but can also be used with the 8086/88 or 80186/ 188. Three DMA controllers are available for use with the 68000: the 68430 single-channel DMA controller, the 68440 two-channel controller, and the 68450 four-channel controller.

Intel's 8089 I/O processor combines the functions of a DMA controller and a specialized microprocessor and is described in Chap. 10.

5.8 DESIGN EXAMPLE: 68901 MFP

In this section, we add the 68901 multifunction peripheral (MFP) to the example system. This chip provides four counter/timers, an interrupt controller, a serial communications interface, and an 8-bit parallel I/O port. The I/O capabilities are covered in later chapters; this section covers the bus interface and the counter/timers.

Figure 5.21 shows the bus interface to the 68901 MFP. The five register select lines enable direct selection of any of the 32 internal registers, making programming simpler than with peripherals that require multibyte sequences to access numerous internal registers with only one or two address lines. The CLK input is used to synchronize the bus interface signals and must be between 1 and 4 MHz. The 10-MHz system clock is divided by 4 to produce a 2.5-MHz clock. The MFP provides an open-drain $\overline{\text{DTACK}}$ output, so it is easily interfaced to a 68000-family system operating at any clock rate. The assertion of the $\overline{\text{CS}}$ signal is delayed by the flip-flop circuit until the first clock edge after $\overline{\text{AS}}$ is asserted, for reasons described in the following subsection.

The MFP includes an interrupt vector register, which is initialized by the system software with the desired base interrupt vector type number. The least-significant four

Figure 5.21. Design example 68901 interface.

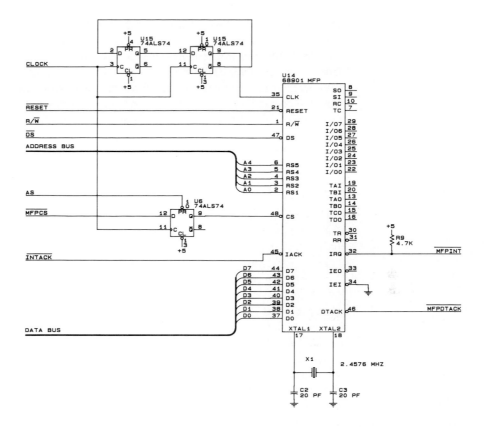

bits of this vector are modified by the MFP according to the source of the interrupt. Possible interrupt sources include any of the eight parallel I/O lines, any of the four timers, and the serial communications interface. Each of these sources can be individually enabled or disabled, and the parallel I/O lines can be programmed to produce an interrupt in response to either a rising or a falling edge.

The MFP includes an $\overline{\text{IEI}}$ input and an $\overline{\text{IEO}}$ output that operate similarly to the Z80-family peripherals' pins of the same name, as described in Chap. 3. These signals can be connected in a daisy-chained manner when more that one MFP is used in a system, allowing the $\overline{\text{IRQ}}$ output of all the MFPs to connect to the same interrupt level. A pull-up resistor is required, since the $\overline{\text{IRQ}}$ output is open-drain. The interrupt enable daisy chain establishes priority among the MFPs.

When an enabled interrupt condition occurs and the MFP's $\overline{\text{IEI}}$ input is asserted, the $\overline{\text{IEO}}$ output is negated and the $\overline{\text{IRQ}}$ output is asserted. The microprocessor responds with an interrupt acknowledge cycle, which is decoded by the logic described in Chap. 3 to produce the $\overline{\text{IACK}}$ signal. This causes the MFP to place the interrupt vector on the data bus, and the microprocessor then executes the selected interrupt service routine.

The clock from the timers is derived from the signal on XTAL1 rather than from the CLK input. This allows the timer clock to be independent of the system clock. For the simplest configuration, XTAL1 can be connected to the CLK pin. Alternatively, a separate crystal oscillator can be connected to XTAL1 and XTAL2, as shown in Fig. 5.21.

The seemingly odd clock frequency of 2.4576 MHz is 300×2^{13} Hz, which divides down exactly to produce standard serial data rate signals as described in Chap. 8.

Each of the four timers is based on an 8-bit down counter. In addition, there is a separate prescaler for each timer. Timers A and B are multimode counter/timers and can operate in an event-count mode, in which transitions of the signal at the TAI or TBI input are counted, or in a pulse-width measurement mode. In addition, all four timers can operate in timer mode. In this mode, the counter is clocked by the prescaled XTAL1 signal. The prescaler can be programmed to divide by 4, 10, 16, 50, 64, 100, or 200. Each timer channel has a time constant register, which must be loaded to start the timer. This value is loaded into the down counter, which is decremented until it reaches 1. An interrupt is then generated (if enabled), the timer output is toggled, and the down counter is reloaded from the time constant register. Thus, this mode can be used to generate periodic interrupts or to produce a square-wave output of a programmable frequency. One of the timers is typically used to provide the data rate clock for the serial communications interface.

Figures 5.22 and 5.23 show the read and write timing for the MFP, and Table 5.1 lists the timing parameter values. Because the MFP does not assert its $\overline{\text{DTACK}}$ output until data is available for a read cycle, or until the data setup time has been met for a write cycle, the required access time and read and write pulse widths are guaranteed to be met, regardless of the speed of the microprocessor. $\overline{\text{DTACK}}$ is asserted time 5 after the second falling CLK edge following the assertion of $\overline{\text{CS}}$.

While the MFP is in most respects a well-behaved 68000-family peripheral, there is one potential timing problem. The MFP specifies a minimum register select (address) setup time of 30 ns (parameter 2). Since the $\overline{\text{CS}}$ output from the 74ALS138 is asserted as soon as the decoder's propagation delay time elapses, this setup time will not be met

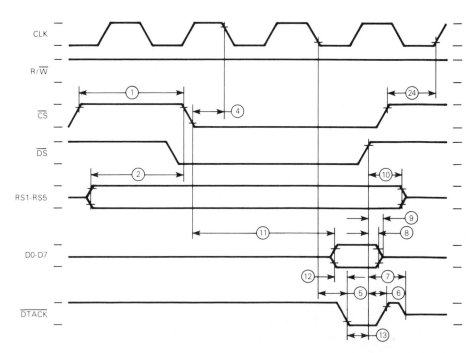

Figure 5.22. The 68901 read cycle timing. *(Courtesy of Motorola, Inc.)*

Figure 5.23. The 68901 write cycle timing. *(Courtesy of Motorola, Inc.)*

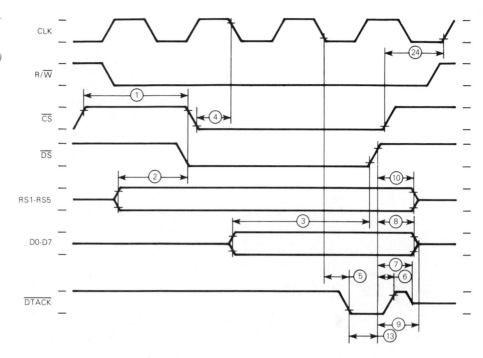

Table 5.1 The 68901 Read and Write Cycle Timing Parameters

No.	Characteristic	Time, ns	
		Min	Max
1	$\overline{CS}$, $\overline{IACK}$, $\overline{DS}$ width high	50	
2	Address valid to falling $\overline{CS}$ setup time	30	
3	Data valid prior to rising $\overline{DS}$ setup time	280	
4*	$\overline{CS}$, $\overline{IACK}$ valid to falling clock setup time	50	
5	Clock low to $\overline{DTACK}$ low		220
6	$\overline{CS}$ or $\overline{DS}$ high to $\overline{DTACK}$ high		60
7	$\overline{CS}$ or $\overline{DS}$ high to $\overline{DTACK}$ high impedance		100
8	$\overline{CS}$ or $\overline{DS}$ high to data invalid hold time	0	
9	$\overline{CS}$ or $\overline{DS}$ high to data high impedance		50
10	$\overline{CS}$ or $\overline{DS}$ high to address invalid hold time	0	
11	Data valid from $\overline{CS}$ low		250
12	Read data valid to $\overline{DTACK}$ low setup time	50	
13	$\overline{DTACK}$ low to $\overline{DS}$ or $\overline{CS}$ high hold time	0	

*If the setup time is not met, $\overline{CS}$ will not be recognized until the next falling clock.
Source: Motorola.

if the address decoder output drives $\overline{CS}$ directly. Gating the address decoder output with $\overline{AS}$ helps, but not enough, since the 68008 guarantees only 20 ns of address setup before $\overline{AS}$ is asserted. (This solution would likely work but does not work worst-case. The setup time provided to the MFP would be the setup time provided by the 68008, plus the delay of the gate. With a minimum gate delay of a few nanoseconds, if the 68008 provided 5 to 8 ns more setup time than is guaranteed, the resulting setup time would be adequate.)

One solution to the setup-time problem is to delay the $\overline{CS}$ signal with two inverters in series. However, this solution depends on minimum gate delays. A better solution that provides proper timing even in a worst-case situation is shown in the schematic. The flip-flop is held set when $\overline{AS}$ is negated, and it is cleared (thus asserting the $\overline{CS}$ signal) at the first rising clock edge after $\overline{AS}$ is asserted if $\overline{MFPCS}$ is also asserted. This delays $\overline{CS}$ sufficiently to ensure that the register select setup time is met. The calculation of the actual setup time provided is left as an exercise for the reader.

5.9 SUMMARY

Peripheral chips supplement the microprocessor's capabilities. In addition to providing basic I/O capability, they are useful for timekeeping functions. Programmable timers can serve as frequency generators, frequency counters, or time-base interrupt generators. For applications requiring calendar time, clock/calendar chips keep time even when the system power is off and eliminate the need for the software to deal with the peculiarities of incrementing seconds, hours, minutes, days, months, and years. When long-term unattended operation is important, watchdog timers put the system back on track in case a noise spike or other uncommon event causes the system to malfunction.

DMA controllers increase the rate at which the microprocessor system can move data and reduce the load on the microprocessor. They are most useful when used with high-speed peripherals that transfer blocks of data. Since they must perform all the bus read and write operations that the microprocessor itself performs, compatibility with the microprocessor used is essential.

Many microprocessor families include a variety of peripheral chips that are designed for easy interfacing to that microprocessor. However, some peripheral chips are designed to be general-purpose, and it is sometimes desirable to use a chip from another microprocessor family. In this case, additional logic is required to translate the control signals, and a careful timing analysis must be performed to ensure compatibility.

5.10 EXERCISES

5.1. A peripheral chip has the following registers:

  Data register   (read/write)
  Command register   (write only)
  Status register   (read only)
  Interrupt Vector register (write only)

    a. List the control and address signals needed for the interface.

    b. Assuming that there is one bit available in the command register, design an interface scheme that does not require any address lines. Assume an 8-bit data bus.

5.2.   A microprocessor-based instrument must write to its display every 25 ms. Assuming a 4-MHz system clock, what values must be written to the registers of a Z80-CTC for it to provide an appropriate interrupt signal?

5.3.   In the instrument described in Exercise 5.2, it is also necessary to read an input port exactly once per minute. How can this time interval be generated with the Z80-CTC?

5.4.   A security system must operate reliably for long periods of time, so a watch-dog timer circuit is included. The clock for the timer is 2 MHz, and the software can reset the timer no more frequently than once every 100 ms. The output required in case of a failure is a 10-ms minimum reset pulse. Design the circuit for the watchdog timer. How many counter stages are required?

5.5.   Draw a flowchart for a program to implement a clock/calendar function, using an interrupt from a programmable counter/timer as the time base. Select either 12- or 24-hour time format. The program must account for the varying length of the months, but leap years may be ignored.

5.6.   A personal computer includes a floppy disk interface that provides bursts of data at a rate of 62,500 bytes/s. A program to perform the transfer requires 45 clock cycles to read each byte and prepare for the next. What is the minimum clock rate required for the system to operate without a DMA controller?

5.7.   A microprocessor-based laboratory instrument collects data from a data acquisition system (DAS). The DAS buffers data from a variety of sources, and every 100 ms a block of 1024 bytes is available to be read. The data can be read at any rate, since it is buffered by the DAS, but all 1024 bytes must be read within the 100-ms period. A program to read and store one byte of data takes 10 μs to execute.

    a. Is a DMA controller required?

    b. The instrument can use all the available processing time to perform calculations based on the data. A DMA controller is used that reads the data at a 1-Mbyte/s rate. What is the percent increase in available processing time as compared to a non-DMA configuration (if it is possible without DMA)?

    c. In different applications, the DAS provides 8192 or 16,384 bytes of data every 100 ms. Repeat parts a and b above for each of these data block sizes.

5.8.   Draw a complete timing diagram for the 68901-to-68008 interface as used in the design example. How many wait states are produced during 68901 accesses? What is the register-select-to-chip-select setup time?

5.11   SELECTED BIBLIOGRAPHY

For detailed information on any of the peripheral chips described in this chapter, refer to the manufacturer's data sheets.

"Microcomputer Support Chip Directory," *EDN*. Annual directory of microprocessor support chips. An excellent reference for finding out what is available to perform a given function.

Mein, John C. "Real-Time LSI Clock Chips Ease μP Control Tasks," *EDN*, Jan. 6, 1983, pp. 138–142. Describes many of the clock/calendar chips and shows some interfacing details.

Sherer, Victor A., and William G. Peterson. "Parallel Interface/Timer Chip Simplifies Peripheral Control," *EDN*, Jan. 20, 1982, pp. 131–136. Describes the use of the 68230 chip as a parallel printer interface.

THE USER INTERFACE

6.1 INTRODUCTION

The user interface consists of input and output devices that allow the user to control, and receive response from, the system. The most common input device is a keyboard, which may range from a few push buttons to a full typewriter-style alphanumeric keyboard. Other input devices, such as joysticks, trackballs, digitizer tablets and "mice," allow arbitrary XY (i.e., two-dimensional) positioning to be performed more readily. Speech recognition systems allow spoken commands to replace more traditional input techniques.

On the output side, displays are the most common device. A wide variety of displays are available for use in microprocessor systems, from simple on/off indicators to large graphics displays. Because of the number of display types and the relative complexity of some of their interfaces, they are covered in a chapter of their own, which follows this one.

Output devices other than displays are covered in this chapter. Printers are the primary alternative to displays, conveying similar information but in a more permanent form. Sound generation is an important part of many applications, from simple beeps to complex sounds. One common complex sound is speech, which can be readily synthesized under microprocessor control.

Note that there are a variety of input and output devices that are not user interface devices, such as stepper motors, temperature sensors, and A/D converters. For more information on such devices, refer to the Selected Bibliography at the end of Chap. 1.

6.2   USER INTERFACE DESIGN

The design of good user interfaces is a complex subject and involves many software as well as hardware considerations. While a comprehensive treatment is beyond the scope of this text, we will provide an overview of some of the considerations. This is important for the system's hardware design, as user interface considerations have considerable influence on the selection of I/O devices.

Ergonomics is the science of matching systems to their users for optimum ease of operation. It requires a detailed understanding of the physical and perceptual characteristics of the product's user. Ergonomics covers all aspects of system design, from the size and placement of the keys to the color of the display. It has become an advertising buzzword, particularly for CRT terminals. In that context, it has come to mean a low-profile keyboard with good tactile response and a clear, stable display with a nonglare faceplate and an adjustable stand.

6.2.1   Friendly Systems

The design of the user interface is, of course, a key factor in the user's perception of a product. There are two aspects to this design: hardware and software. In this book we are concerned primarily with the hardware. Both are equally important and are dependent on one another. Without good software, the most sophisticated hardware is useless. Conversely, even the best software will be very limited with a poor hardware interface. It is important that the hardware have sufficient capability for the software to realize its goals.

For example, the selection of the display type greatly affects the "friendliness" that can be achieved. As microprocessor-based products become more complex, they can become very intimidating and difficult to use if the user interface is not carefully designed. If a seven-segment type display is used, it is limited to numeric characters and a few alphabetic characters. Thus, when a user presses an invalid key, the best response possible is often something like "Err 27," which the user then looks up on a list that has a description of each error code.

A full alphanumeric display, on the other hand, allows the text of the error messages to be displayed directly. "Err 27," for example, can become "Function key expected" or "Voltage out of range." Taken one step further, a multiline display such as a CRT allows a menu of the possible commands to be displayed, and extensive "help" features can be implemented.

Thus, while the friendliness of a system is primarily a function of the software, the hardware determines how much the software can do. When an alphanumeric display is not needed for the basic functions of the system, it may still be justified for the improvement it makes possible in the user interface.

6.2.2   Keyboard Approaches

While the display type determines how the system outputs data to the user, the keyboard is the primary user input device in most systems. The most flexible keyboard is

Figure 6.1. Function selection menu.

```
1 - Set Measurement Parameters
2 - Measure Voltage
3 - Measure Current
4 - Measure Resistance
5 - Display Measurement Results
6 - Print Measurement Results
7 - Analysis Menu


Press Number for Desired Action
```

the full typewriter-style arrangement, which allows an indefinite number of different command words and options and permits new commands to be added with only a software change. It is particularly attractive for users who can touch-type, which speeds input by eliminating the need to visually search for the desired key. The drawback of this approach is that the user must remember the commands or refer to a reference card. One way to lessen this problem is through the use of menus. Even though there may be hundreds of possible commands in the system, usually only a relatively small number are meaningful at any time. These can be listed on the display as a menu, as shown in Fig. 6.1.

A well-designed set of menus can make systems with typewriter-style keyboards much easier to use, since they relieve the operator of having to remember commands. One problem with menus is that they tend to be burdensome to experienced users who know the commands, especially when several levels of menus may be required to fully specify a complex command. Thus, there should be a way to bypass the menus and enter a command directly so that an experienced user can use the system more efficiently.

At the opposite end of the spectrum, a dedicated-function keyboard as shown in Fig. 6.2 does not require the user to remember any commands. A glance at the keyboard shows the user all the options. This approach is often best for instruments and similar applications with a relatively small number of commands, but it has several disadvantages. To add a new function, the physical keyboard must often be changed, which makes it difficult to add a new feature when producing a new revision of the software. For systems requiring many commands, the number of function keys becomes large and can confuse the user.

One solution to these problems is the use of *soft keys*. These are function keys that are defined by the software; they are "soft" because they can be dynamically changed. The legend, rather than being molded in the keycap, is shown on the system display, adjacent to the keys. Figure 6.3 shows an example of a system using soft keys. Soft keys provide many of the same features as a menu, and can be used along with full alphanumeric keyboards or with simple numeric and/or dedicated-function keyboards. The definitions of the soft keys can be changed each time a key is pressed. This approach prompts the user with the available choices at each step in a complex command and has been called *guided syntax*.

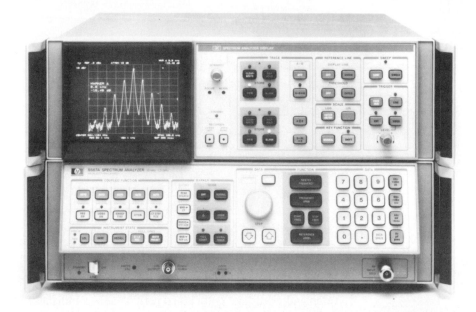

Figure 6.2. Complex instrument using dedicated-function keys. *(Photo courtesy of Hewlett-Packard Company.)*

Figure 6.3. System using soft keys. *(Photo courtesy of Hewlett-Packard Company.)*

A similar type of user interface is implemented in systems with mice using "pop-up" or "pull-down" menus. The user triggers the display of the menu by pointing to a selection word or icon. The desired item in the menu is then selected by pointing to it with the mouse and pressing (or releasing) one of the mouse buttons. Apple's Macintosh is the best-known example of such an interface approach, which originated at Xerox's Palo Alto Research Center, and is now used in a wide range of software for many personal computers.

6.3 KEYBOARD INTERFACING

Keyboards and other switches can be interfaced to the microprocessor in several ways. Some methods are preferable for small numbers of switches, and others for larger numbers. The software burden imposed on the processor for monitoring the keyboard also varies with the interfacing approach. This section describes a variety of approaches and their advantages and disadvantages.

6.3.1 Nonmultiplexed Interface

The simplest technique for interfacing a small number of switches to a microprocessor system is to connect each to an input port bit. Figure 6.4 shows eight switches connected in this way. Pull-up resistors provide a high level when a switch is open, allowing single-throw switches to be used. When a switch is closed, the input is held low, and the corresponding bit is 0 when the microprocessor reads the input port.

This simple interface requires very little software. It is often used to read system configuration (DIP) switches. It can also be used for small numbers of keyboard

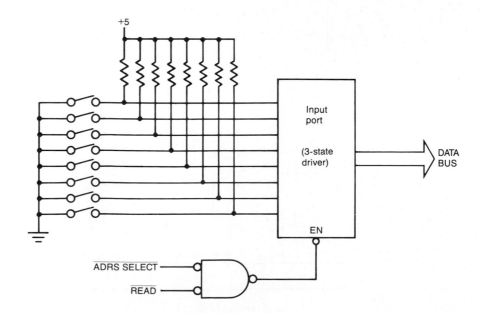

Figure 6.4. Basic nonmultiplexed switch interface.

switches. However, it is impractical for a large number of switches such as in a typical alphanumeric keyboard, since one input port bit is required for each switch.

6.3.2   Multiplexed Switch Interface

A *multiplexed,* or scanned, interface greatly reduces the number of I/O port bits needed for large numbers of switches. Figure 6.5 shows an interface for 16 switches, using one 4-bit input port and one 4-bit output port. As with the nonmultiplexed interface, pull-up resistors provide a high level at the input port when no keys are pressed. (In the context of keyboards, the terms *switch* and *key* are used interchangeably.) The keyboard is read one row at a time, a process called *scanning.* One of the output port bits is set to 0, and all the others are set to 1. Each output port bit drives one row of keys. The rows connected to output bits set to 1 are effectively disabled, since pressing the key would only connect the high-level output port bit to an input port bit that is already pulled high by the pull-up resistor. Only the row driven by the bit set to 0 is active; pressing any key in this row will pull the input port bit in the corresponding

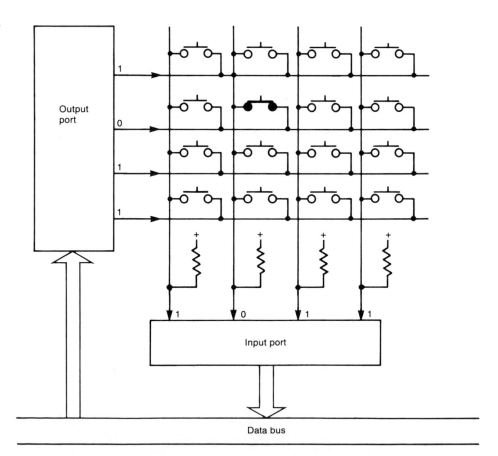

Figure 6.5.   Multiplexed keyboard interface.

column low. Thus, the output port allows the keyboard to be read one row at a time via a single input port.

To read the entire keyboard, each row is read in turn. The sequence is as follows:

1. Data 0111 written to output port.

2. Input port is read. If no keys are pressed in that row, the value read will be 1111. If any keys are pressed, there will be a 0 in the corresponding bit.

3. Data 1011 written to output port, shifting the 0 to the next row.

4. Input port is read. The figure shows a key pressed in this row, which causes the data 1011 to be read at the input port.

5. Data 1101 written to output port, and input port read.

6. Data 1110 written to output port, and input port read.

This sequence is repeated indefinitely.

The keyboard must be fully scanned (all rows read) frequently enough so that if the user quickly presses and releases a key, it will be detected. If, for example, there are eight rows, and one is read each millisecond, then 8 ms is required to read the entire keyboard. The shortest key press that must be detected varies from 20 to 100 ms, depending on the application and the keyboard type.

One way to implement the software for keyboard scanning is to use a programmable timer to generate an interrupt once each millisecond or so. At each interrupt, the data in the output port is shifted, and the input port is read. If the data read has a 0 in any bit position, then a key is pressed. The exact key can be determined by decoding the combination of the row and column data.

The size of the keyboard is easily increased. Eight-bit input and output ports provide a 64-key interface. Adding a second output port provides another eight rows and doubles the number of keys that can be supported. (Alternatively, another input port can be added for additional columns.) With 16-bit input and output ports, 256 keys can be supported.

One problem with a simple matrix keyboard is that it cannot always correctly detect which keys are pressed when more than one is pressed at a time. If more than one key is pressed in the same column or row, there is no problem. However, consider the situation shown in Fig. 6.6. Three keys labeled A, B, and D are pressed. When row 2 is read, column line 1 is pulled low by switch D. However, since the switch B is also pressed, row 1 is pulled low. (Actually, the row 1 driver is trying to pull the line high, and the row 2 driver, via column 1, is trying to pull the line low. With most TTL devices, the low level will win.) Row 1 is therefore enabled, even though the software expects to be reading only row 2. Switch A brings column 0 low, causing the software to erroneously think that switch C is pressed. This is called a *ghost key*.

In most applications using special-function keyboards (i.e., not typewriter-style), this is not a problem. Ghost keys do not appear unless three or more keys are pressed at the same time, which is unlikely to happen if the user is using a single finger. If certain keys, such as a "shift" key, are expected to be pressed in combination with other keys, they should be connected to a separate input port bit and should not be included in the matrix.

However, a fast typist on a typewriter-style keyboard may have several keys pressed at a time, even though they are pressed and released in sequence. In other words, there

Figure 6.6. Ghost key error when three keys are pressed.

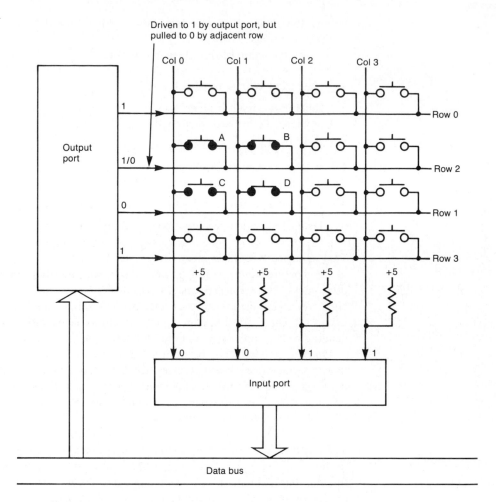

may be some overlap between keys. The ghost key effect can be eliminated by placing a diode in series with each switch, allowing a row to pull down a column, but not vice versa.

6.3.3 Switch Bounce

When a switch is closed, it does not make a single, clean transition from open to closed. Rather, it "bounces" back and forth from open to closed before finally settling in the closed position. A similar effect occurs when the switch is released. The length of the bounce period depends on the construction of the switch. Good-quality switches generally have bounce periods of 1 to 5 ms. Inexpensive switches with lower contact force can bounce for tens of ms. There are also bounce-free switches, which usually use mercury-wetted contacts, but they are much more expensive than conventional switches.

If bounce is not taken into consideration, the microprocessor may think that the switch has been pressed and released several times when in fact it has only been pressed once. You may have noticed this effect on older hand-held calculators. As the inexpensive keypads age, the bounce time increases. If it grows beyond the time the system is designed to account for, the bounce becomes apparent to the user as repeated digits from a single key press.

There are many ways to *debounce* a switch. Four hardware-based methods are shown in Fig. 6.7. The RS latch approach is effective and will work with any amount of bounce, but it requires double-throw switches and two gates per switch. The simplified latch uses only one-third of a hex inverter IC, and requires no resistors. The resistor-capacitor solution requires a careful selection of values to ensure that bounce pulses are filtered out but short key presses are not, and the resistor values must be chosen to maintain good logic levels in both states. When the switch is pressed, the capacitor quickly discharges through resistor R_1, which is usually a relatively low value. When the switch is released, the capacitor slowly charges through resistor R_2, which is relatively large. The buffer must be a Schmitt-trigger device (i.e., a buffer with hysteresis) so that the slowly charging capacitor will not cause the output to oscillate. CMOS devices work best, since their high input impedances allow the use of relatively large resistors and consequently smaller capacitors.

Switch debouncer ICs, such as the MC14490, are a good alternative for small numbers of switches. This CMOS chip can debounce six separate switches. A single capacitor sets the frequency of an internal oscillator, which determines the bounce time that can be tolerated. The inputs are clocked into an internal shift register, and only when the input has remained unchanged for several clock cycles is the output changed.

All these techniques are most useful for reset switches and other applications in which the switch is not read by software. For the usual applications in which the switches are read by software, the debouncing can be performed entirely by the program.

The basic software debounce algorithm is to keep a count of the length of time each key has been pressed or released. Only when the count exceeds a predetermined value (such as 10 ms) is the switch considered to have been pressed or released. This is easily implemented with an interrupt-driven multiplexed interface as previously described. When a key is detected, software stores the key code in a temporary location. If this key is still pressed the next time that row is read, then the switch is considered to be pressed, and the key code is passed to the appropriate service routine. If the bounce time is longer than the scan time, then the number of scans that the key has been pressed (or released) must be counted, and only when the count reaches a predetermined value is the key code passed to the processing routine.

Note that it is not necessary to debounce both the opening and closing of the switch. Figure 6.8 shows the effect when only the release is debounced. As soon as the switch is closed for even a moment, the switch is acknowledged to be closed. However, when the switch is released, it must remain open for 10 ms before it will be considered released. Thus, the bounce when the switch is first closed is ignored, since the brief open periods do not meet the time limit for acknowledging the release of the key. When the switch is opened, there are brief open periods, alternating with the bounce back to the closed state. Each of the brief open intervals is ignored, since they are under the 10-ms limit. Finally, when the switch has stopped bouncing for 10 ms, it is acknowledged to be released.

Figure 6.7. Switch-debouncing techniques: *(a)* RS latch, *(b)* Simplified RS latch, *(c)* RC debounce with Schmitt-trigger inverter, and *(d)* CMOS debouncer IC.

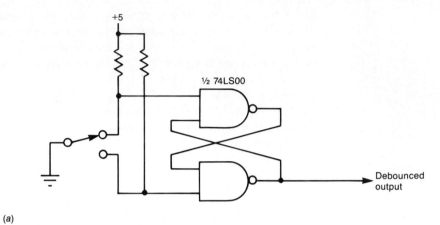

(a)

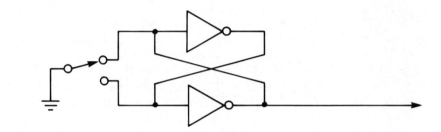

(b)

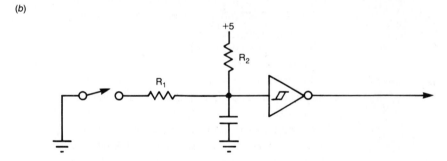

(c)

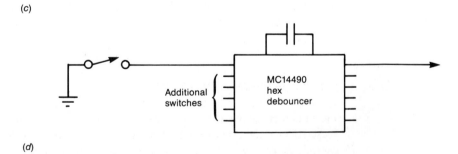

(d)

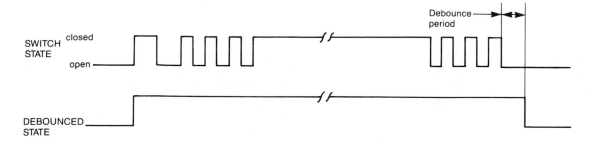

Figure 6.8. Effect of trailing-edge-only debouncing.

6.3.4 Rollover and Lockout

Assuming that the hardware used has the ability to properly detect when multiple keys are pressed, the software must determine how this is handled. The simplest technique is called *two-key lockout*. When any key is pressed, all others are ignored until the first key is released. This is simple to implement and is acceptable for special-function keyboards. The following example shows how this method responds:

Key action	Program action
A pressed	A pressed
B pressed	none
B released	none
A released	A released

Thus, the B key is entirely missed.

A more desirable approach is *two-key rollover*. Two-key rollover acknowledges each key as it is pressed and will detect both keys in the preceding example. A generalization of this method is *n-key rollover,* which allows any number of keys to be pressed at the same time. Each key is acknowledged as it is pressed. *N*-key rollover is generally used for typewriter-style keyboards.

6.3.5 Hardware-Based Interfaces

The keyboard interfaces we have described up to this point are software-intensive. The software must continuously scan the rows and columns of the keyboard, decode the data to determine which key is pressed, debounce the keys, and provide some sort of lockout or rollover to handle multiple keys pressed at the same time. All this software consumes processing time even when no keys are pressed and also adds to the software development burden. By using a keyboard controller IC, these tasks can be shifted to the hardware.

One example of a keyboard controller IC is Intel's 8279. This chip includes keyboard scanning and debouncing logic as well as a display driver and is described further in Sec. 7.2.5. It interfaces directly to a matrix keyboard of up to 64 keys. An internal oscillator clocks the keyboard scan counter. The keys pressed are debounced, and when a valid key is detected, the key code is stored in an 8-byte FIFO buffer. This buffer allows up to eight keys to be stored while waiting to be read by the microprocessor. Either two-key lockout or *n*-key rollover can be selected.

A variety of other keyboard controller ICs are also available. The SMC 3600 is typical of the simpler devices. It can scan a matrix of up to 90 keys and provides debouncing and two-key lockout or *n*-key rollover. An on-chip oscillator drives the scan counter, and a ROM decodes the row-column patterns to produce key codes. Each time a key is pressed, a strobe output is pulsed, and the key code is output on the data lines.

This type of chip is commonly packaged with a typewriter-style keyboard and sold as an "ASCII" keyboard, named for the data output code used. (See Sec. 8.2.1 for a description of the ASCII code.) For many applications, purchasing a keyboard in this format is more economical than designing your own.

Interfacing this type of keyboard to a microprocessor system is relatively simple, as shown in Fig. 6.9. When a key is pressed, the strobe line is pulsed and the ASCII code for the key is read by the input port. The strobe input can be connected to an input port bit, which is frequently polled by the software. For best system performance, the strobe can drive an interrupt input, allowing the microprocessor to ignore the keyboard except when a key is pressed. If a latching input port is used, the response time to the interrupt is not critical. Parity is provided by some standard keyboards but is unnecessary in most applications since the connection path is short and not particularly noise-prone.

Another alternative is to use a single-chip microcomputer as a keyboard controller. Software in the microcomputer's on-chip ROM provides the instructions to scan and debounce the keyboard inputs. The I/O port pins of the microcomputer serve as the row drive and column-sense ports. In many microcomputers, the input ports have built-in pull-up resistors, simplifying the interface further. One advantage of using a microcomputer as the keyboard controller is that a serial interface to the main micro-

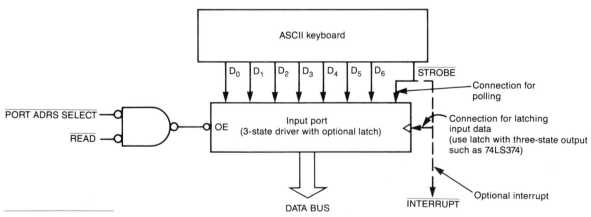

Figure 6.9. ASCII keyboard interface.

processor can be used. Only the "output" side of the serial interface is needed, and this is easily implemented in software. Using a serial interface allows the keyboard to be physically separate from the computer or main system unit and requires only a few wires in the cable. The microcomputer in the keyboard assembly can also buffer several characters, reducing the rate at which they must be read by the main processor. In this case, a bidirectional serial link (or a "request" line from the host to the keyboard processor) is used to allow the main processor to poll the keyboard processor. This type of keyboard interface is used in many personal computers and CRT terminals.

6.3.6 Selecting a Keyboard Interface Approach

As described in the preceding sections, there are several ways to implement a keyboard interface. The software-based approach uses only input and output ports for hardware and therefore has the lowest manufacturing cost. Using a keyboard controller IC relieves the microprocessor of the burden of continuously scanning the keyboard and increases the available processing time. For applications using standard typewriter-format keyboards, the entire keyboard and controller can be purchased as a single module. This saves design time, and the very high production volume of standard keyboard products keeps costs relatively low.

In cost-sensitive applications that can spare some of the processor's time for keyboard scanning, the software-intensive approach remains best. When the keyboard requirements are unusual, or a serial interface is desired, a single-chip microcomputer with the appropriate software makes a versatile and inexpensive keyboard controller.

The worst-case response time of the software to a key press must also be considered. If the software cannot always respond to a key press quickly, some key presses may be lost when several keys are pressed in quick succession. This is annoying to the user and can cause undesirable functions to be performed. This problem is solved by adding a *type-ahead* FIFO buffer that stores key strokes, which can be implemented in either hardware or software.

6.3.7 Keyswitch Technology

A variety of technologies are used to implement keyswitches and keyboards. They can be categorized by the amount the key top moves and by the mechanism used to implement the switch itself. Standard typewriter-style keyboards use *full-travel* switches, whose keycap moves approximately 0.15 in. when pressed. Full-travel switches are preferable from a human-factors point of view; users prefer the relatively large motion.

The oldest type of full-travel switch is the standard mechanical push-button switch, often called a "hard" mechanical switch. These switches use a spring and cam to move two gold-plated contacts together. A small contact area allows a large contact pressure to be developed, providing a low-resistance connection.

Standard mechanical switches have inherent long-term reliability problems. They are susceptible to contamination from liquid spills and other sources, and eventually the contact resistance increases as the switch wears out. A variety of other technologies are used to improve the reliability and/or decrease the cost of keyboards. Reed-switch keyboards use a magnetic reed switch at each key position. Pressing the key moves a magnet near the reed switch, thus causing it to close. Reed switches are more reliable than standard mechanical switches, since the reed-switch contacts are sealed inside a glass tube and are thus protected from contamination.

Even higher reliability can be obtained by replacing the reed switches with Hall effect sensors. A Hall effect sensor is a semiconductor device that detects the presence of a magnetic field. This allows keyboards to be built with no mechanical contacts whatsoever and thus increases their reliability. Unfortunately, it also increases the price significantly, limiting Hall effect keyboards to applications willing to pay a premium price for high reliability.

Capacitance keyboards are a popular technology for implementing moderate-cost keyboards. When a key is pressed, two conductive plates are moved closer together. This changes the value of the capacitor formed by the two plates, which is detected by sensing circuitry. This approach is particularly attractive for applications such as typewriter-style keyboards that have a relatively large number of keys. Each key mechanism is simple and inexpensive, and the capacitance sensing circuitry can be shared among the matrixed keys.

At the opposite end of the spectrum, flat-panel keyboards have very little motion. The most common is the membrane type, a sandwich of three layers of plastic. The outer layers have metallization patterns on the inside surfaces that form the switch contacts. The middle layer has a hole at each switch position. When a switch position is pressed, the top layer is pushed down onto the bottom layer, the metallized patterns make contact, and the connection is made. There is very little travel, since the separating plastic layer is thin. One disadvantage of this type of keyboard is that there is no *tactile feedback*; the user does not receive any feeling in his or her finger to indicate that the switch has been actuated. Thus, systems using membrane keyboards usually produce some other form of feedback when a key is pressed, such as a beep or click. Most users strongly prefer keyboards with tactile feedback.

One popular switch technology is the *dome* switch. As shown in the cross section in Fig. 6.10, the metal dome provides a spring action, and when pressed it snaps to the

Figure 6.10. Metal dome switch operation. *(a)* Switch not pressed; *(b)* Switch pressed.

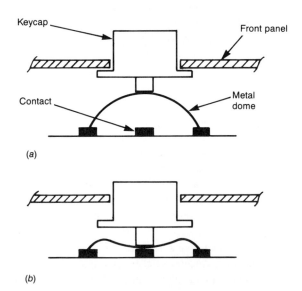

Figure 6.11. Metal dome switches in a membrane keyboard. *(Courtesy of Texas Instruments.)*

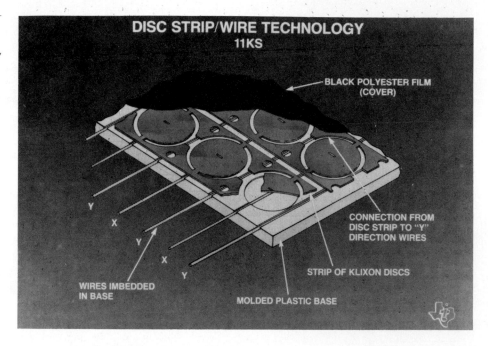

closed position. This provides some travel and good tactile response. Dome switches are available as a single push button and in a keyboard matrix.

A combination of membrane and metal dome technologies is widely used. It combines the low cost and environmental immunity of the membrane technology with the tactile response of the dome switches. The metal dome mechanisms are sealed between a rigid plastic base and a flexible plastic cover, as shown in Fig. 6.11. This is one of the most attractive keyboard alternatives when full travel is not required.

The advantage of membrane switch technology, with or without metal domes, is that the surface of the keyboard is a single sheet of plastic and is thus immune to contamination. The keyboard surface can be silk-screened to provide all the legends and other markings for the front panel. Figure 6.12 shows an instrument that uses a membrane keyboard as its front panel. The display filters are fabricated as an integral part of the panel.

Standard plastic keycaps can be also placed on top of a membrane keyboard with internal metal domes, which produces a conventional-appearing keyboard with discrete keys but retains the sealing benefits of membrane technology. This approach is used in many of the better hand-held calculators.

Flat-panel keyboards have also been made that sense the capacitance to ground of the user's body when he or she touches the switch area. These keyboards have had limited success due to the difficulty of working reliably with a wide range of users and environmental conditions.

Conductive elastomer technology provides another approach to limited-travel keyboards. Keys are molded from silicone rubber, with a dot of conductive rubber (elastomer) on the lower surface of the key top. Figure 6.13 shows a cross section of a

Figure 6.13. Cross section of conductive elastomer switch.

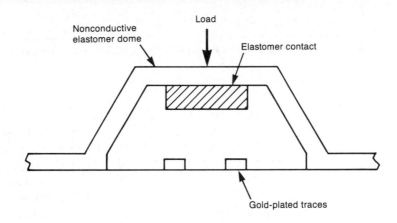

conductive elastomer push-button switch. When the key is pressed, the elastomer contact is pressed down on the printed circuit board, where it shorts two traces together.

Conductive elastomer keyboards are very inexpensive in high volume. The tooling costs for a custom keyboard layout are higher than for a membrane keyboard, but the production costs are lower. The legends can be molded into the rubber keycaps. Alternatively, standard plastic keycaps can be placed over the rubber keys, as shown in Fig. 6.14. Most conductive elastomer keys do not have much tactile feedback; there is some travel, but no "click." However, some elastomer switches do produce a click by designing the rubber key top to snap like the metal dome switches. The click is not as sharp as a metal dome keyboard, but it is acceptable for many applications.

Most switch types are available in a variety of formats. Standard mechanical switches, metal dome switches, and conductive elastomer switches are available as

Figure 6.14. Keyboard assembly using keycaps and conductive elastomer switches. *(Courtesy of Texas Instruments.)*

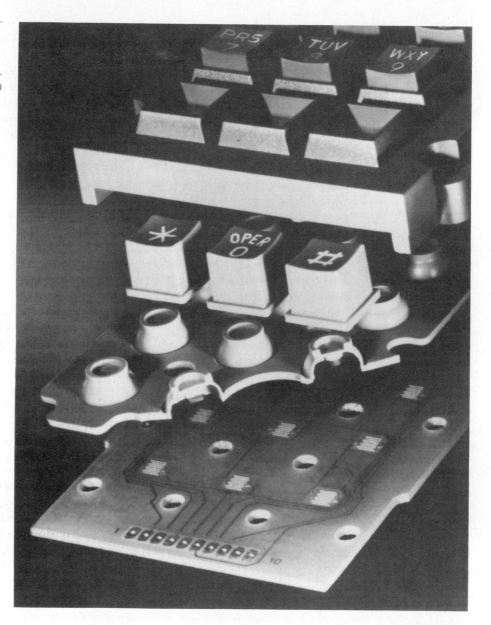

single units, in groups of two or more in a row, in small keyboards of typically 12 to 20 keys, or as full typewriter-style keyboards. Hall effect, reed, and capacitive switches are most common in encoded typewriter-style keyboards with parallel ASCII outputs.

Membrane switches are not generally available as single switches but are usually used for moderate-sized keyboards. They are available in a variety of standard matrix arrangements (such as 3×4, 4×4, 5×4, etc.) and are generally customized with the key legends for a specific application.

6.4   GRAPHIC INPUT AND POINTING DEVICES

While keyboards are a natural input device for alphanumeric data, they are not very effective for graphic input. Cursor keys can be used to position a cursor on a display, but this is a slow method when much graphic input is required. A variety of devices are available that are specifically designed for this task. The following sections describe the most common devices and the methods used to interface them to microprocessor systems.

Graphic input devices can also be used as pointing devices. Any device that can position a cursor at an arbitrary point on the screen can be used as a function selection device. A list of items to be selected is displayed, or a "keyboard" can be drawn on the display. Many systems now use *icons,* which are graphic representations of a function that can be selected. By positioning the cursor over the desired menu item, "key," or icon, the function can be selected.

Another application for cursor positioning is text editing. To move, delete, or otherwise manipulate a block of text, the start and end of the block must be indicated. This is done by positioning the cursor at the start of the block, providing some indication that this is the start, and then positioning the cursor at the end of the block.

6.4.1   Joysticks

The joystick is the least expensive graphic input device. Two potentiometers are connected to a control stick via a mechanism. When the joystick is moved on one axis (e.g., forward and backward), one potentiometer is rotated. When it is moved on the other axis (e.g., left and right), the other is rotated. Thus, one potentiometer indicates the X-axis position and the other the Y-axis position. The position of the potentiometer is detected via an A/D converter, which allows the microprocessor to read the position.

Figure 6.15 shows a low-cost circuit for interfacing a joystick to a microprocessor system. Each potentiometer serves as the frequency-determining element of a simple oscillator, which is implemented in this figure with an IC timer chip. The output of each oscillator connects to an input port bit. The microprocessor measures the frequency of each input signal by counting the time between transitions. Since the frequency is proportional to the potentiometer position, this effectively implements a low-cost A/D converter. This type of interface is widely used in personal computers and video games.

The way the system responds to the joystick is determined by the software. Joysticks are frequently used as velocity inputs; the position of the joystick determines the direction and speed of the cursor motion. When the joystick is returned to the center position, the cursor stops moving. This method is used because the range of motion of the joystick is not adequate to directly position the cursor at any point on a reasonably sized screen with good resolution.

Joysticks frequently include one or more push buttons located near the positioning lever. These allow some action to be initiated when the cursor has been positioned at the desired spot. Examples of actions include marking the start of a text block, selecting a menu item, and firing a missile at an enemy spaceship.

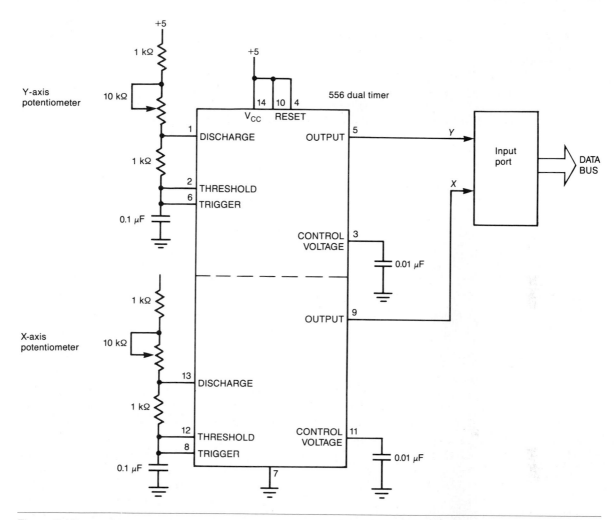

Figure 6.15.   Joystick interface using dual timer as voltage-to-frequency converters. Values shown give period range of approximately 210 to 830 μs.

6.4.2   Trackballs

Figure 6.16 shows a graphic input device called a *trackball*. A metal or plastic ball is mounted in a frame, with only a small portion protruding through the opening in the top of the frame. The ball is supported by two perpendicular rods so that when the ball is rotated left or right, one rod rotates, and when it is rotated forward or backward, the other rod rotates. The position of each rod is then sensed.

The rod position can be sensed by a special potentiometer that can rotate continuously. However, this produces an analog signal, which must be translated to a digital signal for the microprocessor. Many trackballs use optical encoders instead. An optical

Figure 6.16. Track-ball. *(Courtesy of Honey-well/Disc Instruments.)*

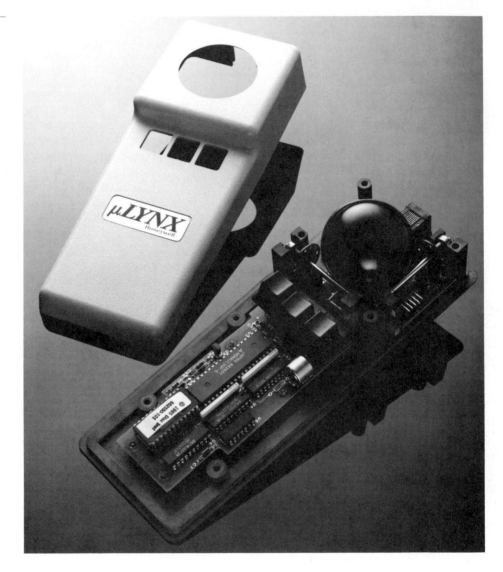

encoder consists of a transparent disk with an opaque striped pattern. An LED on one side of the disk shines a light through it, which is detected on the opposite side by a phototransistor or photodiode. As the disk rotates, the beam of light is interrupted, and the photosensor produces pulses. These pulses are then counted to determine how much motion has occurred.

To allow the direction of motion to be sensed, two sets of patterns are used on the disk, along with two sets of LEDs and sensors, as shown in Fig. 6.17. (The same signals can be produced with a single striped pattern on the disk and a slotted mask for each sensor. The two masks are positioned 90° out of phase with respect to each other.)

Figure 6.17. Optical encoder with quadrature outputs.

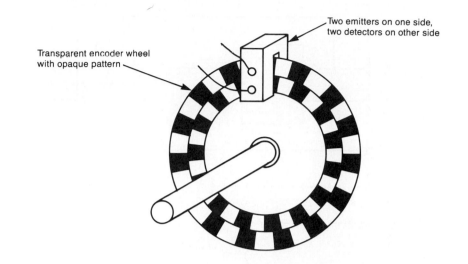

Transparent encoder wheel with opaque pattern

Two emitters on one side, two detectors on other side

Figure 6.18. Quadrature signals.

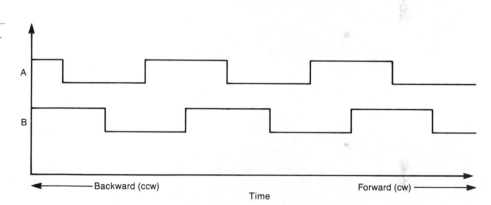

A

B

Backward (ccw)　　　　　　　Forward (cw)

Time

The output is two *quadrature* signals, as shown in Fig. 6.18. The direction can be sensed by examining the phase relationship of the two signals. If signal *A* is high when a rising edge occurs on signal *B,* then the motion is in the forward direction. The signals can be connected directly to an input port and all decoding and counting performed in software if the microprocessor is fast enough.

However, unless a relatively fast microprocessor is used which does not need to perform many other tasks while reading the encoder signals, rapid motion may be missed. A hardware implementation of the quadrature decoder, as shown in Fig. 6.19, removes the speed-critical tasks from the microprocessor. The flip-flop detects the direction of motion by sensing the state of signal *A* at the rising edge of signal *B*. The flip-flop output provides a direction control signal to a counter, which counts the pulses. The counter can be cleared by the microprocessor by writing to the selected address. The counter then accumulates pulses, counting up or down depending on the phase rela-

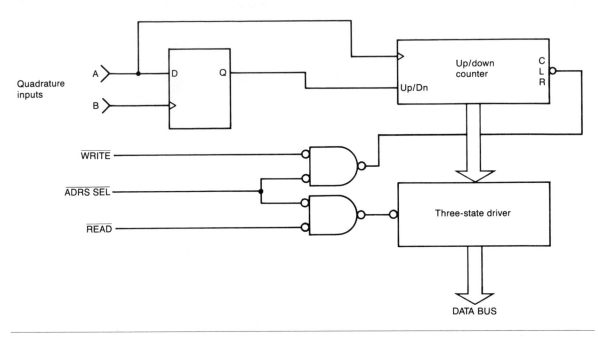

Figure 6.19.   Basic quadrature decoder and position counter.

tionship of the two inputs. The microprocessor can read the position via the three-state buffer (a basic input port) and then clear the count. The size of the counter determines how much motion can be accumulated between reads.

This simple circuit demonstrates the basic approach but has a number of weaknesses. If there is some jitter in the signals, erroneous counts can be accumulated. In addition, only one-fourth the available resolution is used. For maximum resolution, the counter should count both rising and falling edges on both the *A* and *B* input signals. For more sophisticated circuits, refer to the references at the end of this chapter.

Hewlett-Packard's HCTL-2000 IC provides a single-chip solution for interfacing quadrature signals to a microprocessor system. It includes digital noise filters, quadrature decoders for full 4× resolution (both edges of both signals counted), and a 12-bit up/down counter. An 8-bit bus interface is included, which allows the counter to be read in two parts.

Note that while we have described optical encoders in the context of trackballs, they have many more uses. They are one of the best methods for measuring the movement or position of a shaft in robotic and other mechanical applications. They are also useful as replacements for potentiometers for front panel controls in microprocessor-based instruments. When the user turns the knob, pulses are sent to the microprocessor, which then takes the appropriate action (such as moving the position of an oscilloscope trace or adjusting the gain of an input amplifier). In this type of application, an optical encoder is sometimes called a *rotary pulse generator (RPG)*.

Trackballs can be used to input relatively large motions with high accuracy and are therefore more suited to high-resolution direct positioning applications than are joysticks. However, they are relatively expensive and not as natural to use.

6.4.3 Mice

The most popular cursor positioning device is the *mouse*, a small, hand-held device that rolls along a tabletop. You can think of a mouse as an upside-down trackball: rather than moving the ball, the ball serves as a wheel, and the box is moved. Mice are widely preferred as the most rapid, accurate positioning device.

Many mice are built very similarly to trackballs. These mechanical mice are the least expensive but have potential reliability problems since the ball tends to pick up dirt from the surface it rolls on. (Like most trackballs, these "mechanical" mice generally use optical sensors to detect the rotation of the ball, so they are really hybrid optical-mechanical devices.) In addition, the ball sometimes slips, causing a loss of motion. Optical mice solve these problems by using photosensors to pick up signals from a grid pad. A variety of innovative techniques have been developed for optical mice. All require a special surface for the mouse to roll on. One approach uses a reflective surface with lines of two colors ruled on it, one color horizontally and the other vertically. The mouse contains a light source and two sensors, one sensitive to each color. Each sensor thus produces a pulse each time a line of the appropriate color is crossed.

Mechanical mice often have quadrature outputs as described for trackballs. Even some optical mice have quadrature outputs. However, many mice are now built with internal microcomputers to track the motion and maintain X and Y position counts. The mouse then interfaces to the microprocessor system via a standard serial interface. The position can be transmitted each time the mouse moves or only in response to a "send position" command from the microprocessor.

Mice are commonly rated by their resolution, typically stated as counts per in. (cpi) of travel. Most mice have a resolution of 100 to 200 cpi. The higher the resolution, the less motion is required to move the cursor a given distance, but the harder it is to position the mouse on an exact point. The resolution can be decreased by the software to make accurate positioning easier by dividing the count from the mouse.

Mice generally include one to four push buttons on the upper surface of the housing. A button is pushed to select the object pointed to, such as an item in a menu, or to mark a position, such as the start of a text block to be moved. Push buttons can also be used for other application-dependent functions.

Mice, like nearly all other nonkeyboard cursor positioning devices, require that the user remove his or her hands from the keyboard to position the cursor. This is awkward in applications such as word processing that involve much keyboard activity, so cursor-positioning arrow keys on the keyboard are often preferred in such applications.

6.4.4 Touch-Sensitive Displays

One of the most direct methods of positioning a cursor on a display is to simply point at the spot where you want the cursor to be. Touch-sensitive displays make this possible. Several different technologies are used to implement them. One of the most common and straightforward is the light beam approach. Rows of LEDs are placed along two adjacent edges of the display, and photosensors are placed along the opposite edges. This creates a matrix of light beams covering the display area. When the user points to a spot on the screen, two beams are broken, one vertical and one horizontal. This identifies the position of the pointer. A finger is the most commonly used pointer, although anything opaque (such as a pen or pencil) will work as well. (Note that although they are called *touch* screens, screens using this optical sensor approach do not have to be actually touched; only the light beam must be blocked.)

Another approach uses a resistive coating on a glass plate covering the screen. A conductive Mylar overlay is positioned so that there is a small gap between the glass and the Mylar. A voltage is applied across the resistive coating on the glass. When a point on the screen is pressed, the conductive Mylar contacts the resistive surface on the glass. The voltage on the Mylar indicates the position of contact, which is converted to digital form by an A/D converter. The voltage is alternately applied to the horizontal and vertical sides to allow the position on both axes to be detected.

Some advantages of the conductive overlay approach are that higher resolutions are theoretically possible, and there is some tactile feedback since some pressure must be applied to make the Mylar move. However, a significant portion of the display's light output is blocked by the coatings on the glass and Mylar.

Several other technologies have been used to implement touch screens, including capacitive sensing and surface acoustic waves. Each approach requires its own particular sensing electronics and has advantages and disadvantages. From a systems viewpoint, all are similarly interfaced. The output of the sensing electronics is an X and Y position value, which may be presented as parallel or serial data.

Touch screens are most effective for use as selection devices. A list of items is displayed, and the user touches the one of interest. Because of the relatively coarse resolution, touch screens are less effective than mice or other cursor positioners for actual graphic input. Dirt buildup on the screen can also be a problem in some environments.

6.4.5   Light Pens

A *light pen* performs a very similar function to a touch-sensitive screen. Instead of having sensors around the display to detect the position of the pointer, the pointer (the light pen) detects its position on the screen. CRT displays are scanned, so that each point on the display is lit at a different moment. The light pen contains a fast-response photodiode, which produces a pulse when the beam scans by the spot on the screen that it is pointing to. The CRT controller (as described in the following chapter) contains a set of counters that indicate the current beam position. Thus, by storing the state of the counters when a pulse arrives from the light pen, the position of the light pen on the screen is determined. The system then displays a cursor at the corresponding position, creating the illusion that the light pen is writing the spot on the screen.

Since the light pen senses the light from the screen, a "tracking pattern" must be displayed to allow the detection of the pen when it is pointing to a black area. This pattern is displayed at a rate that is infrequent enough so that it does not produce a noticeable image but still provides a signal for the light pen to detect.

Light pens are less expensive to implement than touch screens. However, while the touch screen is nearly invisible to the user, the light pen is a special device that must be used to point with. A finger is certainly a more convenient pointer, although dirty fingers can create problems. When alternating between keyboard entries and light pen actions, the constant picking up and putting down of the light pen can be cumbersome.

6.4.6 Digitizers

A digitizer, also called a *graphics tablet,* is similar to a touch screen or a display with a light pen but is separate from the display. A flat surface, which may be as small as a piece of notebook paper or as large as the largest drafting paper, serves as the input device. A pointer allows any point on the surface to be selected, and the digitizer outputs the coordinates of the selected point. The pointer may be a pen-shaped stylus or a mouselike object with a clear window with cross hairs.

Many technologies have been used to build digitizers, and a description of them is beyond the scope of this text. Regardless of the technology employed, the output is the same: a coordinate pair indicating the position of the pointer. This information is commonly transmitted via a serial link to the microprocessor system.

Digitizers can be used for positioning the cursor on a display. They are less fatiguing to use than a light pen, since the user's arm does not have to be raised. However, their primary use is in digitizing information from a paper document, as their name implies. The digitizer's pointer (often called a *cursor*) is positioned over the desired spot on the drawing or other document, and a switch is pressed. The meaning of the point being entered must be provided via a keyboard or other means. For example, when digitizing a printed circuit board design, the cursor is positioned over each component pin on the board, and the operator enters on a keyboard a designation to identify that pin.

6.5 SPEECH INPUT DEVICES

Talking to computers has long been a science fiction fantasy and is gradually becoming reality. There certainly is no more natural method for providing user input (except perhaps pointing for graphic input). However, there are many technical difficulties in implementing speech recognition. There are also practical problems; many people are uncomfortable talking to machines, and you can imagine the confusion of a roomful of people talking to their computers. Background noise also creates difficulties for speech recognition systems.

Human speech is very complex. Certain sounds mean different things in different contexts, and different people say the same word quite differently. While speech recognition systems are now readily available, they have many limitations. A few very expensive systems are somewhat less limited, but we will concentrate on systems whose price is within reason for microprocessor-based systems.

The current state of the art (at reasonable cost) in speech recognition is isolated-word speaker-dependent systems. *Isolated-word* means that an individual word must be spoken, isolated by pauses. This is necessary because it is extremely difficult to analyze a spoken sentence and determine where the word boundaries are, not to mention figuring out what the words are. *Speaker-dependent* means that the system works with only one user. Before the system can be used, the user must speak each word that is to be recognized several times. This training of the system allows a pattern to be stored in memory for each word. For recognition, the unknown pattern is compared to the patterns previously stored in memory, and the best match is chosen. These systems thus have a limited vocabulary, since they must be trained to recognize each word. With very large vocabularies, memory requirements increase, training and recognition time increases, and the chance of making an error increases due to the number of similar-sounding words.

Some systems can recognize a very limited speaker-independent vocabulary. This is not too difficult to implement if all the words in the vocabulary have distinctive characteristics and none is very similar to another. Typical speaker-independent vocabularies are "yes" and "no" and the digits 0 to 9.

A variety of speech recognition systems are available as single-board subsystems. They typically interface to a microprocessor system via a standard serial interface. To train the system, a "learn" command is sent to the subsystem, followed by the text for the first word. The microprocessor system then instructs the user to speak the word, and the speech recognition subsystem stores the pattern. For recognition, the microprocessor system sends a "recognize" command, and the subsystem responds with the text that it learned for the most closely matching pattern.

Because of its limited capabilities, speech recognition is not yet widely used. Its main applications are in situations where the user's hands are busy and normal input devices are thus inadequate. Examples include quality control inspection and inventory data collection. Another area of applications is telecommunication systems, where speech recognition makes it possible for a user to provide inputs to a computer from a standard telephone. However, these applications require speaker-independent systems, so are currently limited to applications in which a limited vocabulary will suffice.

As speech recognition technology advances, its uses will become more widespread. Single-chip speech recognizers are becoming available, and continued research and application of VLSI technology will bring costs down and make speaker independence and connected speech recognition practical. User resistance to the technology may further delay its implementation.

6.6   AUDIO OUTPUT

Audio output is important in many systems. Even simple beeps are invaluable for getting a user's attention, warning of an error or indicating the completion of a task. Complex sound generation is used in many entertainment applications, such as video games. A sophisticated form of audio output is speech synthesis, which is fortunately much simpler than speech recognition.

6.6.1   Tone Generation

Simple tones can be generated from a microprocessor system in several ways. The least expensive approach is a speaker or other transducer connected directly to an output port bit. (Depending on the type of device used for the output port, a simple one-transistor amplifier may be required.) By toggling the output port bit on and off with software, a tone is generated.

Piezotransducers are particularly attractive for this type of application. These de-

Figure 6.20. Piezo-transducer.

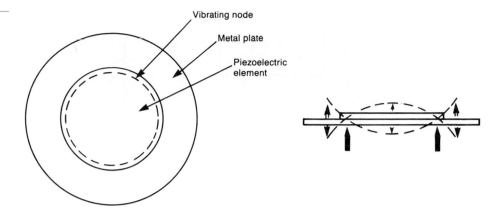

vices consist of a metal disk with a piezoelectric material attached, as shown in Fig. 6.20. The disk is mounted (typically in a cylindrical plastic case) in such a way that the edges are fixed but the center is free to move. Applying a voltage to the piezoelectric material causes the disk to bend. Applying an ac signal causes the disk to vibrate, producing a tone.

The transducer can be driven directly from an output port bit. One factor that must be considered is that the piezoelectric effect will also cause the transducer to *generate* a voltage if a mechanical shock is applied. The voltage produced can be high enough to damage a MOS output device. Thus, a zener diode should be used to protect the output stage, as shown in Fig. 6.21*a,* if there is any chance of a mechanical shock occurring. This prevents the voltage at the driver output from exceeding the breakdown voltage of the diode, and also from becoming more negative than one forward diode drop below ground.

For higher volume, the circuit shown in Fig. 6.21*b* can be used. The transistor supplies additional current drive, and the inductor acts as a "booster" coil. This booster coil increases the drive voltage applied to the transducer to several times the supply voltage. A capacitor can be added in parallel with the coil, which will reduce the volume but produce a milder-sounding tone.

A software-generated square wave is adequate for many applications. It allows a variety of frequencies to be generated, and siren and chirp effects can be produced with appropriate software. However, the software cannot control the waveshape, so characteristics other than frequency (such as attack and decay times) cannot be changed. (Actually, some degree of control is available by modifying the duty cycle of the signal. This effectively produces a pulse-width modulated signal, which is filtered by the response characteristics of the transducer.) A more flexible approach is to drive the speaker or transducer via a digital-to-analog (D/A) converter. The software must then do much more work to generate a tone, but all aspects of the tone can be controlled. This is appropriate for applications in which the tone quality is an important part of the overall product but is not necessary for most applications. Because the microprocessor must output a new value to the converter many times during each cycle of the output signal, the microprocessor may not have much time left for other functions.

Figure 6.21. Piezo-
transducer drive circuits
(a) Direct drive from MOS
device; *(b)* transistor drive
with booster coil.

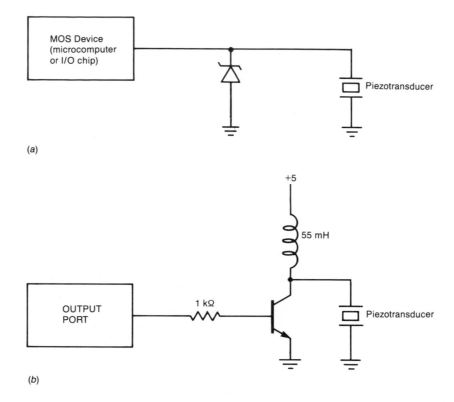

Special tone generator ICs are available for applications such as video games that require a range of complex sounds. The software needs only to send a command to the sound generator, and it then produces the sound continuously without further processor support. This greatly reduces the software burden, which is important in video games and other applications in which the microprocessor is kept busy with other events. Examples include General Instrument's AY-3-8910 and Texas Instruments' 76489.

Figure 6.22 shows the block diagram for General Instrument's AY-3-8910. A bank of 16 registers allows the microprocessor to control the characteristics of the tones produced. The chip is designed to interface to GI's single-chip microcomputers, and the bus interface is nonstandard. The two pins labeled A8 and $\overline{A9}$ are really just chip selects, one active-high and one active-low. A multiplexed address/data bus is used, and the BDIR and BC1 pins control the interface function, as shown in the figure.

The chip includes three programmable tone generators, a noise generator, and programmable amplitude controls. The tones are produced by programmable dividers. Several standard amplitude envelopes are available, which allow attack, sustain, and decay periods to be produced with only a single command from the microprocessor. For complex sounds, the three tone generators and the noise generator can be mixed together. The noise generator is useful for producing bomb explosions and other percussive sounds. In most applications, the three analog outputs are tied together and drive a single audio amplifier.

6.6.2   Speech Synthesis

Speech synthesis is far simpler than speech recognition, and a wide variety of low-cost products are available. This section describes several common techniques used for speed synthesis.

Waveform Digitization Techniques

The simplest way to produce speech digitally is to first digitize the speech via an A/D converter and store the digitized sequence in memory. The speech can then be played back by outputting the sequence via a D/A converter, followed by a low-pass filter. This is called *pulse-code modulation (PCM)*. The disadvantage of PCM is that large amounts of memory are required. The speech must be sampled at least 8000 times per second to produce an audio bandwidth approaching 4 kHz, the minimum required for acceptable speech quality. Each sample consists of 8 to 12 bits, depending on the quality required. The minimum data rate is therefore 64 to 96 kbits/s.

The data rate can be reduced by storing only the change in amplitude from one sample to the next rather than the full magnitude of each sample. This is called *delta modulation*. An elaboration of this technique is *continuously variable slope delta (CVSD)* modulation. CVSD modulation reduces the data rate to 16 to 32 kbits/s while maintaining excellent quality. However, this data rate is still too great to allow storage of a reasonable vocabulary on a ROM chip. CVSD modulation is most useful in speech transmission or recording systems where relatively large amounts of memory are available.

A dramatic reduction in data rate can be obtained by using the *Mozer technique,* named for its inventor, Forrest Mozer. This technique takes advantage of the fact that the ear is insensitive to the phase of the speech signal and to low-amplitude components. A series of manipulations are performed on the input signal to produce a symmetrical waveform that looks different than but sounds similar to the input waveform. Taking advantage of this symmetry reduces the amount of data that must be stored by 50 percent. Low-amplitude components of the waveform are zeroed-out, further reducing the data requirements. The end result is good-quality speech that requires a data rate of approximately 2400 bits/s. This technique is used in National Semiconductor's Digitalker chips.

Parameter Encoding

An alternative approach to waveform digitization is *parameter encoding,* also called *analysis/synthesis.* An impulse generator and white-noise generator provide the sound sources, which are then passed through a complex filter that models the vocal tract. By controlling the amplitude and frequency of the sound sources and the parameters of the filter, speechlike sounds can be produced. These parameters vary slowly in time as compared to the speech waveform itself and therefore require a relatively slow data rate. The most difficult task in analysis/synthesis methods is analyzing the speech to be encoded to produce the sets of parameters to be stored.

Many parameter encoding methods have been devised. Examples are the channel vocoder, formant synthesis, and linear predictive coding. *Linear predictive coding*

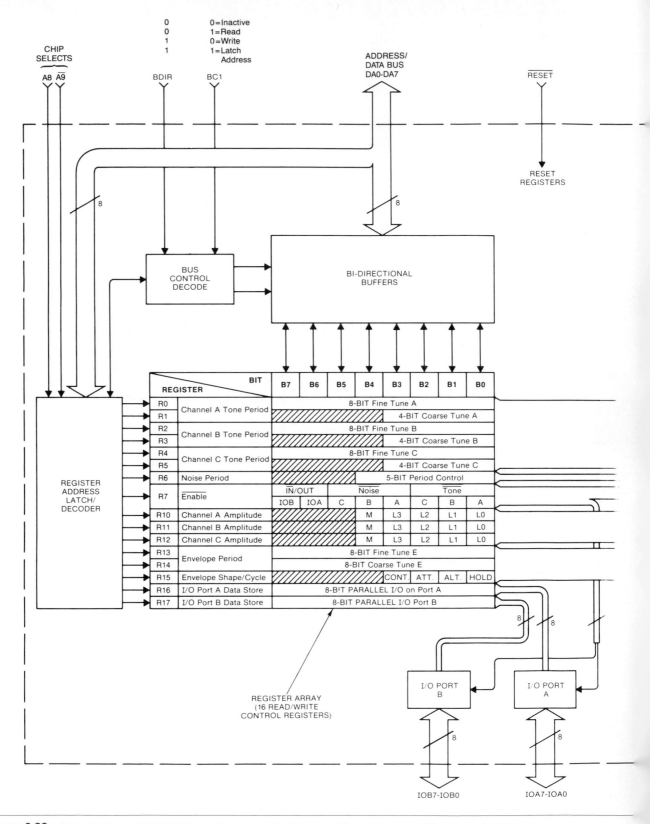

Figure 6.22. General Instrument's AY-3-8910 sound generator chip. *(Courtesy of General Instrument, Microelectronics Division.)*

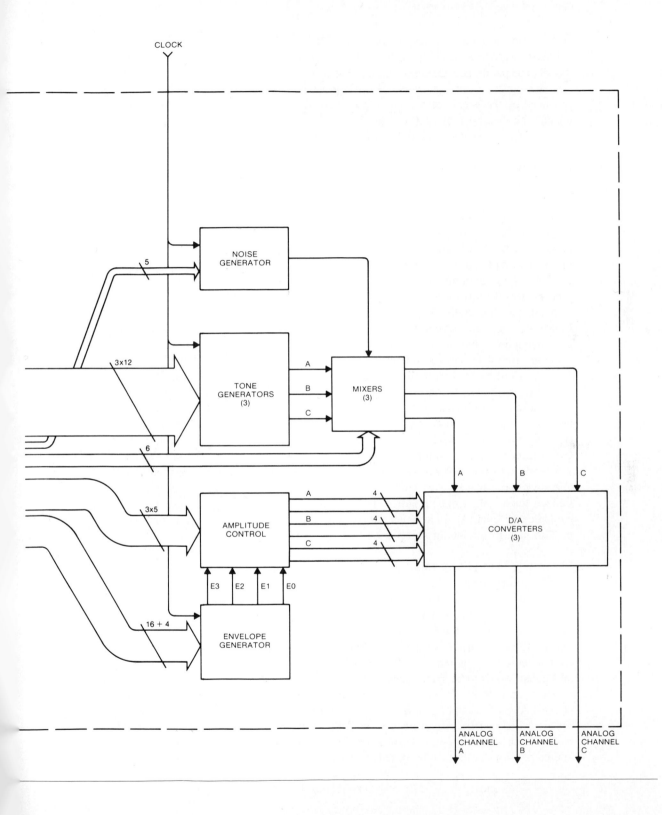

(LPC) is one of the most widely used methods. It is, in effect, a mathematical model of the human speech generation mechanism. A 10- or 12-pole filter is usually used in the model. The parameters that must be stored are the filter coefficients, the filter gain, the frequency of the excitation source, and whether the sound is voiced or unvoiced (i.e., produced by the vocal cords or the lips and breath). Good-quality speech can be obtained with data rates of 1200 to 2400 bits/s. Texas Instruments' TMS5220 is an example of speech synthesis chip that uses this technique.

Encoding Speech

For both parameter encoding and the Mozer technique, generating the compressed data is a very complex process. The encoding process is typically performed by relatively large, high-speed computer systems. It is not performed in real time; that is, considerably more than 1 s of processing time is required to encode 1 s of speech. Once the parameters have been determined, they are stored in a ROM. The ROM is then included in the end product along with the speech synthesis chip, which reproduces the speech from the stored parameters. The synthesis process is much simpler than the analysis process, which makes it possible to implement it in a low-cost IC.

Most speech encoding is performed by the synthesis chip manufacturers. Standard ROMs are available with common words, phrases, and numbers. However, many applications require some custom words or phrases. Phrases sound best when they are encoded as complete phrases rather than as individual words strung together. Parts of phrases can often be used in different sentences, but careful attention must be paid to intonation or the result sounds awkward. Most synthesis chip manufacturers use professional announcers, whose voices are known to work well with their synthesis approach. The customer provides a list of the words and phrases required, and for a fee of typically $100 to $150 per word, the manufacturer provides an EPROM with the encoded speech. For high-volume applications, mask-programmed ROMs are used.

Speech encoding systems are also available that can be purchased by users who want to encode their own speech. These are often based on bit-slice processors that are optimized for the algorithms required. In some cases, they are based on standard minicomputer systems. These systems are cost-effective only for users with a continuing need for a large amount of speech encoding.

Phoneme-Based Synthesis

All the synthesis approaches described to this point are limited in vocabulary. The only words that can be synthesized are those that have been previously encoded and stored in the ROM. An alternative synthesis technique uses the basic units of speech, called *phonemes*. All words in the English language can be constructed from a set of approximately 40 phonemes. A larger set of sounds called *allophones* includes variations in the phonemes as required by different contexts. Approximately 125 allophones allow all English words to be synthesized.

Thus, an unlimited vocabulary synthesizer can be made by storing only the allophones. Any word can be synthesized by stringing together the appropriate allophones. This is called *constructive synthesis,* since the words are constructed from a library of basic sounds. Phoneme-based synthesizers assign a binary code to each phoneme or allophone. Words can then be stored in memory as a sequence of binary codes representing allophone sequences. Much less memory is required for each word as compared to parameter or waveform encoding, and the bit rate can be less than 100 bits/s.

The real power of phoneme-based synthesis is that it is possible to algorithmically translate English text to phoneme strings which can then be fed to the synthesizer. Thus, by adding a microprocessor with the appropriate software, text-to-speech synthesis is possible. This eliminates the need for the time-consuming and expensive encoding process and allows unlimited vocabularies. This approach has been used to make talking computer peripherals, such as CRT terminals and optical-scanning printed book readers, which are an invaluable aid to blind users.

The drawback of this approach is that the resulting speech is quite mechanical sounding. While it is understandable, it lacks the natural-sounding quality possible with parameter- and waveform-encoding approaches. Phoneme-based synthesis is used primarily in applications in which the need for unlimited vocabulary outweighs the desire for a natural-sounding voice.

A phoneme-based synthesizer can be implemented with any of the encoding approaches simply by encoding a set of phonemes (or allophones) rather than entire words. Standard ROMs with the phoneme data are available for some synthesizer ICs. In addition, several synthesizer ICs are designed solely for use with the phoneme-based approach. Votrax's SC-01 and SC-02 were the first such devices, and Silicon Solutions' SSi263 is an enhanced device based on the SC-02.

Speech synthesis has not been widely adopted, and many IC manufacturers have suspended active marketing and new product development for speech synthesis ICs. It seems that most people don't want inanimate devices talking to them.

6.7 PRINTERS

This section describes the most common printer types used in microprocessor-based systems and methods for interfacing them.

6.7.1 Printer Types

Most printers used with microprocessor systems print one character at a time. They are often called *serial* printers; this designation does not refer to the interface, which may be serial or parallel, but to the fact that characters are printed one at a time. Other types of printers print a line or a page at a time.

Printers can be classified according to the method used to produce characters on the paper. *Dot-matrix* printers use an array of dots, which may be as small as 5×7, and generate characters with dot patterns. With a small array, each dot is clearly visible. By increasing the number of dots and overlapping them, the individual dots can be made almost indistinguishable. Many dot-matrix printers can operate in two or more modes that trade off speed for quality. For fastest printing, the print head makes only one pass for each character line. For high-quality printing, the print head makes several passes across each character line, and the paper is moved slightly between each pass. This produces a matrix with a large number of overlapping dots and can produce very high-quality print. Most low-cost dot-matrix printers use a 9-wire print head, while faster high-quality printers use a 24-wire print head to print more dots in each pass of the head. Dot-matrix printers can produce graphics as well as alphanumerics.

Formed-character printers use the same principle as a typewriter, pressing an image of the character to be printed against the ribbon and paper. These produce the highest print quality but are relatively slow. The most common type of formed-character printer is the daisy wheel, which uses a plastic or metal wheel with a spoke for each character. The wheel is positioned so that the desired character is at the top, and a hammer pushes that character against the paper. Another similar type uses a thimble, which is basically a daisy wheel folded into a cup shape. Formed character printers are often called *letter-quality* printers. Speeds typically range from 10 characters per second (cps) for inexpensive models to 55 cps for high-end models. Formed-character printers are limited in their graphics capabilities but are often used when top-quality characters are required. As dot-matrix printers improve, formed-character printers will become less common.

Another fundamental division is between *impact* and *nonimpact* printers. An impact printer presses an inked ribbon against the paper, thereby transferring ink to the paper. Formed-character printers are all impact printers. Dot-matrix printers are available in impact and nonimpact types.

Dot-matrix impact printers use a column of solenoid-driven print wires that press against the ribbon and paper when the solenoid is energized. Each wire produces one dot on the paper. The column of wires (called the *print head*) is moved across the paper to produce a line of text or a strip of a graphics printout. They are faster than formed-character printers, with typical speeds from 80 to 300 cps, and are generally less expensive. Print quality is not as high, but as the dot density is increased, this difference is narrowed.

A variety of technologies are used in nonimpact printers. All share the advantage of quiet operation. The simplest is the *thermal* printer. The print head contains resistive heating elements, which heat a spot on the paper. A special chemically treated paper is used that turns dark when heated; thus, the print head can selectively produce dark spots on the paper. Thermal printers are always dot-matrix. The head typically contains a column of individual elements and is moved across the paper to produce a row of characters.

Some printers (both thermal and impact) have a print head that is only one dot high but is the full width of the paper. This allows fast, reliable printing, since many dots are printed at the same time and the print head does not move.

The *thermal-transfer* printer is a variation on this technique. It is a thermal printer that uses standard paper and a special thermal ribbon. The ribbon is made of a plastic material coated with a pigment that is transferred to the paper when the ribbon is heated. This provides the high speed and quiet operation of thermal printers without their major disadvantage—the need for special paper.

Another type of nonimpact printer is the *ink-jet* printer, which operates by actually squirting droplets of ink at the paper. A variety of different technologies are used for ejecting the droplets and positioning them at the desired place. Although they can use plain paper, a short-fiber or coated paper is often required to prevent the drops from spreading out on the paper. Low-cost ink-jet printers compete with thermal and thermal-transfer printers.

The most sophisticated nonimpact printer is the *laser electrostatic* printer, which uses a mechanism similar to that of a photocopy machine. The image is written on a photosensitive drum by a laser. Toner is attracted to the areas on the drum that have been written by the laser, and the toner is transferred to the paper to produce the printout. Because laser printers print an entire page at a time and the laser can scan the drum very quickly, they are much faster than most other printer types. The mechanism and interface electronics are considerably more complex, however. The interface must have enough memory to store all the data for one page. For an alphanumeric printer, only a few thousand bytes are required. For high-resolution graphics, however, over a megabyte of RAM is required. Storing multiple character fonts can also require a megabyte or more of ROM.

6.7.2 Printer Interfacing

The control of a printer mechanism is complex and depends on the characteristics of the mechanism. Dot-matrix printers require logic to energize the appropriate solenoids (or thermal elements) as the head moves across the paper. Daisy wheel printers require a precise method of rapidly positioning the rotating wheel to select the desired character. All printer types must control the paper motion.

The detailed design of the printer control logic is often complicated, and is not usually done by the system designer. This task is best left to the manufacturer of the printer mechanism, who can benefit from high-volume production and has intimate knowledge of the requirements of the mechanism. The user or system designer generally purchases the print mechanism with the basic control logic. It can be purchased as a bare mechanism and a printed circuit board with the control logic or as a complete packaged printer with power supply and enclosure.

Once the printer control logic is taken care of, the printer interface is relatively independent of the printing technology used. The most common interfaces are RS-232 serial and Centronics-type parallel. Serial data communication is discussed in detail in Chap. 8. Serial printers often include a buffer that allows them to receive data to be printed at a rate independent of the actual print rate. The buffer may be as small as a single line of characters but is commonly 2K to 4 Kbytes. If data is sent faster than can be printed, the buffer will fill up, and some mechanism must be provided for stopping the data transmission to prevent the buffer from overflowing. One common method of doing this is with the XON-XOFF protocol. XON and XOFF are two ASCII control characters, also called DC1 and DC3. (These characters correspond to control-S and control-Q, respectively, on a standard alphanumeric keyboard.) When the printer buffer is nearly full, the printer transmits an XOFF character to the computer to indicate that it should stop sending data. When the printer is ready to receive more data, it sends an XON character, and the computer resumes transmission.

The Centronics-type interface is not an official standard but is widely used. The name is taken from one of the major printer manufacturers that had an early market lead. Since this is not a true standard, there is no universal set of signals. Table 6.1

Table 6.1   Centronics-Type Parallel Interface Signals

Pin No.	Signal	Direction	Description
1	DATA STROBE	To printer	When this signal changes from low to high level, input data is sampled.
2	DATA BIT 1		
3	DATA BIT 2		
4	DATA BIT 3		
5	DATA BIT 4	To printer	Data lines
6	DATA BIT 5		
7	DATA BIT 6		
8	DATA BIT 7		
9	DATA BIT 8		
10	ACKNOWLEDGE	From printer	Low level indicates completion of data input or function operation.
11	BUSY	From printer	High level indicates that the printer cannot receive data.
12	PAPER END	From printer	High level indicates that the paper has run out.
13	SELECT	From printer	High level indicates that the printer is in select (online) state.
14, 16, 33	GND		Signal ground.
17	CHASSIS GND		Frame ground.
18	NC		Not used.
19–30	GND		Return for the wires of pins 1 to 11.
31	INIT	To printer	Low level initializes printer.
32	FAULT	From printer	Low level indicates printer error.
15, 34, 35, 36	NC		Not used.

shows the basic signals that are used by most parallel interfaced printers. The pin numbers shown are for the most commonly used 36-pin connector, but again there is no true standard.

A character is sent to the printer by supplying the data on the eight data lines and pulsing the STROBE signal. Figure 6.23 shows the timing diagram. (Note that the times shown in this figure are simply an example and are not standardized.) As soon as the printer detects the strobe pulse, it asserts BUSY to indicate that it is not ready for another character. When the character has been printed (or stored in a buffer), BUSY is negated, and the acknowledge signal (ACK) is pulsed. The time T as shown in the figure is the time required for the printer to accept the character and be ready for another. This time varies according to the speed of the printer. Most printers include at least a small data buffer, so the time T may be much less than the time required to print a character (when the buffer is not full). The computer can determine when it can send another character either by polling busy until it is negated or by waiting for ACK to be pulsed.

The length of time the printer is busy depends on the speed of the printer and also on the type of printer and the character being printed. Many printers buffer an entire line

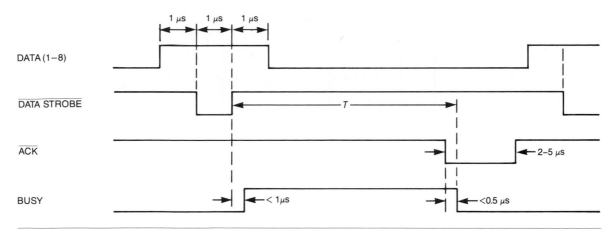

Figure 6.23. Centronics-type parallel interface timing.

of characters before actually printing anything. In this case, the busy period will be brief for each character up to the carriage return (CR) character that terminates the line. When the CR is received, the busy period will be relatively long since the entire line must be printed before the printer can receive another character (assuming the printer buffers only a single line).

Other control signals provide more general control functions. The $\overline{\text{INIT}}$ signal initializes the printer and is asserted by the computer at power-up. Most printers have a few control switches, such as "line feed" and "form feed." In addition, a "select" switch (often labeled ON LINE, or conversely, LOCAL) allows either the printer's control switches or the computer interface to be enabled. To use the paper movement control switches, the printer must first be "deselected" by the select switch. It must then be reselected before the printer can receive data from the computer. The SELECT signal from the printer indicates to the computer that the printer is on-line and ready to receive data. The OUT OF PAPER signal is asserted by the printer when its paper detect switch indicates that no paper is present. Not all printers include this sensor.

A typical interface circuit is shown in Fig. 6.24. All signals except $\overline{\text{ACK}}$ are connected to input or output port bits, so the interface is fully software-controlled. The software first outputs the data and then asserts and negates $\overline{\text{DATA STROBE}}$. $\overline{\text{ACK}}$ is connected to an interrupt input, so the software does not need to continually poll BUSY. When the interrupt occurs, the software outputs another character. Some interfaces ignore the SELECT signal, and the $\overline{\text{INIT}}$ signal may be driven directly from the microprocessor system's reset signal. Note, however, that the printer may require a relatively long reset pulse.

Another technique sometimes used to simplify the interface is to provide only seven data bits and use the eighth bit of the output port as the strobe signal. This reduces the basic interface hardware to a single 8-bit output port for the data and strobe and an interrupt input for the acknowledge signal. Seven data bits are adequate for many alphanumeric printers, since the ASCII code uses only seven bits. However, this simplification can cause problems. In graphics applications, eight-bit words are generally

Figure 6.24.
Centronics-type parallel
interface circuit.

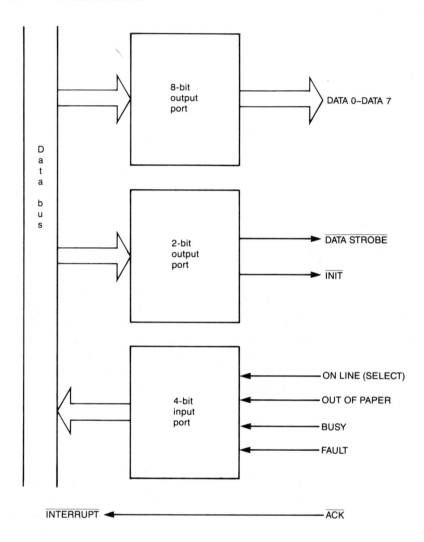

used. Some printers use the eighth data bit even for printing alphanumerics, for additional control characters, or to access extended character sets.

When a small printer mechanism is built-in to an instrument or control system, buying a printer mechanism with a full Centronics-type interface may not be the most cost-effective route. Some printer mechanisms are available with minimum control logic to handle timing-critical functions but do not include character-generation logic or other higher-level functions.

Fixed-head thermal printers, which have a print head that prints an entire dot row at a time, are one example of a printer type often provided with such minimum control logic. These mechanisms have simpler control requirements than moving-head printers. The print head typically includes a shift register with one bit for each dot position. The processor loads this shift register with all the dots for one line, pulses a "head load" signal, and enables the print head to "burn" to dot row. The burn time is typically controlled by the printer's control logic rather than the microprocessor, since keeping the print head on for too long will damage it. The processor then pulses a "motor step" signal to move the paper to the next dot row, and repeats the process. The printer control logic may include an 8-bit parallel-to-serial converter, so the microprocessor can output a series of bytes which the printer control logic feeds to the print head as a serial data stream. The hardware interface required is not much more complex than a standard Centronics-type interface but includes more control signals. Also, unlike a typical "packaged" printer, character generation must be performed by the host microprocessor.

6.7.3 Software Interfacing

When printing simple text, most printers are identical from a software viewpoint. However, many printers allow enhancements such as boldface, various type sizes, and superscripts or subscripts. These are often controlled by using the nonprinting control characters that are part of the ASCII character set. Often, *escape sequences* are used. These are multiple character sequences, beginning with the ASCII "escape" character (1B hex). This allows a large number of control functions to be implemented with only a single control character. The printer knows that the character(s) following the escape character are control functions and not characters to be printed, so any character codes can be used. The details of these control functions vary widely between printers and are often the source of much grief when changing printers in a system.

6.8 DESIGN EXAMPLE

Figure 6.25 shows the circuitry to connect a 4 × 4 matrix keypad to our design example system. The keypad interface itself is identical to that described in Sec. 6.3.2. The 74HCT273 output port drives the rows, and the 74HC244 input port reads the columns. HC-family devices are used because their power consumption is significantly lower than equivalent LS or ALS TTL devices. Note that the output port must be an HCT device unless pull-up resistors are added to the data bus to provide a CMOS-compatible logic high level. The input port can be HC or HCT, however, since the input high level will be very near the positive supply voltage.

A four-input DIP switch and four LEDs share the input and output ports with the keyboard. The software must combine the keyboard row data with the LED control bits when it writes to the output port, and separate the DIP switch data from the keyboard column data when it reads the input port. This type of small DIP switch is useful in many applications for selecting options, such as the serial I/O baud rate or other application-related functions. The I/O lines could be used for other application-dependent signals if the DIP switches or LEDs were not needed.

The 74ALS138 provides the write strobes for the output ports and also provides the display write signals for the display interface described in Chap. 7. The decoder is enabled only when $\overline{\text{IOCS}}$ and $\overline{\text{DS}}$ are asserted and R/$\overline{\text{W}}$ is low. The display interface requires a range of four addresses for each select signal, so A_0 and A_1 are ignored by the decoder.

The input port is minimally decoded by ANDing together $\overline{\text{IOCS}}$, $\overline{\text{R}}$/W, and $\overline{\text{DS}}$,

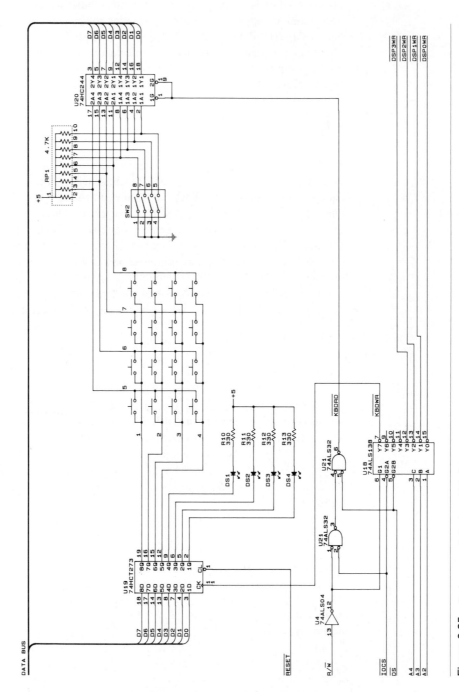

Figure 6.25. Design example keyboard interface.

Figure 6.26. Design example I/O address map.

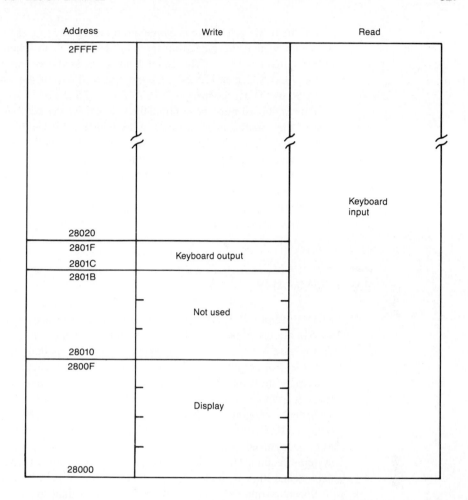

making the input port appear at every address decoded by $\overline{\text{IOCS}}$. If additional input ports are needed, this gating could be replaced by another 74ALS138, enabled by R/$\overline{\text{W}}$.

Figure 6.26 shows the memory map for these ports. The portion of the address space to which the decoder responds is determined by the $\overline{\text{IOCS}}$ signal, which is generated by the address decoder described in Chap. 4. Since address bits A_5 to A_{14} are ignored in the decoding, there is a large "shadow" area. Because there is so much unused address space still available, this is not of concern.

Because of the fast response of the HC devices (as compared to LSI I/O chips), the keyboard interface bus timing is not critical. For the output port, the only parameter of concern is the hold time from the negation of $\overline{\text{KBDWR}}$. (The data setup time required by the 74HCT273 is only 25 ns, and the minimum clock pulse width is only 20 ns, so these parameters are not even close to being limiting.) The 68008 provides 25 ns of data hold time from the negation of $\overline{\text{DS}}$, and the 74ALS138's delay from the negation of its enable to the negation of its outputs is 17 ns. Thus, 3 ns of hold time is available. The 74HCT273 specification calls for 3 ns of hold time, so this is just adequate.

For the read cycle, there is ample timing margin. From the timing analysis in Chap. 4, we know that the time from the assertion of $\overline{DS}$ to when data is required at the 68008's inputs is 185 ns. The actual delay of the keyboard input port circuit is the delay of the 74ALS32 gate (12 ns) plus the enable delay of the 74HC244 (38 ns), which totals 50 ns. Thus, the margin is $185 - 50 = 135$ ns.

This keyboard must be continually scanned by the software to detect a key press. One of the counter/timer channels in the 68901 MFP would typically be programmed to generate a periodic interrupt. Each time this interrupt occurs, the next keyboard row is enabled, and the keyboard columns are read. Thus, the entire keyboard is read every four interrupts. A 10-millisecond interrupt period would therefore produce a 40-millisecond scan time. This is a convenient value, since it is short enough that keys do not have to be pressed for long, yet long enough that if a key is in the same state for two successive scans, it can be considered to be debounced.

6.9 SUMMARY

Many different devices can be used for the user interface. Keyboards of some type are used in almost all products. Many different switch technologies are available; the selection is based on the relative importance of environmental immunity, tactile feedback, and cost. For graphic input and cursor positioning, mice, joysticks, touch screens, and trackballs are used. In addition to cursor positioning, digitizers provide the ability to transfer graphic information from an existing document.

Speech recognition, while an attractive choice for ease of use, is practical today only in a limited form. Most economical systems must be trained by the speaker who is to be recognized, have limited vocabularies, and require pauses between words. Most systems require dozens of ICs and are thus board-level (rather than chip-level) products. Some limited single-chip speech recognizers are available.

Speech synthesis is fortunately much simpler than speech recognition. A variety of techniques are used. Simple digitization provides maximum quality but requires large amounts of memory, while compression and analysis/synthesis schemes reduce the memory requirements greatly with a small loss in fidelity. However, the memory patterns cannot be generated in real time and require special hardware, so the vocabulary is limited to the preencoded words stored in the system's memory. Phoneme-based synthesizers are more mechanical sounding but have unlimited vocabularies when used with the appropriate software.

Sound generation can be performed entirely in software (using an output port bit driving a speaker or piezotransducer) for simple sounds. To produce complex sounds, the software burden on the microprocessor becomes large, and sound generator peripheral chips are used to produce complex sounds with minimal processor requirements.

Printers are the primary device for producing permanent output. Both impact and nonimpact types are available. Another major distinction is between dot-matrix and formed-character printers, although the best dot-matrix printers approach formed-character quality. Regardless of the print mechanism employed, the printer interface is similar. The most common interfaces are Centronics-type parallel and RS-232 serial.

The selection of the proper set of interface devices is critical for a product to be easy to use. The pros and cons of each possible device type must be carefully weighed in the context of each application. Once the devices are selected, the interfaces must be designed, making the tradeoffs between cost, processor burden, and performance.

6.10 EXERCISES

6.1. Make a list of functions for a multipurpose electronic instrument, with at least 10 different capabilities.

    a. Design a user interface using a dedicated-function keyboard.
    b. Design a user interface using a CRT display with menus or soft keys.
    c. List the advantages and disadvantages of each interface.

6.2. A simple instrument uses a keyboard with only 16 keys.

    a. Draw a schematic diagram for a nonmultiplexed interface. How many I/O port bits are required?
    b. Draw a schematic diagram for a multiplexed interface. How many I/O port bits are required?
    c. Draw a flowchart for the software required for each type of interface, including debouncing.
    d. List the advantages and disadvantages of each interface type.

6.3. Repeat Exercise 6.2 for an 80-key keyboard.

6.4. An instrument uses a multiplexed keyboard arranged as a matrix of 8 rows and 8 columns. One row is read each millisecond, and the maximum key bounce time is 20 ms. For how many scans must a key be detected before it can be assumed to be valid?

6.5. Draw a diagram that shows why a diode in series with each key prevents the "ghost key" effect in a matrixed keyboard.

6.6. Draw flowcharts for the algorithms for two-key rollover and n-key rollover.

6.7. Select a keyswitch technology for each of the following applications.

    a. A low-cost instrument to be used in a dusty environment, with a small dedicated-function keyboard.
    b. A high-quality computer terminal.
    c. A printer with only three control switches (push buttons).

6.8. A computer-aided drafting system needs a cursor-positioning device for producing drawings on the CRT screen. What device would you recommend, and why? If data must also be captured from existing noncomputerized drawings, what device would you use?

6.9. A 24 × 80 character display requires a touch screen that can select any single character.

    a. If the LED-photosensor approach is used, how many LED-photosensor pairs are required?
    b. If the resistive-film approach is used, what is the required resolution for the A/D converter that processes the voltage from the film?

6.10. Define the terms speaker-dependent and isolated-word as they relate to speech recognition.

6.11. An electronic game needs to produce a variety of sounds. Suppose that the audio output device is a speaker connected to a D/A converter. To control the waveshape, a table in memory lists a series of 10 values to be output to the converter for each cycle of the tone to be generated. Twenty microprocessor clock cycles are required to output a value to the converter, update the pointer to the table, and jump back to the start of the output routine.

    a. Assuming a microprocessor clock rate of 3 MHz and an output tone of 5 kHz, what percentage of the microprocessor's time is used to produce the output tone?

    b. What is the highest-frequency tone that can be produced, assuming no other tasks need to be performed simultaneously?

    c. Suggest alternative designs to reduce the amount of the microprocessor's processing time used in generating the tone.

6.12. Assuming simple digitization (no compression), a sample rate of 15 kHz, and a word size of 8 bits, how many seconds of speech can be stored in a 256-Kbit ROM? On a 360-Kbyte floppy disk? On a 20-Mbyte hard disk?

6.13. Repeat Exercise 6.12 assuming that linear predictive coding is used to reduce the data rate to 1800 bits/s.

6.14. What are the two main classes of printer types? What are the common types within each class?

6.15. Is a daisy wheel printer a nonimpact printer? What about an ink-jet printer?

6.16. A printer controller includes a 4-Kbyte buffer. The average print speed is 160 characters per second, and the data rate for the serial interface is 9600 baud.

    a. Approximately how long will it take for the buffer to fill up?

    b. Assuming an XON-XOFF protocol is used, describe the series of actions that occur during the printing of a 10,000-character document.

6.17. Modify the design example keyboard interface for a 100-key keyboard. What effect does this have on the software timing? If this is a typewriter-style keyboard, what additional hardware and software considerations are there?

6.11   SELECTED BIBLIOGRAPHY

Keyboards and Other Input Devices

Comerford, Richard. "Pointing-Device Innovations Enhance User/Machine Interfaces," *EDN*, July 26, 1984, pp. 54–66. Describes implementations of touch-screens, mice, trackballs, and digitizers.

Johnson, Roger. "Designing with Optical Shaft Encoders," *Robotics Age*, May/June 1983, pp. 27–34. Describes the problems of reliably decoding quadrature signals and presents a solution using a PROM-based state machine.

Odom, James A. *Applying Manual Controls and Displays.* Minneapolis: Micro Switch, 1984. A general guide to keyswitch selection and panel layout, with (of course) an emphasis on Micro Switch's products.

Sniger, Paul. "Designer's Guide to Keyswitches," *Digital Design,* May 1982, pp. 70–77. An overview of keyswitch technology.

Speech Input and Output

Bursky, Dave. "New Algorithms, Chips Bestow Human Qualities on Synthesized Speech," *Electronic Design,* May 16, 1985, pp. 113–129. Describes approaches to speech synthesis and several chip- and board-level products.

Gargagliano, Tim A., and Kathryn Fons. "Text Translator Builds Vocabulary for Speech Chip," *Electronics,* Feb. 10, 1981, pp. 118–121. Describes the use of phoneme-based synthesizers for text-to-speech systems.

Hoff, Marcian E., and Daniel F. Fink. "Tackling Speech Response: The Complete Picture," *Electronic Design,* Sept. 2, 1982, pp. 179–183. Describes basic concepts of speech recognition.

Morgan, Nelson. *Talking Chips,* New York: McGraw-Hill, 1984. A comprehensive and entertaining text on all aspects of speech synthesis theory and implementation.

Sound Generation

General Instrument Microelectronics Division. *Programmable Sound Generator Data Manual,* Hicksville, NY, 1981. Includes detailed descriptions of the design and applications of GI's sound generator chips.

Printers

Teja, Ed. "Sophisticated OEM Printer Mechanisms Expand System Design Options, Lower Costs," *EDN,* Feb. 9, 1984, pp. 55–62. Describes several printer mechanisms and includes a list of suppliers.

CHAPTER

7

DISPLAYS

7.1 DISPLAY FUNDAMENTALS

Many different display types and technologies are available for use in microprocessor-based systems. This section introduces display-related terminology and describes display characteristics that are independent of the display technology, to provide a background for the descriptions of specific technologies that follow.

7.1.1 Display Types

Displays can be categorized by the amount and type of information that they can display. All displays fall into one of the following categories:

On/off indicator

Numeric display

Alphanumeric display

Graphic display

An example of an on/off indicator is a single lamp. It can convey more information if it is associated with a word or "legend," which indicates the meaning of the lamp. Numeric displays are more general, and while they may be able to display some letters and symbols, they are not generally useful for text messages. Alphanumeric displays provide much greater flexibility, allowing unlimited message capability. Finally, graphic displays can be used to display charts, pictures, and other nontextual information. They can also be used for text, since characters are simply a set of graphic images.

7.1.2 Display Technologies

The technology used for a display determines not only the appearance of the display but also its cost, reliability, power requirements, and the interface circuits needed. Figure 7.1 shows the major display technologies. One of the oldest technologies still in widespread use is the cathode ray tube (CRT), familiar to all as the display used in televisions and in nearly all computer terminals. The CRT uses a vacuum tube type of construction, so it is relatively fragile and bulky. Other technologies are used to produce thinner displays and are often called *flat-panel* displays. Some flat-panel displays have reached the size and information density of the CRT, although they are more expensive for a comparable display capability.

Displays can be classified as *active* or *passive*. Active displays emit light, whereas passive displays simply reflect or absorb light. The most common active display types are vacuum fluorescent (VF), gas discharge, electroluminescent (EL), and light-emitting diode (LED). Incandescent displays are used only in certain applications demanding very high brightness.

The most common passive display type is the liquid crystal display (LCD). Electromechanical displays are used for large billboard-type displays.

This chapter describes the principles of operation and interfacing requirements for each of the major display types. The summary section describes the considerations for choosing a display technology.

7.1.3 Display Terminology

The amount of light emitted by a display is technically called *luminous intensity*, commonly called simply *intensity*. Brightness is the subjective perception of intensity and

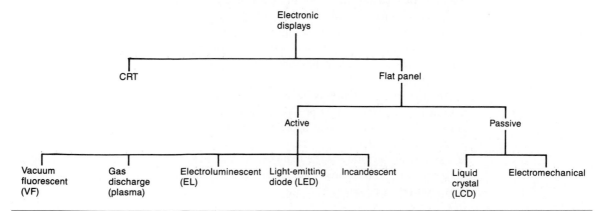

Figure 7.1. Principal display types.

is affected by the color of the light and environmental factors. The unit of intensity is the *candela* (*cd*). The old unit was the candle, which referred to the amount of light produced by a specific-size candle made from sperm whale oil. The candela has a more precise, if rather obscure, definition. It is the amount of light emitted from a small hole of a specific size in a platinum-coated ceramic box that is heated until the platinum melts and then cooled until it just solidifies.

Illumination is the amount of light falling on a given area, and is inversely proportional to the square of the distance from the source. The *footcandle* (*fc*) is the unit of illumination. The *lumen* (*lm*) is the unit for measuring the amount of energy in the beam of light itself. A one-candela source produces a one-lumen beam, which produces one footcandle of illumination on a one-square-foot area that is one foot from the source.

Because the intensity of small displays is only a fraction of a candela, the unit usually used is the *microcandela* (*μcd*) or the *millicandela* (*mcd*). Typical values for LED lamps range from a few hundred microcandelas (that is, a few tenths of a millicandela) to a few millicandelas. These units are commonly used for specifying the brightness of point sources such as LED lamps.

The larger a display, the more light it produces. Thus, to compare display intensity without regard to size, brightness per unit area, called *luminance,* is used. The most common unit of luminance is the *candela per square meter* (cd/m^2). The unit *nits* is sometimes used: one nit equals one candela per square meter. Another commonly used unit is the *footlambert* (*fL*). One footlambert equals 3.426 candelas per square meter.

Color is the other major characteristic of light. Color is the perception of the frequency (or wavelength) of the light. It is commonly specified as the wavelength in *angstroms* (*A*) or *nanometers* (*nm*). The visible range is from approximately 400 nm (violet) to 700 nm (red). Some displays, such as LEDs, produce light of a single color. Others, such as vacuum fluorescent displays, produce a mixture of various wavelengths.

Another important parameter is *contrast*. This refers to the ratio of the brightness of the displayed information to the background. It is often defined as the ratio of the luminance of an "on" dot or segment to that of an "off" dot or segment. Some display types, such as gas discharge displays, have intrinsically high contrast. Others, such as LEDs, require filters to increase the contrast. The inherent contrast of a display with no ambient light is called *intrinsic* contrast. Ambient light often reduces the perceived contrast; the contrast with ambient light striking the display is called *extrinsic* contrast.

Passive displays do not produce any light. Thus, brightness is not an issue. Contrast and viewing angle are the most important parameters for passive displays. Acceptable contrast is a major issue for LCD displays. While a display with a 2:1 contrast ratio is readable under favorable conditions, a contrast ratio of 8:1 or greater is required for easy viewing.

Another important display parameter is *efficiency*. The efficiency of a display is the ratio of the amount of light produced to the energy required and can be expressed as *lumens per watt*. Efficiency applies only to active displays, since passive displays produce no light at all.

Ultimately, legibility is the real concern for most displays. Legibility is not something that can be measured objectively but is a combination of the font, size, brightness, contrast, and color.

7.1.4 Display Fonts

Most displays form digits or characters with a combination of discrete elements, either dots or segments. The arrangement of these elements is called the display *font*. A display with a small number of elements is inexpensive but is not as attractive or flexible as a more complex font.

The most common format for numeric display is the *seven-segment* font shown in Fig. 7.2. By selecting the appropriate combination of segments, any digit (and some other characters) can be displayed. Figure 7.3 shows a 10-segment font, which is still restricted to primarily numeric characters but allows the digit 1 to be centered and can display a "+" sign.

To display alphanumeric data, a more complex display is required. One widely used approach is the 16-segment font, as shown in Fig. 7.4, sometimes called a *starburst*

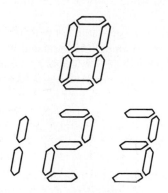

Figure 7.2. Seven-segment font.

Figure 7.3. Ten-segment font allows centered "1" and "+" sign.

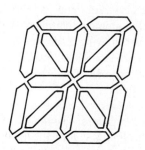

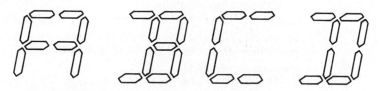

Figure 7.4. Sixteen-segment starburst font.

Figure 7.5.   Dot-matrix fonts: *(a)* 5 × 7 and *(b)* 7 × 9 (7 × 11 including descenders). *(Courtesy of Standard Microsystems Corp.)*

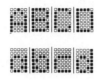
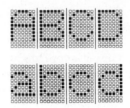

display. This font is sufficient for uppercase characters but does not work well for lowercase. It is sometimes simplified by not dividing the top and bottom horizontal bars to form a 14-segment font.

The best-looking and widest variety of characters are produced by dot-matrix displays. Figure 7.5 shows two common dot-matrix sizes. The larger the matrix used for each character, the better the appearance, and the higher the system cost. The 5 × 7 font is common in low-cost systems, while 7 × 9 or larger fonts are used when appearance is more important.

Graphic displays can be thought of as very large dot matrices. Each dot in a graphic display is called a *picture element,* commonly abbreviated as *pixel* and sometimes shortened to *pel.* The size of a graphic display is stated as the number of pixels horizontally by the number of pixels vertically. For example, a 640 × 400 display has 400 rows of 640 pixels each.

7.1.5   Display Sizes and Configurations

Many different display sizes are available. The height of each character may be as small as 0.1 in. or larger than 1 ft. The size required depends primarily on the distance from which the display must be viewed, but there are a variety of other factors. The minimum size that is comfortable to read is several times larger than the absolute minimum size and also varies considerably from one person to another. The type of display and the level of ambient lighting also affect the required size. Table 7.1 shows typical sizes for various viewing distances.

Numeric displays are available as single digits or in multiple-digit clusters. Individual digits are most common with LED displays. Most numeric displays are no larger than 16 digits.

Alphanumeric displays are rarely useful as single characters and are thus usually packaged in groups. The number of characters in each physical package varies with the display technology; for LED displays, four- or eight-character "clusters" are common, and several clusters are typically used together to form a larger display. Most other technologies include all the characters needed for typical applications in a single package. Single-line alphanumeric displays commonly have 16 to 40 characters. Multiple-line displays are available in many configurations, ranging from 2 lines of 20 characters to 25 lines of 80 characters. Most multiline displays are dot-matrix, and many have graphics capabilities.

Most displays with more than a few digits or characters are *multiplexed.* In a multiplexed display, only one part of the display (such as one character or one digit) is on at

Table 7.1 Comfortable Viewing Distances for Various Display Sizes

Character height, in.	Comfortable viewing distance, ft.
0.1	2
0.15	3
0.2	4
0.3	6
0.43	9
0.56	11
0.8	16
1.0	20

any instant. The control logic switches from one to the next quickly enough so that all parts of the display appear to be lit simultaneously. This significantly reduces the number of interconnections and driver circuits required. Several multiplexing techniques are illustrated in this chapter.

7.2 LIGHT-EMITTING DIODE DISPLAYS

Light-emitting diodes (LEDs) are available as individual (discrete) devices for use as simple on/off indicators, or in groups to form numeric or alphanumeric characters. In addition to their widespread use as numeric displays, LEDs have taken over the role of the small incandescent indicator light.

LEDs have many advantages. They are semiconductor devices; since there is no filament to burn out or glass to break, they are very reliable and rugged. They are inexpensive, easily interfaced to digital logic, and do not require high voltages. They have a wide operating temperature range and are easily multiplexed. The viewing angle is good, and displays of arbitrary numbers of digits are easily assembled. They are an excellent choice for discrete indicators and reasonably small numeric and alphanumeric displays, as long as power consumption is not critical.

One key weakness of LED displays is their relatively high power consumption. In addition, they are uneconomical for displays consisting of large numbers of characters. Another problem with LEDs in some applications is their tendency to "wash out" in very bright light (particularly direct sunlight). Some very high-brightness LEDs are available for such situations, but they are more expensive and require relatively large drive currents.

7.2.1 LED Types and Colors

The actual LED "chip" in an LED display is relatively small. Figure 7.6 shows the construction of a typical discrete LED. Some LEDs are encapsulated in clear epoxy

Figure 7.6. LED lamp construction. *(Courtesy of Hewlett-Packard Company.)*

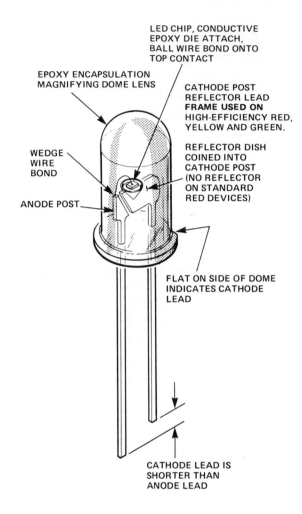

LED CHIP, CONDUCTIVE
EPOXY DIE ATTACH,
BALL WIRE BOND ONTO
TOP CONTACT

EPOXY ENCAPSULATION
MAGNIFYING DOME LENS

CATHODE POST
REFLECTOR LEAD
FRAME USED ON
HIGH-EFFICIENCY RED,
YELLOW AND GREEN.

WEDGE
WIRE
BOND

REFLECTOR DISH
COINED INTO
CATHODE POST
(NO REFLECTOR
ON STANDARD
RED DEVICES)

ANODE POST

FLAT ON SIDE OF DOME
INDICATES CATHODE
LEAD

CATHODE LEAD IS
SHORTER THAN
ANODE LEAD

and are called *point sources* because the light is emitted directly from the small "point" that is the LED chip. They are useful as light sources in emitter-detector systems and similar applications, but the narrow angle of the light they produce makes them unsuitable for displays. Display LEDs are packaged in epoxy with a diffusant and tint added, which provides the familiar diffused glow. Hermetic LEDs packaged in glass and metal are also available for high-reliability applications.

The two most common sizes for LED lamps are called T-1 and T-1¾. The number after the "T" indicates the diameter of the lamp in units of eighths of an inch; thus, the diameter of the T-1 is 0.125 in., and the T-1¾ is approximately 0.22 in.

LEDs are available in red, yellow, and green. Red LEDs were the first ones available, and they still have many advantages. They are the least expensive and most efficient (most light for a given current) of the colors. High-efficiency red LEDs are also available, which produce more light at lower currents and are a slightly deeper red.

Yellow LEDs vary in color from pale yellow to deep amber. Because the human eye is very sensitive to slight changes of color in this range, it is difficult to match many yellow LEDs that are together on a panel. Yellow (or amber) is generally preferred over red for ease of viewing, but the color matching problem, the higher price, and greater current requirements have kept yellow LEDs from becoming as common as red ones.

Green LEDs have many of the same problems as yellow LEDs. They are commonly used when the "go" or "OK" connotation of green is preferred to the "stop" or "fail" connotation of red. Blue LEDs are available but are much more expensive than other colors and are not generally used for displays.

Both yellow and green LEDs are also available in high-performance versions, which are more efficient but also more expensive. In addition to using different semiconductor materials, high-efficiency LEDs have a reflector behind the LED chip so that all the light is projected forward.

Two-color LEDs are also available, which combine a red and a green LED in a single three-pin package. This allows a single lamp to display red, green, or yellow (by turning on both the red and green LEDs).

7.2.2 Numeric and Alphanumeric LED Displays

Seven-segment LED displays are the most commonly used numeric displays for small numbers of digits. They are available as individual digits with digit heights ranging from 0.2 in. to 1.0 in. Diffusers spread the light from the source across the area of the segment. In some displays, more than one LED chip is used per segment.

Small digits are available in groups of four to twelve in a single package. Typical digit heights are 0.1 in. to 0.22 in. Magnifying lenses are often molded into the plastic above the display to increase the apparent digit size, although this reduces the viewing angle.

Sixteen-segment displays are the most common alphanumeric format for LEDs. Because they use fewer elements than dot-matrix displays, they are simpler to drive and consume less power. They are most common in the smaller digit sizes, such as 0.112 in. and 0.16 in. high. Groups of four or eight characters in a single package are available with built-in controller chips, as described in Sec. 7.2.6. These modules are much easier to interface than "bare" displays.

Dot-matrix LED displays are also available and have better character appearance than 16-segment displays. They are also available in a wider range of sizes, including characters over 1 in. high. However, they tend to be more expensive, more difficult to interface, and require more power, so they are less commonly used. Intelligent dot-matrix displays are available, which eliminate the control complexity and make the dot-matrix format more practical. They are also available in several colors, whereas the 16-segment displays are generally available only in red.

7.2.3 Basic LED Interfacing

LEDs are electrically similar to a regular diode. They will pass current only in one direction, and there is a threshold voltage at which they begin conducting (and generating light). As the voltage is increased beyond the threshold, the current (and light output) increases rapidly. This threshold voltage (also called *turn-on* voltage) is typically

Figure 7.7. Current vs. voltage characteristic for typical red LED.

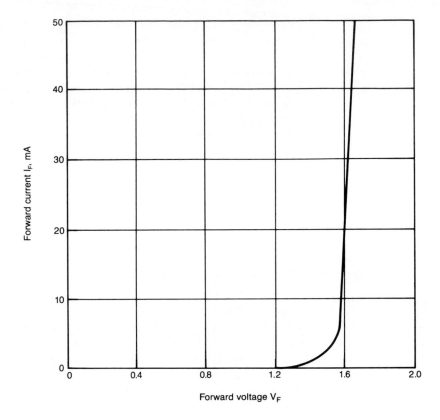

Forward voltage V_F

Figure 7.8. Basic LED drive circuit.

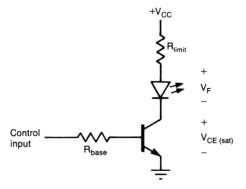

1.5 to 1.7 V, depending on the type and color of LED. Figure 7.7 shows a graph of voltage vs. current for a typical red LED.

Figure 7.8 shows a basic LED drive circuit. The transistor acts as a saturated switch, and the resistor in series with the LED limits the current. The base resistor is not critical and is chosen to ensure that the transistor remains saturated. If the desired current is known, the proper resistor value can easily be calculated by using Ohm's law as follows:

$$R_{limit} = \frac{V_{CC} - V_F - V_{CE(sat)}}{I}$$

where V_{CC} = power supply voltage
         V_F = forward voltage of LED at desired current
         $V_{CE(sat)}$ = transistor's collector-emitter saturation voltage
         I   = LED current

The saturation voltage of the transistor is typically 0.2 V. If the desired brightness is known, then the brightness-vs.-current graph in the LED data sheet will indicate the required current. Frequently, the resistor value (and thus the LED current) is determined by trial and error. High-efficiency red LEDs can operate on as little as 2 mA; 10 to 20 mA is common for larger or less efficient LEDs.

The forward voltage of the LED (V_F) can be read from the voltage-vs.-current graph in the LED data sheet. Because of the diodelike characteristic, the voltage changes little over a wide range of currents for most standard LEDs. Some LED types have a series resistance inherent in the fabrication and packaging process. This causes a relatively linear (but steep) voltage-vs.-current characteristic above the threshold voltage.

The maximum light output is determined by the maximum continuous current specification (sometimes labeled maximum dc current) in the LED's data sheet. In most applications, a lower current is satisfactory. If the device is operated near its maximum current, then the temperature limits must also be considered. This is specified as the maximum junction temperature, which refers to the temperature of the LED chip itself. Junction temperature is a function of the drive current, the ambient temperature, and the thermal resistance of the LED package. If the maximum junction temperature is exceeded, the LED may fail. Thus, if operating near the maximum continuous current or at high ambient temperatures, the junction temperature must be calculated. (For a description of the appropriate thermal calculations, refer to Hewlett-Packard's *Application Note 1005* listed at the end of this chapter.)

TTL ICs with high-current outputs can also be used to drive LEDs, as shown in Fig. 7.9. The 74ALS273 latch, for example, can sink 24 mA at each output, which is sufficient for all but the brightest LEDs. It is particularly convenient for use as an output port and LED driver in a single package. When a simple buffer is desired, the 74LS240 or 74LS244 are often used as LED drivers. High-efficiency LEDs can also be driven

Figure 7.9. LED drive from TTL output port.

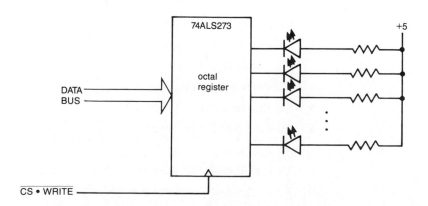

from standard LS TTL gates. Note that, when using TTL drivers, the LED should always be driven as shown in the figure, with a low level at the TTL output turning the LED on. This is necessary because TTL devices cannot source nearly as much current as they can sink. To calculate the limit resistor, the equation described above is used, with the logic low output voltage replacing the transistor's collector-emitter saturation voltage.

High-speed CMOS latches and buffers can also be used to drive low-current LEDs. Standard HC devices can sink or source 4 mA, and for high-current devices such as the 74HC244, this is increased to 6 mA. These devices can source current as easily as sink it, so LEDs can be driven in either direction (i.e., with the noncontrolled end connected either to the positive supply or to ground). This allows each LED to be either on or off when the output driving it is low, which is convenient for choosing the desired default state when an output port register is reset.

7.2.4   Multiplexing LED Displays

The basic drive circuits described in the previous section work well for discrete LEDs or for a single digit or character. However, for multiple-character displays, the number of drive signals becomes large quickly. A single numeric digit requires seven drive signals, one for each segment (plus one for the decimal point, if used). A 20-character 16-segment display, if driven in the same manner, would require 320 drive signals!

To reduce the number of drive signals required, multidigit displays are usually multiplexed. Figure 7.10 shows the basic circuit. All the digits' segment lines are connected in parallel, so only one set of seven segment drivers (eight if a decimal point is used) is needed. This figure shows a *common-cathode* display, in which the cathodes of all segments in each display are connected together. This requires a current source for the segment drivers and a current sink for the digit drivers. *Common-anode* displays are also available and have the opposite requirements.

If all the digits were turned on at the same time, they would all show the same digit. However, digit driver transistors allow each digit to be turned on separately. The control hardware and/or software must turn on each digit in turn and provide the segment data for each digit at the appropriate time. Only one digit is on at a time, but if each is "refreshed" frequently enough, they all appear to be steadily on.

Multiplexed displays require control logic, implemented in hardware or software, to perform the multiplexing. The following tasks must be performed repeatedly:

1. Output segment data for digit 1.

2. Turn on digit 1 digit driver.

3. Wait while digit 1 is on.

4. Turn off digit 1 digit driver.

5. Output segment data for digit 2.

6. Turn on digit 2 digit driver.

7. Wait while digit 2 is on.

8. Turn off digit 2 digit driver.

9. Repeat for each digit, and then go back to digit 1.

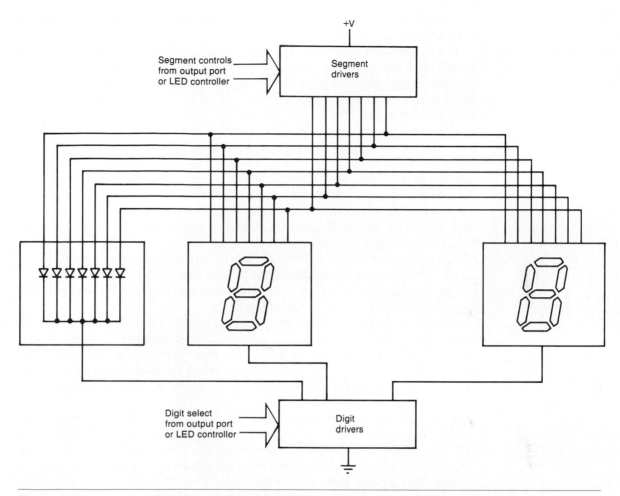

Figure 7.10.   Basic multiplexed LED interface.

Note that the digit driver for the previous digit must be turned off before the segment data is changed for the next digit to prevent "ghosting" (partially lit segments that should be off).

The multiplexing rate is determined by several factors. Each digit must be refreshed more than 30 to 60 times per second to avoid flicker. (Lights flashing faster than this rate appear to be steadily lit.) Display operation is most efficient if the refresh rate is much higher, in the range of 1 kHz. Above approximately 1 kHz, the LED's temperature is proportional to the average current; each LED is not on long enough to heat up to the temperature it would reach if the current were continuous. Below approximately 1 kHz, the LEDs in the display do heat up and cool off with each pulse, and the power dissipation at the peak current must be considered.

The number of digits in the display must also be taken into consideration. For each digit in a 10-digit display to be refreshed at a 1-kHz rate, the multiplexing rate (the rate at which the active digit is changed) must be 10 kHz. The absolute minimum multiplexing rate for a 10-digit display is 10 digits × 30-Hz refresh rate = 300 Hz. A 30-Hz refresh rate is marginally adequate, and 50 to 60 Hz should be considered the minimum for best display appearance.

In a multiplexed LED display, each digit is rapidly pulsed on and off. In a 10-digit display, each digit is on only 10 percent of the time. Since the human eye responds to the average light level, the instantaneous light level when the digit is on must be 10 times what it would be if the display were not multiplexed. Thus, the drive current must be much greater.

LEDs have the unusual characteristic that the higher the current (within limits) the more efficient the display. An LED that is pulsed at 100 mA with a 10 percent duty cycle will be brighter than one that is driven steadily at 10 mA. Thus, multiplexing provides an additional benefit of increased display efficiency. The peak current required for a 10-digit display is somewhat less than 10 times the continuous current required for the same brightness. Most LED data sheets include a graph of light output vs. current. Typical displays are 20 percent to 50 percent more efficient at high peak currents than at their nominal continuous current.

If the peak current is greater than the maximum continuous current rating for the display, the display may be damaged if the multiplexing is stopped and a single digit is left on. Care must be taken in this situation to ensure that the display is turned off at all times when the multiplexing may be stopped.

The driver transistors in a multiplexed display must be able to handle the peak currents. Suppose that a 10-digit display is designed for an average current of 5 mA per segment. To obtain an average current of 5 mA in a 10-digit display, the peak current must be 50 mA. The digit driver must be able to sink the current from all seven segments plus the decimal point. Thus, the total current that the digit driver must sink is 50 mA $\times$ 8 segments = 400 mA.

Because of this relatively high peak current, Darlington transistors are generally used for digit drivers. Each segment driver in this example must be able to handle 50 mA peak current, and Darlington transistors are often used for these drivers as well. Darlingtons are required to ensure that the transistors remain saturated; the base drive current times the beta of the transistor must be greater than the maximum collector current. Darlington transistors are available in quad and octal arrays in DIP packages from Sprague and other manufacturers. For small displays, high-current TTL devices, which can typically sink 48 mA, can be used for the segment drivers. Since their current sourcing capability is relatively low, common-anode displays must be used.

The calculations for the limit resistor are similar to those for nonmultiplexed displays:

$$R_{limit} = \frac{V_{CC} - V_F - V_{CE(sat)} - VD_{CE(sat)}}{I_{peak}}$$

where V_{CC} = power supply voltage
V_F = forward voltage of LED at desired current
$V_{CE(sat)}$ = segment driver's saturation voltage
$VD_{CE(sat)}$ = digit driver's saturation voltage
I_{peak} = peak LED current

The average current is the peak current divided by the number of characters. While the average current is the primary determinant of the display's brightness, the peak current has an indirect effect in that its relatively high value increases the efficiency of the display.

7.2.5   Multiplexed Display Implementations

The control of a multiplexed LED can be implemented entirely in software. The only hardware required for such an implementation is output ports to control the segment and digit drivers. The control software must periodically switch from digit to digit as described previously. This is most commonly implemented by using an interrupt from a programmable timer. At each interrupt, the next digit is turned on, and the segment data is changed. In simple systems, the timing can be implemented with software timing loops instead of interrupts.

Software-refreshed displays use a minimum amount of hardware but have several disadvantages. The amount of processing time available for other tasks is reduced by the time spent processing display interrupts. The software must also translate the character to be displayed into the segment pattern to produce that digit.

Another alternative is to use a display controller chip. One example is Intel's 8279, which supports up to 16 display digits. This device is both a display controller and a keyboard controller; Fig. 7.11 shows the block diagram, and Fig. 7.12 shows a typical configuration. The 8279 uses a standard bus interface, with one address line to distinguish between control register and data memory accesses. A 16-byte display RAM in the chip contains 1 byte for each digit. No translation to segment codes is performed; the software must perform this translation before writing the data to the chip.

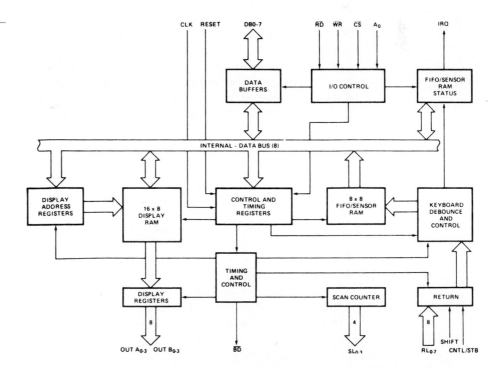

Figure 7.11. The 8279 keyboard/display controller block diagram. *(Courtesy of Intel Corporation.)*

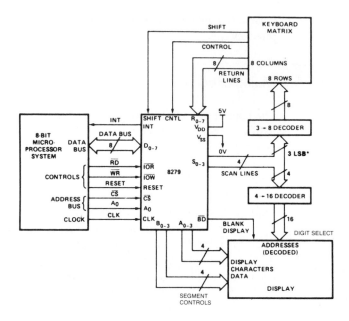

The 4-bit scan counter provides the number of the digit currently displayed. An external 4-to-16-line decoder is required to produce the digit select signals.

The microprocessor can write to the display in several ways. The mode is selected by writing a command to the chip; A_0 high indicates that a command, rather than data, is being written. In the "left entry" mode, the first digit written appears in the leftmost digit. Each successive digit written appears in the next digit to the right. In the "right entry" mode, each digit written appears in the rightmost digit position, and all digits previously written are shifted one position to the left. Alternatively, a specific digit position can be directly addressed by first writing a command to address that position.

The 8279 is a keyboard controller as well and can support a 64-key matrix. The scan counter selects one row of the keyboard at the same time it selects one digit of the display. The 8279 reads the column data each time the scan counter is changed. It debounces the keys and stores the code for the key pressed in an internal 8-byte FIFO buffer. This buffer allows up to eight keys to be stored before the microprocessor must read them from the controller chip, reducing the real-time demands on the software.

The 8279 considerably reduces the software burden in systems using keyboards and displays. Software does not need to be written to perform the display multiplexing function, and the microprocessor spends no time refreshing the display or scanning and debouncing the keyboard.

Other LED display controllers are available that perform the BCD-to-seven-segment conversion as well as the multiplexing functions. One example is Motorola's 14499, which uses a serial interface to the microprocessor. Including the segment decoding function in the display controller relieves the software of this burden, but it also eliminates the flexibility to produce nonstandard characters (such as limited alphabetic characters).

7.2.6 LED Display Modules

LED display modules include a display and control logic in one package and provide a simple interface to the microprocessor. Some display modules consist of standard displays and controller chips mounted on a printed circuit board. Others, such as Siemens' DL-1414 shown in Fig. 7.13, include a controller chip in the same package as the display itself.

The DL-1414 is a four-character alphanumeric display. Each digit is 0.112 in. high and has 17 segments: the standard 16-segment starburst format plus a decimal point. Figure 7.14 shows the block diagram of the DL-1414. All multiplexing circuitry is included in the module, and an internal oscillator sets the multiplexing rate. The internal memory stores the ASCII code for each character, which is decoded by the ROM to determine which segments to illuminate.

The DL-1414 interfaces to the microprocessor system as a write-only memory (WOM). There is no chip select input, so the $\overline{WR}$ input must be driven by a combination of the write strobe and the address decode. Each memory location controls one character in the display. Since only uppercase characters can be displayed, only six bits are needed to represent the character.

In a typical application, several DL-1414s are connected together to form a larger display. The design example at the end of this chapter shows such an interface and describes the timing considerations.

The DL-2416 is a similar display that has larger characters (0.16 in.) and a few additional features. It has two chip select inputs to simplify address decoding and has

Figure 7.13. Four-character alphanumeric LED display module with integral controller. *(Courtesy of Siemens Components Inc.)*

Figure 7.14. DL-1414
LED display module block
diagram. *(Courtesy of Siemens Components Inc.)*

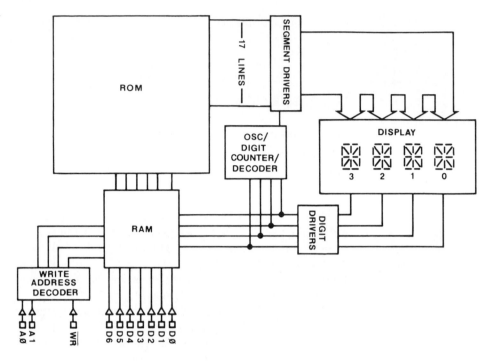

Figure 7.14. DL-1414 LED display module block diagram. *(Courtesy of Siemens Components Inc.)*

provisions for displaying a cursor consisting of a digit with all segments on. Hewlett-Packard manufactures compatible displays as the HPDL-1414 and HPDL-2416. The HP versions have significantly improved bus timing.

The Siemens PD-2816 is an eight-character module that is similar to the DL-2416. It has some additional features, such as an additional segment for an underline cursor and programmable blinking and brightness control. The memory can also be read, so the software can determine what characters are displayed without keeping a separate image in memory. One warning, however: the PD-2816 requires a setup time for address, chip select, and data before $\overline{\text{WRITE}}$ is asserted, and a hold time for all these signals after $\overline{\text{WRITE}}$ is negated. This makes it awkward to interface to most microprocessors, except via I/O ports.

Intelligent alphanumeric LED display modules using a 5 × 7 dot matrix are also available from Siemens and Hewlett-Packard.

7.3   LIQUID CRYSTAL DISPLAYS

Liquid crystal displays (LCDs) offer a number of unique advantages. They are the unchallenged champions when power consumption is critical; a typical display consumes only microwatts of power, over a thousand times less than an LED display. LCDs can operate on voltages as low as 2 to 3 V, and because they require extremely small drive currents, they are easily driven by MOS IC drivers.

LCDs were first used in calculators and watches. While these are still common applications for LCDs, their range of application has been greatly broadened. Numeric and alphanumeric displays are available using seven-segment, sixteen-segment, and dot-matrix formats. Dot-matrix LCDs are also used for graphics. LCD displays are inexpensive to customize, allowing custom patterns of segments, dots, or other symbols to be used. An entire word or abbreviation, such as *volts* or *AM,* can be a single segment.

LCDs also have their disadvantages. Unlike most other display types, LCDs do not emit light; they simply reflect or absorb ambient light. Thus, they cannot be seen in a dark room. This problem can be alleviated by lighting the display, but the power consumption is then greatly increased. One benefit of this characteristic is that LCDs are easily read in very bright light, even direct sunlight, where most light-emitting displays wash out.

LCDs have a limited temperature range. At low temperatures, the display changes state very slowly. At high temperatures, the display does not function due to a chemical change in the liquid crystal material. Typical commercial LCDs have operating temperature ranges of approximately 0 to 55°C, although these limits vary from one display type to another. Wide temperature range versions are also available, with temperature ranges as wide as −40 to 85°C possible. The temperature range is determined primarily by the liquid crystal material used and the level of multiplexing, as described later in this section.

Some LCDs also have poor contrast and a limited viewing angle. This is most common in large dot-matrix displays and is being steadily improved.

LCDs can be more difficult to design with than LEDs. There are many different types and variations of LCDs, and the tradeoffs are complex. In addition to display selection being more complicated, the interface electronics is more complex, and the physical mounting and connection of the display is more involved. LCDs are therefore most common in moderate- to high-volume products where the engineering costs are easily amortized. For low-volume applications, LCD modules containing the display and the drive electronics make the technology more practical.

7.3.1 LCD Operation

There are several types of LCDs. We will cover in detail only the most common type, called *twisted nematic field effect (TNFE)*. Other important types are dichroic, super-twisted, and dynamic scattering displays. *Dichroic* displays are a relatively recent development, providing improved contrast and viewing angle. They also provide color capability, but require higher drive voltages. *Supertwisted* displays are another relatively recent development that improve the contrast of large displays. They use a liquid crystal molecule that has a 270-degree twist rather than the 90-degree twist of conventional TNFE displays. However, supertwisted displays are more difficult to manufacture than conventional TNFE displays. *Dynamic scattering* displays are an older type, now used primarily for very large displays. Dynamic scattering LCDs have a relatively high power consumption.

The heart of all LCD displays is the liquid crystal material itself. A liquid crystal is a substance that flows like a liquid but whose molecules orient themselves in the man-

Figure 7.15. LCD
construction.

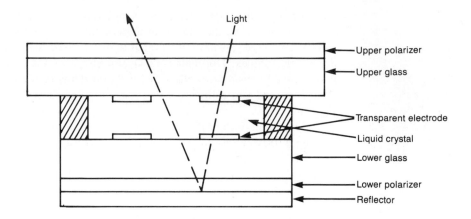

ner of a crystal. Figure 7.15 shows the construction of a typical LCD. Two sheets of glass form the main structure. Between the sheets of glass is a very thin layer of liquid crystal material. The inner surface of each piece of glass is coated with a transparent, conductive layer of metal oxide. The sandwich is completed with a polarizer on the outside of each piece of glass and a reflector on the back of the display.

The two polarizers (front and back) are rotated 90° from each other, so normally no light would pass through both polarizers. However, the liquid crystal material has a very unusual property: it rotates the polarization of light passing though it by 90°. Thus, the polarized light that passes through the front polarizer is rotated by the liquid crystal material so that it passes through the rear polarizer. The light is then reflected by the reflector at the back of the display and passes back through the display. Thus, the display appears as a silver mirror. The reflector is often textured to improve the background appearance.

When an electric field is applied to liquid crystal material, the molecules are straightened out and the polarization of light passing through them is not affected. The display then absorbs the light striking the rear polarizer and appears black instead of silver.

This effect is used to create a useful display by etching the metal oxide on the glass to form the individual dots or segments of the display. In the simplest LCD type, in which every segment is individually driven, one sheet of glass has all segments connected together; this is called the *backplane*. The other sheet of glass has each segment brought out to a separate connection. If the backplane is then connected to ground (0 V), then each segment can be individually turned on by applying to the desired segments a voltage beyond the threshold required to change the state of the liquid crystal molecules.

LCDs do not have a sharp threshold voltage at which they turn on or off. Figure 7.16 shows a graph of contrast vs. voltage for a typical display. For this display, an applied voltage up to approximately 1.5 V has little effect. Above that voltage, the segment begins to get darker until it is near maximum darkness at approximately 2.8 V. Since there are no well-defined on or off points, the 10- and 90-percent contrast levels are usually used as the maximum off and minimum on voltage when designing display drivers. These thresholds also change with temperature, which must be compensated for in most types of drive circuits. There are many different liquid crystal materials, each with different thresholds and temperature characteristics.

LCDs can be fabricated with pins for direct mounting on a circuit board. However, this type of construction can have reliability problems and is also more expensive. The most common approach is to fabricate the display without pins and use a conductive elastomer connector to connect the LCD to the circuit board. Figure 7.17 shows a typical mounting arrangement. The upper piece of glass in the LCD display is larger that the lower piece, so there is an overhang at the top and bottom edges. Each of the LCD connections is made via a metallized pad on the back surface of the overhangs. These

Figure 7.16. Contrast vs. voltage for typical LCD.

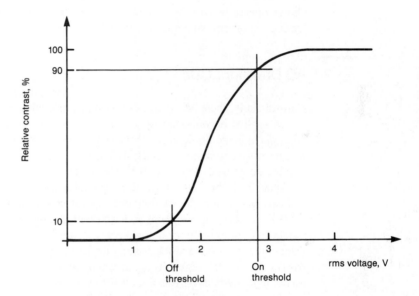

Figure 7.17. LCD mounting with conductive elastomer (Zebra) connectors. Metallized pads on the lower surface of the top piece of glass contact the connector. *(Courtesy of Tecknit.)*

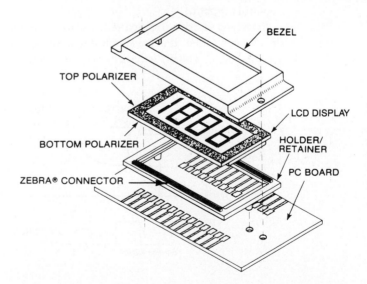

pads are connected to the circuit board via conductive elastomer connectors that consist of strips of rubber with alternating conductive and insulating stripes. The stripes are thin enough so that there is at least one conductive stripe for each connector pad and at least one insulating stripe between each connector pad. The circuit board has a pad pattern matching that of the display. A connector frame holds the elastomer strips in place, and a bezel mounts the entire assembly to the circuit board. The bezel compresses the elastomer strips slightly to ensure a good connection.

When LCDs must be read in darkness, some form of lighting is required. They can be lit from the edge or backlit. Backlighting is the most common approach, as it provides the most even illumination. The reflector on the back surface of the LCD display is replaced with a *transflector,* which reflects some light and passes some light. This allows operation with or without the backlight. The backlight is usually an electroluminescent lamp, which is very thin and provides an even light over its entire surface.

7.3.2   AC Drive for LCDs

Unfortunately, there is an additional complication in driving LCDs. If a steady dc voltage is applied between the backplane and segment lines, a gradual chemical change takes place in the liquid crystal material, greatly reducing the life of the display. Thus, it is necessary to apply an electric field to the desired segments while maintaining an average dc voltage of close to 0 V. This is done by using *ac drive.*

Figure 7.18 shows the basic ac drive implementation. The backplane is connected to a square-wave signal. The frequency is not critical and is typically between 30 and 1000 Hz. Each "on" segment is driven with the inverse of the backplane signal. This produces a continually reversing electric field, with zero average dc voltage. The LCD display is not sensitive to the polarity of the signal but responds to its root-mean-square (rms) value. "Off" segments are driven by the same signal as the backplane, so there is no net field applied. (If it is not clear to you that the circuit in the figure performs this function, consider the function of an XOR gate. It can be thought of as a buffer that can be programmed to invert or not; one input is the "data" input, and the other is the "control" input.)

This type of drive is called *direct drive* (or nonmultiplexed), since each segment is directly controlled. It is the simplest to implement and provides optimum contrast and viewing angle. The off voltage is very near zero and the on voltage can be as high as

Figure 7.18. Basic ac drive circuit for LCD.

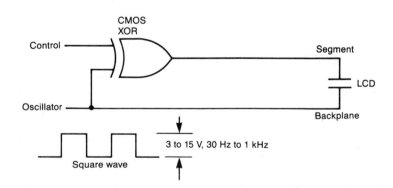

desired, so the exact thresholds of the LCD are not important. Thus, temperature compensation is not necessary in direct-drive systems.

7.3.3   Direct-Drive LCD Interfaces

A number of ICs are available for direct LCD drive. Standard CMOS XOR gates can be used, but for most applications a more complex driver is desirable. (A quad XOR gate can drive only four segments, resulting in a large chip count for even a moderate-size display.) A variety of display drivers are available with ac drive outputs. One common device for simple displays is a BCD-to-seven-segment decoder with ac drive outputs, such as RCA's CD4056.

Figure 7.19 shows a more complex LCD driver chip, Hughes' H0438A. This chip drives up to 32 segments of a nonmultiplexed LCD display. Thus, it can drive a four-digit seven-segment display with decimal points. Multiple chips can be cascaded for longer displays. No decoding is performed by the chip; the microprocessor individually controls each segment. This allows custom displays, whose segment patterns may not match any standard decoder, to be driven. Even if standard seven-segment displays are used, there is an advantage to having the microprocessor software perform the display decoding. When using hardware decoders, the character set for a seven-segment display is typically limited to numeric characters only. By performing the decoding in software, special-purpose characters can be defined, providing more flexibility.

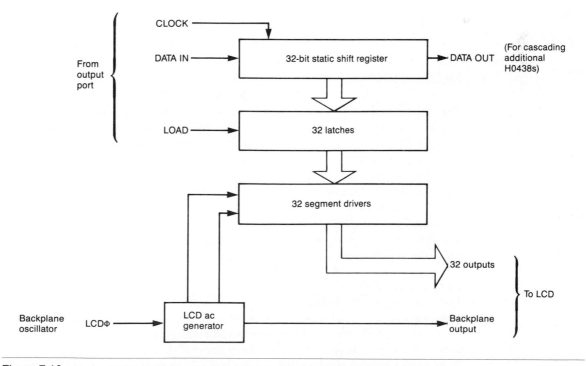

Figure 7.19.   Hughes' H0438A LCD driver IC. *(Courtesy of Hughes Aircraft Co., Semiconductor Division.)*

The microprocessor interface consists of only three signals: CLOCK, DATA IN, and LOAD. Each of these signals is typically connected to an output port bit. At each falling edge of the clock, one bit is shifted into the 32-bit shift register. The microprocessor software outputs a bit of data and pulses the clock line 32 times (outputting the next data bit at each clock pulse) to load the shift register with the data for each segment. When the shift register is loaded, LOAD is pulsed to transfer the data to the 32-bit latch. Multiple H0438As can be cascaded by connecting the DATA OUT signal of the first chip to the DATA IN of the next chip. This allows a larger display to be driven, which appears to the microprocessor as one long shift register.

This type of clocked serial interface is commonly used by display driver ICs to minimize the number of pins needed for the microprocessor interface, allowing more pins to be used for display drive signals. From the microprocessor's point of view, this interface requires only a few output port bits. However, software is required to produce the clock and data signals, and the time to output a given amount of data is relatively long. This approach is ideal for use with single-chip microcomputers that have no external buses, but only output ports. The simple interface used by the H0438A requires the microprocessor to output all 32 bits to change any one; there is no way to address an individual segment. Other devices have more complex serial interfaces, in which commands can be sent to select individual digits or segments.

The segment drivers are basically XOR gates that combine the backplane clock signal with data from the latches to produce the segment drive signal. The backplane clock can be produced by the H0438A by connecting a small capacitor to the LCDΦ input. Alternatively, this input may be driven by an external clock source. The backplane clock is a square wave of the same frequency as the input clock. "On" segments are driven with the complement of the backplane signal, and "off" segments are driven with a signal identical to the backplane signal.

7.3.4   Multiplexed Liquid Crystal Displays

The major disadvantage of direct drive is the number of signals that must connect to the display: one for each segment, plus one for the backplane. For a four-digit seven-segment numeric display with decimal points, a total of 33 connections are required. For an eight-character sixteen-segment alphanumeric display, 129 connections are required, which not only creates a mechanical interconnection problem but also requires many drivers. With dot-matrix displays, direct drive is completely impractical. Even a small matrix of 64×64 dots has 4096 elements, far too many to consider driving individually. A standard panel for displaying 25 lines of 80 characters has 200 lines of 480 dots each, or a total of 96,000 dots. This section describes the methods of LCD multiplexing and an example of a multiplexed LCD controller.

Principles of LCD Multiplexing
LCDs are much more difficult to multiplex than most other display types. Most multiplexing schemes work by turning on one digit or display element at a time, switching from one element to the next so quickly that all display elements appear to be on at the same time. This is not possible with LCDs because of the relatively long period of time (tens or hundreds of ms) required to turn an LCD element on or off. LCDs change

slowly because the molecules in the liquid crystal material must physically move, and the material is extremely viscous. The lower the temperature, the slower the display changes.

The technique used for LCD multiplexing is called *rms multiplexing,* since it is the rms (root-mean-square) value of the applied drive signals that the display responds to. This is an analog multiplexing approach, as compared to the digital approach used with most other display types. The simplest form is 2:1, called *duplex,* or *biplex,* multiplexing, in which the backplane is divided into two sections. The segments are connected in pairs, with one segment of each pair in front of each backplane.

This approach can be expanded to 3:1 *(triplexed),* 4:1 *(quadriplexed),* and higher multiplexing rates. The higher the level of multiplexing, the fewer connections are needed. Unfortunately, both contrast and viewing angle are reduced as the multiplexing rate increases.

Triplexed and quadriplexed displays are commonly used and have acceptable viewing angle and contrast for most applications, although they are not as good as non-multiplexed displays. For dot-matrix displays, multiplexing rates of 8:1 and 16:1 are common, and 32:1, 64:1, and higher rates are used in the largest displays. However, these high multiplexing rates result in displays that must be viewed from a relatively narrow range of angles for acceptable contrast.

Figure 7.20 shows the waveforms for a triplexed display. The three common (backplane) signals are in the middle, and three of the segment drives are shown at the top. At the bottom are the signals obtained by subtracting a segment signal from a common signal; this is the voltage seen by a particular segment.

This is called a *one-third drive* scheme because the voltage step is one-third the maximum dc voltage, resulting in three separate levels (plus the "ground" level). Notice that the complex waveform of each of the common signals is identical and repeats after six time periods. Each common signal is delayed two time periods from the previous one. The voltage applied to an individual segment is the difference between the signal on the common (backplane) and the segment signal. At the bottom of the figure, an example of an on and an off segment is shown. The LCD responds to the rms voltage difference signal. For an off segment, there is an ac signal, but the amplitude is below the threshold at which the LCD turns on. The on segment has larger transitions in the difference signal, and thus a higher rms voltage.

The rms on and off voltages can be calculated by using the following formulas:

$$V_{on} = \frac{V_{LCD}}{A} \sqrt{\frac{A^2 + (N - 1)}{N}}$$

$$V_{off} = \frac{V_{LCD}}{A} \sqrt{\frac{(A - 2)^2 + (N - 1)}{N}}$$

where A = number of voltage levels
N = number of backplanes
V_{LCD} = maximum voltage swing

For the triplexed scheme just described, $A = N = 3$, and the values calculated from the above equations are $V_{on} = 0.64 V_{LCD}$ and $V_{off} = 0.33 V_{LCD}$. If $V_{LCD} = 4.0$ V, then $V_{on} = 2.56$ V and $V_{off} = 1.33$ V. The difference between the on and off voltages is approximately 1.2 V. Remember from the LCD transfer characteristic that there is range of a

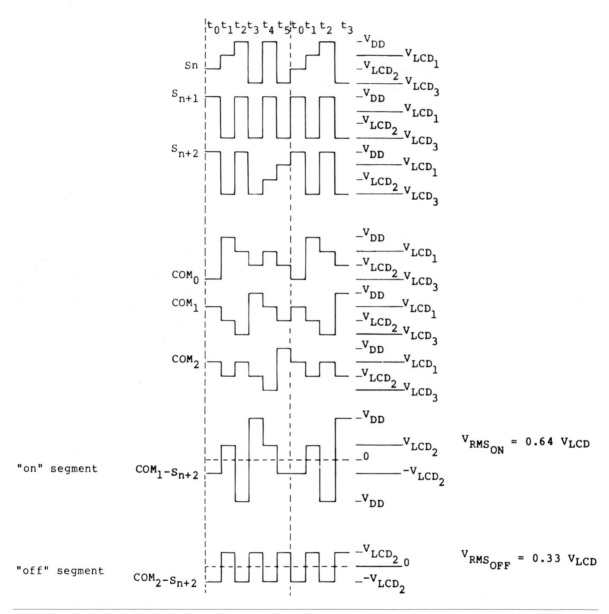

Figure 7.20. Triplexed LCD drive waveforms. *(Courtesy of NEC Electronics Inc.)*

volt or more over which the display gradually goes from on to off. Thus, there is just enough spread between the on and off voltages produced by the multiplexed drivers to switch the display state.

Note that the equations for the rms on and off voltages both approach the same value as N (the number of backplanes) approaches infinity. Thus, the margin between the on and off voltages gets smaller and smaller as the level of multiplexing (the number of backplanes) is increased. As this margin is decreased, the LCD operates in the "slightly on" state when it is logically off and in the "mostly on" state when it is logically on. Thus, the contrast of the display is decreased. In addition, multiplexing reduces the viewing angle. Multiplexing levels of 128 : 1 and higher are used, but display appearance is sacrificed. Large panels are often divided into several separately multiplexed sections to reduce the level of multiplexing and improve display appearance.

Because the on and off voltages in a multiplexed LCD display are close to the 10- and 90-percent contrast points, the voltage levels of the drive signals must change with temperature to match the change of the LCD thresholds. If the off voltage exceeds the 10 percent point, off segments will appear to be slightly on, producing a "ghosting" effect. If the on voltage is less than the 90 percent point, the on segments will appear gray instead of black, reducing the contrast.

Multiplexed LCD Controllers

A variety of controller ICs are available for interfacing to multiplexed LCD displays. Some use serial interfaces such as that described for the H0438 nonmultiplexed LCD driver, and some use parallel bus interfaces similar to those used by most microprocessor peripheral chips. Many are limited to a single form of multiplexing, such as triplexed, but some can be programmed for several different types. Some decode ASCII characters into dot-matrix or segmented patterns, and some require this function to be performed by the host processor.

An example of a particularly flexible multiplexed LCD driver IC is NEC's μPD7225. Figure 7.21 shows a block diagram of the chip. A serial interface to the microprocessor is used to maximize the number of pins available for the LCD interface. The SI pin is the serial data input, and the $\overline{\text{SCK}}$ pin is the serial clock. The chip select ($\overline{\text{CS}}$) input enables the chip to respond to the serial input. This allows the serial inputs of more than one 7225 to be connected together, with one of them selected via the chip select inputs. The command/data ($\overline{\text{C/D}}$) input determines whether the serial data is intended as data or as a control word. Each of these four inputs is typically connected to an output port bit. The $\overline{\text{BUSY}}$ output is typically connected to an input port bit and indicates (when it is high) that the chip is ready to receive commands or data. This is an open-drain output, active only when $\overline{\text{CS}}$ is asserted. This allows the $\overline{\text{BUSY}}$ signal from multiple 7225s to be tied together to a single input port bit.

Commands and data are sent to the 7225 as 8-bit words, as shown in Fig. 7.22. When $\overline{\text{CS}}$ is first asserted, $\overline{\text{BUSY}}$ goes low momentarily while the chip clears its internal bit counter and prepares to receive the byte. The eight bits of the command or data word are then clocked into the 7225, and on the eighth clock, the $\overline{\text{C/D}}$ bit is read to determine how the byte should be treated. $\overline{\text{BUSY}}$ is then asserted while the 7225 processes the command or data byte.

The 7225 includes two memory arrays of 32 4-bit words each. In each array, there is one bit for each display segment. The "display RAM" bit determines if the segment is on or off. If the segment is on, and if the corresponding bit in the "blinking RAM" is set, then the segment is automatically turned on and off at a preset rate. This allows blinking digits to be displayed without the microprocessor having to repeatedly turn the digit on and off.

The 7225 contains a data pointer that provides the address to these RAMs. When $\overline{\text{CS}}$ is asserted, the data pointer is cleared. After a data byte is written to the 7225 (via the serial interface, as previously described), the data pointer is incremented. By holding $\overline{\text{CS}}$ asserted while a series of bytes are written, any number of segments can be turned

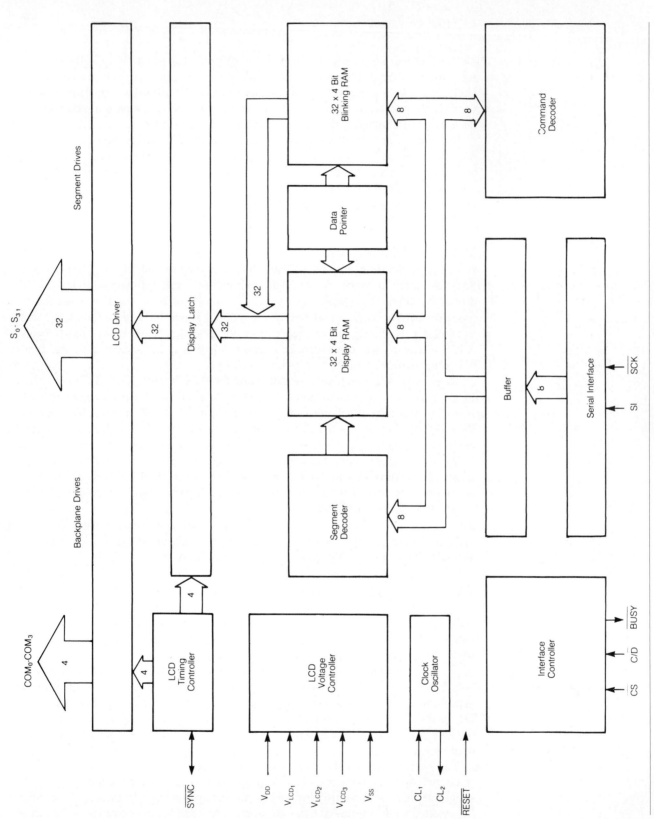

Figure 7.21. NEC 7225 LCD controller block diagram. (*Courtesy of NEC Electronics Inc.*)

Figure 7.22. Timing diagram for microprocessor interface to 7225. *(Courtesy of NEC Electronics Inc.)*

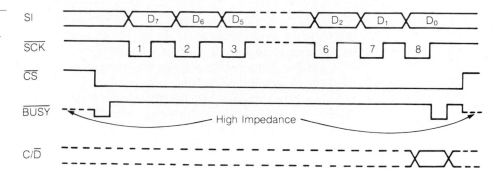

Figure 7.23. The 7225 system configuration. *(Courtesy of NEC Electronics Inc.)*

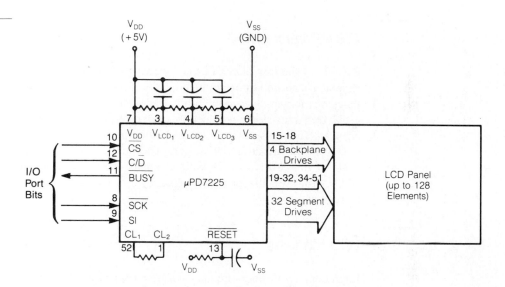

on or off. A specific memory location can also be written by first sending a "set data pointer" command.

A number of other commands are available for controlling the device's operation. A variety of LCD drive configurations can be selected, including static, biplexed, triplexed, or quadriplexed. The internal segment decoder can also be enabled. Two types of decoding can be selected: 7-segment numeric or 14-segment alphanumeric. When one of the decoders is enabled, the microprocessor writes a BCD digit or an ASCII code to the 7225. The segment decoder then writes the appropriate segment pattern to the display RAM. The microprocessor software loses the flexibility of individual control of every segment but is also relieved of the burden of decoding each character to the desired pattern.

Figure 7.23 shows a typical system configuration. The 7225 is interfaced to the microprocessor via five I/O port bits, as previously described. An on-chip oscillator provides the LCD multiplexing clock and requires only an external resistor to set the frequency. Four backplane signals are provided, although all four are used only when operating in the quadriplexed mode. Thirty-two segment signals are available, regardless of the mode. Thus, in the static (direct-drive) mode, 32 segments can be controlled. In the quadriplexed mode shown, 128 segments can be controlled, allowing a display of up to 16 numeric digits or 8 alphanumeric characters.

A resistive divider chain provides the intermediate voltage levels required for the multiplexing waveforms. The value of these resistors depends on the particular display to be used. The capacitors help hold these levels constant as the loading on the resistor divider changes during the multiplexing cycle. The resistor configuration shown is for quadriplexed drive; for lower multiplexing levels, one or more of the resistors are eliminated.

Dot-matrix LCDs require different controllers. An example of a dot-matrix LCD interface is presented in Sec. 7.3.6.

7.3.5 Active-Matrix LCDs

Because of the loss of contrast and viewing angle at high multiplexing rates, another approach is needed for large, high-quality LCDs. *Active-matrix* displays solve the multiplexing problem by using thin-film transistors fabricated on the rear glass of the LCD itself. One transistor is provided for each pixel, providing direct drive for each display element. The transistors can be easily multiplexed, since they have a sharp switching threshold and turn on and off quickly. This provides the high contrast and wide viewing angle of direct-drive LCDs with a simpler interface than conventional multiplexed LCDs. However, the inherent complexity of active-matrix displays makes them much more expensive.

7.3.6 LCD Modules

Liquid crystal displays are also available as modules with built-in control and driver circuits. This makes the user's interfacing task simple and eliminates the need for the end user to understand the intricacies of driving the display directly. LCD modules are particularly popular for larger dot-matrix displays, which are more complex to control than small segmented displays.

Figure 7.24 shows a typical alphanumeric dot-matrix display module. The control electronics are built with surface-mounted components on a circuit board at the rear of the display. Thus, the entire module is only slightly larger than the bare display. The module also includes the mounting bezel and connectors for the LCD, so the user is relieved of these considerations as well.

Figure 7.24. Dot-matrix alphanumeric LCD display module. *(Courtesy of PCI, Inc.)*

Figure 7.25. Block diagram of dot-matrix LCD display module. *(Courtesy of Hughes Aircraft Co., Semiconductor Division.)*

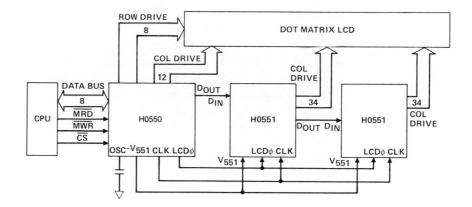

Figure 7.25 shows the block diagram of a typical LCD module. A display controller IC (Hughes' H0550) provides the interface to the microprocessor and the basic control for the display. Additional column drivers (Hughes' H0551) provide the drive signals required for the full display. (Larger displays also require additional row drivers.) The circuit shown drives an 8-row by 80-column display, which can display one line of 16 characters. All of this circuitry, plus temperature compensation for the thresholds, is part of the display module. A standard microprocessor peripheral interface is used. The module connects to the data bus, the read and write lines, and a chip select line (from the system address decoder). Note that there are no address lines in this interface. To write to a particular digit, the microprocessor first writes a command to select the desired digit and then writes the value for the digit. Other commands allow the display to be shifted left or right, or cursors to be displayed. The interface is very similar to that for the 8279 display controller described earlier.

Alphanumeric modules include character generator ROMs so that the microprocessor can simply specify an ASCII code and the display controller will produce the appropriate dot pattern. Graphic display modules require a byte of data for each eight dots, allowing full control of the display image.

For large graphic display modules, addressing every dot on the display can be a problem. Some displays use a serial interface. Data is provided serially, one dot at a time, along with a clock signal to indicate when the data is valid. Each dot is displayed in sequence, from left to right across the display. A "horizontal sync" input is asserted at the end of each line, and a "vertical sync" input is asserted at the end of a full display. These signals keep the controller and the display synchronized. This interface is very similar to that used for video displays, as described in Sec. 7.7.

7.4 VACUUM FLUORESCENT DISPLAYS

Vacuum fluorescent (VF) displays are a variation on the triode vacuum tube. Their high brightness makes them attractive for applications with high ambient lighting. Their power requirements are moderate, although much higher than LCD displays. They are not as easy to interface as LEDs, but specially designed driver ICs and power converter modules help ease the interfacing task.

Most VF displays emit a blue-green light, which is a nearly optimum color because it is near the peak of the human eye's response. The light emitted actually contains energy all across the visible spectrum and can be filtered to other colors. Some VF displays use different phosphors to obtain different colors, but they are much less efficient.

VF displays can operate over a wide temperature range and have a good reliability record. These characteristics, plus their high brightness and non-red color, have made them favorites for automobile dashboards. (Red is generally used only for warning indicators in automobiles.) They are easily multiplexed, since each digit can be rapidly turned on or off.

7.4.1   Vacuum Fluorescent Display Technology

Figure 7.26 shows a cutaway view of a typical VF display. The filament of thin, oxide-coated tungsten is heated enough to emit electrons, but not so much that it is visible itself. The control grid is an open wire mesh placed between the filament and the anode. The anode is divided into individual display segments or dots. It is formed by depositing conductive material on a glass base. The anode is then covered by a phosphor that glows when hit by electrons with sufficient energy.

Individual segments are turned on or off by controlling the anode voltage with respect to the filament. If an anode segment is more positive than the filament, it attracts

Figure 7.26.   Vacuum-fluorescent display construction. *(Courtesy of NEC Electronics Inc.)*

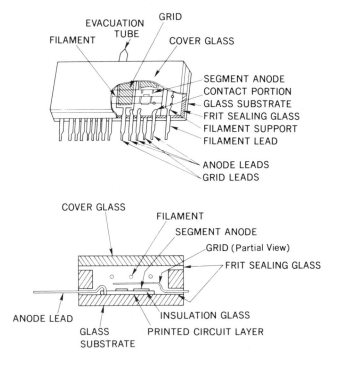

electrons emitted by the filament. When electrons strike the phosphor on the anode, light is produced.

The entire display is packaged in an evacuated glass tube. The viewer actually looks past the filament and through the grid to see the anodes.

There may be a single cathode for the entire display, or there may be a number of cathodes, one for each digit or dot row. The basic nonmultiplexed (also called static) VF display has only a single grid. It is held more positive than the filament to accelerate the electrons. Because it is an open mesh, most of the electrons pass through it.

Most VF displays are multiplexed (also called dynamic) and use separate grids for each digit. The segment lines for each character are connected together. Thus, an eight-character 16-segment display would have 16 anode connections, eight grid connections, and two connections for the filament. Each digit is turned on in turn by holding the associated grid positive, while the segment information for that digit is provided on the anode lines. All nonselected digits are turned off by holding their grids negative. The digits can be turned on and off quickly, so multiplexing rates of several hundred cycles per second can be used, eliminating flicker. Dot-matrix VF displays employ a similar approach, using separate grids for each row and separate anodes for each column.

7.4.2 Interfacing VF Displays

Figure 7.27 shows a basic VF display interface. The VF display's filament is driven by an ac source, which is required for even display brightness; if direct current were used for the filament, the intensity of the display would vary from one end to the other. The

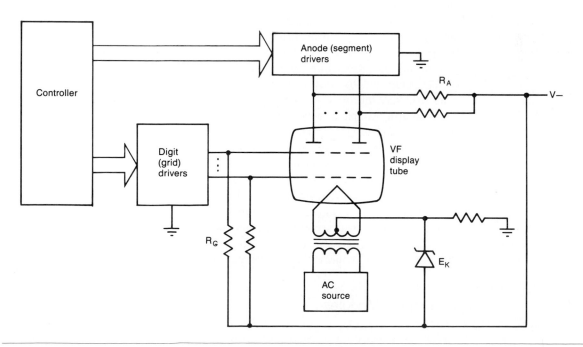

Figure 7.27. VF display interface.

filament is commonly driven by an inverter module specifically designed for this purpose, which converts the system's 5-V supply to the ac filament drive and also supplies the high-voltage direct current.

The center tap of the filament drive transformer is connected to a bias voltage produced by the zener diode (E_K). The bias voltage on the filament keeps the filament more positive than the grid, ensuring that electron flow is cut off. The value of E_K (called *cathode cut-off bias*) is determined by the particular display and is typically 2 to 10 V.

Each anode (segment) and grid (digit control) is pulled to the negative supply by the resistors R_A and R_G. The negative supply voltage required depends on the size of the display and is typically 25 to 60 V for segmented displays. Dot-matrix displays require a higher voltage, typically 70 to 100 V.

When all the anode and grid drivers are off, they are all pulled to the negative supply by the cathode cut-off bias and are more negative than the cathode. Electrons are therefore repelled by the grids, and the display is dark. To display a digit, that digit's grid driver is enabled, pulling the grid voltage to ground. Thus, the grid is more positive than the cathode, and electrons are drawn to it. Specific segments are turned on by enabling the corresponding anode drivers, pulling those anodes to ground.

The display is multiplexed in the same fashion as an LED display, turning on each digit in sequence. (Dot-matrix displays are scanned in a similar fashion, with each row or column turned on in sequence.) Since the display elements do not turn off instantly, some interdigit blanking time is required, during which all anode drivers are off.

The anode and digit drivers may be implemented with simple transistor switches. However, most displays require a large number of drivers, so multiple-output IC implementations are preferable. Many different drivers are available, ranging from 8 to 64 outputs. Most use a serial interface to the microprocessor, similar to that described previously for the H0438 LCD driver. This allows the maximum number of pins to be used for driver outputs. One example of such a driver is TI's 75518, which has 32 outputs. Some drivers are open-collector or open-drain devices and require pull-down resistors as shown in Fig. 7.27. Others include internal pull-down resistors or have active pull-up and pull-down transistors, eliminating the need for external resistors. One critical parameter that varies among drivers is the maximum voltage they can work with; relatively few drivers can handle the voltage required for dot-matrix displays.

When using simple drivers such as the 75518, the microprocessor (or other control hardware) must provide all multiplexing control, including switching from one digit to the next, enabling the required segments for each digit, and providing interdigit blanking. VF display modules often use a single-chip microcomputer for this task. Some single-chip microcomputers are available with on-chip VF display drivers.

For small displays, single-chip VF display controllers are available. National's COP470, for example, directly drives a four-digit, eight-segment display with voltages of up to 35 V. It accepts segment data from the microprocessor via a serial interface and stores the segment data for each digit. An internal counter and decoder scan the digits, and a multiplexer connects the appropriate segment data to the anode output drivers.

7.4.3   VF Display Modules

Because VF displays are complex to drive, they are commonly purchased as display modules. The display modules contain all the drive circuitry described above. They typically include an inverter for the filament and a dc-to-dc converter for the negative supply voltage. This allows the module to operate from a single dc supply voltage (typically 5 V), greatly simplifying the use of the display.

VF display modules interface to the microprocessor in the same way as LED and LCD modules described previously, using either parallel or serial interfaces. Large dot-matrix displays often use serial video-style interfaces.

VF display modules are available in a wide variety of formats. Digit heights range from 0.1 in. to 1.0 in. Both 7-segment and 16-segment formats are common in single-line displays of 4 to 32 characters. Dot-matrix displays are commonly used for single-line and multiline alphanumeric displays with up to 80 characters per line. Dot-matrix graphic displays typically range from 128×128 to 512×256.

7.5 GAS DISCHARGE DISPLAYS

The simplest *gas discharge* display is a neon bulb. Two electrodes are sealed in a glass bulb filled with a mixture of neon and argon gas. When a high enough voltage is applied (typically 100 to 200 V), the gas ionizes and emits an orange-red light. The ionized gas is called *plasma,* and gas discharge displays are therefore often called *plasma displays*.

The neon bulb is in fact so primitive that it is not generally considered a display, but it serves to illustrate the principle. (Neon bulbs were widely used as ac power indicators but have largely been replaced by LEDs connected to the dc power supply output.) There are many varieties of gas discharge displays, and the technology is complex. The most basic type is called *dc plasma*. Figure 7.28 shows the construction of a simple display. The anode can be made from a transparent oxide coating on the front surface of the display, as shown in the figure, or from a wire mesh next to the glass. When a voltage above the ionization threshold is applied between the anode and a selected cath-

Figure 7.28. Basic gas discharge display construction.

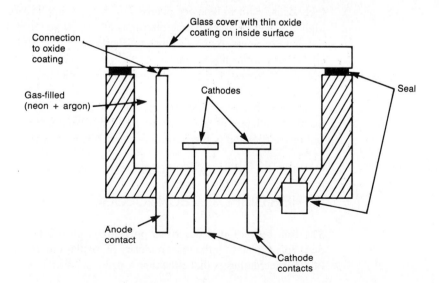

ode, the gas between the two ionizes. The anodes can be arranged as segments to form a segmented numeric or alphanumeric display.

Most gas discharge displays are dot matrix. The cathode is divided into stripes in one direction, and the anodes are stripes in the perpendicular direction. The display is then driven in a multiplexed fashion by driving one cathode at a time. By controlling the anode voltages, dots are formed at the desired intersections. The display size that can be produced by this technique is limited because as the display size increases, each dot is on for a shorter period of time. Thus, the brightness decreases as display complexity increases. This type of display also requires one driver for each row and each column. Unlike LCD displays, the drivers must be able to switch high voltages, which makes them expensive. One improvement on the basic multiplexed dc plasma display is the *Self-Scan* display, developed by Burroughs Corporation. These displays use a more complex physical construction to reduce the number of drivers needed.

DC plasma is a mature technology. Vacuum fluorescent displays are generally less expensive and easier to drive and are available in sizes comparable to those of dc plasma displays.

The future of gas discharge displays lies in *ac plasma* technology. In ac plasma displays, a dielectric is added between the electrodes and the gas, effectively forming a capacitor. Thus, an ac field is required to cause the gas to ionize. A continuous ac voltage that is just below the threshold required to ionize the gas is applied to all the electrodes. By applying an additional voltage pulse to an individual anode/cathode pair, the gas at the intersection is ionized. The continuous ac voltage is sufficient to keep this gas ionized, so the cell stays on after the pulse ends; the display has inherent built-in memory. The display therefore does not require refresh, and a separate refresh memory is not required as with other multiplexed displays. However, the drive circuitry is complex and must control high voltages, resulting in a relatively expensive display.

In spite of its complexities and high cost, plasma displays have a number of advantages. They are very bright, the contrast is high, and very large panels can be built. With ac plasma, the brightness is independent of the number of display elements. AC plasma is the only technology that can produce thin, bright displays as large as several feet square with millions of pixels. For military applications and others in which the high cost can be tolerated, ac plasma is an attractive technology.

There are numerous variations on these basic approaches, including ac/dc hybrids and other approaches to improving the performance of dc displays. Further information can be found in the sources listed in the Selected Bibliography at the end of this chapter.

Because the drive circuitry for gas discharge displays is quite complex, they are usually purchased as modules with built-in drive electronics. The interface may be serial or parallel and is similar to those described for other display technologies.

7.6   OTHER DISPLAY TECHNOLOGIES

The four technologies described previously, plus CRT displays that are discussed in Sec. 7.7, account for the great majority of displays in use. However, there are a number of other technologies that either show promise of increased importance in the future or

Figure 7.29. AC thin-film electroluminescent display construction.

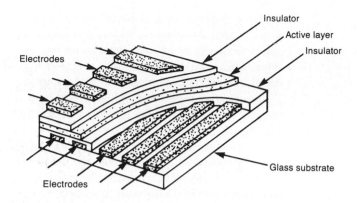

are now widely used in certain types of applications. The more common of these technologies are described briefly in this section.

One potential competitor to gas discharge, vacuum fluorescent, and LCD displays is the *electroluminescent* (EL) display. The specific type that shows the most promise is the ac thin-film electroluminescent (TFEL) display. Unlike other display types in which a glass envelope is filled with a gas or a fluid, TFEL displays are entirely solid-state. Figure 7.29 shows the basic TFEL construction. It is similar in concept to an ac plasma display, except that the gas-filled area is replaced by a thin film of electroluminescent material. When a sufficiently large ac voltage (typically 150 to 200 V) is applied between the front and rear electrodes, the material between them emits light. One material commonly used is zinc sulfide doped with manganese.

The advantages of TFEL displays include very thin and rugged construction, very high brightness, high resolution, wide operating temperature range, and moderate power consumption. Another unique benefit is the ability to control the brightness of each pixel to create gray-scale displays. The light emitted by most TFEL displays is yellow. Their principal disadvantage is the need for a high-voltage driver for each row and column. In addition, the process for fabricating the displays is complex, and the competing ac plasma displays have had the benefit of many more years of development. TFEL displays are rapidly evolving and may become a significant competitor for large dot-matrix applications.

A related technology is thick-film electroluminescent panels. These are most commonly used as lamps for backlighting and similar applications.

Electromechanical displays are well-established in certain applications. These displays use "pixels" made from circular metal disks, which are painted black on one side and a bright light-reflecting color (typically orange) on the other. The disks are mounted on one axis and latched in position by a permanent magnet. Applying a pulse to an attached electromagnet flips the disk to the opposite side. Thus, pixels are turned on by facing the colored side out and turned off by facing the black side out. In either position, the permanent magnet holds the disk in place, so no power is required to maintain the display and no refreshing is required. Significant amounts of power are required in brief pulses to change the state of the display. Large dot-matrix arrays usually are changed in a sweep from one end to the other to limit the instantaneous power requirements.

These displays are popular in stock exchanges, airports, and other situations in which a large alphanumeric display is required. They are also widely used for destination signs on city buses. One major manufacturer of these displays is Ferranti-Packard. While segmented displays are available (in which metal segments are used instead of disks), dot-matrix displays are far more common.

Incandescent displays use a filament for each display segment. Since they use basically the same technology as incandescent light bulbs, very high brightness is possible. The light emitted has a wide spectrum and can be filtered to any color. Their high power consumption limits them to applications that demand very high brightness.

Many other display technologies are used experimentally or in limited application areas. For a comprehensive review of display technologies, refer to the texts by Tannas and Sherr listed in the Selected Bibliography at the end of this chapter.

7.7 CRT DISPLAYS

Cathode-ray-tube (CRT) displays are one of the oldest display technologies and remain one of the most popular. They are unmatched for high-resolution displays of moderately large size. On a per-character basis, they are the least expensive of all display technologies, assuming, of course, that the application needs a display with the number of characters the CRT can supply (typically 2000 or more). No other technology can produce a 2000-character display at comparable cost. CRT displays also have the advantage of graphics and full-color capability.

The primary disadvantage of CRT displays is their relatively large physical size. Typical CRT displays are at least as deep as they are wide; thus, CRT alternatives such as LCDs are often called flat-panel displays due to their drastically thinner shape. CRT displays are vacuum tubes, and are therefore relatively fragile. They require high voltages, and the microprocessor interface is relatively complex. Despite these drawbacks, CRTs remain the preferred display type for a wide variety of microprocessor applications.

7.7.1 CRT Fundamentals

CRT displays use the same basic technology originally developed for television. Figure 7.30 shows the key components of a typical CRT display. Electrons are emitted at the base of the tube by an indirectly heated cathode. The flow of electrons from the cathode is controlled by the grid. These electrons are accelerated toward the faceplate by a high voltage (called the *accelerating potential*) applied to the anode. When the electron beam strikes the phosphor coating on the inside of the faceplate, the phosphor emits light at the point of impact.

The electron beam is aimed at a particular spot on the faceplate by the deflection coils. One coil provides horizontal deflection, and the other vertical deflection. By applying the appropriate voltages to each, the electron beam can be aimed at any spot on the faceplate. (This is called *electromagnetic deflection.* An alternative technique is *electrostatic deflection,* which uses deflection plates inside the CRT. This technique is used in oscilloscope CRTs, but not usually in data display CRTs.) There is also a focus

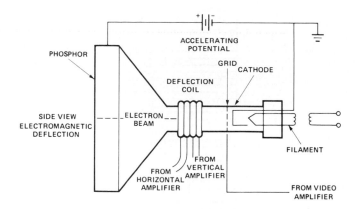

Figure 7.30. CRT display construction. *(Courtesy of Intel Corporation.)*

mechanism in the neck of the tube (usually electrostatic, but can be electromagnetic) that focuses the electron beam.

There are two methods used to generate an image on the screen. In one approach, called *vector, stroke,* or *XY,* the beam is directed to exactly trace each line that makes up the desired image. Because the phosphor glows for only a short period of time after the electron beam strikes it, the image must be continually retraced. To avoid flicker, the entire image must be retraced more than 30 times per second, which places a limit on the complexity of the image that can be displayed. To avoid this limit, special storage CRTs are used that retain the image on the phosphor until it is erased. This, however, requires that the entire image be erased and redrawn to make any change. Storage CRTs are also very expensive. There are also *write-through* storage CRTs that allow some information to be stored and some to be refreshed, but these are even more expensive.

The more common technique is *raster-scan.* Rather than having the beam trace the desired pattern, the beam always traces a standard pattern of horizontal lines. Figure 7.31 shows the trace pattern. Beginning at the top left corner, the beam traces across to the right side and then returns quickly to the left edge. This *retrace* line is blanked (that is, not displayed) by turning off the electron beam via the control grid. The next scan line follows a path parallel to the first, but slightly lower. This repeats until the entire screen has been filled with closely spaced horizontal lines. At the end of the last line, the beam is quickly returned to the top of the screen; this is called *vertical retrace.* The set of horizontal lines is called the *raster.* By turning the electron beam on and off as each line is scanned, the desired image is created on the display.

Raster-scanned displays are by far the most common type of CRT display. They are less expensive than vector displays and can use television-type CRTs and control circuitry. Vector displays require high-speed control of the horizontal and vertical deflection, whereas for raster displays the deflection pattern is always the same. The display information is all contained in the single signal that modulates the electron beam. This signal must be synchronized to the deflection signals, but the deflection signals themselves are not modified regardless of the information displayed. Vector displays have the advantage that sharp diagonal lines can be drawn, whereas in a raster display a diagonal line appears as a stair-step pattern. Because they are by far the most common, the remainder of this chapter covers only raster-scanned displays.

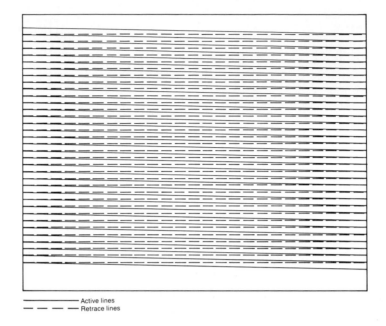

—————— Active lines
— — — — Retrace lines

So-called *flat CRT* displays have recently been developed that greatly reduce the required depth. They do this by placing the neck containing the electron gun at a right angle to the usual position (i.e., parallel to the front of the screen), and use additional deflection elements to bend the beam around the corner. While they are not as compact as most other flat-panel technologies, they have the potential for high performance at a relatively low cost. The interface is the same as for standard CRT displays.

7.7.2   CRT Monitors

Interfacing directly to a cathode ray tube requires the generation of the high voltage for the anode and sweep signals for horizontal and vertical deflection. These functions are common to all CRT applications, and CRT displays are generally purchased as a CRT tube with the associated circuits to perform these functions. This is often called a *CRT monitor*. The physical form may be a complete packaged unit, as is commonly seen with personal computers, or open-frame for integration into custom products. For special situations or very high-volume applications, the "bare" CRT tube can be purchased and the supporting circuitry designed, but for most applications this is an unnecessary task.

Figure 7.32 shows the basic elements of a CRT monitor. The horizontal and vertical oscillators provide the sawtooth-wave sweep signals. The horizontal and vertical sweep signals are both sawtooth waves, with the slow rise causing the scan across (or down) the display and the quick fall causing the retrace. The horizontal sweep goes through many cycles during a single cycle of vertical sweep; the number of cycles is the number

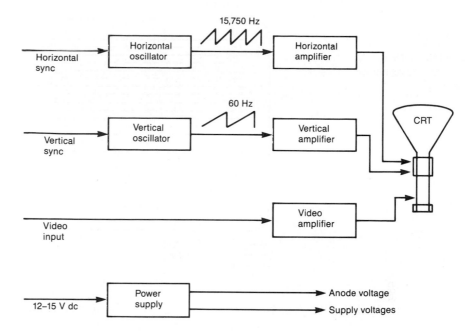

Figure 7.32. Basic CRT monitor elements.

of lines that are displayed, called a *field*. The CRT monitor also includes high-voltage-generation circuitry. Open-frame units typically require a single dc supply of 12 or 15 V, while packaged monitors connect to the ac power line.

CRT displays generate strong electromagnetic fields and can cause interference in sensitive circuits placed near the display. CRT displays are also sensitive to external magnetic fields that can deflect the beam and cause distortion in the display. Careful positioning of components that generate magnetic fields, such as power transformers, can be effective, but shielding of the CRT tube is sometimes required.

7.7.3 CRT Interface Signals

The circuit that interfaces the microprocessor buses to the CRT monitor is called the *CRT controller*. The three basic signals that must be provided to the CRT monitor are the video information, horizontal sync, and vertical sync. Each time horizontal sync is asserted, the electron beam retraces to the left edge of the screen. Each time vertical sync is asserted, the beam retraces to the top of the screen. These signals are usually provided by the CRT controller to synchronize the sweep oscillators in the monitor to the video information. For special applications, such as overlaying of computer-generated video on television images, the CRT controller may accept the sync signals as inputs and synchronize the computer-generated video to them.

Some CRT monitors use signals called *horizontal drive* and *vertical drive* instead of the sync signals described above. These signals have the same period as sync signals but different pulse widths and polarity.

Figure 7.33. Interlaced raster pattern. The solid lines are the even fields, the dashed lines the odd fields.

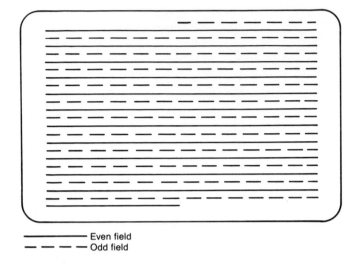

— Even field

— — — Odd field

For standard broadcast format television in North America, the horizontal sweep rate is 15,750 Hz, and the vertical sweep rate is 60 Hz. The vertical rate is chosen to match the power line frequency, which eliminates any waviness in the display due to deflection of the beam by stray electromagnetic fields. The horizontal frequency determines the number of lines per field. A horizontal rate of 15,750 Hz results in 262.5 lines per field. For standard television monitors, the horizontal scan rate must be close to this standard. However, many commercial applications use higher scan rates, such as 18.4 kHz. This provides more lines per field and thus higher resolution. In addition, it raises the scan frequency out of the hearing range of most people; 15,750 Hz is audible to many people, and CRT monitors at this frequency produce an annoying whine. This is not so objectionable with televisions, since the viewer is usually across the room and the television voice channel is generating lots of intentional noise that tends to block out the whine from the scanning.

The fact that the 15,750-Hz scan rate produces an extra half a line is not accidental. It results in *interlacing,* as shown in Fig. 7.33. Each alternate field is offset by one-half the line spacing. This effectively produces a display with twice as many lines, only half of which are scanned each time. Two fields are required to produce a complete image, which is called a *frame*. This is the technique used by standard broadcast television.

Interlacing is used because it doubles the effective resolution without increasing the scan rate. However, the refresh rate for each field is reduced to 30 Hz, which is slow enough to cause flicker. This is not noticeable on television displays because both fields (that is, adjacent lines) are usually quite similar. On computer displays, however, the full resolution is often used, and one scan line may be completely different from the adjacent ones, resulting in flicker. Thus, noninterlaced displays are preferred for computer display applications. Obtaining comparable resolution without interlacing is more expensive, however, so interlaced displays are sometimes used in cost-critical applications.

The sweep oscillators in the CRT monitor are synchronized to the sync signals from the CRT controller. The sync signals must be within a range that the monitor can accept; the width of this range varies depending on the type of monitor. Most monitors can operate in an interlaced or noninterlaced mode; this is determined by the sync signals. In an interlaced system, every other vertical sync pulse occurs in the middle of a horizontal scan.

7.7.4 Composite Video

Many monitors accept separate video, horizontal, and vertical signals as described previously. For broadcast television and some CRT monitors, these signals are all combined into one *composite* signal. As a first step, the horizontal and vertical sync signals are combined. The horizontal sync pulses are typically 3 to 5 μs wide, while the vertical sync pulses are much longer, typically over 150 μs. Because of the difference in frequency, they are easily separated with low-pass and high-pass filters.

The combined sync signals are then combined with the video information by using different voltage levels. Figure 7.34 shows the waveform of a composite video signal for one line. The black, or off, video level is represented by a level of approximately 0.5 V. The white, or on, video level is represented by the maximum voltage, typically 1.5 to 2 V. Intermediate voltages can be used for varying intensity levels. The sync signals appear as pulses below the 0.5-V black level.

The video information is blanked (i.e., set to the black level) for a period before, during, and after the sync pulses. This prevents the retrace of the beam from being displayed and also provides blank borders. Most CRT displays have considerable distortion near the edges and especially near the corners, and blanking prevents these areas from being used. (Standard television is *overscanned*, with the scan lines extending beyond the edges of the tube, so there are no blank borders. This is acceptable because some distortion is not noticeable for most television video images.) The blanking time before the sync pulse is called the *front porch*, and the blanking time after the sync pulse is called the *back porch*.

Figure 7.34. Composite video signal for one line.

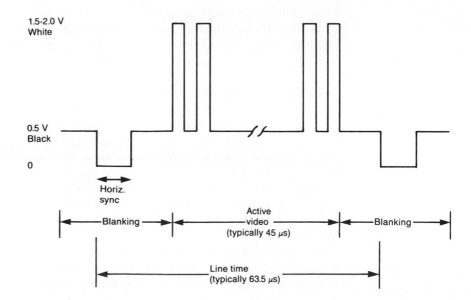

Figure 7.35. Composite video signal for one frame.

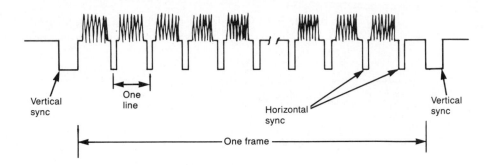

Figure 7.35 shows the composite signal for an entire frame. The vertical sync pulses are distinguished by their length. The number of horizontal sync pulses between each pair of vertical sync pulses determines the number of lines in the field.

There are additional complications in composite sync, such as an additional group of pulses called *equalizing pulses* and serrations in the vertical sync pulse. Fortunately, CRT controller ICs (discussed in Sec. 7.7.7) generate the sync and blanking signals, and the system designer does not need to be intimately concerned with them. It is important to remember, however, that only a portion of the scan time is available for active video. Typically 20 to 30 percent of each scan line is blanked and thus not available for video information. Similarly, a percentage of the vertical scan time is used for blanking and retrace, so some of the scan lines (approximately 20) are not displayed.

For many computer display applications, there is no reason to use composite video. It makes little sense to add circuitry to the CRT controller to combine several signals, which requires additional circuitry in the CRT monitor to separate them again. CRT monitors that accept composite video are generally more expensive than those requiring separate video and sync signals, since the "sync separator" is an additional cost.

There are several standards that apply to CRT monitors, although they are not universally followed. RS-170 specifies the basic interface signals as described previously for television-format displays. For higher-resolution displays, RS-343 defines the interface signals and certain display characteristics.

7.7.5   Display Resolution and Size

The resolution of a CRT display is a combination of two factors: the number of scan lines and the number of dots that can be displayed on each line. As previously described, the number of scan lines is determined by the horizontal scan rate (assuming a fixed vertical scan rate). This determines the resolution in the vertical direction. The resolution in the horizontal direction is determined by the rate at which the electron beam can be turned on and off; this is called the *video bandwidth*.

For example, consider the standard scan rate of 15,750 Hz. This results in a line time of 63.5 μs, of which typically 45 μs is available for active video (the remainder being used for retrace and blanking). Suppose that the desired resolution is 640 dots per line. This implies a dot rate of 640 dots per 45 μs, or approximately 70 ns per dot, which is equivalent to a dot rate of approximately 14.3 MHz. As Fig. 7.36 shows, the worst-case video signal, which is produced by alternating on and off dots, is a square wave at one-half the dot rate. Thus, the worst-case signal is a square wave with a 140-ns period, or a frequency of 7.15 MHz.

Thus, the CRT monitor must have a video bandwidth of at least 7.15 MHz to display 640 dots per line with a 45-μs active line time. However, monitor bandwidth is specified as *sine wave* bandwidth. If a 7.15-MHz square wave is fed to a monitor with a 7.15-MHz bandwidth, only the fundamental sine wave will be displayed, resulting in dots with fuzzy edges. To obtain sharper edges on each dot, the monitor must pass the third harmonic of the fundamental frequency. (The Fourier transform of a square wave is an infinite series of odd harmonics.) Thus, the required bandwidth for a high-quality display is 3 × 7.15 MHz, or 21.45 MHz. Many applications get by with monitor bandwidths equal to the dot rate (twice the maximum square wave frequency), since monitor cost is proportional to bandwidth.

As resolution increases, the bandwidth required increases drastically. In addition to the increased number of dots per line, increasing the number of lines per field decreases the line time, and thereby further increases the bandwidth requirements. In high-resolution systems, bandwidths of 60 to over 100 MHz are common. Standard televisions, on the other hand, have a bandwidth of under 5 MHz, which limits them to approximately 40 characters per line when used for text display. They produce acceptable "real" (i.e., camera-originated) images because their analog nature provides a wide spectrum of colors (or gray levels for monochrome). This spectrum is more important than high resolution for producing appealing displays of such images.

The standard 15,750-Hz horizontal scan rate provides only 262 lines if interlacing is not used, and blanking and retrace reduce the number of usable lines to approximately 240. This is adequate for many computer display applications but not for high-resolution graphics. Thus, faster scan rates are used in these applications to achieve greater numbers of lines. One high-resolution format in general use is 1024 lines, with a horizontal rate of 64 kHz. This results in a line time of 15.6 μs for a 60-Hz vertical rate noninterlaced display. With 1280 dots per line, the dot time is a mere 12.2 ns, which is equivalent to a dot rate of 82 MHz.

CRT display size is measured by the diagonal size of the screen. A wide range of sizes is available, from 5 in. to 25 in. The standard aspect ratio is 4:3; that is, the width is four-thirds the height. Some displays are used with the long axis in the vertical direction. This is particularly popular for text displays, since the format more closely

Figure 7.36. Worst-case video frequency.

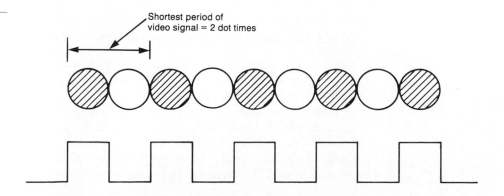

matches that of a sheet of paper. The raster is sometimes scanned vertically in this display orientation, since it is most efficient to scan along the longest axis.

Yet another variable in CRT monitors is the phosphor. Different phosphors produce different colors and also have different *persistence,* the amount of time the phosphor glows after it is struck by an electron. The P4 phosphor is the black-and-white television standard, and has the familiar white glow. It has medium-short persistence; it decays to 10 percent of its maximum luminance in 60 μs. Green and amber phosphors are most commonly used for computer displays. P31 is a short-persistence green phosphor (40-μs decay) that is suitable for noninterlaced displays. For interlaced displays, the longer-persistence P39 (150-μs decay) is preferable. The longer persistence eliminates flicker, but produces some "smearing" of the display when scrolling or otherwise moving images. P134 is a common amber phosphor.

7.7.6 Color CRT Monitors

Color CRTs use the same basic scanning approach but have several additional components. There are many different approaches to the construction of color CRTs, and we will describe only the basic idea. Color displays use a matrix of red, green, and blue phosphor dots (or stripes in some versions). For each pixel, there is a phosphor dot of each color. There are three electron guns, one for each color. All three beams are scanned in the manner of the single beam in a monochrome display. Specific colors are created at each pixel location by using a mixture of red, blue, and green of varying intensities.

There are several important implications of this. First, three video signals are required instead of one. Most color monitors used with computer systems are called *RGB* (red-green-blue) monitors, since they have separate video inputs for each of the colors. There is also a form of composite video for color displays, called *NTSC composite.* The NTSC format was developed for color television and designed to be compatible with both color and monochrome receivers. The color information in the NTSC signal has a smaller bandwidth than the luminance information; in other words, the brightness can be changed with greater resolution than can color. This is acceptable for typical video images but not for most computer applications. Therefore, most computer color CRT displays use RGB monitors, which provide the full video bandwidth for each color signal.

Color monitors also have additional resolution limitations. For each pixel, there must be three spots of phosphor. Therefore, the physical construction of the tube sets a limit on how close the pixels can be, regardless of the video bandwidth. This limitation is specified as *dot pitch,* which is the spacing between phosphor triplets. High-resolution color CRTs typically have a dot pitch of 0.31 mm or less. Note that the concept of dot pitch does not apply directly to monochrome displays, which do not have discrete phosphor dots. The effective dot pitch in such displays is limited by the bandwidth of the beam modulation circuitry.

There are two different types of RGB interfaces in common use. The *analog* interface interprets the voltage levels on each of the R, G, and B inputs as representing the brightness of that color, similar to the manner in which a monochrome CRT monitor interprets the video signal. This allows an infinite number of hues to be produced. On the other hand, *TTL-interface* monitors do not allow different levels on these signals;

each is treated as a digital input, turning the corresponding color on or off. Thus, only eight colors can be displayed, corresponding to the eight possible patterns of three bits. This interface is often extended to 16 colors (actually two shades of eight colors) by adding an "intensity" signal. This is also a digital signal, and allows the selection of a high- or low-intensity version of each color. This interface is used by the IBM personal computer color-graphics adapter (CGA) and enhanced-graphics adapter (EGA).

Note that these variations affect only the number of colors that can be displayed at each dot location, not the total number of dots (i.e., the resolution of the display).

Yet another variation in color monitors is the format of the sync signals. Some monitors have separate inputs for the sync signals, and some accept a composite signal on the "green" video input that includes the sync signals.

7.7.7   Character-Oriented CRT Controllers

The most flexible CRT displays allow the microprocessor to individually control each dot on the screen. This is called a *bit-mapped* display, since one bit (or several bits) of memory controls each dot on the screen. This is the common approach for graphics displays, which are discussed in Sec. 7.7.8. This section describes character-oriented (alphanumeric) displays, in which the microprocessor views the screen not as an array of dots but as an array of character positions.

While character-based display controllers do not allow full graphics, they require much less memory than bit-mapped display controllers, which reduces the cost of the controller. The software burden is also much lower for displaying text on a character-oriented display, since the software needs only to specify the character code rather than all the dots that make up the character. This allows the software to manipulate the text much more rapidly. However, bit-mapped displays are much more flexible and (in addition to providing full graphics) allow different fonts and character sizes to be displayed. They are becoming more popular due to the decreasing cost of memory, increasing processor speed, and the demand for Macintosh-style user interfaces that require them.

Character Generation

Characters are formed on a CRT display by using a dot matrix. For minimum cost, a 5×7 matrix can be used, but the character appearance is poor. Higher-quality displays use a 7×9 basic matrix, which is extended to 7×11 to allow for the descenders in the lowercase characters g, j, p, q, and y.

Many characters go all the way to the edges of the dot matrix, and one or more additional dot spaces are required between characters, both horizontally and vertically. For the horizontal spacing, one dot is acceptable, but two dots is preferred for better legibility. For vertical spacing, two dots is the minimum acceptable and three dots is preferred. The area required by a character, including the spaces and the dot matrix, is called the *character cell*. As Fig. 7.37 shows, a 7×11 matrix with two spaces between characters and three between character rows requires a 9×14 character cell. Each dot row within a character row is called a *cell line*.

The height of the character cell, along with the number of character lines, determines the number of scan lines required in the display. A 25-line display with a 9×14 character cell requires $25 \times 14 = 350$ usable scan lines. Allowing for an additional 25 scan lines for retrace and blanking, a total of 375 scan lines are needed. This, in turn,

Figure 7.37. A 7 × 11
character matrix in a
9 × 14 cell.

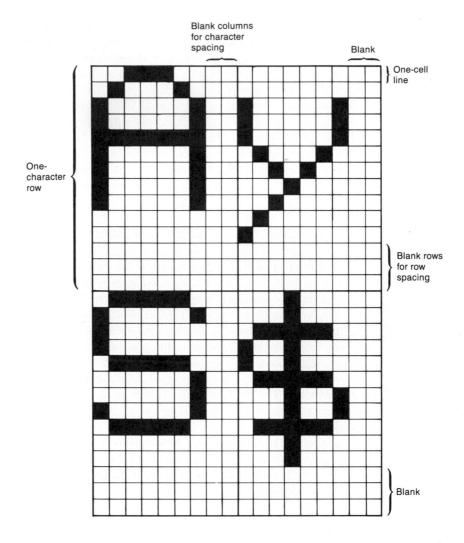

dictates the required horizontal scan rate. If the vertical rate is 60 Hz, then the horizontal rate must be 60 × 375 = 22.5 kHz for a noninterlaced display.

The width of the character cell, along with the number of characters per line and the horizontal scan rate, determines the dot rate required. For example, consider a standard 80-column display with a 9 × 14 character cell. The number of dots per line is 80 × 9 = 720. With a 22.5-kHz scan rate as determined above, the line time is 44.4 μs. Allowing 20 percent for blanking and retrace reduces the active video time to 35.6 μs. Thus, the dot rate is 720 dots per 35.6 μs, or 20.2 MHz.

The dot patterns for each of the characters that can be displayed are stored in a special-purpose memory called a *character generator*. Figure 7.38 shows the inputs and outputs of a typical character generator and the associated shift register. One part of the address specifies the character to be displayed, the other part specifies which cell line is needed. The outputs of the character generator memory provide all the bits for

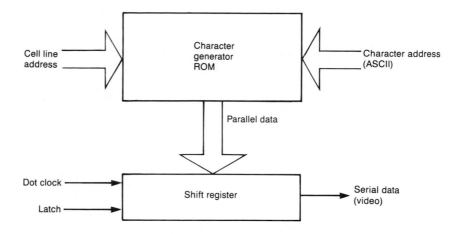

that cell line. These bits are loaded into the shift register and clocked out at the dot rate to produce the basic video signal.

The key task of the CRT controller is providing the appropriate character codes and cell line addresses to the character generator as the electron beam scans the raster pattern. Only one cell line of each character is needed for each horizontal scan line. Figure 7.39 shows the sequence required to display a character row. For the first scan line, the first cell line of the first character is displayed, followed by the first cell line of the second character, and so on, through the first cell line of the last character in the row. After the horizontal sync pulse and blanking, the next scan line is begun. For this line, the second cell line of the first character is displayed, followed by the second cell line of the second character, and so on. This is repeated until the last cell line is displayed, completing the character row. Then, after two or three blank lines for separation, the first cell line of the next character row is displayed.

The ASCII code is typically used for the character selection input to the character generator. The ASCII code is a 7-bit code and includes many nondisplayable *control characters*. These codes are often used for other symbols, such as greek letters, math symbols, or graphics characters. The eighth bit can also be used to access another set of 128 characters, allowing a wide variety of special symbols to be generated. This is also useful for international character sets.

Character generators can be purchased as ROMs with standard character patterns. This is the least expensive approach if the standard character set is acceptable. EPROMs or custom mask-programmed ROMs can be used for nonstandard character generators. For maximum flexibility, RAM can be used for the character generator, which is initialized by the system software with the desired character patterns. This increases the system cost but allows character patterns to be dynamically redefined.

The size of the character-generator memory is determined by the matrix size and the number of characters. As a minimum, a 5×7 matrix implies a 3-bit cell line address (to select one of seven cell lines). The minimum ASCII character set (assuming both uppercase and lowercase are supported) requires a 7-bit character select address. Thus, a total of 10 address lines are needed, which implies a 1-Kword memory. Each word needs five bits, but to use standard memory chips eight bits are used. Thus, the mini-

Figure 7.39. Raster-scan character genera-tion. *(Courtesy of Intel Corporation.)*

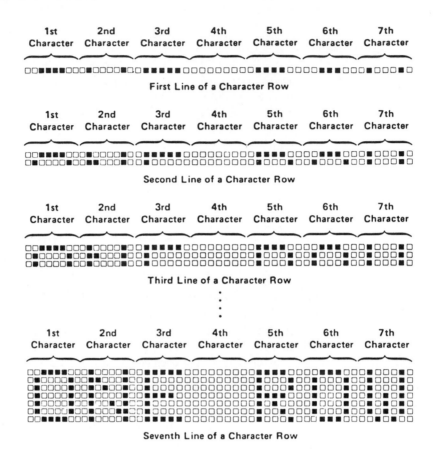

mum character generator is a 1-Kbyte memory. For a more flexible, higher-resolution system, a considerably larger memory is required. A 7 × 11 matrix requires four cell line address bits, and 256-character capability requires eight character select address lines. This results in a total of 12 address lines, or a 4-Kbyte memory. Some memories specifically designed as character generators include circuitry to shift characters up or down, thereby reducing the number of memory bits required by eliminating the need for extra matrix rows for descenders.

Most character generators are MOS devices. National Semiconductor makes a family of character generators, such as the 86S128, that are implemented in bipolar technology. These devices include the input character address latch and the output shift register in the same chip as the character generator memory. They also include a scan line counter and therefore require only a line rate clock instead of a cell line address. This combination of functions not only combines what would normally require several chips into a single device, but also requires only a 16-pin package since the row address inputs and parallel data outputs are eliminated.

CRT Interface Functions

Figure 7.40 shows a general block diagram of a CRT controller. The CRT display RAM (also called the *screen memory*) contains one location for each possible character position. The microprocessor writes the characters to be displayed to this memory, and the CRT controller reads them at the appropriate times. Because the microprocessor and the CRT controller both require access to the same memory, memory contention logic is required to determine which of them can access the memory at what time. There are several approaches to this, which are covered later in this section. Some approaches do not include the entire screen memory in the CRT controller system but use microprocessor system memory for the screen memory.

The CRT controller provides the horizontal and vertical sync signals for the CRT monitor. For each character to be displayed, the CRT controller supplies the appropriate address to the screen memory. The output of the screen memory is the ASCII code for the character to be displayed. This character code is stored in the data latch, which provides the character address to the character generator. The CRT controller provides the cell line address to the character generator. The character generator outputs the dot pattern for the selected line of the selected character, which is loaded into the shift register. The shift register is clocked at the dot rate, and its output is the basic serial video data. Note that the shift register must be reloaded with the next word of data as soon as the last bit of the previous word is shifted out, since the video data stream must be continuous.

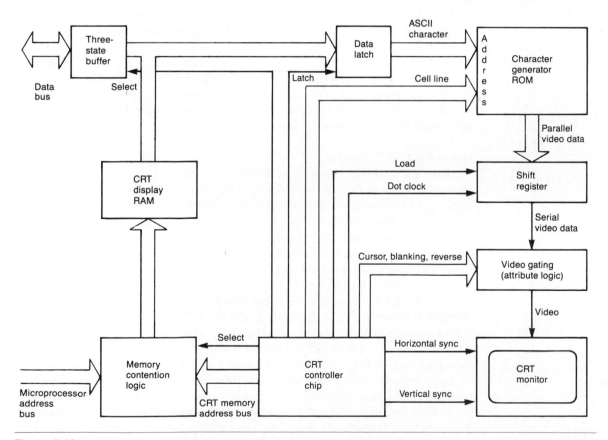

Figure 7.40. CRT interface block diagram.

The attribute logic modifies the basic video data for special character attributes such as reverse video (black on white), blinking, or half-bright. These attributes are stored in the screen memory along with the character codes. In many systems, 7-bit ASCII character codes are stored in 8-bit memory locations, conveniently leaving one bit for attribute control. For more than one possible attribute, additional bits are required. The attribute logic also modifies the video data at the cursor location to produce a blinking underline, white box, or other cursor shape. The cursor position is determined by the CRT controller under the direction of the microprocessor.

The dot rate of the system and the size of the character matrix determine the timing requirements for the system. As the example earlier in this section showed, a 25-line by 80-character display using a 9×14 character cell and a 60-Hz vertical rate requires a dot rate of 20.2 MHz. Since there are nine dots across in each character cell, the character rate is 20.2 MHz / 9 = 2.25 MHz. The character time is the inverse of this, or 445 ns. This determines the access time requirements for the screen memory and the character generator, since each must process each character in that time.

The data latch between the screen memory and the character generator is called a *pipeline latch,* which allows one character to propagate through the screen memory while the previous character is being decoded by the character generator. Because of the pipeline latch, the 445-ns access time requirement applies to the screen memory and the character generator individually; each must have an access time less than this value. Without the pipeline latch, the combined access time of both devices would have to be less than 445 ns. This would increase the cost of these devices, since higher-speed memory chips would be required.

The output shift register effectively provides another level of pipelining. While the character in the shift register is being displayed, the next character is being decoded by the character generator, and the one after that is being accessed from the screen memory. Because of these pipeline delays, the attribute control signals must be two characters behind the screen memory address.

Inside the CRT Controller

As described in the previous section, the CRT controller chip provides the address for the screen memory, the cell line address for the character generator, attribute control signals, and horizontal and vertical sync signals. The heart of all CRT controllers is the counter chain, from which all of these signals are derived. Figure 7.41 shows the basic counter chain and the associated logic. Except for the dot rate clock and dot counter, all this logic is included in most CRT controller chips.

An oscillator provides a clock input at the dot rate. This frequency must be selected so that it produces the desired horizontal and vertical rates for the display format chosen. The dot counter counts the number of horizontal dots per character (i.e., the width of the character cell). The load signals for the character pipeline latch and the shift register are generated by decoding the appropriate states of this counter. The dot counter and its associated logic are often not included in the CRT controller chip, since most CRT controllers are NMOS ICs that cannot operate at the relatively high dot rate.

The carry output of the dot counter is at the character rate and clocks the character counter. This counter counts the number of characters per line. By decoding character positions beyond the active line, the horizontal blanking and sync signals are produced. The carry from the character counter is a clock at the horizontal line rate that clocks the

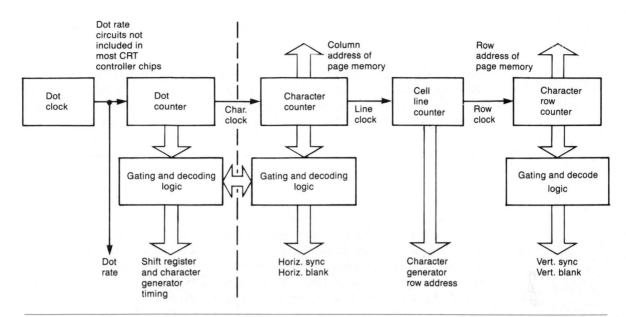

Figure 7.41. CRT controller counter chain and associated logic.

cell line counter. The cell line counter counts the number of cell lines per character row, i.e., the height of the character cell. The output of this counter provides the cell line address to the character generator. Finally, the character row counter counts the number of character rows in a full screen. The vertical sync and blanking signals are generated by decoding character rows past the end of the active video area.

The address for the screen memory can be taken from the character counter, which indicates the column of the character to be displayed, and the character row counter. While this approach minimizes the logic required, it has several disadvantages. Since these counters also produce the sync and blanking signals, they must keep counting through the blanking times, in addition to counting during active video. Thus, the screen addresses they produce continue to increment during the blanking at the end of each line and frame. This wastes memory, since approximately 20 percent of the screen memory locations are never displayed (corresponding to the 20 percent of the scan time that is blanked). In addition, the addresses produced are fixed; a given location in the screen memory always corresponds to the same physical location on the CRT screen. This makes display changes such as scrolling awkward: each character in the entire screen memory must be moved to scroll the display one line.

One solution to these difficulties is to add an additional counter explicitly for screen memory addressing. This counter is clocked by the character clock but is inhibited from counting except during active video. A "top of screen" address register stores the address of the memory location that corresponds to the first character of the first row. During vertical sync, the screen address counter is loaded from this register. Thus, scrolling requires only changing the address in the top-of-screen register. In addition, the screen memory can be larger than one physical display screen. By changing the value in the top-of-screen register, different sections of the screen memory (often called *pages*) can be selected for display.

Memory Arbitration Techniques

Both the microprocessor and the CRT controller must have access to the screen memory. The CRT controller requires access during the active video time, and if it is denied this access, the image on the screen cannot be maintained. The microprocessor is less demanding of immediate access to the screen memory, but if it has to wait for access often, the system performance can suffer. There are a variety of approaches to this problem, each with different cost and performance characteristics.

The simplest approach is to let the microprocessor access the screen memory whenever it wants. This provides maximum performance, since the microprocessor never has to wait for access. However, the CRT controller must continue to produce the video signal, and if the microprocessor is accessing the screen memory, then the CRT controller cannot access the desired location. The result is snow, which is black or white dots scattered across the screen. The amount of snow is small for a single access by the microprocessor, since the screen memory is removed from the CRT controller for less than 1 μs, which is about 2 percent of one line in a typical display. However, the microprocessor frequently needs to access many locations to perform a screen modification, and this creates proportionally more snow. This approach is used in some low-cost systems, in which the aesthetic drawbacks are considered justified by the low cost. For most applications, however, the snow is bothersome, and it is worth a few extra dollars in control circuitry (and perhaps some reduction in CPU performance) to get rid of it.

The simplest technique that produces a snow-free display is for the microprocessor to access the screen memory only when the display is normally blanked. The major blanking periods are the horizontal and vertical blanking times, although it is also possible to make use of the blank dots between characters and the blank lines between character rows. This can be implemented with any CRT controller by connecting the blanking signal to an input port bit or an interrupt input. The microprocessor then polls this input bit (or waits for an interrupt) to determine when it can access the screen memory. Some CRT controller chips include a status register that can be read by the microprocessor to determine when blanking is active.

Some CRT controllers do not allow the microprocessor to ever access the screen memory directly but perform the access for the microprocessor. The microprocessor writes the desired data (or a request to read data) to the CRT controller. The CRT controller then waits for a time when it does not need to access the screen memory and performs the access for the microprocessor. A status bit in the CRT controller is read by the microprocessor to determine when the transfer is complete.

The disadvantage of the wait-for-blanking approach is that the microprocessor can spend a significant amount of time waiting for access to the screen memory. This reduces the amount of time available for other processing tasks and slows screen updating. In applications such as a CRT terminal in which data to be displayed may be received at a high data rate, the wait-for-blanking approach is unacceptable, since the system will likely be unable to keep up with the incoming data. For applications that do not access the display frequently and can afford some performance reduction, this approach is an inexpensive way to implement a snow-free display.

Another approach is to use the microprocessor's main memory for the screen memory. A DMA controller transfers data to the CRT controller. The CRT controller typically includes two *row buffers* that store the screen data for two rows of characters. While one row buffer is being displayed, the other is filled by the DMA controller by reading from the screen memory area in the microprocessor's main memory.

The DMA/row buffer approach has the advantage that the microprocessor thinks it always has access to the screen memory. However, the microprocessor is being stopped frequently to allow the DMA controller to read the next row. These frequent DMA accesses significantly reduce system performance. One benefit of this approach is that a separate screen memory is not required; a portion of the microprocessor's main memory serves this function. The only screen memory in the CRT controller system is the row buffers, which are small enough to be built in to the CRT controller chip.

The highest-performance technique is to use a *dual-ported* screen memory. This is a memory that allows access by both the microprocessor and the CRT controller at any time. Thus, there is no snow, and the microprocessor never waits. The disadvantage of the dual-port approach is cost. (See Chap. 10 for examples of dual-port memory implementations.) Nevertheless, the dual-port memory approach is preferred from a performance viewpoint and is often used when cost is not critical.

Dual-port memory is often easier to implement with microprocessors such as the 6800 and 6502, since they have symmetrical two-phase clocks that define when the microprocessor needs access to the memory. Since the microprocessor requires access to the memory only during one phase of the clock, the CRT controller can be given access on the opposite phase. However, this approach requires that the microprocessor clock be synchronous to the CRT controller clock, and it is not easily extended to other common microprocessors such as the Z80, 8086, and 68000 families.

CRT Controller Example: 6845

There are many CRT controller chips available, each of which provides a slightly different set of functions. This section describes the 6845, and the 9118 and 7220 are described in Sec. 7.7.8. The background material presented earlier in this chapter, along with an understanding of these example devices, should enable the reader to evaluate other CRT controllers.

The 6845 CRT controller was originally developed by Motorola as a 6800-family peripheral chip. It is now second-sourced by Hitachi and is often used with other microprocessors. There are several CRT controllers that are minor variants of the 6845, such as AMI's S68045. While intended primarily for alphanumeric displays, it can be used for graphics displays. It is used in the original IBM PC monochrome text and color graphics display adapters.

Figure 7.42 shows a block diagram of the 6845. While it appears complex at first, it is simply a programmable implementation of the counter chain previously described. The clock input is at the character rate; this chip, like most CRT controller chips, is too slow to operate at the dot rate, so the dot timing must be performed externally. The horizontal counter counts the number of characters per line. The 6845 allows the number of characters per line and many other display parameters to be programmed by the microprocessor. The registers are shown at the right side of the block diagram. Register R0 sets the total number of characters per line (including blanked character positions). The blocks labeled "CO" are comparators, which test the values in the counters against the limits programmed in the registers. The horizontal counter, for example, is reset by the comparator when the value in the counter equals the limit set in R0.

The output of the horizontal comparator is a pulse at the horizontal rate, which

Figure 7.42. The
6845 CRT controller chip
block diagram. *(Courtesy
of Motorola, Inc.)*

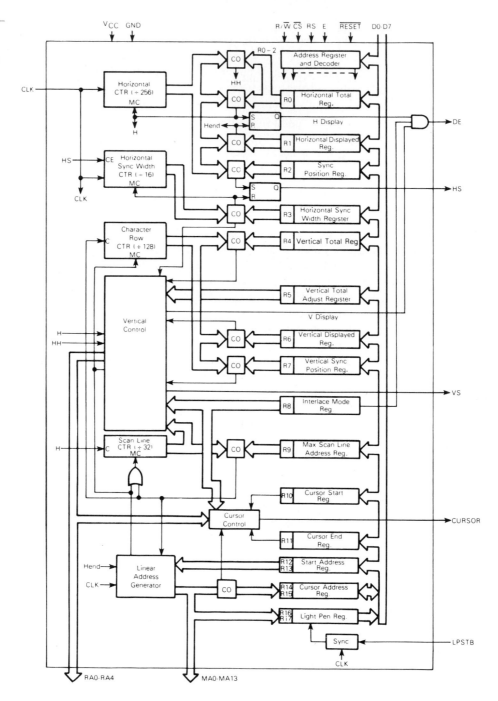

clocks the scan line counter. The scan line counter is reset when its count reaches the value in R9, as detected by the associated comparator. This comparator output clocks the character row counter and the linear address generator. The linear address generator provides the screen memory address.

Thus, the screen format is determined by the values in the registers. Registers R0 to R3 determine the timing within each line, as shown in Fig. 7.43. The DE (display enable) signal is high during active video; it can also be thought of as an active-low blanking signal. The horizontal total register (R0) determines the number of character clocks that make up an entire scan line, including blanking and retrace. The horizontal displayed register (R1) sets the number of actual characters displayed; the difference between R0 and R1 determines the horizontal blanking time. The position of the horizontal sync pulse is independently set by R2, and the width of the sync pulse is set by R3. The unit for all these settings is one character time.

Registers R4 to R7 set the vertical timing in a similar manner. Figure 7.44 shows the relationship of the register values to the signals produced. The vertical total register (R4) sets the total number of character rows in the complete raster, including rows that are blanked. Because this register is set in units of one character row (which is typically

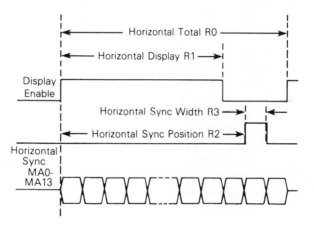

Figure 7.43. Relationship of 6845 registers to horizontal signals. *(Courtesy of Motorola, Inc.)*

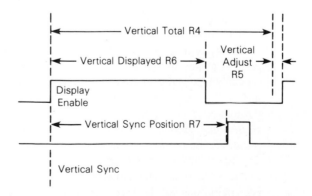

Figure 7.44. Relationship of 6845 registers to vertical signals. *(Courtesy of Motorola, Inc.)*

Figure 7.45. The
6845 sync formats. *(Courtesy of Motorola, Inc.)*

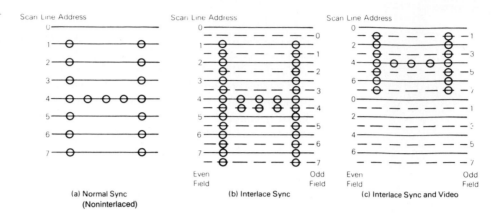

(a) Normal Sync
(Noninterlaced)

(b) Interlace Sync

(c) Interlace Sync and Video

9 to 14 scan lines), it will usually not be possible to specify the exact number of scan lines required for the complete raster. The vertical adjust register (R5) sets the number of additional lines needed to make the complete raster. Register R6 sets the total number of character rows displayed, and R7 sets the number of character rows of delay before the vertical sync pulse is begun. The sync pulse width is fixed at 16 scan lines.

The 6845 can produce interlaced or noninterlaced sync signals. If interlaced sync is used, there are two options for video generation. Figure 7.45 shows the three formats. Interlaced sync and video provides maximum vertical resolution, displaying all the even lines in one field and odd lines in the other. However, this will produce flicker unless a long-persistence phosphor is used. The other interlace mode provides interlaced sync but supplies the same video signal in both fields. This mode drives the monitor in interlaced mode, but the odd and even lines are the same. This eliminates the flicker problem, and the greater number of lines can provide a better display appearance than a noninterlaced display. The desired mode is selected by register R8.

The height of the character cell is set by register R9, and may be up to 32 lines. This sets the maximum count of the scan line counter. The output of the scan line counter provides the row address signals RA0 to RA4.

The cursor size is selected by registers R10 and R11. These registers set the starting and ending scan lines of the cursor. For a 7×9 character matrix, the start line would typically be set to 0 and the end line to 8 to produce a block cursor the size of a normal character. Alternatively, the start and end lines could both be set to 9, which produces an underline cursor. Register R10 also contains a bit that specifies whether or not the cursor blinks.

The 12 registers described above are set by the microprocessor's initialization program at power-up to determine the screen format and mode of operation; they are not typically changed once they are initialized. The registers used during operation all relate to the linear address generator. This is a counter that counts character clocks only during active video; thus, it provides an address for the screen memory that does not require any unused locations for blanked character positions. At each vertical sync pulse, the linear address generator is loaded with the value in the start address register. The linear address generator is a 14-bit counter, allowing addressing of up to 16K memory locations. The registers associated with the address generator are actually register pairs, one for the least-significant 8 bits and one for the upper 6 bits. Registers

R12 and R13 form the start address register. These registers can be changed at any time, and the new start address will take effect at the start of the next field. This allows easy and rapid display scrolling.

The cursor position is set by registers R14 and R15. When the screen memory address matches the address in these registers, the CURSOR output is asserted.

The last register pair, R16 and R17, is for use with a light pen. Light pens, as described in Chap. 6, use photodetectors that produce a pulse when the CRT's electron beam scans past the point the light pen points to. This pulse latches the value of the address generator into the light pen registers. Thus, these registers indicate the character position at which the light pen detects the CRT beam. The delay of the light pen response plus the sync latch in the 6845 must be taken into account in interpreting this value; the address in the registers will typically be a few characters past the actual position.

The microprocessor interface to the 6845 is straightforward, but since it is designed for 6800-type microprocessors, some additional logic is needed for Intel-style processors. The 6845 connects directly to an 8-bit data bus. All transfers are timed by the E (enable) signal, which is driven by the $\Phi 2$ or E signal in 6800-family systems, or by DS, UDS, or $\overline{LDS}$ in a 68000-family system. For most other microprocessors, it can be driven by $\overline{READ\text{-}OR\text{-}WRITE}$; this produces a signal that provides timing for either type of transfer. (Note than an active-high signal is required.) All transfers occur on the falling edge of the E signal. The transfer direction is set by the R/$\overline{W}$ signal. The $\overline{CS}$ input is typically driven by the address decoder; if $\overline{CS}$ is false, then no transfers occur regardless of any activity on the E signal.

There is only one address input, called RS (register select). RS is typically connected to A0 of the system address bus. Rather than use five address pins to allow direct addressing of any of the 18 registers, an internal address register is used. When RS is low, the address register is accessed. To read or write any of the other registers, the number of the desired register is first written to the address register by performing a write with RS low. The selected register is then accessed by performing a read or write with RS high.

Figure 7.46 shows a block diagram of a system based on the 6845. The dot rate oscillator provides the timing source for the system. This clock is divided by the dot counter to provide the character rate clock to the 6845. The CRT controller and the microprocessor share access to the screen memory via the address multiplexers. This example shows the simplest arbitration approach, in which the microprocessor gets access to the screen memory whenever it requests it. The screen memory may be as small as 2K $\times$ 8 for a standard 24 $\times$ 80 display, or additional memory can be used for multiple pages of memory or larger displays. Byte-wide static RAMs are typically used for screen memory in character-oriented systems. For larger screen memories, dynamic RAMs can be used. The memory address is constantly incremented, so refresh circuitry is not needed.

The character output from the screen memory is latched, and the latch output provides the address for the character generator. The CRT controller chip's row address outputs provide the scan line address to the character generator. The output of the character generator is loaded into the shift register by the character clock and is clocked out of the shift register by the dot clock. By grounding the last two inputs to the shift register, two blank dots are added between characters.

The basic video signal from the shift register must be combined with the cursor and

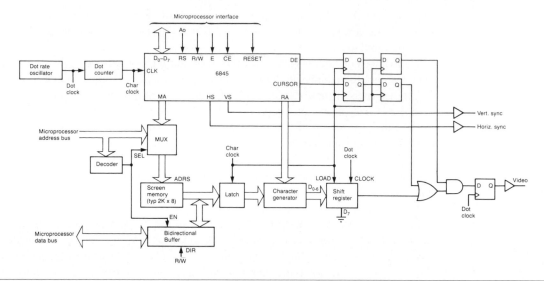

Figure 7.46. Block diagram for 6845-based CRT controller system.

display enable (DE) signals. The DE signal is low when the display should be blanked, and the cursor signal is high when the cursor should be displayed. However, these signals are synchronous with the character address, which is two characters ahead of the character being displayed. Thus, these signals must be delayed by two character times. The video from the shift register is ORed with the delayed cursor signal and ANDed with the delayed DE signal. The resulting signal is resynchronized with the dot clock and buffered to drive the video monitor.

Other Character-Oriented CRT Controllers

Most character-oriented CRT controllers provide functions similar to those of the 6845 described previously. Some, such as Intel's 8275, include character row buffers on the CRT controller chip. These devices use the DMA approach described earlier, in which the screen memory is part of the main system memory.

Most CRT controllers operate only at the character rate and require external logic for dot timing. One CRT controller that does provide the dot rate timing is National's 8350, which is a bipolar chip and can therefore handle the high clock rate. It is also unusual in that the screen parameters are mask-programmed rather than set by the system's initialization software. This simplifies the chip, but it requires that the user pay a mask charge and purchase a minimum quantity of devices for each screen format and does not allow the format to be changed once the system is built.

The most sophisticated character-oriented CRT controllers, such as Intel's 82730 and 82731 chip set, include built-in DMA controllers and access the system memory directly for display information. The memory is not organized as a simple matrix of rows and columns but as a linked list of character strings. This allows rapid editing and manipulation of the display contents, since only pointers need to be changed. This chip set can also display proportionally spaced characters, in which the width of the character cell varies for each character. The character generator memory contains an additional group of bits for each character code that specifies the width of the character. It can also shift characters up or down by modifying the row address output to produce subscript and superscript characters.

7.7.8 Graphic CRT Displays

Several techniques are used to generate raster-scan graphics displays. This section describes several common techniques and the hardware required to implement them.

Graphics Generation Techniques

One simple extension of character-oriented displays is the addition of graphic characters, which provides limited graphics such as boxes and other simple line drawings or symbols. The ultimate in character-oriented graphics is the use of RAM for the character generator, allowing character patterns to be defined at will by the software. However, character graphics are inherently limited and are more an extension of the capabilities of character-oriented displays than a true graphics display. When character graphics are used, the character generator must supply data for the entire character cell, rather than providing blank dots between characters.

Full graphics capability is obtained by using a *bit-mapped* display, in which there is 1 bit (or more) of screen memory for each possible dot (pixel) on the display. For monochrome displays, only 1 bit/pixel is needed. For color or gray scale, additional bits are required. For example, using 8 bits/pixel provides 256 different colors or gray levels. As Table 7.2 shows, the memory requirements for graphics displays increase rapidly as resolution increases. Note that the terms high-resolution and low-resolution are relative and depend on the application. In a home computer, 640×400 may be high-resolution, but to qualify for that designation in a computer-aided design application, 1280×1024 is required.

The requirements for display resolution and number of colors (or shades of gray) vary widely depending on the type of image displayed. In a computer-aided design application, high resolution is important, but a relatively small number of colors will suffice. In applications displaying photographic-type images, on the other hand, a wide range of colors with subtle shading is more important than high resolution.

Graphics CRT Controllers

Graphics CRT controllers are very similar to alphanumeric CRT controllers in many respects. All the same requirements for scan sychronization, memory addressing, ar-

Table 7.2   Bit-Mapped Graphics Display Memory Requirements

Resolution	No. of pixels	Memory in bytes for various numbers of bits per pixel		
		1 bit	4 bits	8 bits
240×200	48,000	6K	24K	48K
480×400	192,000	24K	96K	192K
640×512	372,680	40K	160K	320K
1280×1024	1,310,720	160K	640K	1280K

Figure 7.47. Mono-
chrome graphics video
generation.

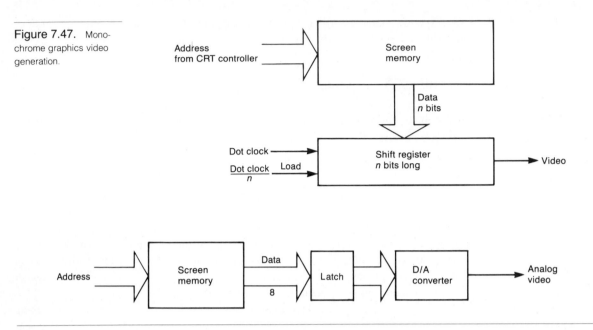

Figure 7.48.   Graphic video generation for 256 gray levels.

bitration, and dot clocking apply. The major difference is that the data from the screen memory, rather than passing through a character generator, is used directly for the dot pattern. Figure 7.47 shows the video generation portion of a basic monochrome bit-mapped graphics display. The eight bits from each location in the screen memory specify the state of eight successive pixels. In this example, no gray levels are supported.

Special dynamic RAMs are available that are explicitly designed for use as display memories in bit-mapped graphics systems. Texas Instruments' 64-Kbit TMS4161 is an example of such a device. This two-port RAM chip has one port that is identical to a standard dynamic RAM. An internal 256-bit shift register provides a separate serial data output at rates up to 25 MHz. This shift register replaces the external shift register shown in Fig. 7.47. Use of these *video RAMs* eliminates the contention between the microprocessor and the CRT controller, since each has a separate port for access to the RAM. In addition, since the shift register is simultaneously loaded with several bytes at a time, the RAM access time requirement for video generation is greatly reduced.

To provide gray levels, more than 1 bit/pixel is required; 8 bits/pixel provides 256 gray levels, enough for virtually any application. The number of bits per pixel is often referred to as the number of *bit planes,* since the memory can be visualized as a number of memory planes, each with 1 bit/pixel. Figure 7.48 shows the video generation circuit for 256 gray levels. Each byte in the screen memory corresponds to a single pixel. All 8 bits are combined by the digital-to-analog converter to produce one of 256 possible video signal levels. Note that this dramatically increases the speed requirements of the screen memory. When using 1 bit/pixel, only one memory access is required for each group of 8 pixels. For example, at a pixel rate of 24 MHz, the memory access rate is $24/8 = 3$ MHz, corresponding to an access time of 333 ns. When an entire byte is used for each pixel, however, the memory access rate is equal to the 24 MHz pixel rate, corresponding to an access time of only 41.7 ns. This would require very fast (and therefore expensive) memory chips. A high-speed D/A converter is also required.

The solution to this access time requirement is to build a "wide" memory array for the screen memory. For example, a 512 × 512 display with 8 bits/pixel requires 256 Kbytes of screen memory. The memory can be organized as 32K × 64, rather than 256K × 8. During each read cycle, all 64 bits are latched into an output register. By reading 64 bits in each access, 4 pixels (of 8 bits each) are read at a time. As shown in Fig. 7.49, a multiplexer selects each of the 4 pixels in turn. This allows four times the access time for the screen memory as compared to an 8-bit-wide organization. The memory array must also be designed to match the size of the microprocessor's data bus when it is accessed by the microprocessor; e.g., for a 16-bit processor, the screen memory must appear to be no more than 16 bits wide when accessed by the microprocessor.

Color CRT controllers must produce three video signals: red, green, and blue. The simplest implementation uses one bit for each of these signals and allows a total of eight different colors. Figure 7.50 shows a block diagram for the video-generation por-

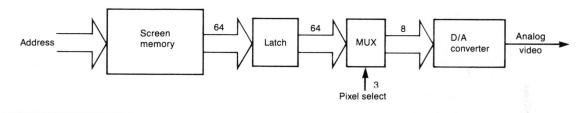

Figure 7.49. Use of wide-word memory to reduce access time requirements.

 **Figure 7.50.** Video generation for digital RGB plus intensity control bit.

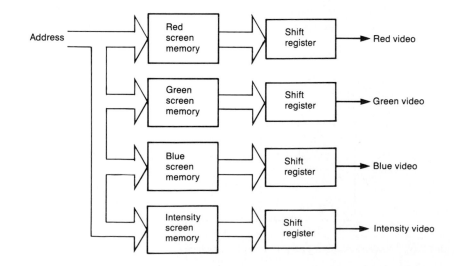

tion of an eight-color CRT controller. A separate memory array is used for each color. All three arrays are accessed in parallel, and the three video signals are clocked out of the shift registers simultaneously. Since only 1 bit/pixel is used from each array, the shift registers reduce the access time requirements of the memory.

The eight-color technique described above is easily extended to 16 colors by adding a fourth bit for luminance. For more colors, analog RGB monitors are used, and more than one bit per color is required. There is one memory array and one D/A converter for each color. This is similar to the gray scale display described previously, except that there are three memory arrays and D/A converters instead of just one. If four bits are used for each color, a total of 2^{12}, or 4096, different colors can be displayed. While 4096 colors are adequate for most applications, more are needed for realistic (true-to-life) color rendition. High-end systems use as many as 8 bits per color (24 bits/pixel), for a total of over 16.8 million different hues.

The memory access time requirements for such displays are the same as for a gray scale display, requiring use of a wide-word memory organization with output multiplexers to reduce the access time requirement for the memory chips.

Graphics displays require high-performance D/A converters. The D/A converter (DAC) must produce a new output level for each pixel; in a high-resolution system, this implies a bandwidth of over 100 MHz. A variety of *video DACs* are available that are optimized for this application. Bandwidth is typically 40 to 200 MHz, and word size is usually 4 or 8 bits. Triple-DACs are also available, which include one D/A converter for each color in a single IC. Many video DACs include sync inputs and provide outputs that can directly drive standard monitors.

Color Lookup Tables

Although it is desirable to have a large number of hues available, most images use a relatively limited selection. A *color lookup table* can be used to take advantage of this characteristic to reduce the amount of screen memory required. Figure 7.51 shows a system using a color lookup table. The lookup table consists of high-speed RAM that is written by the applications program. (The figure does not show the multipexers required on the connections to the lookup table RAM to allow access by the microprocessor.) The lookup table translates a "color number" from the screen memory to RGB data for the DAC. In the example shown, four bits of screen memory are used for each pixel. Thus, only 16 different colors can be displayed simultaneously. However, these 16 colors are not fixed; by writing the desired values to the lookup table, any of 4096 colors (called the *palette*) can be assigned to each of the 16 color numbers. This

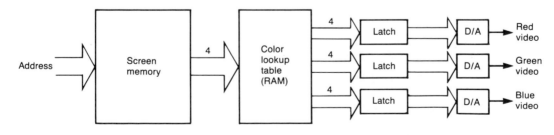

Figure 7.51. Analog RGB video generation with color lookup table.

requires only one-third as much screen memory as compared to the 4096-color display without a lookup table. The lookup table itself is a small memory, requiring only 16 words of 12 bits each. However, it must be fast, since its access time must be less than one pixel time.

A more expensive system could use 8 bits/pixel in the screen memory and provide 8 bits for each color from the lookup table. This would require a 256×24 lookup table and would allow any 256 from a palette of 16.8 million colors to be displayed. The relatively small lookup table greatly reduces the amount of screen memory that would be required for a comparable choice of colors without using a lookup table.

Color palette ICs are available that combine the color lookup RAM and D/A converter in a single chip. AMD's Am8151 was the first such IC, and it includes a 256×8 lookup table and an 8-bit D/A converter. Three of these ICs (one for each color) produce a display with 256 active colors from a palette of 16.8 million. The palette can be reloaded between frames or even between lines to increase the number of colors available, although this significantly increases the software overhead.

Generation of Graphic Images

Bit-mapped displays allow complete flexibility, but the demands placed on the system software are considerable. Consider, for example, what is required to move a graphic object from one position on the screen to another. First, the object must be erased from its old position, pixel by pixel. This may also require replacing the background color "behind" the old position. Each pixel of the object must then be written to the new location. These functions are often called *raster ops*. Moving a block of pixels, which may not be aligned with a memory byte boundary, is called a *bit boundary block transfer,* or *bitblt* (pronounced "bit-blit") for short.

By providing hardware in the CRT controller for functions such as drawing a line between two points or a circle of a specified radius at a specified location, the drawing task can be significantly sped up. High-performance graphics systems often include specialized "graphics engines," which are high-speed processors designed to perform a variety of graphics manipulation tasks. In the past, high-end graphics systems have typically used bit-slice microprocessors for these tasks. Several specialized microprocessors are now available that are designed to perform high-speed bit-mapped graphics manipulations. Examples of such processors are TI's TMS34010 and Intel's 82786. Some high-end graphics CRT controller ICs also include drawing and image manipulation functions.

A few graphic display controller chips, such as TI's 9118 described in the following section, support sprites. A *sprite* is an object that can be moved around the display without rewriting each pixel. It is basically a graphics character that is defined by the application program and positioned on the screen by the display controller. Its key attribute is that it can be moved to any location on the display simply by setting position registers. This allows moving a relatively complex object by changing only a single set of values (the horizontal and vertical positions), therefore providing much faster motion than pixel-by-pixel moves.

Video Display Generators

Video display generators are single-chip CRT controllers that provide more functions than typical CRT controller chips. Most can operate in alphanumeric or graphic modes. They typically provide a direct composite video output and require only external screen memory. Unlike standard CRT controller chips, they include all the dot timing logic on the chip and also have on-chip character generators. In exchange for combining all these functions in one low-cost chip, several things are sacrificed. The programmability of these devices is limited: they are intended for television-standard scan rates, and they have fixed resolution (or a choice among a few fixed resolutions). The maximum dot rate (and thus the resolution) is relatively low, since all dot-rate functions are included in the chip. They are intended for home computers, video games, and similar applications and provide a cost-effective method for interfacing a microprocessor to a standard color television or inexpensive monitor. (They are not generally used with high-performance monitors, since their moderate resolution does not require one.)

One example of a video display generator is Texas Instruments' TMS9118. This device evolved from the 9918 and is part of a family of chips with slightly different characteristics. The large number of functions incorporated in this chip simplifies the system hardware design, but its capabilities are complex.

The 9118 is designed for use with color televisions, and includes a number of features to reduce the processing and memory requirements for animated displays (such as for video games). The display resolution is 256 × 192, and 15 colors plus "transparent" are supported.

The display it produces can be thought of as a series of planes, one behind another, as shown in Fig. 7.52. (Note that these *planes* are different than the more common use of the term *bit planes*. The 9118's planes each have different characteristics and are "ordered" from front to back, whereas the usual bit planes are all combined to form a single pixel.) The first 32 planes are sprite planes. Sprites can be defined in an 8 × 8,

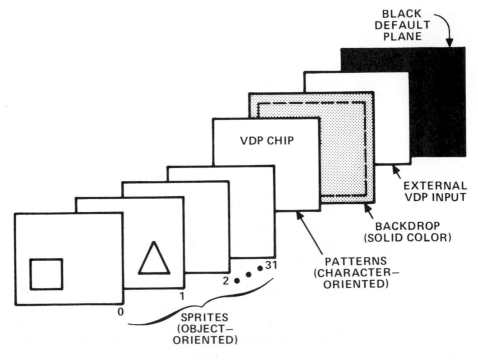

Figure 7.52. Display planes for 9118 video display generator. *(Courtesy of Texas Instruments.)*

16 × 16, or 32 × 32 matrix. Each sprite can be moved anywhere on the screen by changing only its position register. The planes are prioritized, so that if a sprite on one plane overlaps a sprite on another plane further back, it will obscure the part it overlaps. This produces a three-dimensional effect without requiring software to determine which areas are overlapping and which image should be masked.

Behind the sprite planes is the pattern plane. This plane can operate in several modes. All modes are block-oriented; the 9118 is not a bit-map-oriented device. In Graphics I and Graphics II modes, the screen is divided into 768 blocks of 8 × 8 pixels. In Graphics I mode, 256 different graphics patterns can be defined, and each pattern can use any two colors. Each of the 768 blocks on the screen is assigned one of the 256 patterns. Graphics II mode is more flexible, allowing 768 different patterns, so each block can be unique, and more colors can be used. Each line of each pattern can use any two colors. A bit-mapped display can be produced by using Graphics II mode and assigning a different pattern number to each position. The pattern definitions then form the bit map. However, this does not allow arbitrary color assignments. A third graphics mode, the Multicolor mode, reduces the resolution to 64 × 48 by treating groups of 4 × 4 pixels as a single display element. In this mode, each element can be any of the 16 possible colors. Finally, the Text mode produces 24 lines of 40 characters each. Sprites are disabled in this mode.

Behind the pattern plane is the backdrop, which can be set to any color. Two 9118s can be connected together, and the planes of the second 9118 are behind the backdrop. (The backdrop color of the first 9118 would be set to "transparent.") The backdrop is larger than the active display area, so it can be used to produce a colored border.

Figure 7.53 shows the basic circuit configuration for the 9118. The 9118 is designed to work with dynamic RAMs and directly provides the multiplexed address and control signals needed by these memories. This allows the complete subsystem to be implemented with three ICs: the 9118 and two 4416 RAMs. The 4416 is a 16K × 4 dynamic RAM. One-bit-wide dynamic RAMs are more common, but wider-word devices are preferable for this application since only 16 Kbytes of RAM are needed.

The 9118 provides a direct color composite output. The only external video circuit required is a buffer to provide higher drive current. An RF modulator can be added to allow direct connection to the antenna terminals of a television. The 9128 and 9129 are similar to the 9118 but produce "color difference" signals that can be encoded into NTSC composite or RGB signals. The advantage of using an external encoder, rather than the internal encoder of the 9118, is that a higher-quality NTSC or RGB signal can be produced. The 9129 produces a 625-line raster for use in systems conforming to the PAL standard (the European television standard, which is different from NTSC).

The microprocessor interface is fairly standard. There is no chip select input, so the address decode must be gated with the read and write strobes to produce the $\overline{CSR}$ and $\overline{CSW}$ signals. The MODE input is connected to an address line and determines the type of access as described in the following paragraph. The interrupt output, if enabled, is asserted at the start of each vertical blanking period. This indicates that the microprocessor can write to the screen memory with minimum delay times. The 9118 connects directly to the data bus via the CD0 to CD7 pins. However, TI numbers the most-significant data bit as CD0 and the least-significant as CD7, which is the reverse of the standard used by all other microprocessor manufacturers. Thus, unless used with a TI microprocessor, CD0 must be connected to data bus bit 7, CD1 to data bus bit 6, etc.

There are eight write-only registers and one read-only status register in the 9118.

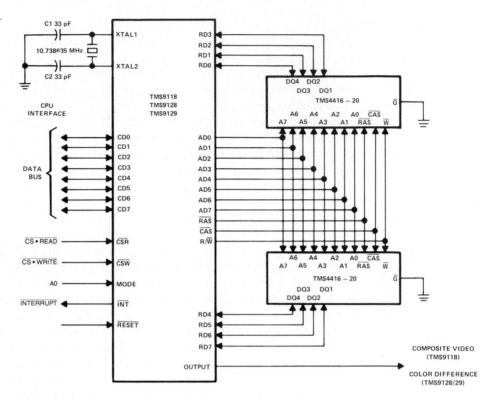

Figure 7.53. Basic 9118 circuit configuration. *(Courtesy of Texas Instruments.)*

All registers are accessed with MODE high. A two-byte sequence is used to write to a register. The first byte is the data to be written, and the second byte specifies the register number. Only one register, the status register, can be read, so any read with MODE high reads this register directly.

The microprocessor accesses the screen memory via the 9118 with a three-byte sequence:

1. Microprocessor writes two bytes to the 9118 to specify the memory address to be accessed.

2. MODE input is set low.

3. Memory data byte is read or written.

Internal registers store the memory address and data, and when the screen memory is not needed for display generation, the data is transferred to the screen memory. Successive locations can be accessed with a single-byte transfer; the address is automatically incremented after each transfer.

The 9118 includes memory contention logic; snow does not appear on the screen during microprocessor accesses to the screen memory. There is a delay between when the microprocessor requests an access and when the transfer occurs, since the 9118 must wait for an "access window" during which the screen memory is not needed for video generation. A status bit indicates when the transfer is completed.

Thus, the 9118 allows a very small number of chips to produce a complex color graphics display. Although the various modes and block orientation make it more awkward to use than a bit-mapped display, the memory requirements are significantly reduced. The sprites allow much faster and smoother motion than would be possible with a typical bit-mapped display, while reducing the demands on the software.

Another popular video display generator is Motorola's 6847. This chip is generally similar to the 9118 but does not provide sprites or prioritized bit planes. However, it provides a wider variety of display modes, including two alphanumeric modes, two "semigraphics" modes (similar to the block-oriented graphics of the 9118), and eight bit-mapped graphics modes. Bit-mapped display modes vary from 64×64 with nine colors to 256×192 with two colors. It is designed to use static RAMs for the screen memory.

Bit-Mapped Display Controllers

High-performance bit-mapped display controllers have traditionally been implemented with custom-designed bipolar controllers that are often built with bit-slice processors. This approach is still used for the most demanding applications. However, CRT controller chips designed for high-resolution bit-mapped displays are now available and provide adequate performance for most applications.

The first such device was NEC's 7220. This chip is second-sourced by Intel as the 82720, and NEC produces an enhanced version called the 7220A. Figure 7.54 shows a block diagram of the 7220. The functions provided by the 7220 are similar to those of alphanumeric CRT controllers, plus there are a number of additional functions. It can support a screen memory of 256K words of 16 bits each for a display resolution of 2048×2048 with 1 bit/pixel or of 1024×1024 with 4 bits/pixel. It is designed to work with dynamic RAM for the screen memory, and although external logic is required to produce the RAS and CAS timing and address multiplexing, the 7220 ensures that sufficient accesses occur to guarantee that the memory remains refreshed.

The 7220 can zoom in on any area of the display, with a magnification factor of up

Figure 7.54. The 7220 graphic CRT controller chip block diagram. *(Courtesy of NEC Electronics Inc.)*

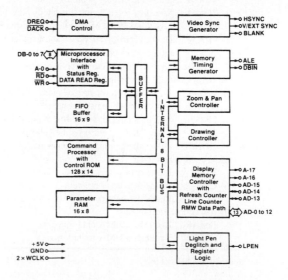

to 16. This is implemented by slowing the dot rate and repeating the same information on successive scan lines. When zoomed in on a portion of the display, the displayed area can be panned to move the displayed window to other areas of the image. The display can be divided into two separate areas, each of which can be independently scrolled.

The microprocessor accesses the screen memory by writing requests to the 7220, which then performs the transfer. For increased performance when drawing geometric images, the 7220 can draw figures in the screen memory as requested by the microprocessor. The figures that can be drawn include lines, arcs, circles, and rectangles. The microprocessor supplies only the parameters of the figure to be drawn, such as its position, radius of a circle, or end points of a line. These figures are drawn at a rate of 800 ns/pixel with a 5-MHz clock. The 7220A can operate with a clock up to 8 MHz, which increases the drawing rate to 500 ns/pixel.

The 7220 connects to an 8-bit data bus and accepts the usual read and write strobes. There is no chip select, so these signals must be gated with the output of the address decoder. The DREQ and $\overline{\text{DACK}}$ signals provide direct connection to a DMA controller, allowing images to be rapidly transferred from the microprocessor's main memory to the screen memory.

Rather than provide direct access to the internal registers, the 7220 uses a high-level command set. Each command is a single byte and is followed by parameter bytes as necessary. Table 7.3 lists the commands. Commands are stored in the on-chip FIFO,

---

Table 7.3   The 7220 Command Set

Video control commands
    RESET: Resets the GDC to its idle state and specifies the video display format.
    VSYNC: Selects master or slave video synchronization mode.
    CCHAR: Specifies the cursor and character row heights.
Display control commands
    START: Starts the display scanning process.
    ZOOM: Specifies zoom factors for the display and writing of graphics characters.
    CURS: Sets the position of the cursor in display memory.
    PRAM: Defines starting addresses and lengths of the display areas and specifies the bytes for the graphics character.
    PITCH: Specifies the width of the X dimension of display memory.
Drawing control commands
    WDAT: Writes data words or bytes into display memory.
    MASK: Sets the mask register contents.
    FIGS: Specifies the parameters for the drawing processor.
    FIGD: Draws the figure as specified above.
    GCHRD: Draws the graphics character into display memory.
Data read commands
    RDAT: Reads data words or bytes from display memory.
    CURD: Reads the cursor position.
    LPRD: Reads the light pen address.
DMA control commands
    DMAR: Requests a DMA read transfer.
    DMAW: Requests a DMA write transfer.

Source: NEC Electronics.

allowing the command and all its parameter bytes to be written in quick succession without waiting for the 7220 to be ready to use the information. The A0 input distinguishes between command and parameter bytes during write cycles. During read cycles, it selects data from the FIFO or the status register.

The interface to the screen memory is via a multiplexed address/data bus. The ALE signal strobes the address into an external latch, and $\overline{DBIN}$ enables the data read buffer. External timing logic is required to produce the $\overline{RAS}$ and $\overline{CAS}$ signals for the RAM chips.

Another example of a high-resolution bit-mapped display controller is Hitachi's HD63484 advanced CRT controller. This device includes all the key functions of the 7220, plus additional functions such as clipping an image to fit in a "window." In addition, the screen memory can be accessed by using XY coordinates rather than actual memory addresses. Bit maps as large as 4096 × 4096 (2 Mbytes) can be supported. A 16-bit bus interface is provided and is designed for use with 68000-family microprocessors.

7.8 DESIGN EXAMPLE

The display system for the design example uses four HPDL-1414 four-character alphanumeric display modules to produce a 16-character display. This provides a moderately priced, easy-to-interface display that requires no software support and is physically compact. The display appears to the software as a 16-byte write-only memory; it simply writes the ASCII code of the desired character to the desired location.

The 0.112 in. character height is rather small but is adequate when the operator is within a few feet of the instrument. The HPDL-2416 is a similar display with a 0.16 in. character height for applications requiring a slightly greater viewing distance. Both of these displays are alternate sources for Siemens' displays of the same part number, without the "HP" prefix. The HP displays are faster, however, and additional wait states must be added to use Siemens' displays in the design example circuit.

These displays have the advantages of fitting in a very small space and having moderately high brightness and good viewing angle. If power consumption were critical and ease of viewing in poor lighting and good viewing angle were not, then an LCD display would be a good alternative. If larger characters or many more characters were desired, then vacuum fluorescent or gas discharge displays should be considered.

Figure 7.55 shows the interface circuit. The displays do not have any chip select input, so the signal on the $\overline{WR}$ pin must be a combination of the write strobe and the address select signals. The write strobes are generated by the I/O address decoder described in Chap. 6.

Figure 7.56 shows the display's timing diagram. Although the displays are theoretically bus-compatible, they require a 50-ns hold time for address and data after the negation of $\overline{WR}$. This problem is solved in this example by latching the address and data at the start of every bus cycle. The data is clocked into the register each time $\overline{DS}$ is asserted. (An active-high version of $\overline{DS}$ is used, since the register is positive-edge-triggered.) The two address bits are latched in a similar manner when $\overline{AS}$ is asserted. The displays also require an address setup time before $\overline{WR}$ is asserted. This is not a problem, since $\overline{AS}$ is asserted one clock cycle before $\overline{DS}$ during a write cycle.

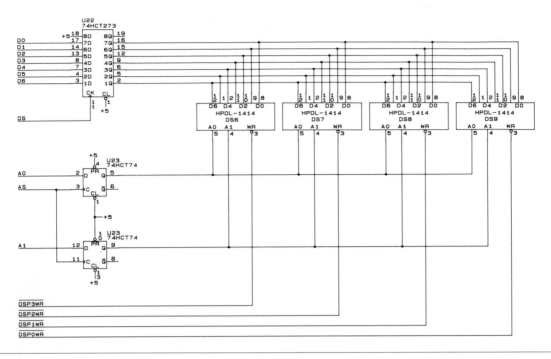

Figure 7.55. Design example 16-character alphanumeric display interface.

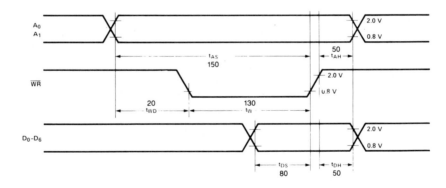

Figure 7.56.

HPDL-1414 display module timing. *(Courtesy of Hewlett-Packard Company)*

Although the timing calculations use only simple arithmetic, they are complex and can be difficult to follow. It is helpful to follow along in the timing diagram as you read the text, since the visual image is easier to grasp.

Figure 7.57 shows the timing diagram for the interface. The presentation of data to the displays is delayed from the start of S4 by:

The 68008 delay in asserting $\overline{DS}$ (55 ns)

The 74ALS04 delay in generating DS (11 ns)

The 74HCT273 propagation delay from clock (46 ns)

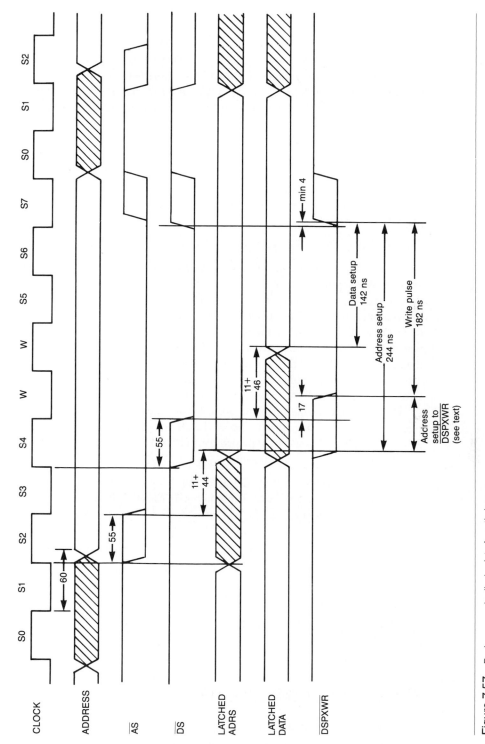

Figure 7.57. Design example display interface timing.

The soonest the write strobe can be negated is the minimum disable delay of the 74ALS138 (4 ns) after the end of S6. Thus, the minimum data setup time to the displays is 2.5 clock cycles minus the delays listed above plus 4 ns, or $250 - 55 - 11 - 46 + 4 = 142$ ns. This comfortably exceeds the 80-ns data setup time required.

The situation for the address is similar. $\overline{AS}$ is asserted one clock earlier than $\overline{DS}$ and the clock-to-data-out delay of the 74HCT74 is 44 ns, so the address setup time to the negation of $\overline{WR}$ is $350 - 55 - 11 - 44 + 4 = 244$ ns, well in excess of the 150 ns required.

The address setup time to the assertion of $\overline{WR}$ is trickier to calculate. The worst-case setup time is one clock cycle, minus the 68008's maximum delay from clock to the assertion of $\overline{AS}$, minus the maximum delay of the 74ALS04 that produces AS, minus the maximum delay of the 74HCT74 flip-flop, plus the 68008's *minimum* delay from clock to $\overline{DS}$, plus the *minimum* enable delay of the 74ALS138 that produces the display's $\overline{WR}$. This is

$$100 \text{ ns} - 55 \text{ ns} - 11 \text{ ns} - 44 \text{ ns} + 0 \text{ ns} + 5 \text{ ns} = -5 \text{ ns}$$

The negative result means that, in the worst-case situation, the address may change after the $\overline{WR}$ signal is asserted. However, this analysis is too conservative. The 68008's delays from the clock to the assertion of $\overline{AS}$ and $\overline{DS}$ are nominally the same, since the maximum for both is 55 ns. The minimum is not specified, so it must be assumed to be 0. The preceding analysis assumed that the delay for $\overline{AS}$ was 55 ns and the delay for $\overline{DS}$ was 0 ns. In this case, the two delays differ by 55 ns and the setup time is 25 ns less than is needed. Thus, if the two delays differ by less than 30 ns, then the required 20 ns setup time will be provided. There is no specification provided for this skew, but it is likely to be less than 10 or 15 ns. From one batch of 68008s to another, the clock-to-$\overline{AS}$ or -$\overline{DS}$ delay may change considerably, but for any particular IC the two delays are likely to be close. Thus, the timing of the circuit shown is acceptable. To be a little safer, the 74HCT74 could be replaced by a faster flip-flop such as a 74ALS74.

The minimum write pulse width is

> 2.5 clock cycles $-$ 68008 $\overline{DS}$ assertion delay
> $-$ 74ALS138 enable time $+$ minimum 74ALS138 disable time
> $= 250 \text{ ns} - 55 \text{ ns} - 17 \text{ ns} + 4 \text{ ns}$
> $= 182 \text{ ns}$

Thus, this easily exceeds the 130-ns requirement.

Since the data and address are present until the next time $\overline{DS}$ and $\overline{AS}$ are asserted, the hold times are easily met. The calculation of the guaranteed hold time is left as an exercise for the reader.

This display circuit can be easily modified for larger or smaller numbers of characters by simply using more or fewer display modules.

7.9   SUMMARY: DISPLAY SELECTION

Given the wide variety of display alternatives available, making an intelligent selection can be an intimidating task. The first step, as in any selection process, is to consider the needs of the application. The following factors should be considered:

Information to be displayed

Distance from which display must be read

Amount of power available

Size constraints

Operating environment

Cost constraints

The most basic consideration is the amount and type of information that must be displayed. For numeric displays, the number of digits required must be determined. For alphanumeric displays, the number of characters per line and the number of lines is the measure of information content. The font must also be selected. For small, minimum-cost displays that do not require lowercase characters, the 16-segment font is a good choice. When lowercase characters are required, dot-matrix fonts are necessary. The larger the matrix used, the better the character appearance, but the higher the system cost. The distance from which the display must be read determines the required character size.

For graphics displays, the number of pixels required horizontally and vertically must be determined, as well as the number of colors or shades of gray. If it is acceptable for the number of colors displayed simultaneously to be less than the total number of possible colors, a color lookup table can significantly reduce screen memory requirements.

The amount of power available is a very important consideration. In applications requiring minimum power consumption, LCDs are currently the only viable choice.

Size constraints are also important. CRT displays, for example, are limited to applications that can tolerate their depth. When CRTs are too large but comparable display capability is required, a selection must be made between vacuum fluorescent, gas discharge, liquid crystal, and electroluminescent displays.

The operating environment can also limit the options. LEDs, for example, can operate over a much wider temperature range than LCDs. On the other hand, LCDs are much more legible in bright sunlight. Thus, all the aspects of the operating environment must be considered, and the tradeoffs among different technologies can be complex.

Cost constraints can easily eliminate certain options. If cost is critical and size and power are not, then a CRT display is likely to win out over any flat-panel display of comparable capability. Cost tradeoffs change rapidly as the various technologies progress, so it is difficult to make many generalizations in this area that are valid for very long.

For small numeric displays, LEDs or LCDs are natural choices. The choice between the two is usually based on power availability and the ambient light in the application environment. The ability to inexpensively customize LCDs can sway the choice in their favor. LEDs, on the other hand, have better viewing characteristics except in very bright light, operate over a wider temperature range, and are generally more reliable.

For moderate-size multiline alphanumeric displays, LCDs, VF displays, and gas discharge displays are usually the prime candidates. Gas discharge displays are becoming less common in these applications. The comparison between LCDs and VF displays is similar to the preceding comparison between LCDs and LEDs, with VF displays taking the part of the LED displays.

For large alphanumeric or graphic displays, CRTs remain the most common choice. When size or power consumption is critical, then the various flat-panel technologies come into play. Large multiplexed LCDs are less expensive than other flat-panel displays and require little power, but display appearance is poor. AC plasma displays are available in very large arrays and are sharp and bright, but are expensive and require much more power. Also competing for these applications are electroluminescent, VF, and active-matrix liquid crystal displays.

To make a display selection, it is necessary to first eliminate those technologies that are unacceptable for one reason or another. The tradeoffs between the remaining technologies must then be carefully considered. Because of the rapid advancements in display technology, it is essential to have current literature and pricing information on the display types being considered. In some cases, the final choice ultimately becomes one of aesthetic preference.

7.10   EXERCISES

7.1.   Which of the following fonts can display uppercase alphanumerics?

   a.   7-segment
   b.   10-segment
   c.   16-segment
   d. 5×7 dot matrix
   e. 7×9 dot matrix
   f. 7×11 dot matrix

7.2.   Which of the fonts listed in Exercise 7.1 can display lowercase characters?

7.3.   A dot-matrix graphic display is built with individual LEDs. Each LED has an intensity of 1 mcd. The LEDs are mounted on 0.2-in. centers in each direction. What is the luminance of the display?

7.4.   One display has a luminance specification of 30 cd/m², another is 42 nits, and a third is 15 fL. Which is the brightest? The least bright?

7.5.   Which of the following is *not* an advantage of LED displays?

   a.   High reliability
   b.   Low cost for small numbers of digits
   c.   Low cost for large numbers of digits
   d.   Low-voltage operation
   e.   Low power consumption
   f.   Easily interfaced

7.6.   The interface for a multiplexed 12-character, 16-segment LED display has the following specifications: $V_{CE(sat)} = 0.2$ V for the segment driver and 0.3 V for the digit driver, power supply = 5.0 V, and average current = 5 mA per segment. Assume the forward voltage of each segment is 1.6 V.

   a.   What is the peak current through the segment driver?
   b.   What is the peak current through the digit driver?
   c.   What is the proper value for the limit resistor in series with each segment driver?

7.7. A 16-digit LED display is multiplexed under software control. A programmable counter/timer produces an interrupt at a rate sufficient to refresh each digit 60 times per second. The interrupt service routine changes the display to the next digit and requires 15 μs to execute. What percentage of the microprocessor's time is spent refreshing the display?

7.8. Draw a schematic diagram for the microprocessor interface for a 64-digit display using the DL-1414 module described in this chapter.

7.9. LCD displays require little power because:

    a. They are very efficient
    b. They produce a small amount of light
    c. They are passive
    d. They use CMOS technology

Which of the above statements is true?

7.10. Using a direct-drive display and H0438 LCD driver chips, draw a schematic for a 10-digit numeric display with decimal points.

7.11. Repeat Exercise 7.10, using a 7225 LCD controller and a multiplexed display. Using only one 7225 chip, can a biplexed display be used? A triplexed or quadriplexed display? What are the advantages and disadvantages of each possible implementation, including the one in Exercise 7.10?

7.12. The H0438 display driver uses a serial interface to the microprocessor. If an 8-bit parallel interface were used, what is the minimum number of additional pins that would be required on the H0438?

7.13. Which of the following is *not* an advantage of VF displays?

    a. High brightness
    b. Easily multiplexed
    c. Operates from low-voltage direct current
    d. Solid-state technology

7.14. What is the least expensive display type for a 2500-character alphanumeric display?

7.15. A CRT display system specification calls for a 640 × 480 display and a vertical rate of 60 Hz. Twenty percent of each scan line is used for blanking and retrace, and 30 line times are used for vertical blanking and retrace. Assuming a noninterlaced display, calculate the following parameters:

    a. Horizontal sweep frequency
    b. Line time
    c. Dot rate
    d. Minimum monitor bandwidth

7.16. Repeat Exercise 7.15 for an interlaced display. What are the advantages and disadvantages of using interlacing?

7.17. An alphanumeric CRT display is to display 44 lines of 132 characters each, using a 5 × 7 dot matrix in a 7 × 9 character cell. Assuming a noninterlaced display, a 60-Hz vertical rate, and the same blanking requirements as in Exercise 7.15, calculate the following parameters:

    a. Number of pixels required per scan line
    b. Number of active lines
    c. Horizontal rate
    d. Line time
    e. Dot rate
    f. Minimum monitor bandwidth

7.18. Repeat Exercise 7.17 for a 7×9 character matrix in a 9×14 cell.

7.19. Draw a block diagram of the counter chain for a CRT controller to implement the display in Exercise 7.18. Show the clock rate of the oscillator, the maximum count for each counter, and what the outputs of each counter are used for.

7.20. A CRT controller system is designed to allow the microprocessor access to the screen memory only during horizontal and vertical blanking. Assume television-standard scan rates, 25 percent blanking on each scan line, and 32 line times of vertical blanking. If each microprocessor access to the screen memory takes 1 μs, how many accesses can be performed per second?

7.21. A bit-mapped graphics system has a resolution of 1280×1024. Calculate the memory requirements for each of the following configurations:

    a. Monochrome, no gray levels
    b. Monochrome, 64 gray levels
    c. Color, 256 possible colors
    d. Color, 4096 possible colors
    e. Color, 16 colors from a palette of 4096
    f. Color, 256 colors from a palette of 16.8 million
    g. Color, 4096 colors from a palette of 16.8 million

7.22. Draw a block diagram of the video generation circuits for each of the displays in Exercise 7.21.

7.23. Modify the design example circuit to provide a 32-character display, using the same display modules. Be sure to provide adequate address decoding for the keyboard interface (see Chap. 6) as well as for the displays.

7.24. Calculate the address and data hold times for the design example display interface.

7.11 SELECTED BIBLIOGRAPHY

Periodicals

Electronic Display World, published by Stanford Resources, Inc., 1095 Branham Lane, Suite 201, San Jose, CA 95136. A monthly newsletter covering display technology and markets. Provides projections of display markets and analyses of display research. Stanford Resources also publishes a variety of specialized reports on display technologies.

Information Display, published by the Society for Information Display (SID), 8055 West Manchester Ave., Suite 615, Playa Del Rey, CA 90293. SID is an organization devoted to displays and related topics. In addition to the monthly journal, proceedings are published quarterly.

The annual conference is the premier meeting for information on state-of-the-art displays, and digests and copies of lecture notes are available from the society.

General

Bylander, E. G. *Electronic Displays,* New York: McGraw-Hill, 1979. A technical review of all common display types. Describes the basic technologies, although it is somewhat dated.

Conrac Corp. *Raster Graphics Handbook,* 2d ed., New York: Van Nostrand Reinhold, 1985. A useful book written by a manufacturer of CRT displays. Briefly describes all common display technologies, with emphasis on graphic CRT displays.

Hess, Kenneth L. "Picking the Best Display: An Easy-to-Follow Guide," *Electronic Design,* Aug. 19, 1982, pp. 139–146. Reviews the characteristics of the basic display types and the requirements of various applications.

Masten, Larry B., and Billy R. Masten. *Understanding Optronics,* Dallas: Texas Instruments, 1981. A very readable introduction to display principles. Also covers light detectors and lasers.

Newman, William M., and Robert F. Sproull. *Principles of Interactive Computer Graphics,* 2d ed., New York: McGraw-Hill, 1973. A classic text covering the algorithms for manipulating graphics data.

Refioglu, Ilhan H. (ed.). *Electronic Displays,* New York: IEEE Press, 1983. An extensive collection of articles on display technology.

Sherr, Sol. *Video and Digital Electronic Displays,* New York: Wiley, 1982. Covers human factors in display systems, all major display types, and the measurement of display performance. This text is oriented toward the end user, and technology and interfacing details are somewhat sketchy.

―――. *Electronic Displays,* New York: Wiley, 1980. A technical description of all common display technologies. Covers the detailed physics and chemistry of display operation.

Tannas, Lawrence E., Jr. (ed.). *Flat-Panel Displays and CRTs,* New York: Van Nostrand Reinhold, 1985. A comprehensive, in-depth description of display technologies.

The Report Store. *The Design of Interactive Computer Displays: A Guide to the Select Literature,* Lawrence, KS, 1985. An extensive (and expensive) annotated bibliography covering a wide range of topics, including human factors, display engineering, cognitive psychology, and standards. A second volume covers related periodicals.

Flat-Panel Displays

Peterson, Robert E. Jr. "Flat-Panel Displays," *EDN,* Nov. 24, 1983, pp. 102–127. A survey of commercially available flat-panel displays and interfacing circuits.

Texas Instruments. *Display Driver Handbook,* Dallas. In addition to data sheets for TI's display driver ICs, this handbook includes descriptions of the technology and interfacing of vacuum-fluorescent, gas-discharge, and electroluminescent displays.

LED Displays

Hewlett-Packard Optoelectronics Division. *Optoelectronics Application Manual,* New York: McGraw-Hill, 1982. An extensive text on the theory and application of LED displays. Also covers optoisolators, photodiodes, and related subjects.

Hewlett-Packard. *Application Note 1005: Operational Considerations for LED Lamps and Display Devices,* Palo Alto, CA. Describes current, power, and thermal calculations for optimum display operation.

Liquid Crystal Displays

Brody, Peter, et al. "Active Matrix Addressing Enhances Flat Panels," *Electronics,* July 12, 1984, pp. 113–117. Describes Panelvision's active matrix panel, one of the first commercially available.

NEC. *μPD7225 Intelligent Alphanumeric LCD Controller/Driver Technical Manual,* Mountain View, CA. A detailed description of the operation of this flexible LCD controller. Includes drive waveforms and voltage calculations for various multiplexing levels.

Peterson, Robert. "High-Capacity, -Contrast LCDs Become Viable CRT Alternatives," *EDN,* July 26, 1984, pp. 132–144. A survey of available large dot-matrix LCD panels.

Vacuum Fluorescent and Gas Discharge Displays

Lieberman, David. "Vacuum Fluorescent Displays Flex Their Muscles," *Electronic Products,* Apr. 20, 1984, pp. 51–54. A survey of commercial VF displays.

———. "Plasma Display Tradeoffs," *Electronic Products,* Nov. 17, 1983, pp. 65–72. Describes the various gas discharge display technologies and the advantages and disadvantages of each. Includes list of display manufacturers.

CRT Displays

Kane, Gerry. *CRT Controller Handbook,* Berkeley, CA: Osborne/McGraw-Hill, 1980. Describes principles of CRT controller operation and five common CRT controller chips.

Leibson, Steven H. "Graphics Controller ICs," *EDN,* Feb. 6, 1986, pp. 104–118. Includes listings of CRT controllers, graphics processors, video RAMs, and video D/A converters.

Murray, John, and George Alexy. *AP-32: CRT Terminal Design Using the Intel 8275 and 8279,* Santa Clara, CA: Intel, 1977. Includes a good overview of basic raster-scan CRT operation and controller functions. Describes an application of Intel's 8275 CRT controller with internal row buffers.

Rogers, William. *AN-822: The Video Display Generator as a Color Television Interface,* Phoenix: Motorola, 1981. Describes the application of Motorola's 6847 video display generator chip.

Scalea, Robert S., and William R. Stronge. "Raster Graphics Systems Use Lookup Tables to Meet Many Needs," *Computer Technology Review,* Spring-Summer 1982, pp. 123–133. A good description of the use of color lookup tables.

Texas Instruments. *TMS9118/9128/9129 Data Manual,* Dallas. A complete description of the 9118 family of video display generators.

Volk, Andrew M. "Build a Workstation that Displays a Greater Variety of Characters," *EDN,* May 3, 1984, pp. 297–314. Describes the use of Intel's high-end alphanumeric CRT display controller, the 82730.

Wise, Jeffery L., and Henryk Szejnwald. "Display Controller Simplifies Design of Sophisticated Graphics Terminals," *Electronics,* Apr. 7, 1981, pp. 153–157. Describes NEC's 7220 graphics controller chip.

Wright, Maury. "Color Monitors," *EDN,* May 31, 1984, pp. 107–123. A survey of color CRT monitor technology and performance. Includes a list of manufacturers.

Yonezawa, Hiroshi, et al. "CRT Chip Controls Bit-Mapped Graphics and Alphanumerics," *Electronic Design,* June 14, 1982, pp. 247–256. Describes Hitachi's sophisticated graphics controller chip, the HD63484.

CHAPTER 8

DATA COMMUNICATION

8.1 INTRODUCTION

Data communication is the transmission of encoded information. It generally refers to *serial* data transmission, in which one data bit is transmitted at a time via a single signal wire or communication channel (such as a telephone line). While parallel data connections (which have one wire per bit) can also be considered to be data communication systems, the larger number of wires required restricts them to relatively short distances. One standard parallel bus, the IEEE-488 GPIB, is designed for communication between systems and is covered in Sec. 8.5.

When transmitting data for tens of feet, the use of a single wire instead of eight results in a small savings in cost and bulk. When the transmission distance is thousands of feet, the savings are significant. And when the data must be transmitted via telephone lines, serial communication becomes imperative; using eight telephone lines to send parallel bytes of data is most impractical.

There are several aspects to data communications interfaces. Since the microprocessor's buses are parallel, data must be converted to serial form at the transmitter and then back to parallel at the receiver. The receiver must determine the location of the bit and byte boundaries. These tasks are performed by the serial interface circuitry connected to the microprocessor system.

If the data is to be sent over a reasonably short distance over a dedicated line (i.e., not a telephone line), then it can be transmitted directly in digital form. Various standards exist for logic levels and signal definitions used for digital data transmission, such as RS-232 and others described later in this chapter.

Digital signals have fast rise and fall times and can be in one state for a long period of time. This implies a very wide frequency spectrum, from dc to harmonics of the bit rate. Telephone lines cannot transmit dc levels or high frequencies. Thus, if the data is to be sent via a telephone line, it is necessary to convert the digital signals to an analog form that can be transmitted in a relatively narrow bandwidth. The circuit that performs this function is called a *modem,* which is a contraction of modulator-demodulator.

Once the basic task of getting the bits from one location to another is accomplished, the receiver must know how to interpret the data and possibly detect errors. This is the function of data communication *protocols,* of which there is a wide variety to choose from.

The data communication techniques described in this chapter assume a point-to-point connection between two devices. A more complex subject is computer networks, which allow multiple computers to communicate. While the basic principles are the same, more complex protocols are required for networks.

This chapter discusses each of these aspects of data communication. Since this is a very large topic, the emphasis is placed on the type of communications most common in microprocessor applications. The discussion of the interface to microprocessor systems is toward the end of the chapter, so the reader will have the background to fully understand the functions that must be performed.

8.2   DATA COMMUNICATION BASICS

8.2.1   Information Coding

Information sent between systems may be in any of several forms. It is often alphanumeric information, such as text in a natural language (such as English) or a programming language. It can also be data representing a machine code program, a graphic image, or numeric information. Alphanumeric information is most commonly transmitted by using the ASCII code (American Standard Code for Information Interchange), which is a 7-bit code. Table 8.1 lists the ASCII code assignments. Note that in addition to the alphanumeric characters, there are a number of *control characters,* represented by codes 00 to 1F (hex). Several uses for these characters are described later in this chapter.

Most IBM equipment (other than personal computers) uses an 8-bit code called *EBCDIC* (extended binary-coded decimal interchange code). Older teletype systems use a 5-bit code called *Baudot,* which is not an acronym but is named after Emile Baudot, a pioneer in telegraphy. Some other special-purpose systems and systems outside the United States use other codes. In this text, we assume the use of ASCII, although other codes could be used.

Binary information can be transmitted without coding. However, many systems are designed primarily to transmit ASCII data and, since ASCII is a 7-bit code, may not be able to transmit arbitrary 8-bit data bytes. Even though the interface hardware is usually capable of 8-bit transmission, the interface software provided as part of the operat-

Table 8.1   ASCII Codes

Second hex digit	First hex digit							
	0	1	2	3	4	5	6	7
0	NUL	DLE	SP	0	@	P		p
1	SOH	DC1	!	1	A	Q	a	q
2	STX	DC2	"	2	B	R	b	r
3	ETX	DC3	#	3	C	S	c	s
4	EOT	DC4	$	4	D	T	d	t
5	ENQ	NAK	%	5	E	U	e	u
6	ACK	SYN	&	6	F	V	f	v
7	BEL	ETB	'	7	G	W	g	w
8	BS	CAN	(	8	H	X	h	x
9	HT	EM	)	9	I	Y	i	y
A	LF	SUB	*	:	J	Z	j	z
B	VT	ESC	+	;	K	[	k	{
C	FF	FS	,	<	L	\	l	|
D	CR	GS	–	=	M	]	m	}
E	SO	RS	.	>	N	^	n	~
F	SI	US	/	?	O	_	o	DEL

Definitions of control symbols

NUL	Null	DLE	Data link escape
SOH	Start of heading	DC1	Device control 1
STX	Start of text	DC2	Device control 2
ETX	End of text	DC3	Device control 3
EOT	End of tape	DC4	Device control 4
ENQ	Enquiry	NAK	Negative acknowledge
ACK	Acknowledge	SYN	Synchronize
BEL	Bell	ETB	End of transmitted block
BS	Backspace	CAN	Cancel
HT	Horizontal tab	EM	End of medium
LF	Line feed	SUB	Substitute
VT	Vertical tab	ESC	Escape
FF	Form feed	FS	File separator
CR	Carriage return	GS	Group separator
SO	Shift out	RS	Record separator
SI	Shift in	US	Unit separator
SP	Space	DEL	Delete

ing system may not support such transmission. One common solution to this problem is to represent each byte with two ASCII characters that form the hexadecimal representation for the byte. For example, the byte 11000101 (hex C5) would be transmitted as the ASCII code for the letter C (43 hex) followed by the ASCII code for the digit 5 (35 hex). This is not particularly efficient, since two characters must be sent for each byte, but has some advantages. Most importantly, it allows use of hardware and software that is designed to process ASCII codes. If binary data is transmitted in a straight binary format, it cannot be printed or displayed on a device accepting ASCII input, and binary data patterns that correspond to ASCII control codes may have undesirable effects.

The transmission of graphic information is considerably more complicated. Transmission of the complete bit map representing an image is rarely desirable, since the number of bits can be very large. In addition, bit map information cannot be readily scaled to other resolutions. One protocol that has been developed for transmitting graphic information is the *North American Presentation Level Protocol Syntax (NAPLPS,* pronounced "nap-lips"). This protocol encodes graphic information as a geometric description of the aspects of the image, and allows graphic images to be represented by a relatively small amount of data. NAPLPS is commonly used in videotex systems.

8.2.2   Terminology

In data communications parlance, the terms *mark* and *space* are used to indicate the logic 1 and logic 0 levels of a signal, respectively. Depending on the logic levels used, either may be the more positive level.

A system that can transmit data in only one direction is called a *simplex* system. If data can be sent in either direction, but not in both directions simultaneously, it is called *half-duplex*. A *full-duplex* system (sometimes called simply *duplex*) can send data in both directions simultaneously.

The basic measure of the rate of data transfer is *bits per second (bits/s,* or *bps)*. A related measure is *baud rate*. The baud rate is a measure of the number of signalling units per second. When simple modulation techniques are used, bits per second and baud are equal; for each bit, there is one possible state change of the signal line. However, when complex techniques such as phase modulation are used, more than one bit can be encoded in each state change. Thus, each signalling unit (change of state) can transmit more than one bit of data, and the bit rate is higher than the baud rate. This is of interest only in the design of high-speed modems; from the user's point of view, the important specification is bits per second. Be aware, however, that the two terms are often used interchangeably but are not equivalent in all cases.

8.2.3   Asynchronous Data Communication

Figure 8.1 shows the waveform for the asynchronous transmission of one character. Each bit is transmitted for one bit time, which is the reciprocal of the bit rate. When no data is being transmitted, the signal is in the *marking,* or logic 1, state. At the beginning of each character, the signal is set to the logic 0 state for one bit time. This is the *start bit,* which provides a timing reference for the receiver. After the start bit, each data bit is output for one bit time, usually starting with the least-significant bit. The number of data bits is commonly seven to correspond with the ASCII code, but five, six, or eight bits can also be used. Parity can be used for error detection, and if it is used, the parity bit follows the last data bit. After all the data and parity bits, one or more *stop bits* are sent. The stop bit is simply a bit forced to the mark state.

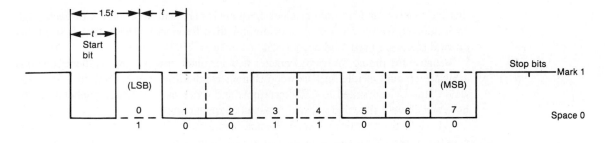

Figure 8.1. Asynchronous serial data waveform.

The stop bit performs two functions. First, it provides a guaranteed minimum delay between characters. This was important for early electromechanical transmitters and receivers (such as teletypes), which required two stop bits for the encoding wheels to rotate back to the start position. Most modern systems require only one stop bit. The second, and most important, function of the stop bit is that it, in combination with the start bit, guarantees that there will be a transition from mark to space at the start of every character. If either the start or stop bit were deleted and two successive characters were transmitted, there would be no transition at the start of the second character for certain character sequences.

For the transmitter, producing the serial data stream is a simple process. It simply outputs each of the required bits, including start and stop bits, for one bit time. The receiver, however, has a more difficult task. In *asynchronous* transmission, which is the type described here, the receiver and transmitter have independent clocks. Thus, the receiver must determine the location of each bit boundary. Typically, the receiver has a clock at 16, 32, or 64 times the bit rate. Although this clock is asynchronous with the transmitter's clock, the frequency must be within a few percent of the transmitter's clock.

To find the first bit cell, the receiver waits for a mark-to-space transition, which occurs at the beginning of the start bit. Most serial receivers include *false start bit detection,* a verification that the line is in the space condition in the middle of the start bit, which is one-half bit time following the mark-to-space transition. This prevents a noise glitch from triggering the receiver. The receiver samples the data line to capture the first data bit 1½ times after the mark-to-space transition, which should place it close to the middle of the data bit. By using a clock at 16 times the bit rate, the receiver can count 24 clocks after the starting edge to find the center of the first data bit. Use of a 32 or 64 times clock provides even more accurate timing. After the first data bit is read, the receiver samples the signal once each bit time until all data bits have been read.

Thus, the timing for data reception is derived from the edge that marks the beginning of the start bit. From that point on, the location of bit cells depends on the receiver's clock being close to the transmitter's clock frequency. Since the data can be sampled anywhere within the bit time, some error in the bit rate clock can be tolerated (typically 3 to 5 percent). (Note, however, that the system's tolerance to slow signal transitions or signal distortion is decreased as the bit rate error increases.) To ensure that the receiver and transmitter clock frequencies are within 3 percent of each other, each must be within ± 1.5 percent of the intended frequency. Typically, crystal-based clock circuits are used, and accuracy is better than ± 0.1 percent.

Because the timing for each character is determined independently, there can be an arbitrary amount of idle time between characters; the line simply remains in the mark state. This is well suited to CRT terminals and other user interface applications that have a relatively slow and unevenly spaced character stream.

When the transmitter may send characters at a rate faster than the receiver can process them, the receiver must be able to tell the transmitter to stop transmitting temporarily. This is called *flow control* and is commonly implemented with the *XON/XOFF* protocol. Two ASCII control characters, called DC1 (or XON) and DC3 (or XOFF), are used to start and stop transmission. When the receiver cannot accept any more data, it sends an XOFF character. In response, the transmitter ceases transmitting until it receives an XON character. For an example of an application of this protocol, see Sec. 6.7.2. (Pressing control-S on a standard CRT terminal or computer keyboard sends XOFF, and pressing control-Q sends XON, so these keys are often used to start and stop the display.) Hardware flow control, using handshake signals instead of control codes, can also be used and is described in Sec. 8.3.1.

8.2.4 Synchronous Data Communication

Asynchronous data transmission does not make maximum use of the available signal bandwidth, since at least two out of every ten bits (the start and stop bits) carry no information. Thus, 20 percent of the bandwidth of the communications link is wasted. In theory, the efficiency could be increased by placing more bits between each pair of start and stop bits. However, since all timing is based on the first transition, any error in the clock frequency accumulates until another stop-start sequence occurs. The clock frequencies of the transmitter and receiver would therefore have to be closely matched. Another problem with asynchronous communication is that high data rates are not practical, since the receiver typically requires a clock of at least 16 times the bit rate.

The solution to these drawbacks is to use *synchronous* communication, in which the clock is transmitted along with the data. The clock can be transmitted as a separate signal, or a *self-clocking* encoding scheme can be used that allows the clock to be extracted from the received data (encoding techniques are described in Sec. 8.2.6). Whichever technique is used, the result is that the receiver is provided with a bit rate clock that is synchronous with the transmitter's clock. This eliminates the need for start and stop bits, as well as the need for a receiver clock that is a multiple of the bit rate. Thus, higher data rates can be achieved.

Figure 8.2 shows the timing differences between asynchronous and synchronous signals. In an asynchronous system, there is always at least one start bit and one stop bit between each pair of characters. When there is no data to be transmitted, the signal remains in the mark state. In a synchronous system, no idle time between characters is allowed. When there is no data to be sent, a *sync* character is transmitted. This character carries no information but maintains the receiver's character synchronization.

Because its primary advantage is the high data rate that can be achieved, synchronous communication is usually used for communication between computers. Several protocols have been defined for use in synchronous communication systems. These pro-

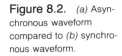

Figure 8.2. (a) Asynchronous waveform compared to (b) synchronous waveform.

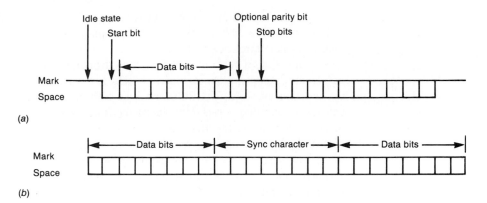

Opening flag (F)	Address field (A)	Control field (C)	Information field (I)	Frame check sequence (FCS)	Closing flag (F)
0 1 1 1 1 1 1 0	8 bits	8 bits	Variable length (only in I frames)	16 bits	0 1 1 1 1 1 1 0

Figure 8.3. SDLC frame format.

tocols provide a method of addressing a specific computer in a network to receive a message and also allow errors to be detected and retransmission requested if an error occurs.

8.2.5 SDLC Protocol

One of the most common protocols is IBM's Synchronous Data Link Control (SDLC). This protocol is widely used in the United States, and is very similar to the international standard protocol called High-level Data Link Control (HDLC). It has built-in mechanisms for checking the integrity of data received and requesting retransmission when an error occurs. SDLC networks consist of a single *primary* station and up to 256 *secondary* stations. The following description is intended to convey only the basic concepts of SDLC operation, not the details of the protocol. For a fully detailed description, refer to the IBM document listed in the Selected Bibliography at the end of this chapter.

The basic unit of transmission in SDLC is a *frame,* as shown in Fig. 8.3. Each frame begins and ends with a *flag* pattern of 01111110. These flags mark the boundaries of the frame. For successive frames, the ending flag of one frame serves as the starting flag of the next.

The address field identifies the secondary station. Depending on the direction of transmission, this may be the sending or the receiving station. Secondary stations cannot communicate directly with each other; all transfers are between the primary station and one of the secondary stations.

The control field indicates the type of frame. Data is transferred by using the *information* frame type. Other types of frames, called *supervisory* and *nonsequenced,* provide network control functions.

The information field contains the actual data to be transmitted. This field can be of any length. Following the information field is the *frame check sequence,* which is a cyclic redundancy check (CRC) for all the information in the frame. The transmitter calculates this value as it is transmitting the frame, and the receiver recalculates it during reception. If the calculated and received values match, then there is a very high probability that the data is correct. If an error occurs, the receiver detects a mismatch in the CRC and ignores the information in the frame.

Each information frame carries a sequence number in the control field. This allows the receiver to determine if any frames are missed and to identify a specific frame to be retransmitted. The control field also includes a bit called *poll/final* (P/F). When one station is sending a series of frames to another station, it sets the poll/final bit to 0 in all frames except the last, in which it is set to 1. When the receiving station receives this frame, it responds with a supervisory frame that indicates if all the frames were received without error, and if not, it specifies which frames should be retransmitted. The transmitting station must keep all frames in its internal buffer until they are acknowledged, in case they must be retransmitted.

Note that there is no byte count or bit count transmitted in the frame. Thus, the only way the receiver can identify the end of the frame is by recognizing the ending flag. It then knows that the 16 bits before the flag were the frame check sequence and that the bits before that were the information. This creates a potential problem: what if the data in the information field contained the pattern 01111110, the same as the ending flag?

The solution to this problem is a technique called *zero bit insertion.* When transmitting the information frame, the transmitter constantly looks for five ones in a row. If it finds five in a row, then it inserts a zero into the transmitted bit stream after the fifth 1. Thus, the transmitter will never allow six ones to be transmitted in a row unless it is sending a flag. The receiver strips out the extra zeros; whenever it receives five ones followed by a zero, it deletes the zero.

8.2.6   Digital Encoding Techniques

Basic serial data encoding, in which the signal remains at the state for each bit during the bit time, is called *non-return-to-zero (NRZ),* since the signal level does not return to zero after each bit. While this is the most common technique for asynchronous communication, it is not self-clocking; it is not possible to derive a bit rate clock from an NRZ signal. In addition, an NRZ signal can be in the same state for an indefinite period of time, so dc coupling is required.

For an encoding method to be *self-clocking,* there must be guaranteed signal transitions regardless of the data pattern transmitted. There need not be transitions at every bit cell boundary; as long as there are transitions every bit or two, a phase-locked loop (PLL) can be used to recover the clock information.

One example of an alternative encoding method is *NRZI.* (This is generally said to stand for non-return-to-zero inverted, although that is not a good description; it is not the inverse of NRZ.) Figure 8.4 shows a single data pattern in several different encod-

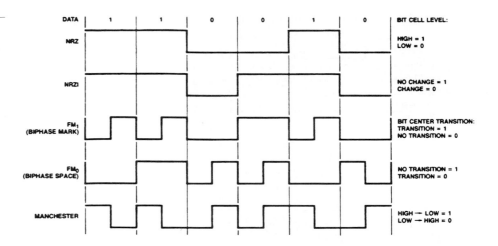

Figure 8.4. Data encoding methods. *(Courtesy of Advanced Micro Devices, Inc.)*

ings. NRZI encoding uses a transition at the start of a cell to indicate a 0, and no transition to indicate a 1. Thus, it is not completely self-clocking; a continuous string of ones would create no transitions.

Manchester encoding is an example of a fully self-clocking encoding technique. There is a transition at the center of every bit cell; a high-to-low transition indicates a 1, and a low-to-high transition indicates a 0. Transitions are used at the bit cell boundaries when necessary to provide the correct transition at the next bit cell center. Thus, there is always one transition, and sometimes two, per bit time. This makes clock extraction simple and limits the signal bandwidth. However, encoding and decoding Manchester signals is more difficult than for NRZ signals.

There are numerous variations on these encoding techniques. *Biphase* encoding uses a transition at every bit cell boundary. The presence or absence of a transition at the center of each bit cell determines the state of the bit. A transition at the center of the cell indicates a 1, and no transition at the bit cell center indicates a 0. The opposite polarity can also be used, with a transition at the bit cell center indicating a 0.

8.2.7 Modems

Modems are used when digital data must be transmitted over long distances or via an analog medium, such as a telephone line. Figure 8.5 shows a block diagram of a basic modem. Serial digital data to be transmitted is modulated, filtered, and amplified for transmission. Analog data received is amplified, filtered, and demodulated to produce a serial digital data signal. Modems often include ring detectors so they can automatically answer a telephone call and dialing tone *(dual-tone multifrequency, or DTMF)* generators for originating a call. In addition to the serial data inputs and outputs, there are several handshake signals for control purposes, which are discussed in Sec. 8.3.1.

The simplest form of modulation is *frequency-shift keying,* or *FSK*, in which one frequency represents a 0 and another a 1. Figure 8.6 shows examples of FSK and phase encoding. *Phase encoding*, also called *phase-shift keying (PSK)*, uses only a single

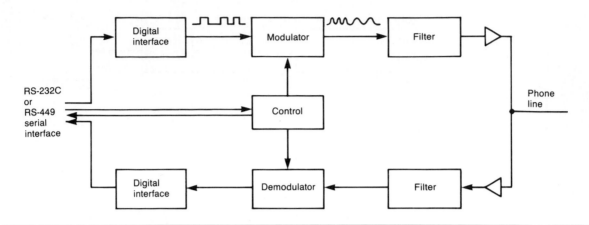

Figure 8.5. Modem block diagram.

Figure 8.6. FSK and phase modulation waveforms.

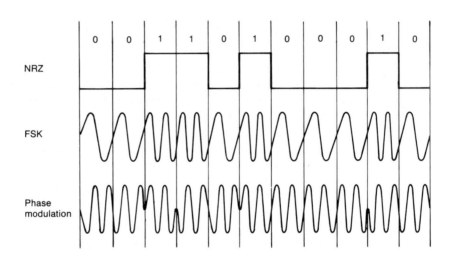

frequency, and phase shifts convey the data. Phase encoding requires less analog bandwidth for a given bit rate (or can transmit a higher bit rate in a given bandwidth) but is more complex to implement. In the waveform shown in the figure, the bit rate is equal to the carrier frequency, a 0 is encoded as no phase change, and a 1 is encoded as a 180° phase change.

The limited bandwidth of telephone lines (300 Hz to 3 kHz for a standard dial-up line) restricts the rate at which data can be transmitted. Half-duplex modems can transmit in only one direction at a time and thus can use all the available bandwidth. Full-duplex modems, however, must transmit in both directions simultaneously. Unless two separate lines are used, the bandwidth must be shared. Each end transmits using different frequencies. To identify which end should transmit using which frequencies, a distinction is made between the originating modem and the answering modem.

The oldest modem standard in common use is the Bell 103, which uses FSK modulation to transmit up to 300 bps, full-duplex. It uses the following frequency assignments:

Originate Modem: 0 = 1070 Hz   Answer Modem: 0 = 2025 Hz
                   1 = 1270 Hz   1 = 2225 Hz

Each modem contains receiver filters that allow only the signals from the other modem to be received, so the modem is not confused by its own transmissions.

Another common standard is Bell 212A, which provides 1200 bps full-duplex operation. Note that it is not possible to use the Bell 103 FSK encoding for higher bit rates because there must be enough time in each bit period to transmit one cycle of the modulation frequency so that the receiver can detect it reliably. Bell 212A-type modems include a 103-compatible FSK mode for 300 bps communication. For 1200 bps operation, Bell 212A-compatible modems use *dibit phase modulation*. The transmit carrier frequency is 1200 Hz for the originate modem and 2400 Hz for the answering modem. The term *dibit* refers to the fact that two bits are encoded in each phase shift. Figure 8.7 shows the four phase shift angles used in 212A-type modems and an example waveform with a 2400-Hz carrier. The baud rate of the phase-encoded signal is the rate of the phase changes. Since two data bits are encoded into a single phase change, the 1200-bps data stream produces a 600-baud analog signal.

The Bell 103 and 212A standards described above are the most common for use on dial-up voice-grade telephone lines. The standards were set by Bell Telephone, and Bell and others make modems that follow these standards. There are also some non-Bell standards in fairly wide use, most notably the Vadic 3400 (which is similar to Bell 212A in its capabilities). Modems operating at 2400 baud generally follow the CCITT V.22 bis standard. Modems operating at 4800 to 9600 baud and even higher are also available but are expensive and more error-prone when using standard telephone lines.

Some modem standards are intended for use with dedicated telephone lines that are not part of the dial-up network but are permanent connections between two points. These can be more economical when long, frequent communications between two fixed locations are required. Dedicated lines are often four-wire lines, with one pair for each direction. This allows bit rates to be increased for full-duplex operation, since it is not necessary to share the bandwidth. Dedicated lines are also available with wider bandwidths for very high-speed data transmission.

An *acoustic coupler* is a modem that connects acoustically to a standard telephone handset, using a microphone and speaker in rubber cups. They were commonly used when non-Bell equipment was not allowed to be connected to the telephone network. As a result of the landmark 1968 "Carterphone" lawsuit and subsequent actions, any device that passes the FCC certification procedure, as described in the FCC's Part 68 regulation, can be connected directly to the telephone network. Since these court decisions, acoustic couplers have become relatively rare.

Figure 8.7. Bell 212A phase modulation dibit definitions and waveform for 10001101 bit pattern.

Dibit	Phase shift
00	90°
01	0°
10	180°
11	270°

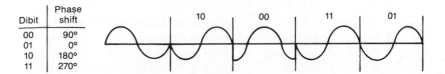

Most modern modems are "intelligent" and are microprocessor-controlled. In addition to simply sending and receiving data, such modems have the ability to respond to commands from the host computer and automatically connect, disconnect, and generate dialing tones on the telephone line. Since there are no signals in the RS-232C standard to allow the host computer to initiate such actions, a software protocol is used. The most widely used protocol, first used by Hayes Microcomputer Products in their Smartmodems, is commonly called the *AT protocol* because the command strings sent to the modem begin with the ASCII characters AT.

8.3   DATA COMMUNICATION STANDARDS

There are many types of standards for data communication. We are concerned here only with *physical-level* standards, which specify the voltage levels and signal definitions for getting bits from one place to another. Higher-level standards, such as Bisync, SDLC, and X.25, are concerned with defining the bits as packets of information and include error-checking protocols and other control functions.

This section describes five data communication standards: RS-232, RS-422, RS-423, RS-449, and RS-485. These standards are defined by the Electronic Industries Association (EIA), which publishes the official definitions. These are the most widely used standards in the United States. There are also international standards, administered by the Comité Consulatif International Téléphonique et Télégraphique (CCITT). Most of the EIA standards described here have an equivalent CCITT standard. The CCITT names for these standards begin with "V."; for example, the equivalent for RS-232 is V.24.

The following descriptions cover only the basic functions and applications of these standards. For a complete description of these standards, refer to the EIA standards documents or the texts listed in the Selected Bibliography at the end of this chapter.

8.3.1   RS-232

RS-232C is the most widely used data communication standard for short distances and moderate data rates. (The "C" indicates that this is the third revision of the standard; earlier versions are no longer used, so the C is sometimes dropped, as it is in most of this text. "RS" stands for "recommended standard.") RS-232 was originally intended for relatively short connections between data terminal equipment (DTE), such as computers or terminals, and data communication equipment (DCE), such as modems. (DCE was redefined in later standards to stand for "data circuit-terminating equipment.") Figure 8.8 shows the basic communication link for which the standard was intended, consisting of two DTEs communicating via DCEs connecting to a transmission line.

RS-232 is both an electrical and a functional standard; that is, it specifies both the electrical levels used to represent a 1 and a 0 and the function of each signal in the interface.

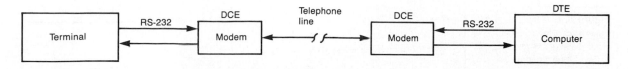

Figure 8.8. Standard RS-232 configuration: terminal connected to computer via modems and telephone line.

Table 8.2   Electrical Characteristics of Common EIA Standards

Specification	RS-232C	RS-423A	RS-422A	RS-485
Mode of operation	Single-ended	Single-ended	Differential	Differential
No. of drivers and receivers	1 driver,	1 driver,	1 driver,	32 drivers,
allowed on one line	1 receiver	10 receivers	10 receivers	32 receivers
Maximum cable length	50 ft	4000 ft	4000 ft	4000 ft
Maximum data rate	20 kbps	100 kbps	10 Mbps	10 Mbps
Max. voltage under any				
condition	±25 V	±6 V	−0.25 to 6 V	−7 to 12 V
Driver output signal:				
Minimum	±5 V	±3.6 V	±2 V	±1.5 V
Maximum	±15 V	±6 V	±5 V	±5 V
Driver load	3 to 7 kΩ	450 Ω min	100 Ω min	54 Ω min
Max. driver output current				
(high-impedance state):				
Power on	NA	NA	NA	±100 μA
Power off	$V_{max}/300$ Ω	±100 μA	±100 μA	±100 μA
Output slew rate	30 V/μs max	*	NA	NA
Receiver input voltage				
range	±15 V	±12 V	±7 V	−7 to 12 V
Receiver input sensitivity	±3V	±200 mV	±200 mV	±200 mV
Receiver input resistance	3 to 7 kΩ	4 kΩ min	4 kΩ min	12 kΩ min

*min depends on bit rate; max not specified

Electrical Characteristics of RS-232

Table 8.2 lists the basic electrical characteristics of RS-232 signals, along with the characteristics for other standards described later in this section. The signals are *unbalanced* (also called *single-ended*) as opposed to *balanced* (also called *differential*), which means that each signal requires only one wire and all signals are referenced to a common ground. The standard specifies a maximum cable length of 50 ft, but much longer cables can be used in many applications. The maximum data rate is 20 kbps; the highest standard bit rate that is used is 19.2 kbps. (The most common data rates are 300, 1200, 2400, 4800, 9600, and 19,200 bps.)

The electrical levels used in RS-232 are shown graphically in Fig. 8.9. The transmitter must produce a level between −5 and −15 V for a 1, and +5 to +15 V for a 0. The receiver must respond to a signal more negative than −3 V as a 1, and more positive than +3 V as a 0. Thus, there can be a voltage drop (or noise) of up to 2 V, even if

Figure 8.9. RS-232
signal levels. Noise margin
includes margin for re-
sistive voltage drops in
cable.

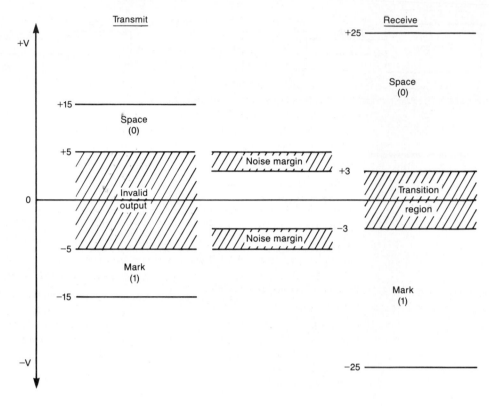

the transmitter is at the minimum output voltage, without any errors. The range from
+3 to −3 V is called the *transition region* and is an invalid level. Although the highest voltage allowed under normal use is ±15 V, all components are required to tolerate
voltages as high as ±25 V. Many systems use a voltage swing of ±12 V. The exact
voltages are not important and are often determined by the power supply voltages
available.

Another important specification is slew rate. The transitions of the signals must be
controlled to limit crosstalk. If very fast transitions are allowed to occur, excessive
noise is induced in adjacent wires. On the other hand, if the transition time is too slow,
the signal will not be stable long enough during each bit time.

RS-232 Drivers and Receivers
A variety of driver and receiver ICs are available for converting TTL levels to RS-232,
and vice versa. One common pair is the 1488 quad driver and 1489A quad receiver.
Figure 8.10 shows the pinout for the 1488 driver. The 1488 requires supply voltages of
±9 to ±15 V. Only the inputs are TTL-level-compatible; the output voltage swing is
determined by the power supply voltages. Three of the four drivers have two inputs,
and the fourth (due to pin limitations) has only one. The two inputs of each driver are
typically tied together, since they are used primarily as level translators and not as logic
gates.

The output slew rate of the 1488 is much faster than allowed by the RS-232 standard. To slow down the transitions, a capacitor is added from each output to ground. A 300-pF capacitive load will limit the slew rate to the specified maximum of 30 V/μs. However, this capacitive load includes both the slew rate limiting capacitor and the capacitance of the cable attached to the output. The value of the output capacitor required therefore depends on the length of cable attached to the driver. Cable capacitance depends on the construction of the cable and is typically 10 to 20 pF/ft. Thus, a cable of over 15 to 30 ft (depending on cable capacitance) will provide adequate slew rate control, and no output capacitor is needed. Selecting a proper capacitor value when the cable length is not known is problematic. If the capacitor is chosen to work with a short cable, it will be too large for a long cable; if it is chosen to work with a long cable, it will be too small to work with a short cable. Many systems get by with no capacitor at all, regardless of the cable length.

Figure 8.11 shows the logic diagram for the 1489A quad receiver. Each receiver has a "response control" input which allows the input thresholds to be modified. The hysteresis is constant, approximately 1 V. (The older 1489, as compared to the 1489A, has much less hysteresis.) With the response control input left open, the input high threshold is typically 1.95 V, and the input low threshold is typically 0.8 V. Thus, this receiver does not require that the input swing negative (as RS-232 requires). It will, of course, work with an RS-232 level input, but it does not require it. By connecting a resistor between the response control input and the positive or negative supply, the thresholds can be modified. A capacitor to ground can also be connected to the response control input for noise filtering. In most RS-232 applications, the response control input is left open.

Figure 8.10. The 1488 RS-232 quad driver IC. *(Courtesy of Motorola, Inc.)*

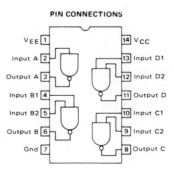

Figure 8.11. The 1489 quad RS-232 receiver IC. *(Courtesy of Motorola, Inc.)*

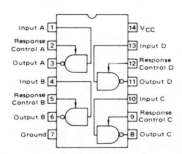

Figure 8.12. RS-232
data link.

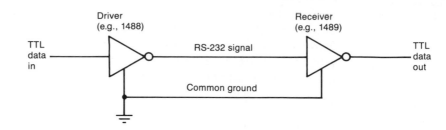

Figure 8.12 shows a complete single-signal RS-232 link. The 1488 translates the TTL levels to RS-232 levels, and the 1489A converts them back to TTL. The single ground wire can serve as the common for any number of signals.

The 1488 and 1489A are widely used because of their low cost and availability from many manufacturers. More modern devices are also available that have several advantages. Pin-compatible CMOS versions of the 1488 and 1489 are available for applications in which power consumption is critical. Another example of a CMOS RS-232 interface IC is Motorola's 145406. This chip includes three receivers and three drivers in a 16-pin package. Slew rate control is provided internally, so no external capacitors are required. CMOS drivers also have the advantage of being able to operate from a ± 5-V supply. The output swing under full load is approximately ± 4 V with a ± 5-V supply. Although this does not meet the RS-232 specification, it is adequate unless long cables are used or noise levels are high.

RS-232 Signal Definitions

The previous section described the electrical aspects of the RS-232 specification. In addition, RS-232 specifies the functions and pin numbers of a group of signals that constitute a complete interface. Table 8.3 lists these signals. The official EIA signal designations are not mnemonic and are rarely used. The first letter of the designation indicates the type of circuit: A for grounds, B for data, C for control signals, and D for clocks. In addition to the primary data channel, a secondary channel is included; these circuit names are prefixed with the letter S. The last letter in the circuit designations indicates a particular signal within the type, starting with A for the most important signal. Because these designations are difficult to remember, an unofficial set of mnemonics has evolved that is generally used instead of the official designations. These mnemonics are also shown in the table for the commonly used signals.

Of the 25 pins in the RS-232 connector definition, only 20 are defined, and many fewer are used in most applications. The minimum set of signals for bidirectional communication is TxD, RxD, and signal ground. In many simple applications, this is all that is needed.

The next most commonly used lines are the handshake signals. The basic handshake pair is Request To Send (RTS) and Clear To Send (CTS). RTS is an output from the data terminal equipment (DTE), and CTS is an output from the data communications equipment (DCE). When the DTE wishes to transmit, it first asserts RTS and then waits for CTS to be asserted. These signals are used by half-duplex modems to control the direction of transmission. The DTE (computer or terminal) asserts RTS when it wants to transmit, and the DCE (modem) reverses the direction of the communication channel. When the modem is ready to transmit data, it asserts CTS, and the computer can then

Table 8.3   RS-232C Signal Names

Pin no.	EIA designation	Mnemonic	Source	Description
1	AA			Protective ground (shield)
2	BA	TxD	DTE	Transmitted data
3	BB	RxD	DCE	Received data
4	CA	RTS	DTE	Request to send
5	CB	CTS	DCE	Clear to send
6	CC	DSR	DCE	Data set ready
7	AB			Signal ground (common return)
8	CF	DCD	DCE	Received line signal detector (carrier detected)
9				Reserved for testing
10				Reserved for testing
11				Unassigned
12	SCF		DCE	Secondary received line signal detector
13	SCB		DCE	Secondary clear to send
14	SBA		DTE	Secondary transmitted data
15	DB		DCE	Transmitter signal element timing
16	SBB		DCE	Secondary received data
17	DD		DCE	Receiver signal element timing
18				Unassigned
19	SCA		DTE	Secondary request to send
20	CD	DTR	DTE	Data terminal ready
21	CG		DCE	Signal quality detector
22	CE	RI	DCE	Ring indicator
23	CH or CI		DTE or DCE	Data signal rate selector
24	DA		DTE	Transmitter signal element timing
25				Unassigned

begin transmitting. Thus, CTS indicates the state of the communication channel. For full-duplex modems or connections not involving modems, RTS and CTS are often connected together in the DCE or in the cable, so CTS is automatically asserted whenever RTS is asserted.

The CTS signal is sometimes used for flow control: the receiver negates CTS when it cannot accept additional data. However, this is an unspecified use of this signal; CTS is intended only to indicate when transmission may start and is not normally negated until RTS is negated. Not all systems will stop transmitting quickly in response to the negation of CTS, so software flow control (such as the XON/XOFF protocol described in Sec. 8.2.3) is preferable. Software flow control also has the advantage that it can be used between two devices connected by modems. Hardware flow control (using CTS) cannot, since the modems interpret this signal for their own use.

The other commonly used handshake pair is Data Terminal Ready (DTR) from the DTE and Data Set Ready (DSR) from the DCE. This pair functions in the same manner as the CTS/RTS pair, except that it indicates the readiness of the equipment rather than the communications channel. For example, DSR may be asserted whenever the modem power is on and the modem is not in a test or voice transmission mode. Modems that include automatic dialers may not assert DSR until dialing has been completed. As with RTS/CTS, in applications not using modems the signals are often connected together so that DSR is asserted whenever DTR is asserted. DTR is often used to instruct a modem to answer or release the telephone line, as described below. DSR or DTR is sometimes used for flow control, but as with CTS, this is an unspecified use and is not recommended.

The signal on pin 8, Receive Line Signal Detector, is generally called Data Carrier Detect (DCD). This is an output from the modem which indicates that it is receiving a carrier tone from another modem.

Ring Indicator (RI), on pin 22, is commonly used in modem interfaces (but not by other peripherals using RS-232). This signal is an output from the modem that is asserted when the ringing tone is present. For "auto answer" operation, the computer counts one or more rings (by counting pulses on RI) and then asserts DTR to instruct the modem to answer the call. When the call is complete, the computer negates DTR to instruct the modem to release the line.

The remainder of the signals are not usually used in asynchronous communications applications. For a complete description of these signals, refer to the EIA standard or one of the texts listed in the Selected Bibliography at the end of this chapter.

All RS-232 control signals use the opposite logic polarity as the data signals. Control signals are asserted when they are at a positive voltage level, whereas logic 1 is represented by a negative logic level on the data lines.

The connector generally used for RS-232 interfaces is the 25-pin "D" type with one row of 13 pins and another of 12 pins. The EIA standard does not actually specify the physical connector characteristics at all, but this connector is a nearly universal de facto standard. Some systems use the nine-pin version of this connector, since nine signals are more than adequate for most applications.

Difficulties with RS-232 Interfaces

While RS-232 is a standard interface, it unfortunately does not guarantee that any two devices designed to the standard can be directly connected together. First, one of the devices must be configured as DTE and the other as DCE. The pin named Transmit Data, for example, is an output from the DTE and an input to the DCE. If two devices are connected that are both DCE (or both DTE), both will transmit on the same line, and the interface will not work. This was not a problem when RS-232 was used primarily for connecting computers or terminals to modems; it is then clear which device is DTE and which is DCE. However, when RS-232 is used to connect a computer directly to a terminal or printer, problems can occur. The terminal is likely to be configured as DTE. The computer may be configured as DTE if it expected that its RS-232 port will be used to connect to a modem, or it may be configured as DCE if it is expected to be connected to a terminal. Thus, a very confusing situation has resulted.

The solution for connecting two devices that are both configured the same is to use a cable that swaps the appropriate signal pairs. Figure 8.13 shows the wiring diagram for such a cable, often called a *null modem* since it allows two devices to be connected to each other when each is designed to be connected to a modem.

Another problem that often arises is the lack of consistent support for the handshake signals and DCD. Some devices that are intended for direct connection to a computer (not via a modem) cut their costs by not connecting to these lines. This causes a problem if the computer is waiting for the handshake line to be asserted before it will trans-

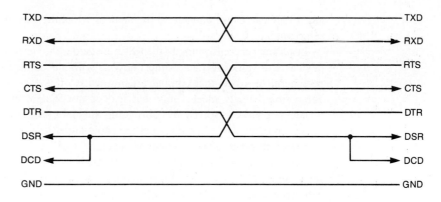

Figure 8.13. Null modem cable.

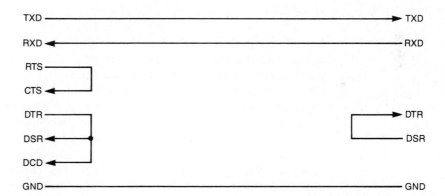

Figure 8.14. RS-232 cable connections to ignore handshake signals.

mit. The problem can be solved by wiring the signals together in the cable, as shown in Fig. 8.14 for a DTE to DCE connection. With this type of cable, both devices receive the needed handshakes, even if the other device does not provide them. This cable can be modified to provide the null modem function as well. Of course, this type of cable must not be used when the handshake signals are used to perform a control function.

The RS-232 specification states that the DCE shall have a female connector and that the DTE shall be supplied with a cable terminated in a male connector. However, when the distinction as to which is the DCE and which is the DTE becomes blurred, the situation is not so simple. In addition, many DTE devices do not include a cable at all, but only a connector, which is typically female. In this case, a cable with male connectors on both ends serves to connect the two units. However, it is not uncommon to require cables with one male and one female end, or even two female ends. So much for standardization!

There are many potential areas for incompatibility that are not covered by the RS-232 specification. The specification makes no mention of data format, so it is up to the user to ensure that the data rate, number of stop bits, parity type, and other parameters are compatible between the two devices attempting to communicate. Some systems use spare pins on the RS-232C connector for power or other application-specific signals. This can cause damage to the devices if conflicting signals are connected to the same pin.

In summary, conforming to the RS-232 standard is far from a guarantee that any two devices will work together. Almost anyone who has connected a serial printer or other peripheral to a personal computer can attest to this fact. Calling a device "RS-232 compatible" really means only that it does not violate the standard. Most interface problems can be resolved by fabricating special cables. There are also a variety of patch boxes available that intercept the cable and allow signals to be disconnected and jumpered to other signals. There are even "smart" cables that configure their inputs and outputs according to the signals they sense at the connectors. Another useful tool for solving RS-232 connection problems is a *gender changer,* which converts a male connector to a female, or vice versa.

8.3.2 RS-449

The RS-232 standard, adopted in August 1969, has remained static while the use of digital communications has rapidly expanded, making the standard inadequate for many current applications. The stated maximum data rate of 20 kbps and maximum cable length of 50 ft are both severe restrictions. In addition, additional control signals are needed in high-speed modem applications. To address these problems, the RS-449 standard was adopted in November 1977. The stated intention at that time was that it should gradually replace RS-232, but this has not occurred.

RS-449 replaces the 25-pin connector used for RS-232 interfaces with a 37-pin connector of a similar type. In addition, the secondary channel, which was part of RS-232's 25-pin connector, is placed on a separate 9-pin connector. Thus, the number of pins is significantly increased. This increases the connector cost, and since most RS-232 applications use only three to eight signals, there is no direct benefit from this increase. For this reason and others, RS-449 has been largely ignored in typical microprocessor-based systems; it is used primarily in high-end modems and related equipment. Thus, RS-449 will not replace RS-232 but will coexist with it.

Since RS-449 is not widely used in microprocessor-based systems, we will not describe it here but only mention a few important characteristics. Ten control signals are added to the RS-232 signals, all of which are concerned with modem control. New mnemonics are assigned to all signals, even those that are identical to RS-232 signals. The biggest contribution of RS-449 is not included in the standard itself. RS-449 contains no electrical specifications; the voltages for logic 1 and logic 0 are not specified. The electrical specifications are provided by two alternative companion specifications, RS-422 and RS-423, which are described in the following sections.

8.3.3 RS-422

Differential Transmission
RS-232 uses *unbalanced,* or *single-ended,* drivers and receivers, in which one wire is used per signal. Each signal is referenced to a common ground. RS-422, on the other hand, uses *balanced,* or *differential,* drivers and receivers, which require two wires per signal. The logic state of a signal is determined not by its voltage with respect to a

Figure 8.15. RS-422 balanced (differential) data link.

common ground but by the relative voltages of the two wires. Figure 8.15 shows a balanced driver/receiver pair. A logic 1 is represented by any voltage on wire A that is greater than the voltage on wire B. Thus, the voltage with respect to ground is not relevant.

This approach has several advantages. Noise induced in the cable by electromagnetic interference affects both wires equally, so the logic state represented is not affected. Similarly, any voltage drop in the cable will affect both wires equally (assuming equal input currents at both inputs of the receiver), so this drop also does not affect the data integrity. Because of these immunities, wide voltage swings between logic 1 and logic 0 are not needed for noise immunity. By keeping the voltage swings to a minimum, less charging and discharging of the cable capacitance is needed. Smaller voltage swings also mean less crosstalk between adjacent wires. Thus, longer cables can be used. Smaller voltage swings can also be made more quickly, allowing the use of higher data rates.

An important advantage of differential transmission is its immunity (within limits) to ground voltage differences between the sender and the receiver. When a long distance separates the two, the ground voltage can vary significantly between them. Using unbalanced transmission, any ground voltage differences change the voltage seen by the receiver and can cause valid levels at the transmitter to be invalid at the receiver. With differential transmission, the ground voltage is irrelevant to the logic state of the signal, since only the relative voltages of the two differential signals is important. There are limits, of course; the receiver has a limit to the voltage above ground it can tolerate at its inputs; this is called the *common-mode* voltage range.

Allowable Cable Lengths for RS-422

Figure 8.16 shows the relationship between data rate and maximum cable length for RS-422 connections. This graph is from the appendix to the EIA standard, and it is not a formal part of the standard but is intended to serve as a conservative guideline. The conditions assumed are 24-gauge twisted-pair cable with a capacitance of 16 pF/ft and a 100-Ω termination resistor at the receiver.

At data rates below 90 kbps, the limiting factor is the resistive loss in the cable. The maximum indicated length of 1.2 km provides a maximum voltage loss of 6 dB. Note that this length limit is higher for smaller-gauge cable and lower for larger-gauge (thinner) cable.

Above 90 kbps, the limiting factor is the cable capacitance's effect on the signal's slew rate. The cable lengths shown in the graph provide a maximum rise and fall time of one-half the bit time. The slope of this curve depends on the capacitance of the cable. Rates as high as 10 Mbps can be used for cables less than approximately 12 m long.

The termination resistor is frequently omitted. As a rule of thumb, it is not needed when the rise time at the receiver is greater than four times the one-way propagation

Figure 8.16. *Maxi-mum data rate vs. cable length for RS-422. (Courtesy of Electronic Industries Association.)*

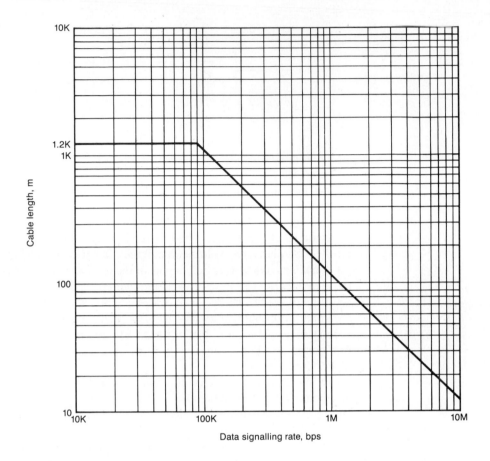

Figure 8.16. Maximum data rate vs. cable length for RS-422. *(Courtesy of Electronic Industries Association.)*

delay time of the cable. Adding the termination resistor preserves the signal rise time at the expense of reduced amplitude.

RS-422 Electrical Characteristics

The key electrical specifications of RS-422 are shown in Table 8.2. The driver must provide a minimum differential output voltage of 2 V under the maximum specified load, and the receiver must have a sensitivity of at least 200 mV. Thus, up to 1.8 V of differential noise (including any difference in voltage drops between the two wires) can be tolerated. All voltages are above ground in normal operation, so no negative power supply is needed. This reduces system costs, since many systems do not require a negative supply for any other purpose except serial interface drivers.

The driver must be able to drive a load as low as 100 Ω, allowing a termination resistor to be used. The receiver input impedance must be greater then 4 kΩ, so by using a slightly larger terminator (or no terminator at all) several receivers can be connected to one driver. This is not possible with RS-232, since the specifications for driver output capability and receiver input loading are the same. Although the RS-422 standard specifies a maximum of 10 receivers, in practice this limit can be higher. At high data rates, the inability to properly terminate a line with multiple receivers can be a problem.

Figure 8.17. The 26LS31 quad differential driver for RS-422. *(Courtesy of Advanced Micro Devices, Inc.)*

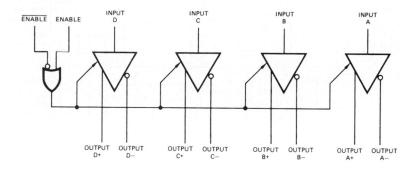

Figure 8.18. The 26LS32 quad differential receiver for RS-422 and RS-423. *(Courtesy of Advanced Micro Devices, Inc.)*

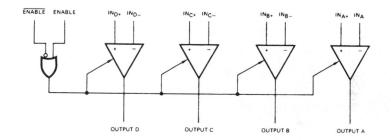

RS-422 Drivers and Receivers

Figure 8.17 shows the logic diagram for a typical RS-422 driver, AMD's 26LS31. These drivers have a common enable; when disabled, the output is in a high-impedance state. This allows them to be used in systems with multiple drivers, as described later in Sec. 8.3.6. (Under RS-422 specifications, there can be only one driver per line, so there is no reason to ever disable the driver.) For each driver there are two outputs, forming the differential signal pair. The inputs are TTL-compatible. The output voltages are 0.5 V maximum for a low level and 2.5 V minimum for a high level. The two outputs from each driver are always the complement of each other. Thus, the minimum differential output voltage is $2.5 - 0.5 = 2.0$ V, as required by the specification.

Figure 8.18 shows the logic diagram for an RS-422 receiver, AMD's 26LS32. The input sensitivity is 200 mV and the common mode input range is ± 7 V, as required by the specification. The outputs are TTL-compatible and can be disabled via the enable inputs. In most applications, the receivers are always enabled.

8.3.4 Ground Isolation

Systems that are widely separated or are in factory environments with devices using large amounts of ac power may have ground potential differences that exceed the common mode input range of the RS-422 receivers. This problem can be solved by isolating the receivers and transmitters from the system ground with optoisolators, as shown in Fig. 8.19. For simplicity, the figure shows optoisolators with built-in amplifiers that provide logic-level outputs, but other types could be used with appropriate output circuits. An isolated power supply, which may be a separate supply connected to the ac

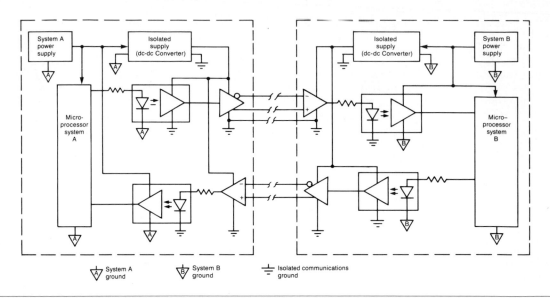

Figure 8.19. Fully optoisolated serial link.

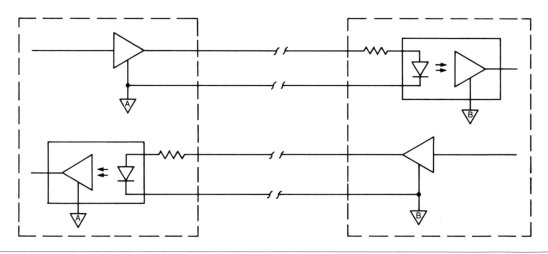

Figure 8.20. Receiver-isolated, self-powered serial link.

line but is typically a dc-to-dc converter connected to the main dc supply, powers the transmitter and receiver to provide isolation. The communication link's ground signal is not connected to either system's ground, so ground potential differences are not a problem as long as they do not exceed the breakdown voltage of the optoisolator, which is typically several thousand volts.

A simpler optoisolated system, as shown in Fig. 8.20, isolates only the receiver.

Both systems' ground signals are passed through the cable to the receiver at the other end, but the two grounds are not connected. No isolated power supply is needed, since the LED in the optoisolator is powered by the signal. This approach, which is better-suited for RS-232 or RS-423 systems than for RS-422 systems (due to the relatively low RS-422 signal levels), is much less expensive but has some disadvantages. The receiver requires relatively large amounts of current, which limits the ability to have multiple receivers on the line. The previous fully isolated approach also provides the system with additional noise immunity, since both the transmitter and receiver are isolated. The system's ground signal is thus not connected to the communications cable and can be kept within the more controlled environment of the system's enclosure.

Isolation can also be implemented with transformers. However, since transformers do not pass direct current, an encoding scheme (such as Manchester encoding) must be used that guarantees a minimum signal frequency, regardless of the data pattern.

8.3.5 RS-423

While RS-422 has many advantages over RS-232, the use of differential transmission does require twice as many wires as unbalanced transmission. The RS-423 specification is intended for those applications in which the lower performance of unbalanced transmission is adequate. For example, RS-449 interfaces that use RS-422 for data and clock signals can generally use RS-423 for the slower control signals. While RS-423 is generally similar to the electrical specifications of RS-232, it contains several improvements.

RS-423 Electrical Characteristics

The RS-232 standard was written at a time when ICs were in their infancy, and most systems were built with discrete semiconductors and had relatively high power supply voltages. RS-423 updates the basic approach of RS-232, using voltage levels and switching speeds more appropriate for modern systems.

Table 8.2 shows the key electrical characteristics of RS-423. The most significant changes are the reduction in voltage swings and increase in receiver sensitivity. The minimum required voltage swing is reduced from ± 5 (for RS-232) to ± 3.6 V, and the maximum allowed swing from ± 15 to ± 6 V. The driver must be able to drive a relatively small load resistance of 450 Ω, allowing multiple receivers on the same line. The receiver sensitivity must be at least 200 mV, as compared to ± 3 V for RS-232. These changes allow the maximum cable length to be increased to 4000 ft, and the maximum data rate to 100 kbps.

RS-423 Cable Lengths and Data Rates

Figure 8.21 shows the relationship between signal rise time, cable length, and data rate. This graph is based on a cable capacitance of 16 pF/ft and an output signal of 12 V peak to peak. The limiting factor for cable length using unbalanced transmission is crosstalk between signals, which is inversely proportional to rise time. The graph is based on a maximum allowable crosstalk of 1 V.

Two methods can be used to control rise time. The simplest is exponential wave-shaping, which is achieved by connecting a capacitor from the signal line to ground. This is not optimal, since the rise time is much faster at the start of the transition than

Figure 8.21. Rise time vs. maximum data rate and cable length for RS-423. *(Courtesy of Electronic Industries Association.)*

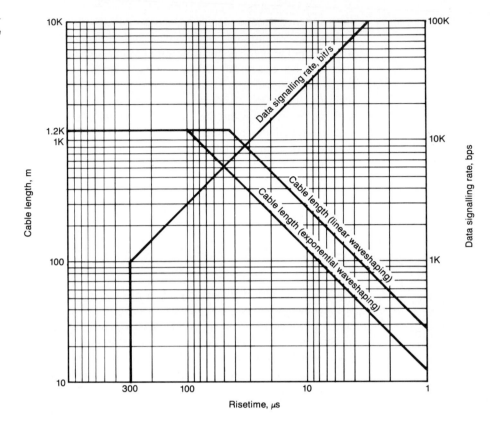

at the end and is used primarily at low data rates. A better approach is to limit the slew rate to a fixed value, producing a linear rise time waveshape. This is implemented by many of the RS-423 driver ICs.

To determine the maximum cable length for a specific data rate, first read from the chart the maximum rise time for that data rate, using the line marked *data signalling rate*. For example, at 20 kbps, the maximum rise time is approximately 14 μs. Then, using one of the lines marked *cable length,* read the maximum cable length for that rise time. For example, using linear waveshaping, the maximum cable length with a 14-μs rise time is approximately 400 m. Using exponential waveshaping, the limit is approximately 190 m. The maximum data rate for a given cable length can be determined by using the reverse process.

RS-423 Drivers and Receivers

Figure 8.22 shows the logic diagram for AMD's 26LS29 quad RS-423 driver. This chip operates from ±5-V power supplies, unlike RS-232 drivers that typically require ±9 V or more. There is a common enable, and a slew rate control connection for each driver. By connecting a capacitor between the slew rate control pin and the output as shown in Fig. 8.23, linear waveshaping is provided. As described previously, this is preferred to the exponential waveshaping that results when a capacitor from the output to ground is used.

Figure 8.22. The 2SLS29 quad RS-423 driver. *(Courtesy of Advanced Micro Devices, Inc.)*

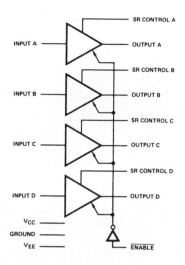

Figure 8.23. RS-423 data link.

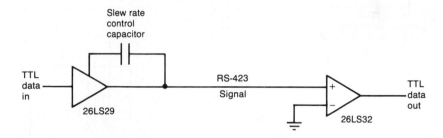

The receiver specification for RS-423 is the same as for RS-422, and the same receivers are generally used for either standard. Figure 8.23 shows receiver and transmitter circuits for RS-423 operation. The inverting input of the receiver is grounded, and the noninverting input serves as the signal input.

RS-423 drivers and receivers can be used for RS-232 interfaces, provided that a few precautions are taken. RS-423 drivers guarantee an output swing of only ± 3.6 V, as compared to ± 5 V for RS-232 drivers. However, RS-232 receivers must respond to a signal of ± 3 V, and most receivers are more sensitive than required. Thus, unless there is a significant level of noise or voltage drop in the cable, RS-423 drivers can be used for RS-232 interfaces. They have the advantages of operating from lower power supply voltages and providing better waveshaping. However, RS-232 drivers are inverting and RS-423 drivers are not, so an inverter is often required at the input of the RS-423 driver when used for RS-232 operation.

Figure 8.24 shows an RS-422/423 receiver used as an RS-232 receiver. There is a potential problem with the maximum voltage at the receiver input, since RS-422/23 receivers are required to withstand only ± 12 V, but RS-232 drivers may produce voltages as high as ± 15 V, and RS-232 receivers are supposed to tolerate voltages as high as ± 25 V. Some RS-422/423 receivers can handle the higher voltages; if not, the resistive divider shown in the figure guarantees that the receiver will not be presented with voltages higher than it is designed for. Since the sensitivity of the RS-422/423

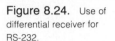

Figure 8.24. Use of differential receiver for RS-232.

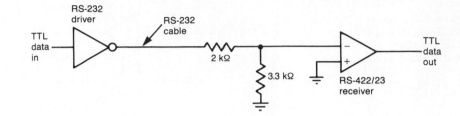

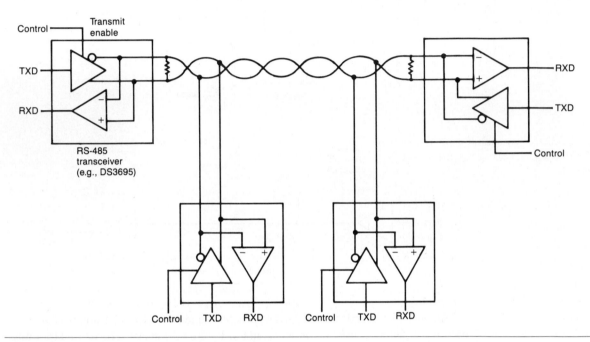

Figure 8.25. Half-duplex RS-485 multidrop network.

receiver is much greater than that required for RS-232, the loss of signal level is not a problem.

8.3.6   RS-485

RS-485 is an enhanced version of RS-422 for use in systems with more than one transmitter. By increasing the drive requirements for the driver and the input impedance of the receiver, up to 32 drivers and 32 receivers can be connected together. This allows the creation of a bidirectional bus connecting up to 32 devices. RS-485 transceiver chips are available in an eight-pin package. They provide a single pair of pins for the RS-485 connection, separate TTL-level input and output pins, and separate receiver and transmitter enable inputs. One example of such a device is National's DS3695.

Figure 8.25 shows a half-duplex RS-485 system using this type of transceiver. Termination resistors are typically included at both ends of the pair. Note that there must also be a ground connection among all the transceivers to provide a common mode reference. If a shielded twisted-pair cable is used, the shield can serve as the common ground. Optical isolation can be added if ground isolation among the systems is desired.

Some form of addressing must be provided to ensure that only one driver is enabled at a time. One simple approach is a polled master/slave protocol. For example, consider a system in which one master device must collect data from several other slave devices. Normally, the master's transmitter is enabled and all others are disabled. When the master wants to read data from one of the peripherals, it outputs a command that includes a slave address. The master then disables its transmitter. The addressed slave recognizes its address and enables its transmitter. When the slave has sent all the data requested, it disables its transmitter, and the master reenables its transmitter. Intel's Bitbus, described in Chap. 10, is an example of a network protocol that uses RS-485 for the physical-layer protocol.

8.3.7 Current Loop Interfaces

The EIA standard interfaces described previously are all voltage-based. Another type of interface is the *current loop,* which uses the presence of current flow, rather than a specific voltage level, to indicate the state of the signal. The current loop interface originated in telegraphy, for which it was necessary to send data for long distances. Telegraphy interfaces used a 60-mA loop. Most computers and peripherals that use a current loop interface use a 20-mA loop; this type of interface was made popular by the ASR 33 Teletype, which was a common computer terminal and printer until the development of low-cost CRT terminals and dot-matrix printers. The current does not need to be exactly 20 mA; it varies depending on the resistance of the wire and other factors.

While current loop interfaces are still in use, they are generally obsolete. Current loop interfaces were popular before the development of inexpensive interface ICs because they were simple to implement and could be used with long lines. They are also relatively insensitive to voltage-induced noise. However, there are several disadvantages. The current transitions tend to cause crosstalk in nearby wires, limiting current loops to low data rates. There is no standard for which end is passive and which is active, the voltage levels used, or the connector type. With the inexpensive interface ICs now available, RS-423 or RS-422 is generally more appropriate for new designs.

Figure 8.26 shows a basic current loop interface. The transmitter switches the current on or off to send a 1 or 0. The battery voltage and resistor value are chosen to set the current in the loop. Note that a 20-mA current can be obtained with a 10-V source and a 500-Ω resistor or with a 100-V source and a 5000-Ω resistor. A high-voltage source allows data to be sent over long distances, since the system can be designed to operate with a large loop resistance. Suppose, for example, that the resistance of the wire in the loop is 500 Ω. This would reduce the current in the loop with a 10-V source to 10 mA, while the current in the loop with a 100-V source is reduced to 18.2 mA. In addition, if the loop is designed to operate with a minimum wire resistance, the current-limiting resistor can be reduced.

In a current loop interface, the current source can be in either the transmitter or the receiver. The end that contains the current source is called *active,* and the other end is

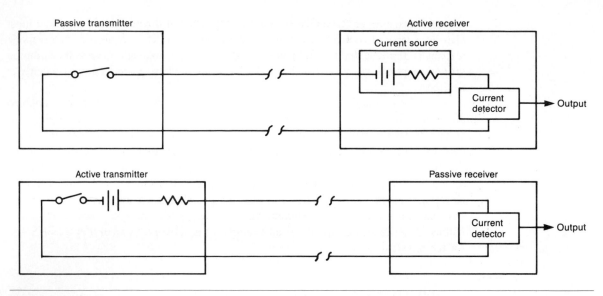

Figure 8.26.   Current loop interfaces.

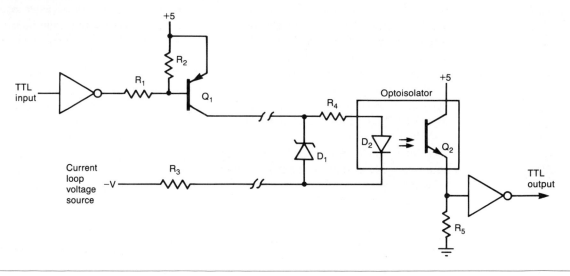

Figure 8.27.   Current loop interface implementation.

called *passive*. There is no standard as to whether the transmitter or the receiver is active, but for the system to operate, one of them must be active and the other passive.

Figure 8.27 shows a typical current loop implementation, using an active transmitter and a passive receiver. The TTL input turns on Q_1 to enable the loop current, which is limited by resistor R_3. The receiver uses an optoisolator to detect the loop current. Zener diode D_1 limits the voltage across the LED and resistor, and R_4 sets the LED current. When current flows in the loop, the LED is lit and the optoisolator's phototransistor conducts. The optoisolator provides ground isolation between the transmitter and receiver, which is important when they are far apart and their system grounds may be at different voltages. An optical isolator can also be used in the transmitter to provide full isolation.

8.4 INTERFACING SERIAL DATA TO MICROPROCESSORS

Previous sections of this chapter have described the basic methods of serial data transmission and the relevant standards. This section describes the logic required to connect serial interfaces to the microprocessor's parallel buses.

8.4.1 USARTs

Figure 8.28 shows a block diagram of the logic required to interface a microprocessor's parallel bus structure to a serial data link. The functions are commonly included in a single IC, called a *universal asynchronous receiver and transmitter,* commonly abbreviated as *UART,* pronounced "you-art." If it is capable of synchronous operation as well, it is called a *USART* (universal synchronous and asynchronous receiver and transmitter), pronounced "use-art."

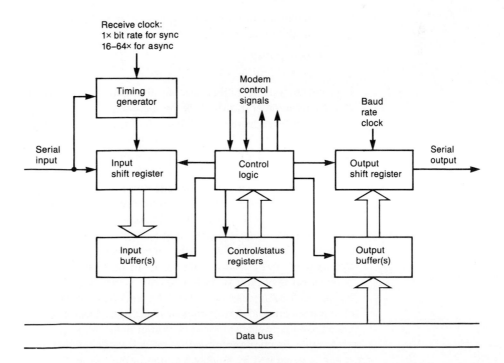

Figure 8.28. UART block diagram.

Basic Functions

The main task of a UART (or USART) is parallel-to-serial and serial-to-parallel conversion. It is basically a pair of shift registers with associated buffers and control logic. Data to be transmitted is loaded into the output shift register, which is clocked at the bit rate. Thus, each bit is output for one bit time. For asynchronous communication, start and stop bits are added surrounding each data word. A parity bit may also be inserted. The output buffer stores the most recent data word written by the microprocessor, while the previous word is output from the shift register.

Receiving data is the reverse of transmitting. The serial data input feeds a shift register, which is clocked at the center of each bit time. For synchronous operation, the position of the bit cell centers is determined by the baud rate clock. For asynchronous operation, a clock at 16 times (or 32 or 64 times) the bit rate sets the bit duration, and the center of the bit cell is determined by measuring the time from the beginning of the start bit (as described earlier in Sec. 8.2.3). When a full word is received, parity is checked (if used), and the word is transferred to the input buffer. The input buffer is often a two- or three-byte FIFO, which allows the UART to store several received words in sequence. This reduces the response time required from the microprocessor to prevent loss of data.

Control registers in the UART (or USART) allow the microprocessor to set various operating parameters, including:

> Number of data bits
>
> Number of stop bits
>
> Even, odd, or no parity
>
> Enable interrupt on received data available,
> transmit buffer empty, or error conditions
>
> Clock divisor

For synchronous operation, several other parameters must be set, including the sync character and other details of the protocol used.

Status registers in the UART indicate if the input buffer is full, meaning that a word has been received, or if the transmit buffer is empty, indicating that another word can be sent. There are also several error flags. If parity is used, errors in a single-bit (or in an odd number of bits) are detected. During asynchronous operation, the UART checks for a stop bit at the end of each word; after receiving the expected number of data (and parity) bits, the next bit received should always be a "mark" (1). If it is not, the *framing error* bit is set. Usually this occurs when the baud rate is incorrect or when noise causes an error in detecting the start bit.

If the input buffer is full and the microprocessor fails to read the data before the next byte is ready to be loaded from the input shift register, a byte of data is lost and an *overrun* error occurs. If the transmitter is empty and there is no data in the output buffer, an *underrun* error occurs. An underrun is really an error only during synchronous operation; during asynchronous transmission, arbitrary amounts of idle time are allowed between words, so the buffer does not need to be kept full.

Another function performed by most UARTs is break generation and detection. A *break* is generated by holding the line in the "space" condition for a relatively long time, more than one character time at the slowest baud rate supported. This provides a mechanism for a baud-rate-independent and code-independent interrupt function. By its very nature, a break cannot be generated via the usual transmit path, so additional logic is required in the UART. Most UARTs provide a status bit that is set when a break is detected at the receiver. For UARTs that do not provide such a status bit, a break will cause a framing error.

In addition to the basic serial input and output functions, most UART and USART chips include connections for the modem control handshake signals for RS-232 operation. These are essentially input and output port bits that are controlled by writing to a control register and read by reading a status register. Most chips also have an "auto enable" function that automatically inhibits operation if the proper handshake signals are not present. In some chips, such as the 8251A, the CTS input functions only as a transmitter enable and cannot be disabled or read by software. This is an undesirable limitation, and in systems using such chips it is best to also connect the CTS signal to an input port bit so that it can be read by software. If the auto-enable function is not desired, then the USART's CTS input should be permanently asserted.

Baud Rate Generation

Although not part of the basic UART functions, some form of baud rate generator is always required. Many ICs include the baud rate generator on the same chip with the UART. For synchronous operation, only a transmit clock is required; the receive clock is provided from the communications link. Asynchronous operation requires a clock at 16, 32, or 64 times the baud rate for reception.

When the baud rate generator is not included in the UART chip, there are several alternative methods for producing the baud rate clock. One channel of a programmable counter/timer chip (as described in Chap. 5) is often used as a baud rate generator. Baud rate generator ICs are also available. These consist of an oscillator (with an external crystal) and a programmable divider, and they are also available as dual devices that can produce two different baud rates simultaneously.

For minimum cost, the same oscillator can be used for the main system (microprocessor) clock and to derive the baud rate clock. There are some disadvantages to this approach, however. Even clock rates, such as 4, 8, or 10 MHz, cannot be precisely divided to create a full range of standard baud rates, although they can come close enough for most applications. One frequency that does divide exactly into all standard baud rates is 2.4576 MHz. Using a clock rate such as this (or two or four times this rate) generally results in running the microprocessor slightly slower than its maximum speed, so some performance is sacrificed. Conversely, if the maximum microprocessor clock rate is used, precision of some baud rates may be sacrificed. Another consideration is that if a separate oscillator is used for baud rate generation, the microprocessor clock rate can be increased for a higher-performance version without affecting the baud rate timing.

Synchronous Operation

Synchronous operation requires most of the functions of asynchronous operation (except the use of start and stop bits), plus several additional functions. A sync detector is required to find the start of a data packet. Each packet starts with two or more sync characters. The sync detector in the USART is a shift register that constantly examines the serial data input, shifting in one bit at each clock. When the contents of the sync register matches the specified sync character, the USART synchronizes its timing to the character boundary.

USARTs also perform zero bit insertion and deletion as required for protocols such as SDLC. Some USARTs also include CRC generator and checker circuits. CRC generation and checking can also be performed by an external chip, or in software (if slow speed is acceptable).

Most USARTs use NRZ encoding. Some are programmable, allowing the use of other encoding techniques such as NRZI, biphase, or Manchester. Some chips include digital phase-locked loops to extract the clock signal from these self-clocking formats.

The amount of software required to implement synchronous protocols such as SDLC varies considerably depending on the controller chip used. The simpler USARTs require software for all protocol functions, while the more complex devices, often called *data link controllers,* include higher-level protocol functions that reduce the software burden.

Microprocessor Compatibility

UARTs and USARTs interface to the microprocessor bus in the same manner as other peripheral chips. Address lines allow different control, status, or data registers to be selected. Read and write (or read/write and data strobe) inputs control bus transfers. The UART appears to the microprocessor as a series of I/O ports or memory locations.

It is generally desirable to use interrupt-driven software for data communications, since fast response is needed when a received character is detected (and also when the output buffer is empty during synchronous operation). Most UARTs and USARTs can be programmed to produce interrupts on one or more conditions, such as receive buffer full, transmit buffer empty, errors, or other conditions such as a change in a handshake line.

Interrupts from high-speed serial data links can cause performance problems, however. At 9600 baud, one character is received approximately once per millisecond. If both transmit and receive interrupts are used, the average time between interrupts is reduced to half a millisecond. This is a reasonable interrupt rate for most microprocessors. At 56 kbaud, however, interrupts occur every 179 μs, or every 89 μs if both transmit and receive interrupts are used. (These values assume an 8-bit character with 1 start bit and 1 stop bit.) Because of the overhead in responding to an interrupt (fetching the interrupt vector and saving and restoring registers), this can exceed the processing capability of many microprocessors even if the interrupt service routine is short. If the microprocessor cannot keep up with the interrupt rate, characters will be lost.

Thus, for high-data-rate applications, the load on the microprocessor must be carefully considered. One possibility is to dedicate a microprocessor or single-chip microcomputer to the serial channel. By using polling rather than interrupts, the interrupt response overhead is eliminated, and a higher data rate can be handled (although the microprocessor may not have any time to do anything else but service the serial channel). The processor dedicated to the serial channel passes data in blocks to and from the main system processor. (See Chap. 10 for an example of such a system). Another alternative is to use a DMA controller to transfer data directly between the USART and the system memory.

Another factor to consider is that the actual character rate on a serial channel may be far less than the maximum rate implied by the baud rate. If the source of the data is a person typing at a keyboard, then even if individual characters are sent at a high data rate, the character rate will be relatively low. Since the U(S)ART handles all activity at the bit rate, the microprocessor is affected only by the character rate. If, on the other hand, the source of the data is another computer, the actual character rate may well be the maximum possible.

Some U(S)ARTs have interrupt vector registers and can supply the vector on the data bus during an interrupt acknowledge cycle. Most devices can also modify the vector depending on the cause of the interrupt. This is one area where microprocessor compatibility can be important. The Z80 family, for example, requires considerable logic in each peripheral chip for interrupt functions. The Z80-SIO, a dual USART designed for use with the Z80, provides all the necessary logic. Using most other USARTs with the Z80 requires more logic for full interrupt support.

The other aspects of microprocessor compatibility are the same as those for other peripherals (as described in Chap. 5): bus drive capability, read and write pulse lengths, access time, and setup and hold time.

Many different acronyms are used for UARTs, USARTs, and related devices. Originally, U(S)ARTs were not designed to interface to microprocessor buses. When microprocessor manufacturers began producing microprocessor-compatible versions, each made up their own name. Thus, there are, among others, Motorola's Asynchronous Communications Interface Adapter (ACIA) and Zilog's Serial Input/Output (SIO) chip. Devices with added capability for handling synchronous communication protocols are often called data link controllers, or multiple protocol communications controllers. Zilog's dual USART that includes baud rate generators and other additional functions is called a serial communications controller (SCC).

UARTs and USARTs in Single-Chip Microcomputers

Many single-chip microcomputers include on-chip UARTs, and a few include USARTs. In general, these UARTs are less programmable than separate UART chips; some do not even provide parity generation and checking. One feature that many single-chip microcomputer UARTs do have is a *wake-up* mode. This is useful when the serial port is used to connect several microcomputers together in a network. (See Chap. 10 for a description of wake-up mode operation. For examples of single-chip microcomputers with on-chip serial interfaces, see Chap. 2.)

8.4.2 The 8250 Asynchronous Communication Element

The 8250 is a UART with an on-chip baud rate generator, and goes by yet another acronym, ACE. It was originally developed by National Semiconductor and is also produced by Western Digital. It is used for the asynchronous communications adapter in the IBM PC family, and has therefore been used in many other personal computers for compatibility with communications software written for the IBM machines.

The 8250 is a typical example of a peripheral chip that has a variety of bugs, which are corrected in the newer 8250A version. However, the 8250's case is particularly complicated. One troublesome situation arises when an interrupt (such as receive buffer full) occurs while another interrupt from the same 8250 (such as transmit buffer empty) is still being processed. The original 8250 will briefly negate its interrupt output when the first interrupt is serviced, and then reassert the interrupt output if another interrupt is pending. This was not the intended behavior, so when National revised the 8250 to fix a variety of bugs, they fixed this problem. The 8250A interrupt output remains asserted as long as there is an interrupt pending. This "fix" caused another problem, however. The IBM PC uses an edge-triggered interrupt controller. Thus, the fix in the 8250A can cause the IBM PC to miss the second interrupt, since no edge is generated between successive interrupt services. This can be corrected with software modifications, but to run standard IBM PC software, the "corrected" 8250A cannot be used. (For complete details, refer to National's "Comparison Guide" listed in the Selected Bibliography at the end of this chapter.)

Further adding to the confusion is that the 8250-B is a slower (and therefore cheaper) version of the 8250 and does not include the changes made in the 8250A. The 16450 is a faster CMOS version of the 8250A and is used in the IBM AT and compatible computers. Intel's 82510, also a CMOS device, is software-compatible with the 8250 but includes many additional features, including higher data rates, dual baud-rate generators, four-byte transmit and receive FIFO buffers, and the ability to generate interrupts when specific control characters are received.

8250 Functions

Figure 8.29 shows the block diagram of the 8250. Ten registers provide the microprocessor's connection to the serial data interface. The receiver buffer register holds the last word received, and the transmitter holding register holds the word waiting to be transmitted. The line control register sets the mode of operation, and the line status

Figure 8.29. The 8250 UART with baud rate generator block diagram. *(Courtesy of National Semiconductor Corporation.)*

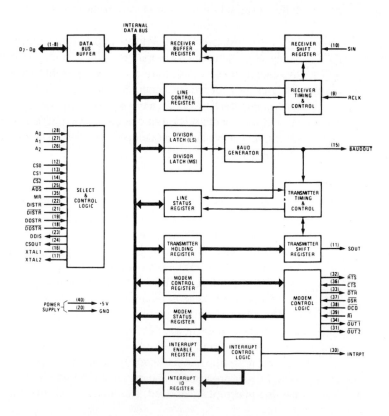

register allows the state of the buffers and error flags to be read. The divisor latch is accessed as two 8-bit registers, which form the 16-bit divisor for the baud rate generator. The modem control register controls the handshake output signals, and the modem status register allows the handshake inputs to be read. Finally, the interrupt enable register determines under what conditions an interrupt will be generated, and the interrupt ID register provides information about the cause of the interrupt.

8250 Connections

Figure 8.30 shows an RS-232 interface based on the 8250. Many UARTs are in 24- or 28-pin packages; the 8250 is in a 40-pin package, providing many control pins. There are three chip select inputs, two active-high and one active-low. When all three are asserted, the chip is selected and the CSOUT output is asserted. In the example, the chip select inputs are used to perform a coarse address decoding, enabling the chip for addresses beginning with 011. If a more complete address decoding is required, one of the CS inputs is connected to the address decoder output.

There are two write strobes called DOSTR and $\overline{\text{DOSTR}}$(data output strobe). They are ORed together, so if either is asserted a write operation occurs. This allows strobes of either polarity to be used without external inverters. Similarly, there are two read

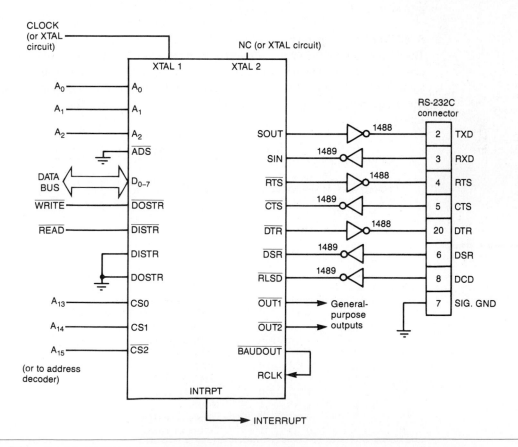

Figure 8.30. Circuit for RS-232 interface using 8250.

strobes, DISTR and $\overline{\text{DISTR}}$ (data input strobe). The figure shows the more common active-low control signals.

Three address lines select one of the internal control, status, or data registers. These inputs are latched at the rising edge of the address strobe ($\overline{\text{ADS}}$) input, so they can be connected directly to a multiplexed address/data bus. In nonmultiplexed systems, $\overline{\text{ADS}}$ is tied low. The interrupt output (INTRPT) is active-high. Since the 8250 does not provide an interrupt vector, the interrupt output will typically connect to an interrupt controller or an autovectored interrupt input.

The master reset (MR) input must be asserted after power-up to initialize the chip's internal state. The XTAL1 and XTAL2 inputs can be connected to a quartz crystal to provide the clock for the baud rate divider. Alternatively, a clock signal can be provided on the XTAL1 input.

The transmit clock is internally connected to the baud rate generator, but the receive clock is connected to an external input (RCLK). To use the same clock for both, $\overline{\text{BAUDOUT}}$ is connected to RCLK.

SOUT and SIN provide the serial data connections. Two handshake outputs are provided, $\overline{\text{DTR}}$ and $\overline{\text{RTS}}$. There are three handshake inputs: $\overline{\text{RLSD}}$ [receive line signal detect, often called data carrier detect (DCD)], $\overline{\text{DSR}}$, and $\overline{\text{DTR}}$. (Refer to Sec. 8.3.1 for descriptions of these signals.) Two additional general purpose outputs are also provided.

8250 Control Registers

The 10 registers of the 8250 are selected by three address inputs and one bit of the line control register, called the divisor latch access bit (DLAB). Table 8.4 shows the register addressing. The DLAB is set to 1 to access either byte of the baud rate divisor latch. The frequency generated (which is 16 times the actual baud rate) is determined as follows:

$$\text{Clock frequency} = \frac{\text{input frequency on XTAL1}}{2^n}$$

where n = 16-bit value in baud rate divisor latch

Table 8.4   The 8250 Register Addressing

DLAB	A_2	A_1	A_0	Register
0	0	0	0	Receiver buffer (read), transmitter holding register (write)
0	0	0	1	Interrupt enable
X	0	1	0	Interrupt identification (read only)
X	0	1	1	Line control
X	1	0	0	MODEM control
X	1	0	1	Line status
X	1	1	0	MODEM status
X	1	1	1	None
1	0	0	0	Divisor latch (least-significant byte)
1	0	0	1	Divisor latch (most-significant byte)

Source: National Semiconductor Corporation.

The maximum clock rate input is 3.1 MHz. Two frequencies that produce accurate baud rates are 1.8432 and 3.072 MHz. For example, suppose a 3.072-MHz clock is used and the desired data rate is 9600 baud. The UART requires a clock at 16 times the baud rate, so the required frequency is $16 \times 9600 = 153.6$ kHz. A divisor of 20 produces this value. The maximum baud rate is 56 kbaud, requiring a divisor of 3 with a 3.072-MHz crystal.

Table 8.5   The 8250 Register Bit Assignments

Bit No.	Register Address										
	0 DLAB=0	0 DLAB=0	1 DLAB=0	2	3	4	5	6	7	0 DLAB=1	1 DLAB=1
	Receiver Buffer Register (Read Only)	Transmitter Holding Register (Write Only)	Interrupt Enable Register	Interrupt Ident. Register (Read Only)	Line Control Register	MODEM Control Register	Line Status Register	MODEM Status Register	Scratch Reg-ister	Divisor Latch (LS)	Latch (MS)
	RBR	THR	IER	IIR	LCR	MCR	LSR	MSR	SCR	DLL	DLM
0	Data Bit 0*	Data Bit 0	Enable Received Data Available Interrupt (ERBFI)	"0" if Interrupt Pending	Word Length Select Bit 0 (WLS0)	Data Terminal Ready (DTR)	Data Ready (DR)	Delta Clear to Send (DCTS)	Bit 0	Bit 0	Bit 8
1	Data Bit 1	Data Bit 1	Enable Transmitter Holding Register Empty Interrupt (ETBEI)	Interrupt ID Bit (0)	Word Length Select Bit 1 (WLS1)	Request to Send (RTS)	Overrun Error (OE)	Delta Data Set Ready (DDSR)	Bit 1	Bit 1	Bit 9
2	Data Bit 2	Data Bit 2	Enable Receiver Line Status Interrupt (ELSI)	Interrupt ID Bit (1)	Number of Stop Bits (STB)	Out 1	Parity Error (PE)	Trailing Edge Ring Indicator (TERI)	Bit 2	Bit 2	Bit 10
3	Data Bit 3	Data Bit 3	Enable MODEM Status Interrupt (EDSSI)	0	Parity Enable (PEN)	Out 2	Framing Error (FE)	Delta Data Carrier Detect (DDCD)	Bit 3	Bit 3	Bit 11
4	Data Bit 4	Data Bit 4	0	0	Even Parity Select (EPS)	Loop	Break Interrupt (BI)	Clear to Send (CTS)	Bit 4	Bit 4	Bit 12
5	Data Bit 5	Data Bit 5	0	0	Stick Parity	0	Transmitter Holding Register (THRE)	Data Set Ready (DSR)	Bit 5	Bit 5	Bit 13
6	Data Bit 6	Data Bit 6	0	0	Set Break	0	Transmitter Empty (TEMT)	Ring Indicator (RI)	Bit 6	Bit 6	Bit 14
7	Data Bit 7	Data Bit 7	0	0	Divisor Latch Access Bit (DLAB)	0	0	Data Carrier Detect (DCD)	Bit 7	Bit 7	Bit 15

*Bit 0 is the least significant bit. It is the first bit serially transmitted or received.

Source: National Semiconductor Corporation.

All other registers are accessed with DLAB set to 0. (Actually, the state of DLAB is irrelevant when accessing registers 2 to 7.) Data is read and written via register 0; writing to this address writes to the transmit holding register, and reading from this address reads the receiver buffer register. Table 8.5 shows the bit functions for each register.

When the LOOP bit in register 4 is set, the chip enters a diagnostic mode. The output of the transmitter is internally connected to the input of the receiver. This allows software to perform a self-test by sending a word and checking the received word.

8.4.3 The 8530 Synchronous Communications Controller

Figure 8.31 shows the block diagram of Zilog's Z8030 SCC. The SCC is a dual USART with on-chip baud rate generators, CRC generator and checkers, and digital phase-locked loops (DPLLs) for clock extraction. It was designed as a peripheral for the Z8000 family of microprocessors. The 8530 is a version of the 8030 with a non-multiplexed bus structure designed for easier interfacing to other microprocessors. It is faster than many other USARTs, allowing data rates up to 1.5 Mbps for synchronous operation when an external clock is supplied. The 8530 is used in Apple's Macintosh. AMD is an alternate source for both the 8030 and 8530, and Intel provides the 8530 as the 82530. The 8531 is an asynchronous-only version.

Figure 8.32 shows a simplified block diagram of one channel of the SCC. The chip contains two sets of the logic shown in the figure. A 16-bit programmable divider

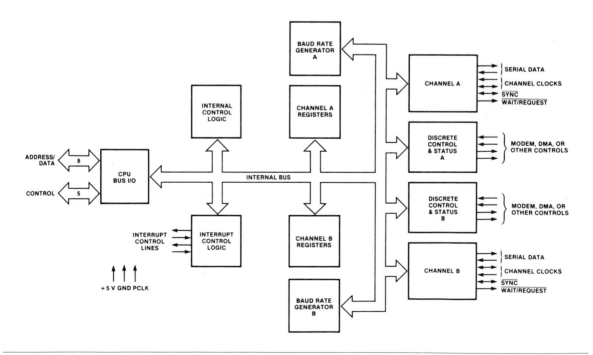

Figure 8.31. The 8530 serial communications interface block diagram. *(Courtesy of Advanced Micro Devices, Inc.)*

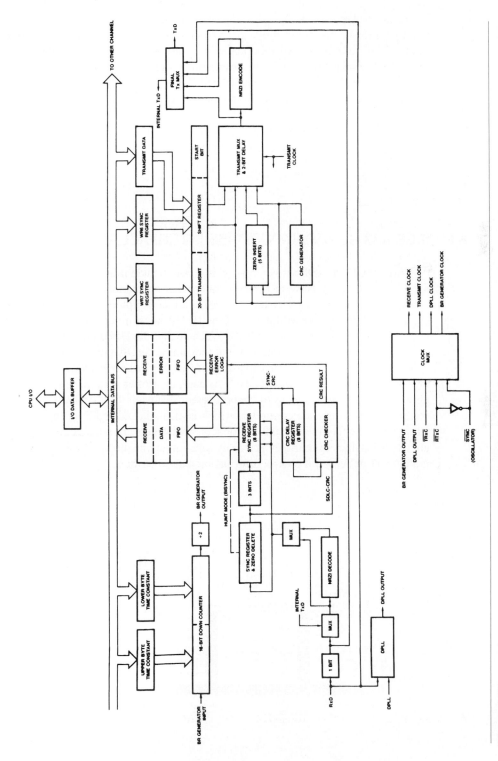

Figure 8.32. SCC channel block diagram. *(Courtesy of Advanced Micro Devices, Inc.)*

serves as a baud rate generator. The chip supports NRZ and biphase in addition to the usual NRZ encoding. It can also generate and check several different CRC codes. There is a 3-byte FIFO buffer for received data, reducing the real-time demands on the microprocessor. A clock multiplexer allows several different sources to be selected under software control. All this flexibility does not come without some drawbacks; there are 15 control registers to be programmed, and 6 status registers.

The bus interface is fairly standard and is easily interfaced to a variety of microprocessors. Some additional logic is required to support all interrupt functions with most processors, and wait states are usually required. The bus interface logic for a 68000-family microprocessor can be implemented with a PAL programmable logic chip; both MMI and AMD provide a description of this interface as an application note for their PALs.

8.5   IEEE-488 GENERAL-PURPOSE INTERFACE BUS

Although the IEEE-488 bus is a parallel bus, we include it in this chapter because it is used for connections between systems, rather than to connect boards within a system. The bus was designed by Hewlett-Packard and then adopted as an IEEE standard. HP calls it the Hewlett-Packard Interface Bus (HPIB); most other manufacturers call it the General Purpose Interface Bus (GPIB). Technically, the HPIB definition is more comprehensive than the GPIB definition, but they are generally equivalent.

Figure 8.33 shows a system consisting of four devices connected via the GPIB. Devices in a GPIB system can be a talker, listener, controller, or some combination of the three. The bus was designed to connect test instruments to a desktop computer. The computer is typically the controller (which is also a talker and a listener), and the instruments are either talkers, talker/listeners, or listeners. In practice, most instruments are talker/listeners even if they primarily function in one direction only, so status information can be read and control information can be written.

Figure 8.33. GPIB system showing signal groups and device types. *(Courtesy of Hewlett-Packard.)*

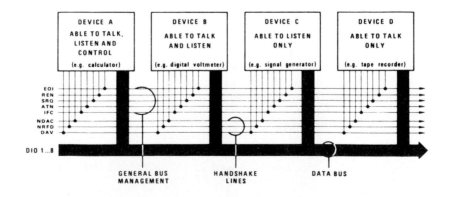

Table 8.6   GPIB Bus Management Signals

Name	Mnemonic	Description
Attention	ATN	Causes all devices to interpret data on the bus as a controller command and activate their acceptor handshake function.
Interface clear	IFC	Initializes the HPIB system to an idle state (no activity on the bus).
Service request	SRQ	Alerts the controller to a need for communication.
Remote enable	REN	Enables devices to respond to remote program control when addressed to listen.
End or identify	EOI	Indicates last data byte of a multibyte sequence; also used with ATN to parallel poll devices for their status bit.

Source: Hewlett-Packard.

The bus consists of eight data lines, three handshake lines, and five bus management (control) lines. Table 8.6 lists the functions of the bus management lines, and the handshake lines are described later in this section. Electrically, all signals are at TTL levels, but high-current (48 mA) drivers are required.

The GPIB uses a special connector that allows cables to be piggybacked. The front of the connector plugs into the device, and another connector can be plugged into the back of the connector. This allows any number of connectors to be stacked together. The maximum total cable length in the system is 2 m times the number of devices in the system, up to an absolute maximum of 20 m.

Note that unlike backplane buses, there are no address lines. However, there can be up to 15 devices on the bus, and each device must have a unique address. Initially, the system controller is the only device that drives the data lines. When it asserts the ATN (attention) control signal, this indicates to all devices on the bus that they should pay attention to the data on the data lines. This data is a command. Although there are a variety of commands, we will cover only the two basic commands that provide the addressing function: address to talk and address to listen. Each of these commands includes a 4-bit address field, which allows any one of the 15 devices on the bus to be selected.

To send data to one or more devices, the controller performs the following sequence:

1. ADDRESS TO LISTEN command sent, with address of device that is to receive the data. ATN is asserted when the command is sent, so all devices examine the command to see if it is intended for them.

2. ADDRESS TO LISTEN command repeated with address of other devices to receive data, if any.

3. Data is sent. Devices that have not been addressed to listen ignore the data.

4. UNLISTEN command sent, which tells all devices that were addressed to listen that they should now ignore all data transfers unless ATN is asserted.

Figure 8.34. GPIB
data transfer timing.
*(Courtesy of Hewlett-
Packard.)*

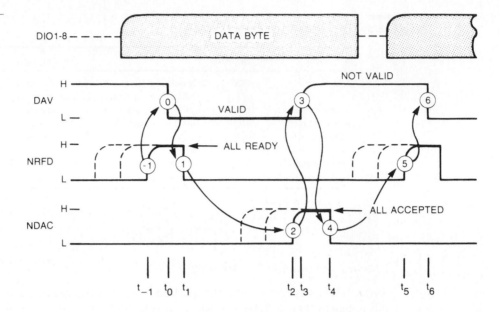

To receive data from another device, the controller follows a similar sequence, except that an ADDRESS TO TALK command is used. Only one device can be addressed to talk at one time. However, several other devices can be addressed to listen, so the data is transferred directly to them; it does not need to pass through the controller.

Thus, the GPIB allows data to be sent from any device on the bus to any number of other devices on the bus simultaneously. To coordinate this transfer, a three-wire handshake is used. Figure 8.34 shows the timing for a data transfer. The DAV (data valid) line is asserted by the talker and functions as the data strobe. The NRFD (not ready for data) and NDAC (not data accepted) signals are driven by the addressed listeners. (The terminology here can be confusing. The signals are active-low, and should really be called $\overline{\text{NRFD}}$ and $\overline{\text{NDAC}}$. The double negation means that when NRFD is high, the device is ready for data.) Since there can be more than one listener, these signals are driven by open-collector (or three-state) drivers. When a listener is not ready to accept data, it drives NRFD low. If there is more than one listener, all will drive NRFD low when they have just received a data byte and are not ready for the next. As each device becomes ready, it releases (stops driving) NRFD. Only when all devices are ready will the line float high; thus, the talker sees the OR of the NRFD signals (which can also be thought of as the AND of the RFD signals) from all the addressed devices.

When all devices are ready for data, the talker drives the data on the data lines and asserts DAV. In response, each listener asserts NRFD. When each listener has stored the data, it releases NDAC. The talker sees NDAC negated when all listeners have accepted the data. The talker then negates DAV and removes the data from the bus. When each listener is ready for another byte, it releases NRFD, and when all listeners are ready, the next byte is sent.

This relatively complex handshaking protocol allows fast and slow devices to be mixed on the bus, and the bus automatically slows to the speed of the slowest device currently addressed to listen. Incidentally, this handshake protocol is patented by Hewlett-Packard. If you purchase a GPIB interface IC or board, the manufacturer has paid the patent fee, and the purchaser can use it freely. However, if you design your own logic to implement this protocol, a nominal license fee is due to Hewlett-Packard.

A variety of ICs are available to implement GPIB interfaces. Examples of talker/listener ICs are Fairchild's 96LS488 and Intel's 8291. Intel's 8292 adds controller functions to the 8291, but since it is a preprogrammed single-chip microcomputer, it is slow. TI's TMS9914A and NEC's μPD7210 are examples of single-chip talker/listener/controller ICs. These ICs require external buffers to provide the required bus drive. They interface to the microprocessor as standard peripheral chips, accepting commands and data and returning status and data via registers that may be memory-mapped or I/O mapped. For high-speed data transfers, DMA controllers are generally used.

One compatibility problem not addressed in the IEEE-488 specification is the format of the data transferred. For example, are values sent in binary or BCD? If BCD is used, is the most-significant digit sent first or last? To help resolve these and other conflicts, an additional standard, IEEE-728, was published that addresses the code and format issues.

8.6 DESIGN EXAMPLE

Figure 8.35 shows the 68901 multifunction peripheral with the RS-232 interface circuitry added. The MFP interface to the 68008 was described in Chapter 5. The RS-232C interface consists primarily of line drivers and receivers. The threshold select inputs of the 1489 receivers are left open. Capacitors are shown on the 1488 outputs to reduce the slew rate when used with short cables. The capacitors can be deleted if the cable length is relatively long. In fact, although the RS-232 slew rate may be exceeded, the capacitors can be eliminated in most applications.

Five of the parallel I/O lines are used for handshake lines. Since each of the parallel I/O bits is programmable as an input or output port, the bit assignments are arbitrary. The pin numbers shown are for a DTE configuration. For a DCE configuration, each pair of signals is reversed, and the DCD signal is an output instead of an input. For maximum flexibility, jumpers can be added to allow the use of either configuration. Since the handshake inputs are all input port bits (and are not monitored by the UART circuitry), there is no auto-enable function, so the the software can decide to ignore the handshake signals if appropriate.

The clock for both transmit and receive is provided by one of the timer channels. Since timers A and B are the most flexible, it is best to leave them available for other functions. For 19.2-kbaud operation, a clock at 16 times that rate, or 307.2 kHz, is required. Since the clock input to the MFP is 2.4576 MHz, a divisor of 8 provides exactly the correct rate. As described in Chap. 5, the timers are clocked by a prescaler. The smallest prescale value available is 4. The timer output pin is driven by a flip-flop that is toggled each time the timer "times out," so the prescaler divide-by-4 and the output divide-by-2 result in an overall divisor of 8, with no division at all by the main

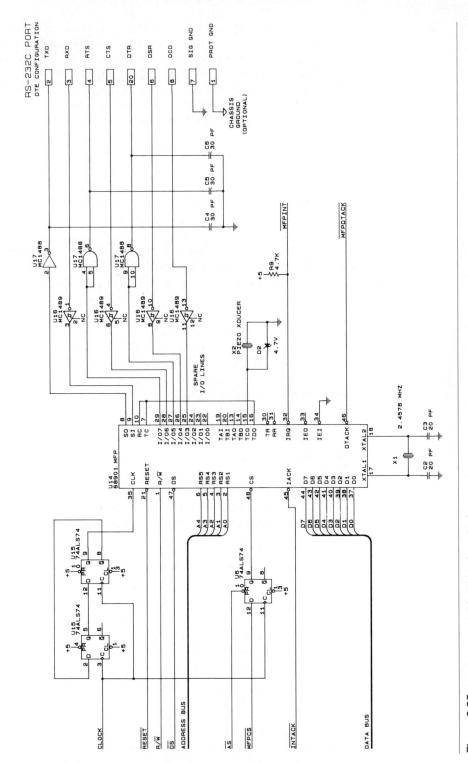

Figure 8.35. Design example RS-232 interface circuit.

Figure 8.36. The 68901 bit rate clock generation.

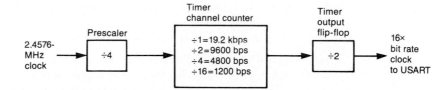

timer counter. Figure 8.36 illustrates this division. This main counter is effectively disabled by setting the time constant value (the value loaded to this counter) to 1, which causes the output flip-flop to be clocked directly by the prescaler. Thus, 19.2 kbaud is the highest data rate that can be used. For 9600 baud the divisor is set to 2, for 4800 baud it is set to 4, for 1200 baud it is set to 16, and so on.

8.7 SUMMARY

Serial data communication allows data to be transferred with a single signal. In addition to reducing wiring requirements, this makes transmission via telephone lines and other communications links possible. Several standard interface specifications, such as RS-232, provide a set of logic level and signal definitions for interconnecting digital devices. U(S)ARTs provide the logic needed to interface the microprocessor's parallel bus structure to a serial data link.

8.8 EXERCISES

8.1. An asynchronous data communications line is operating at 56 kbps. The format used is seven data bits, odd parity, one start bit, and one stop bit. What is the maximum number of characters per second that can be transmitted?

8.2. In Exercise 8.1, what percentage of the time is spent transmitting actual data bits?

8.3. An SDLC synchronous data communications line is transmitting a packet whose information field is 1024 bytes long at 56 kbps. How long does it take to transmit the packet, including the flags, control field, address field, and CRC? What percentage of the time is spent transmitting the data itself?

8.4. A binary data file must be sent via a communications link using the ASCII code. Thus, only seven data bits are available. How can the binary data be transmitted? Describe the conversion process required to send and receive the data.

8.5. A serial data signal has voltage levels of +3.5 V for a space and −4.5 V for a mark. Will this work properly with an RS-232 receiver? Does it meet the RS-232 specification? Will it work with an RS-422 receiver?

8.6. An application requires that data be sent through 500 m of cable at a rate of 10 kbps. Which interface standards could be used?

8.7.   An RS-423 data link is experiencing occasional errors. The rise time of the signals is measured and found to be 10 μs with linear waveshaping. What is the maximum data rate that can be reliably used?

8.8.   A UART has a two-byte received character FIFO buffer in addition to the receive shift register. Assuming 9600-baud operation (960 characters per second), how long does the microprocessor have to respond to an interrupt indicating a character is available before a character is lost? What is this time at 56 kbaud? At 375 kbaud?

8.9.   A synchronous communications link uses 8-bit words and is operating at 100 kbps. The transmitter consists of a data holding register and the output shift register. When an interrupt arrives telling the microprocessor that the buffer is empty, what is the maximum response time allowable to prevent an underrun error?

8.9   SELECTED BIBLIOGRAPHY

General Reference

Friend, George E., et al. *Understanding Data Communications,* Indianapolis: Sams, 1984. Provides more details on protocols and transmission methods than most introductory books but does not describe interface hardware.

Intel. *Microcommunications Handbook,* Santa Clara, CA. Includes data sheets and application notes for Intel's USARTs, protocol controllers, and LAN interface ICs.

McNamara, John E. *Technical Aspects of Data Communication,* 2d ed., Bedford, MA: Digital Press, 1982. A very useful reference, describing asynchronous and synchronous protocols, standards, error detection, electrical interfaces, networks, and multiplexers.

Nichols, Elizabeth A., Joseph C. Nichols, and Keith R. Musson. *Data Communications for Microcomputers, with Practical Applications and Experiments,* New York: McGraw-Hill, 1982. One of the more technical of the many books aimed at users of personal computers.

Sherman, Kenneth. *Data Communications: A Users Guide,* 2d ed., Reston, VA: Reston Publishing Co., 1985. Provides good descriptions of the telephone network, communication protocols, and modem operation.

UARTs and USARTs

For detailed information on individual devices, refer to the manufacturer's data sheets.

Cormier, Denny. "Datacom Protocol ICs," *EDN,* Apr. 3, 1986, pp. 103–114. Includes a directory of common UARTs and USARTs.

National Semiconductor. *Comparison of the INS8250 and NS16450 Series of Asynchronous Communications Elements,* Santa Clara, CA, 1985. Describes the bugs in the original 8250, the differences in the "A" version, and approaches to the interrupt-handling compatibility problems.

Standards

Copies of the "RS" standards are available from the EIA, 2001 Eye St. N.W., Washington, DC 20006. They are also available from National Standards Association, Inc., Bethesda, MD, and from Global Engineering and Documents, Santa Ana, CA, or as part of the compilations listed at the end of this section.

RS-232-C. *Interface Between Data Terminal Equipment and Data Communication Equipment Employing Serial Binary Data Interchange,* 1969.

RS-422-A. *Electrical Characteristics of Balanced Voltage Digital Interface Circuits,* 1978.

RS-423-A. *Electrical Characteristics of Unbalanced Voltage Digital Interface Circuits,* 1978.

RS-449. *General Purpose 37-Position and 9-Position Interface for Data Terminal Equipment and Data Circuit-Terminating Equipment Employing Serial Binary Data Interchange,* 1977.

EIA Industrial Electronic Bulletin No. 9. *Application Notes for RS-232,* 1971.

EIA Industrial Electronic Bulletin No. 12. *Application Notes on Interconnection Between Interface Circuits Using RS-449 and RS-232,* 1977.

IBM Publication No. GA27-3093-2. *General Information —IBM Synchronous Data Link Control,* IBM Systems Development Division, Publication Center.

Folts, Harold C., (ed.). *McGraw-Hill's Compilation of Data Communications Standards,* 3d ed., New York: McGraw-Hill, 1986. Includes the full text for all data communications standards from several U.S. and international organizations, including EIA, CCITT, ANSI, and ISO. Very expensive but comprehensive.

Telebyte Data Communications Standards Library, Greenlawn, NY: Telebyte Technology, Inc. A less-expensive compilation than the one above, including the most-common standards.

IEEE-488 GPIB

Hewlett-Packard. "Tutorial Description of the Hewlett-Packard Interface Bus," Palo Alto, CA, 1984. A general description of HP's implementation of the GPIB.

IEEE 488-1978. *Digital Interface for Programmable Instrumentation,* Piscataway, NJ. The official IEEE-488 standards document.

IEEE 728-1982. *Code and Format Conventions for IEEE-488,* Piscataway, NJ. Provides additional definitions to aid in compatibility among GPIB instruments.

9

MASS STORAGE

9.1 INTRODUCTION

In Chap. 4, we described various types of semiconductor memory: RAMs, ROMs, EPROMs, and EEPROMs. All these memory devices are directly addressable; that is, any location can be selected by providing the corresponding address. Thus, they are called random-access memories. They are often referred to as *main memory,* or *working storage. Mass-storage* devices, the topic of this chapter, differ from main memory devices in several ways. They are:

> Not directly addressable
>
> Low in cost per bit
>
> Nonvolatile
>
> Relatively slow to access

Main memory is intended for storing data and programs in active use; thus, all locations must be directly addressable. Mass storage, on the other hand, is used for programs and data that are not in active use at the moment. For the microprocessor to get at this data, it must first perform some preliminary operations (such as positioning a read/write head over the desired track) to access the desired data, and data must generally be read in a block. Thus, programs cannot be executed directly from a mass-storage device due to the lack of random access. Instead, programs are read from the mass-storage device and stored in main memory while they are needed.

The lack of direct addressability is not entirely a disadvantage. All microprocessors have a limited direct addressing range; for many, this range is 1 Mbyte or less. Since mass-storage devices are not directly addressed, they do not use up large amounts of the addressing capability, and the capacity of the mass-storage devices in a system often far exceeds the system's direct addressing capability.

Mass-storage devices have a relatively low cost per bit. Because of their large capacity the system price may be high, but on a per-bit basis mass storage is less expensive than main memory. In general, the mass-storage devices with the largest capacity have the lowest cost per bit.

A key characteristic of mass-storage devices is that they are nonvolatile. Since they are intended primarily to store programs and data not in current use, they are often expected to retain their contents for a long period of time. Some main memory devices (EPROMs and EEPROMs) are also nonvolatile, but they have a much higher cost per bit.

Mass-storage devices typically have a relatively slow access time. A random-access memory device (such as a ROM or RAM) provides rapid access to any location. Mass-storage devices, on the other hand, require a relatively long time to locate a block of data, and this time is different for different blocks. Once a block is located, it can be read relatively rapidly; the process of locating the data does not need to be repeated for each byte. Thus, there are two separate performance parameters for mass-storage devices: access time and transfer rate. The *access time* is the time it takes to locate a block of data and be ready to transfer the first byte, and the *transfer rate* is the rate at which data can be read or written once the block is located. These two parameters often differ by orders of magnitude.

In this chapter, several mass-storage devices and techniques for interfacing them to a microprocessor system are described. All use magnetic media for storage. The oldest magnetic recording medium still in use is magnetic tape. Tape cartridges are used in certain mass-storage applications but suffer from very slow access times. The most common mass-storage device is the floppy disk. Floppy disks are widely used in personal computers and other applications requiring storage of moderate amounts of data at a moderate cost. *Winchester* (also called *hard,* or *rigid*) disks store more data but are more expensive and usually have nonremovable media.

Magnetic media are always subject to failure from contamination, mishandling, stray magnetic fields, or accidental modification of data. Thus, it is important to be able to easily make copies of each disk or tape. With floppy disks, this is easily accomplished, since they can be removed and stored for safekeeping. Backup disks are easier to make if there are two drives, since data can be read from one and written to the other. Winchester disks, which have nonremovable media, create a more serious backup problem. Floppy disks can be used, but their much smaller capacity makes them a slow and awkward solution. Tape cartridges are a better (but more expensive) solution for hard-disk backup.

Magnetic bubble memory is a type of magnetic storage that, unlike disks or tape, is solid-state. Bubble memory uses semiconductorlike processing techniques, but the storage mechanism is magnetic. Unlike other types of magnetic storage, there are no moving parts in a bubble memory. Rather than moving a magnetic medium (such as a disk or tape) with fixed bit locations past a read/write head, bubble memory uses a stationary medium and moves the bits within the medium.

9.2   MASS-STORAGE TECHNOLOGY

There are three levels at which magnetic data storage can be described:

1.   The fundamental magnetic effects that are the basis of magnetic storage.
2.   The method for encoding data bits into magnetic flux reversals.
3.   The organization of bits in the mass-storage device into useful blocks of data.

Knowledge of these basic principles allows the designer to better understand the characteristics of mass-storage devices and the possibilities for increased storage capacity and performance. This section describes these mass-storage fundamentals to provide a background for the following discussion of specific devices.

9.2.1   Magnetic Recording Principles

Mass-storage devices using magnetic recording are inevitably dependent upon the physics that govern the recording process. To understand the evolution of mass-storage devices and their interfacing requirements, it is helpful to have a basic understanding of magnetic recording principles. This section provides a brief overview of these principles, which are applied in later sections to standard tape and disk drives.

Magnetic recording is by far the most commonly used technology for mass storage. It has a long history, dating back to 1898 when Valdemar Poulsen first demonstrated a magnetic recording and playback apparatus. The first magnetic storage device was the wire recorder, which used spools of steel wire for the recording medium. By passing the wire rapidly past an electromagnet, the wire was magnetized. Varying the signal supplied to the electromagnet varied the force of the field and also the magnetization strength of the wire. When the magnetized wire was again moved past the electromagnet's coil, but with no signal applied to the coil, the coil produced a replica of the signal that was originally written on the wire.

The basic principle used in wire recorders, and most other magnetic recording devices, is that an electromagnet will magnetize a piece of ferrous material that is moved past it. When the magnetized material is moved past an unenergized coil, it induces a voltage in the coil. Steel wire was replaced by paper (and then plastic) strips coated with powdered iron oxide; thus, magnetic tape was born. The read/write head is basically an electromagnet with a highly focused magnetic field.

Figure 9.1 shows the basic read/write head structure, called a *ring head*. It consists of a ring of easily magnetized material (typically ferrite) with a small gap adjacent to the recording surface. Each side of the gap is effectively one pole of the electromagnet; the small size of the gap produces a highly concentrated field. In addition to gap size, other critical parameters are the distance between the head and the medium, and the thickness of the magnetic coating on the medium. Within limits, the smaller these parameters are the more densely data can be stored.

It is easiest to visualize the recording process by imagining that the oxide coating is made up of millions of tiny bar magnets, or *dipoles*, each randomly oriented. Because

Figure 9.1. Basic ring head, showing key dimensions and flux lines. *(Courtesy of Krieger Publishing Co.)*

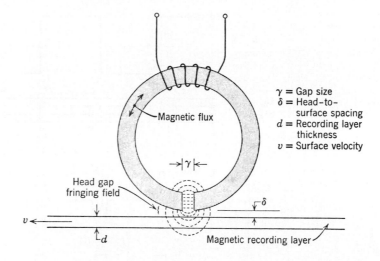

γ = Gap size
δ = Head-to-surface spacing
d = Recording layer thickness
v = Surface velocity

Magnetic flux

Head gap fringing field

Magnetic recording layer

of their random orientation, the net magnetic field is zero. When they are subjected to a magnetic field (such as from an electromagnet), the dipoles align themselves with the external field. When the field is removed, some of the dipoles return to their random orientation, but many remain aligned with the field's direction. Thus, the material has become magnetized.

If a weak magnetic field is applied, many of the dipoles will revert to their random positions when the field is removed. As the field is increased, more and more of the dipoles (and thus the magnetic field) will remain oriented when the external field is removed. Past a certain point, however, increasing the field strength makes no difference; this is the *saturation* level. The amount of magnetization remaining after the field is removed is called *remanence*. The field strength (of opposite direction) required to demagnetize the material is called *coercivity*. A high coercivity is desirable in magnetic media to preserve the data in the presence of stray magnetic fields. However, a high coercivity also indicates that the material requires a strong field to magnetize it, thus making recording more difficult.

Small areas in a magnetic medium, called *domains,* can be magnetized independently of adjacent areas. Each domain can have the opposite magnetic polarity as the adjacent domains. The change from one domain to another of reverse magnetic polarity is called a *flux reversal.* The storage density of a disk or tape can be expressed as *flux reversals per inch (frpi),* commonly called *flux changes per inch (fci).*

In most recording systems, the flux lines are parallel to the direction of motion; this format is called *longitudinal recording.* Another method is *vertical,* or *perpendicular,* recording, in which the flux lines are perpendicular to the surface of the media. Perpendicular recording is more difficult to implement, but flux transitions can occur much closer together than for longitudinal recording, and the potential storage capacity is thus much higher.

Analog recording uses varying field strengths to directly store the analog signal; the magnetic material is not saturated. Digital recording, on the other hand, uses *saturated* recording. Each domain is magnetized as much as possible to one polarity or the other. This provides higher speed and greater noise immunity.

Figure 9.2. Relationship of write current, flux reversals, and read signals.

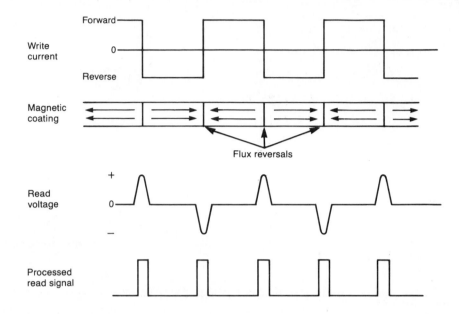

Figure 9.2 shows the relationship between the write signal, flux reversals, and read signal in a saturated recording system. The write signal selects the direction of current flow in the write head, which determines the polarity of the medium's magnetization. A flux reversal occurs when the direction of the write current is reversed. When the data is read, a pulse is produced from the read head at each flux reversal. The direction of the flux change is usually not important, so the analog signal from the read head is amplified and processed to produce a digital signal containing only positive pulses.

One cause of distortion in the reading of magnetic media is a phenomenon called *peak shift,* or *bit shift.* Several factors, including random noise and amplifier non-linearity, contribute to bit shifting. The major cause, however, is the mixing of signals from adjacent flux transitions, as illustrated in Fig. 9.3. The pulse produced at each flux change has finite rise and fall times. When two flux changes occur close together, the signal produced by the read head is the sum of the pulses that would be produced by each flux change individually. The effect of this summation is that the peaks of the resulting signal are farther apart than the flux changes. As long as the peak shift is a small fraction of the spacing between flux transitions, it does not cause any problem. With high-density recording, however, peak shift can cause errors if it is not taken into consideration. The most common approach to eliminating such errors is *precompensation.* Closely spaced flux transitions are recorded closer together than normal bit cell timing would require, so that peak shift will cause the peaks to occur where they were intended to be to begin with.

9.2.2   Data Encoding

Data can be encoded into flux changes in many ways. The problem is similar to that of serial data transmission; a serial bit stream must be written in such a way that the bit

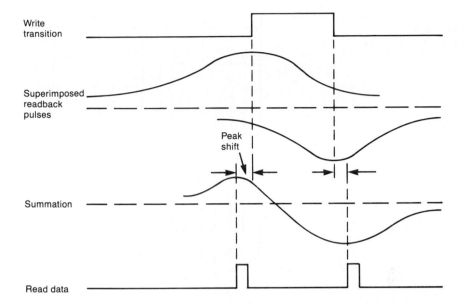

Figure 9.3. Peak shift caused by summation of overlapping signals.

cell positions can be determined when the data is read back. (Some tape drives used in large computer systems record data in parallel, with one channel per bit.) Data density is measured in *bits per inch (bits/in., or bpi)*.

There are two conflicting requirements for encoding data for magnetic recording. First, it is desirable to encode as many data bits as possible in a given number of flux changes. Second, the encoded data must be self-clocking, so the read circuitry can determine the location of each bit. As long as the distance between flux transitions is not too great, a phase-locked loop can be used to extract a bit rate clock from the encoded data stream.

Figure 9.4 shows several possible encoding methods. For all methods, a unit called a *bit cell* is used to encode each bit. A bit cell is a unit of space on the surface of the magnetic medium, and it is a unit of time with respect to the read and write signals. The simplest and most efficient technique is *NRZ,* as is used for serial data communication. However, NRZ is not self-clocking; the signal can be high or low for an arbitrary period of time, making it impossible to create a synchronized clock from the data. Thus, NRZ is not generally used for magnetic recording. *NRZI* encodes data by producing a flux transition for each 1 bit and no transition for each 0 bit. This code is self-clocking only if the data does not contain a long series of zeros.

Phase encoding (PE) is a simple self-clocking encoding method. There is a flux transition at the center of every bit cell, and the direction of the flux transition indicates if the data is a 1 or a 0. Flux transitions occur at bit cell boundaries as needed to allow the proper flux transition at the next bit cell center. Since there is at least one flux transition per bit cell, this code is self-clocking. However, it is inefficient, requiring as many as two flux transitions per bit. Phase encoding is the only common format in which the direction of the flux change is significant. It is used primarily in older tape drives of larger computer systems.

Frequency modulation (FM) has the same efficiency as phase encoding but does not

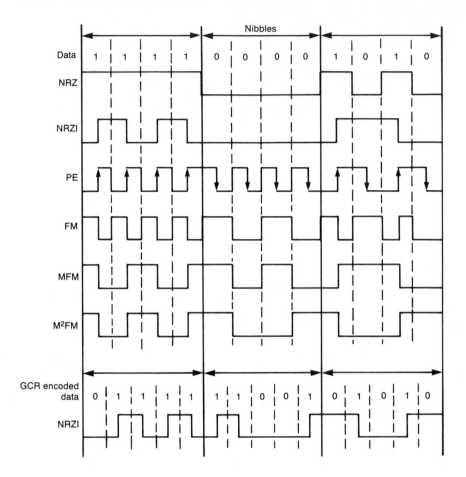

depend on the direction of the flux changes. (FM in this context should not be confused with frequency-shift keying, or FSK, which is commonly thought of as FM. This encoding method is called FM because there are twice as many flux changes for a 1 as for a 0.) FM is similar to NRZI in that a 1 is encoded as a flux change at the center of the bit cell, while a 0 produces no flux change. In addition, a flux change occurs at every bit cell boundary, making it self-clocking. FM was the first encoding method widely used for floppy disks, and it is often called *single-density* recording in that context. It requires up to two flux changes per bit.

Modified frequency modulation (MFM) uses the same basic approach as FM but eliminates most of the flux transitions at bit cell boundaries. A flux transition occurs at a bit cell boundary only if the preceding bit and the following bit are both 0. This encoding method guarantees that no more than two bit cells can occur without a flux transition and is thus self-clocking. MFM is the most commonly used encoding technique for floppy disks, and it is often called *double-density* recording in that context. It requires an average of one flux change per bit.

Modified MFM (M^2FM) further eliminates some of the bit cell boundary transitions in MFM. In addition to the MFM rules, flux transitions at bit cell boundaries are de-

Table 9.1   GCR Translation Table

Data nibble	Run-length code	Data nibble	Run-length code
0000	11001	1000	11010
0001	11011	1001	01001
0010	10010	1010	01010
0011	10011	1011	01011
0100	11101	1100	11110
0101	10101	1101	01101
0110	10110	1110	01110
0111	10111	1111	01111

leted if there was a flux transition at the start of the preceding bit cell. Although this technique was originally recommended by Shugart Associates for double-density floppy-disk drives and was used in some systems, IBM used MFM and the rest of the industry followed.

NRZI can be modified to be self-clocking by using a technique called *group-coded recording (GCR),* as shown at the bottom of Fig. 9.4. First, each group of 4 bits is translated into a 5-bit code. Thus, this is also called the 4/5 code. Table 9.1 lists the translation table. This translation increases the number of data bits by 20 percent, so at first it seems to be inefficient. However, the 5-bit codes are defined such that the resulting data stream is guaranteed never to contain more than two consecutive zeros. Thus, GCR encoded data can be recorded using NRZI, and is guaranteed to be self-clocking. No additional clock transitions are required, as with FM or MFM. Thus, GCR is more efficient than MFM and is widely used in high-density disk and tape recording. The disadvantage of GCR is the relatively high complexity of the encoding and decoding logic.

GCR is called a *run-length-limited (RLL)* code, since it limits the number of zeros that can occur in a row. Other RLL codes with more complex translation schemes have even higher efficiencies and are used in high-performance hard disks. One widely used code is called *RLL 2,7.* The numbers refer to the minimum and maximum number of zeros that can occur in a row; 2,7 means that the number of successive zeros between ones is a minimum of two and a maximum of seven. In this terminology, GCR is an RLL 0,2 code. The RLL 2,7 code can store 60 percent more data than MFM in the same space. Using NRZI recording, only ones produce flux changes. Since RLL 2,7 guarantees a minimum of two zeros between ones, the bit density can be increased without increasing the flux change density. RLL codes use an average of less than one flux change per bit.

FM and MFM are the most commonly used data encoding methods for disk drives. Figure 9.5 shows FM and MFM signals as read from and written to the drive. The disk drive electronics generally includes a flip-flop whose state determines the direction of the write current. Each time the write signal to the drive is pulsed, the state of the flip-flop is changed. For FM, a clock pulse occurs at every bit cell boundary. For a 1 data cell, there is a pulse at the center of the cell; for a 0 data cell, there is no pulse between

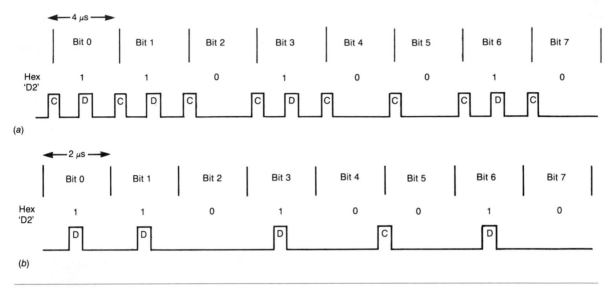

Figure 9.5. *(a)* FM and *(b)* MFM signals as they appear at disk drive interface. C = clock pulse; D = data pulse.

the clock pulses. Generating a clock signal from this format is quite simple, since there is a clock pulse at every bit cell boundary. With MFM encoding, clock pulses are present only at the boundary between two cells that are both 0.

9.2.3 Recording Formats

To make it possible to access individual portions of a magnetic recording, the data must be divided into sections. These sections are generally called *blocks* for tapes, or *sectors* for disks. Each section begins with an identification field and ends with an error detection code (typically a cyclic redundancy check, or CRC). Gaps between sections are required to allow one section to be modified without affecting neighboring sections. (Gaps serve other purposes as well, as described later in this chapter). This arrangement of data is called the *format*. The total number of bits that can be recorded on the media is called the *unformatted* capacity. The amount left for actual data (subtracting the overhead for gaps, ID fields, and CRCs) is the *formatted* capacity. The formatted capacity is the number of interest to the end user, since this is the amount of user data that can be stored. Specific formats for tape and disk recording are described later in this chapter.

In most applications, many different files are stored on a single tape cartridge or disk. To locate a file, a *directory* is needed. The directory is an area at the start of the tape (or a track on a disk) that contains a list of all the files and indicates the point on the disk or tape where each file begins. The structure of the directory is determined by the operating system software. Part of the disk or tape may also be used to store the operating system software itself. Thus, the usable capacity as seen by the system user is the formatted capacity of the disk or tape minus the portions used for the directory and system software.

Most systems include software in ROM or EPROM that allows the system to read the operating system software from the disk at power-up. This is often called the *boot-strap*, or *boot*, ROM, and the process of loading the operating system from the disk is called *booting* the system. The boot ROM contains only enough software to read the operating system software, which is generally stored on a specific track of the disk; the operating system software itself provides the capability to perform more general read/ write accesses. A *BIOS* (*basic input/output system*) ROM includes the boot function and a collection of subroutines to provide a standard software interface for the system.

9.3 MAGNETIC TAPE RECORDING

Magnetic tape has been widely used for both analog and digital recording. Although its use in digital systems has been greatly reduced by the advent of low-cost disk drives, it is still useful in certain applications. This section describes types of disk drives and media and one formatting and interface standard.

9.3.1 Types of Tape Drives

A variety of tape drives are available, ranging from under-$50 audio recorders to high-performance reel-to-reel digital drives costing over $10,000. The reel-to-reel drives commonly used in minicomputer and mainframe computer systems are generally too expensive for use in microprocessor-based systems.

Digital tape recording has had an ironic relationship with disk drives. When floppy disks were introduced, the market for low-cost digital tape recorders was significantly reduced. Then, when Winchester-type hard disks became popular, a backup medium was needed. Tape cartridges serve this need well, and Winchester disk backup is now the primary application of digital tape cartridges. Tape is generally used for archival storage, in which the data stored is unlikely to be used in the near future.

Tape drives can operate in one of two modes. *Start-stop* (also called *incremental*) drives can start and stop for each block of data. The data is divided into blocks with identification headers and gaps between them, which allows any block to be selectively located and read or written. *Streaming* tape drives, on the other hand, are designed to read and write long, continuous streams of data. The tape does not stop between blocks, and no space is wasted on gaps. This mode of operation is most efficient for copying the entire contents of a disk for backup purposes. Streaming drives are less expensive than start-stop drives because of the simpler drive mechanism, which cannot start and stop the tape quickly. Streaming drives pack more data onto the tape and read and write at higher data rates.

The common audio cassette (often called the *Philips* cassette after its originator) can be used for digital data, but its performance is often poor. A very low cost digital storage system can be built by using a standard audio cassette recorder and a simple frequency-shift keyed (FSK) modulator/demodulator. This technique is commonly used in low-end home computers. The modulator and demodulator are similar to a telephone-line modem. Data rates are limited to 300 to 1200 bps, so read and write times are long. Access to an arbitrary point on the tape can take several minutes.

Higher-performance digital cassette drives using saturated recording are also available. These drives use cassettes that are similar to audio cassettes, but they incorporate higher-quality construction and tape to improve reliability.

Because of the performance and reliability limitations of Philips cassettes, a family of tape cartridges was designed by 3M explicitly for digital recording and has become an industry standard. These cartridges use ¼-in.-wide tape, rather than the ⅛-in.-wide tape used in Philips-type cassettes. There are two standard physical sizes of 3M-type ¼-in. tape cartridges, originally called the DC-100 (with 100 ft of tape) and the DC-300 (with 300 ft of tape). The overall dimensions of the larger tape cartridge are 4 by 6 in. Extended-length cartridges are available, with 450 or 600 ft of tape in a DC-300-type cartridge; the DC-100-type cartridges commonly contain 140 ft of tape.

As shown in Fig. 9.6, a rubber belt inside the cartridge controls tape motion and automatically maintains tension. The drive requires only a single motor and drive roller, which presses on the capstan roller in the cartridge. Small holes in the tape near each end allow the drive to sense the end of the tape and stop before it is reached. A write protect tab allows the contents of the tape to be protected from accidental writing.

The DC-1000 and DC-2000 are newer variations on the DC-100-type cartridges. The DC-1000 uses 0.15-in.-wide tape and the DC-2000 uses ¼-in.-wide tape. The original capacities were 10 and 20 Mbytes, respectively, but these have now been more than doubled. Figure 9.7 shows a DC-300 and a DC-1000 cartridge.

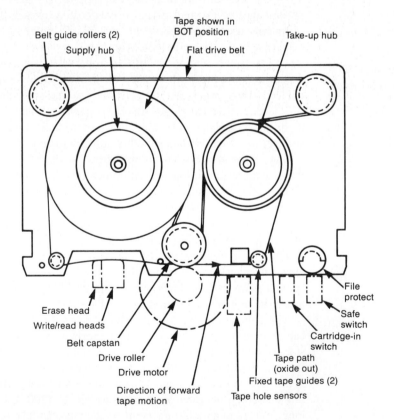

Figure 9.6. Data cartridge internal structure and drive mechanism.

Figure 9.7. The 3M-type data cartridges. *(Courtesy of 3M.)*

9.3.2 Quarter-Inch Cartridge Standards

Many different formats have been used for recording data on 3M-type tape cartridges, and many systems are incompatible with virtually all others. Even though they can accept the same physical cartridge, one system often cannot read data written by another type of system.

To address compatibility problems, an industry group called the "Working Group for Quarter-Inch Cartridge Drive Compatibility" (QIC for short) was formed, and developed several standards. As of this writing, the QIC standards are being followed as de facto standards while they are considered for adoption by ANSI and other formal standards organizations.

The QIC-02 standard defines the interface between the host computer and the tape controller. This interface is designed for use with an "intelligent" controller; the host computer sends relatively high-level commands, such as read block or write block, and the controller must perform all the functions necessary to implement the command.

Figure 9.8. QIC-02 and QIC-36 interfaces, showing signals for QIC-02 interface.

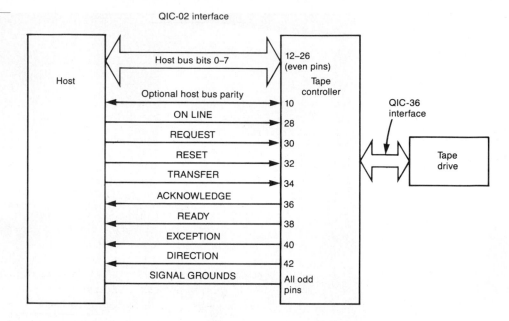

Figure 9.8 shows the signals in the QIC-02 interface. It is an 8-bit parallel, bidirectional interface with handshake and control lines. The precise meaning of each control signal depends on the current mode of operation, which is selected by sending a command via the data bus. The basic data handshake is performed by the TRANSFER and ACKNOWLEDGE signals. In write mode, the host asserts TRANSFER when it has placed data on the bus, and the controller asserts ACKNOWLEDGE when it has read the data. In read mode, the functions of the two signals are reversed. This interface is easy to implement in any microprocessor system using parallel I/O ports and a small amount of control logic. The QIC-02 standard defines both this electrical interface and the commands and data that are sent via the interface.

The QIC-36 interface standard defines the signals between the controller and the tape drive itself. This is a low-level interface, and assumes no intelligence in the tape drive. The QIC-24 standard specifies the format of the data on the tape to allow interchange of tapes between systems. These standards are of concern primarily to manufacturers of tape drives and controllers. System designers will, in most cases, purchase the drive and controller and need only provide the QIC-02 interface to the controller. For lowest cost, however, an interface can be built directly from the host system's bus (such as the Multibus or IBM PC bus) to the QIC-36 drive interface, bypassing the QIC-02 interface.

The QIC-24 data format uses *serpentine* recording, as shown in Fig. 9.9. Only one track is recorded at a time. At the end of the track, the direction of the tape is reversed, and the next track is recorded in the reverse direction. The head is repositioned as necessary. For example, a two-track head used to record a nine-track tape needs five different positions to access all nine tracks. The QIC-24 format allows for either four or nine tracks, recorded at a bit density of 10,000 fci. Group-coded recording is used to achieve a high bit density. Since GCR produces five flux transitions for every four data bits, the data density is 8000 bits/in. Tape speed is 30 or 90 in./s (ips). The maximum

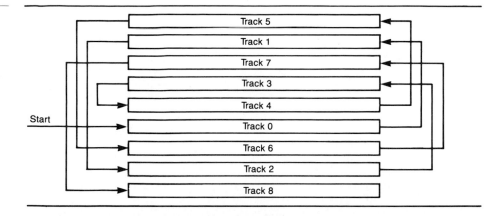

Figure 9.9. QIC-24 nine-track serpentine recording format.

Track 5
Track 1
Track 7
Track 3
Track 4
Start
Track 0
Track 6
Track 2
Track 8

data transfer rate at 90 ips is 90,000 bytes/s. A cyclic redundancy check is used at the end of each 512-byte block for error detection, providing the data integrity essential for a backup application. A read after write can be performed to verify that the write was successfully completed. Standard data capacities are 20, 45, and 60 Mbytes, depending on the length of the tape and number of tracks.

9.4 DISK FUNDAMENTALS

While cartridge tape drives can provide large capacities at a moderate cost, they suffer from one serious drawback: very slow access time. In the worst-case situation, the tape must be rewound (or fast-forwarded) nearly the entire length of the tape to access the desired information, which can take over a minute. Disk drives have much faster access times and are thus more suitable as a general-purpose mass-storage device. Tape cartridges are most useful for secondary, long-term (archival) storage. This section describes the types of disk drives, their operation, and factors that affect performance.

9.4.1 Disk Types

Two fundamentally different disk technologies are in common use: flexible, or *floppy,* disks, and rigid, or *hard,* disks. A floppy disk is made of the same materials as magnetic tape: an iron oxide coating on a Mylar base. As with tape recording, the read/write head is in direct contact with the medium.

Hard disks use a highly polished aluminum substrate coated with iron oxide or plated with a thin metallic film. Because the disk is rigid, the head cannot be allowed to contact the disk during normal operation or catastrophic damage can occur (commonly known as a *head crash*). The head actually "flies" over the surface of the disk, using aerodynamic effects to keep it off the surface. To maintain high recording density, the distance from the head to the disk (the *flying height*) must be very small: typically tens of microinches. As Fig. 9.10 shows, this distance makes a very clean environment

Figure 9.10. Relationship of Winchester disk head flying height to various particle sizes.

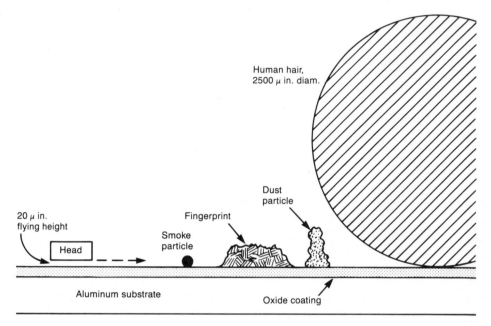

critical. Even a dust particle or a fingerprint is gigantic when compared to typical flying heights, and their presence can cause failure of the disk.

The advantage of rigid disks is that they are more mechanically stable than floppy disks. This allows the tracks to be spaced much more closely together and therefore increases the amount of data that can be stored. It also allows the disk to spin much faster, which provides a higher data transfer rate.

All floppy disks and some hard disks have removable media, which allows an unlimited amount of *off-line* storage (boxes of disks on the shelf). Only one disk can be accessed at a time (per drive), but the total amount of storage available is unlimited. The most common hard disks, called *Winchester* disks, use nonremovable media. Thus, the total storage capacity and the on-line capacity are the same. This is a limitation, but it is necessary to keep down the cost of the drives. Winchester disks are described in detail in Sec. 9.6.

Floppy disks and hard disks are available in a variety of sizes. The most common floppy sizes are 8 in., 5¼ in. (often called *minifloppy*), and 3½ in. (often called *microfloppy*). The 8- and 5¼-in. disk drives are available in *full-height* and *half-height* configurations. Microfloppy drives are less standardized and are available in several heights.

The first floppy-disk drives were *single-sided,* using only one side of the disk. *Double-sided* drives use both sides of the disk, thus doubling the storage capacity. Double-sided drives have two read/write heads, one for each side.

The medium in a hard disk is often called a *platter*. Each side of the platter has its own read/write head. Most hard-disk drives have multiple platters attached to a single spindle.

In a disk drive with more than one recording surface, only one head is active at any time. All heads are positioned together. The group of tracks that are accessed with the heads in any given position is called a *cylinder*. For a double-sided floppy-disk drive, a cylinder consists of two tracks on opposite sides of the disk.

9.4.2 Disk Drive Operation

All disk systems, whether flexible or rigid, have many features in common. Data is recorded in concentric circles on the disk, called *tracks*. The length of each track is shortest near the center of the disk and longest near the outside edge. In most systems, the disk spins at a constant speed and the data rate is also constant, so each track stores the same number of bits and the bit density is highest on the innermost tracks. Such systems limit the bit density based on the length of the inner tracks, and the outer tracks operate at a lower density. A few systems vary disk rotation speed to maintain the same bit density on all tracks, thus increasing the total capacity by allowing more data to be stored on the outer tracks. However, this complicates the drive and the interface.

The disk is spun by the spindle motor, which may be an ac or dc motor depending on the type of drive. Drives with ac motors typically spin the disk continuously, while floppy-disk drives with dc motors allow the rotation to be stopped except when the disk is being accessed. Hard disks spin much faster and require considerable time to reach operating speed, and also depend on the disk rotation to keep the heads off the disk surface, so they are not stopped between accesses.

Once the flux density has been set, the speed of rotation determines the data transfer rate. Data transfer rates vary from 125 kbps for a single-density minifloppy to 5 to 10 Mbps for most hard disks.

The positioning mechanism positions the read/write head over the desired track, as shown in Fig. 9.11. In most disk drives, a stepper motor is used for head positioning,

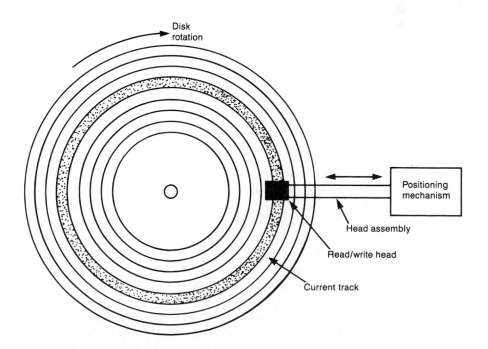

Figure 9.11. Selection of track by positioning mechanism.

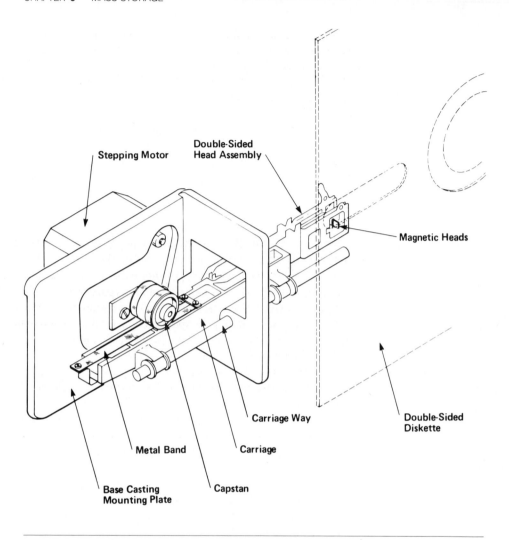

Figure 9.12.   Split-band head positioning mechanism.

with one step moving the head one track. Since the stepper motor produces rotary motion, some mechanism must be used to convert this motion to linear motion for positioning the head. One common approach, called a *band* positioner, is shown in Fig. 9.12. A steel band wraps around the stepper motor shaft and pulls the carriage (to which the head is attached) in the desired direction.

A stepper motor provides accurate relative motion but does not provide any indication of absolute position. A *track 0 sensor* detects when the head is positioned over track 0 (the outermost track) and provides the absolute position reference. When the drive is first turned on, the head is stepped out until the track 0 sensor is actuated, and the head is then stepped in to access the desired track.

Track density, unlike bit density within the track, is not limited by magnetic considerations. Instead, the limiting factor is how accurately and repeatedly the head can be positioned over a specified track. In a floppy drive, the thermal and hygroscopic (humidity-related) expansion and contraction of the disk is the most troublesome problem. The larger the diameter of the disk, the more movement can occur on the outer tracks. Thus, track density is generally higher on smaller floppy disks. This effect negates for the most part the advantage of larger floppy disks and is one reason why a reduction in disk diameter often does not require a reduction in storage capacity.

A basic stepper motor positioning mechanism is an *open-loop* system, since there is no feedback signal telling the controller how far the head has actually moved. Open-loop positioning systems are adequate for all standard floppy disks, which have a track density of 48 or 96 tracks per in. (tpi), and for hard disks with track densities up to approximately 250 tpi. For high track densities or high-speed operation, *closed-loop* positioning mechanisms are used. A closed-loop positioner operates as a servo-mechanism. Servo information is typically stored on the disk to provide the position feedback. The positioning mechanism adjusts the head position until the feedback signal indicates that the head is located over the desired track. Closed-loop positioning systems are rarely used on floppy-disk drives but are common in high-performance hard-disk drives. Hard-disk drives with removable media use closed-loop positioning systems to ensure compatibility of media among drives.

A *dedicated* servo uses an entire disk surface to provide this position information, and is commonly used in hard disks with multiple platters. Another approach is the *embedded* servo. An embedded servo stores servo information in selected areas of the same disk surface used for data. In some systems, servo information is stored only at a few places on each track. The most sophisticated systems have servo information combined with the data along the entire length of every track. This *track-following* type of servo is the most accurate, since it can continuously compensate for variations in track position. It is used primarily in hard disks with track densities in the 1000-tpi range.

Closed-loop positioning systems usually use a *voice-coil* positioner rather than a stepper motor. This device operates similarly to a voice coil in a speaker, moving forward or backward depending on the current through the coil. Voice-coil systems are completely dependent on the servo information for determining the position of the head. Another type of positioning system uses a rotary (nonstepper) motor. Disk drives with closed-loop positioning systems are significantly more expensive than open-loop drives but provide faster seek times and higher track densities.

9.4.3 Disk Performance

The time required to move from one track to an adjacent track is called the *track-to-track access time*. A typical value for a minifloppy-disk drive is 3 ms, although this varies depending on the drive construction. This parameter is key to the performance of the system, since it is the main determinant of the overall access time. The track-to-track access time must be multiplied by the number of tracks to be moved to determine the overall positioning time. At the end of the positioning time, a *settling time* delay must be added to allow the head position to stabilize.

The time to access a specific location on a disk is composed of two parts: the *seek time*, which is the total head positioning time including the settling time, and the *rotational latency*, which is the time for the disk to rotate to the desired position.

In the worst case, to seek a particular track the head must be moved from the outermost to the innermost track; on the average, the head must be moved over a third of the total number of tracks. Thus, the average seek time is one-third the total number of tracks multiplied by the track-to-track access time, plus the settling time. For an 80-track minifloppy with a 3-ms track-to-track access time and a 15-ms settling time, the average seek time is

$$\frac{80 \text{ tracks}}{3} \times 3 \text{ ms (track-to-track)} + 15 \text{ ms (settling)} = 95 \text{ ms}$$

The rotational latency is determined by the rotational speed of the disk. In the worst case, one full rotation is required; on the average, one-half rotation is needed. Thus, for a minifloppy rotating at 300 rpm, the average latency is 100 ms. For a hard disk rotating at 3600 rpm, this is reduced to 8.3 ms.

To determine the total average access time, the seek time and latency must be added together. For the typical floppy drive used in the preceding examples, a 95-ms average

Table 9.2   Key Characteristics of Common Disk Drive Types

	Floppy Disks				**5¼-in. Hard Disks**	
	8 in.	Standard 5¼ in.	High-density 5¼ in.	3½ in.	Low to middle range	High end
Rotational speed, rpm	360	300	360	300/600	3600	3600
Av rotational latency, ms	83.3	100	83.3	100/50	8.3	8.3
Av seek time, ms	90	90	90	150–350	65–120	25–45
Transfer rate, MFM, bits/s	500K	250K	500K	250K/500K	5M	5M–10M
Flux density, fci	6530–6820	5870–5925	9646	8187–8717	9000–10,000	10,000–15,000
Track density, tpi	48	48/96	96	135	250–600	500–1100
Typical formatted capacity, MFM double-sided, bytes	1.0M–1.2M	250K–360K/ 500K–720K	1.2M	720K	5M–70M	60M–380M
No. of tracks (per side for floppy)	77	40/80	80	80	612–8162	7500–18,500

seek and settling time plus a 100-ms latency equals 195 ms. A typical low-cost hard disk has a slightly faster average seek time, but its much smaller rotational latency reduces the total average access time to less than half that of a minifloppy.

Table 9.2 shows several key parameters for various types of disk drives. The values in this table are typical but do not cover all models and manufacturers.

Floppy-disk drives generally spin the disk only when an access is requested. Thus, the motor start-up time also adds to the total access time. This ranges from a few tenths of a second to 1 s, depending on the drive. The disk is typically kept spinning until there are no requests for a second or two, so the motor turn-on delay affects only the first access of a series.

Another aspect of disk performance is reliability. Three error specifications are commonly provided: seek errors, soft read errors, and hard read errors. Common values are 1 in 10^6 seeks, 1 in 10^9 bits, and 1 in 10^{12} bits, respectively. A seek error is recoverable by restoring to track 0 and then repeating the seek (in response to a seek error indication from the disk controller). A soft read error is recoverable by reading the data again, and a hard read error is unrecoverable. Error-correcting codes can be used to decrease effective error rates, but they reduce the available storage (unless the bit density is increased).

9.5 FLOPPY DISKS

9.5.1 The 8- and 5¼-Inch Floppy Disks

The first floppy disk developed used an 8-in.-diameter disk. It was developed by IBM not as a general-purpose storage device but only as a program loading device for the System 370 mainframe computer. The floppy disk stored the system's microcode, which was loaded into RAM when the system was turned on. Shugart Associates first marketed the floppy-disk drive as a general-purpose mass-storage device for small computer systems.

The 5¼-in. minifloppy disk was developed by Shugart Associates to provide a less expensive alternative to 8-in. drives. Originally, minifloppies had a smaller storage capacity, but advanced versions of the minifloppy now have the same storage capacity as standard 8-in. disks. The 8-in. disk capacities have not continued to grow because of the problems of media expansion over the larger diameter and because the popularity of the smaller drives eliminated the incentive for further development.

Figure 9.13 shows an 8-in. floppy disk and a minifloppy disk. A plastic jacket encloses the Mylar media. The read/write head contacts the media through a long slot in the jacket. The jacket has a circular opening in the center which is slightly larger than the circular hole in the center of the media, thus exposing a ring of the media. The drive spindle, which is attached to the drive motor, clamps on to this ring. The drive spindle, and thus the disk medium, rotates at 360 rpm for an 8-in. drive or at 300 rpm for a standard minifloppy.

The index hole is a small hole in both the medium and the jacket. Once per revolution these holes are aligned, which provides a rotational position reference.

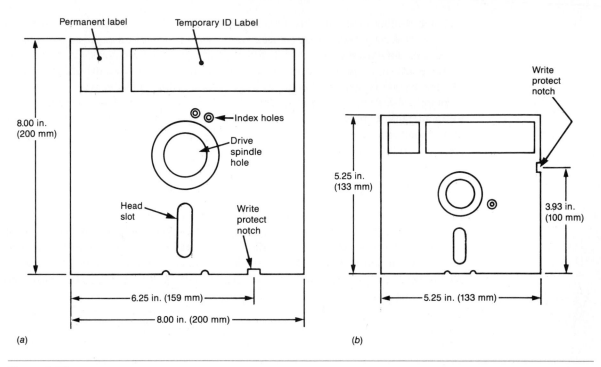

Figure 9.13. *(a)* 8-in. floppy disk and *(b)* 5¼-in. minifloppy diskette.

The write protect notch is a notch in the jacket, which for an 8-in. disk is covered to allow writing on the disk or uncovered to *write-protect* the disk. Write protection prevents accidental loss of data and is particularly useful for master program disks. The write protect notch on a minifloppy has the opposite polarity; it is covered to write-protect the disk. One advantage of the 5¼-in. approach is that disks can be manufactured without the write protect notch for use as program distribution disks. This prevents them from being written by a normal drive. The software manufacturer uses a special drive which allow writing on the "protected" disk, but the user cannot accidentally (or purposely) write on the disk.

Early 8-in. disk drives used synchronous ac motors that operated directly from the ac power line and ran continuously. One problem with such drives is that they require modification for different power line frequencies. Some 8-in. drives and all minifloppy drives use a dc motor with a servo speed control. The dc motors start relatively rapidly and can be turned on and off each time the drive is used.

Standard 8-in. disks have 77 tracks. Double-sided drives have a total of 154 tracks, or 77 cylinders of two tracks each. The original minifloppy drives used 35 tracks. This was soon extended to 40 tracks by simply using a wider area of the disk. The track density in both cases is the same as for 8-in. disks, 48 tpi. Minifloppy drives are also available with twice the track density, with 80 tracks at a density of 96 tpi. The magnetic density within each track (flux changes per in.) is the same for the 40- and 80-track drives, so no fundamental changes are required to the heads or the media. The 80-track drives do require a more accurate head positioning mechanism and are more sensitive to disk expansion and contraction due to temperature and humidity changes.

High-density minifloppy drives use a higher flux density and rotate at 360 rpm to achieve a capacity (1.2 Mbytes) and transfer rate (500 kbps) identical to a double-sided, double-density 8-in. floppy. The higher bit density requires not only a different read/write head but also an improved medium with higher coercivity. Some high-capacity drives are available with dual-speed operation for 300 or 360 rpm operation to allow compatibility with standard minifloppy disks and controllers. The first product to use these high-capacity minifloppy drives in large volume was IBM's PC/AT, which established them as a new standard.

9.5.2 Microfloppy Disks

Minifloppy disks have largely replaced 8-in. floppy disks because of their lower cost and smaller size. Smaller microfloppy disks were a natural next step after minifloppies matured. Disks were developed with diameters of 3.0, 3.25, 3.5, and 3.9 in. Some used a soft jacket similar to those used for 8- and 5¼-in. disks, while others used a rigid plastic shell. The 3.9-in. disk was IBM's entry, which was introduced after most of the other competitors. IBM was too late to set the standard as they did with the 8-in. disk, and in a rare move IBM withdrew the drive from the market in the face of poor acceptance. Sony's 3½-in. disk in a rigid shell was the first to be introduced, and after a long struggle (and several modifications) the Sony-type disk now dominates the microfloppy market.

Figure 9.14 shows the Sony 3½-in. disk. There are several notable departures from earlier disk designs. The shell is rigid, providing protection for the medium inside. A spring-loaded shutter automatically covers the head access slot when the disk is

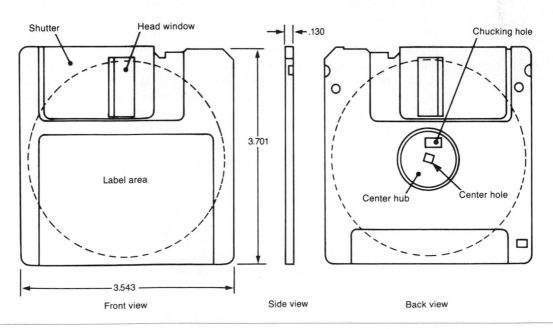

Figure 9.14. Microfloppy disk: *(a)* side view; *(b)* back view.

removed from the drive. Instead of a removable write-protect label, a permanently attached plastic tab can be rotated to protect or unprotect the disk. A metal "chucking hole" on both sides of the disk aligns with pins in the drive, providing a better linkage to the drive motor than the clamping technique used with larger disks. Each of these changes makes the disk more rugged and easier to use than larger, soft-jacketed disks. Ruggedness is particularly important with microfloppies, since they are small enough to be carried in a shirt pocket or purse.

Sony's 3½-in. disk achieved de facto standard status when it was incorporated into Apple's Macintosh and Hewlett-Packard's personal computers. However, the exact characteristics of the medium, the speed of rotation, and the format of the data on the disk have eluded complete standardization. Both HP and Sony used proprietary versions of the disk and drive in their initial products.

The original Sony drive spins the disk at 600 rpm and provides data transfer speeds identical to 8-in. floppy drives. However, the desire for compatibility with minifloppy controllers led to a version with a 300 rpm speed, which is now the most common. The data on the disk is the same regardless of the speed of the rotation; only the transfer rate changes.

The Sony microfloppy drive represents not only a reduction in size but improvements based on years of experience with larger drives. The drives are not only much smaller than earlier drives but also require much less power and have fewer components. The reduction in drive size is much greater than the simple reduction in disk diameter. All dimensions are reduced, resulting in a significant reduction in volume. The volume of a microfloppy drive is approximately one-fourteenth that of a standard 8-in. drive, and one-third that of a half-height minifloppy drive.

Microfloppies use a track density of 135 tpi to pack 80 tracks on the disk. Double-sided microfloppies have 160 tracks. This is a higher track density than even the high-density minifloppies. This is possible in part due to improved positioning mechanisms and the improved alignment of the hard shell case. A major factor making this track density possible is the small diameter of the disk. The smaller the diameter, the less thermal and hygroscopic expansion and contraction, which is generally the limiting factor in determining track density.

Microfloppy disks use the same number of tracks as 96 tpi minifloppy disks. The track length on the microfloppies is shorter, but they use a higher flux density to store the same number of bits per track. At 300 rpm, the microfloppy has the same data rate as standard minifloppies. Thus, microfloppies can be compatible with disk controllers and software designed for minifloppies. However, some systems manufacturers sacrifice this compatibility to obtain a higher transfer rate or larger storage capacity.

9.5.3   Floppy-Disk-Drive Operation

Figure 9.15 shows the key components of a floppy-disk drive and the primary interface signals. The interface signals are described in detail in Sec. 9.5.6. Except as indicated in the following descriptions, the basic operation is the same regardless of the size of disk.

Data is read and written by the read/write head via the read and write logic. The controller provides the encoded data stream during a write operation and receives the encoded data stream during a read operation. No data buffering is performed by

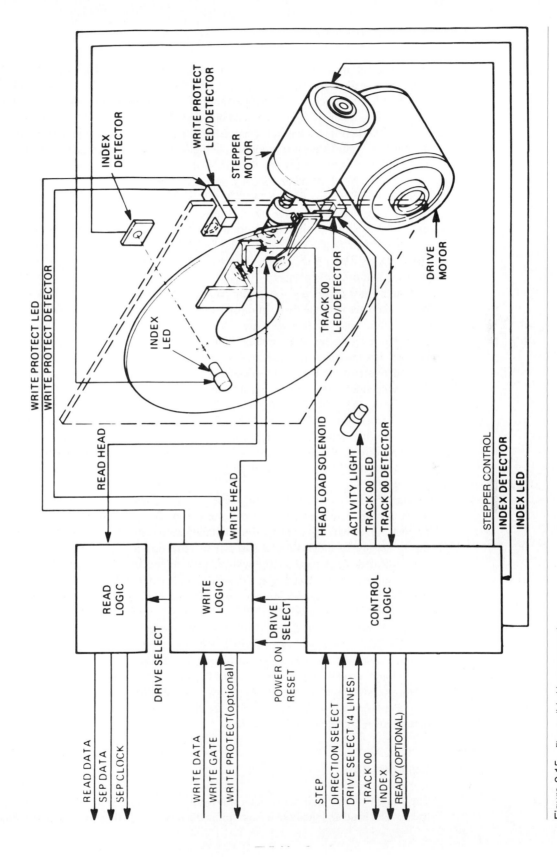

Figure 9.15. Floppy-disk-drive components.

the drive; data must be transferred as the desired part of the disk is passing under the read/write head. Before performing a read or write operation, the head is positioned over the desired track by the stepper motor. The controller provides a series of step pulses, each of which moves the head one track.

An LED illuminates the index hole, and when the holes in the jacket and the media are aligned, a photodetector produces the index pulse. A similar LED-sensor pair (or a mechanical switch) detects whether the disk is write-protected, and if so, the write current is inhibited. Another optical sensor detects when the head is positioned over the outermost track to provide the TRACK 00 signal.

In a microfloppy drive, the index hole is a cutout in the metal hub. There is no hole in the disk medium itself. The cutout is detected by a Hall-effect sensor in the drive.

Some drives produce a "drive ready" signal that indicates that the motor is up to speed. Depending on the drive, the "ready" signal may indicate only that a disk is installed and power is present.

Single-sided drives use a pressure pad on the opposite side of the disk to keep the head in contact with the disk. In most 8-in. disk drives, a *head load solenoid* engages this pressure pad. When read/write operations are not in process, the head can be unloaded to reduce wear on the media. Most minifloppy and microfloppy drives leave the head always loaded, since the disk does not rotate when it is not being accessed. Thus, these drives have no head load solenoid or head load control signal.

Double-sided drives have a head on both sides of the disk, so no pressure pad is needed. One head is fixed, and the head load solenoid (for drives with a head load control) loads the other head against the disk. Early double-sided drives had problems with disk wear, but through innovative mechanical design (and several years of trial and error) reliable double-sided drives were developed. The most common approach, originally developed and patented by Tandon, uses one fixed head and one gimballed head.

The physical size and mounting holes for each size of drive are standardized to allow easy interchange of drives from various vendors. For 8- and 5¼-in. drives, the original full-height drives have been gradually replaced with half-height drives that require only half as much vertical space. This reduction in size is the result of improved mechanical design, particularly with respect to the drive motors. Two half-height drives can be installed in a space designed for a single full-height drive. For 3½-in. microfloppies, the original Sony drives are 2.0 in. high, and slim-line drives 1.6 or 1.2 in. high are also available.

Minifloppy and 8-in. floppy drives use a spring-loaded mechanism to eject the disk from the drive when the door is opened. Microfloppy drives have no door, and the eject button provides an electrical signal which in turn activates the eject solenoid. Standard microfloppy drives do not provide control of this signal from the controller. However, custom versions such as used in Apple's Macintosh allow the disk controller to control the eject solenoid, making it possible for the system software to prevent removal of disks until it completes its transactions.

9.5.4   Disk Formats

The design of the disk drive determines the track spacing and thus the number of tracks. The head and medium design limits the flux change density. The arrangement of the data within the tracks, however, is determined by the controller. The first commercial product to use a floppy disk was the IBM 3740, and the format used by this system became the de facto standard for 8-in. disks. This format uses FM encoding. IBM subsequently used MFM in their System 34, which established a double-density format. However, many other vendors use different double-density formats (although nearly all use MFM encoding), and the only universal standard is the single-density 3740 format. Many 8-in. disk systems use the 3740 single-density format to allow for data interchange with other computers and use a proprietary double-density format for general use.

Figure 9.16 shows the IBM formats for 8-in. floppy disks. Since minifloppy formats are derived from this format, we will explain it first, even though 8-in. disks are rarely used now. Each track is divided into 26 sectors, with gaps between each sector and additional gaps around the index area. Special marks called *address marks* are written on the disk at the beginning of each field. Address marks are unique patterns that have missing clock pulses, which allows them to be identified as address marks and not data. An index address mark is written immediately after the end of the physical index pulse.

Gaps between fields serve three purposes. First, they allow for variations in the speed of rotation. If the disk is rotating slightly faster than nominal, a given number of bytes will consume a larger area on the disk. If there were no gaps, the end of one field might overwrite the start of the next if the disk speed varied slightly. Second, the gaps provide time for the write current to be turned on and off without affecting adjacent fields. Finally, gaps filled with specific data patterns provide a predictable series of pulses that allow the data separator in the disk interface to synchronize to the bit cell boundaries.

For each sector, there is an identification (ID) field and a data field, separated by a gap (gap 2). The ID field begins with an ID address mark. The bytes following the ID address mark specify the track number, side number (if double-sided), sector number, and sector length. Only four standard sector lengths are allowed: 128, 256, 512, or 1024 bytes. The IBM standard uses 128 bytes for FM and 256 bytes for MFM. (Many systems use 512- or 1024-byte sectors with MFM to maximize the disk capacity.) At the end of the ID field is a two-byte cyclic redundancy check (CRC) which allows the controller to verify that it read the field correctly.

After gap 2, the data field begins. The data field starts with either the data address mark or the deleted data address mark. Any field with valid data begins with the data address mark. Fields that have not been written or that contain data which has been deleted begin with the deleted data address mark. Thus, to delete data, it is not actually erased; only the address mark is changed. Following the address mark is the actual data, whose length is 256 bytes in the IBM System 34 standard. At the end of the data is a two-byte CRC for error detection.

Gap 3 fills the space before the next ID field and provides time for the write current to be turned off without affecting the ID field. Gap 4 fills all the space after the last sector and before the index pulse.

Thus, it is apparent that there is a considerable difference between the raw number of bits in the track (the unformatted capacity) and the actual number of data bits (the formatted capacity). A double-sided double-density 8-in. disk has an unformatted capacity of 1.6 Mbytes; using the IBM format, the formatted capacity is approximately 1 Mbyte (26 sectors × 256 bytes × 77 tracks × 2 sides = 1,025,024 bytes).

486

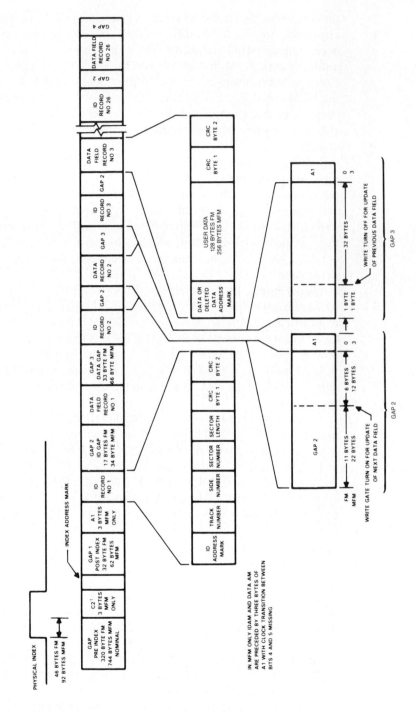

† Missing clock transition between bits 3 and 4

Figure 9.16. IBM 8-in. floppy-disk format. *(Courtesy of Western Digital Corp.)*

Since there is a considerable overhead for each sector, the formatted capacity can be increased by using longer sectors. For example, if eight 1024-byte sectors are used instead of 26 256-byte sectors, the formatted capacity is increased to approximately 1.2 Mbytes for a double-sided double-density drive. There is a drawback to larger sector sizes, however. The disk is generally used to store a number of files, each of which may use several sectors. The space left at the end of the last sector is not used. Suppose a file is 1025 bytes long. Using 256-byte sectors, five sectors are required, and 255 bytes are wasted. Using 1024-byte sectors, two sectors are required, and 1023 bytes are wasted. On the average, each file wastes half a sector. Thus, larger sectors waste more bytes per file. If the disk is used for many small files, this inefficiency negates the advantage of the larger sectors. If the average file size is much larger than 1024 bytes (as it is in many applications), then the percentage of wasted space is lower, and the larger sectors are justified.

The IBM standard format uses one track for the directory and reserves two tracks as spares in case any of the tracks are defective. Thus, the number of available tracks is reduced by three per side.

Minifloppy disks did not have the benefit of an IBM standard until they had been in use for several years, causing a proliferation of formats. Most are variations of the IBM 8-in. format. This allows standard LSI floppy disk controller chips to be used, since these chips were designed for the IBM standard formats. The main variations from the 8-in. format are a reduction in the number of sectors, since the tracks are shorter, and the use of smaller gaps. The format used by the IBM PC has become the most common. This format uses nine sectors of 512 bytes each, for a capacity of 4608 bytes per track. The total capacity for a 40-track double-sided drive (as used in many personal computers) is thus 368,640 bytes (360 Kbytes). The usable space is reduced by tracks used for system software and directory information. An 80-track double-sided drive doubles the capacity to 720K.

High-density minifloppies, which use different heads and media for a higher flux density, can use the same format as 8-in. disks. IBM's PC/AT formats each track with 15 sectors of 512 bytes each. The double-sided 96-tpi drive has a total of 160 tracks for a formatted capacity of 1,228,800 bytes (1.2 Mbytes).

Most systems use *soft-sectored* disks, on which the preceding discussions are based. The "soft" designation refers to the fact that the sectors are defined by patterns written on the disk, and their size and position are thus controlled by the formatting software. This allows the floppy-disk controller to format the disk with any desired sector length and gap length. *Hard-sectored* disks have a hole in the disk at the start of each sector, which is sensed by the same sensor as the index hole. In principle, this allows more data to be stored on the disk, since sector marks can be eliminated, and simplifies the controller. However, hard-sectored disks require that the sector and gap lengths be fixed when the disk is manufactured. LSI floppy disk controllers include all the logic for soft sectoring in a single chip (along with most other interface functions), so the controller complexity is not an issue. Thus, hard-sectored disks are rarely used.

The simplest way to arrange the sectors within the track is in numerical order: sector 1 is followed by sector 2, which is followed by sector 3, etc. However, this is often not the optimal arrangement. A single file generally uses several sectors. When reading a series of sectors, the system hardware and software need some time between sectors to store the data from the previous sector and prepare to read the next. If the gap be-

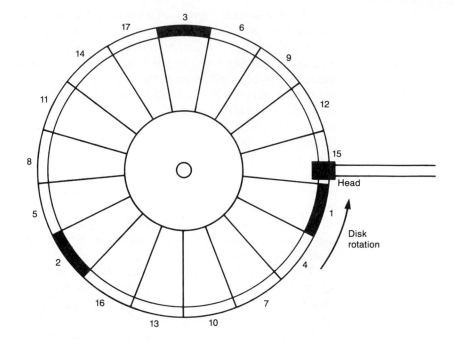

Figure 9.17. Disk with 6:1 interleave factor.

tween the sectors does not provide enough time, the system must wait for a complete revolution of the disk (200 ms for a standard minifloppy) to read the next sector.

This additional latency between sectors can be reduced by *interleaving* the sectors, as shown in Fig. 9.17. This example shows a 6:1 interleaving factor. Six revolutions are required to read all the sectors in a track sequentially. Rather than being directly adjacent, there are five sectors between sectors 1 and 2. Thus, the system has the time required for five sectors to pass by to be ready to read the next sector. Ideally, the next sector should be approaching the read/write head just as the system is ready to read (or write) that sector. The optimum interleaving factor depends on the system's hardware and software design. If the interleaving factor is too small, the system will not be ready for the next sector and will have to wait a full revolution. If the interleaving factor is too large, time is wasted waiting for the next sector.

9.5.5 High-Capacity Floppy Disks

The preceding sections have described the types of floppy disks that are most widely used. A variety of techniques has been used to produce floppy-disk drives with higher storage capacities, but due to their increased cost (and possibly lower reliability), they have not been as widely used. By using closed-loop head positioning mechanisms to achieve high track density and improved heads and media for high bit density, several megabytes have been stored on a minifloppy. Specialized drives have been produced with storage capacities as high as 10 Mbytes.

In the early development of floppy disks, most of the attention centered on faster and more accurate positioning mechanisms to increase the number of tracks, on reliable double-sided operation, and on reducing size and power requirements. Improved heads and media first appeared in wide use in the high-performance minifloppies. Additional improvements in these areas, combined with encoding techniques such as RLL 2,7, promise further capacity increases. Perpendicular recording, which requires a new medium and radically different head, promises flux densities as high as 100,000 fci and minifloppies with capacities of 5 to 10 Mbytes.

9.5.6 Floppy-Disk Interface Signals

Figure 9.18 shows the standard minifloppy interface signals. Two connectors are used: one for power and one for all other signals. The signal cable is typically a ribbon cable, and alternate wires are grounded to prevent crosstalk between signals. Up to four drives can be connected in parallel with a single cable. Each drive contains several jumpers that allow one of the four drive select signals to be selected as the enable signal for that drive. Each drive connected to the same cable must be jumpered to use a differ-

Figure 9.18. Minifloppy interface signals.

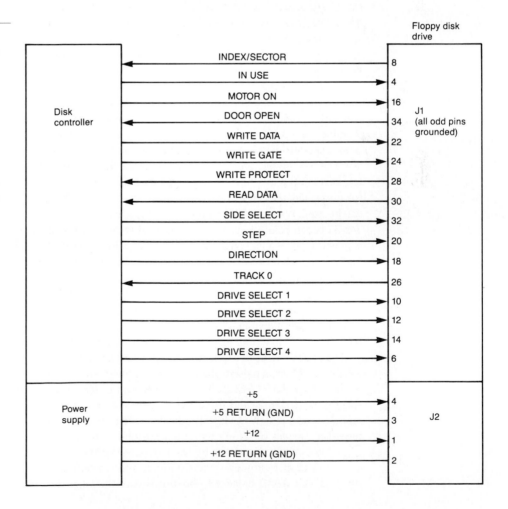

Figure 9.19. Driver and receiver for floppy-disk interface signals.

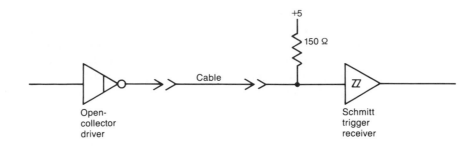

ent drive select signal. Only the drive that is enabled responds to the output signals from the controller or drives the input signals to the controller.

As shown in Fig. 9.19, each signal is driven with an open-collector driver and is terminated at the receiving end with a 150-Ω pull-up resistor and a Schmitt-trigger receiver. This applies to signals in both directions: signals from the drive are driven with open-collector drivers and terminated in the controller, and signals from the controller are driven with open-collector drivers and terminated in the drive. If more than one drive is connected to the interface cable, only the drive at the end of the cable should include the termination resistors. The termination resistors are generally in a DIP resistor pack in a socket, which is removed in all drives except the last one in the chain.

Most disk drive specifications indicate a 48-mA sink current requirement for the driver, and the 7438 is the device usually recommended. The 7438 is a quad NAND gate driver, and since the logic function is not usually needed, both inputs are tied together. In many applications, a 7406 hex driver can be used, although its 40-mA output specification is below the recommended value. (Even if the 150-Ω pull-up resistor is 5% low in value, it requires no more than 33 mA of sink current for a 0.4-V low level. With a 40-mA driver, 7 mA is left to drive logic inputs, which is adequate for four standard TTL loads.) For the receiver, the 74LS14 hex Schmitt-trigger inverter can be used, but most floppy controller chips require noninverting receivers. Either two 74LS14s can be used in series, or an octal receiver such as the 74LS244 can be used.

The MOTOR ON signal enables power to the drive motor. Depending on the particular drive and jumper options selected on the drive, this signal may operate in combination with or independently of the drive select signals. After turning on the motor, the controller must wait for the drive to reach full speed before performing any read or write operations. This time can be determined from the READY line, if provided, or by waiting the maximum specified start-up time. Alternatively, the spacing between index pulses can be measured to determine the drive speed.

The read/write head is positioned via the STEP and DIRECTION SELECT signals. Each time STEP is pulsed, the head moves one track in or out, depending on the state of the DIRECTION SELECT signal. The controller must generate step pulses with a spacing no less than the drive's track-to-track access time, or some pulses may be missed. The TRACK 00 signal indicates when the head is positioned over track 0 and provides a means of setting the initial position of the head.

Data is written to the disk by asserting the WRITE GATE signal to enable the write current, and then providing the data to be written on the WRITE DATA signal. Each time WRITE DATA is pulsed, the direction of the magnetic field written on the disk is reversed. This signal must include both clock and data pulses as required by the encoding method used (typically FM or MFM). The WRITE PROTECT signal is asserted if the disk is write-protected (as indicated by the notch on the disk being covered). If the disk is write-protected, the WRITE GATE signal is ignored, so data cannot be written. Some drives provide a WRITE FAULT signal that is asserted if for any reason the drive is unable to perform the requested write operation.

The READ DATA signal is the combined clock and data pulses as read from the disk. A pulse appears on this signal at every flux transition. Some drives include an internal data separator, in which case a clock that changes state at each bit cell boundary is also provided.

The INDEX/SECTOR signal is asserted each time the disk rotates to the position that aligns the index holes in the jacket and the disk. For hard-sectored disks, which have an additional hole in the disk at the start of each sector, a pulse is also produced for each sector.

Double-sided drives have a SIDE SELECT signal (sometimes called HEAD SELECT) that determines the side of the disk to be read or written. Some drives provide a DOOR OPEN signal, which indicates that the drive door is open and the disk cannot therefore be accessed. Some drives also have an IN USE input signal that illuminates an LED on the front of the drive. More commonly, the combination of the drive select and motor on signals controls the LED.

Eight-inch disk drives use the same basic set of interface signals. A 50-pin connector is used rather than a 34-pin connector, but most of the additional pins are unused. The 34 signals of the minifloppy interface are placed on pins 17 to 50, so the pin numbers are different. Eight-inch drives with ac motors have no MOTOR ON signal, since the motor is always on. Many 8-in. drives have a HEAD LOAD signal to cause the head(s) (or pressure pad) to be loaded against the disk. Some 8-in. drives have an input called TG43 (track greater than 43), which is used to reduce the write current on the inner tracks due to the higher flux density.

Microfloppy drives use nearly the same interface as minifloppy drives. One difference is the addition of a DISK CHANGED output from the drive, which is asserted whenever a disk is removed. A CHANGE RESET input to the drive resets this signal. Pin 2, which is unused in the minifloppy interface, is used for DISK CHANGED, and pin 1, which is a ground pin in the minifloppy interface, is used for CHANGE RESET. Although the signals and pin numbers are the same as for a minifloppy interface, the physical connector is different. Minifloppy and 8-in. floppy drives use a printer circuit edge connector, whereas microfloppy drives use a pin-and-socket connector.

While most drives adhere to this standard interface, there are small variations among vendors and models. Before designing an interface, the interface specifications for the drives to be used should be consulted. By adding a few jumpers to the disk controller circuit, it is possible to allow the interface to be configured for most commonly used drives.

9.5.7 Disk Controller/Formatter Functions

Figure 9.20 shows a block diagram of a disk controller and formatter (often called simply a disk controller). The microprocessor interface provides the connection to the microprocessor buses. The microprocessor initiates an action by writing a command

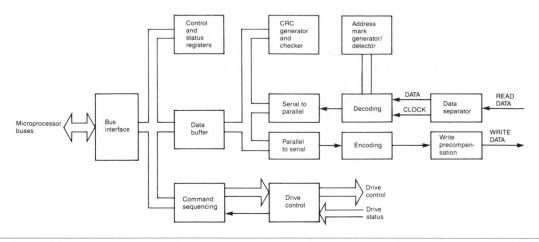

Figure 9.20.   Floppy-disk controller block diagram.

and any required parameters to the registers. The controller then provides the detailed sequencing needed to implement the command.

The data buffer stores data being read from or written to the disk. It may be as small as one byte or as large as several sectors. The data transfer rate is determined by the speed of the disk and the encoding method. If the data buffer is only a single byte, the microprocessor interface must be able to transfer data at the disk's transfer rate. If the buffer can store an entire sector of data, then the microprocessor interface is relieved of this requirement, since all the data for the current read or write operation can be stored in the buffer. Alternatives for implementing the microprocessor interface are described in Sec. 9.5.11.

The controller must perform a variety of drive control functions. It must provide the motor control and drive select signals to enable the drive. Step pulses must be produced at the required rate to move the head from one track to another, and the index pulse and write protect signals must be sensed.

Reading and writing data are the most complex functions performed by the controller. The encoding and decoding logic performs the parallel-to-serial and serial-to-parallel conversions and also adds clock pulses as required by the encoding method used. The write data pulses may be shifted slightly earlier or later by the write precompensation circuit to precompensate for the effects of peak shift.

The read data from the disk includes both clock and data pulses. The data separator extracts a clock signal from this combined data stream, which informs the decoder of the boundaries of each bit cell. The data separator can be one of the most difficult aspects of the controller to design. Fortunately, single-chip data separators and controllers with built-in data separators are now available. Some disk drives include the data separator in the drive and provide both the clock and data signals.

The read/write logic must perform several additional functions. Each time a data or ID field is written, the CRC is calculated and written at the end of the field. The CRC is then verified when the field is read. To generate address marks, the encoder modifies the encoding algorithm to delete certain clock pulses. The decoder then detects these missing clock pulse patterns.

The command sequencing logic coordinates the activities of all portions of the controller. For example, consider the sequence required to seek a particular track. The current track number is compared to the desired track number, and the direction select output is set accordingly. Step pulses are then generated, ideally at the maximum rate acceptable to the disk drive. The number of step pulses generated is the difference between the current and desired track numbers. After the last step pulse, the controller must wait for the duration of the head settling time before reading or writing.

9.5.8 LSI Floppy-Disk Controller Chips

Early floppy-disk controllers required over 100 TTL ICs. LSI floppy-disk controllers (FDC's) were soon developed that drastically reduced the total number of chips required. The first floppy controller ICs, such as Western Digital's 1771, required external logic for data separation, write precompensation, and address mark generation and detection. The next generation, such as Western Digital's 179X series and NEC's 765, includes the address mark circuitry on the chip and support MFM in addition to FM. External logic is still required for data separation and write precompensation with these controllers, and support chips are available to perform these functions. In the third generation, the data separation and write precompensation were incorporated into the controller chips, producing nearly complete single-chip floppy-disk controllers. External chips are required for the interface drivers and receivers and for some bus interface functions. One example of such a third-generation controller chip is Western Digital's 279X series, which is described in the following section.

Even in the third-generation devices, only a single byte of data buffering is included in the controller chip. Thus, the microprocessor bus interface must transfer data at the disk's data transfer rate, requiring the use of DMA or other techniques as described in Sec. 9.5.11. Some advanced controller chips include a DMA controller in the disk controller chip so that it can transfer data directly to the main system memory.

All the common floppy-disk controller chips are designed for IBM standard soft-sectored disk formats. The data rates, type of CRC and address marks, and encoding methods cannot be changed. Most controllers allow sector lengths of 128, 256, 512, or 1024 bytes and support 8-in. floppy or minifloppy data rates with FM or MFM encoding. The number of sectors per track, number of tracks, and gap sizes can be changed within limits.

9.5.9 Western Digital 279X Floppy-Disk Controller

Western Digital's 279X series is an example of a third-generation FDC. It evolved from the 1771 and 179X series and is software-compatible with those devices. The main improvement from one generation to the next is a reduction in external logic required. The last digit of the part number specifies a particular device within the series. The 2791 and 2795 use an active-low data bus, while the 2793 and 2797 use an active-high data bus. The 2791 and 2793 include a clock divider to allow a single clock oscillator to be used for 8-in. floppy and minifloppy interfaces. The 2795 and 2797 do not include this divider but instead provide a side-select output for double-sided drives. (The

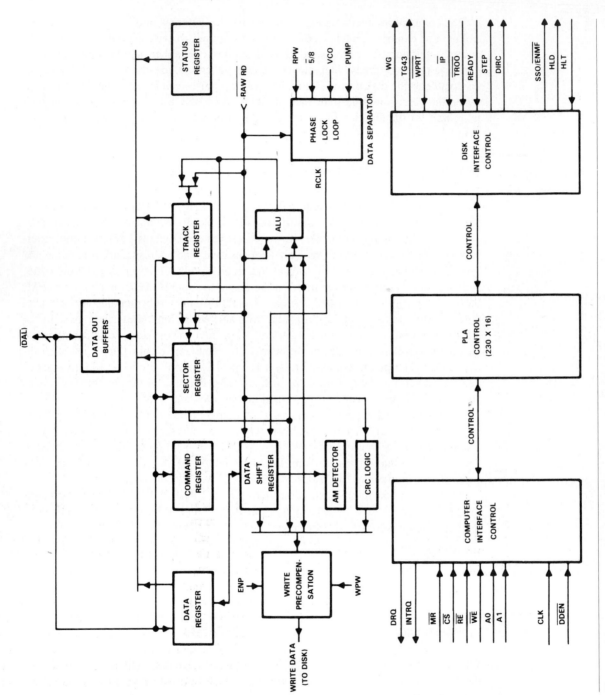

Figure 9.21. Western Digital 279X FDC block diagram. *(Courtesy of Western Digital Corp.)*

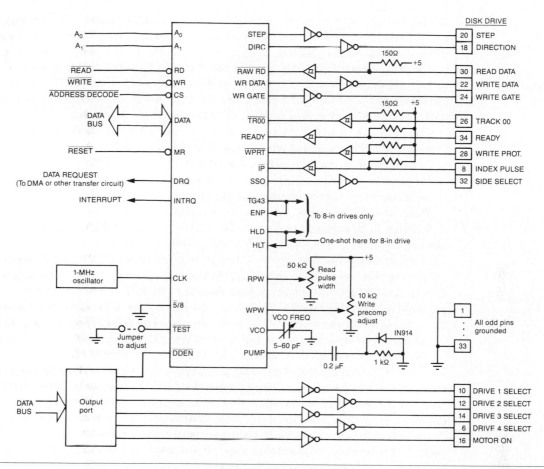

Figure 9.22. Minifloppy controller circuit using the 2797 FDC.

277X series is similar but has an improved data separator. The 1770 and 1772 are similar to the 279X series but are less expensive and support 5¼ disks only.)

Internal Structure and Circuit Connections

Figure 9.21 shows a block diagram of the 279X, and Fig. 9.22 shows a typical application circuit. The microprocessor interface is a standard peripheral interface, consisting of a chip select, read and write strobes, and two address lines to select one of the internal registers. Two additional signals are DRQ (data request), which is asserted when the FDC is ready for a read or write transfer, and the interrupt output (INTRQ), which is asserted at the completion of each command.

There are five registers accessible by the microprocessor. The track register stores the track number at which the head is currently positioned and is generally set by the FDC and only read by the microprocessor. The sector register is set by the microprocessor to specify a sector to be read or written. The command register stores the current command and is a write-only register. The status register is a read-only register sharing the same address as the command register. The data register holds parameters for commands (such as the track number to seek) and also serves as the data buffer during read and write operations.

The programmed logic array (PLA) control section provides the sequencing logic for command execution. The arithmetic and logic unit (ALU) increments (or decrements) the track number when positioning the head and is also used to compare the track and sector numbers read from ID fields to those in the registers.

The 279X connects directly to the signals to and from any standard floppy-disk drive, requiring only external buffers. The $\overline{\text{RAW READ}}$ signal is the combined clock and data signal from the drive. This connects to the data input of the data shift register and to the phase-locked loop (PLL) data separator. The data separator provides a clock signal at the center of each bit cell to clock the data into the data shift register.

When writing to the disk, the FDC automatically precompensates the data for bit shift during double-density operation. The enable precomp (ENP) input allows this function to be enabled or disabled. Precompensation is often used only on the inner-most tracks (track numbers above 43 on an 8-in. drive or an 80-track minifloppy drive). The FDC provides an output signal indicating that the current track is greater than 43 (TG43), and this signal can be connected to the ENP input to enable precompensation only on those tracks. Some 8-in. disk drives have a TG43 input, which reduces the write current when writing on the inner tracks. The ENP input can also be connected to an output port bit for full software control.

Two parameters must be set to match the disk drive: the stepping rate and the head load time. The stepping rate is set under program control. The head load time is determined by an external one-shot. When the head load (HLD) signal is asserted, the FDC waits for the head load time (HLT) input to be asserted before proceeding with the operation. For most minifloppy disk drives, in which the head is always loaded, HLD can be connected directly to HLT. The HLD signal is not needed for such drives. For drives that have a head load control, a one-shot whose delay is equal to the head load time must be connected between HLD and HLT.

The internal PLL data separator includes an oscillator that normally runs at the nominal bit rate (250 kHz for a minifloppy with MFM encoding). The trimmer capacitor connected to the VCO pin adjusts this free-running frequency. When data is being read from the drive, the PLL circuitry attempts to adjust the frequency of the oscillator to match the data rate of the signal from the disk. The frequency is adjusted by varying the voltage on the PUMP pin. The phase locked loop circuitry outputs positive or negative pulses to this pin, whose duration is proportional to the difference between the oscillator frequency and the data rate from the disk. The RC network connected to the PUMP pin filters these pulses. The diode is needed to compensate for differences between the pump-up and pump-down pulses produced by the FDC.

The $\overline{5}/8$ input selects minifloppy or 8-in. floppy operation, and the $\overline{\text{DDEN}}$ (double-density enable) input selects FM or MFM operation. These pins can be connected to jumpers, but for maximum flexibility they should be connected to output port bits. The system software can automatically determine whether a disk being read is FM or MFM, since reading in the wrong mode will cause persistent CRC errors.

The 2795 and 2797 require a 1-MHz clock for minifloppy operation and a 2-MHz clock for 8-in. floppy operation. The 2791 and 2793 will work with either type of disk, using a 2-MHz clock input. The $\overline{\text{ENMF}}$ (enable minifloppy) pin is asserted to enable the internal divide-by-two circuit for minifloppy operation. On the 2795 and 2797 this pin is used for the side select output signal. If using the 2791 or 2793 with a double-sided drive, the side select signal must be provided by an output port bit.

Three adjustments are required. The VCO frequency adjust was described earlier. The other two adjustments are for the read pulse width and the amount of write pre-compensation. To make these adjustments, the $\overline{\text{TEST}}$ input is grounded. This causes the VCO output frequency to appear on the DIRC output, a precompensation adjustment pulse on the WR DATA output, and a read pulse width adjustment pulse on the TG43 output. These signals are monitored with a frequency counter or oscilloscope while the corresponding adjustments are made. The $\overline{\text{TEST}}$ input is then opened (and will float high), allowing normal operation.

The 279X chips do not provide drive select signals, so an output port is required to produce them. Each drive select can be taken directly from an output port bit, or two output port bits can be decoded into four drive select signals by a two-to-four line decoder.

Commands

Table 9.3 lists the 279X commands, and Table 9.4 shows the status bit definitions for each command. Each command includes bit fields to specify stepping rates and other required parameters. The following description is limited to the general operation of the commands; for details of each command code and options, refer to the 279X data sheet.

Table 9.3 The 279X FDC Commands

RESTORE	READ SECTOR
SEEK	WRITE SECTOR
STEP	READ ADDRESS
STEP-IN	READ TRACK
STEP-OUT	WRITE TRACK
	FORCE INTERRUPT

Table 9.4 The 279X FDC Status Bits

Bit	STEP and SEEK commands	READ ADDRESS	READ SECTOR	READ TRACK	WRITE SECTOR	WRITE TRACK
S7	NOT READY	NOT READY	NOT READY	NOT READY	NOT READY	NOT READY
S6	WRITE PROTECT	0	0	0	WRITE PROTECT	WRITE PROTECT
S5	HEAD LOADED	0	RECORD TYPE	0	0	0
S4	SEEK ERROR	RNF	RNF	0	RNF	0
S3	CRC ERROR	CRC ERROR	CRC ERROR	0	CRC ERROR	0
S2	TRACK 0	LOST DATA	LOST DATA	LOST DATA	LOST DATA	LOST DATA
S1	INDEX PULSE	DRQ	DRQ	DRQ	DRQ	DRQ
S0	BUSY	BUSY	BUSY	BUSY	BUSY	BUSY

Source: Western Digital Corporation.

The RESTORE command causes a series of step-out pulses to be generated until the TRACK 00 input is asserted. This is used to recalibrate the drive at power-up or whenever the system gets off track for any reason. This command is automatically executed when the FDC is reset.

The SEEK command is used to seek a particular track. The microprocessor writes the desired track number to the data register. The FDC subtracts this number from the value in the track register and issues the appropriate number of step pulses (with direction select set to the required state) to position the head over the specified track. A "verify" option can be selected, which causes the FDC to read an ID field when it reaches the specified track and verify that the track number in the ID field corresponds to the expected track number. If not, the FDC sets the SEEK ERROR status bit.

The STEP, STEP-IN, and STEP-OUT commands move the head a single track and are used primarily when formatting the disk.

The READ SECTOR and WRITE SECTOR commands are the primary commands for accessing data on the disk. To read a sector, the following sequence is performed:

1. Microprocessor writes track number and SEEK command to FDC to position head over desired track.

2. Microprocessor writes desired sector number to FDC sector register.

3. Microprocessor writes READ SECTOR command to FDC.

4. FDC reads ID fields until it finds one with requested sector number and no CRC error. If FDC does not find valid matching ID field within five disk revolutions, it terminates command and sets record not found (RNF) status bit.

5. FDC reads data from disk until data address mark is read.

6. FDC begins reading data from disk into data shift register.

7. When complete byte is assembled, FDC transfers it to data register, sets DRQ status bit, and asserts DRQ output.

8. When microprocessor reads data register, FDC negates DRQ status bit and output signal. If DRQ is still set when next byte is ready to be transferred (indicating that previous byte was not read quickly enough), byte that was not read in time is lost and LOST DATA status bit is set.

9. When entire sector has been read, FDC negates BUSY status bit and asserts INTRQ output.

10. Microprocessor reads CRC ERROR status bit to make sure that the sector was read correctly.

The WRITE SECTOR command functions similarly, except that DRQ is asserted each time the FDC is ready for another byte of data to be written.

The READ ADDRESS command causes the FDC to read the first ID field encountered and transfer the six bytes of the ID field to the microprocessor interface in a manner similar to a read sector operation. This is useful in systems that have multiple disk drives under the control of a single FDC, so the FDC track register may not represent the state of the currently selected disk.

The READ TRACK command is used primarily for verifying the disk formatting.

The WRITE TRACK command is used to format the disk. The WRITE TRACK command operates similarly to the WRITE SECTOR command, except that the entire track is written instead of only a single sector. The microprocessor's software must provide every byte to be written, including gaps, address marks, and ID fields. Certain data patterns are treated as commands. For example, writing the data F7 causes the CRC to be written to the disk. Other data patterns are used to initialize the CRC generator and to write address marks. Thus, the WRITE TRACK command cannot be used to write arbitrary data patterns; it is used only for formatting.

The FORCE INTERRUPT command terminates the command in progress.

Software Interface to Application Programs

Several layers of software generally mediate between an application program and the FDC. The basic low-level routines that directly access the FDC are:

Format a disk

Read sector

Write sector

Seek a track

Subroutines that perform these functions are typically part of the system's basic input/output system (BIOS) stored in ROM or EPROM. The operating system software uses these routines to provide higher-level functions (such as reading or writing a selected file) to application programs. The operating system is responsible for maintaining the directory so that it can locate files by name, reading and writing the necessary sectors for the requested file name, and handling errors.

9.5.10 Other Floppy-Disk Controller Chips

Another FDC in wide use is NEC's μPD765, second-sourced by Intel as the 8272. This chip is used in the IBM PC family and is thus used in many other personal computers for software compatibility. Its capabilities are generally similar to the 179X series. Write precompensation and data separation circuits are not included and must be provided externally.

One advantage of the μPD765 over the Western Digital family is a higher-level command set. For example, a FORMAT TRACK command formats the entire track based on a few parameters; there is no need to provide every byte to be written, as with the Western Digital devices. Commands are also available to scan tracks for specified data sequences.

Other features of the μPD765 include drive select outputs, interface signals designed for direct compatibility with an 8257 DMA controller, and better resolution for the step rate specification. The head load time is also software programmed, eliminating the need for the head load one-shot timer.

Standard Microsystems' 9266 combines the best features of the μPD765 and the 279X. It is software-compatible with the μPD765 but includes on-chip write precompensation and data separation.

Many other floppy-disk controller chips are available. Some are optimized for use with a particular microprocessor, such as Rockwell's 68465 for the 68000 family. Most include the same basic functions as those described here, and an understanding of these chips should allow the reader to evaluate other devices.

9.5.11 Disk Controller-to-Microprocessor Interfacing

Since most floppy disk controller chips include only a single-byte data buffer, transfers to and from the controller chip must occur at the disk's data transfer rate. Table 9.5 shows the data rates for various types of disks and encoding methods. The most demanding drives are 8-in., 5¼-in. high-density, and 3½-in. 600 rpm. For these drives, a byte is read or written nominally every 16 μs (using MFM encoding). Because of variations in disk speed and delays within the controller circuitry, the worst-case time between bytes is slightly shorter. For the 279X FDC, the minimum time between bytes is specified as 11.5 μs.

Polled data transfers are the simplest to implement. The software polls the data request bit in the FDC's status register, and the data request output signal is not used. To read a sector of data, the following tasks must be performed:

1. Write sector number and read sector command to FDC.

2. Read loop repeated for each byte in the sector:

    a. Until the data request bit is set, repeatedly read disk controller's status register.
    b. When the data request bit is set:
    (1) Read the byte.
    (2) Store it in memory.
    (3) Increment the memory pointer.
    (4) Test to see if the transfer is complete.
    (5) Jump back to the beginning of the loop.

The worst-case execution time for this loop must be less than the shortest possible time between bytes, or data may be lost. A high-speed microprocessor such as a 68000 can execute this loop in under 16 μs, but many 8-bit microprocessors cannot. Even if the microprocessor can execute the loop in the required time, the system must not have

Table 9.5   Floppy-Disk Bit Times and Data Transfer Rates

Disk type	Encoding	Bit rate, kbits/s	Bit cell, μs	Byte rate, kbytes/s	Byte time, μs
8-in., or 5¼-in. high-density, or 3½-in. 600 rpm	FM	250	4	31.25	32
	MFM	500	2	62.5	16
5¼-in. or 3½ in. 300 rpm	FM	125	8	15.625	64
	MFM	250	4	31.25	32

any interrupts (such as an interrupt for software refresh of dynamic RAM) that cannot be disabled for the duration of the transfer. If such an interrupt were to occur during the transfer, data would be lost.

One solution is to use DMA to transfer the data directly from the FDC to the system RAM. The data request output from the FDC is used as the transfer request to the DMA controller. The main drawback to this approach is the requirement for a DMA controller, which is a relatively expensive function to add.

There are several other techniques that can be used to perform disk data transfers that are less expensive than a DMA controller. The best technique depends on the particular microprocessor used and on other system requirements.

When using a microprocessor (or a system bus) that has a READY signal to accommodate slow memory or I/O devices, this signal can be used to coordinate the data transfers. Figure 9.23 shows a circuit that illustrates the basic approach, and Fig. 9.24 shows the timing diagram for a read cycle. The purpose of this logic is to eliminate the need for the software to test the data request bit of the FDC's status register and wait for it to be set. The microprocessor begins the read cycle before the data is available. The microprocessor is held in a wait state by the READY signal. When the FDC has a byte of data ready, it asserts its DATA REQUEST output, and the READY flip-flop is set. The microprocessor then reads the data and terminates the read cycle. The termination of the cycle resets the READY flip-flop and the DATA REQUEST output of the FDC. The microprocessor stores the data in memory, increments the memory pointer, and begins the read cycle for the next byte. This continues until the entire sector is read.

A control signal from an output port bit is needed to allow the ready logic to be

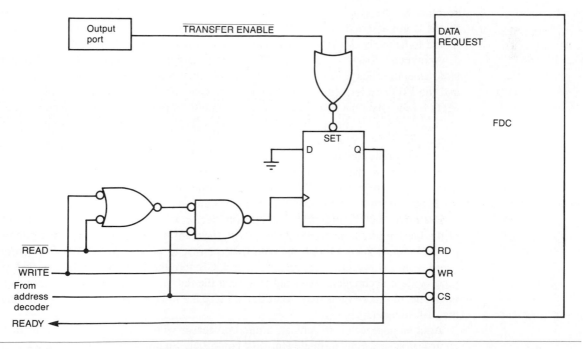

Figure 9.23. Data transfer synchronization circuit using ready signal.

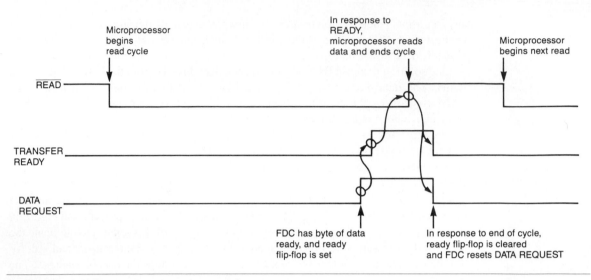

Figure 9.24.   Read cycle timing for ready synchronization circuit.

disabled to permit access to the control registers in the FDC, since DATA REQUEST is not used for these accesses. The circuit shown illustrates the basic approach, but additional logic is required in most applications, depending on the FDC chip and the microprocessor used. One problem is that the DATA REQUEST signal may never be asserted by the FDC if a read cycle is already in progress when the data becomes available. This problem can be avoided by gating the chip select signal to the FDC with READY so that it is not asserted until the READY signal is active. Additional logic may be required to delay the READY signal to allow for the access time of the FDC.

Another approach is to include a FIFO buffer memory in the disk controller that can store an entire sector. Simple control logic coordinates the transfers between the FDC and the FIFO buffer. This control logic must generate read (or write) pulses for the FIFO buffer when the FDC asserts its data request output. To perform a sector write, the microprocessor first writes the data to the FIFO and then issues the write sector command. For a sector read, the microprocessor issues the read sector command and then waits for the command to be completed. The FIFO buffer stores the data as it is read from the disk, so there are no time constraints on the rate at which the microprocessor reads the data from the FIFO buffer. The microprocessor communicates directly with the FDC when writing commands or reading status.

Even if the FIFO buffer is smaller than one sector, it still relieves the microprocessor of the burden of constantly keeping up with the transfer rate. On average, the microprocessor must keep up with the data transfer rate to prevent the FIFO buffer from overflowing. However, the microprocessor can ignore the FIFO buffer for a period of time while it accumulates data and then read the data in bursts. This is helpful when interrupts or other events may occur that require the microprocessor's attention during the disk transfer.

Another approach is to dedicate a microprocessor with a buffer memory to the disk control task, creating an intelligent disk controller. Figure 9.25 shows the block diagram for one possible architecture. The dedicated disk control microprocessor accepts

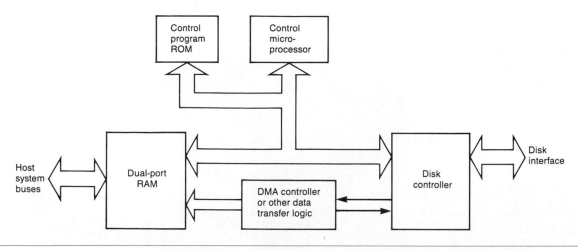

Figure 9.25. Intelligent disk controller block diagram.

commands from the host microprocessor, issues commands to the FDC, and transfers data between the FDC and the buffer memory. The dual-port memory provides the interface to the host system. The host writes commands and data to this memory and reads status and data from the memory. Commands sent from the host microprocessor can be higher-level commands, such as reading or writing a file by name; the disk controller microprocessor performs the required sequence of commands. The controller microprocessor can perform additional tasks such as automatically repeating a command if an error occurs. This relieves the host microprocessor of all detailed control of the FDC. Note that the disk controller microprocessor must be able to read and write data at the rate required by the disk.

If more than one sector can be stored in the buffer, additional performance improvements can be obtained. If the host microprocessor requests to read a sector that is already in the buffer memory, no disk access is required. The task of the dedicated FDC microprocessor is to keep the buffer filled with the sectors most likely to be needed by the main microprocessor. The trick is figuring out which sectors these are. This type of buffer is called a *disk cache* and is often used in high-performance systems.

9.6 HARD DISKS

9.6.1 Winchester Disk Technology

Rigid-disk drives have been used for many years as mass storage in mini and mainframe computer systems. In traditional rigid disks, the disk platters are removable, either as cartridges holding a single platter for smaller drives or as disk packs containing multiple platters for larger drives. Because of the extremely clean environment required for hard disks, extensive filtration systems are required for such drives. The

mechanical requirements imposed by removable media require complex systems to guarantee that the tracks can be located with sufficient accuracy after the disks have been removed and replaced.

In 1973, IBM introduced the 3340 disk drive, the first to use the technology called *Winchester*. Figure 9.26 shows a typical Winchester drive with the protective cover removed. Winchester technology deviates from the previous approach in a variety of ways. The head and disk are hermetically sealed in a single assembly, and the medium is not removable. This allows the cleanliness of the disk's environment to be guaranteed by building the head/disk assembly in a clean room. Filtration is required only to extract any particles produced by the drive's operation.

The read/write head technology is also different for Winchester drives. Winchester heads have a very low mass, and only a small force is needed to keep them in position. Combined with the very clean environment, this allows the heads to fly closer to the disk than was practical for earlier rigid disks, which in turn allows higher density recording.

Another significant departure from earlier hard disk technology is the method used to load and unload the heads when the drive is turned on or off. Conventional drives require complex mechanisms to gradually bring the head toward the disk at power-up and to remove them when the drive is turned off. If the heads were allowed to touch the disk, a *crash* occurred, damaging the disk and/or the head. In a Winchester drive, the low-mass heads are allowed to land on the disk when power is removed, and they "take off" from the disk when it is turned on. A lubricating film, combined with the low mass, prevents damage to the disk or the head. When landing the head, many Winchester drives force the head to a specific area of the disk that is not used for data storage for an extra measure of safety; this is often called *parking* the head. For drives that do not do this automatically, the head can be parked by software (by sending a head positioning command to the disk controller) when the system is to be moved.

Thus, Winchester technology made possible the production of low-cost hard-disk drives with increased bit density. Many variations of the technology are now in use, but most share the above mentioned characteristics. A few removable-media Winchester disk drives are available, which require more extensive filtration systems, but in most other respects they use Winchester technology.

Because of the high track and bit densities used in hard disks, it is difficult to manufacture disk platters that are 100 percent error-free. The cost of the platters is greatly reduced if they are allowed to have some areas that may not be used. The specified capacity for a hard-disk drive usually does not assume that the entire surface is defect-free; rather, some number of defects are allowed. When the drive is shipped, a *defect map* is included that indicates which sectors of which tracks should not be used. The controller must avoid these areas; this task is called *defect management*.

9.6.2   Drive Types

The first commercially available Winchester drives used a 14-in. platter. Smaller drives were then developed, using the package size of standard floppy disks. These disk drives are named not for the exact diameter of the platter but for the size of the floppy-disk drive whose external dimensions they use; 8-, 5¼- and 3½-in. hard disk drives are available. As with floppy disks, half-height drives are also available. Hard-disk drives in the 5¼-in. minifloppy package are the most widely used, with larger drives reserved for high-end applications.

Removable hard disks are available in 3.9- and 5¼-in. diameters but have not achieved widespread standardization.

As with floppy-disk drives, one of the key aspects of the drive is the head positioning mechanism. Most low-cost hard disk drives use a stepper-motor-driven mechanism similar to that used in standard floppy-disk drives. Unlike floppy-disk drives, most hard-disk drives use two or more platters, each with a head on each side, so the positioning mechanism moves a group of heads. A single track is accessed by positioning the heads to the desired cylinder and then selecting one of the heads. High-performance hard disk drives use closed-loop positioning systems with voice-coil actuators to achieve high track densities and faster seek times.

Most low-cost hard disk drives use oxide-coated media and ferrite heads, similar to those used in floppy disk drives. High-capacity drives often use a medium that is plated or *sputtered* to obtain a thinner, smoother coating than is possible with the composite coatings of iron oxide and a binder. Plated media are also more rugged, and are preferred for removable disks and for drives used in portable applications.

Most low-cost hard-disk drives use miniature ferrite heads, which use basically the same magnetic structure as tape and floppy-disk heads. The principal difference is the small size and mass of the head and the aerodynamic design of the mounting, which allows it to fly over the disk surface. Thin-film heads, which are fabricated with semi-conductor processing techniques, are often used in high-capacity drives.

9.6.3 Interface Standards

Due to the market dominance of the original supplier (Shugart Associates), the floppy disk drive interface became a universally used de facto standard. Minor changes were made for 5¼- and 3½-in. drives, but the basic interface remained unchanged. For hard-disk drives, the situation is somewhat more complicated. The most common interface for small hard-disk drives, the so-called ST506 interface, was standardized in the same manner as the floppy-disk interface: by the dominance of the first major manufacturer, Seagate Technology. However, there are many other interfaces in use. Some are minor variations of the ST506 interface that increase performance, and others are completely different, providing a higher-level "intelligent" interface. This section describes these interfaces.

ST-506 and Related Standards

The most common size for hard-disk drives in microprocessor-based systems is 5¼ in. The first such mini-Winchester was the ST506 from Seagate Technology. The ST506 interface set a de facto standard that has been widely used for low-cost hard-disk drives.

The ST506 has a capacity of 6.38 Mbytes unformatted or 5 Mbytes formatted. Even though this disk drive was quickly replaced by higher-capacity drives, it is important because it established a standard that many other drives have followed. The disk spins at 3600 rpm, producing a data rate of 5 Mbps. There are 612 tracks of 10,416 bytes each. Each track is typically formatted as 32 sectors of 256 bytes each. Gaps and ID fields are similar to those used in the IBM standard floppy formats. The track density is 255 tpi, and the flux density is 7690 fci. Two platters are used, providing four recording surfaces. The newer ST412 is similar to the ST506 in most respects but uses a track density of 345 tpi and a flux density of 9074 fci to store 10 Mbytes (formatted) on the same number of platters. The average seek time for both drives is 85 ms.

The ST412 uses the same interface as the ST506, with the addition of buffered seek (described later). This de facto standard interface is commonly referred to as the ST506/412 interface. The interface is derived from the standard minifloppy interface and is very similar in many respects. Because of the much higher data rate (5 MHz vs. 500 kHz), the data signals cannot be daisy-chained from one drive to the next, so they are in a separate cable. Figure 9.27 shows the typical cabling for a multidrive system.

Figure 9.28 shows the control signals. Except for a few new signals, these are the same as the signals in the floppy-disk interface. Since there are more than two heads, more than one head select signal (often called *side select* in a double-sided floppy-disk drive) is needed. The interface provides a 3-bit head select code, allowing one of up to eight heads to be selected. (The ST412 needs only two of these signals, since it has only four heads. Higher-capacity drives have six to eight heads and thus require the third bit.)

The only other new control signal is SEEK COMPLETE. This allows the drive to inform the controller when the head is in the requested position. ST412-type drives allow a *buffered seek* operation, in which the controller can issue step pulses at a rate higher than the maximum stepping rate. The disk drive remembers how many pulses were received and steps the head at the maximum rate. This decreases the seek time,

Figure 9.27. Connectors and cabling for ST506-type Winchester interface.

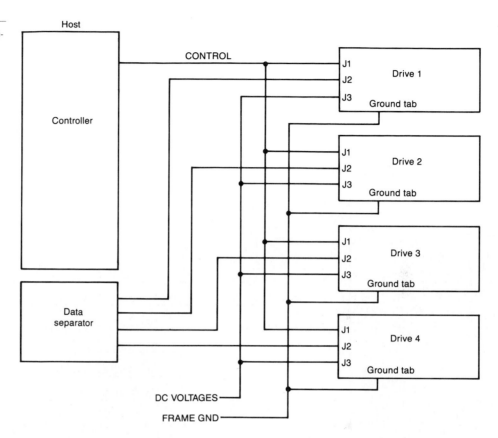

since the drive can take advantage of the stepper motor's acceleration characteristics if it knows in advance how many steps it has to move.

As with floppy-disk drives, all control signals are driven by TTL-level open-collector drivers. The only change is in the termination; instead of a 150-Ω pull-up resistor, a 220-Ω pull-up and a 330-Ω pull-down are used.

Figure 9.29 shows the signals on the data connector. One signal pair is used for write data and one for read data. Because of the high data rate, open-collector drivers are too slow. Instead, RS-422 differential drivers and receivers are used for the data signals. (Refer to Chap. 8 for a description of RS-422 levels and interface ICs.) The encoding method is MFM, the same as is used for double-density floppy disk drives.

Higher-Performance Hard-Disk Interfaces

The standardization of the hard-disk-drive interface was essential for the growth of the industry, since it allowed systems designers to design their interface circuitry without limiting themselves to a single disk drive vendor. Standardization also allows semiconductor manufacturers to invest in the development of LSI controller chips, knowing that there will be a wide market.

However, standardization is also limiting. To be compatible with the ST506/412 standard, the data rate must be 5 Mbps. That effectively limits the flux density that can

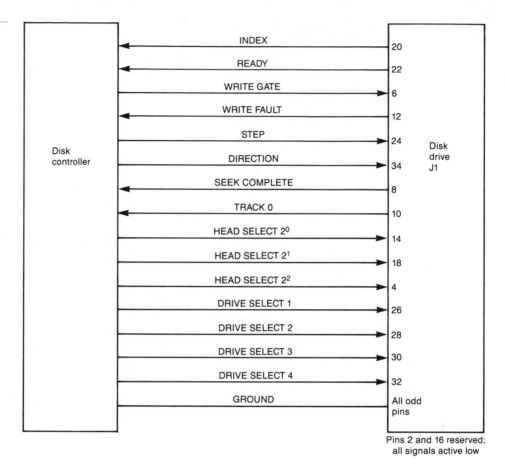

Figure 9.28. ST506/412 control signals.

Pins 2 and 16 reserved; all signals active low

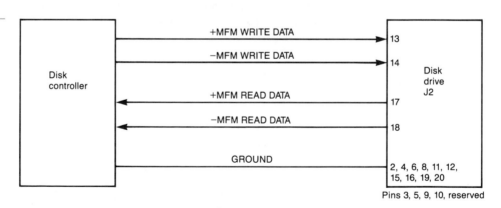

Figure 9.29. ST506/412 data signals.

Pins 3, 5, 9, 10, reserved

be implemented, since increasing the flux density increases the data rate. The primary method of increasing capacity while remaining compatible with controllers designed for the standard is to increase the number of tracks. This can be done by increasing the track density, using a wider area of the disk, or increasing the number of platters. Many high-performance drives do use the ST506/412 interface standard and accept the

5 Mbps limitation. In many applications, access time is more significant than data transfer rate; by using the standard ST506/412 interface but providing an access time of 30 ms or so, performance is considerably increased without requiring a new interface.

However, as technology developed to allow a higher flux density, the need for a modified standard became clear. Unfortunately, not all manufacturers were able to agree on the best approach, and none dominated the market enough to set a de facto standard. Thus, several standards have emerged.

Seagate's high-performance standard is the ST412HP, which is essentially the same as the earlier standard but allows data rates up to 15 Mbps. The high-performance standard also has an additional head select line to allow up to 16 recording surfaces (eight platters).

Another approach is the *Enhanced Small Disk Interface (ESDI),* a more complex standard intended for larger-capacity drives. In addition to the usual control signals, ESDI has a serial command line via which 17-bit serial commands can be sent to the drive. Another significant departure from the ST506/412 approach is that the data separator is placed in the disk drive instead of in the controller. This relieves the controller designer of the most difficult aspect of controller design. The data passed between the controller and the drive is NRZ, and the drive encodes and decodes the data into the desired format. This allows the drive designer to deviate from the MFM encoding required by the ST506/412 standard without affecting the controller or the interface. The RLL 2,7 encoding is commonly used in high-capacity drives.

The *Storage Module Device (SMD)* interface was developed by Control Data Corporation and is widely used in large disk drives (typically over 100 Mbytes). It is not generally used with low-cost hard disks. The *Intelligent Peripheral Interface (IPI)* is a more recent interface standard used by some high-capacity high-performance drives.

SCSI Intelligent Interface

The *Small Computer System Interface (SCSI)* is designed to provide a standard interface between the host system and the disk controller, as shown in Fig. 9.30. The *host adapter* interfaces the SCSI bus to the controller. The SCSI bus is a true bus in that up

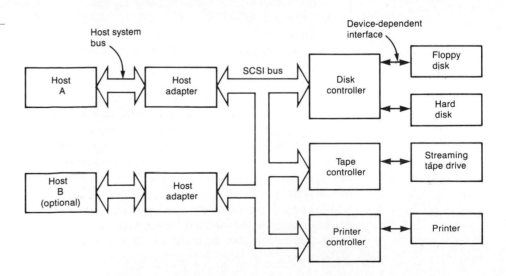

Figure 9.30. SCSI system architecture.

to eight devices can be connected in parallel on the bus. A typical system might include one host adapter and several device controllers. (Device controllers are called *formatters* in SCSI terminology.) Thus, the single host adapter can provide the microprocessor system's interface for several peripherals. More than one host adapter can also be connected to the SCSI bus, allowing sharing of peripherals among systems.

The design of the SCSI bus originated at Shugart Associates and was called the Shugart Associates Standard Interface (SASI). The name was changed to SCSI in the ANSI standard definition to avoid inclusion of a company name. The basic concepts of the bus originate from IBM's I/O channel used in their mainframe computer systems. Although Shugart Associates designed the bus as an interface for hard-disk controllers, it is applicable to any device that performs block data transfers. Such devices include hard- and floppy-disk drives, tape drives, printers, and communications network interfaces.

The SCSI standard uses the term *initiator* for the device requesting a transfer on the bus and the term *target* for the other device in the transfer. Most commonly, the host adapter is the initiator and one of the device controllers is the target, but this is not necessarily true.

Table 9.6 lists the 18 signals that constitute the SCSI bus. There are eight data lines plus a parity line, and nine control signals. The standard provides two alternative definitions for the electrical characteristics: single-ended or differential. The single-ended configuration can be used for cable lengths up to 6 m, while the differential configuration allows cables up to 15 m.

The SCSI definition consists of more than the definition of the bus signals. It also includes command definitions to support a variety of peripheral devices, status message definitions, and error-handling procedures. This makes it a very powerful but complex standard. We will describe only the basic functions of the SCSI bus; for information on the detailed operation, refer to the references listed in the Selected Bibliography at the end of this chapter.

The initiator begins a bus transaction by arbitrating for access to the bus. If there is only one host adapter and one device controller, it will always "win" the arbitration. Otherwise, the highest-priority device wins and gains access to the bus. It then selects the target with which it wants to communicate. This establishes the path between the initiator and the target, and commands, status, and data can be transferred between them.

One powerful feature of the SCSI bus is the ability of a target (such as a device controller) to disconnect from the bus when it is not ready to transfer data but is executing a command. When executing a disk read command, for example, the disk must first seek the required track. After receiving this command, the disk controller can disconnect from the bus. When it is ready to transfer data, it reconnects to the bus. This disconnect capability significantly increases the available bus time when multiple devices are sharing the bus. In a system with multiple hard-disk drives, it allows a seek to be initiated on one drive while a seek is in progress on another. This *overlapped seek* can significantly improve performance in a multiple-drive system with a large amount of disk activity.

SCSI also allows data to be transferred from one device on the SCSI bus to another device on the bus without intervention from the host adapter. The host adapter must initiate the transfer, but the transfer of data proceeds directly between the two device

Table 9.6   SCSI Bus Signals

Bus signal	Definition	Single-ended option pin number
DB0*	Data bus bit 0	2
DB1*	Data bus bit 1	4
DB2*	Data bus bit 2	6
DB3*	Data bus bit 3	8
DB4*	Data bus bit 4	10
DB5*	Data bus bit 5	12
DB6*	Data bus bit 6	14
DB7*	Data bus bit 7	16
DBP*	Data bus parity	18
ATN*	Attention (indicates INITIATOR has message to send TARGET)	32
BSY*	Busy (SCSI bus is busy)	36
ACK*	Acknowledge (ACK of REQ/ACK pair used for information transfer on data bus)	38
RST*	Reset (clears SCSI bus of all activity)	40
MSG*	Message (indicates bus is in message transfer phase)	42
SEL*	Select (used to select/reselect an SCSI Device)	44
C/D	Command/Data (indicates command/ status information transfer or data in/out transfer)	46
REQ	Request (REQ of REQ/ACK pair used for information transfer on data bus)	48
I/O	Input/output (indicates direction of data flow on data bus)	50

controllers. A typical application of this "copy" operation is backing up a hard disk onto a streaming cartridge tape.

The full SCSI implementation described above requires bus arbitration logic in the host adapter(s) and device formatter(s). Some lower-cost implementations do not include the arbitration logic, which is specified as optional in the SCSI standard. Formatters without arbitration cannot disconnect during a command execution, since they cannot reacquire the bus to complete the command. Host adapters without arbitration can be used only in single-host systems.

Some hard-disk drives include the controller and SCSI interface as part of the drive electronics, eliminating the need for a separate controller. Using this high-level interface results in an intelligent disk drive, which eases the system designer's task by removing the need to deal with the disk drive at the primitive control level. Functions such as defect management can be performed in the drive, so the system software does not need to be aware of defective areas on the disk. This approach also eliminates the inefficiency of having two interfaces in the system (the SCSI bus and the drive interface). In a system with multiple drives, however, the replication of the SCSI formatter function in each drive is inefficient.

9.6.4 Hard-Disk Controllers

Hard-disk controllers must perform the same tasks as a floppy-disk controller. The primary difference is that the data rate is much higher for a hard disk than for a floppy disk. The 5 to 15 Mbps serial data rate makes the design of the data separator more difficult and requires faster shift registers and other logic for converting the data to parallel format. All logic in the data path must operate at least 10 times faster than required for the fastest floppy disks. The interface to the microprocessor bus must use either a full-sector buffer memory or a high-speed DMA channel. Even the minimum 5 Mbps serial data rate produces a 625 kbyte/s data transfer rate, or one byte every 1.6 μs.

Hard-disk controller chips are available and have command sets and capabilities similar to floppy-disk controller chips. Because of the higher data rate, the data separation and write precompensation circuits are provided in separate ICs. Some hard-disk controller chip sets also place the parallel-to-serial and serial-to-parallel converters in separate ICs. Some hard-disk controllers include a sector buffer on-chip, and some include DMA logic to transfer data between the disk and the host system's main memory. Because many systems include both hard and floppy disks and the control functions for each are similar, many disk controller chips can control both types of drives.

Standard floppy-disk formats use 16-bit CRC codes to check for errors in each data block and ID field. This code does not allow errors to be corrected, however. Many hard-disk controllers use a longer error checking code of 32 to 40 bits, which allows certain errors to be corrected.

A hard-disk controller with an intelligent interface such as the SCSI bus generally requires a dedicated microprocessor to provide the intelligence. The architecture of such a controller is similar to that of the intelligent floppy-disk controller described earlier in this chapter. Firmware stored in ROM translates SCSI commands from the host system into the more detailed command sequences required by the disk controller chip.

9.7   MAGNETIC BUBBLE MEMORY

Although disk drives are effective mass-storage devices, they are far from ideal in one respect: they are precision mechanical devices. As a result, they are less rugged and more expensive to manufacture than semiconductor devices. The ideal mass-storage device would have a capacity and cost per bit comparable to a disk drive but would have no moving parts and use semiconductor technology for fabrication. *Bubble memory* is the only technology that has approached this goal.

9.7.1   The Saga of Bubble Memory

The first bubble memories were demonstrated at Bell Laboratories in 1967. After a decade of development, commercial products appeared. In 1978, Rockwell, TI, and Fujitsu introduced the first commercial products, with capacities from 92 to 256 Kbits. In 1979, Intel entered the market with a 1-Mbit device. National Semiconductor and Motorola also introduced bubble memory products. For several years, each year was predicted to be the "year of the bubble," and many expected bubble memories to widely replace floppy disks.

However, the early 1980s were not kind to bubble memory. The bubble memory chips required large investments by their manufacturers for development costs and capital equipment, and the market for the devices developed slowly due to their high prices. The development of the complex LSI chips required to interface bubble memories to microprocessor systems was also a stumbling block. In the face of large short-term losses, a weak economy, and an uncertain future, Rockwell, National, TI, Motorola and Intel abandoned the bubble memory business, leaving Fujitsu and Hitachi as the primary suppliers.

Bubble memory capacity has now increased to 4 Mbits per chip, and prices have fallen steadily. Had floppy disk technology stood still while bubble memories were developed, they would have been a major competitor. However, floppy disks steadily improved their capacity and performance while reducing their costs, and bubble memory has thus been relegated to a niche market. It is used primarily in applications in which its small size, high reliability, and ruggedness outweigh its higher price.

One limitation of bubble memory is that it has a relatively limited temperature range. Low-cost devices typically have a temperature range of approximately 0 to 60°C; some are as limited as 15 to 35°C. Wider temperature range devices are available, but the cost increases dramatically as the temperature range is widened. This has limited the military applications of bubble memory, which could otherwise have been a major use.

Bubble memory cartridges can be used as removable media, providing the functions of a floppy disk with the advantages of bubble memory. However, bubble memory cartridges are much more expensive than floppy disks, restricting their use to applications in which bubble memory's unique advantages are needed.

9.7.2   Bubble Memory Technology

As described earlier in this chapter, a magnetic material can be viewed as a large number of magnetic domains. When the material is not magnetized, each domain points in a random direction, and the sum of all the domains produces no net magnetic field. In an extremely thin film of certain materials, the magnetic domains can be constrained to be oriented perpendicularly to the surface of the film. Thus, there are only two possible orientations: the north pole of the domain facing the top surface of the film or facing the bottom surface of the film. As Fig. 9.31 shows, in these materials the domains tend to be long and snakelike. If a small magnetic field is applied, the domains oriented

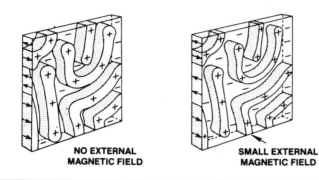

Figure 9.31. Magnetic bubble formation in a thin film. *(Courtesy of Intel Corporation.)*

Figure 9.32. Bubble propagation using asymmetric chevrons. *(Courtesy of Intel Corporation.)*

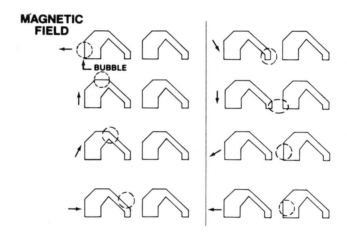

opposite the applied field shrink. As the field is increased, a point is reached where the domains contrary to the applied field are reduced to small cylindrical areas. These are the bubbles, which appear as circles when viewed from above.

To control the positions of the bubbles, a pattern of easily magnetized metal (generally permalloy, an alloy of iron and nickel) is laid over the film containing the bubbles. The asymmetric chevron, as shown in Fig. 9.32, is one common pattern. If a rotating magnetic field is applied, the poles of the chevron-shaped areas move with the field. The bubbles are drawn to the nearest pole of opposite polarity to that of the bubble. As the field rotates, the bubble is pulled over the top of the chevron, down the other side, and finally is transferred to the next chevron. Thus, a shift-register-type structure is created. The presence of a bubble indicates a 1, and the absence indicates a 0.

Bubble memory chips are fabricated from nonmagnetic garnet wafers. A thin magnetic garnet layer is deposited on the wafer, and it is in this film that the bubbles exist. Nonmagnetic conductors and magnetic permalloy layers are then deposited in the desired patterns, with intermediate insulating layers. The manufacturing process is similar to that used for silicon semiconductors.

Figure 9.33 shows the construction of a bubble memory device. The garnet chip,

Figure 9.33. Bubble memory packaging. *(Courtesy of Intel Corporation.)*

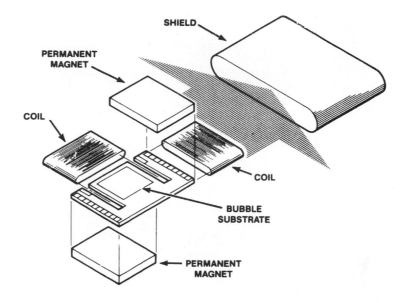

processed as described above, is mounted on a substrate. This substrate is then mounted in a package with the other magnetic components. Permanent magnets provide the *bias field,* which shrinks the snakelike magnetic domains into cylindrical bubbles. Two coils surround the bubble chip, and when properly driven provide the rotating magnetic field. The entire assembly is enclosed in a metal shield to prevent external magnetic fields from affecting the device. Both leaded and leadless packages have been used.

The rotating magnetic field supplied by the coils stops when power is removed. This stops the motion of the bubbles, but as long as the bias field is present (which is supplied by the permanent magnets), the bubbles remain in the position they were in when the rotating field stopped. Thus, bubble memories are nonvolatile, like other forms of magnetic storage.

Because the bubbles are very small, the data storage density is higher than for semiconductor devices. Fewer processing steps are required than for semiconductor devices. However, the garnet wafers are much more expensive than silicon wafers, and the package (including the permanent magnets and coils) is more complex, increasing the cost of the bubble memory device.

9.7.3 Bubble Memory Architecture

In principle, a bubble memory could be built as a single long shift register. However, the rate at which the bubbles can be shifted is limited, and the time to access a selected bit in a shift register millions of bits long would be excessive. Thus, bubble memories are divided into a number of smaller shift register structures, called *storage loops,* which are accessed via input and output loops. This is the *major loop—minor loop* architecture. A variation on this architecture, as shown in Fig. 9.34, uses input and output tracks instead of an access loop. A bubble generator provides bubbles at the

Figure 9.34. Bubble memory architecture. *(Courtesy of Intel Corporation.)*

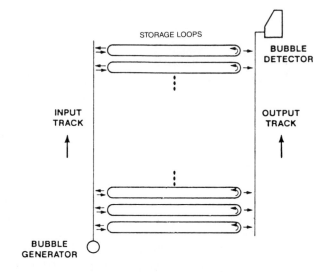

start of the input track. These new bubbles (representing new data to be written) are exchanged with bubbles from the storage loops. The bubbles from the storage loops (representing data that has been overwritten) are shifted to the end of the input track and destroyed. To read data from the memory, bubbles from the desired storage loop are copied to the output track, where they are shifted out to the bubble detector. The bubble detector provides an electrical signal indicating the presence or absence of a bubble. Bubbles are copied (or *replicated*) to the output track rather than simply transferred, so data in the storage loop is not affected.

Bubble memories require a complex controller. The controller and its associated circuitry must provide the signals for the coils to produce the rotating field, generate signals to produce bubbles for the writing of data, sense the signals from the bubble detector, and time all these operations to properly move data along the input and output tracks. To access a particular point in a storage loop, the controller must wait for the bubbles in the loop to shift along the loop until the desired bubble is next to the input or output track. These functions require an LSI controller chip and several support chips to provide the interface to a microprocessor system.

To obtain acceptable production yields, bubble memories are fabricated with a number of extra storage loops. During production testing, all tracks are tested to determine which are good. The list of good and bad loops is then stored in a special loop called the *boot loop*. The controller circuitry must read this boot loop and use only the good loops for data storage.

9.8   SUMMARY

Mass-storage devices provide large amounts of nonvolatile storage at a low price per bit. The most common mass-storage devices use rotating magnetic media. Floppy disks of several sizes provide removable media and low cost. Winchester disks provide large capacity and fast access and transfer rates but generally do not have removable media. Tape cartridges store large amounts of data in removable media and are widely used as backups for nonremovable disks.

Disk technology is rapidly advancing, and capacity can be expected to double several times before fundamental limits are approached. Capacity increases can be obtained in any of the following ways:

More efficient codes, which store more data with the same magnetic density

More accurate positioning mechanisms, which allow more tracks per inch

Improved heads and media for increased magnetic density within each track

A steady stream of new products with advances in one or more of these areas can be expected.

Bubble memory is unique among mass-storage devices in that it is solid-state. Thus, it is compact, very reliable, and tolerant of dirty environments and vibration. The cost per bit for bubble memory remains relatively high, restricting its use to applications in which its unique advantages justify the higher price.

All the mass-storage technologies described in this chapter are based on magnetic storage. Optical storage, using tiny marks read and written by lasers, is now challenging magnetic recording in high-capacity applications.

9.9 EXERCISES

9.1. Suppose a new semiconductor memory technology is developed that can store 10 Mbits on a single chip, which is directly addressed like a RAM but is nonvolatile and has a cost per bit comparable to a hard disk. Should this be considered a mass-storage device?

9.2. What units are used to specify the magnetic density for a given head and medium?

9.3. What units are used to specify the data density for a given head and medium? What is the relationship between magnetic density and data density?

9.4. A four-track streaming tape drive has a flux density of 10,000 fci and uses FM encoding. The usable length of the tape is 300 ft. What is the unformatted capacity of the tape?

9.5. Which of the following is a distinguishing difference between floppy and rigid disks? (Select as many as applicable.)

a. Medium in direct contact with head during read/write operations.
b. Medium is not removable.
c. Both sides of medium are used.
d. Closed-loop head positioning system allows higher track density.
e. Medium is flexible.

9.6. A double-sided floppy disk with 40 tracks per side has how many cylinders?

9.7. A disk drive has a track density of 255 tpi. Due to thermal and hygroscopic effects, the outermost track can move as much as $\pm.005$ in. from its nominal position. Can this drive operate with an open-loop head positioning system?

9.8. Given an arbitrarily fast head positioning mechanism, what sets the limit on the average access time for a disk drive?

9.9. An 80-track high-density minifloppy drive rotates at 360 rpm and has a track-to-track access time of 3 ms. The settling time is 15 ms. What is the average access time? What is the maximum access time?

9.10. A hard-disk drive rotates at 3600 rpm and has an average seek time (including settling) of 35 ms. What is the average total access time, including rotational latency?

9.11. For a disk using MFM encoding and the IBM standard format with 26 sectors of 256 bytes each, what percentage of the disk capacity is lost due to formatting? What is this percentage if eight sectors of 1024 bytes are used instead?

9.12. Draw a detailed block diagram for a circuit to implement the head position control portion of a floppy-disk controller using standard TTL components (no floppy-disk controller chip). Assume that the desired track is provided from an output port.

9.13. For a microprocessor that you are familiar with, write the assembly language program required to perform a polled data transfer for a sector read. Can it keep up with a standard double-density minifloppy? An 8-in. double-density disk? An ST506-type hard disk?

9.14. What allows Winchester disks to use a higher track density than floppy disks?

9.15. Assuming an 85-ms access time and a 5-Mbps data rate, how long does it take to access and transfer a 10,000-byte file (disregarding time lost in reading gaps and ID fields)? What is the total time if the data rate is increased to 10 Mbps? What if the data rate remains 5 Mbps but the access time is reduced to 35 ms?

9.16. Suppose a 1-Mbit bubble memory is organized as one long storage loop. If the data transfer rate is 200 kbps, what is the average access time?

9.17. A floppy disk has a hard-error rate of one error per 10^{12} bits. Assuming that the data transfer rate is 250 kbps and data transfers are in progress an average of 10 percent of the time, how many hours will elapse (on average) between errors?

9.10   SELECTED BIBLIOGRAPHY

Magnetic Recording Fundamentals

The Hoagland and White books are not for the casual reader, but if you want to know how magnetic recording *really* works, these are the sources.

Hoagland, Albert S. *Digital Magnetic Recording,* Malabar, FL: Krieger Publishing Co., 1983. A classic text on digital recording theory. Originally published in 1963 but still useful since the emphasis is on the fundamental theory.

Jorgensen, Finn. *The Complete Handbook of Magnetic Recording,* Blue Ridge Summit, PA: Tab Books, 1980. Oriented toward analog recording but does cover basic digital recording. Good coverage of tape and tape drive theory and of magnetic recording theory.

White, Robert M. *Physics of Magnetic Recording,* Palo Alto, CA: Xerox, 1984. A thorough and up-to-date treatment of recording theory, including thin-film heads and perpendicular recording. Available from Xerox Palo Alto Research Center, 3333 Coyote Hill Road, Palo Alto, CA 94304. Publication number GSL-84-01.

Tape Cartridges and Hard Disk Backup

Archive. *Streaming,* 1982. Available from Archive Corp., 3540 Cadillac Ave., Costa Mesa, CA 92626. Covers streaming tape drive operation, plus an overview of mass storage in general.

Warren, Carl. "Tape Unravels Secondary Storage Knots," *Electronic Design,* Aug. 18, 1983, pp. 119–130. An overview of magnetic tape technologies.

QIC-02: Proposed 1/4 Inch Cartridge Tape Drive Intelligent Interface Standard, Rev. D, September 1982, and *QIC-24: Proposed Standard for Data Interchange on the Streaming 1/4 in. Magnetic Tape Cartridge Using Group Code Recording at 10,000 FRPI,* Rev. D, April 1983. Available from Freeman Associates, 311 E. Carrillo St., Santa Barbara, CA 93101.

Disk Drives and Controllers

For specific information on disk drives and controller chips, refer to the manufacturer's data sheets. The technical reference for disk drives is called an *OEM Manual* by most manufacturers.

ADSI. *SCSI Guide,* 2d ed., 1985. Available from Adaptive Data Systems, Inc., 2627 Pomona Blvd, Pomona, CA 91768. A thorough description of the SCSI standard and its applications.

ANSI. *X3.131M SCSI Standard,* 1430 Broadway, New York, NY 10018. The official SCSI standards document. (Until this standard is accepted by ANSI, the draft standard is available from X3 Secretariat, CBEMA, 311 First St. NW, Suite 300, Washington, DC 20001.)

Di Bianca, Gaetano. "Ingenious Data Encoding Fills Floppy Disks Twice as Full," *Electronics,* Apr. 7, 1983, pp. 155–157. Describes several encoding techniques, including GCR.

Disk/Trend. *Disk/Trend Report,* Published annually by Disk/Trend, Inc., 5150 El Camino Real, Suite 20, Los Altos, CA 94022. The authoritative (and expensive) report on who's selling how many of which disk drives, including projections for the future.

Eidsmore, Doug, and Bob Hirshon. "Designer's Guide to Disk Drives," *Digital Design,* November 1983, pp. 40–63. A good review of Winchester disk drive technologies.

Marshall, Trevor G., and John A. Attikiouzel. "Floppy Disk Data Transfer Techniques," *IEEE Micro,* December 1983, pp. 17–23. Describes alternatives to DMA controllers for data transfer.

National Semiconductor. *APPS Handbook 1: Mass Storage,* Santa Clara, CA. In addition to data sheets for National's disk controller ICs, this handbook includes application notes that cover mass-storage technology, interface standards, and controller design.

Nesin, Richard. "One Chip Controls Both Hard and Floppy Disks," *Electronic Design,* Dec. 8, 1983, pp. 151–159. Describes Standard Microsystems' HDC9224 universal disk controller chip. Includes a typical application circuit.

Teja, Edward R. *The Designer's Guide to Disk Drives,* Reston, Virginia: Reston Publishing, 1985. Describes both floppy and hard disks, with the emphasis on the latter. Aimed at systems integrators, so technical detail on controllers and interfaces is lacking, but provides a useful overview.

Teja, Edward R. "5¼-in. Winchester Disk Drives," *EDN,* Aug. 18, 1983, pp. 118–131. An overview of commercially available mini-Winchesters. Includes a list of manufacturers.

Travis, Bill. "Disk-Drive-Controller ICs Provide Board-Level Performance," *EDN,* Dec. 13, 1984, pp. 42–58. An overview of hard disk controller chips.

Weiner, Richard, and Gregory York. *Application Note 8: A Single/Double Density Floppy Disk Controller Using the μPD765,* NEC Microcomputers, Inc., Mountain View, CA. Describes data separators and other circuits for use with the 765 controller chip.

Western Digital. *Storage Management Products Handbook,* Irvine, CA. Includes data sheets on controllers for floppy disks, hard disks, and tape drives, plus data separators and other associated devices.

Bubble Memory

Bobeck, Andrew H., and H. E. D. Scovil. "Magnetic Bubbles," *Scientific American,* June 1971, pp. 78–90. An early paper by Bell Labs scientists describing basic bubble technology and the first devices that were built.

MULTIPLE MICROPROCESSOR SYSTEMS

10.1 MOTIVATIONS

Traditional computer architectures are based on the sharing of a powerful, expensive processor. The microprocessor has changed the design rules, however, by decreasing the cost of the processor itself to a small fraction of the system cost. The additional cost of using two or more microprocessors is therefore relatively small, particularly in light of potential increased system performance and other benefits.

There are several motivations for using multiple processors:

Increased performance

Increased reliability/availability

Functional modularity

Physical distribution of processing power

Depending on the particular application, one or more of these factors may be the primary motivation.

Using multiple microprocessors increases performance without pushing the limits of the technology. To build a single-processor *(uniprocessor)* system with higher performance than the fastest available microprocessor requires the use of bit-slice or custom processors based on relatively small-scale high-speed ICs. Price, complexity, and power consumption for such systems are much greater than for microprocessor-based systems. Using multiple microprocessors increases performance beyond that possible with a single microprocessor with a more modest increase in cost and complexity, assuming that the problem can be divided into two or more parts that can execute in parallel.

The price/performance ratio for microcomputers is generally much better than that for large computers. It therefore seems attractive to consider using large numbers of microprocessors to build large computers. This is a difficult task, and there are few commercial products using this approach. One key difficulty is the division of the software: how one program is divided among numerous processors. Current multiple microprocessor applications typically use a few microprocessors with each dedicated to a specific task.

Multiple processor *(multiprocessor)* systems can be designed for high system reliability. Such systems include multiple identical processor units. If a failure is detected in any unit, another can take over its tasks. One way to detect such failures is to operate two processor units in parallel, using the same software and input data, and compare their outputs. If the outputs ever differ, then an error has occurred. If three modules operate in parallel, then a majority vote can determine which module is in error.

Rather than concentrating all the processing for an application in a single processor, multiprocessor systems divide the tasks into groups that can be handled by separate processors. Thus, the processing load is distributed among several processors; this is called *distributed processing*. This term often refers to systems in which the processing elements are physically distributed such that each is a separate box, and there may be some distance between the units. This is not necessarily the case, however; processing may be distributed among several microprocessors on a single circuit board.

In a functionally partitioned multiprocessor system, each microprocessor is assigned a relatively independent task. This breaks the system into isolated modules and allows development work to be easily divided among team members. The communication between modules is via high-level commands, so each module is independent of the detailed operation of the others. A module can be modified or even redesigned with a new microprocessor without affecting other modules.

Multiple microprocessors are used in a number of ways in personal computers. Many systems use a single-chip microcomputer to scan and decode the keyboard. Others use one processor to handle the keyboard, display, and communications overhead and another to execute the application software. Many disk controllers have their own dedicated microprocessor, and high-performance graphics systems dedicate a processor to display functions.

Multiprocessor systems promise to continue to provide more powerful systems as microprocessor technology reaches its limits. Other ways to increase performance are to increase the clock rate, to use more sophisticated architectures, and to use longer word lengths. However, these factors cannot continue to increase at the rate of the last decade. Clock rates much beyond 25 MHz would greatly complicate system design, even if the ICs were capable of higher speeds. While 16- and 32-bit microprocessors provide much greater throughput than 8-bit microprocessors, it is unlikely that 64-bit or wider word lengths would be generally useful; the nature of most data is such that 16 or 32 bits provide sufficient representation. Sophisticated architectures using pipelining and instruction caches increase performance but can do only so much. Using multiple microprocessors is one approach that does not so clearly reach a practical limit.

10.2 APPLICATIONS

Applications for multiple microprocessor systems range from instruments and dedicated control systems to large *supercomputers*. In the middle of this range is the high-performance multiuser *super-microcomputer*. The techniques described in this chapter apply to the lower and middle ranges; in keeping with the rest of this book, the design of large general-purpose computers is not covered.

Any application that needs more performance or faster response time to external events is a candidate for a multiprocessor implementation. For example, consider an instrument that is sampling an input from a sensor 1000 times per second and performing a series of calculations on that measurement to determine if a limit has been exceeded and an alarm should be set. The 1000-sample-per-second rate dictates that each sample must be processed within 1 ms. At a minimum, the microprocessor must be able to do the required processing within this 1 ms interval. For the moment, let us assume that this is within the capability of a standard microprocessor.

There are, however, additional requirements for this instrument. It must scan the keyboard for user input and respond to commands from a computer connected via a serial interface. These tasks also have response time requirements. If the input processing task requires only a fraction of the 1 ms available for its execution, then it may be possible for the same microprocessor to perform these tasks and the input processing. However, the user (keyboard) and computer interface tasks can also be handled by a separate processor. This allows the input processor to devote all its time (except that required for communication with the other processor) to processing the input signal, while the user and computer interface processor is freed from the input processing requirements. The result is that faster response times can be obtained for the user and computer interface, and less powerful processors can be used than would have been required if one processor were handling all functions. Software design is also easier when the microprocessor's performance is not being stretched to its limits.

A slightly different situation occurs if the input processing requires more than 1 ms for an inexpensive microprocessor. This leaves two alternatives: a single higher-performance microprocessor or splitting the task between two or more processors. This split could be performed either by having each of two processors handling alternate samples or by having one processor perform half the processing on each sample and then pass it on to another processor for completion. The optimal partitioning depends on the processing algorithm.

This type of functional partitioning is key to the type of multiprocessor applications described in this chapter. In addition to providing more performance (or requiring a less powerful processor), it provides additional flexibility. For example, multiple input channels could be added to the instrument described above by adding additional input processor subsystems. The performance of each input processor is not affected by the total number of input processors in the system. In a single-processor version of such an instrument, the ability to add additional input channels would be strictly limited by the amount of processor time available.

When evaluating the implementation of a system using multiple microprocessors, first partition the system functions into as many distinct tasks as possible. Then consider the following issues:

1.   What are the real-time requirements? The task requiring the fastest response is a good candidate for a dedicated processor.

2.   How much communication is required between tasks? Those requiring frequent communication of large amounts of data may be difficult to divide among processors.

3.   What are the expansion requirements? Any time-critical task that may have to be duplicated is a good candidate for a dedicated processor.

After this analysis is performed, a specific architecture can be chosen.

10.3   MULTIPROCESSOR SYSTEM DESIGN

The design of a multiple processor system can be divided into logical and physical aspects, as follows:

1.   Logical structure:
     a.   Static or dynamic distribution of tasks
     b.   Master/slave or egalitarian control
     c.   Coordination of processors and shared resources

2.   Physical structure:
     a.   Connection topology
     b.   Global and local distribution of resources
     c.   Interprocessor communication links

This section addresses each of these design issues, except for the last which is covered in detail in Sec. 10.4.

10.3.1   Classifications

Multiple processor architectures can be classified in a variety of ways. One broad classification scheme, devised by M. J. Flynn, divides systems into four types, depending on the number of instruction and data streams:

SISD: *S*ingle *i*nstruction stream, *s*ingle *d*ata stream

SIMD: *S*ingle *i*nstruction, *m*ultiple *d*ata

MISD: *M*ultiple *i*nstruction, *s*ingle *d*ata

MIMD: *M*ultiple *i*nstruction, *m*ultiple *d*ata

Conventional uniprocessor systems are SISD machines; they use a single instruction stream to operate on a single data stream. SIMD machines perform the same operations on a number of data streams and are often called *array processors*. They are used for applications that are naturally array-oriented and require high performance, such as image processing. The MISD classification is rarely used; it is sometimes applied to pipelined machines. Most multiple microprocessor systems are MIMD machines, with each microprocessor operating on its own data using its own instructions, and it is with this class of machine that this chapter is concerned.

10.3.2 Interprocessor Coupling

MIMD systems can be categorized by the degree of coupling between the processors. Figure 10.1 shows a *tightly coupled* system, in which the processors share a common program memory and bus structure and are typically under the control of a single operating system. In a tightly coupled system the processors must be closely synchronized with each other. As described in the section on shared buses later in this chapter, the shared bus becomes a bottleneck, and tightly coupled systems must be very carefully designed to use more than a few processors effectively.

Figure 10.2 shows a *loosely coupled* system, in which each processor has its own local resources and can therefore operate independently of the other processors. Each processor executes its own program from its own local memory, and communication between processors is relatively infrequent. Most multiple microprocessor applications

Figure 10.1. Tightly coupled multiprocessor system.

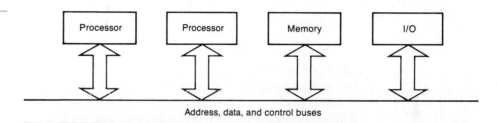

Figure 10.2. Loosely coupled multiprocessor system.

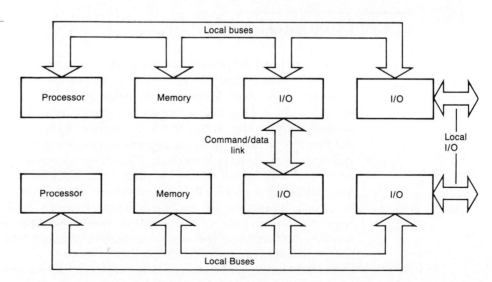

are loosely coupled systems. Relatively independent microprocessors, each dedicated to a particular task, operate simultaneously and communicate only when necessary. This breaks the bottleneck of the shared bus, since each processor has its own local bus.

The terms *loosely coupled* and *tightly coupled* do not have rigid definitions and have been used in different ways by different people. Some consider only those systems described above as tightly coupled to be multiprocessor systems; those systems we have called loosely coupled they call multicomputer systems. Others have also introduced an intermediate category of *moderately coupled* systems. These terms can be applied either to the physical system architecture or to the degree of software interaction among processors.

10.3.3 Logical System Structure

In most functionally partitioned systems, one microprocessor acts as the *master* and has one or more *slaves*. Each slave may in turn be the master to other slaves. Such systems are called *hierarchical*.

Hierarchical systems are generally *asymmetric*, with each processor performing a different function. The task assignment is static, and it is not generally possible for one processor to share another's load. Thus, depending on the processing requirements, one processor may be idling while another is overloaded.

Systems in which all processors have identical capabilities and can therefore be used interchangeably are called *symmetrical*. A list of tasks, in order of priority, is maintained in global system memory. When a processor completes a task, it then proceeds with the next task on the list. This logical structure is readily scalable to any number of processors, providing that the global resources do not get saturated and there are enough tasks to be done to keep all the processors busy. It is also adaptable to high-reliability applications, since no single processor module is essential to the system's operation.

10.3.4 Partitioning of Software

One of the central difficulties in the design of any multiprocessor system is the partitioning of software among the processors. In the general-purpose case, this is a very difficult task. Consider, for example, a multiprocessor system in which a number of processors are used to execute a standard program supplied by the user. For common assembly languages, as well as high-level languages such as BASIC, Fortran, Cobol, and Pascal, it is difficult to devise a general method for splitting up the program to be executed among the various processors. These languages do not make clear which subroutines or tasks may be executed in parallel and which must be executed in series. More recent languages such as Concurrent Pascal and Ada allow programs to be written as independent tasks that can be concurrently executed. Programs written in these languages can thus more easily use multiple processors to execute a single program. However, the number of processors that can be effectively utilized is limited by the number of concurrent tasks in the application program.

In most multiple-microprocessor systems, the various microprocessors are not co-operating to execute parts of one large program but are each executing a program of their own. Each processor is assigned a function (or set of functions) when the system is designed, and that function does not change regardless of the task the system is performing. For example, a general-purpose computer may have a keyboard processor, a disk processor, and a printer processor, but only the main processor executes application programs. The I/O processors and disk processor are dedicated to their respective functions, regardless of the program being executed by the main processor. They increase the performance of the system not by making the application program itself execute faster, but by relieving the main processor of other tasks.

This type of software division implies a loosely coupled hardware architecture. Software development is relatively straightforward, since each processor has a particular task to perform and is isolated from the others. Communication protocols define the interactions among the processors, and each processor needs only to maintain its part of the protocol. It is completely isolated from the internal structure of the other processor systems. Therefore, each processor's software can be separately developed. For testing, each processor can be isolated and its performance separately tested.

Countering this benefit is the additional software required for interprocessor communications. Debugging can also be hampered by subtle interactions between processors that sometimes make bugs difficult to localize. Proper protocol design minimizes these problems.

The principle of *mutual suspicion* helps avoid interaction problems. Each processor should be suspicious of all messages from other processors and not assume them to be valid. By checking each message for validity, interprocessor side effects in which a bug in one processor's software causes an unexpected effect in another processor's software can be minimized.

In addition, messages sent over communication links subject to noise should have a checksum or CRC appended to allow error detection. The receiver can then request retransmission of a message whose checksum fails, providing error tolerance. Examples of such protocols are bisync and SDLC.

10.3.5 Management of Shared Resources

When multiple processors share resources such as memory and I/O devices, a mechanism is needed to control access to these resources. Some program sequences must be performed without any possibility of another processor using the same resource during that sequence; this is called a *critical section*. For example, if one processor is creating or modifying a block of data in the shared memory that will be used by another processor, it is critical that the data not be accessed when it is only partially created or modified. Another example is a shared printer; if one processor is sending a listing to the printer, then the other processors must wait for the printout to complete before attempting to use the printer. In each of these cases, programs running on separate processors must have some communication link that allows them to determine if a shared resource is available or busy.

A *semaphore* is a flag used for this purpose. Basically, it is a flip-flop (or a bit of memory) that indicates the status of a resource. If the semaphore is set, then the resource is busy; if it is clear, then the resource is free. The rules that each processor must follow before using a shared resource are as follows:

Read semaphore.

If semaphore set, read again until clear or defer this task.

Set semaphore.

Use shared resource.

Clear semaphore.

Testing and setting the semaphore is itself a critical section. To test and set the semaphore, most microprocessors must first read the semaphore, execute a second instruction to test it, and then execute a third instruction to set it. Suppose two bus masters simultaneously decide to use a shared resource, and each requests access to the bus to read the semaphore. If they are each granted bus cycles in turn, they will both see that the semaphore is clear, and both will attempt to use the resource simultaneously. Thus, for semaphores to function properly, an *indivisible test-and-set* operation is needed, which cannot possibly be interrupted by any other processor. Any master must therefore be able to obtain several consecutive memory cycles without any other master gaining access to the memory.

This is implemented on the Multibus by the master entering a "bus lock" state, as described in Sec. 10.5.4. In this state, the master refuses to release the bus, effectively locking out all other masters regardless of priority. This state must be used only when necessary, since it indefinitely delays all access to the bus by other masters. It is used only for critical sections of code, such as testing and setting a semaphore, which must be executed as consecutive bus cycles.

The 8086 exchange (XCHG) instruction can be used to implement the test and set operation. This instruction swaps the data in a processor register with the contents of a memory location. Its execution requires two bus cycles, but if the LOCK prefix precedes the instruction, the microprocessor's $\overline{\text{LOCK}}$ output will be asserted for the duration of the instruction execution, causing a bus lock state. Thus, by exchanging the contents of the semaphore with a register that has been previously set to 1, the semaphore can be read and set in an indivisible sequence. After the semaphore is swapped into the processor's register, it is tested, and if it is set then the processor knows not to use the associated resource. The 68000 provides the same capability with a test-and-set instruction. This instruction also requires two bus cycles, but the address strobe output from the 68000 is held asserted during both cycles. The 68000 retains control of the bus as long as $\overline{\text{AS}}$ is asserted.

Another approach to the indivisible test-and-set problem is to build a special memory that automatically sets the semaphore bit whenever it is read. One example of a device that uses this approach is the 68120 slave processor, which is described in Sec. 10.6.3. Semaphores can also be implemented with a flip-flop and a small amount of additional logic.

10.3.6   Interconnection Topologies

The *topology* of a multiprocessor system is the physical arrangement of the processors and communication links. For a two-processor system, there is only one possible topology: a link between the two processors. The link can be implemented with serial ports, parallel ports, a shared memory, or a FIFO, but the topology remains the same.

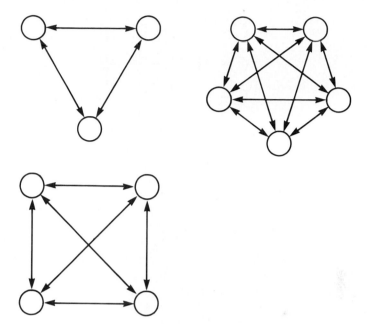

Figure 10.3. Fully connected topology for three, four, and five processors.

Table 10.1   Number of Communications Links and Interfaces per Processor for a Fully Connected Network

No. of processors, n	No. of links	No. of interfaces on each processor
2	1	1
3	3	2
4	6	3
5	10	4
6	15	5
7	21	6
8	28	7

With more than two processors, a choice must be made. Fully connected processors, as shown in Fig. 10.3, provide a conceptually simple and flexible topology. However, the number of connections and the number of interface ports required on each processor increases rapidly as the number of processors increases. The number of interconnections required to fully connect n processors is:

$$\sum_{i=1}^{n-1} i = \frac{n(n-1)}{2}$$

The number of interfaces required per processor is $n - 1$. Table 10.1 lists the results for various values of n.

Figure 10.4. Connection topologies: *(a)* crossbar, *(b)* star, *(c)* ring or loop, and *(d)* bus.

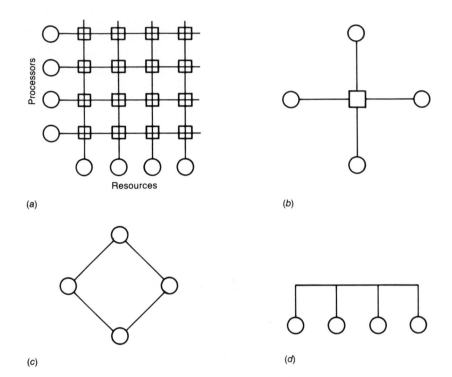

There are a number of alternative interconnection schemes that reduce the number of links required. Figure 10.4 shows four possible configurations: the crossbar, star, ring, and bus.

The *crossbar* switch provides a data path between any of the units on the vertical axis and any of the units on the horizontal axis. Typically, there would be a number of processors on one axis and resources such as memory and I/O devices on the other. The crossbar system has the advantage of providing great flexibility and high throughput but requires complex and expensive circuitry that increases as the square of the number of elements. Although it has been used in several research machines, it is generally considered to be impractical.

The *star* and *ring* topologies use point-to-point connections but are not fully connected. As a result, messages must often be passed along by one or more processors before they reach their destination.

The star configuration is often the simplest to implement but has the disadvantage of relying on a central switch. This central unit must handle all messages, thus becoming a bottleneck. In addition, failure of the central switch disables all communication in the system.

The ring (also called *loop*) arrangement requires relatively few interconnections and does not rely on a central switch. Each processor must check each message it receives to determine the destination address. Each message is likely to be passed along by a number of processors before it reaches its destination. To minimize the message transfer time and the burden on each processor, the ring interface logic must be able to pass along messages and check message addresses without intervention from the main processor. Only when the interface logic detects a message with the proper address is the main processor interrupted. To increase system reliability, it should be possible either to send data in either direction or to bypass any processor; otherwise, the failure of one processor could cause the system to be disabled.

The *bus* topology is one of the most widely used for multiple microprocessor systems. Systems using this topology are covered in detail in Sec. 10.5.

Many other interconnection topologies are possible. One topology that has been explored for general-purpose high-performance computers is the *hypercube*. Originally developed at Cal Tech, it is used by several computer manufacturers. A hypercube is an *n-dimensional* cube with a processor at each corner. The edges of the cube represent the communication links. A three-dimensional cube is easily envisioned, as it is what we all think of as a cube. As Fig. 10.5 shows, a four-dimensional cube can be thought of as two three-dimensional cubes, with a connection between each corresponding corner. This can be extended up to *n* dimensions. A four-dimensional system has 16 processors; a five-dimensional system has 32, a six-dimensional system 64, and so on. An *n*-dimensional system has 2^n processors and requires that each processor have *n* interprocessor communication interfaces.

Figure 10.5. Hypercube topology for three, four, and five dimensions.

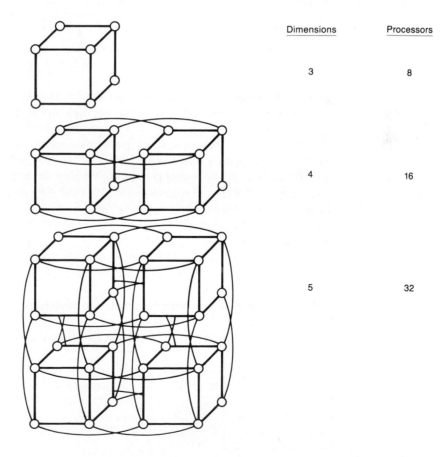

Dimensions	Processors
3	8
4	16
5	32

Functionally partitioned multiprocessor systems generally do not require that all processors be able to communicate with all others, and in these systems the interconnections generally follow the data flow required by the application.

10.4   INTERCONNECTION METHODS

Regardless of the system topology, a variety of interconnection methods can be used. The best type of connection for a particular application depends on the number of microprocessors involved, the speed required when transferring data between microprocessors, the amount of data to be transferred, and physical and economic constraints. Serial or parallel ports can be connected together, and FIFO buffers and shared memories can also serve as the link between processors. When several processors are involved, shared buses (either serial or parallel) are often used.

10.4.1   Interconnected Parallel Ports

A simple approach is to interconnect parallel I/O ports on two processor systems, allowing word-serial communications. A number of variations are possible. The most basic is a unidirectional interface, as shown in Fig. 10.6. One processor's output port drives the other processor's input port. Handshaking signals are required to ensure that the receiving processor has accepted the data before the transmitting processor attempts to output another word.

In most applications bidirectional communication is necessary. Even in a master/slave arrangement in which the master always controls the slave's operation, the master usually needs to read back some status information or data from the slave. One approach is to use two separate unidirectional links, one in each direction. By using programmable I/O ports, a single pair of ports can transfer data in either direction. The master provides a direction control signal to the slave to prevent contention for the data bus, as shown in Fig. 10.7. When the master sends data to the slave, DATA DIRECTION is low, the master's port is programmed for output, and the slave's port is programmed for input. When the master wants to read data from the slave, it programs its port for input and sets data direction high. The slave responds to the high level on DATA DIRECTION by programming its port for output and outputting the desired

Figure 10.6. Unidirectional parallel interface.

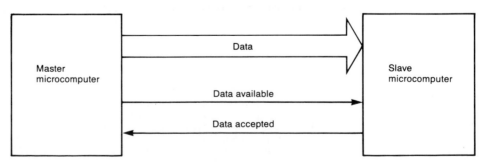

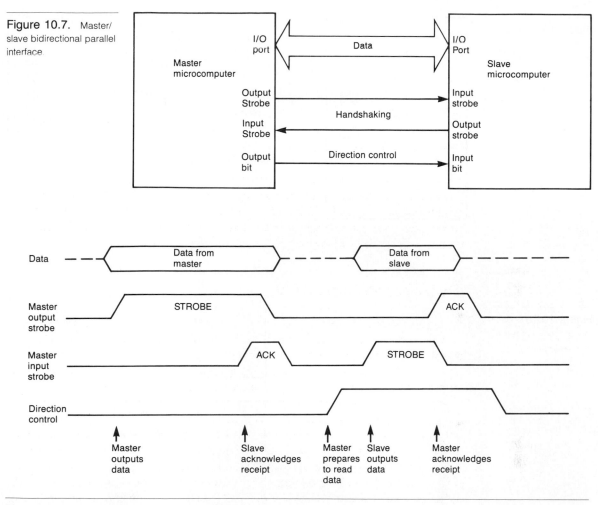

Figure 10.7. Master/
slave bidirectional parallel
interface

Figure 10.8. Timing for master/slave data exchange.

data. The master must know the slave's worst-case response time to a direction change request so that both processors will never attempt to drive the bus simultaneously.

Figure 10.8 shows that the handshake lines change meaning depending on the direction of the data flow. Note that the slave cannot send data to the master except when the master is expecting data and has therefore set DATA DIRECTION high.

Figure 10.9 shows a more flexible approach in which either processor can request to send data at any time. The simple direction control signal is replaced by two REQUEST/GRANT lines. When the system is reset, one processor is initialized as the talker and the other as the listener. Figure 10.10 illustrates the reversal of the talker/listener relationship. When the listener wants to talk, it asserts its REQUEST/GRANT output. When the current talker is willing to relinquish control, it sets its REQUEST/GRANT output low, indicating that it is now listening and the other processor can be the talker. The software to control the interface is identical in both processors, except for the initialization.

Figure 10.9. Half-duplex bidirectional parallel interface.

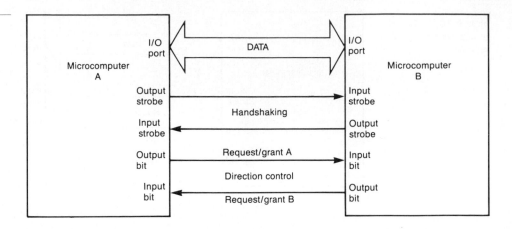

Figure 10.10. Direction control via request/grant signals.

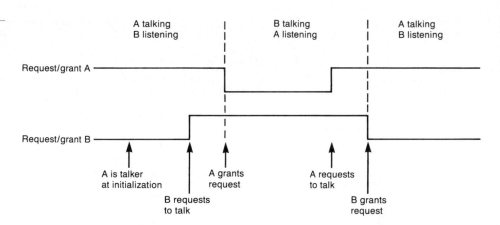

Most single-chip microcomputers include I/O ports with handshake lines that can be used to implement these interconnections. Individual I/O port bits are used for the direction control or request/grant signals. Software determines the functions of these signals. LSI parallel interface chips, such as the Z80-PIO or the 8255, can also be used.

10.4.2   FIFO Buffer Interconnections

One problem with any direct parallel connection is that both processors must remain synchronized word by word. Adding a first-in-first-out (FIFO) buffer between the processors alleviates this problem, since the FIFO buffer can store a block of data from one processor until the other processor is able to read it. FIFO buffers are particularly

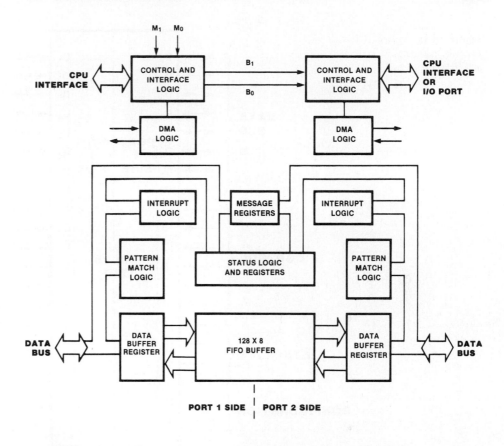

Figure 10.11. Z-FIO interprocessor FIFO buffer block diagram. *(Courtesy of Zilog, Inc.)*

useful when a processor supplying a block of data can send it at a rate faster than the receiving processor can accept it. A number of FIFO ICs are available and can easily be adapted to this use.

FIFO buffers designed explicitly for use as interprocessor connections are also available. Figure 10.11 shows a block diagram of the Z8038 Z-FIO chip, a 128-byte FIFO buffer with a built-in microprocessor interface. Port 1 always connects to a microprocessor bus; port 2 can be configured to connect to a microprocessor bus or to act as an I/O port. Figure 10.12 shows the Z-FIO pin assignments. Each port can be programmed to operate in several different modes. The control signal definitions for each mode are listed in Table 10.2. Port 1 can be configured for a "Z-Bus device" with a multiplexed bus (such as a Z8000 or Z8 microprocessor) or for a "non-Z-Bus device" (most other microprocessors). Port 2 can also be configured in either of these modes, and in addition can be programmed to operate as an I/O port using either a standard two-wire handshake (HS) or a three-wire handshake (as used in the IEEE-488 interface bus).

Figure 10.12. Z-FIO pin assignments. *(Courtesy of Zilog, Inc.)*

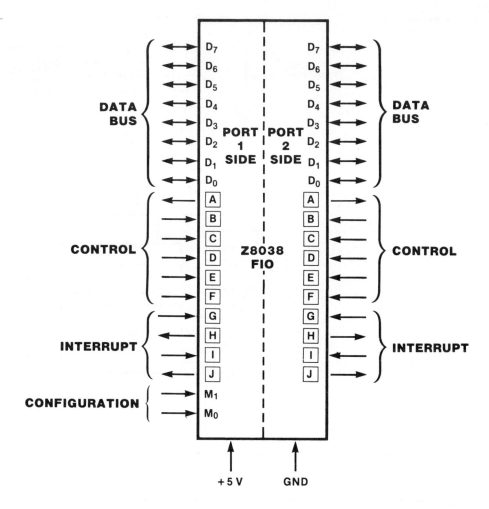

Two control pins, M_0 and M_1, are read at reset to determine the mode of port 1. The microprocessor connected to port 1 must then write the two bits B_0 and B_1 in the Z-FIO's control register to set the operating mode for port 2.

The Z-FIO can be programmed to transfer data in either direction and also to generate an interrupt to either microprocessor when the FIFO is full, empty, or contains a specified number of bytes. Two devices can be used in parallel for 16-bit transfers, and another device (the Z8060 Z-FIFO) can be added to increase the length of the FIFO. Another feature is a pair of "mailbox" registers, which can be used for single-byte communication between the processors, bypassing the FIFO. This is useful for transferring commands separately from data.

Figure 10.13 shows an example of a system using a Z-FIO as the link between a disk control processor and the main system processor. Data read from or waiting to be written to the disk is buffered in the Z-FIO. This relieves the main system processor of continuously keeping up with the disk's data rate.

Table 10.2   Z8038 Z-FIO Pin Definitions

Signal Pins	Z-BUS Low Byte	Z-BUS High Byte	Non-Z-BUS	Interlocked HS Port*	3-Wire HS Port*
A	$\overline{\text{REQ}}/\overline{\text{WT}}$	$\overline{\text{REQ}}/\overline{\text{WT}}$	$\overline{\text{REQ}}/\overline{\text{WT}}$	RFD/$\overline{\text{DAV}}$	RFD/$\overline{\text{DAV}}$
B	$\overline{\text{DMASTB}}$	$\overline{\text{DMASTB}}$	$\overline{\text{DACK}}$	$\overline{\text{ACKIN}}$	$\overline{\text{DAV}}$/DAC
C	$\overline{\text{DS}}$	$\overline{\text{DS}}$	$\overline{\text{RD}}$	FULL	DAC/RFD
D	R/$\overline{\text{W}}$	R/$\overline{\text{W}}$	$\overline{\text{WR}}$	EMPTY	EMPTY
E	$\overline{\text{CS}}$	$\overline{\text{CS}}$	$\overline{\text{CE}}$	$\overline{\text{CLEAR}}$	$\overline{\text{CLEAR}}$
F	$\overline{\text{AS}}$	AS	C/$\overline{\text{D}}$	DATA DIR	DATA DIR
G	$\overline{\text{INTACK}}$	A_0	$\overline{\text{INTACK}}$	IN_0	IN_0
H	IEO	A_1	IEO	OUT_1	OUT_1
I	IEI	A_2	IEI	$\overline{\text{OE}}$	$\overline{\text{OE}}$
J	$\overline{\text{INT}}$	A_3	$\overline{\text{INT}}$	OUT_3	OUT_3

*2 side only.

Source: Zilog, Inc.

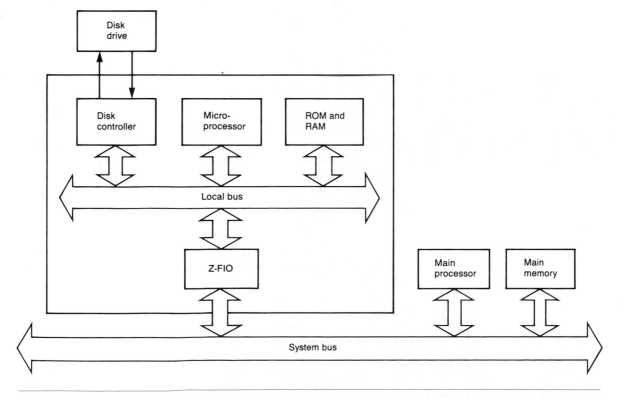

Figure 10.13.   Z-FIO used as interface to intelligent disk controller. Commands transferred via mailbox registers, data transferred via FIFO.

10.4.3   Serial I/O Interconnections

Parallel I/O interconnections are usually limited to short distances due to the number of wires required. Serial I/O allows processors to be connected with only a few wires. This reduces the connector size and cable size and cost and allows processors separated by greater distances to be economically interconnected. The disadvantages are reduced communication speeds and a more complex interface.

Point-to-Point Serial Links

Figure 10.14 shows two processors interconnected via serial I/O ports (UARTs or USARTs). The link is conceptually the same as a parallel link, although the handshaking is different, additional error conditions must be taken into account, and the speed is slower. Many UARTs and USARTs buffer two to four received bytes, easing the synchronization problem slightly.

Interprocessor serial interfaces may be either synchronous or asynchronous. Synchronous interfaces either can use a second wire for the data clock or can use an encoding that allows the clock to be extracted from the data. Refer to Chap. 8 for a discussion of serial interface techniques.

The simplest serial interfaces are unidirectional point-to-point links, which can use standard TTL interface levels or RS-232 or RS-422 levels. For bidirectional point-to-point communication, the most common approach is to use one wire (two for RS-422) for each direction. Half-duplex configurations can also be used, in which a single line is used for both directions. This requires additional logic to allow the direction to be reversed.

A simple example is the computer terminal (or personal computer) shown in Fig. 10.15. The keyboard processor scans and debounces the keyboard and then sends the code for the pressed key to the main processor via a serial link. This enables the keyboard to be physically detached and to connect to the terminal via a small cable. The cable need have only a few wires (power, ground, and serial data, and perhaps a clock). The keyboard assembly can be changed (perhaps for a different language) with no effect on the rest of the system. A performance advantage is also obtained: since the main processor does not need to scan or debounce the keyboard, it has more time for other tasks. In addition, the keyboard processor can maintain a small FIFO buffer, so even if the main processor is busy with some task and ignores the keyboard for a short time, keystrokes are not lost.

For systems involving more than two processors, multiple point-to-point links can be used. A fully connected topology can be used for a few processors, but the number

Figure 10.14. Serial interface connecting two processors.

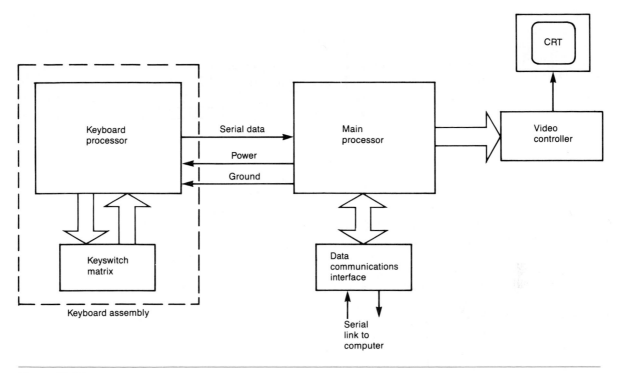

Figure 10.15. Keyboard processor used to scan keyboard and provide serial link to main processor.

of interfaces required on each processor quickly gets out of hand as the number of processors increases. Other topologies, such as the star or ring, can also be used, but these introduce additional complications and limitations (as described in Sec. 10.3.6).

An example of a system using point-to-point serial connections in a star topology is a robotic arm, as shown in Fig. 10.16. This device requires precise control of each joint. One approach is to use a microprocessor at each joint, which monitors a position sensor to provide closed-loop control. In addition, the joint processor can perform some of the computation necessary to execute a motion command. A central microprocessor handles the user interface and gives directions to each of the joint processors. This architecture makes possible a much faster and more accurate arm than would be possible if one microprocessor directly controlled all the joints. Since the joints do not need to communicate with each other, but only communicate with the central microprocessor, the star topology is a natural one. The central microprocessor can send messages to all the joint processors concurrently.

Serial Buses

Figure 10.17 shows a multidrop serial bus. (Such buses are commonly implemented with RS-485 transceivers, as described in Chap. 8.) Only one processor can transmit at a time. Data transferred between processors is formatted into messages. At the beginning of each message is the address of the microcomputer that should receive the message. Each microcomputer must read this address at the beginning of every message. If

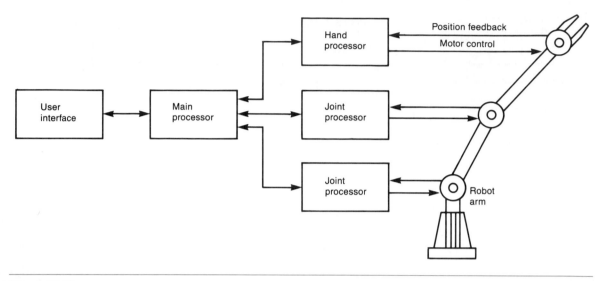

Figure 10.16.   Robot arm using multiple serial links in star configuration.

Figure 10.17.   Multi-drop serial bus.

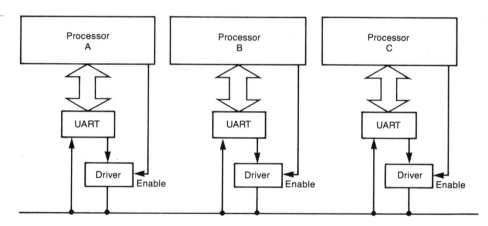

the message is not addressed to that particular microcomputer, it does not need to pay attention to the remainder of the message. In a simple system, one microcomputer may always be the transmitter and the others only receivers.

In the general case, in which each processor must be able to transmit data, a software protocol is required to allow control of the link to be passed from one processor to another. The simplest approach is a polled master/slave protocol, such as that used in the SDLC protocol. One microcomputer acts as the master and periodically polls each slave. The slaves are allowed to transmit only in response to a poll from the master; thus, there is no contention. This is a natural architecture for applications such as distributed data acquisition systems, in which the master collects data from the slaves but there is no interaction among the slaves. Although the physical topology is a bus, the logical topology is a star. For a slave to send a message to another slave, it must first

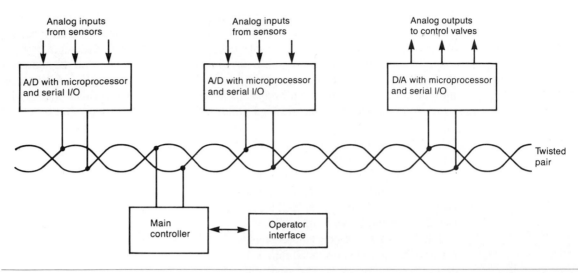

Figure 10.18. Process control system using microprocessor for each group of sensors or actuators, connected by a serial bus.

wait to be polled by the master, and then send the message to the master with an address tag indicating which slave the message is intended for. The master then retransmits the message to the designated slave. Another approach is to use an "address to listen" approach similar to that used in the IEEE-488 interface bus, which allows the master to indicate to one slave that it should receive the message being sent by another slave.

Figure 10.18 shows an example of a system using a serial bus. In a factory automation or process control application, data must be gathered and actions taken at a variety of points. Rather than transferring analog signals in the noisy industrial environment, each analog sensor (or group of sensors) has its own local processor. The local processor digitizes the signal from the sensor and may perform filtering or other preprocessing operations before transmitting the data in serial form to the central processor. A local processor may have control over actuators as well and act on commands from the central processor or in response to conditions at its local inputs.

Serial buses are also used in some multiprocessor systems with shared parallel buses. The serial bus provides a method for sending messages between processors without using the main (parallel) system bus. The VMSbus, designed for use with the VMEbus, is an example of such a serial bus.

Single-Chip Microcomputer Serial Network Support

Serial bus or ring networks require that every processor receive at least the beginning of every message to check to see if it is supposed to receive the message. When there are many processors on the network, monitoring messages intended for other processors can be a considerable burden. Some single-chip microcomputers provide special capabilities in their serial interfaces to ease this burden.

Motorola's 6801-family single-chip microcomputers, for example, include logic to allow the processor to ignore all the message following the address and to be automatically "awakened" when a new message begins. When the processor reads the address at the beginning of a message and determines that the address is not its own, it sets its "wake-up" control bit. This disables the serial receiver for the duration of the message. When the serial line is idle for more than one byte time, indicating the end of the message, the wake-up circuitry enables the serial receiver so that it can read the address at the beginning of the next message. Note that for this scheme to function properly, there must be no idle time during a message and a minimum idle time between messages.

A similar approach is taken in Intel's 8051-family microcomputers. The serial port in these devices has a mode in which each serial character consists of nine bits: eight data bits plus an address/data flag. "Sleeping" microcomputers are awakened when they receive a character with the address/data flag set. This provides the same capability as the 6801's wake-up mode, but does not require that messages not contain gaps or that there be gaps between messages. It does, on the other hand, add an extra bit to every character sent. Motorola's 68HC11A4 single-chip microcomputer includes this mode as well as the 6801's wake-up mode.

Intel's 8044 single-chip microcomputer includes an intelligent serial interface that performs many of the overhead functions required for the SDLC protocol without processor intervention. It can, for example, read a message and check the address and interrupt the processor only if the message address matches the processor's network address. This device is described in Sec. 10.6.4.

Local Area Networks

Serial buses are commonly used for connecting multiple computer systems within a building. These systems are called *local area networks (LANs)*. Because these are multimaster systems, some form of bus arbitration is required to deal with bus contention. The two most common approaches are *token-passing* and *carrier-sense multiple-access (CSMA)*. In a token-passing system, a logical "token" is held by one processor at a time. Only the processor in possession of the token may transmit. When that processor is done transmitting, it "passes" the token to the next processor. Token-passing can be implemented with either a ring or a bus topology. The token-passing ring is the basis for IBM's local area network.

Carrier-sense multiple-access systems use the same principle as a party-line telephone. When one processor wants to transmit, it first listens to the line to see if anyone else is transmitting. If so, it waits until the line is idle. There is still the possibility of two processors both being ready to transmit at the same time, both sensing the line idle and then both proceeding to transmit at the same time. This is called a *collision*. To avoid this problem, most CSMA systems use collision detection; the method is then known as CSMA/CD (CSMA with collision detect). The Ethernet LAN, originally developed by Xerox Corporation, is the best-known example of a CSMA/CD system. During transmission, the transmitter continuously compares the data it intended to transmit with the actual state of the line. If the two differ, it assumes that a collision has occurred. It then stops transmitting, sends a "jamming" sequence to inform all receivers that the transmission has been aborted, and "backs off" (stops transmitting) for a random time. After the back-off time has elapsed, it attempts to repeat the transmission. The back-off time must be random (or in some way different for each processor) to avoid periodic repeated collisions as each processor attempts to retransmit.

While CSMA/CD and token-passing networks are most commonly used for connecting independent computer systems, they can also be used for connecting processors within a single system. This is becoming practical as the cost of LSI interface ICs for these networks decreases.

10.4.4 Multiport Memories

Another way to interconnect microprocessors is via a *multiport* memory. The global memory in a shared-bus system can be considered to be a multiport memory, with the system bus performing the memory arbitration function. However, the term *multiport memory* is generally used to refer to a memory system that has two or more sets of address, data, and control signals and can therefore be connected to two or more different sets of buses.

Figure 10.19 shows a two-port memory connecting two microprocessor systems. One processor transfers data to the other by storing the data in the two-port RAM and then indicating to the other processor (via an interrupt or a flag in the RAM) that a new data block is available. This provides many of the advantages of a FIFO interconnection but is considerably more flexible. The penalty is that the hardware and software required are generally more complex.

The simple two-port memory arrangement in Fig. 10.20 uses a multiplexer to select one processor for access to the memory. If both request simultaneous accesses, then one must wait for the other to complete its access before it can get control. This is

Figure 10.19. Two-port memory connecting two processors.

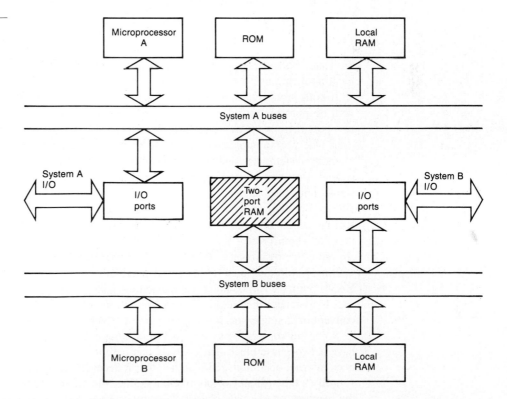

Figure 10.20. Multiplexed two-port memory with request/grant control.

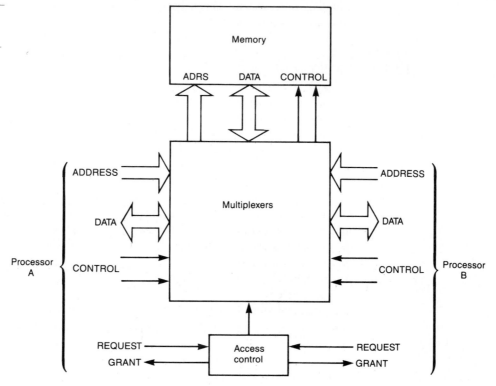

the least expensive type of two-port memory, and provides adequate performance in most applications.

If both processors must have unrestricted access to the two-port RAM at all times with no possibility of delay, then a more complex system is required. A *transparent* two-port memory allows each processor to access the memory as if it were the only user. One way to implement such a memory is to use a high-speed clock to switch the memory system back and forth between the two ports once every memory cycle time so that each port has the impression of sole control of the memory. Latches provide stable inputs and outputs. This is expensive to implement, since not only are additional latches and control logic required, but the RAM's access time must be less than one-half the access time required by either processor. This approach is used in applications in which both processors are performing time-critical tasks and cannot afford to be slowed down by having to wait for access to the shared memory.

Single-chip dual-port RAMs are also available. They are similar to standard static RAMs but have two complete sets of address, data, and control lines. They are easy to use, but because they require a package with many pins and are not as widely used as conventional single-port RAMs, they are relatively expensive.

Some microprocessors, such as the 6800 and 6502 families and their derivatives, have a two-phase clock that controls bus activity. On one phase the microprocessor does internal operations, and on the other it accesses memory or I/O. This can greatly simplify a transparent two-port memory, since the microprocessors can be set up to use the memory on alternate phases. Two microprocessors can share the same buses, and therefore the same memory, by connecting one microprocessor's phase 1 clock to the other microprocessor's phase 2 clock, and vice versa. While one microprocessor uses the buses, the other does its internal operations. However, this technique cannot be used with most microprocessors, including the 8085, Z80, and most 16-bit microprocessors, since they do not use a two-phase clock. It also cannot be extended beyond two processors.

Texas Instruments' TMS9650 Multiprocessor Interface is a dual-port device that includes a 256-byte RAM, but it is not a dual-port RAM in the usual sense. Figure 10.21 shows the block diagram of this device. There are two processor ports, each with an 8-bit data bus and the usual $\overline{WE}$, $\overline{CS}$, and $\overline{OE}$ control signals. One of eight register locations is selected via the register select lines, S_0 to S_2. To access the RAM, the processor first writes the desired memory address to the address register and then reads or writes the data via the data register. The address can be automatically incremented, so it need not be written for every transfer. Separate address registers are maintained for each port. The RAM can be accessed as a FIFO with minimal additional software.

The RAM cannot be accessed concurrently from both ports. If the RAM is being accessed from one port and the other port attempts an access, the READY output for the second port will go low until the first port's access is completed. The CLKIN input allows the READY output to be synchronized to the processor's clock. The $\overline{LOCKIN}$ input allows successive accesses to be guaranteed for critical code sections, such as semaphore testing and setting. When this input is asserted, the RAM will not be made available to the other port. This input can be driven from the $\overline{LOCK}$ output from an 8086-family microprocessor, or the $\overline{AS}$ output from a 68000-family microprocessor, to allow indivisible test-and-set instructions. For longer critical sections, the $\overline{LOCKIN}$ signal can be driven from an output port bit.

In addition to the shared RAM, there are two message registers. One is written from port A and read from port B, and the other is the reverse. The chip can be programmed (by writing to the control register) to produce an interrupt when a message is read or written, or when the other port's memory address register reaches a preset value.

10.5 SHARED-BUS SYSTEMS

The bus topology is widely used for multiple microprocessor systems. This section describes the design considerations for shared-bus systems and then describes the Multibus as a detailed example.

10.5.1 Types of Shared Buses

Both multidrop serial networks and multimaster system buses are examples of the bus topology. Connecting all components of the system to the same set of wires greatly simplifies the interconnections. The failure of any device will not stop other devices from communicating via the bus as long as the failure does not cause illegal activity on the bus. Any device on the bus can, in principle, communicate directly with any other device on the bus.

There are, however, a number of problems that must be dealt with. Since the same

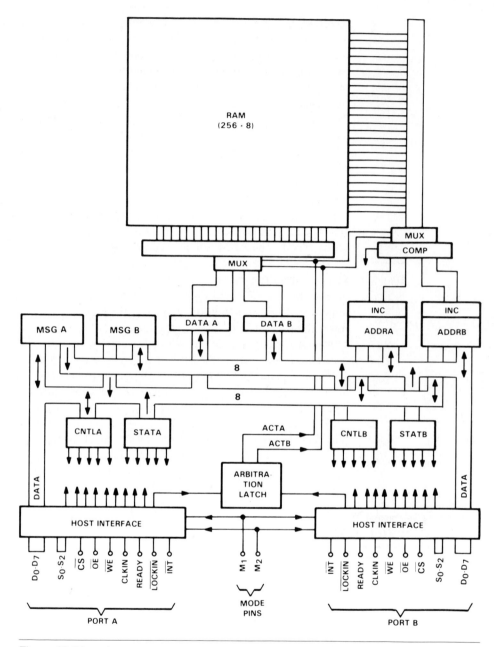

Figure 10.21. TMS9650 Multiprocessor Interface block diagram. *(Courtesy of Texas Instruments.)*

wires are shared by a number of devices, a protocol must be established to provide for bus arbitration. If two devices simultaneously request use of the bus, one must be chosen in a reliable, predictable manner. There are many solutions to these problems; the best approach depends on the application.

Local area networks commonly use a single coaxial cable or twisted pair to connect all the devices. Due to the distances involved, parallel data transfer is impractical, and it is undesirable to have additional control lines. This constraint leads to access control systems such as token-passing and CSMA/CD, as described previously.

Another class of shared-bus systems incorporates several processors in the same enclosure. In this case, the high speed of a parallel bus is generally preferred, and the addition of a few extra bus control lines is not a problem. The use of these control lines provides a relatively simple solution to bus contention problems. Arbitration methods for system buses are described in Chap. 3, and Multibus arbitration is described in detail in Sec. 10.5.4.

10.5.2   Bus Utilization

Tightly coupled shared-bus systems, in which all processors fetch instructions from a global memory, are difficult to implement effectively for more than a few processors. Figure 10.22 shows that as the number of processors increases, actual performance increases much more slowly than the theoretical limit; doubling the number of processors does not double the performance. (Note, however, that even a modest performance improvement may be sufficient to justify the addition of another processor.) Since all processors share the buses and memory, each must wait for the bus to be available before it can access memory or I/O. As the number of processors increases, each spends more of its time simply waiting for the bus to be available, and the perfor-

Figure 10.22. Performance as function of number of processors in tightly coupled shared-bus system.

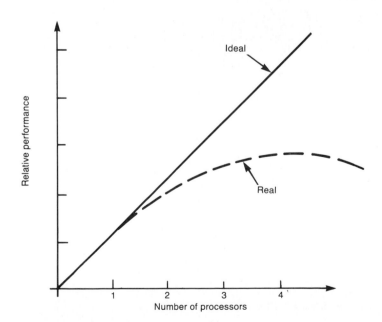

mance improvement is lost. The performance of this type of system is dependent primarily on the percentage of time each processor uses the bus, called *bus utilization*.

A bus utilization of 33 percent, for example, indicates that the processor uses the bus a third of the time. The best possible throughput in such a system is three times the throughput of a single processor, regardless of how many processors are used (assuming that the processors are all identical and are tightly coupled). This performance is achieved only if there is perfect synchronization between processors and interleaving of bus cycles; if each processor requests bus cycles asynchronously with respect to the others, the performance of a three-processor system degrades to approximately twice that of a uniprocessor system. The key to making such a system effective is using relatively few processors whose bus utilization is low, so the total bus utilization for all processors is well under 100 percent.

10.5.3   Shared-Bus Architectures

Several techniques can be used to improve the performance of shared-bus systems. By using a multiple-bus architecture, as shown in Fig. 10.23, the processors are loosely coupled even though they can access a shared bus. Each processor has its own local memory, and a global memory accessible to all processors provides the communication link. The key difference as compared to a tightly coupled system is that each processor has its own local bus and does not need to use the shared bus except when it wishes to communicate with another processor or access a shared resource. This greatly reduces

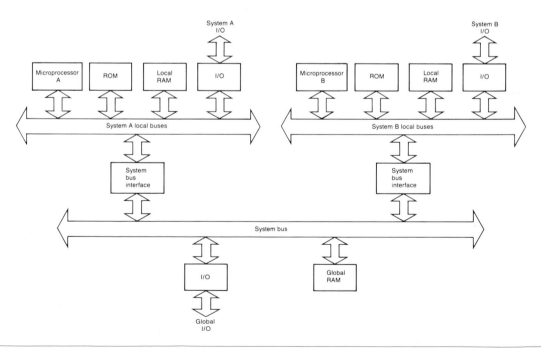

Figure 10.23.   Multiple-bus architecture.

the system bus utilization of each processor subsystem. This can be considered to be a moderately coupled system.

Figure 10.24 shows another possible shared-bus architecture. Rather than using a global memory, each processor has a dual-port local memory that is also accessible from the system bus. This architecture is easily implemented with standard Multibus boards and has therefore been widely used.

The multiple-bus architecture can provide a simple multiprocessor approach to a multiuser computer, as shown in Fig. 10.25. There is one single-board computer for

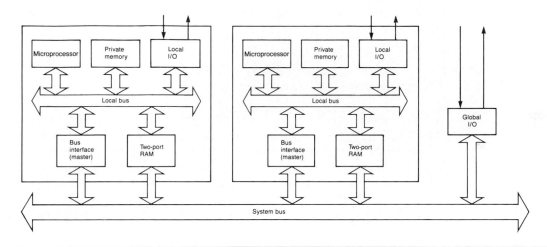

Figure 10.24. Multiple-bus architecture using two-port RAMs on each processor board. Each processor board is a bus master for accessing other devices, and its two-port RAM is a bus slave.

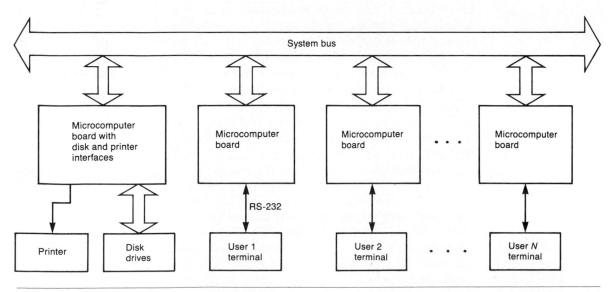

Figure 10.25. Multiuser computer with dedicated microcomputer board for each user.

Figure 10.26. Multi-processor system using cache memory.

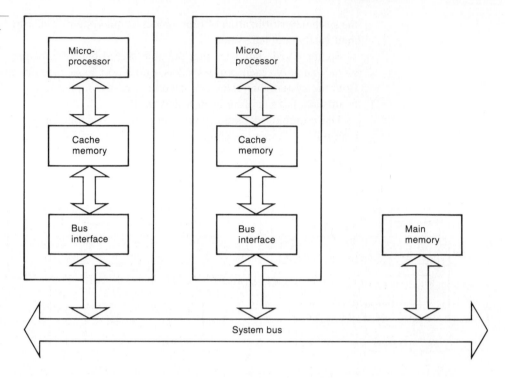

Figure 10.26. Multi-processor system using cache memory.

each user, and an additional processor board manages the printer and the disk. Each single-board computer includes a serial interface for the user's terminal and a parallel bus interface for accessing shared resources such as the disk and printer. Many of these boards can exist in the system, as determined by the number of users. Each board is an independent system and contains its own copy of the operating system. The part of the operating system that would normally access the disk drive is replaced with a program that places a disk request on the shared parallel bus. The disk/printer processor board reads this request and performs the indicated operation, returning data via the shared bus. The printer is handled in a similar manner. This architecture is not particularly efficient, in that the operating system and any common application code must be duplicated for each user and the resources available to each user are fixed. However, it is a simple way to extend single-user architectures and operating systems into a multi-processor, multiuser computer.

A more sophisticated architecture, as shown in Fig. 10.26, keeps bus utilization low while allowing all processors to share a common memory, which in turn allows all processors to share programs and data. The key feature of this type of system is the high-speed cache memory associated with each processor. This cache stores the data most recently accessed, along with a "tag" indicating the main memory address with which the data is associated. Since programs tend to execute the same sections of code and access the same data structures repeatedly, many of the locations accessed will already be stored in the cache if the cache is sufficiently large.

The cache provides two significant benefits. First, because the cache is built with high-speed memory and can be accessed without bus arbitration and buffer delays, an access to a location stored in the cache is much faster than a main memory access. Second, because an access to a location stored in the cache does not require access to the system bus, the bus utilization of each processor is greatly reduced. The *hit rate* is the percentage of accesses that are to locations already stored in the cache. Well-designed systems with moderately large caches can achieve hit rates of over 90 percent. Thus, less than 10 percent of the processor's memory read cycles require access to the system bus. (Memory write cycles always require access to the system bus, as described in the following paragraph.) Cache performance is a complex subject and is dependent not only on the size of the cache but also on the type of software being executed.

There are several problems that must be addressed in the design of a cache for a multiprocessor system. The cache stores a copy of data from the global memory. When the CPU writes to a byte in the cache, the global memory must be updated. In addition, when a write is performed to a global memory location, all caches that contain copies of that location must be updated or invalidated. This problem is called *cache concurrency,* or *cache consistency*. There are two functions required to solve this problem. First, *write-through* logic copies all data written to the cache to the global memory. This ensures that the global memory is always current. The write-through logic can store the data written while it waits for access to the system bus, so the processor's write cycle does not need to be delayed for access to the system bus. Second, *bus watcher* logic associated with each cache monitors the system buses, looking for any write to a global memory location that is stored in the cache. When such a write occurs, the corresponding cache location is invalidated.

Packet-oriented bus protocols can also be used to reduce bus utilization. Standard bus protocols are very inefficient in that the address must be held on the bus for the duration of the memory access time. In addition, many accesses are to sequential bytes of memory, but the address must still be transferred for every cycle. In a packet bus, the microprocessor reads from memory by sending a request for a block of data to the memory subsystem. The bus is then freed while the memory subsystem fetches the required data. When the data is ready, it is transferred in a block. Thus, the bus is not kept busy during the memory access time, and an address is not required for every byte read, only for every block. Since standard microprocessors do not support packet-oriented bus protocols, additional logic must be added to mediate between the processor and the system bus.

Sequent Computer Systems' Balance 8000 computer is an example of a general-purpose multiprocessor computer using this architecture. The system is based on a CPU that consists of a 32032 microprocessor, a floating-point processor, a memory management unit, and an 8-Kbyte cache memory. Two of these CPU systems are included on each processor card, and the system can contain from one to six processor cards (2 to 12 CPUs). The CPUs all share a common global memory; the only local memory on each CPU is the cache. Sequent calls this a *scalable processor pool* architecture, since there is a pool of processors available to execute tasks, and the system is readily scalable by adding more CPUs.

10.5.4   Implementing a Shared-Bus System: The Multibus

While the shared bus approach has many advantages, there is some overhead required to manage access to the bus and shared resources. An arbitration scheme must be implemented to decide which processor can access the bus at any given time. In addition, some mechanism must be provided for one processor to be guaranteed a number of consecutive bus cycles when executing critical sections. Many buses have been designed to meet these needs; Intel's Multibus is one of the most popular, and it is used here as an example of a complete multiprocessor bus implementation. In this section, only the multiprocessor aspects of the bus are considered; refer to Chap. 3 for general information on the Multibus.

In a shared-bus system, any card that can drive the address and control lines (and thus take control of the bus) is called a *bus master*. Bus masters are typically microprocessor or DMA cards. All other cards are *bus slaves*; they cannot control the bus but can only read and write data under the control of a bus master. Typical slaves are I/O and memory cards. A bus slave may contain a microprocessor, as in the case of an intelligent I/O card. Note that a bus master may be a slave in the system hierarchy; the hierarchy is determined by the software.

Bus Arbitration

Each bus master may request the use of the bus at any time. However, since all share the same bus, they must coordinate their bus activities. *Bus arbitration* is the process by which one bus master is chosen to access the bus at any given time.

The system bus must incorporate some form of *priority resolution* logic. When more than one processor is requesting the bus, priority resolution logic determines which processor has the highest priority and thus should be granted access to the bus.

Table 10.3 explains the Multibus arbitration signals. There are two principal methods of implementing priority resolution: serial and parallel. The serial approach is the

---

Table 10.3   Multibus Arbitration Signals

BCLK*	Bus clock. The negative edge of this clock synchronizes signals listed below. Maximum speed is 10 MHz. Independent of microprocessor clock.
BPRN*	Bus priority in. Indicates to a particular bus master that no higher-priority master is requesting the system bus. Not bused on backplane; connections depend on priority resolution scheme.
BPRO*	Bus priority out. Used only with serial priority resolution. Not bused on backplane; BPRO* is connected to BPRN* input of bus master with next-lowest bus priority.
BUSY*	Bus busy. Open-collector line driven by current bus master to indicate that bus is in use. Prevents all other masters from gaining control of bus.
BREQ*	Bus request. Used only with parallel priority resolution schemes. Not bused on backplane; separate signal from each master connects directly to priority encoder and indicates that use of the bus is desired.
CBREQ*	Common bus request. Open-collector line driven by all bus masters when they are requesting bus. Not used for arbitration but to indicate to the current bus master that no other master has requested the bus. This allows master to keep bus for next cycle and save arbitration time.

Figure 10.27. Serial priority resolution.

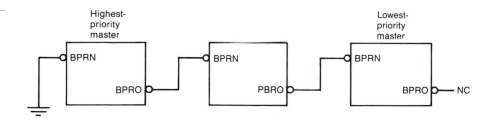

simplest, as shown in Fig. 10.27. Each board has an input called BPRN* (bus priority in) and an output called BPRO* (bus priority out). The highest-priority master's BPRN* is tied low (asserted), indicating to that processor that it can always request use of the bus. Normally, each processor is using only its local bus and sets its BPRO* low. Thus, when all processors are using only their local buses, the BPRN* input to each processor is low, indicating that the system bus is available.

When a master wants to access the system bus, it sets its BPRO* high, causing BPRN* for all masters farther down the line to be high, preventing any lower-priority master from contending for the bus. If a higher-priority master wants to access the bus, it sets its BPRO* high. The master which first made the request will then have its BPRN* driven high and will have to wait for the higher-priority master to complete its use of the system bus.

This priority resolution technique requires that the system backplane include daisy-chained bus priority signals, as described in Chap. 3. Any unoccupied bus slots between occupied slots must have a jumper installed to provide continuity from BPRO* to BPRN*. Slave boards also jumper these signals to each other. The priority of each processor card is determined by its physical location in the backplane.

The bus priority signal must propagate through each card, limiting the number of cards in the chain. The bus clock (BCLK*) controls the arbitration timing. Each master must synchronize its BPRO* output with the falling edge of BCLK*, and by the next falling edge of BCLK* the arbitration must be complete (i.e., all master's BPRN* inputs must be valid). The maximum bus clock frequency is 10 MHz, so 100 ns is available for this process. With standard Multibus arbiter ICs, which have a propagation delay time of 18 to 30 ns, this limits the serial arbitration scheme to systems with no more than five bus masters. BCLK* can be slowed to allow more masters, but this also increases the time to acquire the bus and therefore degrades system performance.

Figure 10.28 shows the circuitry for parallel priority resolution. This approach allows more bus masters to be used without slowing BCLK*. Rather than daisy chaining the priority signals, a bus request (BREQ*) signal from each master connects directly to the priority resolution circuit. The bus request signals are fed to a priority encoder, which responds only to the highest-priority input that is active. The encoder outputs a binary number corresponding to that input. This binary number is then fed to a binary-to-one-of-eight decoder, which generates a BPRN* signal for each master. BPRO* is not used with parallel arbitration. Since all requests are processed in parallel, rather than propagating through each master as in the serial scheme, the number of possible masters is increased. However, the priority resolving logic requires additional circuitry which electrically must be part of the backplane.

In the implementation shown in Fig. 10.28, the binary outputs (address) from the

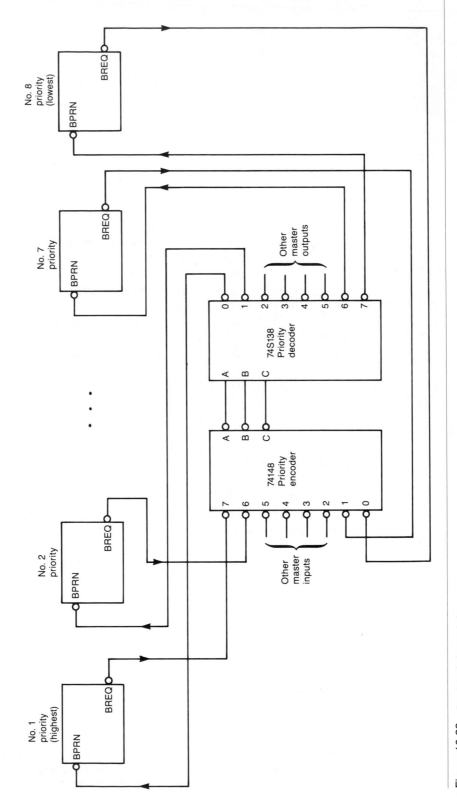

Figure 10.28. Parallel priority resolution.

74148 are active-low, but the address inputs to the 74138 are active-high. This effectively complements the address. Therefore, the request on input 0 of the 74148 is granted by asserting output 7 of the 74138.

Both the techniques described above have a drawback: since the priority of each master is fixed, they do not all have equal access to the bus. A variation of the parallel approach is *rotating priority resolution*. Priorities are dynamically changed, so that each potential master is granted top priority in turn. The simple encoder/decoder circuit used for standard parallel arbitration is replaced with a more complex circuit to change the priorities after each bus access. Due to the increased complexity of this approach, it is less commonly used.

Bus Exchange

Figure 10.29 shows a timing diagram for a Multibus exchange operation, in which control of the bus is transferred from one master to another. Master A is in control of the bus, and Master B wants to take control. Master B's internal transfer request signal is first synchronized with the falling edge of BCLK* and is then applied to master B's BREQ* pin. (This example assumes parallel arbitration.) By the next falling edge of BCLK* the arbitration circuitry negates master A's BPRN*, indicating that it no longer has bus priority. Master B's BPRN* is asserted, indicating to master B that it is next in line to take control of the bus. Master A may be in the middle of a bus cycle, so it does not have to relinquish the bus immediately. When it has completed its bus cycle, it negates BUSY* and disables its bus drivers. Master B, seeing that its BPRN* is asserted and that BUSY* is negated, asserts BUSY*, turns on its bus drivers, and takes control of the bus.

An optional control signal, common bus request (CBRQ*), improves the performance of the bus. This is an open-collector signal that is asserted by any master that is requesting use of the bus (not including the current bus master). The current bus master examines this signal at the end of each bus cycle. If CBRQ* is false, then the current bus master knows that no other device is requesting access to the bus. It can therefore continue with its next cycle without releasing and then reacquiring the bus. This saves the bus exchange overhead for cycles in which no bus exchange is necessary. If CBRQ* is not used, the bus must be released and reacquired after each cycle to allow other potential masters to gain access to the bus.

A bus master can hold the bus for successive cycles by simply keeping BUSY* asserted between cycles. This allows critical sections to be executed without interference from other processors on the Multibus. Many Multibus systems use processor boards with dual-port RAMs that can be accessed by the on-board processor or by other processors via the Multibus. Holding BUSY* asserted prevents other processors on the Multibus from accessing the RAM, but it does not prevent access to a dual-port RAM from the non-Multibus port (i.e., by the processor on the same board with the RAM.)

The LOCK* signal on the Multibus allows this problem to be prevented. When LOCK* is asserted, it indicates that all accesses to the addressed memory must be inhibited, including those from ports other than the Multibus. This signal is not universally supported, however, so if this protection is needed, both the bus masters and the cards containing the dual-port RAM must be checked to be sure they support this function. Cards with dual-port RAMs that do not support the LOCK* signal often provide another mechanism, such as setting a particular output port bit, to lock out accesses to the RAM.

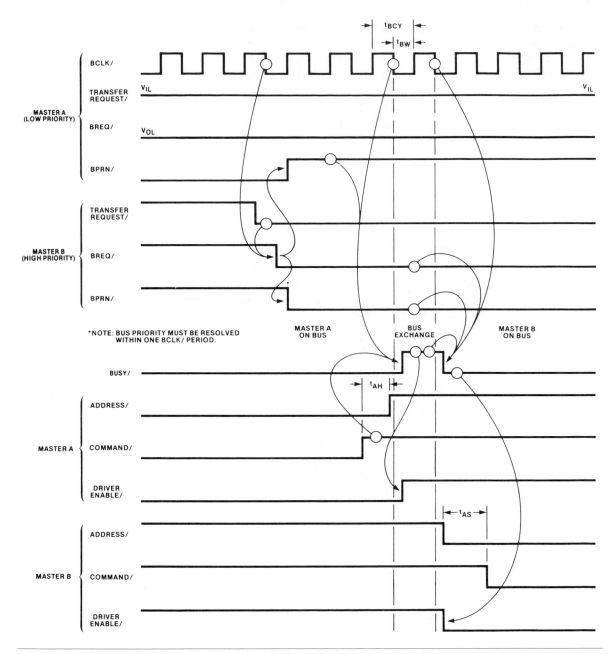

Figure 10.29. Multibus exchange timing. *(Courtesy of Intel Corporation.)*

Hardware Implementation Example

A considerable amount of logic is required to interface a microprocessor to the Multibus. Bipolar ICs called *bus arbiters* are available to simplify this task. These devices provide all the logic and drive circuitry for the interface.

Several different Multibus bus arbiter ICs are available. The 8218 mates to 8080A

Figure 10.30. The
8089 Multibus arbiter
block diagram. *(Courtesy
of Intel Corporation.)*

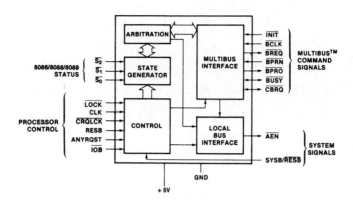

control signals; the 8219 is similar, except that it mates directly to 8085 control signals. The 8289 is a considerably more powerful arbiter, which interfaces to an 8086, 8088, or 8089 processor. Another difference is that while the 8218 and 8219 also provide the bus read and write command signals, the 8289 relies on an 8288 bus controller to provide these signals. The 82289 arbiter is designed for use with the 80286.

Although the Multibus is general-purpose and can be used with virtually any processor, all the available Multibus arbiter ICs are designed for particular Intel-designed microprocessors. Therefore, while Z80, 6809 or 68000 microprocessors can be (and are) interfaced to the Multibus, they require more interface logic. The bus arbiter function must either be implemented with standard TTL ICs, or one of Intel's arbiters must be adapted with additional logic.

Figure 10.30 shows the block diagram of the 8289 bus arbiter. The $\overline{S0}$, $\overline{S1}$, and $\overline{S2}$ inputs connect to the status pins of an 8086, 8088, or 8089 and indicate to the arbiter whether the current bus cycle is read or write, memory or I/O, etc. ANYRQST and $\overline{CRQLCK}$ modify the conditions under which the bus will be surrendered.

The $\overline{LOCK}$ input can be asserted by the processor to cause the bus arbiter to refuse to surrender the bus, regardless of other requests; this is used to provide guaranteed consecutive cycles for critical operations such as semaphore processing (see Sec. 10.3.5). The 8086 and 8088 in maximum mode provide a $\overline{LOCK}$ output, which is asserted during the execution of instructions that are preceded by the LOCK instruction prefix. This allows instructions that require multiple bus cycles to execute to be guaranteed consecutive bus cycles. The 8086 and 8088 support bus lock only for one instruction, however; the LOCK prefix does not guarantee that the bus is held during successive instructions. If an output port bit is used to drive $\overline{LOCK}$, the software can keep the bus locked for as long as desired.

(Note that the $\overline{LOCK}$ input to the arbiter is different from the $\overline{LOCK}$ signal on the Multibus. If dual-port RAMs are used on some processor boards in the system, the $\overline{LOCK}$ signal should connect both to the arbiter input and, via a buffer, to the Multibus LOCK∗ signal.)

The 8289 supports three different types of buses: resident, I/O, and system. A resident bus is the processor's local bus, which is not shared with any other processor. An I/O bus is a bus that is used only for I/O operations; this is to support the 8089 I/O processor, described in Sec. 10.6.5. The system bus is the Multibus. The system bus is always present. The resident and I/O buses may or may not be present; the resident bus

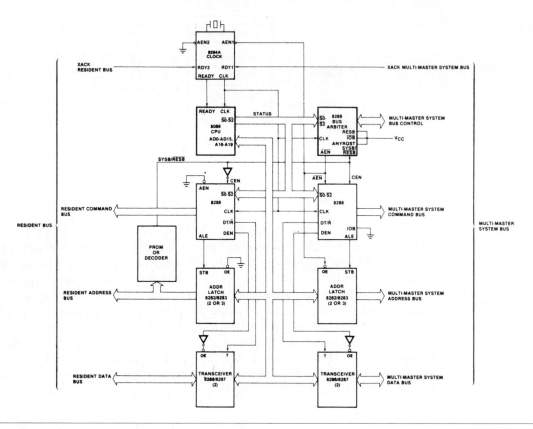

Figure 10.31. The 8086 interface to Multibus and local bus. *(Courtesy of Intel Corporation.)*

(RESB) and I/O bus ($\overline{\text{IOB}}$) pins on the 8289 are wired high or low to indicate the configuration.

Figure 10.31 shows an 8086 CPU interfaced to a local (resident) bus as well as to the Multibus. The local bus connects the CPU to local (on-board) memory and I/O. A typical configuration is a CPU board with some local resources (ROM, RAM, and I/O) and a Multibus interface. The local resources are not accessible to other masters on the Multibus.

The RESB input to the 8289 is tied high to indicate the presence of the local bus. An address decoder determines if the address generated by the microprocessor is of a local (resident) device or a system device and generates the SYSB/$\overline{\text{RESB}}$ signal. Two sets of bus controllers, address latches, and data transceivers are used: one for the local bus and one for the system bus. If SYSB/$\overline{\text{RESB}}$ is low, indicating that the addressed device is local, then the local bus controller, address latches, and data transceivers are enabled; the Multibus is not involved. If, on the other hand, a system device is accessed, SYSB/$\overline{\text{RESB}}$ is high. This instructs the bus arbiter to acquire the Multibus.

The address enable signal ($\overline{\text{AEN}}$) is set low by the 8289 when it has acquired control of the Multibus. This signal enables the system bus controller, address latches, and data transceivers. In addition, it selects (via the 8284 clock generator) the Multibus "ready" signal (transfer acknowledge, XACK*) to synchronize the transfer.

10.6   INPUT/OUTPUT PROCESSORS

Most microprocessor systems consist of a central microprocessor and a number of peripheral controllers. Examples of peripheral controllers include serial interface controllers, disk controllers, CRT controllers, and keyboard/display controllers. Each of these devices removes some software burden from the main processor by including some intelligence in the peripheral interface.

There are many specialized interfaces that can also benefit from intelligent controllers but for which no specially designed interface chip is available. Single-chip microcomputers can be used in these applications to act as programmable intelligent interfaces. However, interfacing a standard single-chip microcomputer to the main processor's bus requires adding an I/O port and handshaking logic to the main processor for communicating with the peripheral processor. To simplify this task, several *slave microcomputers* are available, which are variations of conventional single-chip microcomputers with an added interface to a host processor bus. The 8041 and 68120 described below are examples of slave microcomputers.

10.6.1   UPI-41A Universal Peripheral Interface

The UPI-41A, also called the 8041A, is a version of the 8048 which is designed to be used as a slave microcomputer. Figure 10.32 shows the block diagram of this device. It

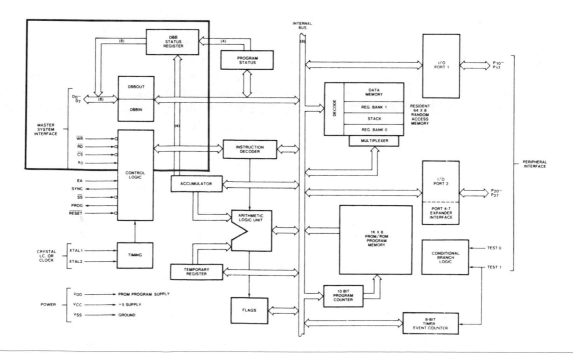

Figure 10.32.   The 8041 slave processor block diagram. *(Courtesy of Intel Corporation.)*

includes the usual ROM (EPROM in the 8741A), RAM, processor, and I/O ports but also has a host (master) processor interface. There are three registers in addition to those in the 8048: data bus buffer in (DBBIN), data bus buffer out (DBBOUT), and status. These registers appear to the host processor as simple I/O ports.

The 8042 is pin-compatible with the 8041A but has twice as much ROM (2 Kbytes) and twice as much RAM (128 bytes). The 8741A and 8742 are EPROM versions of the 8041A and 8042, respectively.

The interface to the host processor is the same as for any other peripheral chip: an 8-bit data bus, a write strobe, a read strobe, a chip select, and an address line. The host processor sends data to the 8041 by writing to the DBBIN register, and reads data from the 8041 by reading the DBBOUT register. These registers appear to the 8041 as its own local registers, which it can read and write directly. Table 10.4 shows how the registers are accessed by the host processor, and Table 10.5 lists the basic instructions used by the 8041 to access the registers.

The status register contains control bits to provide handshaking and other functions. Table 10.6 lists the bit assignments. The OBF bit indicates when the output buffer (DBBOUT) is full. This bit is set automatically when the 8041 writes to DBBOUT and is read by the host processor to determine when there is data available for it to read. The 8041 can also be programmed to output the OBF signal on an output port line so that it can be used to interrupt the host processor.

The IBF bit indicates when the input buffer (DBBIN) is full. This bit is set automat-

---

Table 10.4   The 8041 Register Decoding

A_0	$\overline{RD}$	$\overline{WR}$	Function
0	0	1	Read DBBOUT
1	0	1	Read status
0	1	0	Write DBBIN (data)
1	1	0	Write DBBIN (command)

Table 10.5   The 8041 Instructions for Accessing Interface Registers

Instruction	Function
IN A,DBB	Input DBBIN to accumulator and clear IBF
OUT DBB,A	Output accumulator to DBBOUT and set OBF
MOV STS,A	Copy accumulator bits 4–7 to status bits 4–7
CLR F0	Clear flag F0
CPL F0	Complement flag F0
CLR F1	Clear flag F1
CPL F1	Complement flag F1
JF0 addr	Jump if flag F0 is set
JF1 addr	Jump if flag F1 is set
JNIBF addr	Jump if input buffer not full
JOBF addr	Jump if output buffer full

Table 10.6   The 8041 Status Register Bit Assignments

Bit	Name	Description
D0	OBF	Output buffer full
D1	IBF	Input buffer full
D2	F0	General-purpose flag
D3	F1	Command/data flag
D4	ST4	
D5	ST5	General-purpose status bits
D6	ST6	
D7	ST7	

ically when the host processor writes to DBBIN, and it can either be polled by the 8041 or can generate an interrupt within the 8041. These two bits (IBF and OBF) provide the basic handshaking necessary to coordinate data transfers.

Status bit F0 is a general-purpose flag that can be set, reset, or tested by the 8041. Its use is dependent on the application program in the 8041, but it typically indicates to the host processor that the 8041 is busy or that an error condition has occurred.

Status bit F1 indicates to the 8041 if the data written to DBBIN is intended as a command or as data. Since the two address bits on the 8041 allow four registers to be accessed, and there are actually only three, two addresses are used to access DBBIN. A write to either address writes the data into DBBIN; however, writing to one address sets F1, and writing to the other clears F1. Thus, the 8041 appears to the host processor as if it had one register for commands and another for data. In fact, both commands and data are written to the same register (DBBIN), and the 8041 tests the F1 status bit to distinguish between the two.

The four most-significant bits of the status register are defined by the application program in the 8041. The 8041 sets these bits by loading them from the four most significant bits of the accumulator. These are used for application-dependent status information.

10.6.2   Applications of the 8041

A number of examples of 8041 applications can be found right in Intel's catalog—as standard parts bearing other numbers. The 8294 data encryption unit and 8292 GPIB controller are both preprogrammed 8041s. Intel has simply written an application program, produced a masked ROM version, and provided a data sheet whose specifications are a combination of 8041 specifications and descriptions of functions provided by the program. Pins that may be labeled as application-specific signals are simply I/O port bits whose function has been determined by the application software in the 8041's ROM. Intel is not the only supplier of such devices; Cybernetic Microsystems manufactures a variety of devices including stepper motor controllers, waveform synthesizers, and dot-matrix printer controllers that are also preprogrammed microcomputers. In effect, this is a way of selling software as custom hardware by embedding it in silicon along with the execution engine.

10.6.3   The 68120 Intelligent Peripheral Controller

The 68120 Intelligent Peripheral Controller (IPC) is similar in concept to the 8041 but has a more sophisticated host interface including a dual-port RAM and semaphore logic. It is a version of the 6801 single-chip microcomputer and includes 2 Kbytes of ROM, 128 bytes of RAM, a full-duplex hardware UART, and up to 21 I/O lines in a 48-pin package. (For general information on the 6801, refer to Chap. 2.) The IPC interfaces to the host processor via the on-chip 128-byte RAM, which is dual-ported. Both the IPC and the host processor can access the RAM. Thus the IPC appears to the host as an ordinary 128-byte RAM, except that there is another processor also accessing the RAM.

The 68120 is a mask-programmed device. External EPROM can be connected by using the chip's expansion buses for applications that do not have the volume to justify a mask-programmed device. The 68120 is available as a standard part with a monitor program in ROM, or as the 68121 with no ROM.

To control access to the RAM, six special semaphore registers are included. Figure 10.33 shows the block diagram of the IPC. The CPU, timers, and I/O ports are the same as the 6801's. I/O ports 3 and 4 can be used as I/O ports or expansion buses, just as in the 6801. This allows the 68120 to operate in an expanded mode in which it has its own local buses in addition to connecting to the host's buses. The host processor interfaces to the IPC just as if it were a RAM chip, supplying eight data lines (SD0 to SD7), eight address lines (SA0 to SA7), read/write control (SR/$\overline{\text{W}}$), and chip select. A $\overline{\text{DTACK}}$ output is provided for use with asynchronous-bus microprocessors such as the 68000, as shown in Fig. 10.34.

The $\overline{\text{DTACK}}$ pin also serves as an input; if it is tied low, the 68120 operates synchronously with the system clock (E). This mode is used with microprocessors such as a 6809. The 6809 and the 68120 are both driven by the same clock signal, and no wait states are generated.

The RAM appears to the IPC at addresses 80 to FF hex. It appears to the host processor at addresses XX80 to XXFF; the high-order bits (XX) are determined by the address decoder that drives $\overline{\text{CS}}$. Since the processor and the IPC can both access the RAM simultaneously, semaphores are needed to allow either processor to indicate when a block of memory is in use and must not be accessed by the other processor.

Six semaphore registers are provided. These registers are addressed by the host processor at addresses XX17 to XX1C and by the IPC at addresses 17 to 1C. Each of the six registers can be used to control access to a different part of the RAM. Both the host software and the IPC software must agree on which semaphore controls access to which part of the RAM; the hardware does not enforce this. Only two bits are used in each semaphore register; one is the semaphore bit itself, and the other is the ownership bit, which indicates which processor last set the semaphore.

When either the host or the IPC wants to access the shared RAM, it reads the semaphore register associated with the desired section of RAM. If the semaphore bit is clear (0), then the memory is available, and the bit is *automatically* set after it is read. The data read will have a 0 in the semaphore bit, indicating that the memory is available. The automatic setting of the semaphore bit on any read provides the required indivisible test-and-set operation. If the semaphore is set when the semaphore register is read,

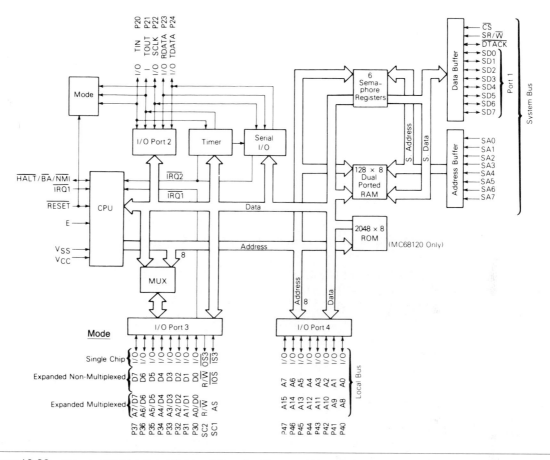

Figure 10.33. Motorola 68120 Intelligent Peripheral Controller. *(Courtesy of Motorola, Inc.)*

Figure 10.34. The 68120-to-68000 interface. *(Courtesy of Motorola, Inc.)*

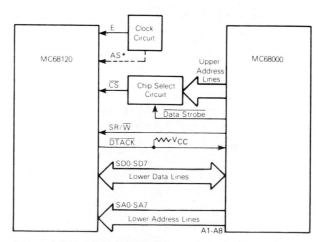

* Only needed in expanded multiplexed modes.

the data read will have a 1 in the semaphore bit, indicating that the memory is not available.

One arbitration problem still remains. The dual-port memory (which includes the semaphore registers) is fully transparent; that is, a memory location (or semaphore register) can be read simultaneously by both the host processor and the IPC. Some protection mechanism must therefore be included to prevent both processors from simultaneously reading (and thus setting) a semaphore, since both processors would then think they had sole access to the memory. The IPC gives this protection by providing *different data* to each processor in such a case. Whenever both processors simultaneously read a semaphore that is clear, the IPC will read the semaphore as clear and the host will read the semaphore as set. Thus, in case of simultaneous requests, the IPC is always given priority.

10.6.4   The 8044 Remote Universal Peripheral Interface

Intel's 8044 RUPI is a slave I/O processor that is designed to interface to the host processor by using a serial interface. Figure 10.35 shows the block diagram of the chip. The 8044 is based on the 8051 single-chip microcomputer. (The 8744 has EPROM instead of ROM.) The primary difference between the 8044 and 8051 is that the 8044 replaces the 8051's asynchronous serial interface with an intelligent synchronous interface. This serial interface unit (SIU) supports a subset of the SDLC protocol, independently of the CPU. (See Chap. 8 for a description of SDLC.)

The 8044 uses the NRZI encoding method. NRZI encodes a 1 as no signal transition during the bit time and a 0 as a signal transition at the start of the bit time. The zero-bit

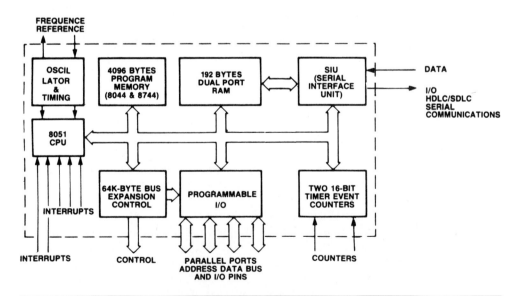

Figure 10.35.   Intel 8044 Remote Universal Peripheral Interface block diagram. *(Courtesy of Intel Corporation.)*

insertion used in SDLC guarantees that no more than five consecutive ones can occur, except during a flag when there are six consecutive ones. Thus, a long period without signal transitions cannot occur, which allows the clock to be recovered from the data stream using a PLL. The 8044 includes an on-chip digital PLL for this purpose. Data rates up to 375 kbps can be achieved with the on-chip PLL. By using an external PLL or transmitting the clock as a separate signal, data rates up to 2.4 Mbps can be used.

The SDLC network can use a multidrop (also called multipoint) or loop topology. The 8044 supports both these modes. In loop mode, the 8044 retransmits data received with a one-bit delay.

The SIU interfaces to the 8044's CPU via a dual-port memory, several control and status registers, and an interrupt signal. The CPU controls the SIU's mode of operation by setting these registers. In an SDLC network, a primary station periodically polls all secondary stations. Each secondary station has a unique address. When the secondary station receives a poll command with its address, it can then send a data block to the primary station.

The SIU handles much of the SDLC protocol without intervention from the CPU. To send a block of data, the CPU stores the data in the shared RAM, and sets the "transmit buffer full" control bit. This indicates to the SIU that a data block is ready to be sent. The SIU receives every frame sent by the primary station. When it receives a poll command that matches its address (as set by the CPU's initialization software), it responds with a frame containing the data in the shared RAM. The SIU automatically appends the flags, address field, frame sequence number, and frame check sequence (CRC). If the SIU receives a negative acknowledge from the primary station, it retransmits the frame. If it receives a positive acknowledge, it interrupts the CPU to indicate that the transmission has been completed. Note that all the CPU must do is place the data in the RAM and request transmission; the SIU independently performs all the data link control and response functions. The CPU continues to operate normally during this time. Thus, this greatly reduces the burden on the CPU as compared to traditional systems in which the CPU must respond to every byte received.

The SIU also automatically handles reception of data blocks from the primary station. The SIU loads the data into the shared RAM. If the CRC is correct, the SIU sends an acknowledge to the primary station and interrupts the CPU to indicate that a new data block is available. If there is an error, the SIU requests retransmission.

The 8044's SIU can also be programmed to operate in a nonautomatic mode, which allows more flexibility but places a greater burden on the CPU. This mode can be used to implement nonstandard protocols or HDLC protocol. It also allows frames to be sent without waiting for a poll, so it can be used to implement a primary station.

The 8044 is an attractive device to use as the remote node controller for distributed control and data collection systems. Since the SIU independently implements the data link protocol, the CPU has most of its processing time available for data collection and control functions. The built-in error detection and retransmission capabilities provide a high level of data integrity. Intel has specified a network they call the *Bitbus*, which uses an RS-485 electrical interface and a subset of the SDLC protocol and is designed to provide a standard network definition for systems using 8044 microcontrollers as nodes on the network. Intel, Data Translation, and other manufacturers provide a variety of standard boards to interface to the network, including analog and digital input and output boards and general-purpose controllers.

10.6.5   The 8089 I/O Processor

Intel's 8089 I/O processor (IOP) is a sophisticated device that has attributes of both a DMA controller and a microprocessor. Unlike the devices described in the preceding sections, it is not a single-chip microcomputer but requires external ROM, RAM, and I/O ports. It is designed to work with an 8086-family microprocessor but can be interfaced to other microprocessors via the Multibus. It relieves the CPU of detailed I/O processing chores, in much the same way as any slave processor. Because it can also perform DMA transfers, large blocks of data can be quickly transferred. For example, a disk controller implemented with the 8089 can read blocks of data from the microprocessor's memory, write them on the disk, check the disk controller status, and automatically repeat the operation if an error occurs. A disk controller chip is still required; the 8089 feeds the controller commands, checks the controller's status, and reads and writes data blocks.

Figure 10.36 shows a block diagram of the 8089 IOP. The 8089 bus interface is identical to that of the 8086, so the same clock generator and system controller ICs can be used. There are two channels that operate independently. The 8089 has a relatively small instruction set that includes the usual arithmetic and jump instructions but is optimized for I/O. Its most unique instruction is XFER, which causes it to perform a DMA transfer. It can thus perform both normal computations and programmed I/O and also perform DMA transfers.

The 8089 uses the two-cycle DMA technique, in which a byte (or word) is first read from the source address and temporarily stored in the 8089. The data is then written to the destination address. This approach allows memory-to-memory transfers and also gives the 8089 a number of special capabilities. It can perform a table lookup translation on the data as it is transferred; for example, data could be converted from ASCII to EBCDIC. It can also transfer between 8- and 16-bit buses. For example, when transferring data from an 8-bit bus to a 16-bit bus, it first performs two 8-bit reads, assembles a 16-bit word, and then performs a 16-bit write.

The 8089 can be used in local or remote mode. In local mode, as shown in Fig. 10.37, it shares the host processor's bus controller and buses. The host for this mode of

Figure 10.36. The 8089 I/O processor block diagram. *(Courtesy of Intel Corporation.)*

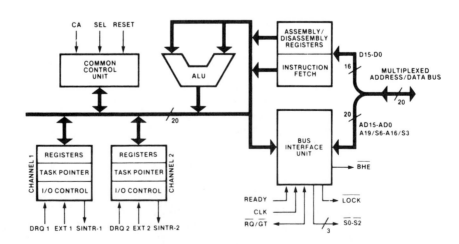

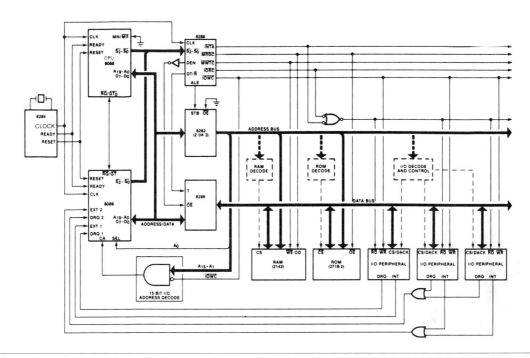

Figure 10.37. Circuit diagram for 8086 with 8089 in local mode. *(Courtesy of Intel Corporation.)*

operation must be an 8086 or 8088 in maximum mode. The RQ/GT line arbitrates use of the system bus. The 8089 adds intelligent DMA capabilities to the system. Because the IOP does not have a private bus in this mode, the full performance potential is not realized; the host CPU cannot use the buses while the IOP is active.

The 8089 is most powerful when used in remote mode. As shown in Fig. 10.38, the remote mode 8089 is an independent processor that interfaces to the system bus. It has its own clock generator, bus controller, and bus arbiter, which interfaces it to the Multibus. In addition, it has its own local bus. The I/O processor board is very similar to an 8086 CPU board except that it has a processor with an I/O-oriented instruction set and DMA capabilities.

Figure 10.39 shows a detailed example of an I/O processor system with local memory and I/O. The 8288 bus controller generates control signals for both the local bus and the Multibus. The memory read and write commands access the system bus (Multibus), and the I/O read and write commands access the local bus. These names do not imply the usual distinctions, however; the 8089 may have local memory, which would be accessed with I/O read and write commands. In other words, the "I/O" bus is the local bus, which can be used for either memory or I/O. Devices on the local bus are not directly accessible from the system bus. The 8089 can support system and I/O buses of 8 or 16 bits in any combination. It can therefore be used with an 8086 or 8088 and can interface to either 8- or 16-bit peripherals.

The interface between the host processor and the 8089 is primarily through blocks of shared memory. There are three interprocessor interface signals: channel attention (CA) and two system interrupts (SINTR-1 and SINTR-2). CA is an input to the 8089 that tells it to look at the control block in shared memory to get a command. CA is

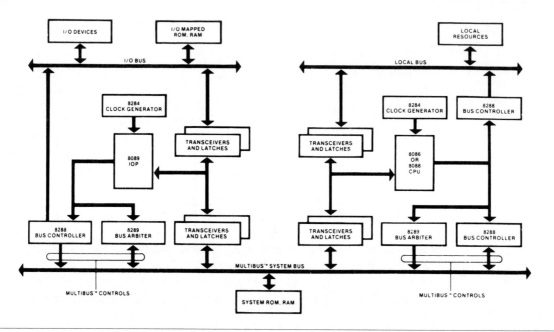

Figure 10.38. System block diagram with 8089 IOP in remote mode. *(Courtesy of Intel Corporation.)*

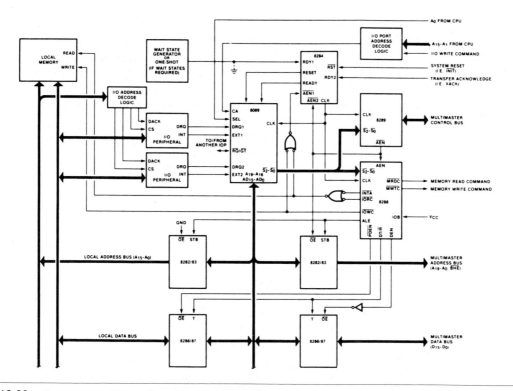

Figure 10.39. Circuit for 8089 IOP in remote mode. *(Courtesy of Intel Corporation.)*

generated when the host processor writes to a particular I/O address on the system bus; only the write pulse is used, and the data written is ignored. SINTR-1 and SINTR-2 are outputs from the 8089 that can be used to interrupt the host processor to indicate completion of a command.

Five control blocks in memory provide all other communications between the host processor and the 8089. This is a very different architecture than in the other I/O processors that have been described previously, which communicate with the host via dedicated registers or RAM in the I/O processor itself. The 8089 approach is more complex and somewhat more difficult to understand but considerably more flexible and powerful. It allows arbitrarily large blocks of data to be passed between the processors with a minimum of overhead.

The top 16 bytes of memory (FFFF0 to FFFFF hex) in 8086-family systems are called the *system configuration pointer (SCP)* and include reset and initialization vectors. The SCP is generally in ROM. The 8089 first reads location FFFF6, which specifies the width of the system bus as 8 or 16 bits. The 8089 then reads from addresses FFFF8 to FFFFB the pointer to the system configuration block (SCB). This pointer consists of a 16-bit base and a 16-bit offset, which are combined into a 20-bit address. The address calculation is the same as that done by any 8086-family processor. The resulting address points to the SCB, which can be located anywhere in memory. The SCB contains a byte called SOC, which determines the width of the I/O bus. The SCB also contains another pointer, which provides the address of the channel control block (CB).

The SCP and SCB are only read immediately after a system reset. Once the system is initialized, the CB address is fixed and the bus widths are set. When the host processor has a command for the 8089, it places the command byte in the channel command word (CCW), which is located at the previously defined CB address. Figure 10.40 shows the format of the channel control block and the associated parameter and

Figure 10.40. Control and parameter blocks for 8089 IOP. *(Courtesy of Intel Corporation.)*

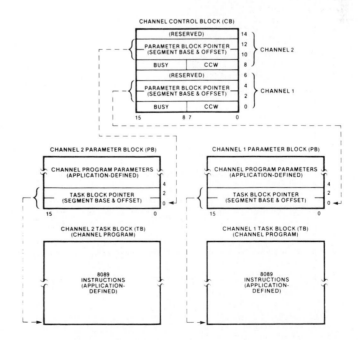

Figure 10.41. CPU/
IOP interaction for disk
transfer. *(Courtesy of Intel
Corporation.)*

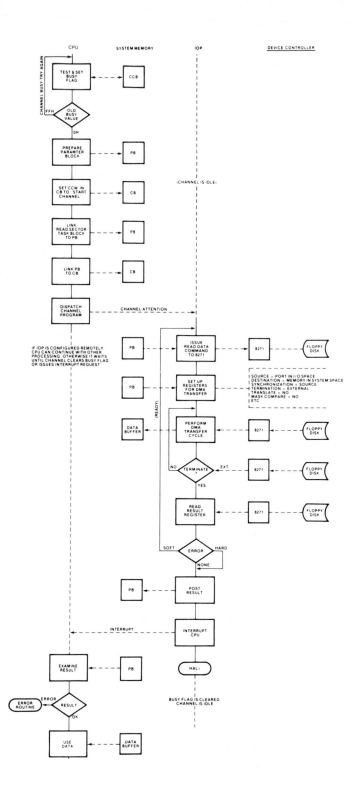

task blocks. The second byte of the CB, called BUSY, is set to 1 by the 8089 when it receives the command and reset to 0 when it is complete. The remaining two bytes in the CB are set by the host CPU to point to the parameter block (PB) for the command. The PB begins with yet another pointer, which points to the task block (TB). The remainder of the parameter block contains the parameters for the command and can be as large as necessary (limited by available memory space). The PB is also used by the 8089 to return results to the host CPU. The final block, the task block, contains the actual program for the 8089.

Figure 10.41 shows a typical host CPU/IOP interaction. In this example, the IOP is controlling a floppy-disk controller (FDC). The host processor waits for the channel to be not busy, sets up the parameter and task blocks, and performs a write to the address that causes CA to be pulsed. In this example, the task block is a routine for reading a sector of data from the disk.

After receiving the CA signal, the 8089 reads the command and follows the pointers to the parameter and task blocks. The task program writes a READ SECTOR command to the FDC and then prepares for a DMA transfer. When the FDC is ready, the transfer begins. The data is transferred directly into the parameter block area. When the transfer is complete, the IOP checks for an error condition, and repeats the read attempt if a soft error has occurred. Finally, the IOP clears its BUSY flag, interrupts the host processor, and halts. The host processor then reads the data from the PB.

The 8089 thus provides very powerful data transfer and control capabilities. The amount of hardware and software required to incorporate an 8089 into a system is considerable, but so is the performance gained. It is used in high-performance I/O-intensive applications, such as disk interfaces, terminal multiplexers, and graphics terminals. Intel's application notes AP-122 and AP-123 provide detailed examples of 8089-based systems.

10.7 COPROCESSORS

The preceding section described several processors that are designed primarily to act as slaves to a host processor. These processors interface to the host processor either via registers or shared memory in the slave processor or via external shared memory. The slave processor is loosely coupled to the host and executes an independent instruction stream.

Coprocessors are designed to operate closely coupled to the host processor. A coprocessor executes instructions from the same instruction stream as the main processor. A coprocessor effectively extends the instruction set and register set of the host processor and may add new data types. The programmer need not be aware of the division of tasks between the main processor and the coprocessor(s); unlike systems using slave processors, communication among the processors is transparent to the programmer.

Most microprocessors are quite slow when it comes to performing floating-point and transcendental calculations, since lengthy iterative subroutines are required. These are therefore natural functions to be provided by a specialized processor for applications that require such calculations. Use of a specialized floating-point processor not only increases the system's speed but eliminates the need to write the routines to implement the floating-point and transcendental algorithms. Thus, floating-point processors are the most widely used coprocessors. This section describes the coprocessor interfaces used by Intel and Motorola.

10.7.1   Intel 8087 Floating-Point Coprocessor

Coprocessors are tightly coupled to the host processor and are usually designed to work in conjunction with a particular microprocessor. Intel's 8087 floating-point processor is designed to work with an 8086-family microprocessor. The 8086/8087 pair forms a powerful two-chip processor. The 8087 is so closely coupled to the 8086 architecture that it is virtually impossible to use it with any other microprocessor family. The 80287 and 80387 are designed to work with the 80286 and 80386, respectively, and are similar in operation.

The 8087 connects directly in parallel with most of the pins on the 8086, including the address and data buses, status outputs, and clock and reset signals. Figure 10.42 shows the internal structure of the 8087, and Fig. 10.43 shows the block diagram for the 8086/8087 combination. Three signals act as control lines between the 8086 and

Figure 10.42. The 8087 floating-point co-processor block diagram. *(Courtesy of Intel Corporation.)*

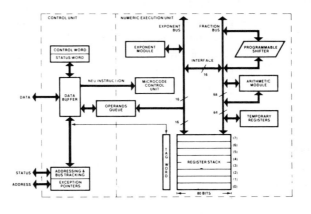

Figure 10.43. Circuit for 8086 CPU and 8087 coprocessor connection. *(Courtesy of Intel Corporation.)*

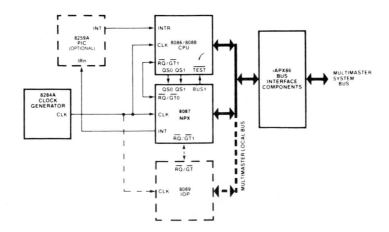

Table 10.7   The 8087 Floating-Point Coprocessor Instruction Types

Class	Instructions
Data Transfer	Load (all data types), Store (all data types), Exchange
Arithmetic	Add, Subtract, Multiply, Divide, Subtract Reversed, Divide Reversed, Square Root, Scale, Remainder, Integer Part, Change Sign, Absolute Value, Extract
Comparison	Compare, Examine, Test
Transcendental	Tangent, Arctangent, $2^X - 1$, $Y \bullet Log_2(X+1)$, $Y \bullet Log_2(X)$
Constants	0, 1, π, $Log_{10}2$, Log_e2, Log_210, Log_2e
Processor Control	Load Control Word, Store Control Word, Store Status Word, Load Environment, Store Environment, Save, Restore, Enable Interrupts, Disable Interrupts, Clear Exceptions, Initialize

Source: Intel Corp.

Table 10.8   The 8087 Coprocessor Data Types

Data Type	Bits	Significant Digits (Decimal)	Approximate Range (Decimal)
Word integer	16	4	$-32,768 \leqslant X \leqslant +32,767$
Short integer	32	9	$-2 \times 10^9 \leqslant X \leqslant +2 \times 10^9$
Long integer	64	18	$-9 \times 10^{18} \leqslant X \leqslant +9 \times 10^{18}$
Packed decimal	80	18	$-99...99 \leqslant X \leqslant +99...99$ (18 digits)
Short real*	32	6-7	$8.43 \times 10^{-37} \leqslant |X| \leqslant 3.37 \times 10^{38}$
Long real*	64	15-16	$4.19 \times 10^{-307} \leqslant |X| \leqslant 1.67 \times 10^{308}$
Temporary real	80	19	$3.4 \times 10^{-4932} \leqslant |X| \leqslant 1.2 \times 10^{4932}$

*The short and long real data types correspond to the single and double precision data types defined in other Intel numerics products.

Source: Intel Corp.

8087. The $\overline{RQ/GT0}$ pin of the 8087 connects to the $\overline{RQ/GT1}$ pin of the 8086 and is used by the 8087 to request use of the buses for reading or writing operands. The BUSY output from the 8087 drives the $\overline{TEST}$ input of the 8086 and indicates to the 8086 when the 8087 is executing an instruction. The 8086 waits for the 8087 to be done by executing a WAIT instruction, which repeatedly reads the $\overline{TEST}$ input until it is asserted. The 8087 also generates an interrupt output, which can be used to interrupt the 8086 in case of an arithmetic error (such as dividing by zero).

The 8087 monitors the 8086 buses and control signals to watch for arithmetic instructions. Table 10.7 lists the 8087's instruction types, and Table 10.8 lists the data types. Instructions intended for execution by a coprocessor are called *escape* instructions and can be identified by the coprocessor because the most-significant five bits are always 11011. The coprocessor must determine when the 8086 is actually executing the escape instruction, which may be several bus cycles after the instruction was fetched due to the 8086's prefetch queue. The 8087 therefore monitors the queue status signals QS0 and QS1 from the 8086 and tracks the operation of the queue.

In the simplest case, in which the operation to be performed by the 8087 uses only its internal registers and does not require any memory accesses, the 8087 simply captures the instruction from the data bus and executes it. However, most instructions require the 8087 to read from or write to memory, since all data transferred between the host processor and the coprocessor is transferred via the system RAM. In the case of an instruction requiring a single word of data to be read, the 8086 reads the data after reading the opcode, and the 8087 captures the data from the bus.

If an instruction for the 8087 requires more than one word from memory, the 8086 reads only the first word. The 8087 captures the data *and the address* from the buses. It then takes control of the buses (via $\overline{\text{RQ/GT}}$) and reads successive data words from the memory as needed. Write operations are handled similarly; the 8086 reads from the address to which the data is to be written so that the 8087 can capture the address. The 8086 must always supply the first address, since the base registers and address calculation logic in the 8086 are not externally accessible.

The 8086 can continue executing instructions from its internal queue while the 8087 is in control of the bus. If the 8086 requires access to the bus, it waits until the 8087 has completed its operation.

A software emulator for the 8087 is also available, which allows programs to be developed with 8086 software subroutines performing the arithmetic computations. The program can then be easily modified to use the 8087 if higher performance is required. The LINK utility in the development software can automatically incorporate code for use with the software emulator or the 8087; no source code modifications are required. For the software emulation, the escape instructions are changed to interrupt instructions, and the interrupt handler emulates the 8087 instruction set. As Table 10.9 shows, the 8087 performs the functions much faster than the 8086 software simulation. The 8087 thus provides an easily used, high-performance solution for floating-point mathematics.

10.7.2   Motorola 68020 Coprocessor Interface

The Motorola 68020's coprocessor interface uses a different approach than Intel's. (The 68000 and 68010 do not include a coprocessor interface.) An Intel-style coprocessor must continuously monitor the data bus and track the operation of the microprocessor's internal queue so that it can recognize a coprocessor instruction and know when the microprocessor is ready to execute it. In Motorola's approach, the coprocessor does not monitor instructions as they are fetched by the microprocessor. Instead, the microprocessor recognizes coprocessor instructions and in response writes a command word to the coprocessor. This requires an extra bus cycle to initiate a coprocessor instruction but simplifies the design of the coprocessor's bus interface. This approach is also dictated by the presence of an on-chip instruction cache in the 68020. It is not possible for

Table 10.9   Execution Times for 8087 Coprocessor Compared to 8086 Software Emulation

Instruction	Approximate Execution Time (μs) (5 MHz Clock)	
	8087	8086 Emulation
Multiply (single precision)	19	1,600
Multiply (double precision)	27	2,100
Add	17	1,600
Divide (single precision)	39	3,200
Compare	9	1,300
Load (single precision)	9	1,700
Store (single precision)	18	1,200
Square root	36	19,600
Tangent	90	13,000
Exponentiation	100	17,100

Source: Intel Corp.

a coprocessor to monitor the instructions fetched by the processor, since instructions fetched from the cache do not appear on the external buses.

Instructions that are intended for a coprocessor are identified by the four most-significant bits of the operation word (the first word of the instruction) being 1111 (hex F). Thus, these are called *F-line* instructions. The F-line operation words include a field to select one of eight coprocessors and also include general information about the type of instruction. The F-line operation word is decoded only by the microprocessor; it is not transferred directly to the coprocessor. Following the F-line operation word is typically a command word, which is not decoded at all by the microprocessor but is transferred to the coprocessor selected in the preceding operation word. This command word can optionally be followed by additional parameters for the coprocessor.

Normal coprocessors, such as the 68881 floating-point coprocessor, are bus slaves and access memory only via the main microprocessor. It is possible, however, for a coprocessor to include DMA capabilities, which would allow it to directly access memory and I/O. Such a coprocessor would request use of the system buses via the usual bus arbitration signals. This would be appropriate for a coprocessor that required access to large blocks of data, since there is additional overhead in transferring data through the main microprocessor.

Figure 10.44 shows the connections between the 68020 and a coprocessor, such as the 68881 floating-point processor. No special signals are used for the coprocessor connection. To address a coprocessor, the microprocessor performs a bus cycle with the address and function code lines as follows:

Figure 10.44. Motorola 68020 coprocessor interface. *(Courtesy of Motorola, Inc.)*

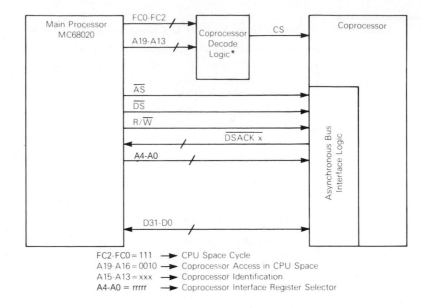

FC2-FC0 = 111 → CPU Space Cycle
A19-A16 = 0010 → Coprocessor Access in CPU Space
A15-A13 = xxx → Coprocessor Identification
A4-A0 = rrrrr → Coprocessor Interface Register Selector

*Chip select logic may be integrated into the coprocessor

Address lines not specified above are "0" during coprocessor access.

$FC_2\text{-}FC_0 = 111$ Indicates CPU space access

$A_{19}\text{-}A_{16} = 0010$ Indicates coprocessor access

$A_{15}\text{-}A_{13} = xxx$ Coprocessor ID number

$A_4\text{-}A_0 = xxxxx$ Coprocessor interface register select

The function code (FC) can be thought of as an address modifier code. The 111 code indicates a *CPU space* operation. This code is used for breakpoints, interrupt acknowledge cycles, and coprocessor access cycles. By decoding the FC signals, normal memory and I/O devices are prevented from responding to this type of cycle. Address bits A_{16} to A_{19} specify the type of CPU space cycle; 0010 identifies the cycle as a coprocessor access rather than an interrupt acknowledge or a breakpoint. Address bits A_{13} to A_{15} select one of eight coprocessors, and address bits A_0 to A_4 select one of 32 interface registers within the coprocessor.

Thus, the coprocessor connects to the buses very similarly to a standard peripheral chip, except that its chip select decoding logic enables the chip only when the function code and address lines indicate a coprocessor access cycle to this coprocessor. The usual asynchronous data transfer acknowledge terminates the cycle, so coprocessors can be designed with bus interfaces that are as fast as the microprocessor or that are much slower.

The coprocessor includes a number of interface registers. The two registers essential to the basic coordination between the coprocessor and the main microprocessor are the command register and the response register. The microprocessor writes to the command register to pass the command word of an F-line instruction to the coprocessor.

The coprocessor indicates its status to the microprocessor and can also make requests of the microprocessor by placing a *response primitive* in its response register. The microprocessor periodically reads this register while the coprocessor is executing an instruction. Response primitives allow the coprocessor to request that the microprocessor calculate an effective address, read or write a memory location, or read or write microprocessor registers.

The following sequence of operations occurs when a coprocessor instruction is fetched:

1. Microprocessor fetches F-line operation word.

2. Microprocessor fetches command word following operation word.

3. Microprocessor writes command word to coprocessor's command register, addressing coprocessor as described previously.

4. Coprocessor begins executing command. If additional parameters are required, coprocessor requests them from the microprocessor by placing appropriate response primitive in its response register.

5. Microprocessor reads coprocessor's response register, and if any action is requested, performs that action.

6. When coprocessor completes instruction execution, it indicates this via its response register.

7. When microprocessor detects completion response in coprocessor's response register, it continues with the next instruction.

The preceding description covers only a subset of the coprocessor interface capabilities. It is a complex and flexible interface, designed to allow the development of a wide variety of coprocessors. Because the coprocessor interface is fully documented, and does not require the coprocessor to track the operation of the main microprocessor, it is possible for custom coprocessors to be developed for specific applications.

The coprocessor communication protocol is fully implemented in microcode in the 68020. Thus, it is transparent to the programmer. It is not necessary to understand the protocol to use a standard coprocessor. The coprocessor simply extends the instruction set and register set of the main microprocessor. A coprocessor can be used with microprocessors such as the 68000 and 68010, which do not have the microcode for the coprocessor protocol. In this case, the coprocessor must be addressed as a standard peripheral, and the communications protocol must be implemented in assembly language. In this case the protocol is not transparent to the programmer, and the overhead for coprocessor communication is much greater. In fact, the coprocessor is no longer a true coprocessor but rather a slave processor.

10.8 SUMMARY

There are many approaches to multiple microprocessor systems, but the goals are the same: to provide increased performance, flexibility, and cost effectiveness. Because of the relatively low cost of the microprocessor, it is often better to use several of them than to use one higher-performance processor. Advantages of modularity, both in design and in physical structure, are also obtained.

The key design issues for multiprocessor systems are the interconnections and the software partitioning. The most effective applications are those for which there is a natural functional partitioning. Interconnections can be as simple as connected I/O ports or as complex as a multimaster bus with command blocks in shared memory.

Single-chip microcomputers are ideal elements for multiprocessor systems. Special versions with host processor or serial interfaces make the interconnection task relatively simple. As these microcomputers become more powerful and less expensive, the number of processors in the average system will steadily increase.

10.9   EXERCISES

10.1.   How has the development of the microprocessor affected multiprocessor system design?

10.2.   What are the advantages of multiprocessor systems other than higher performance?

10.3.   What are the key differences between tightly coupled and loosely coupled systems?

10.4.   A tightly coupled multiprocessor system uses four identical microprocessors, each with a bus utilization of 20 percent. What is the maximum possible system performance as a multiple of uniprocessor system performance? What if five processors are used? Six processors? What factors make this maximum performance unlikely to be achieved?

10.5.   Draw a circuit diagram for a 16-bit bidirectional parallel link between two microprocessor systems. How is the data direction controlled?

10.6.   What is the advantage of adding a FIFO buffer to the link in Exercise 10.5?

10.7.   An industrial control system must control two motors, based on signals from digital tachometers and position indicators. The operator enters motion commands via a small keyboard, and a multiplexed LED display provides position and speed information. How can multiple microprocessors be used?

a.   Draw a block diagram of a system using three microprocessors, and list the functions performed by each.

b.   List the information that must be exchanged between processors.

c.   What type of links should be used between the processors?

10.8.   In a Multibus system, what is the advantage of parallel priority resolution?

10.9.   Is a system using multiple single-board computers connected via the Multibus tightly or loosely coupled? Why?

10.10.   Describe the design approaches that can be taken to reduce bus utilization in a shared-bus system. What are the advantages and disadvantages of each?

10.11.   What is the difference between a slave processor and a coprocessor?

10.12. Motorola's coprocessors do not monitor the instructions fetched by the main microprocessor. Are they truly coprocessors, or are they slave processors? Why?

10.10 SELECTED BIBLIOGRAPHY

General Multiprocessor References

Bowen, B. A., and R. J. A. Burr. *The Logical Design of Multiple-Microprocessor Systems,* Englewood Cliffs, NJ: Prentice-Hall, 1980.

Fathi, Eli T., and Moshe Krieger. "Multiple Microprocessor Systems: What, Why, and When," *Computer,* March 1983, pp. 23–32. A good review of general principles of multiprocessor system design.

Fielland, Gary, and Dave Rodgers. "32-Bit Computer System Shares Load Equally among up to 12 Processors," *Electronic Design,* Sept. 6, 1984, pp. 153–168. Describes Sequent's multiprocessor architecture.

Haynes et al. "A Survey of Highly Parallel Computing," *Computer,* January 1982, pp. 9–24. Surveys various approaches to using large numbers of processors.

Liebowitz, Burt H., and John H. Carson. *Multiple Processor Systems for Real-Time Applications,* Englewood Cliffs, NJ: Prentice-Hall, 1985.

Paker, Y. *Multi-microprocessor Systems,* London: Academic Press, 1983. Describes architecture and software requirements for multiple microprocessor systems but does not provide circuit-level detail.

Satyanarayanan, M. "Multiprocessing: An Annotated Bibliography," *Computer,* May 1980, pp. 101–116. An extensive list of references on multiprocessor systems.

Short, Kenneth. "Multiple Microprocessor Systems," Section 12.6 in *Microprocessors and Programmed Logic,* Englewood Cliffs, NJ: Prentice-Hall, 1981. Covers basic concepts of multiprocessor systems, using the 8041 and the Multibus as examples.

Weitzman, Cay. *Distributed Micro/Mini Computer Systems,* Englewood Cliffs, NJ: Prentice-Hall, 1980.

Interprocessor Communication

Dijkstra, E. W. "Solution to a Problem in Concurrent Programming Control," *Communications of the ACM,* Sept. 1965, p. 569. The original solution to process synchronization using semaphores.

Gable, Melvin. "Communications in Distributed Systems," *Computer Design,* February–April 1980 (3 parts). A series of articles describing communication protocols and interconnection topologies.

Hillman, Daniel L. "Intelligent Buffer Reconciles Fast Processors and Slow Peripherals," *Electronics,* Sept. 11, 1980, pp. 131–135. General description of the Z-FIO.

Motorola. "Serial Communications Interface Wake-Up Feature," and "Dual Processor Interface Modes," Sec. 6.5 and 8.7 in *MC6801 Reference Manual,* Phoenix, 1980. Describes features of the 6801 microcomputer in multiprocessor applications.

Texas Instruments. *TMS9650 Data Manual* and *Interfacing Multiple Microprocessors Using the TMS9650,* Dallas. Descriptions of TI's multiprocessor interface device.

Zilog. *Z8038 Z-FIO Buffer Product Specification* and *Z8060 FIFO Buffer Unit Product Specification,* Campbell, CA.

Multibus Interfacing

The principal Multibus references are listed in the Selected Bibliography in Chap. 3. The following references provide additional information on multiprocessor Multibus systems.

Intel. "Application Note AP-51: Designing 8086, 8088, 8089 Multiprocessing Systems with the 8289 Bus Arbiter," Santa Clara, CA, 1979. Detailed description of the design of Multibus systems using 8086-family microprocessors.

Rector, Russel, and George Alexy. "The Multibus" and "Multiprocessor Configurations for the 8086," in *The 8086 Book,* Berkeley, CA: Osborne/McGraw-Hill, 1980. Tutorial description of 8086-based multiprocessor systems and the Multibus.

I/O Processors

Intel. *8041 User's Manual,* Santa Clara, CA. Reference manual for the 8041 slave processor. The 8041 data sheet is included in the *Microsystem Component Handbook,*

————. *Microcontroller Handbook,* Santa Clara, CA. Includes descriptions of the 8044.

Kop, Hal. "Application Note AP-122: Hard Disk Controller Design Using the Intel 8089" and "Application Note AP-123: Graphic CRT Design Using the Intel 8089," Santa Clara, CA: Intel, 1982. Examples of 8089 system designs.

Motorola. The 68120 data sheet, included in *Single-Chip Microcomputer Data,* Phoenix.

Wiles and Lamb. "Special-Purpose Processor Makes Short Work of Host's I/O Chores," *Electronics,* May 19, 1981, pp. 165–168. General description of the 68120 slave processor.

Coprocessors

Intel. *iAPX 86, 88, 186, 188 Hardware Reference Manual,* Santa Clara, CA. Includes description of 8087 coprocessor operation.

Groves, Stan. "Standard Interface Keys Coprocessor Design," *Electronics,* Nov. 17, 1983, pp. 141–144. A general description of the 68020's coprocessor interface.

Motorola. *68020 User's Manual,* Phoenix. (Also published by Prentice-Hall.) Includes a detailed description of the coprocessor interface.

SUBJECT INDEX

581

PRODUCT NUMBER INDEX

Note: Devices are listed under their root number without prefixes, except when the prefix is an integral part of the number (e.g., Z80).

CREDITS

Figs. 2.5, 2.9, 5.7, 5.8, 5.9, 10.11. 10.12; & Table 10.2: Reproduced by permission. © 1986 Zilog, Inc. This material shall not be reproduced without the written consent of Zilog, Inc.

Figs. 2.7, 2.8, 2.12–2.18, 2.21, 2.23, 2.24, 3.7, 3.17, 3.23, 3.24, 4.16, 4.30, 4.31, 7.11, 7.12, 7.30, 7.39, 9.31–9.34, 10.29–10.32, 10.35–10.43; Tables 10.7, 10.8 & 10.9: Illustrations reprinted by permission of Intel Corp., © 1985.

Fig. 3.35: From *Multibus Design Guidebook* by Johnson and Kassel, © 1984, courtesy of McGraw-Hill Book Co.

Figs. 4.42, 5.19, 5.20, 8.4, 8.17, 8.18, 8.22, 8.31, 8.32; Tables 4.5 & 4.6: Copyright © Advanced Micro Devices, Inc., 1985. Reprinted with permission of copyright owner. All rights reserved.

Tables 9.3 & 9.4; Figs. 9.16 & 9.21: Copyright © 1984 Western Digital Corp. All rights reserved.

KEEP UP TO DATE!

Please send me a free trial subscription to *Microprocessor Report*. This newsletter is edited by Michael Slater, author of *Microprocessor-Based Design,* and is the only periodical dedicated to meeting the information needs of designers of microprocessor-based systems. There is, of course, no cost or obligation.

Name _____ Title _____

Company or School _____

Street _____

City _____ State _____ Zip _____

Telephone (_____) _____

KEEP UP TO DATE!

Please send me a free trial subscription to *Microprocessor Report*. This newsletter is edited by Michael Slater, author of *Microprocessor-Based Design,* and is the only periodical dedicated to meeting the information needs of designers of microprocessor-based systems. There is, of course, no cost or obligation.

Name _____ Title _____

Company or School _____

Street _____

City _____ State _____ Zip _____

Telephone (_____) _____

Place
Stamp
Here

Mail to: **MICRO DESIGN RESOURCES, INC.**
550 California Avenue
Suite 320
Palo Alto, CA 94306

Place
Stamp
Here

Mail to: **MICRO DESIGN RESOURCES, INC.**
550 California Avenue
Suite 320
Palo Alto, CA 94306

F